SOMETHING ABOUT THE AUTHOR®

Something about
the Author *was named
an "Outstanding
Reference Source,"
the highest honor given
by the American
Library Association
Reference and Adult
Services Division.*

ISSN 0276-816X

SOMETHING ABOUT THE AUTHOR®

Facts and Pictures about Authors and Illustrators of Books for Young People

volume 128

GALE GROUP

THOMSON LEARNING

Detroit • New York • San Diego • San Francisco
Boston • New Haven, Conn. • Waterville, Maine
London • Munich

STAFF

Library of Congress Catalog Card Number 72-27107

ISBN 0-7876-4716-0
ISSN 0276-816X

Printed in the United States of America

10 9 8 7 6 5 4 3 2 1

Contents

Authors in Forthcoming Volumes vii
Introduction ix
***SATA* Product Advisory Board xi**
Acknowledgments xiii

v

Authors in Forthcoming Volumes

Below are some of the authors and illustrators that will be featured in upcoming volumes of *SATA*. These include new entries on the swiftly rising stars of the field, as well as completely revised and updated entries (indicated with *) on some of the most notable and best-loved creators of books for children.

*Lloyd Alexander: Alexander is widely regarded as a master of twentieth-century children's literature. He is best known for his fantasy fiction and modern fables: imaginative and adventurous stories, often rooted in historical fact and legend, which explore universal themes such as good versus evil and the quest of individuals for self-identity. Among Alexander's best-known works are the five novels which comprise his "Prydain Chronicles"—culminating with *The High King,* which received the Newbery Medal.

Ken Brown: Brown's realistic yet luminous watercolors highlight his own stories for children as well as titles like Stephen Wyllie's *A Flea in the Ear.* Brown's self-illustrated work *Mucky Pup* was shortlisted for the Kate Greenaway Medal and was the winner of the Sheffield Children's Book Award.

Dia Calhoun: Calhoun has produced two award-winning fantasy titles for teens, *Firegold* and *Aria of the Sea,* novels that explore fantastic realms but which are grounded in the universal issues facing adolescents and teens. Both works earned a Best Book for Young Adults citation from the American Library Association.

Deborah Ellis: Canadian author Ellis's political activism has inspired her writings for young adults. Published in early 2001, before the September 11th attack on the World Trade Center and the ensuing war on terrorism conducted by the United States mainly in Afghanistan, *The Breadwinner* provides a child's-eye view of life under the Taliban regime.

*Susan Jeffers: Jeffers is an award-winning illustrator best known for her pen-and-ink drawings. Specializing in outdoor landscapes populated by both humans and animals, she creates most of her work using the cross-hatch method—an intricate process that involves the intersecting of parallel lines. Jeffers primarily illustrates the works of others, although she has adapted a few tales herself, including her Caldecott Honor Book *Three Jovial Huntsmen.*

*Mercer Mayer: Popular children's author Mayer is well-known for his versatility, humor, and artistic skill. Noted as one of the first creators of wordless picture books, Mayer also writes and illustrates nonsense fiction, fantasy, and folktales. He is perhaps best known for his "Little Critter" series.

Darren O'Shaughnessey: London-born author O'Shaughnessey is the creator of "The Saga of Darren Shan" series, written under the pseudonym Darren Shan. The series follows the adventures of a schoolboy who, after a visit to a freak show, reluctantly becomes a vampire's assistant.

John H. Ritter: Ritter has written two award-winning books about sports for young adults. His debut novel, *Choosing up Sides,* was the winner of the prestigious International Reading Association's Children's Book Award as well as an American Library Association Best Book for Young Adults citation.

Esmeralda Santiago: Santiago moved to New York City from Puerto Rico when she was an adolescent. Part of a planned series of memoirs, *When I Was Puerto Rican* and *Almost a Woman* trace her experiences from her childhood home in Puerto Rico to her life in the United States from the age of thirteen and beyond.

*Mildred D. Taylor: In works such as *Roll of Thunder, Hear My Cry* and *Let the Circle be Unbroken,* Taylor shares pride in her racial heritage and provides historical fiction about life for black Americans. Taylor received the Newbery Medal for *Roll of Thunder, Hear My Cry,* and she is a four-time winner of the Coretta Scott King Award.

*William Wegman: An innovative artist, Wegman won critical praise for photographs and videos of his pet dog, a Weimaraner named Man Ray, made between 1970 and 1982. The artist's subsequent work with another Weimaraner, Fay Ray, and her descendants has continued to both move and amuse audiences, such as in his parodies of the classic children's books, *Cinderella* and *Little Red Riding Hood,* and in his alphabet book, *ABC.*

Introduction

Something about the Author (*SATA*) is an ongoing reference series that examines the lives and works of authors and illustrators of books for children. *SATA* includes not only well-known writers and artists but also less prominent individuals whose works are just coming to be recognized. This series is often the only readily available information source on emerging authors and illustrators. You'll find *SATA* informative and entertaining, whether you are a student, a librarian, an English teacher, a parent, or simply an adult who enjoys children's literature.

What's Inside SATA

SATA provides detailed information about authors and illustrators who span the full time range of children's literature, from early figures like John Newbery and L. Frank Baum to contemporary figures like Judy Blume and Richard Peck. Authors in the series represent primarily English-speaking countries, particularly the United States, Canada, and the United Kingdom. Also included, however, are authors from around the world whose works are available in English translation. The writings represented in *SATA* include those created intentionally for children and young adults as well as those written for a general audience and known to interest younger readers. These writings cover the entire spectrum of children's literature, including picture books, humor, folk and fairy tales, animal stories, mystery and adventure, science fiction and fantasy, historical fiction, poetry and nonsense verse, drama, biography, and nonfiction.

Obituaries are also included in *SATA* and are intended not only as death notices but also as concise overviews of people's lives and work. Additionally, each edition features newly revised and updated entries for a selection of *SATA* listees who remain of interest to today's readers and who have been active enough to require extensive revisions of their earlier biographies.

New Autobiography Feature

Beginning with Volume 103, *SATA* features two or more specially commissioned autobiographical essays in each volume. These unique essays, averaging about ten thousand words in length and illustrated with an abundance of personal photos, present an entertaining and informative first-person perspective on the lives and careers of prominent authors and illustrators profiled in *SATA*.

Two Convenient Indexes

In response to suggestions from librarians, *SATA* indexes no longer appear in every volume but are included in alternate (odd-numbered) volumes of the series, beginning with Volume 57.

SATA continues to include two indexes that cumulate with each alternate volume: the Illustrations Index, arranged by the name of the illustrator, gives the number of the volume and page where the illustrator's work appears in the current volume as well as all preceding volumes in the series; the Author Index gives the number of the volume in which a person's biographical sketch, autobiographical essay, or obituary appears in the current volume as well as all preceding volumes in the series.

These indexes also include references to authors and illustrators who appear in Gale's *Yesterday's Authors of Books for Children, Children's Literature Review,* and *Something about the Author Autobiography Series.*

Easy-to-Use Entry Format

Whether you're already familiar with the *SATA* series or just getting acquainted, you will want to be aware of the kind of information that an entry provides. In every *SATA* entry the editors attempt to give as complete a picture of the person's life and work as possible. A typical entry in *SATA* includes the following clearly labeled information sections:

- *PERSONAL:* date and place of birth and death, parents' names and occupations, name of spouse, date of marriage, names of children, educational institutions attended, degrees received, religious and political affiliations, hobbies and other interests.

- *ADDRESSES:* complete home, office, electronic mail, and agent addresses, whenever available.

- *CAREER:* name of employer, position, and dates for each career post; art exhibitions; military service; memberships and offices held in professional and civic organizations.

- *AWARDS, HONORS:* literary and professional awards received.

- *WRITINGS:* title-by-title chronological bibliography of books written and/or illustrated, listed by genre when known; lists of other notable publications, such as plays, screenplays, and periodical contributions.

- *ADAPTATIONS:* a list of films, television programs, plays, CD-ROMs, recordings, and other media presentations that have been adapted from the author's work.

- *WORK IN PROGRESS:* description of projects in progress.

- *SIDELIGHTS:* a biographical portrait of the author or illustrator's development, either directly from the biographee—and often written specifically for the *SATA* entry—or gathered from diaries, letters, interviews, or other published sources.

- *BIOGRAPHICAL AND CRITICAL SOURCES:* cites sources quoted in "Sidelights" along with references for further reading.

- *EXTENSIVE ILLUSTRATIONS:* photographs, movie stills, book illustrations, and other interesting visual materials supplement the text.

How a SATA Entry Is Compiled

A *SATA* entry progresses through a series of steps. If the biographee is living, the *SATA* editors try to secure information directly from him or her through a questionnaire. From the information that the biographee supplies, the editors prepare an entry, filling in any essential missing details with research and/or telephone interviews. If possible, the author or illustrator is sent a copy of the entry to check for accuracy and completeness.

If the biographee is deceased or cannot be reached by questionnaire, the *SATA* editors examine a wide variety of published sources to gather information for an entry. Biographical and bibliographic sources are consulted, as are book reviews, feature articles, published interviews, and material sometimes obtained from the biographee's family, publishers, agent, or other associates.

Entries that have not been verified by the biographees or their representatives are marked with an asterisk (*).

Contact the Editor

We encourage our readers to examine the entire *SATA* series. Please write and tell us if we can make *SATA* even more helpful to you. Give your comments and suggestions to the editor:

BY MAIL: Editor, *Something about the Author,* The Gale Group, 27500 Drake Rd., Farmington Hills, MI 48331-3535.

BY TELEPHONE: (800) 877-GALE

BY FAX: (248) 699-8054

Something about the Author **Product Advisory Board**

The editors of *Something about the Author* are dedicated to maintaining a high standard of excellence by publishing comprehensive, accurate, and highly readable entries on a wide array of writers for children and young adults. In addition to the quality of the content, the editors take pride in the graphic design of the series, which is intended to be orderly yet inviting, allowing readers to utilize the pages of *SATA* easily and with efficiency. Despite the longevity of the *SATA* print series, and the success of its format, we are mindful that the vitality of a literary reference product is dependent on its ability to serve its users over time. As literature, and attitudes about literature, constantly evolve, so do the reference needs of students, teachers, scholars, journalists, researchers, and book club members. To be certain that we continue to keep pace with the expectations of our customers, the editors of *SATA* listen carefully to their comments regarding the value, utility, and quality of the series. Librarians, who have firsthand knowledge of the needs of library users, are a valuable resource for us. The *Something about the Author* Product Advisory Board, made up of school, public, and academic librarians, is a forum to promote focused feedback about *SATA* on a regular basis. The five-member advisory board includes the following individuals, whom the editors wish to thank for sharing their expertise:

- **Eva M. Davis,** Teen Services Librarian, Plymouth District Library, Plymouth, Michigan

- **Joan B. Eisenberg,** Lower School Librarian, Milton Academy, Milton, Massachusetts

- **Francisca Goldsmith,** Teen Services Librarian, Berkeley Public Library, Berkeley, California

- **Monica F. Irlbacher,** Young Adult Librarian, Middletown Thrall Library, Middletown, New York

- **Caryn Sipos,** Librarian—Young Adult Services, King County Library System, Washington

Acknowledgments

Grateful acknowledgment is made to the following publishers, authors, and artists whose works appear in this volume.

APOSTOLOU, CHRISTINE HALE. Hale, Christy, illustrator. From an illustration in *Mama Elizabeti,* by Stephanie Stuve-Bodeen. Lee & Low Books, Inc., 2000. Illustration copyright © 2000 by Christy Hale. Reproduced by permission./ Hale, Christy, illustrator. From an illustration in *Billy and Emma,* by Alice Mead. Farrar, Straus & Giroux, 2000. Illustration copyright © 2000 by Christy Hale. Reproduced by permission of Farrar, Straus & Giroux, LLC.

BELLER, SUSAN PROVOST. Beller, Susan Provost. From a photograph in her *Never Were Men So Brave: The Irish Brigade During the Civil War.* Simon & Schuster, 1998. Photograph courtesy of the Library of Congress. Reproduced by permission of Simon & Schuster Macmillan./ Blyth, Benjamin, illustrator. From a cover of *Woman of Independence: The Life of Abigail Adams,* by Susan Provost Beller. iUniverse.com, 2000. Cover illustration courtesy of Massachusetts Historical Society. Reproduced by permission.

BENEDUCE, ANN KEAY. Homer, Winslow, illustrator. From an illustration in *A Weekend with Winslow Homer,* by Ann Keay Beneduce. Rizzoli, 1996. Painting titled *Fresh Air,* The Brooklyn Museum, Dick S. Ramsay Fund. Reproduced by permission./ Spirin, Gennady, illustrator. From an illustration in *Joy to the World: A Family Christmas Treasury,* by Ann Keay Beneduce. Simon & Schuster, 2000. Illustration copyright (c) 2000 by Gennady Spirin. Reproduced by permission of Atheneum Books for Young Readers, an imprint of Simon & Schuster Children's Publishing Division.

BLACKMAN, MALORIE. Attard, Karl, photographer. From a cover of *Hacker,* by Malorie Blackman. Corgi, 1993. Reproduced by permission of Transworld Publishers, a division of Random House Group Limited./ Attard, Karl, photographer. From a cover of *A.N.T.I.D.O.T.E,* by Malorie Blackman. Corgi, 1997. Reproduced by permission of Transworld Publishers, a division of Random House Group Limited./ Blackman, Malorie. From a cover of her *Dangerous Reality.* Corgi, 2000. Photograph copyright SuperStock Ltd. Reproduced by permission of Transworld Publishers, a division of Random House Group Limited.

BOUMA, PADDY. Bouma, Paddy, illustrator. From an illustration in *Upside-Down Cake,* by Carol Carrick. Clarion Books, 1999. Illustrations copyright (c) 1999 by Paddy Bouma. Reproduced by permission of Houghton Mifflin Company./ Bouma, Paddy, photograph by Raymond Bouma. Reproduced by permission.

BRESLIN, THERESA. All photographs reproduced by permission of Theresa Breslin.

BRISSON, PAT. Barner, Bob, illustrator. From an illustration in *Benny's Pennies,* by Pat Brisson. Bantam Books, 1993. Illustration copyright (c) 1993 by Bob Barner. Reproduced by permission of Bantam Books, a division of Random House, Inc./ Shine, Andrea, illustrator. From an illustration in *The Summer My Father Was Ten,* by Pat Brisson. Boyds Mills Press, 1998. Illustrations (c) 1998 by Andrea Shine. All rights reserved. Reproduced by permission.

BUSH, CATHERINE. Bush, Catherine. From a photograph in her *Ghandi.* Chelsea House, 1985. Photograph by AP/ Wide World Photos. Reproduced by permission./ Bush, Catherine, photograph by Gaspar Tringale. Reproduced by permission of Catherine Bush.

CANNON, JANELL. Cannon, Janell, illustrator. From an illustration in her *Verdi.* Harcourt Brace, 1997. Copyright (c) 1997 by Janell Cannon. Reproduced in the U.K. by permission of Janell Cannon. In the rest of the world by permission of Harcourt, Inc./ Cannon, Janell, photograph. Reproduced by permission of Janell Cannon.

CHENG, ANDREA. Cheng, Andrea, photograph by Tricia Waddell. Reproduced by permission of Lee & Low Books, Inc.

CLIFTON, (THELMA) LUCILLE. Turkle, Brinton, illustrator. From an illustration in *The Boy Who Didn't Believe in Spring,* by Lucille Clifton. Penguin Putnam, 1973. Illustration copyright (c) 1973 by Brinton Turkle. Reproduced by permission of Dutton Children's Books, an imprint of Putnam Books for Young Readers, a division of Penguin Putnam Inc./ Grifalconi, Ann, illustrator. From an illustration in *Everett Anderson's Year,* by Lucille Clifton. Henry Holt, 1974. Illustration copyright © 1974 by Ann Grifalconi. Reproduced by Henry Holt and Company, LLC./ Lewis, E. B., illustrator. From an illustration in *The Times They Used to Be,* by Lucille Clifton. Random House, 2000. Illustration copyright © 2000 by E. B. Lewis. Reproduced by permission of Random House Children's Books, a division of Random House, Inc./ Lucille Clifton, photograph by Chris Felver. Reproduced by permission.

CRISP, MARTA MARIE. Neidigh, Sherry, illustrator. From an illustration in *Black and White,* by Marty Crisp. Rising Moon, 2000. Reproduced by permission./ Crisp, Marty, photograph. Reproduced by permission.

DEMAREST, CHRIS(TOPHER) L(YNN). Demarest, Chris L., illustrator. From an illustration in *When Cows Come Home,* by David L. Harrison. Boyds Mills Press, 1994. Text copyright © 1994 by David L. Harrison. Illustrations copyright © 1994 by Chris L. Demarest. Reproduced by permission./ Demarest, Chris L. From an illustration in his *Firefighters A to Z.* Simon & Schuster, 2000. Copyright © 2000 by Chris L. Demarest. Reproduced by permission of Margaret K. McElderry Books, an imprint of Simon & Schuster Children's Publishing Division./ Demarest, Chris L. (sitting with Judith Ross Enderle and Stephanie Gordon Tessler), photograph. Reproduced by permission of Judith Ross Enderle.

EHLERT, LOIS (JANE). Ehlert, Lois. From an illustration in her *Fish Eyes: A Book You Can Count on.* Harcourt Brace, 1990. Copyright (c) 1990 by Lois Ehlert. Reproduced by permission of Harcourt, Inc./ Ehlert, Lois. From an illustration in her *Nuts to You!* Harcourt, 1993. Copyright (c) 1993 by Lois Ehlert. Reproduced by permission of Harcourt./ Ehlert, Lois. From an illustration in her *Market Day.* Harcourt, 2000. Copyright (c) 2000 by Lois Ehlert. Reproduced by permission of Harcourt, Inc.

ESPELAND, PAMELA (LEE). Espeland, Pamela. From an illustration in *The Kid's Guide to Service Projects: Over 500 Service Ideas for Young People Who Want to Make a Difference,* by Barbara A. Lewis. Edited by Pamela Espeland. Free Spirit, 1995. Reproduced by permission./ Tolbert, Jeff, illustrator. From a cover of *How Rude!: The Teenagers' Guide to Good Manners, Proper Behavior, and Not Grossing People Out,* by Alex J. Packer, Ph.D. Edited by Pamela Espeland. Free Spirit, 1997. Reproduced by permission.

GAMMELL, STEPHEN. Gammell, Stephen, illustrator. From an illustration in *The Wing Shop,* by Elvira Woodruff. Holiday House, 1991. Illustrations copyright (c) 1991 by Stephen Gammell. Reproduced by permission of Holiday House, Inc./ Gammell, Stephen, illustrator. From an illustration in *Old Black Fly,* by Jim Aylesworth. Henry Holt and Company, 1992. Text copyright (c) 1992 by Jim Aylesworth. Illustrations copyright (c) 1992 by Stephen Gammell. All rights reserved. Reproduced by permission of Henry Holt and Company, LLC./ Gammell, Stephen, illustrator. From an illustration in *The Relatives Came,* by Cynthia Rylant. Simon & Schuster, 1993. Illustration copyright (c) 1985 by Stephen Gammell. Reproduced by permission of Simon & Schuster Books for Young Readers, an imprint of Simon & Schuster Children's Publishing Division./ Gammell, Stephen, illustrator. From an illustration in *Monster Mama,* by Liz Rosenberg. Penguin Putnam, 1997. Illustration copyright (c) 1993 by Stephen Gammell. Reproduced by permission of Philomel Books, an imprint of Putnam Books for Young Readers, a division of Penguin Putnam Inc.

GARRITY, LINDA K. Moore, Jackie, illustrator. From a cover of *Fabulous Fables: Using Fables with Children,* by Linda K. Garrity. HarperCollins, 1991. Copyright (c) 1991 by Good Year Books. Reproduced by permission of Pearson Education, Inc.

GELLIS, ROBERTA (LEAH JACOBS). Gellis, Roberta, photograph. Reproduced by permission.

GETZINGER, DONNA. Getzinger, Donna, photograph. Reproduced by permission.

GILBERT, ANNE YVONNE. Gilbert, Anne Yvonne, illustrator. From an illustration in *A Christmas Star Called Hannah,* by Vivian French. Candlewick, 1997. Illustration copyright (c) 1997 by Anne Yvonne Gilbert. Reproduced by permission of the publisher Candlewick Press, Inc., Cambridge, MA, on behalf of Walker Books Ltd., London.

GOOBIE, BETH. Hitch, Jeffrey, illustrator. From a cover of *Mission Impossible,* by Beth Goobie. Red Deer Press, 1994. Reproduced by permission./ Clark, Dan, illustrator. From a cover of *The Dream Where Losers Go,* by Beth Goobie. Roussan Publishers, 1999. Reproduced by permission.

GUTMAN, BILL. Gutman, Bill. From a photograph in his *BMX Racing.* Capstone, 1995. Photograph by Gork/ABA. Reproduced by permission of the photographer./ Gutman, Bill. From a cover of his *Shooting Stars: The Women of Pro Basketball.* Random House, 1998. Copyright © 1998 by Bill Gutman. Reproduced by permission of Alfred A. Knopf Children's Books, a division of Random House, Inc.

HARRIS, TRUDY. Harris, Trudy, photograph. Reproduced by permission.

HAUTMAN, PETE(R MURRAY). Hautman, Pete. From a cover of his *Mr. Was.* Simon & Schuster, 1996. Copyright (c) 1996 by Pete Hautman. Reproduced by permission of Simon & Schuster Books for Young Readers, an imprint of Simon & Schuster Children's Publishing./ McKeveny, Tom, illustrator. From a cover of *Mrs. Million,* by Pete Hautman. Pocket Books, 2000. Reproduced by permission of Pocket Books, a division of Simon & Schuster, Inc./ Hautman, Pete, photograph by Francisco Photography. Reproduced by permission of Pete Hautman.

HICKMAN, PAMELA (M). Stephens, Pat, illustrator. From a cover of *Animal Senses: How Animals See, Hear, Taste, Smell and Feel,* by Pamela Hickman. Kids Can, 1998. Cover illustration copyright (c) 1998 by Pat Stephens. Reproduced by permission of Kids Can Press Ltd, Toronto./ Hickman, Pamela, photograph. The Photo Shop, Rodney Bay, St. Lucia. Reproduced by permission.

ROOS, STEPHEN. Garro, Mark, illustrator. From a cover of *R.L. Stine's Ghosts of Fear Street: The Ooze,* by Stephen Roos. Parachute Press, Inc., 1996. Reproduced by permission of Minstrel Books, an imprint of Simon & Schuster Children's Publishing Division./ Liepke, Peter, photographer. From a cover of *The Gypsies Never Came,* by Stephen Roos. Simon & Schuster, 2001. Reproduced by permission of the photographer./ Roos, Stephen, photograph by David Wolfe. Reproduced by permission.

SCILLIAN, DEVIN. Carroll, Pamela, illustrator. From an illustration in *A is for America,* by Devin Scillian. Sleeping Bear Press, 2001. Illustration copyright © 2001 by Pam Carroll. Reproduced by permission./ Scillian, Devin, photograph. Reproduced by permission.

STEVENS, CHAMBERS. Preston, Karl, photographer. From a cover of *Magnificent Monlogues for Kids,* by Chambers Stevens. Sandcastle, 1999. Reproduced bypermission./Chambers, Stevens, photograph. Reproduced by permission.

STEWART, JENNIFER J(ENKINS). Stewart, Jennifer J., photograph. Reproduced by permission.

STICKLER, SOMA HAN. Stickler, Soma Han, photograph. Reproduced by permission.

TAYLOR, THEODORE. Dietz, James, illustrator. From a cover of *Air Raid—Pearl Harbor!,* by Theodore Taylor. Harcourt, 1991. Illustration copyright (c) 1991 by Harcourt, Inc. Reproduced by permission of Harcourt, Inc./ Taylor, Theodore. From a cover of *Sniper.* Avon Books, 1991. Copyright (c) 1989 by Theodore Taylor. Reproduced by permission of HarperCollins Publishers./ Taylor, Theodore. From a cover of *Tuck Triumphant,* by Theodore Taylor. Avon, 1992. Reproduced by permission of HarperCollins Publishers./ Thompson, John, illustrator. From a jacket of *A Sailor Returns,* by Theodore Taylor. Scholastic, 2001. Illustration copyright (c) 2001 by John Thompson. Reproduced by permission of Scholastic Inc./ Taylor,Theodore, photograph by James Graves. Reproduced by permission of Theodore Taylor.

WHELAN, GLORIA (ANN). Bowman, Leslie, illustrator. From an illustration in *Night of the Full Moon,* by Gloria Whelan. Random House, 1996. Illustration copyright (c) 1993 by Leslie Bowman. Reproduced by permission of Alfred A. Knopf, a division of Random House, Inc.

WITTLINGER, ELLEN. All photographs reproduced by permission of Ellen Wittlinger.

something about the author

ADAMS, Douglas (Noel) 1952-2001

OBITUARY NOTICE—See index for *SATA* sketch: Born March 11, 1952, in Cambridge, England; died May 11, 2001, in Santa Barbara, CA. Editor, businessman, and author. Adams was best known for his "Hitchhiker's Guide to the Galaxy" series. He studied at Cambridge and received a masters degree in English literature. In 1978 Adams began working for the British Broadcasting Corp. (BBC), where he worked as a script editor for the television show *Dr. Who.* It was after the BBC job that he wrote the *Hitchhiker's Guide to the Galaxy,* which was written as a stage production first; book and television versions came subsequently. Adams also wrote *The Meaning of Life* and *Dirk Gently's Holistic Detective Agency.* He was founder of a computer software company called Digital Village. In 1980 he received recognition on the American Library Association's Best Books for Young Adults list. In 1987 Adams received the Golden Pen Award for *Hitchhiker's Guide to the Galaxy.*

OBITUARIES AND OTHER SOURCES:

PERIODICALS

Los Angeles Times, May 13, 2001, p. B12.
New York Times, May 15, 2001, p. A21.
Times (London, England), May 14, 2001.
Washington Post, May 13, 2001, p. C8.

APOSTOLOU, Christine Hale 1955-
(Christy Hale)

Personal

Born January 21, 1955, in Southbridge, MA; daughter of Harold Charles (a mechanical engineer) and Eunice Sherman (a draftsperson) Hale; married Scott Julian Apostolou, August 31, 1991. *Education:* Lewis and Clark College, B.A., 1977, M.A.T., 1980; Pratt Institute, B.F.A., 1986. *Politics:* Democrat. *Religion:* Protestant. *Hobbies and other interests:* Letterpress printing, playing guitar, traveling, and speaking Spanish.

Addresses

Home—1 Second Place, Apt. 2, Brooklyn, NY 11231.

Career

Willamette Middle School, West Linn, OR, art instructor, 1978-84; freelance designer and illustrator, 1986—; E. P. Dutton, New York, NY, art assistant, 1986-87; Aperture, New York, NY, designer, 1987-88; Putnam/Philomel, New York, NY, senior designer, 1987-89; Bradbury Press, New York, NY, interim art director, 1989; Macmillan, New York, NY, interim art director, 1989-90; Four Winds Press, New York, NY, art director, 1990-94.

Christine Hale Apostolou's illustrations enhance Stephanie Stuve-Bodeen's story of a Tanzanian girl who must care for her baby brother and learns that her experience mothering her doll has not prepared her for this challenging job. (From Mama Elizabeti.*)*

Awards, Honors

Award of Excellence, AIGA Cover Show, 1988; two Merit Awards for photo design, 1988-89; first place award, Bookbinder's Guild, 1989, for special trade book; honorable mention, *How* magazine, 1990, for illustration.

Illustrator

UNDER NAME CHRISTY HALE

William Stafford, *How to Hold Your Arms When It Rains,* Confluence Press (Lewiston, ID), 1990.

Felix Pitre, reteller, *Juan Bobo and the Pig,* Lodestar (New York, NY), 1993.

May Swenson, *The Complete Poems to Solve,* Macmillan (New York, NY), 1993.

T. Obinkaram Echewa, *The Ancestor Tree,* Lodestar (New York, NY), 1994.

Felix Pitre, reteller, *Paco and the Witch,* Lodestar (New York, NY), 1995.

Ali Wakefield, *Those Calculating Crows!,* Simon & Schuster (New York, NY), 1996.

Stephanie Stuve-Bodeen, *Elizabeti's Doll,* Lee and Low (New York, NY), 1998.

Stephanie Stuve-Bodeen, *Mama Elizabeti,* Lee and Low (New York, NY), 2000.

Betsy Hearne, *Who's in the Hall? A Mystery in Four Chapters,* Greenwillow (New York, NY), 2000.

Alice Mead, *Billy and Emma,* Farrar, Straus (New York, NY), 2000.

Rosemary Bray McNatt, *Beloved One: The Black Child's Book of Prayer,* Jump at the Sun/Hyperion (New York, NY), 2001.

Eileen Spinelli, *A Safe Place Called Home,* Marshall Cavendish (New York, NY), 2001.

Some of Apostolou's works have been translated into Spanish.

Sidelights

Children's illustrator Christine Hale Apostolou is the contributor of pictures to a dozen books for young readers. Teaming up with author Felix Pitre, the duo created two picture books retelling traditional Puerto Rican folktales, providing "a unique and playful look at the folk heroes of another culture," according to a *Publishers Weekly* critic in a review of *Juan Bobo and the Pig.* This first work shows Juan left to care for the family pig as his mother attends church. Considered a traditional "wise fool" character in Puerto Rican legend, Juan cannot figure out how to quiet the unhappy pig, even after offering it a pork chop and a soda. Finally, Juan realizes what the pig wants, and proceeds to dress it up and send it off to church as well. Several reviewers noted Apostolou's creative use of color. Calling them "brightly colored and vigorous," *Booklist*'s Julie Corsaro found Apostolou's illustrations to have "a fifties, kitschy feeling," while *School Library Journal* contributor Lauren Mayer remarked that the "linoleum block prints are painted in bleached yet vibrant colors, evoking the sun-drenched Caribbean."

In 1995, the illustrator's second effort with Pitre appeared. In a Puerto Rican version of the Rumpelstiltskin tale, *Paco and the Witch* features young Paco who falls under the spell of an old woman. Actually a witch, Paco's captor will not release him until Paco guesses her name correctly. If he cannot figure out her name in time, the witch intends to use the boy as the main ingredient in her stew. According to Puerto Rican folklore, a crab helps the boy discover the witch's name, and to this day, crabs now fear humans, believing they are sent by the old lady to punish them. According to a *Publishers Weekly* contributor, Apostolou's "distinctive, sultry palette of purples, greens and golden browns is immediately recognizable." Other critics noticed the illustrator's ability to capture Pitre's words in pictures, with *School Library Journal* reviewer Maria Redburn observing that the "illustrations are full of color, relating the ever-changing mood of the story."

Working with other writers, Apostolou provided the artwork for two stories by Stephanie Stuve-Bodeen, *Elizabeti's Doll* and *Mama Elizabeti.* In the first book, a young Tanzanian girl wishes to have a doll of her own to care for, just as her mother provides for her new baby brother. Searching for a suitable doll, Elizabeti finds a smooth rock and names it Eva, bathing, diapering, and burping it just like a real baby. When Eva is mistakenly used by Elizabeti's older sister in the cooking fire, the young girl is distraught, but eventually she finds her doll and sings the toy to sleep. Apostolou "deftly captures the story's mood in softly shaded mixed-media illustrations," claimed a *Publishers Weekly* reviewer. Writing in *Booklist,* GraceAnne A. DeCandido commented favorably on Apostolou's use of textiles and paper to create the character's clothing and other fabrics, going on to call *Elizabeti's Doll* "another triumph for the illustrator."

Elizabeti's story continues in *Mama Elizabeti,* "a perfect book for mothers hoping to spend some quality reading time with their daughters," suggested *Black Issues Book Review* critic Khafre Abif. Here Elizabeti must help care for her toddler brother after their mother has another baby. Thinking that she has plenty of experience after taking care of her doll, the young girl discovers that a wiggly boy is much harder to watch than a lifeless rock. After momentarily losing track of her brother Obedi, Elizabeti fears for his safety, but her worries are quickly relieved as he toddles back to her, walking for the first time. Claiming "the illustrations bring this book alive," *School Library Journal* reviewer Martha Topol thought that Apostolou "perfectly captures the spontaneity and totality of a toddler's love."

Apostolou has also provided the illustrations for Betsy Hearne's *Who's in the Hall? A Mystery in Four Chapters,* an "excellent blend of good writing and fine illustration," remarked Marlene Gawron in a *School Library Journal* review. Left temporarily alone by their caregivers in their apartment building, two separate sets of children refuse to let a mysterious character into their homes. When Lizzy plays with twins Rowan and Ryan later in the day, their respective babysitters team up to figure out who this person could be. Eventually they all discover that the strange person knocking on doors is the newly hired janitor trying to fix residents' broken sinks. Describing the book as a "dandy choice for newly independent readers," *Horn Book* contributor Joanna Rudge Long observed that Apostolou's "dynamic cartoon-style illustrations pick up the story's humor" as well as provide a way for readers to keep track of all the characters in the story.

"I have been interested in 'making books' since I can remember," Apostolou once told *SATA.* "I decided at ten to become a writer and illustrator; although, the writer part hasn't happened yet. I entered into book design through letterpress printing, fine print editioning, paper making, and book binding and am just getting started on my illustration career. From the printer's need to make multiples, I have worked mainly in linoleum and woodcut. I have worked with poets on small chapbooks, and this medium (linocut) has allowed me to become the publisher of limited edition books along with several small books of poetry and illustration.

Brilliantly colored illustrations by Apostolou complement Alice Mead's **Billy and Emma,** *the story of a loyal macaw who bravely sets out to find his kidnaped mate.*

"I enjoy the research involved in illustration. My picture books have been set in other cultures with great riches for me to draw from."

Biographical and Critical Sources

PERIODICALS

Black Issues Book Review, July, 2000, Khafre Abif, review of *Mama Elizabeti,* p. 74.

Booklist, June 1, 1993, Carolyn Phelan, review of *The Complete Poems to Solve,* p. 1805; October 15, 1993, Julie Corsaro, review of *Juan Bobo and the Pig,* p. 447; October 1, 1994, Hazel Rochman, review of *The Ancestor Tree,* p. 331; May 15, 1995, Hazel Rochman, review of *Paco and the Witch,* p. 1650; November 15, 1996, Kay Weisman, review of *Those Calculating Crows!,* p. 596; October 1, 1998, Grace-Anne A. DeCandido, review of *Elizabeti's Doll,* p. 336; February 15, 2001, Henrietta M. Smith, review of *Elizabeti's Doll,* p. 1161; October 1, 2001, Carolyn Phelan, review of *A Safe Place Called Home,* p. 330.

Horn Book, May-June, 1993, Nancy Vasilakis, *The Complete Poems to Solve,* p. 341; July, 2000, review of *Mama Elizabeti,* p. 448; November, 2000, Johanna Rudge Long, review of *Who's in the Hall? A Mystery in Four Chapters,* p. 746.

New York Times Book Review, January 15, 1995, review of *The Ancestor Tree,* p. 25; January 21, 2001, De-Raismes Combes, review of *Who's in the Hall?,* p. 25.

Publishers Weekly, July 12, 1993, review of *Juan Bobo and the Pig,* p. 447; May 29, 1995, review of *Paco and the Witch,* p. 84; July 15, 1996, review of *Those Calculating Crows!,* p. 73; August 24, 1998, review of *Elizabeti's Doll,* p. 56; July 3, 2000, review of *Who's in the Hall?,* p. 70.

School Library Journal, May, 1993, Lee Bock, *The Complete Poems to Solve,* p. 122; November, 1993, Lauren Mayer, review of *Juan Bobo and the Pig,* p. 101; February, 1995, Marilyn Iarusso, review of *The Ancestor Tree,* p. 73; August, 1995, Maria Redburn, review of *Paco and the Witch,* p. 137; December, 1996, JoAnn Rees, review of *Those Calculating Crows!,* p. 109; September, 1998, Martha Topol, review of *Elizabeti's Doll,* p. 183; May, 2000, Susan Hepler, review of *Billy and Emma,* p. 150; July, 2000, Martha Topol, review of *Mama Elizabeti,* p. 88; August, 2000, Marlene Gawron, review of *Who's in the Hall?,* p. 156.*

B

BELLER, Susan Provost 1949-

Personal

Born April 7, 1949, in Burlington, VT; daughter of Edward Roland (a machinist) and Lauretta (a nurse; maiden name, Lamothe) Provost; married W. Michael Beller (a program manager), December 18, 1970; children: Michael, Jennifer, Sean. *Education:* Catholic University of America, B.A., 1970; attended University of Maryland School of Library and Information Sciences, 1973-74; University of Vermont, M.Ed., 1990. *Politics:* Independent. *Religion:* Catholic. *Hobbies and other interests:* Reading, traveling to historic places, visiting with grandchildren.

Addresses

Home—187 Stone Wall Lane, Charlotte, VT 05445-9324. *E-mail*—Kidsbks@aol.com or kidsbks@msn.com.

Career

Fairfax City Adult Education, Fairfax, VA, genealogy instructor, 1980-82; Christ the King School, Burlington, VT, librarian, 1982-86; Bristol Elementary School, Bristol, VT, librarian, 1986-93; full-time writer, 1993—. Instructor, University of Vermont, 1993—; created and conducts a hands-on history program for schools; member of teachers' advisory board, Shelburne Museum. *Member:* Society of Children's Book Writers and Illustrators, Author's Guild.

Writings

NONFICTION

Roots for Kids: A Genealogy Guide for Young People, Betterway (White Hall, VA), 1989.
Cadets at War: The True Story of Teenage Heroism at the Battle of New Market, Shoe Tree Press (White Hall, VA), 1991.
Woman of Independence: The Life of Abigail Adams, Shoe Tree Press (White Hall, VA), 1992.

Mosby and His Rangers: Adventures of the Gray Ghost, Betterway (Cincinnati, OH), 1992.
Medical Practices in the Civil War, Betterway (Cincinnati, OH), 1992.
To Hold This Ground: A Desperate Battle at Gettysburg, Margaret K. McElderry Books (New York, NY), 1995.
Never Were Men So Brave: The Irish Brigade During the Civil War, Margaret K. McElderry Books (New York, NY), 1998.
Confederate Ladies of Richmond, Twenty-First Century Books (Brookfield, CT), 1999.
Billy Yank and Johnny Reb: Soldiering in the Civil War, Twenty-First Century Books (Brookfield, CT), 2000.
The Revolutionary War, Benchmark Books (New York, NY), 2001.
American Voices from the Revolutionary War, Benchmark Books (New York, NY), 2002.
American Voices from the Civil War, Benchmark Books (New York, NY), 2002.
Yankee Doodle and the Redcoats: Soldier in the Revolutionary War, illustrated by Larry Day, Twenty-First Century Books (Brookfield, CT), 2003.

Sidelights

A noted author of nonfiction for children, Susan Provost Beller has written several works exploring Revolutionary War and Civil War history. After first penning a book about helping young people with genealogy, several of Beller's early titles cover various aspects of the Civil War, including the role of young soldiers in *Cadets at War: The True Story of Teenage Heroism at the Battle of New Market,* the famous Confederate guerrilla fighter John S. Mosby in *Mosby and His Rangers: Adventures of the Gray Ghost,* and the advancements of medicine in *Medical Practices in the Civil War.* Also among these early works is *Woman of Independence: The Life of Abigail Adams,* an in-depth look at Abigail Adams, the second First Lady of the United States.

Beller continued her research into Civil War history with *To Hold This Ground: A Desperate Battle at Gettysburg,* where she explains one smaller battle within the larger

Beginning with a description of the hardship that drove many Irish to the United States, Susan Provost Beller relates the story of the formation of the Irish Brigade, admired for their courage during the Civil War. (From Never Were Men So Brave.)

one at Gettysburg. Telling the story about the fight over Little Round Top, Beller relates the struggle over the elevated plot of land in chapters alternating between Confederate and Union points of view. *School Library Journal* reviewer Elizabeth M. Reardon found this aspect "particularly valuable because it tells the story of the Confederate brigade, about which little has been written." Throughout the book, Beller uses primary sources to describe the event, leading *Voice of Youth Advocates* critic Lynne B. Hawkins to remark that "the excitement and anxiety of the battle are revealed through the words of the men who fought it." Further complementing the text are photographs, old and new, which add to the quality of the book, claimed Reardon.

Beller uses the actions of a specific ethnic group, the Irish and Irish Americans, in her 1998 work *Never Were Men So Brave: The Irish Brigade During the Civil War.* Here the author lists the exploits of the unit as a whole as well as investigates in more detail the lives of several individuals, including Commander Thomas Francis Meagher, who eventually became the acting governor of the Montana Territory, and Father William Corby, whose inspirational blessings moved both the hearts of Catholics and Protestants alike. According to *School Library Journal* contributor Starr E. Smith, this additional research "never slow[s] the narrative, which is skillfully organized, fast paced, and compelling." Noting the inclusion of "both vintage and modern photographs,

sketches and maps," *Horn Book*'s Elizabeth S. Watson found *Never Were Men So Brave* both "simply and effectively designed."

Turning toward the feminine efforts in the War between the States, Beller looked to investigate the experience of war through the eyes of the women in the Confederate capital of Richmond, Virginia. *Booklist*'s Carolyn Phelan thought *Confederate Ladies of Richmond* provided "an unusual focus on the war," concentrating less on the men who fought in the war and more on the women "who sewed the uniforms, tended the wounded, and went to funerals." Using actual diaries and letters, the author shares with readers how the lives of women in Richmond changed as they lost their loved ones, struggled to provide for their families, and found their once prosperous city in the hands of Union soldiers. Writing in *School Library Journal,* Renee Steinberg called *Confederate Ladies of Richmond* "a useful resource on the period as well as an excellent nonfiction read."

Furthering her nonfiction efforts to make the Civil War an interesting topic for students, Beller relates the life of a common soldier in *Billy Yank and Johnny Reb: Soldiering in the Civil War.* Called "a good choice for showing a soldier's life during this period of history," by Eldon Younce in a *School Library Journal* review, *Billy Yank and Johnny Reb* explains to readers what life was like for fighters on both sides of the Mason-Dixon line. Through soldiers' own journals and letters, the author presents a picture detailing camp life, medical care, and other everyday concerns the men, and a few women, faced. Calling the book "well-documented," *Booklist* critic Carolyn Phelan observed that Beller "presents a good deal of solid information in an interesting manner."

"I consider myself to be mostly a 'teller of stories,'" Beller once told *SATA*, "and I find the true stories from the adventure of history to be the ones I most enjoy telling. I have always been a reader of history. I especially loved to read biographies during my childhood. As an adult, I began reading more of the primary source material of history—diaries and letters and reminiscences by people who were actually involved in a historical event. The stories I found in this reading, especially the ones from the Civil War, were fascinating and much too interesting to be left to just adult readers. So I became a writer of history, in addition to being a reader of it. All I try to do is to take my favorite stories from history and share them with younger readers, using

Through letters written by the second First Lady, Beller presents Adams's views on the formation of the United States and the everyday concerns of colonial women. (Cover painting by Benjamin Blyth.)

the words of the people who were really there as much as possible.

"There are so many great stories from our history that have fascinated me, and I hope to be able to continue to share them with young readers. History, the real stories of real people, is the most fascinating adventure of them all!"

Biographical and Critical Sources

PERIODICALS

Booklist, May 15, 1992, Patricia Braun, review of *Woman of Independence: The Life of Abigail Adams,* p. 1671; February 15, 1998, Randy Meyer, review of *Never Were Men So Brave: The Irish Brigade During the Civil War,* p. 993; December 15, 1999, Carolyn Phelan, review of *Confederate Ladies of Richmond,* p. 779; October 15, 2000, Carolyn Phelan, review of *Billy Yank and Johnny Reb: Soldiering in the Civil War,* p. 432.
Bulletin of the Center for Children's Books, July, 1991, p. 259.
Horn Book, May-June, 1998, Elizabeth S. Watson, review of *Never Were Men So Brave,* p. 354.
New York Times Book Review, November 12, 1995, Richard E. Nicholls, *To Hold This Ground: A Desperate Battle at Gettysburg,* p. 28.
School Library Journal, June, 1991, David A. Lindsey, review of *Cadets at War: The True Story of Teenage Heroism at the Battle of New Market,* p. 129; September, 1992, Valerie Childress, review of *Woman of Independence,* p. 284; December, 1995, Elizabeth M. Reardon, review of *To Hold This Ground,* p. 132; February, 1998, Starr E. Smith, review of *Never Were Men So Brave,* p. 112; January, 2000, Renee Steinberg, review of *Confederate Ladies of Richmond,* p. 138; December, 2000, Eldon Younce, review of *Billy Yank and Johnny Reb,* p. 154.
Voice of Youth Advocates, April, 1996, Lynne B. Hawkins, review of *To Hold This Ground,* p. 46.

*   *   *

BENEDUCE, Ann Keay

Personal

Born in Maplewood, NJ; daughter of Elmer Scofield (a broker) and Winnifred Houghton Keay (an advertising agency chief executive officer); married Sanford Worth (deceased); married Eugene J. Beneduce (divorced); married Joel L. Lebowitz (a mathematical physicist); children: Wendy Worth, Cynthia Beneduce. *Education:* Attended Bryn Mawr College; Barnard College, B.A., 1946; graduate study at Columbia University. *Hobbies and other interests:* Painting, traveling.

Addresses

Home—52 Locust Ln., Princeton, NJ 08540. *E-mail*—lebowitz@phoenix.Princeton.edu.

Career

Freelance author, translator, and editorial consultant on children's literature and illustration. J. P. Lippincott, New York, NY, apprentice and assistant to Eunice Blake, 1960-63; head of the children's book departments at World Publishing Company, 1963-69, T. Y. Crowell, 1969-77, and Collins and World Publishing, 1977-80; founder of imprint and head of children's books at Philomel Books and G. P. Putnam, 1980-86. Member of several committees, including National Advisory Council, U.S. Committee for UNICEF, executive committee of the U.S. chapter of the International Board on Books for Young People (USBBY), the International Relations Committee of the American Library Association (ALA), art jury for the Biennale of Illustration in Bratislava (BIB), and several committees of the Children's Book Council; member of board of directors of U.S. Committee of UNICEF and the Valida Foundation; member of advisory board for various organizations, including Weston Woods Institute and the Eric Carle Museum of Picture Book Art. *Member:* PEN, Authors' Guild, Women's National Book Association, United States Board on Books for Young People, Association for

As if relating a conversation between the artist and a weekend guest, Ann Keay Beneduce discusses the techniques, major works, and artistic formation of the famous American Impressionist painter Winslow Homer. (Homer's Fresh Air, *reproduced in* A Weekend with Winslow Homer.*)*

Library Services for Children of the American Library Association.

Awards, Honors

Plaque d'Honneur, Biennale of Illustration in Bratislava, 1986, for contributions to the field of international publishing; Carey Thomas Award, *Publishers Weekly,* 1986, for creative publishing (innovative books for visually impaired children); honored in 1987 by the Women's National Book Association.

Writings

A Weekend with Winslow Homer, Rizzoli (New York, NY), 1993.

(Reteller and adaptor) Jonathan Swift, *Gulliver's Adventures in Lilliput,* illustrated by Gennady Spirin, Philomel Books (New York, NY), 1993.

(Reteller and adaptor) William Shakespeare, *The Tempest,* illustrated by Gennady Spirin, Philomel Books (New York, NY), 1996.

(Reteller) *Jack and the Beanstalk,* illustrated by Gennady Spirin, Philomel Books (New York, NY), 1999.

(Editor and author of introduction) *Joy to the World: A Family Christmas Treasury,* illustrated by Gennady Spirin, Atheneum (New York, NY), 2000.

(Reteller) Leo Tolstoy, *Philipok,* illustrated by Gennady Spirin, Philomel Books (New York, NY), 2000.

TRANSLATOR FROM THE FRENCH

A Weekend with Picasso, Rizzoli (New York, NY), 1991.

A Weekend with Renoir, Rizzoli (New York, NY), 1991.

A Weekend with Rembrandt, Rizzoli (New York, NY), 1991.

A Weekend with Velazquez, Rizzoli (New York, NY), 1992.

A Weekend with Leonardo da Vinci, Rizzoli (New York, NY), 1993.

A Weekend with Vincent Van Gogh, Rizzoli (New York, NY), 1994.

Agnes S. Holzapfel, *Petit Claude: The Orphan of Auschwitz,* Xlibris (New York, NY), 2001.

Work in Progress

A collection for children tentatively titled *Kamlyl: Tales from the Arctic Circle,* illustrated by Gennady Spirin, for Atheneum (New York, NY); *Exodus* (retold from the Bible), illustrated by Gennady Spirin, for Orchard Books (New York, NY).

Sidelights

Ann Keay Beneduce told *SATA:* "Writing books for young readers might seem a natural thing for a children's book editor to do, yet it took me more than two decades to make this transition. I loved editing and cherished the opportunities it afforded for working creatively with authors and artists. I liked producing books that young people would enjoy and which would also, I hoped, contribute to their intellectual, social, and artistic growth and provide both hope and inspiration. In 1986 I began a second career as an independent consultant in the field of children's books, advising

In this work, Beneduce compiles a collection of stories, carols, poems, plays, and biblical passages centering on familiar symbols of Christmas. (From Joy to the World, *illustrated by Gennady Spirin.)*

publishers on a variety of projects. But I was still an editor: I continued to work editorially with many of the authors and artists I had come to know over the years.

"As I have spent a great deal of time in Paris, I love all things French and so I was delighted when I was asked by an editor at Rizzoli to translate several French art books in an excellent series. Then the same editor invited me to write a book in the series myself—a book about the life and work of the American artist Winslow Homer. Until then, I had never thought of myself as an author, but I liked the subject and I decided to accept the challenge. Having completed my research, I sat down to write—and suddenly felt a rush of pleasure as my protagonist seemed to come to life on my computer screen, telling his own story in his very distinctive voice, showing his art and explaining his methods and goals. At that moment I realized I had moved to the other side of the desk, from my comfortable position as editor to the more precarious perch of the writer."

As Beneduce explained, *A Weekend with Winslow Homer* is part of a series that relates the stories of artists. The story is usually told via first-person conversations between the artist and a guest, and in this particular book Beneduce uses the conversation to relate the evolution, techniques, and major works of Homer, an American Impressionist known for his paintings depicting nature. Reviewing this book for the *School Library Journal,*

Kenneth Marantz remarked that it delivered a "load of information about a major American artist in an appealing manner."

Beneduce continued for *SATA,* "More writing opportunities followed. The brilliant artist Gennady Spirin, newly arrived from Russia, had a contract to illustrate a book for Philomel, but he needed help with the text. Philomel editor Patricia Gauch asked me to do a retelling of the story for him. Spirin and I found we enjoyed working together. His tastes were classical, and I retold such works as Shakespeare's *The Tempest,* and Swift's *Gulliver's Travels* in versions for young readers, as well as Leo Tolstoy's *Philipok,* and other tales. For Atheneum, we collaborated on *Joy to the World: A Family Christmas Treasury.* Then a French author asked me to translate her book—a moving account of the almost miraculous rescue of a Jewish child from a concentration camp; other books are in progress."

Both *Gulliver's Adventures in Lilliput* and *The Tempest* were published to positive reviews. Calling *Gulliver's Adventures* an "intelligent picture book," a reviewer for *Publishers Weekly* noted that Beneduce is able to minimize the political themes of Swift's work without sacrificing his wit and satire. Kathleen Whalin, writing for *School Library Journal,* also noted this challenge. According to Whalin, although Swift's satire has always held appeal for children, adapting his works is a challenge because of the need to balance the original author's "cynical, political voice" with the story of a merry sea adventurer. For _The Tempest,_ Beneduce and Spirin collaborated to retell William Shakespeare's classic play of the same name. Mary M. Burns, writing in _Horn Book,_ noted that Beneduce "has captured the essence of the story," re-phrasing the complex poetry and language of the original into language that will provide a "beguiling" introduction to Shakespeare.

Beneduce collaborated once again with illustrator Gennady Spirin to edit _Joy to the World: A Family Christmas Treasury._ This book is divided into five sections, each associated with a traditional Christmas symbol, such as the star, the manger, the tree, and so on. Selections such as Bible passages, classic carols, as well as traditionally popular stories and poems are included in each section. _Booklist_ critic Carolyn Phelan called _Joy to the World_ a "fine selection" of stories that will be "accessible to a wide age range."

Beneduce concluded her remarks to _SATA:_ "But not all my time is devoted to writing, although all my professional activities are still related to children's books. Recently, for instance, I organized an exhibit of the art and lifestyle of Tasha Tudor, which is being shown in museums in Japan. I work editorially with Eric Carle on some of his projects and am on the advisory board for his planned museum of picture book art. I have always believed that international publishing and exchange of children's books can be strong factors for promoting peace and mutual understanding among nations, and I devote some time and effort to this cause.

"So far, all my published work has been nonfiction: books of information and commentary; translations; classics retold. Will I ever have the urge to write fiction? Maybe, but right now I'm happy in my niche—I love making classics available to children, as well as sharing my own interest in art and literature with them. I think such retellings are valid and even necessary for children as first introductions to great literature and universal themes which they will later explore in more depth. And sharing one's love of literature or of a particular facet of information is part of awakening a child's creativity as well as extending his or her interests. It is impossible to envision running out of subject matter. For example, there is a story that I recently found in medieval French manuscript, the story of a Prince who fell in love with a servant girl, daughter of a captured enemy. Against all odds, these star-crossed lovers married, but unlike Romeo and Juliet, lived happily and long, and reigned wisely as first king and queen of a great country! It has every element of a fairy tale, but it is true! What if I were to translate it into simple English... ? In my mind's eye, I can already see the illustrations."

Biographical and Critical Sources

PERIODICALS

Booklist, March 15, 1994, Stephanie Zvirin, review of _A Weekend with Winslow Homer,_ p. 1377; September, 1, 2000, Carolyn Phelan, review of _Joy to the World: A Family Christmas Treasury,_ p. 128.

Bulletin of the Center for Children's Books, July, 1996, review of _The Tempest,_ p. 386; December, 1999, Janice M. Del Negro, review of _Jack and the Beanstalk,_ pp. 119-120.

Horn Book, May, 1996, Mary M. Burns, review of _The Tempest,_ p. 329.

Kirkus Reviews, October 15, 1993, review of _Gulliver's Adventures in Lilliput,_ p. 1326.

Publishers Weekly, September 13, 1993, review of _Gulliver's Adventures in Lilliput,_ p. 128; November 1, 1999, review of _Jack and the Beanstalk,_ p. 83; September 25, 2000, Elizabeth Devereaux, review of _Joy to the World: A Family Christmas Treasury,_ p. 68.

School Library Journal, October, 1993, Kathleen Whalin, review of _Gulliver's Adventures in Lilliput,_ p. 132; November, 1993, Kenneth Marantz, review of _A Weekend with Winslow Homer,_ p. 113; May, 1996, Sally Margolis, review of _The Tempest,_ p. 126; October, 2000, review of _Joy to the World: A Family Christmas Treasury,_ p. 56.

*   *   *

BLACKMAN, Malorie 1962-

Personal

Born February 8, 1962, in London, England; daughter of Joe (a carpenter) and Ruby (a linen worker); partner of Neil Morrison (a computer programmer). _Education:_ Thames Polytechnic, H.N.C. (computer science; with distinction), 1984. _Religion:_ Christian. _Hobbies and other interests:_ Playing the saxophone, reading, film, theater, listening to music, collecting horror story comics.

Addresses

Home—London, England. _Agent_—Michael Thomas, A. M. Heath Co., 79 St. Martin's Ln., London WC2N 4AA, England.

Career

Reuters, London, England, computer programmer, 1983-85, database manager, 1986-90; Digital Equipment, London, England, software specialist, 1985-86; full-time writer, 1990—. Has volunteered as a reader's helper at local schools.

Awards, Honors

Feminist Book Fortnight Top 20 Title citation (young adult), 1991, for _Not So Stupid!;_ Young Telegraph/ Gimme 5 Children's Book of the Year citation, and Mind Boggling Book Award, W. H. Smith, both 1994, both for _Hacker._

Writings

FOR CHILDREN, UNLESS OTHERWISE NOTED

Not So Stupid! (for young adults), Livewire Books, 1990.
That New Dress!, illustrated by Rhian Nest James, Simon & Schuster (New York, NY), 1991, published as _A_

New Dress for Maya, Gareth Stevens (Milwaukee, WI), 1992.

Girl Wonder and the Terrific Twins, illustrated by Lis Toft, Dutton (New York, NY), 1991.

Elaine, You're a Brat!, illustrated by Doffy Weir, Orchard Books (London, England), 1991.

Girl Wonder's Winter Adventures, Gollancz (London, England), 1992.

Hacker (for young adults), Corgi (London, England), 1992.

Trust Me (for young adults), Livewire Books, 1992.

Operation Gadgetman!, illustrated by Derek Brazell, Corgi (London, England), 1993.

Girl Wonder to the Rescue, Gollancz (London, England), 1994.

Rachel vs. Bonecrusher the Mighty, Longman Education (London, England), 1994.

Rachel and the Difference Thieves, Longman Education (London, England), 1994.

My Friend's a Gris-Quok!, Scholastic (New York, NY), 1994.

Eddie and the Treasure Hunt Rap, Tamarind Press, 1995.

Thief! (for young adults), Corgi (London, England), 1995.

Deadly Dare, Scholastic (New York, NY), 1995.

Whizziwig, Viking (New York, NY), 1995.

Jack Sweettooth, the 73rd, Viking (New York, NY), 1995.

Mrs. Spoon's Family, illustrated by Jan McCafferty, Andersen (London, England), 1995.

The Mellion Moon Mystery ("Puzzle Planet Adventures" series), illustrated by Patrice Aggs, Orchard (London, England), 1996.

The Quasar Quartz Quest ("Puzzle Planet Adventures" series), illustrated by Patrice Aggs, Orchard (London, England), 1996.

A.N.T.I.D.O.T.E. (for young adults), Corgi (London, England), 1996.

Space Race, illustrated by Colin Mier, Corgi (London, England), 1997.

Pig-Heart Boy (for young adults), Corgi (London, England), 1997.

Dangerous Reality (for young adults), Corgi (London, England), 1999.

Dizzy's Walk, illustrated by Pamela Venus, Tamarind Press, 1999.

Whizziwig Returns, illustrated by Stephen Lee, Viking (New York, NY), 1999.

(Reteller) *Aesop's Fables,* illustrated by Patrice Aggs, Scholastic (London, England), 1998.

Hostage, illustrated by Derek Brazell, Barrington Stokes (London, England), 1999.

Marty Monster, illustrated by Kim Harley, Tamarind Press, 1999.

Animal Avengers (graphic novel; part of "Epix" series), illustrated by Stik, Mammoth (London, England), 1999.

Tell Me No Lies (for young adults), Macmillan (London, England), 1999.

"BETSEY BIGGALOW CARIBBEAN STORIES" SERIES

Betsey Biggalow Is Here!, Mammoth (London, England), 1992.

Betsey Biggalow the Detective, Mammoth (London, England), 1992.

Hurricane Betsey, Mammoth (London, England), 1993.

Vicky must hack into a bank's computers to prove her father is not an embezzler in Malorie Blackman's suspenseful novel. (Cover photo by Karl Attard.)

Magic Betsey, illustrated by Lis Toft, Mammoth (London, England), 1994.

Betsey's Birthday Surprise, illustrated by Lis Toft, Mammoth (London, England), 1996.

OTHER

Also contributor of short stories and poems to anthologies. *Trust Me* and *Not So Stupid!* have been translated into Italian; *Trust Me* has also been translated into Danish.

Adaptations

Hacker has been dramatized on British national radio. *Whizziwig Returns* was recorded as an audiobook, 1999.

Sidelights

British author Malorie Blackman's stories for children, ranging from picture books for preschoolers to adventure novels for teen readers, often draw on her own background as an Englishwoman of color who is both an experienced computer programmer and a software specialist. "Part of the reason I started writing children's books," she once told *SATA,* "was because of the dearth of children's books which featured black children as the protagonists. As a child I was an avid reader and read thousands of books, but not *one* featured a black child like me in any manner, shape, or form that I could recognise. I was invisible." Praised by critics for such books as *Pig-Heart Boy, Thief!,* and her "Betsey Biggalow" series, Blackman was hailed by a *Books for Keeps* reviewer for her "instinct for what . . . readers love . . . and the talent to create unputdownable adventures."

Blackman was born in 1962 in London, where her father worked as a carpenter. The author's unique family history has provided her with ample material to draw upon. "My parents were born in Barbados," Blackman

Thirteen-year-old Elliot hacks into the computer network of a radical environmental-protest organization to determine his mother's involvement in a break-in at a pharmaceutical company. (Cover photo by Karl Attard.)

once explained to *SATA.* "I feel this gives me three sources of inspiration to tap into—Britain, Barbados, and Africa." When she was planning her college education, Blackman wanted to be an English teacher. "I wanted that more than anything else in the world," she recalled. "My careers [counselor] told me that she didn't feel she could give me a good reference for the university I wanted to go to because she didn't feel I would pass my English A-Level examination. My reaction was, 'I'll show you, you old cow!'—and I passed!"

Accepted at Thames Polytechnic, she eventually switched majors and received a computer science degree with distinction. Even during a successful career working in the computer field, she knew she still wanted to be involved with young people. "I'd always written stories and poems for myself but it never occurred to me that I could get anything published," Blackman recalled to *SATA.* "I worked in the computing industry for ten years, becoming more and more unhappy because I wanted to write. So I started sending off my stories to publishers. Eighty-two rejection slips later, I finally got my first book accepted for publication." That "first book," destined to change the course of Blackman's career, was *Not So Stupid!* "I decided [at that point] to go for it," she explained, "so I gave up my job as a database manager and have been a full-time writer ever since." Her typical day still begins at nine o'clock, and lasts for eight to ten hours, but "as I love writing so much, it rarely seems like a chore."

Blackman drew on her Caribbean heritage to form the foundation for her "Betsey Biggalow" books, a series of beginning readers that includes *Betsey Biggalow Is Here!, Betsey Biggalow the Detective, Hurricane Betsey,* and *Magic Betsey.* Betsey Biggalow is a spunky six-year-old Caribbean girl who is being raised in a close family with brothers and sisters, loving parents, and her Gran'ma Liz. Each book contains several episodes which convey life in the Caribbean as seen through Betsey's eyes. In *Magic Betsey,* for example, young readers empathize with Betsey's frustration over not being able to run as fast as her friends, and the fear she experiences after getting lost in a busy local marketplace.

The "Betsey Biggalow" books have been highly praised by reviewers for their ability to imbue everyday events with what a *Junior Bookshelf* reviewer termed "much childhood magic." *School Librarian* reviewer Celia Gibbs noted that "the dialogue and pace are excellent" and added that the "cheerful atmosphere" is one that "many children will enjoy." In *Books for Keeps* an equally pleased critic called Blackman's "Betsey Biggalow" tales "a delight—the books look enticing and the stories are fun, moving and very real."

In addition to easy-readers, Blackman has authored a number of picture books geared toward young children of color. In *Dizzy's Walk* a young boy and his dad are shooed out of the house by Mom and told to walk the family dog. Their trip starts quietly enough but soon escalates into an adventure when the mischievous Dizzy stirs up all sorts of innocent trouble. Called a "funny, engaging story" by a *Books for Keeps* reviewer and featuring humorous illustrations by artist Kim Harley, *Marty Monster* is the story of an imaginative young boy who dreams up all sorts of monsters living in his home on the trip upstairs to fetch his dad for dinner. And in *Mrs. Spoon's Family,* illustrator Jan McCafferty brings to life Blackman's story of a cat, a dog, and an old woman whose peaceful existence is threatened by a battle between rival gangs: the cats against the dogs. Praising the "straightforward storyline, vernacular banter and engaging humour" in Blackman's tale, *School Librarian* reviewer Catriona Nicholson noted that *Mrs. Spoon's Family* contains a worthwhile message about tolerance and friendship.

Among Blackman's favorite books as a reader are "thrillers, adventure stories, mystery stories, humorous stories," so it is no surprise that those are the kinds of stories she writes for teen readers. One of her most successful books, *Hacker,* draws on her experience with computers, as its young protagonist uses her knowledge of computer language to help her solve a mystery. Similar in theme but written for younger readers, *A.N.T.I.D.O.T.E.* finds thirteen-year-old Elliot Gaines worried about his secretary mother's involvement in Action Now Thwarts Immoral Destruction of the Environment, a radical environmental protest organization. His concern deepens after she is caught breaking into a pharmaceutical company and subsequently disappears. Cracking the password on his mother's computer and hacking into A.N.T.I.D.O.T.E.'s database help Elliot sort out the puzzle and determine who to trust to help him find his mother. A *Books for Keeps* contributor called the novel "reminiscent of a TV spy-thriller in pace and style." While noting that Blackman includes a good amount of computerese in her story, a *Junior Bookshelf* reviewer believed it would not deter readers of "a long good read" full of "scares and disappointments in a racy atmosphere."

At the start of Blackman's *Dangerous Reality* Dominic's life seems perfect: His mom is a famous inventor of a robot used in dangerous situations, and he is about to get a new stepdad. Then, suddenly, everything falls apart when the robot breaks down and his mom is suspected as a saboteur. It is soon up to Dominic to put his own computer knowledge to use to save his mom and solve the mystery. This novel was hailed by a *Books for Keeps* critic as "another fast-moving computer-based adventure" from the "highly regarded" Blackman.

Like *Hacker,* Blackman's 1995 novel *Thief!* features a young female protagonist, but in this book the mystery involves human emotions rather than computers. The new girl in a rural Yorkshire school, London-born Lydia soon finds herself the target of someone's animosity when she is framed for stealing the school sports trophy. In an effort to escape her troubles, Lydia runs away onto the moors. She takes shelter during a violent storm, only to find herself suddenly in the year 2032 with England now a police state ruled by an evil tyrant. With her school crime now over forty years in the past and her fellow students now in their fifties, twelve-year-old

In Blackman's thriller, Dominic employs his computer skills to save his mother, a scientist, when the robot she designs becomes dangerous.

Lydia attempts to find a way to change the past to avoid this unpleasant future. Praising the novel as unique and "spellbinding," as well as a "narrative of continuous interest," a *Junior Bookshelf* contributor added that *Thief!* "must surely establish Malorie Blackman as one of today's outstandingly imaginative and convincing writers." Vivienne Grant added her praise for the work in *School Librarian,* calling *Thief!* a "gripping and fast-moving" work of fiction that "deals successfully with issues of betrayal, honesty, friendship and hate."

Other novels by Blackman that explore sensitive issues confronting young people include *Tell Me No Lies,* in which a girl named Gemma turns the pain and anger she feels into hateful acts that hurt another. Called "an absorbing and moving thriller" by a *Books for Keeps* contributor, the novel takes a compassionate stance toward both the hurtful Gemma and her victim, a boy named Mike whom she viciously bullies, by allowing both young people to take turns narrating their story. Harassment of a different sort is the focus of *Pig-Heart*

Boy, as a young teen suffering from heart disease is offered the chance to prolong his life through the implantation of a genetically re-engineered pig's heart when no human hearts can be found. While considering the controversial procedure and its many risks, the young man and his family are hounded by both tenacious reporters and a group of angry animal rights activists. In *School Librarian* contributor Diane Southcombe praised Blackman for forcing readers, through her "clear, unequivocal writing," to think about what they would do in such a difficult situation. Calling the novel "unflinching" in its consideration of right and wrong, Amanda Craig added in a review for *New Statesman* that Blackman's "writing is brisk" and she possesses "a sharp ear for the way this age-group talks."

Whether in picture books or in her more mature novels for teens, Blackman continues to write, in her words, "for the child in myself." As she told *SATA,* "The biggest thrill for me is receiving a letter from a child who has enjoyed one of my books. For me that's what it's all about; that's why I'm doing it." Her advice to aspiring writers: "DON'T GIVE UP! And if writing is really what you want to do, then don't let anyone else tell you that you can't do it. GO FOR IT! Only you know what you're really capable of—and you might even surprise yourself!"

Biographical and Critical Sources

PERIODICALS

Booklist, September 1, 1993, Ouraysh Ali, review of *Girl Wonder and the Terrific Twins,* pp. 59-60.

Books for Keeps, March, 1994, p. 5; May, 1995, review of *Operation Gadgetman!,* p. 11; January, 1996, review of *Deadly Dare,* p. 12; March, 1996, review of *Thief!,* p. 11; May, 1997, review of *Magic Betsey,* p. 22; May, 1997, review of *A.N.T.I.D.O.T.E.,* p. 24; May, 1999, review of *Dangerous Reality,* p. 28; July, 1999, review of *Marty Monster,* p. 20; November, 1999, review of *Animal Avengers,* p. 27; November, 1999, review of *Tell Me No Lies,* p. 29.

Bulletin of the Center for Children's Books, March, 1993, pp. 205-206.

Growing Point, September, 1991, p. 5587.

Junior Bookshelf, April, 1994, p. 63; April, 1995, review of *Thief!,* p. 76; June, 1996, review of *A.N.T.I.D.O.T.E.,* p. 116; August, 1996, review of *Betsey's Birthday Surprise,* p. 145.

New Statesman, December 5, 1997, Amanda Craig, review of *Pig-Heart Boy,* p. 64.

School Librarian, February, 1992, p. 19; August, 1992, p. 100; August, 1995, Vivienne Grand, review of *Thief!,* p. 116; May, 1996, Catriona Nicholson, review of *Mrs. Spoon's Family,* p. 56; August, 1996, Janice Weir, review of *A.N.T.I.D.O.T.E.;* August, 1996, Celia Gibbs, review of *Betsey's Birthday Surprise,* p. 104; February, 1997, Sybil Hannavy, reviews of *The Quasar Quartz Quest* and *The Mellion Moon Mystery,* p. 23; November, 1997, Marie Imeson, review of *Space Race,* p. 190; summer, 1998, Diane Southcombe, review of *Pig-Heart Boy,* p. 99; spring, 1999, Sarah McNicol, review of *Aesop's Fables,* p. 22;

autumn, 1999, Rachel Ayers-Nelson, review of *Tell Me No Lies,* p. 154.*

*   *   *

BOUMA, Paddy 1947-
(Paddy Bouma Niehaus)

Personal

Surname is pronounced "*Bow*-ma"; born April 18, 1947, in Cape Town, South Africa; daughter of Hermanus Johannes (a businessman) and Gwendoline Ivy Celliers (a homemaker) Niehaus; married Jan Raymond Dirk Bouma (an architect), February 21, 1970; children: Nicholas, Catherine. *Education:* University of Cape Town, B.A. (fine arts), 1967; attended École des Beaux-Arts (Paris, France), 1968-69. *Politics:* Democratic Party. *Religion:* Catholic. *Hobbies and other interests:* Landscape gardening, farming.

Addresses

Home—Waterhof Farm, P.O. Box 116, Stellenbosch 7599, South Africa. *Office*—Department of Fine Art, University of Stellenbosch, Victoria St., Stellenbosch 7600, South Africa. *E-mail*—bouma@mweb.co.za.

Career

University of Stellenbosch, Stellenbosch, South Africa, lecturer in lithography and illustration, 1971—. *Member:* Writers and Illustrators Group, South African Children's Book Forum.

Awards, Honors

McIver scholarship, University of Cape Town, 1969; Bursary student of the French government, 1968-69; Kate Greenaway Medal commendation, Library Association (England), 1986, for *Are We Nearly There?*

Writings

SELF-ILLUSTRATED

Nicolaas en die Bere, Qualitas, 1983.

A Knock on the Door, Qualitas, 1984.

Bertie at the Dentist's, Bodley Head (London, England), 1987.

Bertie Visits Granny, Bodley Head (London, England), 1987.

Bertie and the Hamsters, Bodley Head (London, England), 1988.

Bertie in the Bag, Bodley Head (London, England), 1988.

Gideon's Game, Methuen (London, England), 1991.

ILLUSTRATOR

Anna S. du Raan, *Hector Berlioz,* Albertyn, 1969.

Hester Heese, *Op die vensterbank in April,* Qualitas, 1983.

Louis Baum, *Are We Nearly There?,* Bodley Head (London, England), 1986, published as *One More Time,* Morrow (New York, NY), 1986.

One Dark, Dark Night, The Little Library, 1993.

must stay with her grandmother, a kind-hearted woman who watches the child during the day. Only temporarily distracted by baking a batch of Valentine Day's cookies, Heather decides to go with her grandmother to check on the newborn lambs. Cold and near death, one of the little lambs needs immediate care, an activity that keeps Heather occupied until her mother returns. "Accompanied by soft pastel watercolors that adequately reflect the text," wrote Janice M. Del Negro in *Booklist,* "this is a simple, reassuring story." Describing *Valentine* as "a very successful effort that children will relate to and enjoy," *School Library Journal* critic Lee Bock observed that Bouma's illustrations "blend well with the text."

On her working habits, Bouma told *SATA:* "I lecture part-time at the University of Stellenbosch. On days when I am not teaching, I can be found in my attic studio at home. I try to keep office hours, whether I feel like it or not. Once I have settled into the rhythm of working, I find myself enjoying it. We live on a small farm in an area of exceptional natural beauty and going down to organize details of the farm work (we grow lemons) provides a welcome break.

A nine-year-old boy loses his father to cancer in Carol Carrick's **Upside-Down Cake,** *a reassuring tale enhanced with soft illustrations by Bouma.*

"Writers and illustrators who have influenced me? Lewis Carroll was the formative influence of my childhood. I loved the humor and the sense of being turned loose in a world which was all the more intriguing for being so incomprehensibly Victorian! Maurice Sendak, Beatrix Potter, Ron Brooks, Helen Oxenbury, and John Burningham, among many others, influenced me as an adult.

"My books have been translated into Danish, Afrikaans, French for Francophone Africa, and a multitude of African languages, including Zulu and Swahili. I believe the latest book I illustrated is to appear in Korean shortly.

"Currently, I have become very interested in writing comics and graphic novels for a more adult audience. These have an autobiographical or socio-political content. I am also working on an even more ambitious project—a book on human evolution for young adults.

"What do I hope to achieve through the books I write and illustrate? Besides the pleasure gained from something well-made, I hope to make a difference to someone. To share and affirm, perhaps to offer a new perspective, to enable someone to say, 'This confirms what I have always sensed, but could not have put into words.' All my life, books have been my friends and mentors. I hope to be able to give back something of what I have received."

Biographical and Critical Sources

BOOKS

Louis Baum, *Are We Nearly There?,* Bodley Head (London, England), 1986, published as *One More Time,* Morrow (New York, NY), 1986.

PERIODICALS

Booklist, April 1, 1995, Janice M. Del Negro, review of *Valentine,* p. 1422.
Books for Keeps, June, 1987, Helen Pain, "Carnegie and Greenaway: The 1986 Winners," p. 11.
Junior Bookshelf, December, 1988, Marcus Crouch, review of *Bertie in the Bag* and others, pp. 278-279; February, 1992, review of *Gideon's Game,* p. 7.
Publishers Weekly, December 12, 1986, review of *One More Time,* p. 51.
School Librarian, February, 1992, Sue Rogers, review of *Gideon's Game,* p. 15.
School Library Journal, June-July, 1987, Cathy Woodward, review of *One More Time,* p. 76; May, 1995, Lee Bock, review of *Valentine,* p. 82.
Spectator, December 5, 1987, Juliet Townsend, "Children's Books," p. 48.

*   *   *

Carol Carrick, *Valentine,* Clarion Books (New York, NY), 1995.

Carol Carrick, *Upside-Down Cake,* Clarion Books (New York, NY), 1999.

OTHER

Also author and illustrator of comics published in *Bitterkomix,* no. 9, 1999, no. 10, 2000, and no. 11, 2001. Bouma's work has been translated into Danish, Afrikaans, French for Francophone Africa, and several African languages, including Zulu and Swahili. Some of Bouma's early work appeared under the name Paddy Bouma Niehaus.

Work in Progress

A picture book on human evolution.

Sidelights

South African children's author and illustrator Paddy Bouma is the creator of several well-received picture books for young readers. However, as she shared with *SATA,* her early, unprofitable, efforts at publishing initially kept her from choosing writing and illustrating as a career. Bouma said, "I was trained as a painter and a printmaker but was always fascinated by anything to do with books or illustration, without any idea how I might access this magical world. My first illustration commission came along out of the blue while I was studying lithography in Paris—it was for a South African publisher. It proved, however, to be such hard work, so poorly paid and so badly printed that I decided not to be an illustrator after all! It was only years later, when my first child began taking an interest in books that I began to think seriously about doing a book of my own. My early books were based on experiences around bringing up my two children."

As she returned to illustrating children's books in the 1980s, Bouma teamed up with author Louis Baum in the 1986 work *Are We Nearly There?,* published in the United States as *One More Time.* A young boy and his father set out on an event-filled afternoon in the park. Throughout the story, young Simon keeps asking his father to do everything "one more time." Only at the end of the story, as Simon leaves his father and returns to his mother's house, does the reader come to understand that Simon's parents are divorced. According to a *Publishers Weekly* critic, "the phrase 'one more time' takes on new significance as we consider the meaning it holds for both father and son." *School Library Journal* contributor Cathy Woodward remarked upon Bouma's ability to capture a wide range of emotions in her illustrations, saying "a delicately watercolored yet richly shaded panorama of scenes of father and son embellish the tender but dynamic relationship."

One year later, the first of Bouma's self-illustrated books about a stuffed hippo named Bertie and his owner, Thomas, appeared. Though he is lovable, Bertie's inquisitiveness often causes much embarrassment for Thomas. The two take a trip to the dentist in *Bertie at the Dentist's,* while in *Bertie Visits Granny,* the duo

Paddy Bouma

cause trouble in Granny's antique shop. Reviewing both books for *Spectator,* Juliet Townsend noted that "there is plenty to look at in the clear detailed illustrations." *Bertie in the Bag* features young Thomas as he decides to bring Bertie along with him for his first day at a new school. Initially, Thomas feels out of place in the new building, but after a few of Bertie's mishaps, the young boy begins to feel at home. "The soft colours and the naturalistic drawings catch the mood and communicate the fun without exaggeration," claimed *Junior Bookshelf* reviewer Marcus Crouch.

Bouma selected a South African black township setting for her 1991 work *Gideon's Game.* Left in the charge of their next-door neighbor, siblings Miranda and Gideon cannot agree on a game to play. Miranda wants to play hospital, but Gideon does not and, after a brief quarrel, retreats to his bedroom instead. While there, however, the young boy sees a picture of a train and becomes inspired to create a game of his very own. Using items from the house and yard, Gideon begins to assemble a pretend locomotive. Seeing the fun her brother is having, Miranda forgets their earlier squabble and soon joins the game of make-believe. Calling *Gideon's Game* "a simple but effective picture book," *School Librarian* critic Sue Rogers described the illustrations as "large, colourful and appealing."

Little Heather cannot understand why her mother must go to work in Bouma's 1995 title *Valentine.* Heather wishes her mother would stay at home, but instead she

Autobiography Feature

Theresa Breslin

BACKGROUND

I was born in Central Scotland in a small town called Kirkintilloch. The town is located close to Glasgow on the road to Stirling, gateway town to the Highlands and not too far from Edinburgh, the capital of Scotland. Historically the site is a very strategic position, a crossroads of civilisation going back beyond the time of the Roman Empire. The name of the town, Kirkintilloch *(Caer-pen-taloch)* means the fort at the end of the ridge. In the Peel Park in the centre of the town there are the remains of the base of the Roman Wall in Scotland, and when standing at the highest point in the Peel Park one has a tremendous vista towards the hills and overlooking the valley of the River Kelvin. Sunsets viewed from here are breathtaking. It is accepted that this was the site of one of the forts on the Antonine Wall, the boundary wall of the furthest northern territories of the Roman Empire, built in the time of the Emperor Antoninus Pius. The garrison here was one of the string of forts which girdled the waist of Scotland stretching from the River Forth in the east to the River Clyde in the west. Here the mighty Roman Empire sought to defend itself from those they called the barbarians. Some of these were the Caledonian tribes, forerunners of the Scottish clans, and members of the Celtic race. The Celts were great bards and storytellers. It is from them that we have the origins of many of the folk tales and legends which we still tell today, and which are the basis of many modern stories.

It is probably this background of living and growing up in an area suffused in history which has stimulated many of my ideas for stories.

Bullies at School—Chapter 7 has a description of the School Resource Library where the Celtic History Collection is stored. It mentions books on excavation of burial places, books on artwork showing chariots, clothes, jewellery, and collections of tales telling of exciting and mysterious stories of battles, treachery and romance.

I have always found history—local, national and worldwide—a tremendous source of inspiration for stories and have mined it effectively to contribute background and actual incidents for my books.

There is a scene in my first book, *Simon's Challenge,* which illustrates my drawing on specific local history. The main character of the book, Simon, is walking through the town park when he remembers a history lesson from school. His teacher had told the class that their town was

the site of one of the Roman forts on the Antonine Wall which stretched across Scotland from the River Forth in the east to the River Clyde in the west. The Romans had built this wall as a boundary on their mighty Empire to protect their conquered lands of southern Britain from the tribes of Caledonia (Scotland).

Remains of the Roman fort had been found in the park, and the finds had included sandals, pottery, lamps and weapons. Less than a hundred years ago a leather bag with fifty Roman coins in it had been discovered near the bandstand. For days after their teacher told them this piece of news, the park had been infested with boys from Simon's class digging among the flower beds, until eventually the Parks Department had complained to the school and the

Theresa Breslin, 1989

Theresa's parents, Sarah and Thomas Green

Headteacher had forbidden any school pupils to go near the park for a month. However, any time he was in the park Simon always kept a sharp eye out for interesting objects.

Extract from Simon's Challenge—*Chapter 9*

This ancient history also features in *Across the Roman Wall*. The action of this book takes place in Britain in 397 AD, at a time when the power of the Roman Empire is waning. Tribesmen from the North have captured Marinetta, a British girl, and Lucius, the nephew of a Roman official, Titus. They are taken on horseback from the North of England across Hadrian's Wall and through a great wood.

They rode for many miles, until the trees thinned out. Suddenly, in front of them, was a great marshy swamp. In the middle of this were some crannogs, houses built on platforms. The ponies were left tied to the trees as the tribesmen and their prisoners walked across the rough wooden planks to the dwelling places.

'Look,' sneered one of the tribesmen and he pointed northwards to a hill on the horizon.

'There is the wall of Antoninus Pius and your great Roman fort at Cibra. See what remains of it now? Ruins!' He opened a door in what looked like a pigsty and flung them inside.

'Ruffians!' said Lucius, as soon as they were alone. 'That's what they are. All of these Celts are thieves and barbarians living in foul dwellings.'

'Not so,' said Titus. 'These Celtic people have a language and culture of their own. Remember your manners. Marinetta's mother was of this race.'

Lucius's face went red. 'I spoke without thinking,' he admitted.

'As you often do,' his uncle reminded him. 'If you had paid attention to your history lessons then you would know that the great Julius Caesar himself spoke highly of them. Their bards are gifted musicians and storytellers.'

'But Uncle,' protested Lucius, 'they are so undisciplined. Their fighting method has no order.'

*Titus held up his hands which were tied together. '**We** are **their** captives Lucius,' he smiled.*

'Because they don't fight fairly!' protested Lucius. 'They don't follow proper military procedure.'

His uncle laughed out loud. 'Why should they do battle as we do? They fight according to their own rules.'

'And they enjoy it,' said Marinetta. She remembered her mother telling her of the great Celtic warriors, heroes who were honoured. The stories of the wars, with brave and

noble deeds, and then the feasting afterwards which went on for many days and nights.

Extract from Across the Roman Wall—*Chapter 6*

When I read history I find it to be rich with exciting events and peopled with vibrant characters.

My hometown was also the site of the castle given to a loyal subject by the King of Scots, Robert the Bruce, after his success in the Scottish Wars of Independence. I found this fed into my imagination when I wrote *Duncan of Carrick.* In this story the boy Duncan fights alongside Robert the Bruce, helping him keep contact with his people during the struggle to retake the Scottish castles one by one from the occupying force of English soldiers. At the end, King Robert the Bruce gives into the hand of Duncan of Carrick the Declaration of Arbroath, the Scottish claim to Independence. This is the document on which other countries, including the United States of America, have based their own Declaration of Independence.

It is in truth, not for glory, nor riches, nor honour that we fight: but for that which no good man relinquishes but with his life. We fight for freedom—for that alone.

Extract from Duncan of Carrick—*Chapter 14*

EARLY LIFE

My ancestry is Scots and Irish. My father's mother came from County Donegal in the west of Ireland, my mother's father from Waterfoot in County Antrim in Northern Ireland. Both families settled in Scotland before my parents met each other. They chose this area as there was at that time a variety of employment opportunities; canal boat building, coal mining, foundry work, weaving and a clothing mill. It is also a very beautiful place and although I love to travel I cannot imagine living anywhere else. We are tucked in beside the Campsie Hills which protect us from the worst of the weather in the winter and provide a panorama of ever-changing colours throughout the year.

There was certainly a strong Celtic influence at home with family gatherings which involved singing and story-telling. I was almost at the end of a family of six children having one older brother and three older sisters, and one sister my junior by four years. My dad was the caretaker of a large school on the very edge of the town. It took pupils from age four years right through to seventeen years old. Our home was the basement flat of an enormous old house on the school grounds. It had been the original schoolhouse before the "new" school was built. The school property was extensive, with lawns, gardens, playing fields and lots of interesting trees to climb. I particularly remember the trees

School photograph: Theresa is in the second row (third from left) and future husband, Tom, is in the fourth row (third from right)

Theresa (front left, wearing school blazer) with father, brother, and four sisters

as being unusual and beautiful—holly and rowan, willows, monkey-puzzle, oak and chestnut. We also had free run of the school during the holidays and I remember playing in the gymnasium and roller skating in the corridors, which I think were made from granite and sent sparks flying from the wheels of our metal skates. My dad grew an enormous variety of plants and flowers and food—vegetables and fruit and grapes and tomatoes in his greenhouse. The school had lots of cats, and we had budgies and pet mice and a hedgehog and a tortoise. We had five boy cousins who lived in the town and four cousins who visited from England. Beyond the school grounds was open land, the river, the canal, fields and wooded areas. It was a wild free childhood and we cycled and went on picnics and made up little plays which we staged for long-suffering adult relatives.

There were two cinemas in the town, but it was the library where we spent much of our free time. They say that your sense of smell gives your strongest associations. Even now, many years later, the smell of wax floor polish brings back memories of the quiet awe of being in the library, the

lowered tones, the sense of anticipation as to what story might be waiting for me to find on those long shelves. I read all those boarding house books, dreamt I was climbing in the Alps, making gang huts or going on sailing holidays. I was the lost princess of the Chalet School. I knew that soon my real parents would come to claim me and take me away from this rather boring little family and I would be able to claim my rightful place as heir to the throne of Slobonia.

The town library was in an old house situated in the Peel Park. It was established by a local benefactor in memory of his brother, William Patrick. When I went there as a child to borrow books I had no idea that much later in the 1990s, a new civic library would be built on the main street and be named the William Patrick Memorial Library; that it would stock books written by me, and that I would be allocated my own library book classification number. For me this rates on par with a Carnegie Medal!

Our house was full of books and I can now appreciate how much of my parents' income was spent on these. In a tribute to this I wrote a short story called "Notes in the

Margin" (contained in the anthology *Points North*). We also read a variety of journals and magazines, such as the *National Geographic*. In addition to fiction, there were biographies, books on philosophy and music, songs and poetry, folk and fairy tales and traditional ballads. We had an organ and a piano. My father played outdoor bowls on a nearby bowling green. I liked the touch of the smooth turned wood and the sound of the bowls connecting on the flat grass. We seemed to enjoy long hot summers and proper winters when it snowed heavily and we made snowmen and built snow caves.

My grandmother (my father's mother) was very old when she died—ninety-three, but very active until then. She was a little lady who wore mainly black, with perhaps a white blouse or a white lace collar. My father would take us to visit her each week and I always thought it strange that he should call this little lady "Mother." She kept a pile of old brown Victorian pennies (which show the head of Queen Victoria) on her dresser and she would ask each child their age and then count out the same number of pennies.

My father would always protest, saying, "Mother, they have enough. Keep your money for yourself." She would say nothing, and I would hold my breath, and then she would press the pennies into my hand.

She died when I was quite young and at her funeral I had never seen so many people all together in one house. Men and women all in black. The mirror in her house was covered with a lace cloth and candles were lit on either side of the bier as she lay in her coffin.

Granddad, my mother's father, was a tall dignified man with snow white hair, a glorious white moustache and absolutely full of fun. He lived in a room and kitchen with an open fire. He had a bayonet saved from the war with which he split kindling in the hearth. In this tiny house he had a music organ and every year he had a birthday party which all his family attended. They played music, sang songs, told jokes and we were allowed to stay up very late. He visited us often, and we would run home from school each day hoping he would be there to play with us. If we were in the town we would always call in at his house. His door, like his heart, was always open.

Primary School was very strict. Looking back I think it had a restrictive discipline which appeared for the most part to be used to restrain children in order that they would cause the teacher less stress. The Secondary School Department was much more encouraging for pupils. It drew children from right across the central belt of Scotland and was a great mix of urban and rural youth. We had an inspired English teacher, Mr. Kearns, who produced a school magazine, encouraged creative writing, organised theatre trips and opened up our appreciation of literature. A wide range of subjects were taught, including Latin, modern languages, the sciences, history, classics, and it helped foster a love of language and literature which has never left me.

For one year, when I was about nine or ten years old, we had a wonderful teacher called Miss Docherty. She was kind and encouraging and everything a good teacher should be. In my class at that time, although I can't say that I noticed him particularly, was a boy called Tom Breslin . . .

Tom and I were in the same class in upper Primary and also for most subjects in Secondary school. I can't say that I really noticed him much in Primary school apart from the fact that he was usually top of the class, and I certainly wasn't! In secondary school we had this amazing class as part of physical education. It was called "social dancing" and pupils were taught exactly what it says—how to dance socially. There was a strong emphasis on Scottish country dancing and although I am not the most coordinated person, I am now glad that I know the traditional dances of my country. The good thing about many of the Scottish dances is that they do not require a partner. A lot of them involve a group of people and can be (is!) an excuse to play act etc. I suppose when the classes in "social dance" began I took interest in boys in general, and Tom in particular. But it wasn't until we were in fifth year at secondary school (we would be about sixteen or seventeen years old) when we were returning from representing our school in a debating competition that Tom asked me out. We saw each other regularly after that and found that we shared some common interests. We don't have all the same likes and dislikes. Tom loves sport, whereas I prefer reading. We like music but not always the same kind. However, both of us do have a great liking for travel and the theatre.

STUDENT DAYS

I left Secondary School and drifted for a bit. I was working in a café when a friend came in one day and said, "The Mitchell Library is looking for staff. You like books. Why don't you work there?"

So I went to work for Glasgow Public Libraries. The Mitchell Library in Glasgow is the largest public reference

Author while attending University of Aston

library in Europe. It has a fabulous collection of books and archive material. At that time it was mainly closed access and staff had to retrieve books for readers via a warren of corridors which led to basements and different floors. One way of doing this involved staff running up and down the famous metal spiral staircase, later removed as a fire hazard. I had only been there a matter of days when I knew that this is what I wanted to do for the rest of my life—work in libraries. I decided I would be a librarian. Off I went to Birmingham to take the course that would eventually lead to my Charter in Librarianship. I chose Birmingham partly because my aunt was there, but also because it was far enough away from home to prevent me travelling home each night. There is no strong tradition in Scotland for young people to leave home to go to university or college. More often they remain at home while in tertiary education. But I wanted some freedom.

It was the end of the '60s, and my parents were concerned about the effect all that hippie culture might be having on their children. Me, I wanted as much of it as I could absorb. So I hoped to be far away from too much parental input. It was a massive culture shock for me. This was the late sixties. Birmingham was the second city of swinging Britain. I had come from a small town with old-fashioned drapers' shops. Not so long ago coal had been transported along the main street in drays drawn by huge Clydesdale horses. I was now plunged into a world of discos, nightclubs, flashing lights, and boutique style shops with mirrored floors. It was an experience! However I was made welcome by a friendly aunt who gave me a room so that I would not feel too homesick and I made friends whom I still have to this day. My aunt and cousins looked after me well. But I found that I was homesick and missed my town and family and one person in particular . . . Tom.

WORKING DAYS

Eventually I returned to work in the Glasgow libraries. At this time life in the libraries was very formal. Staff addressed each other by second name prefixed by Mr./Miss/Mrs. There was a rigid job division progressing up the ranks with tasks allocated to suit. In branch libraries staff were numbered 1, 2, 3, etc.

MARRIED LIFE

Tom and I got married, and soon after I left work to bring up our four children. Tom went into teaching, became Physics Department Head and eventually a Secondary School Head Teacher. I enjoyed those early years at home with my children and got a lot of life experience looking after them. Far from being non-productive, I felt that my organisational skills were honed to perfection. Anyone who can decorate, shop, clean, cook, wash, clothe, nurse, comfort, counsel, check homework, polish shoes, launder, iron, remember who requires P.E. kit, lunch and/or school trip money on which day is fit to do almost anything else!

RETURNING TO WORK

When the children got to school age, I applied for a job with my local library service—Strathkelvin District

public library service. When I returned to work in the public library service I found lots of things had changed—mostly for the better. Staff on all levels were on first name terms, the working rotas and shift hours were less destructive of family life, and there was a greater emphasis on customer service. More time was devoted to outreach projects and schemes for promoting literature and literacy. There was a firm commitment to encouraging readers, as opposed to the early regimes of preserving our precious books locked up in ivory towers away from grubby hands.

My first promoted post was mobile librarian for the District Library Service. For me, being a librarian was my dream job. I could read books, buy books, promote books—and get paid for doing it! I loved working on the Mobile Service. This was the late 1980s and our mobile libraries were not the streamlined super vans with all facilities that exist now. It was the days before computerisation and mobile telephones. So in effect once the van was loaded up in the morning and we set out on our run, we were free! Untraceable. It was fantastic! No air conditioning meant that we sweltered in summer and froze in winter. Despite this I really enjoyed going around the countryside visiting towns, villages, farms and smallholdings in our book bus with Gavin, legendary driver and wise and generous friend. We brewed our tea in an old kettle on top of a gas ring, with an open gas flame, which rested on the engine casing! We delivered books to the housebound individual and to nursing homes. We stopped at the cattery, and at schools, in hamlets, ex-mining villages and in housing estates. And the names of these are a roll call of communities and friends: Baldernock, Bardowie Loch, Twechar, Harestanes, Waterside. The role of the mobile librarian is unique, occupying a position of trust and privilege, bonding with readers in a very personal way. I often think that local government misses the most amazing opportunity if they do not nurture and support their library services. The library is the one place that people come with their problems, their hopes, their aspirations, their troubles and their worries. They look for information, education and relaxation, and ideally receive encouragement, support, impartial advice and sympathetic non-judgmental help.

WRITING

One of our mobile stops was the village of Gartcosh, just outside Glasgow. Still enough of a village to have dairy herd grazing in fields near the main street but with a huge steel mill on the outskirts. A cold rolling mill, it was a vital link in the production of steel for home use and export. It was placed away from main centres of industry but next to the canal for water supply and close to road links. Lorries came and left, travelling to Germany and Italy, carrying steel for refrigerators and washing machines. The drivers would stop at the local shop (as we did) for a bacon butty or chips on a piece. (I guess that translates as BLT or a sandwich with french fries.) At this time children from the Gartcosh Primary School were working on a local history project and the Library Department produced their work in book form. It was done with care and attention and, among other things, detailed the life of the steel works and its contribution to the area. Particularly interesting was the fact that during the Second World War these children's grandmothers had worked there when their menfolk were

Theresa and Tome with their children at the Fidler Award Ceremony

called up. They had maintained the steel production as this steel was being used for armaments. They were very frightened when in the 1940s, the German bombing raids began on Britain. Some of them recalled running to hide under tables when they heard the Luftwaffe planes passing overhead during the Clydebank Blitz of 1941. Hiding under a table does sound a little inadequate when one considers the size of a parachute bomb. However they did survive until ...

In the late 1980s the news broke that the steel mill was to be closed down. This was a major source of income for the area and the effect was devastating. This event coincided with the starting of a local writers group. I went along to this with my sister and attended a series of lectures by a wonderful writer called Margaret Thomson Davis. We then submitted work for her mini-competition and at the final lecture she would announce the prizewinner. On the evening in question Margaret held up a paper. I recognised my own writing.

"This is NOT the way to submit a manuscript," she declared.

My spirits dropped.

"And this manuscript has a lot of faults," she went on.

My spirits sank lower.

"But ... " She paused. "This person is a storyteller."

It was the first occasion that anyone had used that word about me, and it had a magical effect.

Storyteller.

Seanchaidh (Gaelic).

I did not think anything of it at the time and no one commented on this, but much later I realised that the hero of my very first story is a child. I had instinctively written a children's story.

The writers group was great fun and very supportive and I began to think. Could I actually do this? Be a writer?

Would-be writers are sometimes given advice along the lines of ... "Write about something you know." I would suggest that you write about something you care about. Writing is about emotion, about feelings. You might be travelling on the train and see someone reading a book. Suddenly they laugh out loud. You want to know the title of that book. You want to share that feeling.

I realised that there was something I cared about. Something that had happened, not directly to me, but to those I cared about. Gartcosh steel mill had been closed down. The workers had marched to London to protest, like the hunger marches of the 1930s years of the Great Depression. But ... no one had listened. The workers and their supporters had written to the newspapers with little effect. It suddenly struck me that at least they had a voice. Adults have ways of making themselves heard. But what about the children? Who spoke for the children? Weren't they too feeling the effects of this recession? Didn't their parents' redundancy have an effect on them, their home life, social life, school life? Had it been explained to them? Were any of them feeling the way that children often do when things go wrong in their life? Is this my fault? Was it something I did or said? If I had behaved better would this not have happened? And my progression of thought from there was—could I write about this from a child's point of view?

As I began to write my story it also occurred to me that my own children were reading those same books that I had read so long ago. Wonderful as they were these stories were set in a different culture with little to do with Scotland. Where were my children's school days, their jokes, their concerns, their life? It suddenly struck me that, as a child, I had not existed within the pages of a book. I now saw how reading fiction could validate experience, give a person a sense of identity, promote pride in your heritage and culture. I determined to do this with this book, set it in a modern day Scotland reflecting my own children, their friends, their life.

It became the book *Simon's Challenge.* I showed it to some friends at the writers group and received direct constructive criticism, and the best exhortation any new

aspiring writer can get—"FINISH it and send it away." I did both, sending it to Scottish Book Trust who administered a special award for new writing for children. Months later I was at home and had completely forgotten about my manuscript. The telephone rang. My children were playing, very loudly, I remember, and I yelled, "Be quiet!" as I snatched up the telephone.

I didn't follow the first part of the conversation, but when I realised that it was the Director of Book Trust and she was asking me for my address I thought . . . oh dear, they've lost the address and now need it to return my manuscript. I said my address, having to raise my noise over the bedlam in the background.

"Just checking that I've got the right person," was the reply. "You've won the Book Trust's Kathleen Fidler Award for new writing for young people. There is a cash prize and your book will be published next year. We'll be in touch later with the details."

At the award ceremony established writers such as Anne Fine, Joan Lingard and Terence Dicks congratulated me. I found this tremendously encouraging.

At the ceremony I was asked to do a reading. . .

I asked the question—What was Simon's challenge?

I selected an extract from the book where Simon is in class with his friends being a taught by his teacher Mrs. Davies. The town has just received the news that their local steel mill is to close down. Mrs. Davies reads out the

Theresa Breslin in back row (third from left) with other authors at Carnegie Greenaway shortlist party, 1995

newspaper headline, which states that the workers are to be made redundant, and then she addresses the class.

> *'Pay attention, please, everybody. Simon, would you go and look up this word in the dictionary.'*
>
> *Mrs. Davies walked over to the blackboard and chalked up the word "redundant" in large letters.*
>
> *'Now class. PAY ATTENTION!'*
>
> *Everyone turned around at once. Mrs. Davies seldom shouted.*
>
> *'I have something to tell you and I want you to listen carefully. Last night on the national news it was announced that our Steelworks will close down. I know that you all have relatives who work there, and there is a difficult time ahead. The closure will affect this whole community drastically. Now I am not going to discuss the rights or wrongs of that decision, but there is one thing I would like to say. Simon, please read out the definition of the word which is on the blackboard.'*
>
> *'Redundant,' Simon read out, 'surplus to requirements, unnecessary, or superfluous.'*
>
> *'Thank you, Simon. Go and sit down.' Mrs. Davies turned and pointed to the blackboard. 'This word and its meaning applies to things,' she said, 'not to our workers. Only THINGS, that is machines, or the skill to operate them, can become redundant. The world may no longer have any use for the Works or the steel it produces, but we always have use for human beings. PEOPLE do not become superfluous. Not even when they are little and helpless as a baby is. We always need each other. All of us have something to give. It is very important that you understand this.*
>
> *PEOPLE ARE NEVER REDUNDANT.'*

Extract from Simon's Challenge—*Chapter 2*

The issue of redundancy and the effects on Simon and his family are fed in as background to an adventure-crime-thriller-mystery story.

The BBC took an option on the book and filmed it as a two-part drama. The producer made a statement at the film launch to the effect that he thought he had found some rare "gold dust"—a book that dealt with modern children in modern Scotland.

Thinking back, I now see that I wrote that book because I was upset and annoyed about a situation. When they closed the steel mill at Gartcosh I expressed my anger and frustration in the written word of storytelling. I think good writing can come from writing about what matters to you. If your story is powerful then you can make it matter to someone else. To the "write about what you know" advice for would-be writers I might add "write about what you care about."

This has become a pattern for my writing. Even now that I have an agent, this is still my main method of working. I write about my chosen subject, addressing an issue, exploring themes. Sometimes, if it suits, I will contribute to a series or an anthology on invitation, but mainly I write about what I am interested in and my agent and editors have always supported me in this—bless them!

In addition to tackling big issues, there is a good deal of fun to be had in writing for young people. Very soon after writing *Simon's Challenge* I latched onto some changes that were taking place in our secondary schools.

At the beginning of the '90s the Scottish Education Department decided to allow adults to return to daytime high school. In some cases childcare was supplied in some schools with before and after school care and breakfast served in the morning. These were not separate classes run specifically for older people, but adults in the normal classes of the school day. I had a friend with some artistic talent who had left school early and she decided to return to study art at the local secondary school. Her teenage daughter attended the same school and far from developing a cosy mother-daughter relationship as my friend had hoped might happen, the teenage girl was embarrassed by her mother's presence in the school. Within the school she would not acknowledge her in any way, avoiding her in the corridors and diving into the toilets when she saw her mother walking towards her. She would move quickly ahead as they came out the school gates, accelerating to put as much distance as possible between her and her mother.

It really was too good not to write about it!

> *Katharine Douglas looked out of the bus window at the figure running desperately towards the stop. A big baggy striped shirt flapped over bright pink leggings. High-heeled shoes and a large satchel did nothing to help the runner's progress. Katharine slid further down in her seat and prayed that the driver would not see the woman who was now shouting and waving frantically. As the bus pulled away from the stop and gathered speed, Katharine straightened up and relaxed. Her mother was going to be late for school again.*

Extract from Different Directions—*Chapter 1*

School stories have always appealed to me, both for reading and writing.

New School Blues deals with that first crazy week of first term at high school when pupils from separate primary/junior schools are mixed together.

Bullies at School was written in response to a direct request from a child who was being bullied at school. I was doing a school author visit and he asked me privately to write about the subject as he himself was being bullied. It is one of my most popular books and is frequently used for radio drama and within schools' personal development programmes.

For me one of the most attractive things about writing for young people is the freedom it affords a writer. You are not tied to readers of a certain age group, nor to a specific genre—I can write science fiction, fantasy, historical, adventure, etc. for any age. And the great thing about children's books is their universal appeal—adults can and do enjoy reading them too.

Carnegie Medal Award ceremony at the South Bank, London

THE "KEZZIE" BOOKS

*K*ezzie and *Homecoming for Kezzie* were a tribute to the mining communities and also to my aunt who was brought up in a small mining village. The last of the ponies were taken up from the pits in 1994, and attracted more media attention than the last miner might expect. My aunt always said that her childhood had been happy and interesting. She had amused herself with games, gone berrying, made canal trips and rode donkeys at the seaside. My children could not credit this when they found out she had lived without electricity—no television, computer, radios, and only an open range to cook meals. To them it did not seem possible to survive childhood without these essentials! The two books are set in Britain and Canada just before and during the Second World War. I interviewed men who had been miners and men and women who had been children during the Blitz. The story of the runaway coal hutches deep underground is based on fact—many miners tell of animals giving warning of some danger about to happen. Social conditions, tied houses, women restricted to certain types of employment, and poverty all had an effect on lifestyle. School log books of the day give reasons for children's absence from school—this sometimes being due to poor clothing, bad weather and taking time off in autumn when the harvest must be brought in. It features the stories of migrant workers and their problems, many of which are still relevant today. It shows that emigration can be forced on people, and how immigrants are viewed, and there is a parallel for this in our modern world.

Kezzie was shortlisted for the Children's Book Award. It was then serialised in a popular woman's magazine, which resulted in a mailbag of over fifteen thousand letters.

CARNEGIE MEDAL—WHISPERS IN THE GRAVEYARD

*I*n 1994 a wonderful editor called Miriam Hodgson asked me what I was working on at the moment and I explained to her my ideas for a story about a child who could not read or write very well. While working in the library I was aware of the difficulty of finding this child in a fiction setting. When parents asked for information there was an increasing amount of non-fiction, but I could find no book written from the child's point of view. She also believed that this was a story needing to be told and gave me my first ever contract for an uncompleted work. As I was commissioned for this book I found it a terrifying responsibility. For the first time in my writing career I was working to a deadline. My work as librarian helped give me an insight into the complexities of learning differences. Parents and carers often asked if there were spoken word editions of children's books, audiotapes to help their children enjoy books, both classic and modern. Many information enquiries were from self-help groups seeking help with literacy. Adults were looking for names of special tutors, requests came asking for books about dyslexia and related subjects. Advice was sought by social workers, carers, and teachers and by the children themselves. In addition, our own reading promotion schemes in the library showed up certain things. The children were asked to write a brief summary of a book they had read, one for each month over a period of six months. At the end of this period they received a certificate and a free book. I noticed that some children could read and enjoy a book, but could not cope with writing a review about it. They could not form the letters to make the words they wanted to use. Some needed to have the book read to them, yet they could follow the plot and understand emotional issues within the story. They could discuss the story easily but could not form the letters to make the words to complete their book reviews. I became interested, interested enough to go along to the meeting of the Area Dyslexia Association ...

I went with my notebook and the vague idea in my head that I could get a story out of this, as I like to write books that are relevant to children's lives. The meeting began. I very quickly slid my notebook back into my bag as I felt that I was being rude taking notes in the circumstances in which I found myself. I have never been in a room where there was so much pain. I was moved by the frustration, anger, and despair of parents, adults, children, teachers, social workers, etc., trying to battle the system. It took me some time to collect my thoughts, but when I did I determined to write a book about it.

I chose to write in the first person because the problem is so individualistic that I wanted to get right inside the head of the sufferer, and I wanted to put the reader there too. I decided to write in the present tense because it was ... is ... happening at this moment.

I needed a story ... no point in wittering on about dyslexia without a good going tale. Without a "story" what is there to say? Solomon goes to school, has a rough time, comes home, has a rough time ... so what?

Then the story happened in front of my eyes. A ring road was being built around my hometown, and in the course of clearing older buildings they came across a small old burial ground. The bodies had to be moved out of this old graveyard and relocated. It was discovered that within the burial ground lay a mass grave of smallpox victims (children). There was some concern that disturbing the earth could lead to the infection spreading once again. These fears proved to be unfounded. The opened grave revealed nothing. It had all dissipated into the earth.

Nothing was left. I thought "what a boring end to a promising tale." But being a writer means that I can change the facts to make a more interesting story ... What if? What if? Instead of Point Horror, let's have horror with a point. I did some research into gravestones, symbols, designs, guild marks on burial slabs, codes ... and I began to get a feel for my story. I thought this is it—it is the perfect place for him to hide out, a boy who loves stories. Solomon imagines from the language of the stones. As I began to write and I did more research on both my main subjects, the whole thing locked. It meshed together unlike anything else I've ever known—the solitary grave, his father, the stories, the presence of evil inside everyone, the power of words, the infinite resource of the human mind— it all came together.

In *Whispers in the Graveyard,* the main character, Solomon, is on a journey. As in many fantasy stories where the main character has to choose between different paths, Solomon is faced with difficult choices. Caught up in the awakening evil of the newly opened grave in a derelict graveyard, with his own personal life becoming more troublesome, he could go for the easy way out—ignore what he knows is happening and leave.

Civic reception with Lord Provost

Like many of the protagonists in this type of tale, Solomon's character is flawed. He is capable of human weakness, and this is, I think, why children find fantasy stories so appealing. They see the hero as being similar to themselves, liable to make mistakes, prone to weakness. Solomon's problem is his illiteracy, and the deceit he employs to keep the fact hidden.

The story is essentially a quest, a voyage of discovery, but also of self-discovery, where heroes and heroines are put to the test, find out things about themselves, and ultimately win through. There is the struggle of evil against good, and all that stands between evil triumphant is Solomon. *Whispers in the Graveyard* explores the concept of evil within the imagination, and how people's emotions can be manipulated by circumstances and events. The boy's struggle in the graveyard becomes a gripping metaphor for his relationship with the world in general.

There is evil in all of us; we all have opportunities to choose between good and evil, right or wrong. Sometimes it is not an obvious or straightforward choice; sometimes good is the harder path to take. But Solomon opts to stay and attempts to deal with the situation. He fights to regain Amy's soul, confronts his father, and begins to deal with his own learning challenges. And Solomon's character is altered, strengthened. He comes through the test and decides to face up to his problems. At the end of the book he refers to the mirror which he had held up to confront the evil in the graveyard.... which disintegrated because there was nothing there to see ... the absence of light, the absence of hope.

And then Solomon asks the question... How many others, every drab day, avoid their own reflection? In a moment of self-realisation he knows that ... Ultimately it is yourself you face. If you can.

And finally, as his own breath condenses on the glass in front of him, he traces out the letters and he writes his name.

First, the curved letter, slithering from top to bottom.
S.
Next ... a circle.
The sun by day, and the moon by night.
Now I have to cross my bridge.
I make the letters.
Carefully and complete.
Solomon, my name.

This was one of the most uplifting parts of my writing career. *Whispers in the Graveyard* was published to widespread critical acclaim.

John Hannah who stunned cinema audiences with his rendition of Auden's poem in *Four Weddings and a Funeral* agreed to record the book. He was extremely supportive of the project and agreed to read it word for word so that it could be followed accurately by those who wanted to read and listen and who find the printed word especially challenging.

Then I was placed on the shortlist for the Carnegie Medal.

Of course, friends, family and my hometown were hoping that I would win, but I hardly dared hope. It seemed enough to be there on the shortlist.

To capture the whole essence of the use of words and the reception of the written word into the reader's mind is a challenge. It's interesting to bend the language and manipulate the words to enhance their effect upon the reader. The position of text on page is also important.

'Lies'

The sound hissed in my ear.

Lies. Lies. Lies.

Was there a word written on the chest? Dead leaves from the rowan tree had fallen on the lid. They rustled, disturbed by a small whisper of air. Was that what I heard?

No, there WAS lettering. Their moving had revealed it on the lid. 'HERE LYE ...'

A brief moment, a break in the cloud, allows the moonlight to shine down on me crouched in the earth, and onto the disturbed grave.

'HERE LYE THE ASHES OF ...'

Extract from Whispers in the Graveyard—*Chapter 11*

And again:
Solomon, while on a car journey, sees a street name and recalls the day his mother walked out.

More shades of grey. Buildings and people. Tints and hues of absence of colour. Smirring rain glossing the pavements with an oily sheen.

A name, suddenly, on the wall of a street flashing past. Golden Road. I close my eyes to shut it out. She had made me say it, over and over. Traced the letters with my fingers. 'That's where I'll be.'

She had written it down. I threw the piece of paper in the bin as soon as she left. Crushing it up in my hand. Maybe she knew I would, and that's why she had made me repeat it to her, again and again.

Standing in the hall with her suitcase, by the open front door. I turned my head away so that I did not see her go.

But I heard. 'Solomon, I'm sorry.'

I heard. The door closing.

And she was gone. I was left.

But I didn't care so much. She would never help me do up my tie or my shoelaces, whereas Dad would. She was the boring one who made me try to write my homework over and over. The one who forced me to sound out the spelling words, while he only glanced at my reading book and then told me the story the way it ought to be.

What a dope I am.

She loved me.

Extract from Whispers in the Graveyard—*Chapter 17*

In the summer of 1995, I was informed that I had won the Carnegie Medal!

The medal itself really is a beautiful thing to own. Engraved with the winner's name and book title, it's heavy and very handsome and gleams quietly against the black velvet case. It sits now under the lamp by the window and I look at it from time to time in mild disbelief.

We had lots of celebrations. I was overwhelmed by the number of cards and letters that I received. I was treated to a civic lunch and the Lord Provost of Strathkelvin presented me with my civic award and a beautiful Charles Rennie Mackintosh mirror.

The book is now in translation in various languages, including Thai. The amount of publicity was welcomed by those who work with people with learning differences. It portrays a positive image of a non-literate person. A person who has been limited in expression but does not lack imagination, courage and the strength of character needed to overcome adversity.

Since writing the book I have become involved with many projects and schemes to promote reading, and now I constantly harp on to anyone who will listen about book production. I feel passionate enough about it to mount a one woman campaign to eradicate the old-fashioned lower case printer's "a" and "g" as printed in this Times New Roman type face that I am using at this very moment. What is that all about? We teach children that small letter "a" is a circle with a stick all the way down the right hand side and that small letter "g" is a circle with a longer stick that curves to the left at the end. We show them this in lots of infant books and then slam! We suddenly without any warning or by-you-leave completely change the shape of a crucial vowel sound and that of a much-used consonant. They look nothing like the shapes children have been taught. They are not formed in the same way. I find that "a" irritating and the "g" with the tail and the feather in its cap quite pretentious. I was once informed that most children could distinguish the difference. I dispute that. I think that we have many children who are underachieving because they are being tripped up or blocked. We should be helping more with better book production. Let's have clear type, good leading, proper space between lines, wide margins, adequate gutters, etcetera, etcetera.

It is why I am glad to be involved in projects promoting literacy and books, for example, writing the Power Pack for the Library Association, which was designed to empower young people to acquire information retrieval skills. I had a lot of fun making up the Library Rap, which was performed by local schoolchildren. Youth librarians in Scotland undertake many great literacy initiatives and involve Scottish authors with these—Nursery Picture Book Presentations. And I also love my work with the Federation of Children's Book Groups and our area West of Scotland Children's Book Group.

I am very concerned to help those whom I call "challenged children" and contribute to specific initiatives by publishers to produce material designed to aid reading skills. *Bodyparts* is one such book, part of a series designed and illustrated in the style of a graphic novel.

Also, Barrington Stoke, publishers based in Edinburgh, publish magnificent books especially designed, with typeface, paper and text editing for this purpose. At the moment I have one title there, *Starship Rescue*.

The Master of the Household

has received Her Majesty's command to invite

Ms Theresa Breslin

to a Reception for the Arts to be given

by The Queen and The Duke of Edinburgh

at Windsor Castle

on Wednesday 29th April 1998 at 6.00 p.m.

A reply is requested to :
The Master of the Household,
Buckingham Palace,
London SW1A 1AA.

Dress :
Lounge Suit/Jacket
Day Dress

Guests are asked to arrive at Windsor Castle between 5.15 p.m. and 5.50 p.m.

"I received a very special invitation."

I then took on a serious subject in *Death or Glory Boys* where a terrorist bomb shatters the bright, safe world of a group of friends, and suddenly Sarah and Phil find themselves divided. Is Phil a pacifist at any price? When Sarah decides to join the Army Cadet course, Phil is stunned, *'You're joking. Join the Death or Glory boys?'*

Sarah is determined to keep an open mind, but unknown to them always near, moving in a terrible dance of death, is Cal, waiting to bomb again.

Within this book I sought to challenge responses to terrorism, and to soldiers, who fight to keep the peace with the weapons of war.

MORE WRITING ...

Ideas for books come from all sorts of places. I have to admit to, on at least one occasion, doing the "overheard on the train" source of story idea.

It was while undertaking a train journey that I overheard a conversation between two teenagers on their way to their interview for art school. Looking through their folio of work one commented to the other as to how good her drawings were. The first girl replied.

'Its no use. I'll never be accepted. I'm doomed to be a failure for the rest of my life. It's all my parents' fault. They gave me this stupid name.'

That one sentence sparked the idea. But I like to put in layers in my books so in my mind the girl is thinking. "If I had a different name. My life would be changed. I would be different."

This became the book *Name Games* with its themes of Identity, Self-worth, Perception of Others, Prejudice, Racism, using onomatopoeia, and association by name and yes, you can very aptly quote Shakespeare in a book for younger children!

When her teacher tries to explain to Jane (the main character) that she shouldn't change her name, that "you are what you are, not what you are called" he quotes Shakespeare, *"That which we call a rose, by any other name would smell as sweet."*

But, with the crushing logic of a child, Jane thinks to herself, *'Oh no it wouldn't. Try calling it "dog turd" and see what happens.'*

I think this book says a lot more than it tells. There is the boy, Big Mac, and his relationship with his grandfather who dies. There is also the fact that when Jane changes her name she chooses to be Scheherazade, the Arabian princess, the teller of tales ...

But in all these books the baseline is the story. If you don't have a story, then in my opinion you can pack up and go home. Maybe it's my Celtic roots, perhaps it's my family upbringing, but to me the story is the thing. You can address an issue, explore a theme or themes, but the book has to have a story. Stories like to be told, need to be told. Who can resist it? You meet a friend in the street and they say ... Listen, wait until tell you this ... and you wait, and you listen, because you want to be told ...

Following from this I wanted to write more for younger readers and so evolved the BLAIR stories starring the "middle" child—*Blair the Winner* and *Blair Makes a Splash.* With a pest of a baby brother, and a very bossy big sister this very active little boy strikes a chord everywhere. There are four stories in each book and I have to confess that I did draw on actual incidents involving my children in their early years. It hadn't been published very long, when in Britain Tony Blair became Prime Minister. As you can imagine the title of the first book, Blair the Winner attracted some media attention. The book was featured in *Private Eye,* a satirical magazine, and the diary section of a national newspaper.

And then some mind tricks ...

Have you ever woken up in the middle of a really good dream? Just at the most exciting bit, when something sensational is about to happen? It's happened to me—tons of times. Then, one day **I think** ... *supposing you could get back into your own dream ...?*

When I was in Cairo Museum in Egypt, our guide Heva led us to the tomb relics of Tutankhamun. And ... I looked upon the face of the Boy King.

There stood his Pharaoh Throne with back of beaten gold. It showed Tutankhamun sitting—his Queen anointing him with perfume. On her foot one sandal, while he wears the other. **I wonder** ... *could this be a sign of great affection between two people?*

I love hieroglyphics. Mysterious symbols telling secret things. **I imagine** ... *drawing all those shapes. Were they as hard to form as our alphabet?*

Would it make a difference if you carved out your letters? What if you engraved them into a softer thicker surface?

Extract from The Dream Master

To help Cy practice his writing, Aten shows him the Egyptian Letter Learner. Pressing outlines deep into the wet sand allows Cy to form his letters in another way. A bit like having an extra Dimension ...?

My books are pathways to other Dimensions.

I think .... I wonder .... I imagine ...

That's how I write my stories.

*T*he Dream Master has been hugely popular, picking up good reviews, some quite far afield—in New Zealand and in the USA (audio version) and leading to a follow-up

book ...

Dream Master—Nightmare! This puts Cy in the time of the Vikings meeting a very determined Saxon princess who eventually sails to North America. With this book I thought I could develop a little more the storytelling theme begun in the first book. Part of the reason for doing this was the demand on my time to do author visits. We have a wonderful scheme in Scotland sponsored by the Scottish Arts Council and managed by Scottish Book Trust called the Writers in Scotland scheme. It is used extensively by individuals and organisations to bring authors to a wider audience. I am sometimes overwhelmed by the number of requests to visit libraries, schools, writers' groups, etc. So I thought that as many of the questions I am asked are the same, and the discussions often cover similar lines, perhaps I could work this into the story.

My books have been well served by some gifted illustrators, both for covers and text illustrations. David Wyatt produces intriguing and exciting work for covers and inside chapter headings for my "Dream Master" books— showing Egyptian, Norse and Celtic imagery (soon to be Roman with the third Dream Master adventure where Cy and his Dream Master journey to visit Pompeii at the time of the eruption of Vesuvius). As does Scoular Anderson for *Bullies at School,* where his drawings evocatively capture the body language of aggression, and then the indecision on the face of the victim Siobhan who wants to defend herself but is caught in the quandary of perhaps becoming a bully herself.

Scottish Writers launch

Nineteen ninety-eight was a big year for me. Our last child finished University, and encouraged and supported by Tom, I decided to leave my post in the libraries (not without sadness) and write full time.

I also received a very special invitation ... from the Queen to a reception at Windsor Castle! This was a reception given by the Queen to celebrate the Arts in Britain. Various guests attended from all the different fields: acting, painting, dance, writing, singing, including Joan Collins, Michael Caine and Helena Bonham-Carter. It also marked the reopening of Windsor Castle after a devastating fire. Guests were allowed into rooms not normally open to the public, and many members of the Royal Family were there; the Queen, Prince Philip, Princess Margaret, Prince Edward, and some Dukes and Duchesses.

Windsor is a magnificent castle and it was dazzling evening!

My plans for full-time writing were quickly put on hold as for the year 2000, I became Project Manager for the Scottish Library Association's half million pound lottery funded Scottish Writers Project CD & Web site. This was a promotion of Scottish books to teenagers. Display units, posters, bookmarks and a wealth of books and promotional materials were distributed to secondary schools and public libraries. The CD was nominated for a BAFTA award, in a category with productions of Spielberg and Lucas! As a method of "leading to reading" it is unique. The CD is an information resource of books, subjects, biographies, reviews and authoritative critical text analysis. Authors read from their work talk about reading and writing and give writing tips to students. It is also a spectacular interactive game involving the player rescuing books from planets scattered throughout the galaxy.

In the year 2000 I was awarded lifelong Honorary Membership in the Scottish Library Association for distinguished services to Children's Literature and Librarianship.

CURRENT PROJECTS

At long last I am a full-time writer and during the year 2000 I turned again to concentrate on a "big" book for young adults. *Remembrance* was a massive undertaking, a novel set in World War I and I became immersed in research, which included visits to France and Belgium. The amount of material amassed during this has led to requests for copies of background notes, which I am presently trying to collate.

At the battlefields in France and Belgium teenagers wander soberly around the monuments. They push their poppies into the spaces between the stones of the Menin Gate and the little wooden crosses purchased in Ypres are crowded onto the grave of a young soldier age fifteen—their age.

Nearby runs the Yser Canal where the Canadian John McCrae wrote his poem In Flanders Fields.

At the Somme, around Thiepval and in Beaumont Hamel they walk through preserved trenches and stand looking into the huge mine craters. By the roadside and on the hills they see cemetery after cemetery, collections of headstones among fields fertile with crops.

The white clay clings, and they spend time wiping boots before reboarding the coach.

'Came over this morning, back home to Britain tonight,' the driver tells me.

One is aware of great lies and great truths, a sudden consciousness of youth and vulnerability and a tremendous sense of loss.

Extract from Research Notes—November 2001

NOW

I am still involved in supporting books and libraries. I am a board member of Scottish Book Trust and of the national Public Lending Right Advisory Committee.

I love travelling, and it is a great opportunity to meet adults and young people. I have spoken to audiences in New Zealand, the Orkney Islands, Ireland, Canada, and America. Everywhere there is an enormous enthusiasm for children's books.

It is a very difficult task today to be writer for young people. The days of "duty" reading are gone. If a story doesn't interest them then they will not finish it. To write a good book that is actually read ... to write a worthwhile tale that they enjoy ...

But when I write and it is going well, there is nothing like it. When the story starts to "sing" you can, as one Scottish author put it "see for a hundred miles."

So I hope to go on writing and telling stories to whoever will listen.

FUTURE

I am now working on a book provisionally entitled *Saskia's Journey.* It will reflect the life of the fishing communities, which is where Tom's mother's people are from. Strong principled folk, wresting a living from the sea, living a hard life—a life that has changed, is changing. The book will explore relationships, young adults with each other, with parents, with relatives.

Writing is a journey, a journey of self-discovery. I like research. Now as I am looking at the sea, I think, this planet is mainly water, and we have a strong family history connected to it. I think it is very elemental; our history is tied up with navigation. The stars, the sea and the earth, as writing is for me, is where we are ... who we are.

Writings

FOR CHILDREN

Simon's Challenge, Blackie & Son (London, England), 1988.

Different Directions, Blackie & Son (London, England), 1989.

A Time to Reap, Blackie & Son (London, England), 1991.

New School Blues, Canongate, 1992.

Bullies at School, illustrated by Lynne Willey, Blackie & Son (London, England), 1993.

Kezzie, Methuen (London, England), 1993.

Whispers in the Grave Yard, Methuen (London, England), 1994.

A Homecoming for Kezzie, Methuen (London, England), 1995.

Missing, Mammoth (London, England), 1995.

Death or Glory Boys, Methuen (London, England), 1996.

Across the Roman Wall, illustrated by Michael Charlton, A & C Black (London, England), 1997.

Blair, the Winner!, Mammoth (London, England), 1997.

Name Games, illustrated by Kay Widdowson, Mammoth (London, England), 1997.

Bodyparts (graphic novel), illustrated by Janek Matysiak, A & C Black (London, England), 1998.

Starship Rescue, Barrington Stoke (Edinburgh, Scotland), 1999.

The Dream Master, Doubleday (London, England), 1999.

Blair Makes a Splash, illustrated by Ken Cox, Mammoth (London), 1999.

Dream Master—Nightmare!, Doubleday (London, England), 2000.

Duncan of Carrick, Pearson (Harlow, England), 2000.

Also author of *Alien Force* and *Remembrance.* Contributor to anthologies, including *Adventure Stories for Ten Year Olds, All for Love, Amazing Adventure Stories, A Braw Brew, Just What I Always Wanted, Magic Carpet, Points North, Stories from Scotland,* and *Turning Points. Kezzie* has been translated into Gaelic.

BRISSON, Pat 1951-

Personal

Born February 23, 1951, in Rahway, NJ; daughter of Thomas Francis (a plumber and foreman) and Jane Margaret (Gerity) McDonough; married Emil Girard Brisson (an administrator), May 29, 1971; children: Gabriel, Noah, Benjamin, Zachary. *Education:* Rutgers University, B.A. 1973, M.L.S., 1990. *Politics:* Democrat. *Religion:* Roman Catholic. *Hobbies and other interests:* Gardening, baking.

Addresses

Home—94 Bullman St., Phillipsburg, NJ 08865. *Agent*—Tracey Adams, McIntosh and Otis Inc., 353 Lexington Ave., New York, NY 10016. *E-mail*—brisson@enter.net.

Career

Teacher, librarian, and author. St. Anthony of Padua School, Camden, NJ, elementary school teacher, 1974-75; Phillipsburg Free Public Library, Phillipsburg, NJ, library clerk, 1978-81, reference librarian, 1990—; Easton Area Public Library, Easton, PA, library clerk, 1981-88. *Member:* American Library Association, Society of Children's Book Writers and Illustrators.

Awards, Honors

Kate Heads West was named an American Booksellers Pick of the Lists selection, 1990; *The Summer My Father Was Ten* received the 1998 Christopher Award, The Paterson Prize for Children's Literature, Hodge Podger Award, American Booksellers Pick of the Lists

Selection, IRA-CBC Teachers' Choice Award, and the 1998 National Parenting Publications Awards Honor Book.

Writings

Your Best Friend, Kate, illustrated by Rick Brown, Bradbury Press (New York, NY), 1989.

Kate Heads West, illustrated by Rick Brown, Bradbury Press (New York, NY), 1990.

Magic Carpet, illustrated by Amy Schwartz, Bradbury Press (New York, NY), 1991.

Kate on the Coast, Bradbury Press (New York, NY), 1992.

Benny's Pennies, illustrated by Bob Barner, Doubleday (New York, NY), 1993.

Wanda's Roses, illustrated by Maryann Cocca-Leffler, Boyds Mills Press (Honesdale, PA), 1994.

Hot Fudge Hero, illustrated by Diana Cain Bluthenthal, Holt (New York, NY), 1997.

The Summer My Father Was Ten, illustrated by Andrea Shine, Boyds Mills Press (Honesdale, PA), 1998.

Little Sister, Big Sister, illustrated by Diana Cain Bluthenthal, Holt (New York, NY), 1999.

Sky Memories, illustrated by Wendell Minor, Delacorte Press (New York, NY), 1999.

Bertie's Picture Day, illustrated by Diana Cain Bluthenthal, Holt (New York, NY), 2000.

Star Blanket, illustrated by Erica Magnus, Boyds Mills Press (Honesdale, PA), 2003.

Sidelights

Through her experiences as an elementary school teacher and as a librarian, not to mention as the mother of four boys, Pat Brisson has developed a good instinct for what goes into a successful children's book. Beginning her second career as a children's book author with

Pat Brisson's picture book follows generous Benny McBride, who decides to spend his five new pennies on those he loves.
(From Benny's Pennies, *illustrated by Bob Barner.)*

works that combine geography with a young protagonist curious about other places—from the mysterious-sounding Orient to sections of the United States not yet visited—Brisson has gone on to expand her focus, and she has gained a popular following for her chapter books featuring likeable protagonists who meet everyday obstacles with good humor, imagination, and a dash of hutzpa.

Brisson was born in Rahway, New Jersey, in 1951. As the fourth child in her family, she earned the nickname "the caboose"; as she recalled to *SATA,* "It was quite a shock when I was five and my brother Kevin was born. Over the years I was able to forgive my brother for being born and complicating my life so much. But I also wrote a story in which I stayed the caboose forever—history the way it should have been, I like to call it."

Although Brisson did not have access to a wide variety of books as a child, she cherished the ones she had. Growing up to become a writer was not a childhood ambition, so when her father brought home a used manual typewriter the year she entered the fifth grade,

her first bit of writing—after figuring out how the keys worked—was an essay on strawberries. During high school she took a writing course that combined journalism with creative writing, and it was there that Brisson first had the notion that fiction-writing might be in her future. Enrolling at Rutgers University, she took only one course in writing—a poetry class—late in her senior year. "My teacher, Frank McQuilkan, told me if he had known earlier I could write so well he would have nominated me for the writing prize at graduation," Brisson related. "This meant a great deal to me. Even though I didn't consider myself a writer, it was there for encouragement later on when I decided to write for publication."

Married in 1971, Brisson eventually found herself frequenting the children's section of her local library in search of picture books for her growing family. In 1982 she decided to try her hand at writing a book of her own. Scouring writers' magazines and books on the craft of writing, she began to learn the ropes, and her newly minted articles soon began appearing in magazines. After five years of work, her first book for children,

Your Best Friend, Kate was accepted by Bradbury Press, and Brisson was on her way to a new career.

Focusing on stories that help young listeners learn about geography, Brisson has authored several "Kate" books, beginning with *Your Best Friend, Kate,* about a girl's vacation trip along the East Coast of the United States. Through postcards home to her best friend Lucy, Kate expresses her excitement about her family's four-week round-trip excursion from New Jersey to Florida, a trip peppered with the hijinks of her annoying little brother Brian. Praising the letters as "convincingly childlike," *School Library Journal* contributor Louise L. Sherman added that Brisson includes in her book "those things that would impress" children of the same age as the reader.

Kate Heads West takes readers on a trip through Arizona, Texas, Oklahoma, and New Mexico, this time in the company of friend Lucy and Lucy's family. Kate's notes home to family, friends, and even her teacher are "entertaining and educational," according to Lois Ringquist in *Five Owls.* Noting the book's value in social studies classes, *School Library Journal* contributor Jeanette Larson added that *Kate Heads West* "will be enjoyed by armchair travelers and families planning a similar trip" of their own. In *Kate on the Coast* the

young traveler and her family have moved across the country and now make their home in Seattle, Washington. During their first year on the West Coast, they take numerous vacations, all chronicled by Kate in letters to friend Lucy. Trips to Hollywood, Alaska, and even as far west as Hawaii inspire letters that "effortlessly impart information" and even serve as what *School Library Journal* reviewer Carla Kozak deemed "an exercise in the art of letter writing."

Many of Brisson's books are geared for beginning readers, and their engaging storylines have even captured and held the interest of kids who would rather be doing something besides curling up with a good book. In the three short chapters of *Hot Fudge Hero,* a young boy named Bertie manages to get a mis-hit baseball back from his grouchy old neighbor Mr. Muckleberg (and gets a hot fudge sundae); becomes amazed when his feeble efforts at learning to play the saxophone are rewarded by the appearance of his fairy godfather (and a hot fudge sundae); and overcomes the clumsiness of using a new bowling ball (and winds up with a strike and yet another hot fudge sundae). Praising the book's large type and Brisson's use of short sentences, Christina Dorr noted in *School Library Journal* that *Hot Fudge Hero* captures "Bertie's determination and good nature." *Booklist* contributor Lauren Peterson added her praise,

The next day was Saturday. My father and the old man worked all day together. When they were finished, they had a patch of ground carefully raked and planted with tomato and pepper plants, teeny tiny onions, and seeds for marigolds and zinnias. Now when my father looked at the garden, he didn't get a hard knot in his stomach.

Summer came, and every morning my father and Mr. Bellavista checked their plants. My father carried water from his apartment during dry spells and learned to tell what was a weed and what wasn't.

After a boy's inadvertent act of vandalism destroys his elderly neighbor's garden, the boy makes amends and establishes a friendship with the old man. (From The Summer My Father Was Ten, *written by Brisson and illustrated by Andrea Shine.)*

noting that the "clever tales" penned by Brisson "are excellent for beginning readers," while in *Horn Book* Martha A. Parravano cited the "nice messages" about "not making assumptions" and "the power of perseverence."

Another easy-to-read chapter book, *Little Sister, Big Sister* describes the relationship between young Edna and her older sister Hester. While Hester uses her age and experience to trick young Edna into undertaking horrible tasks like cleaning her room, she also serves as a friend, particularly during thunder storms and when she has a candy bar that needs sharing. According to a *Kirkus Reviews* critic, "Brisson deftly captures the nuances" of the relationship between siblings," while in *School Library Journal* Amy Lilien praised the characters as "real, the language ... accessible." Brisson's "clear sentences ... will draw beginning readers to daily dramas they will recognize," added Hazel Rochman in a *Booklist* review of *Little Sister, Big Sister*. The equally humorous *Bertie's Picture Day* focuses once again on second-grader Bertie and his dismay at losing a front tooth just before school pictures are taken. "The funny situations" combine with the "short, pithy text" to "make this a very readable story," in the opinion of Carolyn Phelan in *Booklist*, while in *School Library Journal* contributor Kay Bowes had special praise for Bertie's "unique irrepressible personality." *Bertie's Picture Day*, Bowes concluded, "is a surefire hit."

Expanding her range beyond chapter books for developing readers, Brisson's first work for the story-hour set was 1991's *Magic Carpet*. The story of a girl named Elizabeth who, with her aunt, imagines the trip taken by several objects now in her parents' home, *Magic Carpet* was praised for its ability to encourage creativity while also "getting [youngsters] acquainted with an atlas," in the opinion of *School Library Journal* contributor Jane Saliers.

The engaging picture book *Wanda's Roses* finds a young optimist determined to brighten up the vacant lot next to her inner city home. The discovery of a scrubby bush with thorns causes her to believe that with enough care the lot can become full of roses. Although her more horticulturally astute neighbors are at first skeptical, they are soon won over by Wanda's enthusiasm and work together to make her vision come true. Praising Brisson's protagonist as "loveable," a *Publishers Weekly* contributor dubbed *Wanda's Roses* an "upbeat urban tale" enhanced by watercolors that "genially depict ... the city's great variety." In *School Library Journal* reviewer Carolyn Jenks hailed the book as "the story of one person's faith against all odds and a caring community," praising Brisson for telling her story "simply and with good humor."

The Summer My Father Was Ten, which was published in 1998, takes a different approach, as Brisson pens "a profoundly moving cross-generational story," according to *Booklist* contributor Hazel Rochman. Illustrated with vivid watercolor renderings by artist Andrea Shine, the story focuses on a ten-year-old boy whose act of inadvertent vandalism results in the destruction of elderly Mr. Bellavista's vegetable garden. When the boy realizes what he has done, he apologizes; the following year he helps till the soil and plant the next crop of vegetables, and remains a friend of Mr. Bellavista until his death. Calling the work "a fine story of intergenerational friendship," a *Kirkus Reviews* contributor praised Brisson for imbuing her characters with "plainspoken, unsentimental, distinct voices."

Supplementing her continued success as a children's book author, Brisson went back to college and earned her master's degree in library science. She continues to write books for young readers in addition to working as a reference librarian in her hometown of Phillipsburg, New Jersey. Although she has written several board books for toddlers and contemplated experimenting with longer chapter books, she continues to find the greatest reward writing stories that help fuel the interest and excitement of children just beginning a lifetime of reading. "I hope to continue writing for a long, long time," she once admitted.

Biographical and Critical Sources

PERIODICALS

Booklist, March 15, 1992, Carolyn Phelan, review of *Kate on the Coast,* p. 1386; December 15, 1993, Ellen Mandel, review of *Benny's Pennies,* p. 762; April 1, 1997, Lauren Peterson, review of *Hot Fudge Hero,* p. 1333; February 1, 1998, Hazel Rochman, review of *The Summer My Father Was Ten,* p. 913; April 15, 1999, Hazel Rochman, review of *Little Sister, Big Sister,* p. 1528; May 15, 1999, Karen Hutt, review of *Sky Memories,* p. 1695; December 1, 2000, Carolyn Phelan, review of *Bertie's Picture Day,* p. 703.

Five Owls, March, 1991, Mary Ann Saurino, review of *Your Best Friend, Kate,* p. 69; September, 1994, Lois Ringquist, "Reading across America," pp. 1-3.

Horn Book, November-December, 1991, Elizabeth S. Watson, review of *Magic Carpet,* p. 733; July-August, 1997, Martha A. Parravano, review of *Hot Fudge Hero,* p. 450.

Kirkus Reviews, May 15, 1994, review of *Wanda's Roses,* p. 696; February 1, 1998, review of *The Summer My Father Was Ten,* p. 193; April 15, 1999, review of *Little Sister, Big Sister,* p. 628.

New York Times Book Review, October 17, 1999, Perry Nodelman, review of *Sky Memories,* p. 31.

Publishers Weekly, June 21, 1991, review of *Magic Carpet,* p. 62; February 17, 1992, review of *Your Best Friend, Kate,* p. 64; July 19, 1993, review of *Benny's Pennies,* p. 251; May 16, 1994, review of *Wanda's Roses,* p. 64; June 14, 1999, review of *Sky Memories,* p. 71.

School Library Journal, July, 1989, Louise L. Sherman, review of *Your Best Friend, Kate,* pp. 61-62; November, 1990, Jeanette Larson, review of *Kate Heads West,* p. 86; January, 1992, Jane Saliers, review of *Magic Carpet,* p. 88; July, 1992, Carla Kozak, review of *Kate on the Coast,* p. 56; January, 1994, Linda Wicher, review of *Benny's Pennies,* pp. 82-83; December, 1994, Carolyn Jenks, review of *Wanda's*

Roses, p. 71; July, 1997, Christina Dorr, review of *Hot Fudge Hero,* p. 60; April, 1998, Susan Pine, review of *The Summer My Father Was Ten,* p. 91; July, 1999, Amy Lilien, review of *Little Sister, Big Sister,* p. 61; August, 1999, Marilyn Payne Phillips, review of *Sky Memories,* p. 125; September, 2000, Kay Bowes, review of *Bertie's Picture Day,* p. 184.

OTHER

Pat Brisson Web Site, http://www.enter.net/~brisson/ (February 2, 2002).

*   *   *

BUSH, Catherine 1961-

Personal

Born August 2, 1961, in Toronto, Ontario, Canada. *Education:* Yale University, B.A., 1983.

Addresses

Home—Toronto, Canada. *Agent*—Denise Bukowski, Bukowski Agency, 14 Prince Arthur Ave., Ste. 202, Toronto, Ontario M5S 1M5, Canada. *E-mail*—catebush@aol.com.

Career

Novelist, journalist, 1983—. Concordia University, Montreal, Ontario, Canada, assistant professor of creative writing, 1997-99; University of Florida, Gainesville, FL, visiting professor of creative writing, 2001. *Member:* Writers Union of Canada, PEN Canada.

Awards, Honors

Minus Time was shortlisted for Smith Books/*Books in Canada* First Novel Award and City of Toronto Book Award, 1993; *The Rules of Engagement* was shortlisted for the City of Toronto Book Award, 2001.

Writings

Elizabeth I (juvenile), Chelsea House (New York, NY), 1985.
Gandhi (juvenile), Chelsea House (New York, NY), 1985.
Minus Time (novel), Hyperion Press (New York, NY), 1993.
The Rules of Engagement (novel), Farrar, Straus (New York, NY), 2000.

Contributor to *All America: The Catalogue of Everything American,* Morrow (New York, NY), 1987.

Sidelights

Canadian writer Catherine Bush's first novel, *Minus Time,* revolves around the activities of the Urie family. David and Barbara are Canadian scientists. David, a seismologist, has gone to Los Angeles to help in the wake of a massive earthquake while Barbara, an astronaut, embarks on a long-term mission in space. The couple's twenty-year-old children Helen and Paul are on their own, searching for identity and fulfillment.

The minus time of the title refers to the countdown before the launch of a rocket and is indicative of the space metaphors that inform the work. "Bush has chosen a strange and remarkable metaphor for the chaos of modern life," remarked Laurie Muchnick in her review of *Minus Time* for the *Voice Literary Supplement,* adding, "What could better represent the fragmentation of the nuclear family than a mother who's in outer space? What better symbol for the anomie and aimlessness of so many twenty-year-olds than minus time, the period that's nothing but a lead-up to something else?" Critic Richard Eder of the *Los Angeles Times* said that the author's use of "space flight as a symbol of the human abandonment of our times is bold, and Bush works it extremely well.... [*Minus Time*'s] strength is mainly allegorical; as fiction it has an initial liveliness that tends to run down. It lasts long enough, though, to let its message come through to the reader." Marie Campbell, writing in *Quill and Quire,* characterized *Minus Time* as a "compelling story" and "an accomplished and confident novel."

Minus Time focuses primarily on Helen. Alternating between chapters written in the third person and in the first person, it recounts Helen's childhood and adolescence in what Rena Jana of the *San Francisco Review of Books* described as a "jarring" style. Calling the work a "dazzling debut" and a "book of stunning originality,"

Catherine Bush

Books in Canada contributor Gary Draper analyzed its style further: "Bush's narrative voice is documentary and largely unemotional; what she records is often surreal. The reader is made to see the familiar as if for the first time: the everyday seems strange, the strange seems everyday." "It's thrilling to read a novel so excited by science, especially one that is so unabashedly literary," stated Muchnick in the *Voice Literary Supplement.* "Bush's prose, full of metaphor and visual description, gives the book its complexity, though sometimes it also drags it down.... Once the book gets moving, though, Bush relaxes and her prose unclots itself, reveling in quirkiness and a sly humor." Barbara J. Graham, writing for *CM: Canadian Review of Materials,* called *Minus Time* "a novel filled with ideas just begging to be discussed." Tibor Fischer in the London *Times* described the book as "an elegant spiritual examination of a woman struggling to find her bearings; *Catcher in the Rye* done female, Canadian."

In her next novel, *The Rules of Engagement,* Bush explores themes of violence, risk, and responsibility through the story of Arcadia Hearne, a thirty-one-year-old Canadian who devotes her life to research on war. Arcadia's obsession with violence stems from an earlier event in her life, when she betrayed her lover with another man and the two rivals engaged in an old-fashioned pistol duel over her. Arcadia fled without even waiting to learn the result of the duel, and she now holds herself distant and aloof from the violence she studies. Her life changes when her sister, a journalist, asks Arcadia to shelter a Somali refugee. Arcadia subsequently becomes involved with a Iranian man with his own dark past, and she is forced to confront her ghosts. It is "an engrossing story," according to Kristine Huntley in *Booklist. Library Journal*'s Ann Irvine gave *The Rules of Engagement* credit for dealing "affectingly with life, death, responsibility, and love," while a *Publishers Weekly* writer deemed the book "eloquent and thoughtful."

Analyzing the novel in *Village Voice,* M. G. Lord noted that nearly all of the book's characters are concerned with how to make their lives have "meaning"; they try to be sure that the risks they take are meaningful. Lord further commented, "Without this constant emphasis on meaning, *Rules of Engagement* might have been just another thriller. With it, the book becomes a sort of secular humanist manifesto. I say secular humanist because oddly—in a book that deals with war and violence—not one single character ever thinks or talks about God.... Bush is ... a graceful, literary writer.... Through rich language, she makes her characters and locations vivid."

Discussing *The Rules of Engagement* with Ron Hogan for *The Beatrice Interview,* Bush commented: "I started with the idea of a woman who writes about war theory and has a duel fought over her. I just loved the coming together of someone who writes about, and intellectualizes, violence and war and also has this bizarre violent event in her own life. I wanted to talk about violence, confront it in myself, to think about it in ways that I had

In her biography for young adult readers, Bush depicts the life of the incomparable Indian nationalist leader. (From Ghandi.)

resisted thinking about it, and a duel seemed to be an interesting angle at which to come at the issue."

Bush, who now lives back home in Toronto, Canada, once remarked: "It's not easy being a novelist at the end of the twentieth century, but I like the challenge of committing to narrative and telling a story in an age of rapid-fire imagery. And I like the challenge of engaging with the world around me—the world of public decisions as well as private, or perhaps the place where the two meet. I like writing about people on the cusp of difficult choices, people who are tugged in two directions at once. Fiction offers me a way to probe ambivalence and ask questions about the world in which we find ourselves. Ambivalence, after all, is what makes life interesting."

Biographical and Critical Sources

PERIODICALS

Belles Lettres, summer, 1994, p. 37.
Booklist, August, 2000, Kristine Huntley, review of *The Rules of Engagement,* p. 2109.
Books in Canada, October, 1993, Gary Draper, review of *Minus Time,* pp. 53-54.
Chatelaine, April, 2000, review of *The Rules of Engagement,* p. 17.

CM: Canadian Review of Materials, November, 1993, Barbara J. Graham, review of *Minus Time,* pp. 212-213.

Entertainment Weekly, September 1, 2000, Daneet Steffens, review of *The Rules of Engagement,* p. 76.

Kirkus Reviews, June 15, 2000, review of *The Rules of Engagement.*

Library Journal, July, 2000, Ann Irvine, review of *The Rules of Engagement,* p. 136.

Los Angeles Reader, August 13, 1993, David Ulin, review of *Minus Time.*

Los Angeles Times, August 12, 1993, Richard Eder, review of *Minus Time,* p. 6; September 11, 2000, Merle Rubin, review of *The Rules of Engagement.*

New York Times Book Review, September 3, 2000, Catherine Lockerbie, review of *The Rules of Engagement,* p. 9.

Publishers Weekly, June 5, 2000, review of *The Rules of Engagement,* p. 69.

Quill and Quire, August, 1993, Marie Campbell, review of *Minus Time,* p. 30.

San Francisco Review of Books, November-December, 1993, Rena Jana, review of *Minus Time,* pp. 20-21.

Times (London), July 20, 1995, Tibor Fischer, review of *Minus Time.*

Times Educational Supplement, November 11, 1988, p. 30.

Village Voice, August 15, 2000, M. G. Lord, review of *The Rules of Engagement,* p. 109.

Voice Literary Supplement, September, 1993, Laurie Muchnick, review of *Minus Time,* p. 30.

OTHER

The Beatrice Interview: 2000, http://www.beatrice.com/ (December 5, 2000), Ron Hogan, interview with Catherine Bush.

C

CANNON, Janell 1957-

Personal

Born November 3, 1957, in St. Paul, MN; daughter of Burton H. and Nancy A. Cannon. *Hobbies and other interests:* Traveling, bicycling, reading.

Addresses

Office—P.O. Box 1362, Carlsbad, CA 92018. *Agent*—Sandra Dijkstra, 1155 Camino Del Mar, Del Mar, CA 92014.

Career

Carlsbad Library, Carlsbad, CA, graphic artist, 1981-93; freelance author and illustrator, 1993—. *Member:* Bat Conservation International.

Awards, Honors

Book of the Year Award, American Booksellers Association, 1994, for *Stellaluna;* Best Book of the Year, *Child* magazine, Children's Choice selection, International Reading Association/Children's Book Council, and Notable Children's Trade Book in the Field of Social Studies, National Council for the Social Studies/Children's Book Council, all for *Verdi.* Cannon's books have received numerous best book of the year awards from regional reading associations.

Writings

SELF-ILLUSTRATED

Stellaluna, Harcourt (San Diego, CA), 1993.
Trupp: A Fuzzhead Tale, Harcourt (San Diego, CA), 1995.
Verdi, Harcourt (San Diego, CA), 1997.
Crickwing, Harcourt (San Diego, CA), 2000.
Little You, Harcourt (San Diego, CA), 2002.

Stellaluna has been translated into other languages, including Portugese, Danish, French, German, Hebrew, Japanese, Korean, Norwegian, Spanish, and Swedish.

Adaptations

Stellaluna has been adapted as a computer game for children, Living Books (San Francisco, CA), 1996; a Grammy-winning audio recording, High Windy Audio, 1996; and a pop-up book and mobile, Harcourt (San Diego, CA), 1997.

Janell Cannon

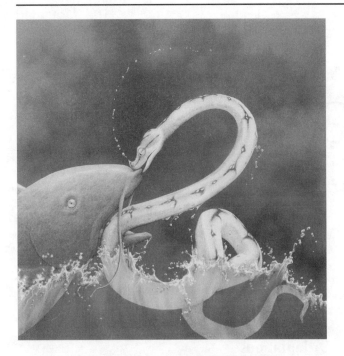

Young python Verdi learns that taking life at a slower pace has its advantages in Cannon's amusing picture book, which includes informative facts about snakes. (From Verdi, *written and illustrated by Cannon.*)

Sidelights

Author and illustrator Janell Cannon broke on to the children's literature scene with the appearance of *Stellaluna,* the tale of a small bat who loses contact with her mother one evening. The winner of numerous awards, this debut picture book, first published in 1993, has gone on to sell over one million copies and has been adapted into a pop-up book, mobile, audio recording, computer read-along game, puzzle, board game, stuffed animal, and greeting card, among other incarnations. In the story, a baby fruit bat is separated from her mother during an attack by an owl. Stellaluna falls into a nest of baby birds and is quickly accepted into the family. The birds teach the little bat to eat worms instead of fruit, to stay awake all day, and to sleep in the nest instead of hanging upside down from a branch. But despite Stellaluna's willingness to attempt this strange behavior, she is neither comfortable nor very good at being a bird. Stellaluna is soon discovered by a group of fruit bats who recognize her as one of their own and help her find her real mother.

Her mother teaches Stellaluna to improve the skills—such as finding fruit to eat—that come more naturally to her as a bat. The book concludes with two pages of facts about bats, an addition that critics note reinforces the usefulness of this picture book as an introduction to the subject for younger children. In a review of *Stellaluna* in *Publishers Weekly,* a critic praised the humor and ease with which Cannon tells this story of tolerance in friendship and the value of self-knowledge. Reviewing the book for *School Library Journal,* Marianne Saccardi called *Stellaluna* "a promising debut" and dubbed the

author's illustrations "lovely." The *Publishers Weekly* critic also praised the author's illustrations, calling Cannon's images "striking" and set off by a "luminous precision."

Two years later, Cannon's next book, *Trupp: A Fuzzhead Tale,* shares the story of a youngster wishing to learn about life in the big city. A peaceful creature resembling a cat, Trupp leaves his Fuzzhead home in the cliffs, setting out to see the rest of the world. Early in his journey, Trupp meets a crow, and together the two reach the city and struggle to comprehend the fast-paced metropolis. Luckily, a flamboyant, homeless woman befriends Trupp, takes him under her wing, and shows him what life in the city is like. While calling the story "deft and accomplished," *Booklist* reviewer Carolyn Phelan observed that *Trupp* did not have the same magic as *Stellaluna,* though she suggested that "readers who adore Cannon's first book may want to see this one." A *Publishers Weekly* reviewer, however, found that the quality of Cannon's second book matched her first effort. "Carefully crafted prose and stunning art," wrote the reviewer, "shape a story that delicately spans the fictional and real, at the same time delivering a message worthy of reflection."

A young python stars in Cannon's 1997 work, *Verdi.* Ready to leave home and tackle the jungle on his own, Verdi vows to never take on the solid green hue of an adult. The youngster prefers his own sporty, yellow racing stripes and tears around the trees, afraid that slowing down will make him "lazy, boring [and] green." But when an injury sends Verdi to the sidelines, the maturing serpent learns to appreciate a slower-paced life, discovering many things in the jungle he missed while going at full speed. For readers interested in learning more, the author/illustrator ends her book with a double-page note on snakes. "Cannon's finely tempered prose is as exquisite as her luminous artwork," wrote a *Publishers Weekly* contributor in a review of the picture book. Much like *Stellaluna, Verdi* combines a child-pleasing story with actual information about science, according to *Booklist*'s Susan Dove Lempke, who went on to say that the "rich greens and shiny yellows of the jacket art are sure to entice youngsters."

In *Crickwing,* Cannon takes another creature most people dislike and creates "a gripping story that also works as an inspiring lesson in compassion," wrote *Booklist* reviewer Connie Fletcher. Crickwing, so named after a run-in with a toad left his wing crooked, is a cockroach who loves to make sculptures out of his food. Unfortunately, other critters continue to steal his creations, leaving Crickwing hungry. The young cockroach decides to take his anger out on some smaller insects, but the leaf-cutter ants instead take him prisoner and intend to give him over to the stronger army ants as a peace overture. After a change of heart by his captors, the clever cockroach comes up with an idea to scare away the threatening band of enemy ants. Several reviewers praised Cannon's ability to match pictures to her text, including a *Publisher Weekly* critic who wrote, "Reeling in her audience with saucy characters and an engaging plotline, she hooks them with her vibrant visuals."

"As a kid, I always was drawing," Cannon once told *SATA*. "In the classroom, doodling was my way of getting through slow lectures without falling asleep. I liked the idea that I appeared to be taking notes. In high school, the habit escalated into carrying an 18" x 24" sketchbook from class to class. It fit perfectly over the desk, and I could wildly draw without marring the desk surface. I loved black Bic pens and did most of my drawings with them. Being a left-hander, the side of my hand tended to drag over the ink while drawing, and so I walked about for most of my school years with an ink-blackened hand. My academic career was not exemplary, but I sure got a lot of practice at my art."

Biographical and Critical Sources

BOOKS

Cannon, Janell, *Verdi,* Harcourt (San Diego, CA), 1997.

PERIODICALS

Booklist, April 15, 1995, Carolyn Phelan, review of *Trupp: A Fuzzhead Tale,* p. 1505; April 15, 1997, Susan Dove Lempke, review of *Verdi,* p. 1434; October 15, 2000, Connie Fletcher, review of *Crickwing,* p. 434.
Kirkus Reviews, April 1, 1997, review of *Verdi,* p. 551.
New York Times Book Review, July 2, 1995, Margalit Fox, review of *Trupp,* p. 13.
Publishers Weekly, April 26, 1993, review of *Stellaluna,* p. 78; February 20, 1995, review of *Trupp,* p. 204; April 24, 1995, "Queen of the Night," p. 19; February 17, 1997, review of *Verdi,* p. 219; May 1, 2000, "Going Batty for *Stellaluna,*" p. 27; August 7, 2000, review of *Crickwing,* p. 95.
School Library Journal, June, 1993, Marianne Saccardi, review of *Stellaluna,* p. 70; July, 1995, Virginia Opocensky, review of *Trupp,* p. 55; May, 1997, Nina Lindsay, review of *Verdi,* p. 93; November, 2000, Barbara Buckley, review of *Crickwing,* p. 110.

OTHER

Harcourt Trade Publishers, http://www.harcourtbooks.com/ (November 17, 2001), "Popular Author Champions Another Unloved Creature."

*   *   *

CHENG, Andrea 1957-

Personal

Born September 19, 1957, in El Paso, TX; married Jim Cheng, 1982; children: Nicholas, Jane, Ann. *Education:* Cornell University, B.A., 1979, M.S., 1982.

Addresses

Home—3928 Red Bud Ave., Cincinnati, OH 45229. *E-mail*—ajcheng@fuse.net.

Andrea Cheng

Career

Cincinnati State Technical and Community College, Cincinnati, OH, instructor in English as a second language and director of English as a second language, 1996—.

Writings

Grandfather Counts, Lee & Low Books (New York, NY), 2000.
Marika, Front Street Books (Asheville, NC), 2002.
When the Bees Fly Home, illustrated by Joline McFadden, Tilbury House (Gardiner, ME), 2002.

Work in Progress

Anna the Bookbinder, for Walker and Co. (New York, NY), completion expected in 2003.

*   *   *

CHEVALIER, Tracy

Personal

Born in Washington, DC; married; children: one son. *Education:* Oberlin College, B.A., c. 1984; University of East Anglia, M.A., 1994.

Addresses

Home—London, England. *Agent*—Jonny Geller, Curtis Brown, Haymarket House, 28/29 Haymarket, London SW1Y 4SP, England. *E-mail*—tracy@tchevalier.com.

Career

Worked as an editor for St. James Press, London, England, early 1990s.

Writings

Virgin Blue, Penguin (London, England), 1997.
Girl with a Pearl Earring, HarperCollins (New York, NY), 2000.
Falling Angels, Dutton/Plume (New York, NY), 2001.

Also editor of reference volumes, including *Twentieth Century Children's Writers,* St. James, 1989, *Contemporary Poets,* 5th edition, St. James, 1991, *Contemporary World Writers,* 2nd edition, St. James, 1993, and *Encyclopedia of the Essay,* Fitzroy Dearborn, 1998.

Sidelights

Tracy Chevalier scored a bestseller with her 2000 novel, *Girl with a Pearl Earring,* set in the Dutch city of Delft in the 1660s. Her heroine, Griet, is a teenager who enters the household of the painter Jan Vermeer as a maid, and finds herself embroiled in a situation that nearly ruins her reputation, but results in one of the artist's most stunning visual images. Critics praised Chevalier for her evocation of seventeenth-century Holland through the eyes of an illiterate servant, a young woman with very few options and few possessions save for her capacity for backbreaking work and a good reputation. As she answered a query about themes in her work, Chevalier reflected that fiction seemed to be guided by what she called "Otherness—how people cope with being the outsider, taking on new values and ways of life. I also seem to write a lot about women in difficult circumstances finding their way forward."

Chevalier grew up in Washington, D.C., and confessed to literary ambitions from an early age. "I always said I wanted to be a writer, but I think that's because I loved books so much—I wanted to be part of something I loved," she noted. "At various points I also said I wanted to be a teacher and a psychiatrist. I wrote a bit, but not really that much."

She was, however, an avid reader. "I read a lot from about age seven onwards," she remembered. "I used to go to the public library every week and bring home a stack of books to read. A librarian there, Mrs. Carney, took me under her wing and set aside a book for me each week. She gently directed me towards all kinds of things. My favorites were the Laura Ingalls Wilder series, the Walter R. Brooks 'Freddy the Pig' series, everything by Zylpha Keatley Snyder (*The Egypt Game, A Season of Ponies*), Madeleine L'Engle (*Arm of the Starfish, A Wrinkle in Time*), Joan Aiken (*The Wolves of Willoughby Chase,* etc.), the 'Dark Is Rising' series by Susan Cooper, the 'Book of Three' series by Lloyd Alexander, Tolkien's *Lord of the Rings,* and C. S. Lewis's *Narnia* series. From that list you can see I liked fantasy."

Her love of books, it seems, was linked to a tragic event in her childhood, as Chevalier revealed. "I was quiet, the kind who lay on my bed and read a lot. My mother got sick when I was three and died when I was almost eight, and I think reading was my means of escape from that." She excelled in school. "I was a good student, that annoying teacher's pet who did her homework and got good grades," the author admitted. "From kindergarten to eighth grade I went to public schools in Washington, D.C. and had the experience of being a white student in a school that was ninety percent black. So I got a little taste of what it's like to be a minority. When I was thirteen we moved to the suburbs—what a shock it was to walk into eighth grade classes to a sea of white faces! Sometimes I wonder if that's why I tend to write about outsiders—people put in situations where they are foreigners."

As a teenager, according to Chevalier, she was "pretty nerdy. I played clarinet from the age of eight and got more and more serious about it as time went on. I was in a youth orchestra program from age nine and started taking private lessons at twelve. At seventeen I had to decide if I wanted to pursue music professionally, and go to a conservatory rather than college. I was pretty good, but I wasn't good enough, so I chose college. I also read a lot still as a teenager and was editor of the high school literary magazine."

Chevalier attended a small liberal-arts college in Ohio. "College was freedom. I loved it. I went to Oberlin and it was the perfect place for me. Ironically given what's happened to my career, Oberlin has an extensive creative writing program but it never occurred to me to take a class in it. I majored in English." She moved to London in 1984 after college. "I went over for a junior semester in London and really loved it," the writer told Gavin J. Grant for another interview published on the Internet site *BookSense.com.* "After I graduated I didn't really know what to do with my life, so a couple of friends and I came over here for six months and I ended up staying."

Her sojourn in Britain was permanently secured by marriage to an English husband, and Chevalier embarked upon a career as editor of literary reference volumes. She wrote short stories on the side, but eventually felt herself drawn further into the creative realm. She pursued a master's degree in creative writing at the University of East Anglia and graduated in 1994. As she recalled, Chevalier said she "had the idea for my first novel, *The Virgin Blue,* during that year. Before that I'd always written short stories, never feeling I had an idea big enough to make into a novel. I began it during the [degree course], and continued it after while I was also working.

"I got it published by finding a good agent. I was very lucky in that regard: someone on the M.A. course found someone who was just starting out as an agent, and I wrote to him and said, 'I know so-and-so, could you read my work too?' And he did, as he didn't yet have many clients, and took me on. Now he's a really hot agent (not because of me—I just got lucky!) and takes on very few writers. Anyway, he found me a publisher for *The Virgin Blue,* and we went from there."

Chevalier's *The Virgin Blue* stretches back to sixteenth-century France and Switzerland. It centers upon a French Huguenot family, recent converts from Catholicism to Protestantism, who find themselves persecuted when the winds of political fortune turn. They flee to Switzerland, and it is their modern descendant, an American woman, who travels there to trace her roots and discovers a long-buried secret history in the family. The novel was published first in Britain in 1997, but after the success of *Girl with a Pearl Earring,* it appeared in North America as well early in 2002.

Despite the achievement of *The Virgin Blue,* it was Chevalier's *Girl with a Pearl Earring* that cemented her career as an author. The title is borrowed from a painting by Vermeer of the same name. The book jacket shows the maiden in question, somewhere in her teens, with the memorable face glancing over her shoulder, "her eyes signaling both anxiety and expectation," noted *Time* writer R. Z. Sheppard. As Chevalier confessed, she had owned a print of the work for many years and had always loved it, she told Grant in the *BookSense.com* interview. "My sister had a poster of the painting. When I was nineteen I visited her in Boston and I saw it and loved it so much. I'd never seen it before so I went out and got one for myself."

In the late 1990s, Chevalier was trying to complete another novel and suffering a bit of writer's block. As she said in another talk with the Web site *Book-browse.com,* "One morning a couple years ago I was lying in bed worrying about what I was going to write next, and I looked up at the painting and wondered what Vermeer did or said to the model to get her to look like that. And right then I made up the story." Vermeer's actual painting hangs in The Hague, and unlike other works by the master, is an unusual close-up of a face, looking directly at the viewer, against a dark background. Art historians have often wondered who the young girl is, for she does not appear in any other works by Vermeer. She is also wearing some rather exotic headgear—unlike other women in Vermeer paintings who are clad in the more conventional garments and accessories of the Dutch bourgeois—save for her pearl earring.

Chevalier imagined that the girl in the painting was a maid in the artist's household in Delft, and came up with her compelling story in a matter of days. The novel opens in the year 1664 by introducing Griet, who is sixteen and in her family's kitchen in Delft when a well-dressed couple come to meet her. Her mother has arranged the brief interview unbeknownst to Griet, who learns that day that she will leave her family home to work as a maid for the couple. She is also astonished to learn that the man who asked her why she arranged the vegetables she was chopping that day according to their color is none other than the city's most famed painter, Jan Vermeer.

Griet's father was a tile glazier, a maker of famed blue tiles for which the city of Delft is known, but a kiln explosion blinded him and plunged the family into poverty. He does belong to the local guild of painters and artisans, which Vermeer heads. Griet was recommended as a maid because of her ability to arrange items in her family's home for her father so that he will know where everything is. Vermeer needs a worker who can clean his studio without disturbing it, and soon Griet is using the techniques she honed at home to dust and mop without rearranging Vermeer's still lifes. At first, she is uneasy about working for a Catholic family, as the Vermeers are. There were few such families in Delft at the time, and the Vermeer household was situated in a part of town called Papists' Corner, to which Griet had never before dared venture before her first day of work.

Besides cleaning the painter's studio, Griet has many other duties in the household, which is dominated by Vermeer's volatile, often-pregnant wife, Catharina, and her formidable, business-minded mother, Maria Thins. Another maid in the home, Tanneke, once posed for the painter, and seems jealous of Griet and her youth. Griet also makes an enemy of one of the young Vermeer daughters, Cornelia, who appears to Griet as spiteful and untrustworthy. Griet sleeps in the cellar and faces a mountain of laundry to wash by hand daily, then iron. She must fetch the water from the canal. She is also sent daily to the Market Square, where a butcher's son begins to court her.

In Chevalier's work, Vermeer seems as intrigued by Griet as she is in awe of him as a painter. He sends her to the apothecary one cold day to buy the plant extracts that he uses in his paints, and then begins showing her how to grind and mix them. The arrival of a nursemaid for another Vermeer child disturbs the sleeping arrangements among the servants, and it is decreed that Griet may sleep in the attic above Vermeer's studio, locked in for the night, and then clean it in morning before heading downstairs for her other duties. She is the only member of the household besides Maria Thins allowed inside the studio—even Catharina is expressly barred from entering, because of her legendary clumsiness.

Griet is unable to read, save for her Protestant prayer book, or write anything but her own name, which her father once taught her. He also explained much to her about art, and she is fascinated by Vermeer's studio and the painting in progress that hangs on the easel. She describes each work to her father when she visits her parents on Sundays to bring them her meager wages. She realizes that her new job in an affluent household is creating a distance between herself and her impoverished family. A plague takes away her beloved younger sister, and her parents sink into a state of permanent despair. They encourage her romance with Pieter, the butcher's son, for a marital match will mean that they might once again enjoy decent food at their dinner table.

Griet is conflicted about Pieter. She tells him that she is too young to think of marriage, but her innermost thoughts seem preoccupied with Vermeer. The grueling duties of her job begin to take their toll on her, and she fears a life of drudgery and the permanent ill humor of Tanneke. Griet is also a little ashamed of her decline in status to that of maid. A *Publishers Weekly* reviewer praised the author for her portrayal of seventeenth-century Holland's "inflexible class system, making it clear that to members of the wealthy elite, every member of the servant class is expendable."

Resented by some members of the household—crafty Cornelia, for instance, hides items among Griet's meager personal belongings in an attempt to portray the maid as a thief—her problems intensify when Vermeer's wealthy patron van Ruijven begins leering at her. The collector once enjoined Vermeer to paint him with a servant from his own household, and the maid's subsequent pregnancy caused a scandal in Delft. Van Ruijven is adamant about having a painting of that "wide-eyed maid," as he calls Griet. Catharina, jealous of Griet's elevated status as her husband's assistant, eagerly agrees to the idea, appearing to believe that the same ignominious fate will befall Griet. Soon, there is gossip in Delft that the tiler's daughter will sit for the Master Vermeer, innuendo that undermines Griet's reputation—of which she is fiercely protective. She attends church every Sunday, and wears a cap that covers all of her hair, since she cannot afford to dress it; she explains that women from the lower classes who left their heads bare were usually prostitutes.

Vermeer agrees to a painting for van Ruijven, but paints Griet alone. At first he tells her to take her cap off, which she refuses, but then suggests that she find something instead in his storeroom full of props. Griet intertwines some blue and yellow cloths into a makeshift turban, and when one end comes loose the first day, Vermeer tells her to leave it. When the portrait is finished, Griet and the artist both adjudge it dull, missing some sort of spark to draw the eye, and Vermeer declares that she must wear Catharina's pearl earrings. Terrified lest Catharina find out that a maid wore a piece of her prized jewelry for a sitting, Griet refuses, but Vermeer insists. She must even pierce her own ears, using some of her precious wages to purchase the clove oil to numb the lobes. She tells her parents that she broke a mirror at the Vermeers' and had to pay for it, which prompts a chastising comment from them.

Maria Thins conspires with Vermeer and takes the earrings from Catharina's jewelry box one day when the once-again pregnant Catharina has left the house for the afternoon. The portrait is then finished, but Cornelia leads her mother up the stairs into the studio before van Ruijven takes it away, and a near-violent confrontation occurs. That same day was Griet's eighteenth birthday, and Pieter proposed to her. Though tensions between the heroine and Vermeer seem to mount toward a more titillating conclusion during the final days of the sitting, the outcome remains as ardently upright as Griet herself: "Chevalier steers her novel deliberately close and tacks abruptly away," noted Richard Eder in his review for the *New York Times*. "The book she has written, despite a lush note or two and occasional incident overload, is something far different and better."

Other reviews of Chevalier's bestselling novel offered similarly admiring words. *Entertainment Weekly*'s Vanessa V. Friedman commended "Chevalier's lustrous prose, which mimics ... the remove of the painting." Writing for *Booklist*, Carolyn Kubisz called *Girl with a Pearl Earring* "a beautiful story of a young girl's coming-of-age, and it is delightful speculative fiction." Critics also commended Chevalier's characterization of her teenaged servant. "Griet establishes herself as a keen observer who sees the world in sensuous images, expressed in precise and luminous prose," stated a *Publishers Weekly* review. Eder commented further about what he termed the "erotic element, but it is never more than implicit" as the story unfolds. "Chevalier's pattern is complex and revealing," the *New York Times* critic noted, and felt that in Griet Chevalier had created an enigmatic heroine. One minor character, Vermeer's kindly friend and microscope inventor Anton van Leeuwenhoek, warns her on one page that women sometimes become "trapped" in Vermeer's hauntingly quiet interiors. "She refuses to be lost, though," Eder noted, "and her refusal is the book's triumph, opening the way to an ending, ten years later, that weaves together, sardonically and exhilaratingly, the social and artistic complexities that Ms. Chevalier has so pungently presented."

Girl with a Pearl Earring seemed to strike a chord with the reading public, and was one of several fictionalized accounts of Vermeer or his artistry that had been published in recent years. It landed on the *New York Times* bestseller list in early 2000, and Chevalier even began to receive mail from women claiming they resembled the girl in the painting. The fascination with Vermeer and his images was in inverse proportion to what was actually known about him. He left nothing revealing about him save for about thirty-five paintings. No writings are extant, and what is known comes from Delft guild and registry records. As Chevalier said in the *Bookbrowse.com* interview, some details were easy to re-create for her novel—names of his wife and children, for instance, or his years as master of the guild, and his takeover of the tavern owned by his family. "Other facts are not so clear-cut and I had to make choices: he may or may not have lived in the house of his mother-in-law (I decided he did); he converted to Catholicism at the time of his marriage but not necessarily because Catharina was Catholic (I decided he did); he may have been friends with the scientist Antony van Leeuwenhoek, who invented the microscope (I decided he was). But there was a lot I simply made up."

Gary Schwartz wrote about the book in an essay for *Art in America* that discussed the spate of books about

Vermeer and his world. Schwartz found only one error in *Girl with Pearl Earring:* the New Church tower, Griet remarks, is visible from Vermeer's street, and she wonders whether such a view is not unusual for a Catholic household, who would never enter the Protestant church. But Schwartz pointed out that the New Church was actually owned by city, and citizens of all faiths were welcome. Still, the art scholar praised the novel for its accuracy. "Chevalier, let it be said, is the most scrupulous of the group as a researcher," Schwartz noted.

Chevalier's next novel, *Falling Angels,* was published in 2001. The work is set in London at the turn of the nineteenth century, and kicks off in Highgate Cemetery, where many well-known figures from history are buried, including Karl Marx. The story centers upon two little girls who meet there, at their families adjoining plots, just after Queen Victoria's death in 1901. Though Maude Coleman and Lavinia Waterhouse hail from different backgrounds, they forge a friendship marked by ups and downs that reflect the changing times. The Waterhouse clan, for example, are conservative and revere the late queen. The Colemans are of a more progressive mind, and are excited about the new century and the new king.

Other characters also provide different perspectives on the times. Simon Field is the son of the gravedigger at Highgate, and his life intertwines with that of Maude and Livy. Maude's mother joins the heated political movement to grant British women the right to vote, and the novel concludes in 1910 with the death of another monarch. Jessica Mann, writing for the *Telegraph,* described *Fallen Angels* "as cleverly atmospheric as its predecessor." It was a sentiment echoed by a *Publishers Weekly* critic who asserted that Chevalier "proves herself an astute observer of a social era, especially in her portrayal of the lingering sentimentality, prejudices and early stirrings of social change of the Victorian age." Mann found a few anachronisms in Chevalier's writing, but commended her talent in creating several separate narrative voices, each of which she termed "perfectly judged, reverberating in the mind's ear and leaving a melancholy echo: death and the means of disposing of corpses pervade the narrative," her *Telegraph* review concluded.

Chevalier admits that her novels require a good deal of legwork in addition to the creative process. They necessitate "loads of research," as she once noted, "since they've all been historical novels. I read books about the time, books written during the time, look at paintings of the time, and of course go to the places. For *Girl with a Pearl Earring* I looked at loads of Dutch paintings (both Vermeer's and others') and spent several days in the town of Delft." She even left open a bottle of linseed oil while writing sometimes; in the novel, Griet's parents become suspicious when she returns for her Sunday visits smelling of this pungent oil used to mix paints, which tells them she has been spending time in Vermeer's sacrosanct studio.

Chevalier described the town of Delft in the interview with Grant for *BookSense.com.* "It's built around a market square, the canal system, and bridges. There are a lot of seventeenth-century houses around, but there's a lot of the twentieth century there: a lot of cars and signs and stuff. You really have to squint to get past that but you do get a sense of [the older city] by being there." She noted that places in her novel like the Market Square, Meat Hall, and eight-pointed star in center of town were very visible still.

In researching the novel, Chevalier also felt compelled to take a painting course, at which she failed abysmally, as she told Grant during the *BookSense.com* interview. "I was really, really not good at it at all! It was very useful to be reminded how hard it is to paint anything, much less a masterpiece like *Girl With Pearl Earring.* It also gave me an idea what it's like to mix and handle paint."

Chevalier lives in London and has a young child who arrived just a few weeks after the manuscript for *Girl with a Pearl Earring* was sent off. She admits that the dual roles of writer and mother have made it more difficult to work. "I work in a room at home," she stated. "It has to be quiet—no music or anything—and I have to be alone. I write longhand, sitting in an armchair with some paper on a big book. Then at the end of the day I type what I've done into the computer. I pin pictures to the wall above the computer to look at—Vermeer paintings for *Girl,* pictures of suffragettes and Victorian children for *Falling Angels.*

"I write part-time and look after my two-year-old son part-time. It's hard to compartmentalize life like that so that life doesn't intrude into writing. I can't write when my son is in the house, as he always comes and finds me. And I have much less mind-space for thinking about my books. Before I had my son I could think about what I was writing anywhere—at the grocery store, walking down the street. Now I'm with him when I do those things, and I'm singing or talking to him or keeping him from picking up trash or putting ten jars of caviar in the shopping basket."

Chevalier still has the poster of *Girl with a Pearl Earring* that she bought in college. "I've carried it with me wherever I go," she told Grant in the *BookSense.com* interview. "It's always hung wherever I've lived, usually in the bedroom, but now she's in the office. Maybe I got her out of my system!" When she went to the Netherlands to research her novel, Chevalier purchased a new print at a museum, but disliked it once she had it home. It was too new, as she told Grant. "I took it down and put the old one back up. I like the old fadedness of it."

Biographical and Critical Sources

PERIODICALS

Art in America, March, 2001, Gary Schwartz, review of *Girl with a Pearl Earring,* p. 104.
Atlantic Monthly, February, 2000, Phoebe-Lou Adams, review of *Girl with a Pearl Earring,* p. 105.

Booklist, December 1, 1999, Carolyn Kubisz, review of *Girl with a Pearl Earring,* p. 684; April 1, 2000, Brad Hooper, review of *Girl with a Pearl Earring,* p. 1444; April 1, 2001, Stephanie Zvirin, review of *Girl with a Pearl Earring,* p. 1460.

Entertainment Weekly, February 4, 2000, Vanessa V. Friedman, review of *Girl with a Pearl Earring,* p. 66.

Library Journal, October 15, 1999, Barbara Hoffert, review of *Girl with a Pearl Earring,* p. 103.

New York Times, January 24, 2000, Richard Eder, "Master Vermeer, Isn't It, Um, Missing a Little Spark?"

Publishers Weekly, October 11, 1999, review of *Girl with a Pearl Earring,* p. 52; February 7, 2000, Dick Donahue; Daisy Maryles, "A Pearl of a Girl," p. 19; July 30, 2001, review of *Falling Angels,* p. 56.

School Library Journal, June 2000, Sheila Barry, review of *Girl with a Pearl Earring,* p. 173; December, 2000, Trev Jones, review of *Girl with a Pearl Earring,* p. 56.

Telegraph (London, England), August 6, 2001, Jessica Mann, "The Intimacy of the Grave."

Time, January 17, 2000, R. Z. Sheppard, "A Portrait of Radiance," p. 94.

OTHER

Bookbrowse.com, http://wwwbookbrowse.com (August 13, 2001), "An interview with Tracy Chevalier."

BookSense.com, http://www.booksense.com (August 13, 2001), "Very Interesting People: Tracy Chevalier," interview with Gavin J. Grant.

Tracy Chevalier Web Site, http://www.tchevalier.com (February 3, 2002).*

*   *   *

CLIFTON, (Thelma) Lucille 1936-

Personal

Born June 27, 1936, in Depew, NY; daughter of Samuel Louis, Sr. (a laborer) and Thelma (a laborer; maiden name, Moore) Sayles; married Fred James Clifton (an educator, writer, and artist), May 10, 1958 (died November 10, 1984); children: Sidney, Fredrica, Channing, Gillian, Graham, Alexia. *Education:* Attended Howard University, 1953-55, and Fredonia State Teachers College (now State University of New York College at Fredonia), 1955.

Addresses

Office—Division of Arts and Letters, St. Mary's College of Maryland, Montgomery Hall #126, St. Mary's City, MD 20686. *Agent*—Marilyn Marlow, Curtis Brown Ltd., 10 Astor Pl., New York, NY 10003. *E-mail*—lclifton@osprey.smcm.edu.

Career

New York State Division of Employment, Buffalo, NY, claims clerk, 1958-60; U.S. Office of Education, Washington, DC, literature assistant for Central Atlantic Regional Educational Laboratory, 1969-71; Coppin State College, Baltimore, MD, poet-in-residence, 1974-79; University of California, Santa Cruz, CA, professor of literature and creative writing, 1985-89; St. Mary's College of Maryland, St. Mary's City, MD, Distinguished Professor of Literature, 1989-91, Distinguished Professor of Humanities, 1991—; Duke University, Durham, NC, Blackburn Professor of Creative Writing, 1998—. Visiting writer, Columbia University School of the Arts; Jirry Moore Visiting Writer, George Washington University, 1982-83; Woodrow Wilson and Lila Wallace/*Readers Digest* visiting fellowship to Fisk University, Alma College, Albright College, Davidson College, and others. Trustee, Enoch Pratt Free Library, Baltimore. Has made television appearances, including *The Language of Life, The Today Show, Sunday Morning with Charles Kuralt, The Power of the Word,* and *Nightline. Member:* International PEN, Academy of American Poets (chancellor, 1999—), Poetry Society of America, American Cancer Society, Global Forum Arts Committee, Authors Guild, Authors League of America.

Awards, Honors

Discovery Award, New York YW-YMHA Poetry Center, 1969; *Good Times: Poems* was cited as one of the year's ten best books by the *New York Times,* 1969; National Endowment for the Arts awards, 1969, 1970, and 1972; Poet Laureate of the State of Maryland, 1974-85; Juniper Prize, University of Massachusetts, 1980; Pulitzer prize nominations for poetry, 1980, 1987, and 1991; Coretta Scott King Award, American Library Association, 1984, for *Everett Anderson's Goodbye;*

Lucille Clifton

named a "Maryland Living Treasure," 1993; Andrew White Medal, Loyola College of Baltimore, 1993; Lannan Literary Award for poetry, 1997, and National Book Award nomination, both for *The Terrible Stories;* inducted into National Literature Hall of Fame for African American Writers, 1998; Lenore Marshal Poetry Prize and *Los Angeles Times* poetry award, both 1998; Phi Beta Kappa, 1998; Lila Wallace/*Readers Digest* Award, 1999. Recipient of honorary degrees from Colby College, University of Maryland, Towson State University, Washington College, and Albright College.

Writings

POETRY

Good Times, Random House (New York, NY), 1969.

Good News about the Earth: New Poems, Random House (New York, NY), 1972.

An Ordinary Woman, Random House (New York, NY), 1974.

Two-headed Woman, University of Massachusetts Press (Amherst, MA), 1980.

Good Woman: Poems and a Memoir, 1969-1980, BOA Editions (Brockport, NY), 1987.

Next: New Poems, BOA Editions (Brockport, NY), 1987.

Ten Oxherding Pictures, Moving Parts Press (Santa Cruz, CA), 1988.

Quilting: Poems 1987-1990, BOA Editions (Brockport, NY), 1991.

The Book of Light, Copper Canyon Press (Port Townsend, WA), 1993.

Terrible Stories, BOA Editions (Brockport, NY), 1998.

Blessing the Boats: New and Selected Poems 1988-2000, BOA Editions (Brockport, NY), 2000.

Clifton's poetry has been translated into Norwegian, Spanish, French, Japanese, Hebrew, and other languages.

FOR CHILDREN

The Black BCs (alphabet poems), illustrations by Don Miller, Dutton (New York, NY), 1970.

Good, Says Jerome, illustrations by Stephanie Douglas, Dutton (New York, NY), 1973.

All Us Come 'cross the Water, pictures by John Steptoe, Holt (New York, NY), 1973.

Don't You Remember?, illustrations by Evaline Ness, Dutton (New York, NY), 1973.

The Boy Who Didn't Believe in Spring, pictures by Brinton Turkle, Dutton (New York, NY), 1973.

The Times They Used to Be, illustrations by Susan Jeschke, Holt (New York, NY), 1974, reprinted with illustrations by E. B. Lewis, Delacorte (New York, NY), 2000.

My Brother Fine with Me, illustrations by Moneta Barnett, Holt (New York, NY), 1975.

Three Wishes, illustrations by Stephanie Douglas, Viking (New York, NY), 1976, illustrations by Michael Hays, Delacorte (New York, NY), 1992.

Amifika, illustrations by Thomas DiGrazia, Dutton (New York, NY), 1977.

The Lucky Stone, illustrations by Dale Payson, Delacorte (New York, NY), 1979.

From **The Boy Who Didn't Believe in Spring,** *written by Clifton and illustrated by Brinton Turkle.*

My Friend Jacob, illustrations by Thomas DiGrazia, Dutton (New York, NY), 1980.

Sonora Beautiful, illustrations by Michael Garland, Dutton (New York, NY), 1981.

Dear Creator: A Week of Poems for Young People and Their Teachers, illustrations by Gail Gordon Carter, Doubleday (Garden City, NY), 1997.

Clifton's works have been translated into Spanish.

"EVERETT ANDERSON" SERIES; FOR CHILDREN

Some of the Days of Everett Anderson, illustrations by Evaline Ness, Holt (New York, NY), 1970.

Everett Anderson's Christmas Coming, illustrations by Evaline Ness, Holt (New York, NY), 1971, illustrations by Jan Spivey Gilchrist, Holt (New York, NY), 1991.

Everett Anderson's Year, illustrations by Ann Grifalconi, Holt (New York, NY), 1974.

Everett Anderson's Friend, illustrations by Ann Grifalconi, Holt (New York, NY), 1976.

Everett Anderson's 1 2 3, illustrations by Ann Grifalconi, Holt (New York, NY), 1977.

Everett Anderson's Nine Month Long, illustrations by Ann Grifalconi, Holt (New York, NY), 1978.

Everett Anderson's Goodbye, illustrations by Ann Grifalconi, Holt (New York, NY), 1983.

One of the Problems of Everett Anderson, illustrations by Ann Grifalconi, Holt (New York, NY), 2001.

OTHER

(Compiler with Alexander MacGibbon) *Composition: An Approach through Reading,* Harcourt (New York, NY), 1968.

(Contributor) Langston Hughes and Arna Bontemps, editors, *Poetry of the Negro, 1746-1970,* Doubleday (Garden City, NY), 1970.

(Contributor) Marlo Thomas and others, *Free to Be ... You and Me,* McGraw-Hill (New York, NY), 1974.

Generations: A Memoir (prose), Random House (New York, NY), 1976.

Also contributor to *Free to Be a Family,* 1987, *Norton Anthology of Literature by Women, Coming into the Light, Stealing the Language,* and other anthologies. Has made numerous sound and video recordings of poetry readings. Contributor of poetry to the *New York Times.* Contributor of fiction to *Negro Digest, Redbook, House and Garden,* and *Atlantic.* Contributor of nonfiction to *Ms.* and *Essence.*

Sidelights

Poet Lucille Clifton "began composing and writing stories at an early age and has been much encouraged by an ever-growing reading audience and a fine critical reputation," wrote Wallace R. Peppers in a *Dictionary of Literary Biography* essay. "In many ways her themes are traditional: she writes of her family because she is greatly interested in making sense of their lives and relationships; she writes of adversity and success in the ghetto community; and she writes of her role as a poet." Clifton's work emphasizes endurance and strength through adversity. Ronald Baughman suggested in his *Dictionary of Literary Biography* essay that Clifton's "pride in being black and in being a woman helps her transform difficult circumstances into a qualified affirmation about the black urban world she portrays." A *Publishers Weekly* critic noted that Clifton "redeems the human spirit from its dark moments. She is among our most trustworthy and gifted poets." Clifton holds dual

Clifton's verse text follows seven-year-old Everett Anderson month by month through one year of school, special events, playtime, and loneliness. (From Everett Anderson's Year, *illustrated by Ann Grifalconi.)*

professorial appointments at St. Mary's College of Maryland and Duke University. She served as the state of Maryland's poet laureate from 1974 until 1985. Her poetry has been translated into Norwegian, Spanish, French, Japanese, Hebrew, and other languages.

Clifton's first volume of poetry, *Good Times: Poems,* which was cited by the *New York Times* as one of 1969's ten best books, was described by Peppers as a "varied collection of character sketches written with third person narrative voices." Baughman noted that the poems "attain power not only through their subject matter but also through their careful techniques; among Clifton's most successful poetic devices ... are the precise evocative images that give substance to her rhetorical statements and a frequent duality of vision that lends complexity to her portraits of place and character." Calling the book's title "ironic," Baughman stated: "Although the urban ghetto can, through its many hardships, create figures who are tough enough to survive and triumph, the overriding concern of this book is with the horrors of the location, with the human carnage that results from such problems as poverty, unemployment, substandard housing, and inadequate education."

In Clifton's second volume of poetry, *Good News about the Earth: New Poems,* "the elusive good times seem more attainable," remarked Baughman, who summarized the three sections into which the book is divided: the first section "focuses on the sterility and destruction of 'white ways,' newly perceived through the social upheavals of the early 1970s"; the second section "presents a series of homages to black leaders of the late 1960s and early 1970s"; and the third section "deals with biblical characters powerfully rendered in terms of the black experience." Harriet Jackson Scarupa noted in *Ms.* that after having read what Clifton says about blackness and black pride, some critics "have concluded that Clifton hates whites. [Clifton] considers this a misreading. When she equates whiteness with death, blackness with life, she says: 'What I'm talking about is a certain kind of white arrogance—and not all white people have it—that is not good. I think airs of superiority are very dangerous. I believe in justice. I try not to be about hatred.'" Writing in *Poetry,* Ralph J. Mills, Jr., said that Clifton's poetic scope transcends the black experience "to embrace the entire world, human and non-human, in the deep affirmation she makes in the teeth of negative evidence."

An Ordinary Woman, Clifton's third collection of poems, "abandons many of the broad racial issues examined in the two preceding books and focuses instead on the narrower but equally complex issues of the writer's roles as woman and poet," according to Baughman. Peppers likewise commented that "the poems take as their theme a historical, social, and spiritual assessment of the current generation in the genealogical line" of Clifton's great-great-grandmother, who had been taken from her home in Dahomey, West Africa, and brought to America in slavery in 1830. Peppers noted that by taking an ordinary experience and personalizing it, "Clifton has elevated the experience into a public confession" which may be shared, and "it is this shared sense of situation, an easy identification between speaker and reader, that heightens the notion of ordinariness and gives … the collection an added dimension." Helen Vendler declared in the *New York Times Book Review* that Clifton "recalls for us those bare places we have all waited as 'ordinary women,' with no choices but yes or no, no art, no grace, no words, no reprieve." "Written in the same ironic, yet cautiously optimistic spirit as her earlier published work," observed Peppers, *An Ordinary Woman* is "lively, full of vigor, passion, and an all-consuming honesty."

In *Generations: A Memoir,* "it is as if [Clifton] were showing us a cherished family album and telling us the story about each person which seemed to sum him or her up best," described a *New Yorker* contributor. Calling the book an "eloquent eulogy of [Clifton's] parents," Reynolds Price wrote in the *New York Times Book Review* that "as with most elegists, her purpose is perpetuation and celebration, not judgment. There is no attempt to see either parent whole; no attempt at the recovery of history not witnessed by or told to the author. There is no sustained chronological narrative. Instead, clusters of brief anecdotes gather round two poles, the deaths of father and mother." Price believed that *Generations* stands "worthily" among the other modern elegies that assert that "we may survive, some lively few, if we've troubled to *be* alive and loved." However, a contributor to *Virginia Quarterly Review* thought that the book is "more than an elegy or a personal memoir. It is an attempt on the part of one woman to retrieve, and lyrically to celebrate, her Afro-American heritage."

Clifton's books for children are designed to help them understand their world. *My Friend Jacob,* for instance, is a story "in which a black child speaks with affection and patience of his friendship with a white adolescent neighbor … who is retarded," observed Zena Sutherland in the *Bulletin of the Center for Children's Books.* "Jacob is Sam's 'very very best friend' and all of his best qualities are appreciated by Sam, just as all of his limitations are accepted. … It is strong in the simplicity and warmth with which a handicapped person is loved rather than pitied, enjoyed rather than tolerated." Critics felt that Clifton's characters and their relationships are accurately and positively drawn in *My Friend Jacob.* Ismat Abdal-Haqq noted in *Interracial Books for Children Bulletin* that "the two boys have a strong relationship filled with trust and affection. The author depicts this relationship and their everyday adventures in a way that is unmarred by the mawkish sentimentality that often characterizes tales of the mentally disabled." And a contributor to *Reading Teacher* stated that "in a matter-of-fact, low-keyed style, we discover how [Sam and Jacob] help one another grow and understand the world."

Clifton's children's books also facilitate an understanding of black heritage specifically, which in turn fosters an important link with the past generally. *All Us Come*

During the summer of 1948, twelve-year-old Sooky sees her first television show, loses her uncle, and gets her share of life lessons. (From The Times They Used to Be, *written by Clifton and illustrated by E. B. Lewis.)*

'*cross the Water,* for example, "in a very straight-forward way … shows the relationship of Africa to Blacks in the U.S. without getting into a heavy rap about 'Pan-Africanism,'" stated Judy Richardson in the *Journal of Negro Education.* Richardson added that Clifton "seems able to get inside a little boy's head, and knows how to represent that on paper." An awareness of one's origins figures also in *The Times They Used to Be.* Called a "short and impeccable vignette—laced with idiom and humor of rural Black folk," by Rosalind K. Goddard in *School Library Journal,* the book was described by Lee A. Daniels in the *Washington Post* as a "story in which a young girl catches her first glimpse of the new technological era in a hardware store window, and learns of death and life." "Most books that awaken adult nostalgia are not as appealing to young readers," maintained Sutherland in the *Bulletin of the Center for Children's Books,* "but this brief story has enough warmth and vitality and humor for any reader."

In addition to quickening an awareness of black heritage, Clifton's books for children frequently include an element of fantasy as well. In *Three Wishes,* for example, a young girl finds a lucky penny on New Year's Day and makes three wishes upon it. Christopher Lehmann-Haupt in the *New York Times Book Review* called the book "an urbanized version of the traditional tale in which the first wish reveals the power of the magic object ... the second wish is a mistake, and the third undoes the second." Lehmann-Haupt added: "Too few children's books for blacks justify their ethnicity, but this one is a winning blend of black English and bright illustration." *The Lucky Stone,* in which a lucky stone provides good fortune for all of its owners, was described by Ruth K. MacDonald in *School Library Journal* as "Four short stories about four generations of Black women and their dealings with a lucky stone.... Clifton uses as a frame device a grandmother telling the history of the stone to her granddaughter; by the end, the granddaughter has inherited the stone herself."

Barbara Walker wrote in *Interracial Books for Children Bulletin* that Clifton "is a gifted poet with the greater gift of being able to write poetry for children." But in a *Language Arts* interview with Rudine Sims, Clifton indicated that she doesn't think of it as poetry especially for children. "It seems to me that if you write poetry for children, you have to keep too many things in mind other than the poem. So I'm just writing a poem," she said. *Some of the Days of Everett Anderson* is a book of nine poems, about which Marjorie Lewis observed in *School Library Journal:* "Some of the days of six-year-old 'ebony Everett Anderson' are happy; some lonely— but all of them are special, reflecting the author's own pride in being black." In the *New York Times Book Review,* Hoyt W. Fuller thought that Clifton has "a profoundly simple way of saying all that is important to say, and we know that the struggle is worth it, that the all-important battle of image is being won, and that the future of all those beautiful black children out there need not be twisted and broken." *Everett Anderson's Christmas Coming* concerns Christmas preparations in which "each of the five days before Everett's Christmas is described by a verse," observed Anita Silvey in *Horn Book.* Silvey added: "The overall richness of Everett's experiences dominates the text." Jane O'Reilly suggested in the *New York Times Book Review* that "Everett Anderson, black and boyish, is glimpsed, rather than explained through poems about him." *Everett Anderson's Year* celebrates "a year in the life of a city child ... in appealing verses," according to Beryl Robinson in *Horn Book.* Robinson felt that "mischief, fun, gaiety, and poignancy are a part of his days as the year progresses. The portrayals of child and mother are lively and solid, executed with both strength and tenderness."

Language is important in Clifton's writing. In answer to Sims's question about the presence of both black and white children in her work, Clifton responded specifically about *Sonora Beautiful,* which is about the insecurities and dissatisfaction of an adolescent girl and which has only white characters: "In this book, I *heard* the characters as white. I have a tendency to *hear* the language of the characters, and then I know something about who the people are." However, regarding objec-

tions to the black vernacular she often uses, Clifton told Sims: "I do not write out of weakness. That is to say, I do not write the language I write because I don't know any other.... But I have a certain integrity about my art, and in *my* art you have to be honest and you have to have people talking the way they really talk. So all of my books are not in the same language."

In Clifton's 1991 title, *Quilting: Poems 1987-1990,* the author uses a quilt as a poetic metaphor for life. Each poem is a story, bound together through the chronicles of history and figuratively sewn with the thread of experience. The result is, as Roger Mitchell in *American Book Review* described it, a quilt "made by and for people." Each section of the book is divided by a conventional quilt design name such as "Eight-pointed Star" and "Tree of Life," which provides a framework within which Clifton crafts her poetic quilt. Clifton's main focus is on women's history; however, according to Mitchell, her poetry has a far broader range: "Her heroes include nameless slaves buried on old plantations, Hector Peterson (the first child killed in the Soweto riot), Fannie Lou Hamer (founder of the Mississippi Peace and Freedom Party), Nelson and Winnie Mandela, W. E. B. DuBois, Huey P. Newton, and many other people who gave their lives to black people from slavery and prejudice."

Enthusiasts of *Quilting* included critic Bruce Bennett in the *New York Times Book Review,* who praised Clifton as a "passionate, mercurial writer, by turns angry, prophetic, compassionate, shrewd, sensuous, vulnerable and funny.... The movement and effect of the whole book communicate the sense of a journey through which the poet achieves an understanding of something new." Pat Monaghan in *Booklist* admired Clifton's "terse, uncomplicated" verse, and judged the poet "a fierce and original voice in American letters." Mitchell found energy and hope in her poems, referring to them as "visionary." He concluded that they are "the poems of a strong woman, strong enough to ... look the impending crises of our time in the eye, as well as our customary limitations, and go ahead and hope anyway."

Clifton's 1993 poetry collection, *The Book of Light,* examines "life through light in its various manifestations," commented Andrea Lockett in a *Belles Lettres* review of the collection. Among the poetic subjects of the collection are bigotry and intolerance, epitomized by a poem about notorious U.S. Senator Jesse Helms; destruction, including a poem about the tragic bombing by police of a MOVE compound in Philadelphia in 1985; religion, characterized by a sequence of poems featuring a dialogue between God and the Devil; and mythology, rendered by poems about figures such as Atlas and Superman. "If this poet's art has deepened since ... *Good Times,* it's in an increased capacity for quiet delicacy and fresh generalization," remarked *Poetry* contributor Calvin Bedient. Bedient criticized the poems in the collection that take an overtly political tone, taking issue with "Clifton's politics of championing difference—except, of course, where the difference opposes her politics." However, Bedient commended the more personal poems in *The Book of Light*, declaring that when Clifton writes without "anger and sentimentality, she writes at her remarkable best." Lockett concluded that the collection is "a gift of joy, a truly illuminated manuscript by a writer whose powers have been visited by grace."

The Terrible Stories and *Blessing the Boats: New and Selected Poems 1988-2000* shed light upon women's survival skills in the face of ill health, family upheaval, and historic tragedy. Among the pieces collected in these volumes are several about the author's breast cancer, but she also deals with juvenile violence, child abuse, and a shaman-like empathy with animals as varied as foxes, squirrels, and crabs. In a *Booklist* review of *Blessing the Boats*, Donna Seaman found the poems "lean, agile, and accurate, and there is beauty in their directness and efficiency." A *Publishers Weekly* reviewer likewise concluded that the collection "distills a distinctive American voice, one that pulls no punches in taking on the best and worst of life."

In her interview with Sims, she was asked whether or not she feels any special pressures or special opportunities as a black author. Clifton responded: "I do feel a responsibility.... First, I'm going to write books that tend to celebrate life. I'm about that. And I wish to have children see people like themselves in books.... I also take seriously the responsibility of not lying.... I'm not going to say that life is wretched if circumstance is wretched, because that's not true. So I take that responsibility, but it's a responsibility to the truth, and to my art as much as anything. I owe everybody that.... It's the truth as I see it, and that's what my responsibility is."

Biographical and Critical Sources

BOOKS

Beckles, Frances N., *Twenty Black Women*, Gateway Press (Baltimore, MD), 1978.
Black Literature Criticism, Gale (Detroit, MI), 1992.
Children's Literature Review, Volume 5, Gale (Detroit, MI), 1983.
Contemporary Literary Criticism, Gale (Detroit, MI), Volume 9, 1981, Volume 66, 1991.
Dictionary of Literary Biography, Gale (Detroit, MI), Volume 5: *American Poets since World War II*, 1980, Volume 41: *Afro-American Poets since 1955*, 1985.
Dreyer, Sharon Spredemann, *The Bookfinder: A Guide to Children's Literature about the Needs and Problems of Youth Aged 2-15*, Volume 1, American Guidance Service (Circle Pines, MN), 1977.
Evans, Mari, editor, *Black Women Writers (1950-1980): A Critical Evaluation*, Doubleday-Anchor (New York, NY), 1984.
St. James Guide to Children's Writers, 5th edition, St. James Press (Detroit, MI), 1999.

PERIODICALS

America, May 1, 1976.
American Book Review, June, 1992, Roger Mitchell, review of *Quilting: Poems 1987-1990*, p. 21.

Belles Lettres, summer, 1993, Andrea Lockett, review of *The Book of Light*, p. 51.
Black Scholar, March, 1981.
Black World, July, 1970; February, 1973.
Booklist, June 15, 1991, p. 1926; August, 1996, Patricia Monaghan, review of *The Terrible Stories*, p. 1876; May 1, 1997, p. 1506; March 15, 2000, Donna Seaman, review of *Blessing the Boats: New and Selected Poems, 1988-2000*, p. 1316; September 15, 2001, Shelley Townsend-Hudson, review of *One of the Problems of Everett Anderson*, p. 230.
Book World, March 8, 1970; November 8, 1970.
Bulletin of the Center for Children's Books, March, 1971; November, 1974, Zena Sutherland, review of *Times They Used to Be;* March, 1976; September, 1980, Zena Sutherland, review of *My Friend Jacob*.
Christian Science Monitor, February 5, 1988, p. B3; January 17, 1992, p. 14.
Horn Book, December, 1971, Anita Silvey, review of *Everett Anderson's Christmas Coming;* August, 1973; February, 1975; December, 1975; October, 1977; March, 1993, p. 229.
Interracial Books for Children Bulletin, Volume 5, numbers 7 and 8, 1975; Volume 7, number 1, 1976; Volume 8, number 1, 1977; Volume 10, number 5, 1979; Volume 11, numbers 1 and 2, 1980; Volume 12, number 2, 1981.
Journal of Negro Education, summer, 1974, Judy Richardson, review of *All Us Come 'cross the Water*.
Journal of Reading, February, 1977; December, 1986.
Kirkus Reviews, April 15, 1970; October 1, 1970; December 15, 1974; April 15, 1976; February 15, 1982.
Language Arts, January, 1978; February 2, 1982.
Library Journal, April 15, 2000, Louis McKee, review of *Blessing the Boats: New and Selected Poems, 1988-2000*, p. 95.
Ms., October, 1976, Harriet Jackson Scarupa, review of *Good News about the Earth*.
New Yorker, April 5, 1976, review of *Generations: A Memoir*.
New York Times, December 20, 1976.
New York Times Book Review, September 6, 1970; December 6, 1970; December 5, 1971; November 4, 1973; April 6, 1975, Helen Vendler, review of *An Ordinary Woman;* March 14, 1976, Reynolds Price, review of *Generations: A Memoir;* May 15, 1977, Christopher Lehmann-Haupt, review of *Three Wishes;* February 19, 1989, p. 24; March 1, 1992, Bruce Bennett, "Preservation Poets"; April 18, 1993, David Kirby, review of *The Book of Light*, p. 15.
Poetry, May, 1973, Ralph J. Mills, review of *Good News about the Earth;* March, 1994, Calvin Bedient, review of *The Book of Light*, p. 344.
Publishers Weekly, July 22, 1996, review of *The Terrible Stories*, p. 236; April 17, 2000, review of *Blessing the Boats: New and Selected Poems, 1988-2000*, p. 71.
Reading Teacher, October, 1978; March, 1981, review of *My Friend Jacob*.
Redbook, November, 1969.
Saturday Review, December 11, 1971; August 12, 1972; December 4, 1973.
School Library Journal, May, 1970; December, 1970; September, 1974, Rosalind K. Goddard, review of

Times They Used to Be; December, 1977; February, 1979, Ruth K. MacDonald, review of *Lucky Stone;* March, 1980; October, 2001, Sally R. Dow, review of *One of the Problems of Everett Anderson,* p. 113.

Tribune Books (Chicago, IL), August 30, 1987.

Virginia Quarterly Review, fall, 1976, review of *Generations: A Memoir;* winter, 1997, p. 41.

Voice of Youth Advocates, April, 1982.

Washington Post, November 10, 1974, Lee A. Daniels, review of *Times They Used to Be;* August 9, 1979.

Washington Post Book World, November 11, 1973; November 10, 1974; December 8, 1974; December 11, 1977; February 10, 1980; September 14, 1980; July 20, 1986; May 10, 1987; February 13, 1994, p. 8.

Western Humanities Review, summer, 1970.

World Literature Today, autumn, 2000, Adele S. Newson-Horst, review of *Blessing the Boats: New and Selected Poems 1988-2000,* p. 817.

OTHER

Academy of American Poets, http://www.poets.org/ (April 23, 2001).

University of Illinois English Department Home, http://www.english.uiuc.edu/ (April 23, 2001), "Modern American Poetry: About Lucille Clifton."

Voices from the Gaps: Women Writers of Color, http://voices.cla.umn.edu/ (April 23, 2001).*

*　　*　　*

CRISP, Marta Marie 1947-
(Marty Crisp)

Personal

Born December 18, 1947, in Baltimore, MD; daughter of Charles Morris (a mechanical engineer) and Doris (a homemaker; maiden name, Herr) Tibbels; married George B. Crisp, May 29, 1977; children: Meribeth Ellen, Matthew Earl, Jonathan William, Joshua Mark. *Education:* Davis and Elkins College, B.A. (English),

Marta Marie Crisp

1969; Guilford Technical Institute, 1977. *Politics:* Independent. *Religion:* Quaker. *Hobbies and other interests:* Collecting teddy bears, traveling, reading, walking.

Addresses

Home—253 Spring Garden St., Ephrata, PA 17522. *Office*—c/o Lancaster Sunday News, 8 West King St., Lancaster, PA 17603. *Agent*—Frances Kuffel, 1350 Avenue of the Americas, Ste. 2905, New York, NY 10019. *E-mail*—mcrisp@dejazzd.com.

Career

Associated Press, Baltimore, MD, reporter, 1969-70; Lancaster Sunday News, Lancaster, PA, reporter and staff writer, 1985—. Lancaster Community Hospital, Lancaster, PA, registered nurse, 1977-79; Lancaster General Hospital, Lancaster, PA, registered nurse, 1979-82; Ephrata Community Hospital, Ephrata, PA, registered nurse, 1982-85. *Member:* Society of Children's Book Writers and Illustrators, WRT4KDZ, Dog Writers Association of America.

Awards, Honors

Black Eyed Susan list, Maryland Education Media Association, 1995, for *Buzzard Breath;* Maxwell Medal for Best Children's Book, Dog Writers Association of America, and IPPY Award finalist, Independent Publisher, both 1999, both for *Ratzo.*

Writings

AS MARTY CRISP

The Stormy Heart, Avalon (New York, NY), 1987.

Teddy Bears in Advertizing Art, Hobby House Press (Grantsville, MD), 1991.

At Your Own Risk, Avalon (New York, NY), 1993.

Buzzard Breath, Atheneum (New York, NY), 1995.

Destiny, Arizona, Heartsong (Bluehill, ME), 1997.

Ratzo, Rising Moon (Flagstaff, AZ), 1998.

My Dog, Cat, illustrated by True Kelly, Holiday House (New York, NY), 2000.

Black and White, illustrated by Sherry Neidigh, Rising Moon (Flagstaff, AZ), 2000.

Totally Polar, illustrated by Viv Eisner, Rising Moon (Flagstaff, AZ), 2001.

Private Captain: A Story of Gettysburg, Philomel (New York, NY), 2001.

White Star, Holiday House (New York, NY), in press.

Contributor of reviews to *Audiofile* magazine. Contributor of articles to *Dolphin Log, Family Circle, Writers' Digest, Highlights for Children,* and *Guideposts.* Short story "Members of the Flock" was anthologized in *More Stories from Guideposts: Friendship at Its Best,* Augsburg, 1987. *Buzzard Breath* has been translated into German.

Work in Progress

Turnspit, "a dog in 1599 England"; *Titanicat,* "a picture book about the ship's cat on the *Titanic*"; *Maggie Mazoo,* "about a St. Bernard living at a zoo as a foster mother to a polar bear cub."

Sidelights

Marta Marie Crisp told *SATA:* "I decided to 'become a writer' in eighth grade when my social studies teacher ran off copies of a poem I'd written, passed it out to the class, and read it aloud—without identifying who wrote it. I loved the feeling of being judged solely on what I wrote—and not all those other teenage criteria for popularity.

"I didn't much like history in school. Thought it was boring. But now that I've starting writing history—I love it. I love all the tiny details that don't make it into history textbooks—like the facts that fat ladies in 1599 were considered beautiful (they had to be very rich to get fat) and carried lap dogs to attract fleas away from their own bodies.

"Dogs fascinate me. I used to want to be a veterinarian and worked in kennels for several years when I was in my early twenties. I loved reading dog books (especially Jim Kjelgaard's) and decided early that it was my 'literary' dream to write dog books myself. I'm working on my sixth (*Turnspit*) right now, and I can't seem to get enough of the subject!"

One of these works featuring canines, *Buzzard Breath,* tells the story of Will Winkle, a sixth-grade student fascinated with dogs. After his parents decide that he may get a pet, Will searches for the perfect pedigreed dog but ends up, temporarily, looking after a common German shepherd named Buzz. After this dog is wrongly accused of biting a toddler, Will decides he must convince everyone of Buzz's innocence, saving the dog from being put to death. While noting a few flaws with the novel, *School Library Journal* reviewer Cyrisse Jaffee nonetheless remarked that "readers will respond to the heartfelt bond between boy and dog and the satisfying happy ending," while a *Publishers Weekly* critic described the book as "full of energy and ripe with thoughtful themes."

Greyhounds are the featured canine in Crisp's 1998 book, *Ratzo.* Out fossil hunting with his friend one day, Josh Marks comes across a group of Greyhounds in the desert. No longer suitable for racing, the dogs were abandoned by their former owner and left to die in the Arizona wilderness. Allowed to keep one of the greyhounds, Josh cares for the animal, learning that he once was the great Raj Ratoon Racer. However, as he tries to restore the dog to his former status, Josh discovers the mistreatment of many animals in dog racing and decides to help his grandfather find the person who tried to dispose of Raj in the desert. Claiming that *Ratzo* "should be popular with dog lovers," *Booklist* reviewer Kay Weisman remarked favorably upon the "well-drawn,

Crisp's picture book tells how Bud brings home a new dog, only to lose it among the animals on the family farm—a situation that gives young readers the chance to discover the dog hiding on each page. (From Black and White, *illustrated by Sherry Neidigh.)*

believable characters with strengths and weaknesses readers will understand."

Other books by Crisp also feature dogs in starring roles. *Black and White* shows, in picture book format, the story of a little boy who brings home a new dog but loses it among all the other animals on his family's farm. Youngsters are challenged to find the black and white puppy hiding among the other animals, including pigs, ponies, and cows. Illustrated by True Kelley, Crisp's 2000 work *My Dog, Cat* introduces another canine-loving protagonist, Abbie, who wishes for a big dog of his own. Presented with the opportunity to watch his Aunt Laura's dog for a time, Abbie looks forward to seeing the animal. Despite his initial disappointment that the dog named Cat is only a small Yorkie, the young boy learns not to judge everything by its appearance.

Crisp has also demonstrated her writing talents with other subjects as well, including the 2001 novel *Private Captain: A Story of Gettysburg.* After his father dies, twelve-year-old Ben sets out to find his older brother, Captain Reuben Reynolds, and bring him home to help the family. Accompanied by his faithful dog and younger cousin Danny, Ben learns first hand about the tragedies of war as they come upon the Battle of Gettysburg and the horrible cost of human life it extracted. Admiring the depth of the novel, *School Library Journal* reviewer Coop Renner commented on Crisp's ability to blend "the well-rounded characterization and vivid attention to detail common to the classic writers of historical fiction" with the "more colloquial and leaner" efforts of contemporary authors.

When speaking about her writing inspiration, Crisp told *SATA*, "When you hear the advice, 'Write what you have a passion for,' that's me and dogs!"

Biographical and Critical Sources

PERIODICALS

Booklist, February 15, 1999, Kay Weisman, review of *Ratzo,* p. 1070; June 1, 2000, Lauren Peterson, review of *Black and White,* p. 1906; January 1, 2001, Ilene Cooper, review of *My Dog, Cat,* p. 958.

Kirkus Reviews, June 1, 1995, review of *Buzzard Breath,* p. 779.

New York Times Book Review, May 21, 1995, Linda Gray Sexton, review of *Buzzard Breath,* p. 30.

Publishers Weekly, July 3, 1995, review of *Buzzard Breath,* p. 61; March 5, 2001, review of *Private Captain: A Story of Gettysburg,* p. 80.

School Library Journal, June, 1995, Cyrisse Jaffee, review of *Buzzard Breath,* p. 110; April, 1999, Linda L. Plevak, review of *Ratzo,* p. 130; August, 2000, Meghan R. Malone, review of *Black and White,* p. 146; April, 2001, Coop Renner, review of *Private Captain,* p. 139.

OTHER

Marty Crisp Web Site, http://www.martycrisp.com (November 16, 2001).

*   *   *

CRISP, Marty
See CRISP, Marta Marie

*   *   *

CUTLIP, Kimbra (Leigh-Ann) 1964-

Personal

Born February 13, 1964, in NJ; daughter of David and Judyth (Delorenzo) Cutlip; married Michael R. Broglie, June 3, 1995; children: Sienna Michelle, Eleanor Alden. *Education:* Syracuse University, B.S., B.A., 1985; graduate study at George Washington University. *Hobbies and other interests:* Sailing, wake-boarding, kite-boarding, biking, pottery.

Addresses

Office—Galesville, MD. *E-mail*—kcutlip@erols.com.

Career

U.S. Peace Corps, Washington, DC, volunteer in Niger, 1985-88; Smithsonian Institution, Washington, DC, videotape producer, 1989-91, assistant diving officer, 1991-96; *Weatherwise* (magazine), associate editor, 1997—. American Academy of Underwater Sciences, codirector, 1986-88. *Member:* National Association of Science Writers, District of Columbia Science Writers Association.

Awards, Honors

Silver Award for excellence in print, Washington Edpress, 1997.

Writings

Sailor's Night before Christmas, illustrated by James Rice, Pelican Publishing (Gretna, LA), 1999.

Contributor to magazines and newspapers.

Sidelights

Kimbra Cutlip told *SATA:* "Like many writers, I've always been compelled to write: journals, letters, ideas scribbled on scraps of paper. My first published book came about when I was living aboard my sailboat. Children always wanted to know how I lived there in the wintertime and, if I really *did* live there in the winter, how Santa Claus got in. *A Sailor's Night before Christmas* is my answer to them.

"While most of my energy is devoted to my primary job as an editor and to raising my two daughters, I meet with a writers' group weekly to share ideas and work on new writing projects. The support and constructive critical feedback is very motivational and keeps me focused on writing for myself. I am interested in writing stories for my girls about young women and girls who take on challenges and adventures on the seas and learn to be strong, independent individuals. I'm also actively involved in science reporting: natural history and environmental news."*

D

DANIELS, Max
See GELLIS, Roberta (Leah Jacobs)

* * *

DEMAREST, Chris(topher) L(ynn) 1951-

Personal

Born April 18, 1951, in Hartford, CT; son of Robert (a salesperson) and Shirley (a librarian; maiden name, Johnston) Demarest; married Larkin Dorsey Upson (a finish carpenter), February 2, 1982 (divorced); married Laura L. Gillespie (a travel/tour director), September 26, 1992; children: Ethan. *Education:* University of Massachusetts, B.F.A., 1976. *Hobbies and other interests:* Sailing, cycling, music/rock 'n' roll, tennis, horseback riding.

Addresses

Home—P.O. Box 1280, Lebanon, NH 03766-4280.

Career

Cartoonist, author, and illustrator of books for children. House painter in Seattle, WA, 1976-77. Has worked as a volunteer fireman. *Member:* Society of Children's Book Writers and Illustrators.

Awards, Honors

Ford Foundation Grant, 1975; Junior Literary Guild selections, 1982, for *Benedict Finds a Home,* and 1983, for *Clemens' Kingdom;* Kentucky Bluegrass Awards, 1991, for *The Butterfly Jar,* and 1994, for *Bob and Jack;* Colorado Children's Book Award nomination, 1991, for *No Peas for Nellie;* Parents' Choice Award, 1992, for *My Little Red Car; School Library Journal* Best Book, 1994, for *Lindbergh;* Children's Choice Award and Reading Rainbow selection, both 1994, for *Smart Dog.*

Writings

FOR CHILDREN; SELF-ILLUSTRATED

Benedict Finds a Home, Lothrop (New York, NY), 1982.
Clemens' Kingdom, Lothrop (New York, NY), 1983.
Orville's Odyssey, Simon & Schuster (New York, NY), 1986.
Morton and Sidney, Macmillan (New York, NY), 1987.
No Peas for Nellie, Macmillan (New York, NY), 1988.
The Lunatic Adventure of Kitman and Willy, Simon & Schuster (New York, NY), 1988.
Kitman and Willy at Sea, Simon & Schuster (New York, NY), 1991.
My Little Red Car, Caroline House (Honesdale, PA), 1992.
Lindbergh (biography), Crown (New York, NY), 1993.
My Blue Boat, Harcourt (San Diego, CA), 1995.
Ship, Harcourt (San Diego, CA) 1995.
Plane, Harcourt (San Diego, CA), 1995.

Chris L. Demarest (center) with fellow authors Stephanie Gordon Tessler (left) and Judith Ross Enderle.

Train, Harcourt (San Diego, CA), 1996.

Bus, Harcourt (San Diego, CA), 1996.

Summer, Harcourt (San Diego, CA), 1997.

Spring, Harcourt (San Diego, CA), 1997.

Let's Go! Soft Cube with Rattle, Harcourt (San Diego, CA), 1997.

All Aboard!, Harcourt (San Diego, CA), 1997.

Farmer Nat, Harcourt (San Diego, CA), 1998.

Zookeeper Sue, Harcourt (San Diego, CA), 1999.

The Cowboy ABC, Dorling Kindersley (New York, NY), 1999.

Firefighters A to Z, McElderry Books (New York, NY), 1999.

Honk!, Boyds Mills Press (Honesdale, PA), 2001.

I Invited a Dragon to Dinner: And Other Poems to Make You Laugh Out Loud, Philomel Books (New York, NY), 2002.

Smokejumpers One to Ten, McElderry Books (New York, NY), 2002.

ILLUSTRATOR

Rose Greydanus, *Tree House Fun,* Troll (Mahwah, NJ), 1980.

Elizabeth Isele, *Pooks,* Lippincott (New York, NY), 1983.

Betty Jo Stanovich, *Hedgehog and Friends,* Lothrop (New York, NY), 1983.

Betty Jo Stanovich, *Hedgehog Adventures,* Lothrop (New York, NY), 1983.

Sue Alexander, *World Famous Muriel,* Little, Brown (Boston, MA), 1984.

Betty Jo Stanovich, *Hedgehog Surprises,* Lothrop (New York, NY), 1984.

Sue Alexander, *World Famous Muriel and the Dragon,* Little, Brown (Boston, MA), 1985.

Jeff Moss, *The Butterfly Jar* (poems), Bantam (New York, NY), 1989.

Joanne Oppenheim, *"Not Now!" Said the Cow,* Bantam (New York, NY), 1989.

Andrew Sharmat, *Smedge,* Macmillan (New York, NY), 1989.

Marvin Varori, *I've Got Goose Pimples: And Other Great Expressions,* Morrow (New York, NY), 1990.

(With others) Joanna Cole and Stephanie Calmenson, compilers, *The Scary Book* (stories, poems, and riddles), Morrow (New York, NY), 1991.

David Kirby and Allen Woodman, *The Cows Are Going to Paris,* Caroline House (Honesdale, PA), 1991.

Stephen Krensky, *The Missing Mother Goose,* Doubleday (New York, NY), 1991.

Jeff Moss, *The Other Side of the Door* (poems), Bantam (New York, NY), 1991.

Joanne Oppenheim, *The Donkey's Tale,* Bantam (New York, NY), 1991.

Bobbye S. Goldstein, editor, *What's On the Menu?* (poems), Viking (New York, NY), 1992.

Jeffie Ross Gordon, *Two Badd Babies,* Boyds Mills Press (Honesdale, PA), 1992.

Jeff Moss, *Bob and Jack: A Boy and His Yak,* Bantam (New York, NY), 1992.

Diana Klemin, *How Do You Wrap a Horse?,* Boyds Mills Press (Honesdale, PA), 1993.

Ralph Leentis, *Smart Dog,* Caroline House, 1993.

Joanne Oppenheim, *"Uh-oh!" Cawed the Crow,* Bantam (New York, NY), 1993.

N. L. Sharp, *Today I'm Going Fishing with My Dad,* Boyds Mills Press (Honesdale, PA), 1993.

David L. Harrison, *When Cows Come Home,* Boyds Mills Press (Honesdale, PA), 1994.

Susan Karnovsky, *Billy and the Magic String,* Troll (Mahwah, NJ), 1994.

Thomas McKean, *Hooray for Grandma Jo!,* Crown (New York, NY), 1994.

Jeff Moss, *Hieronymus White: A Bird Who Believed that He Was Always Right,* Ballantine (New York, NY), 1994.

Marvin Terban, *Time to Rhyme: A Rhyming Dictionary,* Boyds Mills Press (Honesdale, PA), 1994.

Judith Ross Enderle and Stephanie Gordon Tessler, *What Would Mama Do?,* Boyds Mills Press (Honesdale, PA), 1995.

Nancy Lee Charlton, *Derek's Dog Days,* Harcourt (San Diego, CA), 1995.

Cynthia DeFelice, *Casey in the Bath,* Farrar, Straus (New York, NY), 1995.

Larry Dane Brimher, *If Dogs Had Wings,* Boyds Mills Press (Honesdale, PA), 1996.

Missing Cat, Berlitz (Princeton, NJ), 1996.

Jeff Moss, *The Dad of the Dad of the Dad of Your Dad,* Ballantine (New York, NY), 1997.

A Visit to Grandma, Berlitz (Princeton, NJ), 1997.

French Picture Dictionary, Berlitz (Princeton, NJ), 1997.

Italian Picture Dictionary, Berlitz (Princeton, NJ), 1997.

The Five Crayons, Berlitz (Princeton, NJ), 1998.

First 100 German Words, Berlitz (Princeton, NJ), 1998.

First 100 French Words, Berlitz (Princeton, NJ), 1998.

First 100 Italian Words, Berlitz (Princeton, NJ), 1998.

Deborah Heiligman, *Mike Swan, Sink or Swim,* Dell (New York, NY), 1998.

Harriet Ziefert, *Dozens, Dozens,* Viking (New York, NY), 1998.

J. Stuart Murphy, *Beep Beep, Vroom Vroom!,* HarperCollins (New York, NY), 2000.

Harriet Ziefert, *April Fool!,* Penguin Putnam (New York, NY), 2000.

Isaac Olaleye, *Bikes for Rent!,* Scholastic (New York, NY), 2000.

Harriet Ziefert, *Someday We'll Have Very Good Manners,* Putnam (New York, NY), 2001.

Kirsten Hall, *My Best Friend,* Reader's Digest (New York, NY), 2001.

The Philomel Anthology of Humorous Verse, Penguin Putnam (New York, NY), 2002.

Estelle Feldman, *Snowy Winter Day,* Scholastic (New York, NY), 2002.

Also illustrator of greeting cards. Contributor to *Atlantic Monthly, Travel and Leisure, Woman's Day, Town and Country, Reader's Digest, Yankee, Highlights for Children, New York Times, New York Daily News,* and the *Boston Globe.* Also illustrator, with others, of *Free to Be ... a Family,* edited by Marlo Thomas with Christopher Cerf and Letty Cottin Pogrebin.

They somersault
And prance away
And laugh to hear
The donkeys bray.

Cows indulge in merrymaking when people aren't looking in David L. Harrison's picture book **When Cows Come Home,** *with illustrations by Demarest.*

Sidelights

Gentle humor marks the work of Chris L. Demarest, a children's author of dozens of self-illustrated picture books as well as the illustrator for other prominent writers. Demarest has added his award-winning illustrations to the works of Jeff Moss of *Sesame Street* fame, Cynthia DeFelice, Stephen Krensky, Joanne Oppenheim, and Betty Jo Stanovich, among many other well-known authors for children. Noted for a loose, humorous cartoon style, Demarest has worked on wordless picture books, board books, basic-concept number and alphabet books, in addition to picture books with longer texts. His talents have been noted ever since this creator of the greeting-card bird named Benedict produced his first children's book, *Benedict Finds a Home.* His list of accomplishments now includes such popular titles as *Morton and Sidney, Farmer Nat, My Blue Boat,* and *Firefighters A to Z.* Demarest once commented that his "motive is pure entertainment" and that he attempts to leave his "readers with a warm smile and the feeling they've been included in the joke."

Demarest's success is the result of years of practice as well as talent and enthusiasm. As a boy growing up in Connecticut and Massachusetts, he loved cartoons and animation. He once told *SATA* that when he "started drawing, the first images were of many of my cartoon heroes." Demarest earned a painting degree from the University of Massachusetts, but, as he has commented,

he decided to stop painting seriously because he realized that he "found more enjoyment in dashing off a drawing in minutes than in slaving for weeks over one painting, and even then questioning the result." With his training as a painter and his interest in the human form to guide him, Demarest began to develop his cartooning skills.

Demarest launched his career as a cartoonist by creating greeting cards and contributing illustrations to newspapers and magazines. In his first book, *Benedict Finds a Home,* a bird leaves his crowded nest in search of a new place to live. After trying out a shoe in the park, a trumpet, a statue, and a weathervane, Benedict ends up in his old nest. Although Kristi L. Thomas, writing in *School Library Journal,* decided that the book "never quite takes flight," a critic for *Publishers Weekly* admired the "scenes of unusual beauty" and Benedict's "comic adventures."

Clemens' Kingdom tells the story of Clemens, a lion statue who wonders what he is guarding. Clemens leaves his pedestal and ambles inside what turns out to be the library. He settles down in the sunny children's room and reads every book on the shelves. Louise L. Sherman noted in *School Library Journal* that the "whimsical watercolor illustrations" and "simple text" create a "pleasant picture book fantasy." In another imaginative tale, *Orville's Odyssey,* young Orville drops his fishing line into a puddle in the sidewalk while waiting for the bus. A large fish pulls him underwater, and after being snapped at by a crab and nudged by a sea horse, Orville escapes back to the surface in an enormous air bubble and even manages to catch his bus. According to *School Library Journal* contributor Lisa Castillo, the characters in this wordless work "radiate with life."

"Children will delight" in *Morton and Sidney,* wrote Jennifer Smith in *School Library Journal.* Morton is a little boy who finds that the monsters in his closet have evicted Sidney, a pink monster with green horns. Morton tries to find Sidney a new home under a chair and in the laundry basket, but he soon realizes that the monster is too big. When Morton and Sidney dress up as a large, scary monster, Sidney is finally allowed back into the closet. A critic for *Publishers Weekly* enjoyed the moral of the story: "Think twice before rejecting something—what takes its place may be worse."

No Peas for Nellie begins when Nellie refuses to eat her peas. As she tells her mother that she would rather eat a spider, a hunk of wart hog, or even an elephant, Demarest's illustrations show her stalking these animals and preparing to eat them. Ants on these pages carry peas away, and by the end of the book, readers find that Nellie has eaten up her peas. Ann A. Flowers, a reviewer for *Horn Book,* described the illustrations as "ridiculously funny" and enjoyed the "horrified" expressions of the animals as Nellie confronts them.

The Lunatic Adventure of Kitman and Willy and *Kitman and Willy at Sea* feature Kitman, a cat, and Willy, a mouse. In the second book, the pair improvises a boat and sail to an island where a hunter is rounding up all the animals. The cat and mouse come up with a plan to rescue the animals and manage to teach the hunter a lesson. Referring to *Kitman and Willy at Sea,* Debra S. Gold noted in *School Library Journal* that "each page is full of captivating details," and she recommended the book as "a prize selection for summertime story hours." In the opinion of a critic for *Publishers Weekly* about the same book, "children will want to cast off again with this beguiling crew."

With his red toy car in hand, a little boy imagines future adventures in *My Little Red Car.* He motors up mountains, lunches in Paris, and drives to the North Pole. According to a *Publishers Weekly* critic, the "charmingly skewed vision" of *My Little Red Car* is "illustrated with warm zippiness." At the end of the book, the boy cuddles up with his car to sleep.

More transportation is served up in *My Blue Boat,* in which bath time becomes the opportunity for a sea adventure in the imagination of one little girl. Launching her craft on the opening page, the bathing girl dreams of playing with dolphins and navigating storms in scenes that are "adroitly illustrated by sprawling, loosely rendered watercolors," according to a reviewer for *Publishers Weekly. Booklist*'s Ilene Cooper noted that though a childhood fantasy of sailing off into the unknown is nothing new, "Demarest does it with panache." Kathy Mitchell, reviewing the same title in

School Library Journal, observed that Demarest's "expansive illustrations, done in bright watercolors and india ink, flow with the movement of the simple text."

Demarest offers up further travel adventures for young readers with his quartet of board books, *Plane, Ship, Train,* and *Bus.* Using a simple, rhythmic text, Demarest reflects the sound of the vehicle, as in *Train:* "Train chugs / Clickety-clack / Engine up front / Caboose in back." Reviewing *Bus* and *Train* in *School Library Journal,* Lisa Marie Gangemi noted that both "feature creative texts and brightly colored images." A *Kirkus Reviews* critic found Demarest's *Plane* to be "a near-perfect marriage of the board book format to content." Reviewing *Ship* and *Plane,* a critic for *Publishers Weekly* called Demarest's work a "flight of fancy," and an "inventive melange of color, shapes and language." And in a review of *Bus* and *Train* in *Booklist,* Carolyn Phelan concluded that Demarest brings a "sense of style to board books without losing sight of the experience and interests of the very young." In *All Aboard!,* Demarest presents an accordion-folded board book introduction to a train with its dining, sleeping, and passenger cars. Employing cross-sections, the author-illustrator takes the viewer inside to see the passengers,

Employing insider knowledge gained on the job as a volunteer fireman, Demarest uses the revered occupation to explore the alphabet in his self-illustrated **Firefighters A to Z.**

as well. "The simple text evokes the bustle of travel," wrote a contributor for *Publishers Weekly.*

Demarest has also written and illustrated a work of nonfiction for children titled *Lindbergh.* This biography describes famous aviator Charles Lindbergh's youth with text and watercolor pictures. Readers learn how Lindbergh became an excellent mechanic, walked on the wings of airplanes, and flew dangerous U.S. airmail routes. In the words of Barbara Peklo Abrahams in *School Library Journal,* "The clear prose relates the pertinent facts briefly and with verve," and the illustrations are "crisp and light filled." Notes about Lindbergh's later life along with sources for more information are included in the book.

Employing a lift-the-flap technique, Demarest has also created animal books that give toddlers verbal clues of what critter is hidden behind the flap. In *Farmer Nat,* the farmer in question goes about his morning chores, accompanied by a cat. Various barnyard creatures are foreshadowed by a moo, bah, or cluck-cluck. Ann Cook, writing in *School Library Journal,* mentioned the "dashes of quiet humor" to be found on each page, and further commented, "Forget all of those sappy farm-animal books—this one is a keeper." A *Publishers Weekly* writer also praised Demarest's "vivid illustrations," in *Farmer Nat.* Another similar title is *Zookeeper Sue,* in which verbal clues and lift-the-flap again "perfectly [capture] the blend of illustrations and story to spark a child's curiosity," according to Ann Cook in *School Library Journal.* With *Honk!,* Demarest uses the lift-the-flap technique to search for a lost gosling in a "simple but clever story," as Kathy M. Newby described the book in *School Library Journal.*

More innovative board book adventures come in Demarest's *Fall* and *Winter.* Here the artist uses die-cut holes as well as irregularly shaped pages to alter the illustrations. The flip of a page changes the scene to add more detail and intense feeling of the season. "Demarest's deft watercolors of happy, active children make these a cheerful, chunky pair," noted a writer for *Publishers Weekly.*

With *The Cowboy ABC* and *Firefighters A to Z,* Demarest turns his hand to alphabet books. In the former title, he uses the letters of the alphabet to introduce the various elements of a modern cowboy on a cattle drive in a rhyming text that uses two letters in a couplet: "C are the Cattle that follow the trail. / D is the dog, wagging his tail." "Demarest's watercolors evoke the wide-open spaces of the range," wrote Steven Engelfried in *School Library Journal,* who went on to conclude that *The Cowboy ABC* was an "appealing day on the range." A writer for *Kirkus Reviews* felt that Demarest "abandons his familiar minimalist cartoons for a more elaborate style in this tribute to the cowboy mythos," while *Booklist*'s Phelan noted that while "enjoying this colorful alphabet book, young children will long to be home on the range."

Employing insider knowledge as a volunteer fireman, Demarest uses that favorite childhood occupation for a further exploration of the alphabet in *Firefighters A to Z.* Here again the illustrations are more detailed than in most of his other work, depicting the action from the time the alarm rings at the fire station until the final "zip into bed for a rest," as the author concludes his tale. "There's nothing babyish or cute about the robust, action-oriented pastel artwork in *Firefighters from A to Z,* an exciting alphabet book," according to a reviewer for *Horn Book. Booklist*'s Phelan also called attention to Demarest's "large-scale, deeply colored pictures, ablaze with yellows and orange-reds," noting also that the book is a "colorful, dramatic introduction that future firefighters will adore."

Demarest has also provided illustrations for a wide variety of children's authors. Working with Jeff Moss, a writer and music composer for *Sesame Street* and creator of the Cookie Monster, Demarest has illustrated five titles of wacky verse, including *The Butterfly Jar, The Other Side of the Door, Bob and Jack, Hieronymus White,* and *The Dad of the Dad of the Dad of Your Dad.* Reviewing his work for *The Butterfly Jar,* Barbara S. McGinn wrote in *School Library Journal* that "Demarest's cartoon-like sketches complement the verses and are subtly humorous." Reviewing *The Other Side of the Door,* Kathleen Whalin commented in *School Library Journal* that Demarest's "line drawings have genuine verve and humor, extending the comic potential of each poem he illustrates." Linda Greengrass, also writing in *School Library Journal,* felt that *Bob and Jack,* "a story of life and death, growth and loss, has been told with a sense of humor that is punctuated by Demarest's delightful line drawings." The life and times of a plucky bird are recorded in *Hieronymus White,* a further tale accompanied by Demarest's "playful line drawings," as a reviewer for *Publishers Weekly* described them.

Demarest has also provided illustrations for renderings of classic rhymes, as in Stephen Krensky's *The Missing Mother Goose.* "Demarest's winsome cartoon drawings illustrate this waggish volume," noted a critic for *Publishers Weekly.* Dogs—four-legged and other—take center stage in Ralph Leentis's *Smart Dog,* Larry Dan Brimher's *If Dogs Had Wings,* and Nancy Lee Charlton's *Derek's Dog Days.* In the first-named title, simplicity is celebrated in the story of a dog and its master. A contributor for *Publishers Weekly* found that Demarest's "loose sketches, each roughed in with sunny watercolors, achieve an illusion of ease and effortlessness that matches the author's happy leisure." In *If Dogs Had Wings,* another reviewer for *Publishers Weekly* applauded Demarest's illustrations, which "translate this fantasy in a frenzy of loose, squiggly lines and almost expressionistic swaths of color." With *Derek's Dog Days,* a young boy discovers that it really is nice being a boy instead of a dog. "Whimsical watercolor cartoons, funny and bright, adorn this doggie-romp," according to Jacqueline Eisner in *School Library Journal.*

Cows are featured in David Kirby and Allen Woodman's *The Cows Are Going to Paris* and David L. Harrison's *When Cows Come Home*. In the former title, Demarest again departs from his usual cartoon style to come up with "impressionistic watercolor cartoons . . . in the style of Monet and . . . Seurat," according to Nancy Seiner in *School Library Journal. When Cows Come Home* takes a look at the antics of some bovine friends when people are not watching. A critic for *Publishers Weekly* thought that Demarest's "splashy watercolors lend a sense of playful motion and fluidity to his characters." Reviewing the same title in *Booklist*, Janice Del Negro called Demarest's artwork "tremendously appealing."

Working with Cynthia DeFelice on *Casey in the Bath*, a tale of a fantastical bath time aided by magic green goo, Demarest "contributes loose ink sketches, slack strokes of transparent watercolor and dabs of darker paint," according to a writer for *Publishers Weekly*. The same reviewer observed that Demarest's illustrations have a "roughly Seussian appearance." Writing in *School Library Journal*, Lisa S. Murphy thought that Demarest's "goofy, cartoon-style art adds exuberant color to the fantasy." In addition to his collaborative efforts with numerous authors, Demarest has also illustrated several dictionaries, easy dual-language readers, and vocabulary lists for Berlitz.

Children who wonder how Demarest develops his stories will want to know that "the visuals are worked out first—usually in storyboard fashion to allow an overall view." As Demarest once explained to *SATA*, "Seldom is the ending known. What happens is a character is born and sent upon an adventure which keeps developing from page to page. In other words, the story line is very much a puzzle which has to be assembled before the story works."

Demarest emphasizes the role of physical activity in his work. He once explained to *SATA* that sports and "cartooning go hand-in-hand" because his work "involves moving figures," and "having an understanding of body motion helps to translate that to paper. Most of my cartoons are captionless so this too is where motion comes in handy." Demarest also told *SATA* that sports are important because they provide a "physical release. . . . The longer I'm stationary, the shorter my attention-span and thus my work becomes demented."

Most obviously, Demarest does not stay in place for too long, for his work—by turns buoyant, goofy, cartoonish, and full of whimsy—is anything but "demented." As a critic for *Publishers Weekly* noted of Demarest's work for Andrew Sharmat's *Smedge*, his illustrations "are cheerfully bright and busy, creating a rollicking atmosphere." Such a critique could serve as a summation of the author-illustrator's entire body of work, as well.

Biographical and Critical Sources

BOOKS

Demarest, Chris, *Train*, Harcourt (San Diego, CA), 1996.

Demarest, Chris, *The Cowboy ABC*, Dorling Kindersley (New York, NY), 1999.

Demarest, Chris, *Firefighters A to Z*, McElderry Books (New York, NY), 1999.

PERIODICALS

Booklist, July, 1993, pp. 1969-1970; May 1, 1994, Janice Del Negro, review of *When Cows Come Home*, p. 1608; August, 1994, p. 2054; March 15, 1995, Ilene Cooper, review of *My Blue Boat*, p. 1333; October 1, 1995, pp. 325-326; April 1, 1996, Carolyn Phelan, review of *Train* and *Bus*, p. 1371; April 1, 1997, p. 1337; April 15, 1999, Carolyn Phelan, review of *The Cowboy ABC*, p. 1533; February 15, 2000, p. 1125; July, 2000, Carolyn Phelan, review of *Firefighters A to Z*, p. 2036; February 15, 2001, p. 1142.

Children's Playmate, July-August, 1994, p. 8.

Horn Book, July-August, 1988, Ann A. Flowers, review of *No Peas for Nellie*, p. 478; July-August, 2000, review of *Firefighters A to Z*, p. 434.

Kirkus Reviews, August 15, 1995, review of *Plane*, pp. 1186-1187; April 1, 1999, review of *The Cowboy ABC*, p. 531.

New York Times, January 8, 1990, p. 29.

New York Times Book Review, March 4, 1990, p. 33.

Publishers Weekly, February 19, 1982, review of *Benedict Finds a Home*, p. 65; May 20, 1983, p. 236; November 29, 1983, review of *When Cows Come Home*, p. 64; January 16, 1987, p. 73; March 13, 1987, review of *Morton and Sidney*, p. 82; July 14, 1989, review of *Smedge*, p. 77; May 31, 1991, review of *Kitman and Willy at Sea*, pp. 74-75; October 18, 1991, review of *The Missing Mother Goose*, p. 61; January 6, 1992, p. 65; August 17, 1992, review of *My Little Red Car*, p. 498; October 19, 1992, p. 75; December 28, 1992, review of *Smart Dog*, p. 72; August 2, 1993, p. 80; May 2, 1994, p. 307; November 21, 1994, review of *Hieronymus White*, p. 75; January 16, 1995, review of *My Blue Boat*, p. 454; October 2, 1995, review of *Plane* and *Ship*, p. 72; March 4, 1996, review of *Casey in the Bath*, p. 65; August 26, 1996, review of *If Dogs Had Wings*, p. 96, review of *Fall* and *Winter*, p. 99; June 2, 1997, pp. 71-72; October 27, 1997, review of *All Aboard!*, p. 78; April 20, 1998, review of *Farmer Nat*, p. 68; September 18, 2000, p. 113; April 30, 2001, p. 77; December 10, 2001, review of *I Invited a Dragon to Dinner: And Other Poems to Make You Laugh Out Loud*, p. 68.

School Library Journal, August, 1982, Kristi L. Thomas, review of *Benedict Finds a Home*, p. 96; September, 1983, Louise L. Sherman, review of *Clemens' Kingdom*, p. 104; January, 1987, Lisa Castillo, review of *Orville's Odyssey*, pp. 61-62; April, 1987, Jennifer Smith, review of *Morton and Sidney*, p. 80; July, 1990, Barbara S. McGinn, review of *The Butterfly Jar*, p. 86; September, 1990, p. 215; August, 1991, Debra S. Gold, review of *Kitman and Willy at Sea*, p. 144; September, 1991, pp. 262-263; October, 1991, p. 100; December, 1991, Kathleen Whalin, review of *The Other Side of the Door*, p. 125; February, 1992, pp. 82-83; March, 1992, Nancy Seiner, review of *The Cows Are Going to Paris*, p. 216; August, 1992, p. 136; November, 1992, pp. 68-69; April, 1993,

Linda Greengrass, review of *Bob and Jack,* p. 101; June, 1993, p. 78; July, 1993, pp. 1969-1970; October, 1993, Barbara Peklo Abrahams, review of *Lindbergh,* p. 117; November, 1993, p. 90; February, 1994, p. 86; May, 1994, p. 100; May, 1995, Kathy Mitchell, review of *My Blue Boat,* pp. 83-84; April, 1996, Lisa S. Murphy, review of *Casey in the Bath,* p. 106; July, 1996, Jacqueline Eisner, review of *Derek's Dog Days,* p. 57; August, 1996, Lisa Marie Gangemi, review of *Bus* and *Train,* p. 121; June, 1997, p. 69; July, 1997, p. 109; February, 1998, pp. 93-94; August, 1998, Ann Cook, review of *Farmer Nat,* p. 133; October, 1998, Kathy M. Newby, review of *Honk!,* p. 94; April, 1999, Steven Engelfried, review of *The Cowboy ABC,* p. 92; August, 1999, Ann Cook, review of *Zookeeper Sue,* p. 132; March, 2000, p. 220; May, 2000, p. 163; December, 2000, p. 132.

OTHER

Children's Literature, http://www.childrenslit.com (February 3, 2002), author profile of Chris Demarest.*

E

EHLERT, Lois (Jane) 1934-

Personal

Born November 9, 1934, in Beaver Dam, WI; daughter of Harry and Gladys (Grace) Ehlert; married John Reiss, 1967 (separated, 1977). *Education:* Graduated from Layton School of Art, 1957; University of Wisconsin, B.F.A., 1959.

Addresses

Agent—c/o Author Mail, Harcourt Brace, 525 B Street, Suite 1900, San Diego, CA 92101.

Career

Writer and illustrator. Layton School of Art Junior School, Milwaukee, WI, teacher; John Higgs Studio, Milwaukee, WI, layout and production assistant; Jacobs-Keelan Studio, Milwaukee, WI, layout and design illustrator; freelance illustrator and designer, 1962—. Has also designed toys and games for children, a series of basic art books, banners for libraries and public spaces, posters and brochures, and sets for the Moppet Players, a children's theater. *Exhibitions:* Creativity on Paper Show, New York, NY, 1964; Society of Illustrators shows, 1971, 1989, and 1990; International Children's Book Exhibit, Bologna, Italy, 1979. *Member:* American Institute of Graphic Arts.

Awards, Honors

Three gold medals for outstanding graphic art, a best of show citation, and fourteen merit awards, Art Directors Club of Milwaukee, 1961-69; five awards of excellence, five merit awards, one gold medal, and one bronze medal, Society of Communicating Arts of Milwaukee, 1970-72 and 1976; Graphic Arts awards, Printing Industries of America, 1980 and 1981, for posters for Manpower; Paul Revere Award for Graphic Excellence, Hal Leonard Publishing Corp., 1983; grant from National Endowment for the Arts/Wisconsin Arts Board, 1984;

Design Award, Appleton Paper Co., 1985; grants from Wisconsin Arts Board, 1985 and 1987; Award of Excellence citations, Art Museum Association of America, 1985, 1986, and 1987; Best Children's Book citations, New York Public Library, 1987, for *Growing Vegetable Soup,* and 1989, for *Planting a Rainbow;* Pick of the Lists citations, American Booksellers, 1988, for *Planting a Rainbow,* and 1989, for *Color Zoo* and *Eating the Alphabet; Eating the Alphabet* was selected by the Book-of-the Month Club, and as one of the year's ten best books by *Parenting,* 1989; Caldecott Honor Book citation, American Library Association, 1989, for *Color Zoo; Growing Vegetable Soup* was placed on the Museum of Science and Industry book list of children's science books, 1989; *Planting a Rainbow* was placed on the John Burroughs list of nature books for young readers, 1989; Notable Children's Book citation, American Library Association (ALA), 1989, and Book-of-the-Month Club selection, both for *Chicka Chicka Boom Boom,* by Bill Martin, Jr., and John Archambault; Wisconsin Library Association Citation of Merit, 1989; Outstanding Science Trade Book for Children citations, National Science Teachers Association, 1989, for *Planting a Rainbow,* and 1990, for *Color Farm;* John Cotton Dana Award, Summer Reading Program—State of Wisconsin, 1990; *Color Farm* and *Fish Eyes* were named best books by *Parenting,* 1990; *Boston Globe/ Horn Book* Honor Award, 1990, for *Chicka Chicka Boom Boom; Parents' Choice* Honor awards for story book, 1990, for *Chicka Chicka Boom Boom* and *Fish Eyes; Parents' Choice* Award for paperback, 1990, for *Growing Vegetable Soup; Feathers for Lunch* was named one of *Redbook*'s ten best picture books, 1990; *Fish Eyes* was named one of the ten best illustrated books of the year by the *New York Times,* 1990; Certificate of Merit, Graphics Arts Awards, 1990, for *Fish Eyes;* Certificate of Excellence, *Parenting* magazine, 1991, Outstanding Science Trade Book, National Science Teachers Association, 1991, Elizabeth Burr Award, Wisconsin Library Association, 1992, *Boston Globe/Horn Book* Nonfiction Honor Book, 1992, and California Children's Media Award for Nonfiction, 1992, all for *Red Leaf, Yellow Leaf;* Gold Award,

I'd flip down rivers and splash in the sea.

Holes cut in the pages of Lois Ehlert's self-illustrated **Fish** **Eyes** *encourage youngsters to touch the book while they learn about counting.*

Dimensional Illustrators Awards Show, 1991, for *Color Zoo;* First Place, New York Book Show, for Juvenile Trade Specialty, and Reading Magic Award, *Parenting* magazine, the year's ten best books, both 1992, both for *Circus;* New York Public Library Best Children's Books, Notable Book selection, ALA, and *Booklist* Editors' Choice, all 1992, and *Horn Book*'s Fanfare list, 1993, all for *Moon Rope; Boston Globe/Horn Book* Nonfiction Honor Award, 1992, and Outstanding Science Trade Book, National Science Teachers Association, 1993, both for *Feathers for Lunch;* Best Book—Children's Books, Printing Industry of America, 1994, for *Nuts to You!;* Gold Seal Award, Oppenheim Portfolio, 1996, for *Eating the Alphabet;* New York Show Award, 1996, for *Snowballs;* Best Books of 1997, *Book Links,* Reading Magic Award, *Parenting* magazine, and *Booklist* Editors' Choice, 1997, for *Hands.* D.H.L., University of Wisconsin, Milwaukee, 1994.

Writings

SELF-ILLUSTRATED

Growing Vegetable Soup, Harcourt (San Diego, CA), 1987.

Planting a Rainbow, Harcourt (San Diego, CA), 1988.

Color Zoo, HarperCollins (New York, NY), 1989.

Eating the Alphabet: Fruits and Vegetables from A to Z, Harcourt (San Diego, CA), 1989.

Color Farm, HarperCollins (New York, NY), 1990.

Feathers for Lunch, Harcourt (San Diego, CA), 1990.

Fish Eyes: A Book You Can Count On, Harcourt (San Diego, CA), 1990.

Red Leaf, Yellow Leaf, Harcourt (San Diego, CA), 1991.

Circus, HarperCollins (New York, NY), 1992.

Moon Rope: A Peruvian Folktale, translated into Spanish by Amy Prince, Harcourt (San Diego, CA), 1992.

Nuts to You!, Harcourt (San Diego, CA), 1993.

Mole's Hill: A Woodland Tale, Harcourt (San Diego, CA), 1994.

Snowballs, Harcourt (San Diego, CA), 1995.

Under My Nose (autobiography), photographs by Carlo Ontal, Richard C. Owen (Katonah, NY), 1996.

Hands, Harcourt (San Diego, CA), 1997.

Cuckoo: A Mexican Folktale, translated into Spanish by Gloria de Aragon Andujar, Harcourt (San Diego, CA), 1997.

Top Cat, Harcourt (San Diego, CA), 1998.

Market Day: A Story Told with Folk Art, Harcourt (San Diego, CA), 2000.

Waiting for Wings, Harcourt (San Diego, CA), 2001.

ILLUSTRATOR

Patricia M. Zens, *I Like Orange,* F. Watts (New York, NY), 1961.

Edward Lear, *Limericks,* World Publishing (Chicago, IL), 1965.

Mary L. O'Neill, *What Is That Sound!,* Atheneum (New York, NY), 1966.

Mannis Charosh, *Mathematical Games for One or Two,* Crowell (New York, NY), 1972.

Andrea Di Noto, *The Great Flower Pie,* Bradbury (New York, NY), 1973.

Vicki Silvers, *Sing a Song of Sound,* Scroll Press, 1973.

Nina Sazer, *What Do You Think I Saw?: A Nonsense Number Book,* Pantheon (New York, NY), 1976.

Diane Wolkstein, *The Visit,* Knopf (New York, NY), 1977.

Jane J. Srivastava, *Number Families,* Crowell (New York, NY), 1979.

Richard L. Allington, *Shapes and Sizes,* Raintree Publishers, 1979.

Bill Martin, Jr., and John Archambault, *Chicka Chicka Boom Boom,* Simon & Schuster (New York, NY), 1989.

Gene Baer, *Thump, Thump, Rat-a-tat-tat,* Harper (New York, NY), 1989.

Bill Martin, Jr., and John Archambault, *Words,* Little Simon (New York, NY), 1993.

Sarah Weeks, *Crocodile Smile: Ten Songs of the Earth as the Animals See It,* HarperCollins (New York, NY), 1994.

Bill Martin, Jr., and John Archambault, *Chicka Chicka Sticka Sticka: An ABC Sticker Book,* Little Simon (New York, NY), 1995.

Stuart J. Murphy, Jr., *A Pair of Socks,* HarperCollins (New York, NY), 1996.

Ann Turner, *Angel Hide and Seek,* HarperCollins (New York, NY), 1998.

Also illustrator and designer of "Scribbler's" products for Western Publishing. A selection of Ehlert's papers are housed in the Kerlan Collection at the University of Minnesota.

Adaptations

Chicka Chicka Boom Boom was adapted for video, Weston Woods, 2000, employing Ehlert's illustrations.

Sidelights

Known for her vibrant collage artwork which features colored paper and found objects, Lois Ehlert has entertained and educated children for over four decades. Initially providing illustrations for the books of others, Ehlert began writing her own material to accompany her artwork in the mid-1980s and has created books on subjects such as birds, flowers, weather, work, retellings of folktales, and the alphabet. These books include pictures that feature bold colors and clear, crisp shapes. She wrote and illustrated *Color Zoo,* which was named a Caldecott Honor Book in 1989. A year later, her illustrations helped *Chicka Chicka Boom Boom,* written by Bill Martin, Jr., and John Archambault, win a *Boston Globe/Horn Book* Honor Award. She has gone on to win numerous other awards for her artwork and books. In an article for *Horn Book* she discussed her attraction to picture books and described her work: "I didn't want to be gimmicky; I wanted to distill, to get the essence of what it was that was so exciting. I hope I'm still exploring that idea. I don't see any sense in creating books otherwise. I get a lot of joy out of it."

As a child, Ehlert received both the encouragement and the environment to develop an interest in art. Her mother, who liked to sew, supplied her with scraps of cloth, and her father gave her wood from his woodworking projects. They also provided her with a place to work by setting up a card table in a little room in their house. She spent a great deal of time at the table, both as a small child and through high school, working on projects that helped her to develop her talent. Finally, she sent some of her work to the Layton School of Art and received a scholarship that allowed her to become a student there. After taking the table with her to Layton, she made it into a drawing table by placing a wooden breadboard on top of it and then giving the board a slant by propping a tin can underneath it. The table has traveled with her during her career as an artist. "It's got holes drilled in it and ink slopped on it and cuts from razor blades," she noted in *Horn Book,* "but I still use it."

After graduating from art school in 1957, Ehlert did graphic design work and illustrated some children's books. She did not enjoy working on picture books, however, mainly because she could not approve the final color selections for her illustrations when her books went to the printer. In disappointment, she stopped working on picture books and concentrated on graphic design projects. But her friends eventually convinced her to go back to illustrating children's books. In *Horn Book* she acknowledged: "I began to see an emphasis on graphics in picture books, and I thought that the time

Ehlert's bright illustrations and text depict the antics of a feisty squirrel who crawls inside the narrator's apartment window. (From Nuts to You!*)*

Ehlert created collages of traditional and folk art from Latin America, China, and Mali to adorn her picture book about a peasant family's day at the market. (From Market Day.*)*

might be right for my work. I could see that there was a lot more care being taken in the production of children's books."

After providing artwork for many children's books, Ehlert decided to try both writing and illustrating a book of her own. While working as a freelance graphic designer, she created *Growing Vegetable Soup,* a book that combines pictures and words to show the steps involved in growing a vegetable garden. Then she wrote and illustrated *Planting a Rainbow,* which tells the story of a mother and a child who cultivate a flower garden. Both of these books show Ehlert's passion for using bold colors. Andrea Barnet noted in the *New York Times Book Review* that Ehlert's "colors are tropical, electric and hot—the grape purples and sizzling pinks children tend to choose when they paint. Often she pairs complementary hues ... to startling effect, giving her illustrations a vibrant op-art feel, a visual shimmer that makes them jump off the page."

After achieving success with *Growing Vegetable Soup,* Ehlert took a class at the University of Wisconsin and found new ways to design books by using such eye-catching techniques as cutting holes in the pages and using different combinations of light and dark colors in the illustrations. She made use of methods that she learned in this class in *Color Zoo,* a book that introduces children to a wide range of colors and geometrical figures through the use of different-shaped holes cut in sturdy paper and placed on top of a design. Each new cutout shape—circle, square, triangle—is decorated with the features of different animals which make readers think of the whole figure as a tiger, then a mouse, and then a fox. Ehlert repeats this routine with two more sets

of shapes and ends *Color Zoo* with a summary of all of the shapes and colors used in the book. Ehlert reprises this technique with *Color Farm,* another award-winning title in which she "uses an array of brilliant graphics with carefully planned die-cuts to introduce geometric shapes," according to *Horn Book* reviewer Mary M. Burns.

For another self-illustrated work, *Feathers for Lunch,* Ehlert regularly used numerous pieces of paper to create collages that tell the story of a hungry cat at mealtime that chases after a dozen birds. A bell, worn around the cat's neck, alerts the birds of his presence. Ehlert's artwork is accompanied by a rhyming text, a list of the birds that are presented, and printed representations of their calls. In order to create a book that was both educational and attractive, she presents the birds in natural settings with flowers that are harmonious with the birds' actual colors. Since she wanted to make sure that her collages of the birds were the right colors and sizes, she checked them against the skins of birds kept at the Field Museum in Chicago.

Ehlert also wanted to make life-size pictures of the birds for the pages of *Feathers for Lunch,* but that meant that she also had to make a cat that was life-size. Instead of trying to make such a big book, Ehlert decided to show only parts of the cat on certain pages and to replace him entirely with the "JINGLE JINGLE" of his bell on others. Such practice is routine in Ehlert's books. "If I say something with words, I don't need to describe it with the art, and vice versa." she wrote in *Horn Book,* later noting, "I really use typography as just another design form, another element of the art."

In *Fish Eyes* Ehlert uses the patterns and shapes of sea creatures in order to teach kids about arithmetic. Holes cut in the pages encourage youngsters to touch the book while they learn about numbers by counting fish. Ehlert also puts black type on blue pages, hoping that children will find the subtle, hidden text. She explained in *Horn Book*: "I purposely didn't want that design element to be dominant because I already had a dominant theme. So I worked on my layout, and then I stood in front of a full-length mirror to see how close I had to come to the mirror before I could read that second line. I wanted the type to be a surprise to a child discovering it. I try to work on a lot of different levels in every book. Some things are more successful than others." Ehlert's efforts were rewarded by Andrea Barnet, who wrote in the *New York Times Book Review* that *Fish Eyes* has "enough novelty to hold a child's interest, and enough complexity to sustain repeated readings."

Other animals are served up by Ehlert in *Circus, Nuts to You!, Top Cat,* and *Waiting for Wings.* Hugo the elephant, Fritz the wonder bear, and Samu, the fiercest tiger in the world are just part of the amazing menagerie she presents in *Circus,* a book which is "a most joyous use of the graphic-art style which Lois Ehlert continues to expand and refine," according to *Horn Book* critic Margaret A. Bush. With *Nuts to You!* Ehlert presents a cheeky squirrel who gets braver and braver as it approaches an opening in an apartment window and finally goes inside. *Horn Book* reviewer Ellen Fader dubbed this an "imaginatively designed book," calling special attention to the title page and verso which were camouflaged to look like tree bark. A reviewer for *Publishers Weekly* felt that *Nuts to You!* is a "work of extraordinary visual splendor with an effectively simple, active plot."

In *Top Cat* Ehlert features a feline who rules the roost until a striped kitten makes an appearance. At first angry and spitting at the youngster, Top Cat finally figures out that the kitten is here to stay and makes the best of the situation by becoming a teacher and mentor to the younger animal. "Children and other feline fans will quickly warm to this spunky story of rivalry and acceptance," wrote a contributor for *Publishers Weekly.* Reviewing the same title in *Booklist,* Linda Perkins noted, "Ehlert's distinctive collages portray a remarkable range of expression and movement and are sure to tickle funny bones."

A butterfly takes center stage in *Waiting for Wings,* "a marvelous presentation of the butterfly life cycle," according to a reviewer for *Horn Book,* and one that will "engage children curious about a seemingly magical process." Ehlert accompanies her usual cut-paper illustrations in this 2001 title with simple rhymes in large black letters. "Ehlert again spreads her creative wings to deliver this inventively designed picture book," noted a contributor for *Publishers Weekly.* Tracing the development for the metamorphosis of the caterpillar into the graceful flying creature readers will recognize as a butterfly, Ehlert created a "beautifully woven blend of information," according to Lisa Gangemi Krapp, writing

in *School Library Journal,* and an "original and vivid introduction," as *Booklist*'s Carolyn Phelan observed.

For the illustrations in *Red Leaf, Yellow Leaf* and *Snowball,* among other titles, Ehlert constructed her characteristic collages not only out of colored paper, but also from found objects including ribbons, seeds, bottle caps, twigs, and pieces of string and clothing, in addition to layered paper. She also found inspiration in native and folk cultures for her illustrations in several of her books. For the bilingual *Moon Rope* she drew on designs in ancient Peruvian textiles, jewelry, ceramics, and even architecture. For *Mole's Hill,* Ehlert took inspiration from the beadwork designs of Woodland Indians. And in *Market Day,* a celebration of Latin America's rural markets, she follows a peasant family's day at market in text, accompanied with illustrations that come from traditional and folk art of the region, from Guatemala, Bolivia, Peru, and Mexico, as well as from farther afield, from China and Mali. Shirley Lewis, reviewing *Market Day* in *Teacher Librarian,* felt that Ehlert's artwork "blazes through this handsome tour."

Critics and readers alike have responded enthusiastically to such titles. Reviewing her *Moon Rope,* a retelling of a Peruvian folk tale, Fox talks Mole into climbing on a braided grass rope with him—a rope he has hooked to the moon. As Fox climbs, he keeps his eyes upward, but timid Mole keeps looking back to the Earth until he falls, thus explaining his preference for life in solitary tunnels. A critic for *Kirkus Reviews* felt that *Moon Rope* "may be [Ehlert's] handsomest book yet," and appraised the work as "altogether outstanding." *Mole's Hill,* a Seneca Indian tale, is a "whimsical story of overcoming the might of an adversary through ingenuity," according to a reviewer for *Publishers Weekly.* The same reviewer also applauded Ehlert's illustrations, in which she "achieves dazzling effects with simple geometric shapes and strong, pure hues." Fox and Mole are at it once again in this story, in which Fox is so frustrated at having to walk around Mole's hill that he sends Raccoon and Skunk to tell her to move out. However, Mole uses her cleverness to defeat Fox, enlarging the hill and planting seeds to create such a pretty spot that Fox cannot bring himself to destroy it. In a *Horn Book* review, Margaret A. Bush also praised Ehlert's illustrations in *Mole's Hill,* which depict the flowers and trees of Wisconsin woodlands "as primitive abstractions in folk art style." Bush concluded that the book is "vivid and spare . . . a feast for the eye."

From rivalries, Ehlert turned to the natural world in *Snowballs.* "Only an artist as gifted as Ehlert could take so well-worn a topic as building a snowman and make it as fresh as—well, new-fallen snow," remarked a reviewer for *Publishers Weekly* regarding this title. The same critic dubbed *Snowballs* a "joyful and inventive book." In *Cuckoo,* Ehlert retells a folktale about the evolution of the vain cuckoo. "Sombreros off to this innovative artist for yet another eye-catching work," wrote a contributor for *Publishers Weekly.* Carolyn Phelan, reviewing *Cuckoo* in *Booklist,* called it an "exhilarating adaptation" with "arresting artwork, some of [Ehlert's] best to date."

With *Hands* Ehlert celebrates such crafts as gardening and art, through the use of photo-collage. The easy text is told from the point of view of a child who watches his father creating things in his workshop and his mother sewing wonderful creations. *Booklist*'s Stephanie Zvirin felt that *Hands* "is full of lovely surprises," a "thoughtfully designed book, wonderful for lap sharing." A tribute to Ehlert's own parents, both of whom enjoyed working with their hands and who encouraged Ehlert in her pursuit of a career in art, *Hands* grew out of an earlier project "to create a portrait of someone without using photographs" of that person, as she told Connie Goddard in a *Publishers Weekly* interview. Instead of portraits, Ehlert uses mementos, such as pigskin work gloves, screws, and a folding ruler to call up the sense of that person. Approaching the realm of the toy book, *Hands* employs die-cut pages, including one with the image of a tin box with screwdrivers inside. More tools of the trade pop up throughout this innovative book. A *Publishers Weekly* critic noted that Ehlert "works visual magic" in this "inventive effort that deserves nothing less than a big hand."

Although Ehlert wants children to learn from her books, she does not think of herself as an educator. She admitted in *Horn Book* that "it's like being a grandmother in a way—setting down something that might, if I'm lucky, be remembered after I'm gone. And also to communicate what I think is important. Look for those birds! Plant a garden or a tree! They are very homely, ordinary subjects—yet spiritual." Such concerns have made Ehlert one of the key illustrators of her generation. "There is a sense of adventure, fun, and experimentation in all of Ehlert's books that inspires and encourages readers to try their own artistic experiments," concluded a contributor for *St. James Guide to Children's Writers* in a critical assessment of the author-illustrator's work. "Yet, her books are infused with an artistry and design, and a careful attention to detail that makes them much more complex that they at first appear."

Biographical and Critical Sources

BOOKS

Authors of Books for Young People, 3rd edition, Scarecrow Press (Metuchen, NJ), 1990.

Children's Book Illustration and Design, edited by Julie Cummins, Library of Applied Design (New York, NY), 1992.

Children's Books and Their Creators, edited by Anita Silvey, Houghton (Boston, MA), 1995.

Children's Literature Review, Volume 28, Gale (Detroit, MI), 1992.

Cummings, Pat, *Talking with Artists,* Bradbury (New York, NY), 1991.

Ehlert, Lois, *Under My Nose,* photographs by Carlo Ontal, Richard C. Owen (Katonah, NY), 1996.

St. James Guide to Children's Writers, 5th edition, St. James (Detroit, MI), 1999.

PERIODICALS

Booklist, October 15, 1992, p. 423; March 1, 1993, p. 1226; March 15, 1994, pp. 1366-1367; December 1, 1994, p. 675; December 1, 1995, p. 640; September 1, 1996, p. 121; April 1, 1997, Carolyn Phelan, review of *Cuckoo,* p. 1330; November 15, 1997, Stephanie Zvirin, review of *Hands,* p. 558; May 15, 1998, p. 1633; August, 1998, Linda Perkins, review of *Top Cat,* p. 2014; July, 2000, p. 2048; March 2, 2001, Carolyn Phelan, review of *Waiting for Wings,* p. 1276.

Horn Book, May-June, 1989; July-August, 1989; January-February, 1991, Mary M. Burns, review of *Color Farm,* p. 55; November-December, 1991, Lois Ehlert, "The Artist at Work: Card Tables and Collage," p. 695; March-April, 1992, Margaret A. Bush, review of *Circus,* p. 189; November-December, 1992, pp. 732-733; May-June, 1993, Ellen Fader, review of *Nuts to You!,* p. 315; July-August, 1994, Margaret A. Bush, review of *Mole's Hill,* p. 461; January-February, 1996, pp. 61-62; September-October, 1996, p. 613; September-October, 1997, pp. 556-557; March-April, 2001, review of *Waiting for Wings,* p. 346.

Kirkus Reviews, August 1, 1991, review of *Red Leaf, Yellow Leaf,* p. 1019; September 1, 1992, review of *Moon Rope,* p. 1128.

New York Times Book Review, May 20, 1990, Andrea Barnet, review of *Fish Eyes,* p. 40; October 25, 1992, p. 28; September 17, 2000, p. 33.

People Weekly, November 28, 1994, p. 35.

Publishers Weekly, October 13, 1989; February 12, 1992, Connie Goddard, "Alive with Color: An Interview with Lois Ehlert," pp. 18-19; August 17, 1992, review of *Moon Rope,* p. 499; February 15, 1993, review of *Nuts to You!,* pp. 372-373; February 21, 1994, review of *Mole's Hill,* p. 252; October 16, 1995, review of *Snowballs,* p. 60; January 20, 1997, review of *Cuckoo,* p. 401; June 30, 1997, review of *Hands,* p. 76; August 3, 1998, review of *Top Cat,* p. 84; October 18, 1999, p. 86; September 4, 2000, p. 110; April 2, 2001, review of *Waiting for Wings,* p. 63.

School Library Journal, November, 1991, p. 94; April, 1992, pp. 90-91; October, 1992, p. 102; April, 1993, p. 96; May, 1994, p. 92; November, 1994, p. 461; November, 1995, p. 65; December, 1996, pp. 112, 116; March, 1997, p. 174; December, 1997, p. 88; September, 1998, p. 184; July, 2000, p. 71; April, 2001, Lisa Gangemi Krapp, review of *Waiting for Wings,* p. 129.

Teacher Librarian, January, 1999, p. 42; June, 2000, Shirley Lewis, review of *Market Day,* p. 50.

*   *   *

ESPELAND, Pamela (Lee) 1951-

Personal

Born August 19, 1951, in Oak Park, IL; daughter of Jack Ingolf (a carpenter) and Roberta (a housewife; maiden name Ralls) Espeland; married to John A. Whiting (business manager); children Jonah Daniel Klevesahl. *Education:* Attended Harvard University, 1972, and University of Minnesota, 1974; Carleton College, B.A., 1973. *Politics:* Democrat. *Hobbies and other interests:* Reading, traveling (especially to Italy and Quebec), music.

Addresses

Home—5153 Chowen Ave., S., Minneapolis, MN 55410.

Career

Author, copywriter, editor, and owner of Pamela Espeland Associates Inc.

Writings

FOR CHILDREN

The Story of Cadmus, illustrated by Reg Sandland, Carolrhoda (Minneapolis, MN), 1980.

The Story of Arachne, illustrated by Susan Kennedy, Carolrhoda (Minneapolis, MN), 1980.

The Story of King Midas, illustrated by George Overlie, Carolrhoda (Minneapolis, MN), 1980.

The Story of Pygmalion, illustrated by Catherine Cleary, Carolrhoda (Minneapolis, MN), 1981.

The Story of Baucis and Philemon, illustrated by George Overlie, Carolrhoda (Minneapolis, MN), 1981.

Theseus and the Road to Athens, illustrated by Reg Sandland, Carolrhoda (Minneapolis, MN), 1981.

Pamela Espeland edited Barbara A. Lewis's book on volunteer opportunities for young people, which covers topics from the care of animals to literacy programs.

Why Do We Eat?, illustrated by Nancy Inderieden, Creative Education (Mankato, MN), 1981.

(With Marilyn Waniek) *Hundreds of Hens and Other Poems for Children,* illustrated by D. M. Robinson, translated from the Danish by Halfdan Rasmussen, Black Willow Press, 1982.

(With Marilyn Waniek) *The Cat Walked Through the Casserole and Other Poems,* illustrated by Trina Schart Hyman and others, Carolrhoda (Minneapolis, MN), 1984.

(With Jacqulyn Saunders) *Bringing Out the Best: A Resource Guide for Parents of Young Gifted Children,* Free Spirit (Minnesota, MN), 1986, revised edition, 1991.

(With Evelyn Leite) *Different Like Me: A Book for Teens Who Worry about Their Parents' Use of Alcohol-Drugs,* Johnson Institute (Saint Paul, MN), 1987.

(With Gershen Kaufman and Lev Raphael) *Stick Up for Yourself: Every Kid's Guide to Personal Power and Positive Self-Esteem,* Free Spirit (Minneapolis, MN), 1990, revised edition, 1999.

(With Rosemary Wallner) *Making the Most of Today: Daily Readings for Young People on Self-Awareness, Creativity, and Self-Esteem,* Free Spirit (Minneapolis, MN), 1991.

(With Susan Strauss) *Sexual Harassment and Teens: A Program for Positive Change: Case Studies, Activities, Questionnaires, Laws, Guidelines, Policies, Procedures, Resources, and More,* Free Spirit (Minneapolis, MN), 1992.

(With Peter L. Benson and Judy Galbraith) *What Teens Need to Succeed: Practical Ways to Shape Your Own Future,* Free Spirit (Minneapolis, MN), 1995, revised edition, 1998.

(With Craig Mitchell) *Hints to Teach: Over Three Hundred Strategies, Tips, and Helpful Hints for Teachers of All Grades,* Free Spirit (Minneapolis, MN), 1996.

(With Elizabeth Verdick) *Making Every Day Count: Daily Readings for Young People on Solving Problems, Setting Goals, and Feeling Goods about Yourself,* Free Spirit (Minneapolis, MN), 1998.

(With Peter L. Benson and Judy Galbraith) *What Kids Need to Succeed: Proven Practical Ways to Raise Good Kids,* Free Spirit (Minneapolis, MN), 1998.

Succeed Every Day: Daily Reading for Teens, Free Spirit (Minneapolis, MN), 2001.

Knowing Me, Knowing You: The I-Sight Way to Understand Yourself and Others, Free Spirit (Minneapolis, MN), 2001.

OTHER

Also the editor of many books for teens, children, parents and teachers on topics ranging from self-help to mental health, school success to social action, and art to business history, including *The Kid's Guide to Service Projects,* by Barbara A. Lewis, Free Spirit (Minneapolis, MN), 1995, and *How Rude!: The Teenagers' Guide to Good Manners, Proper Behavior, and Not Grossing People Out,* by Alex J. Packer, Free Spirit (Minneapolis, MN), 1997.

Sidelights

An author and editor of educational material as well as the author of her own books for children, Pamela Espeland is especially well regarded for her books that help parents, teachers, and counselors improve children's learning experiences. Frequently working with other authors, Espeland has produced works that encourage students to succeed in school, present teachers with new teaching ideas, and offer parents of gifted children activities to keep their sons and daughters mentally active. For example, *What Kids Need to Succeed: Proven Practical Ways to Raise Good Kids* offers caregivers strategies for helping kids lead healthy, productive, and positive lives, a popular title with over 550,000 copies in print. In other volumes like *Teach to Reach: Over Three Hundred Strategies, Tips, and Helpful Hints for Teachers of All Grades,* the author teamed up with Craig Mitchell to develop a book for educators looking for ideas to capture their students' attention. Assisting parents looking for new challenges for exceptionally talented children, Espeland has written works such as *Bringing Out the Best: A Resource Guide for Parents of Young Gifted Children,* discussing not only projects for children but also ways to keep parents from overloading them with too much activity. In addition to her nonfiction work, Espeland has also written her own fiction, including a series of books on Greek myths, and several volumes of poetry.

Biographical and Critical Sources

PERIODICALS

Publishers Weekly, November 2, 1984, review of *The Cat Walked Through the Casserole and Other Poems,* p. 77; October 24, 1986, review of *Bringing Out the Best: A Resource Guide for Parents of Young Gifted Children,* p. 68.

School Library Journal, April, 1981, C. Nordheim Woolridge, review of *The Story of Cadmus, The Story of Arachne,* and *The Story of King Midas,* p. 126; February, 1982, Laura F. Secord, review of *The Story of Pygmalion, The Story of Baucis and Philemon,* and *Theseus and the Road to Athens,* p. 66; August, 1982,

Espeland served as editor of Alex J. Packer's book, which uses a variety of formats—Dear Alex letters, surveys, and stories—to teach teenagers about etiquette with humor and insight. (Cover illustration by Jeff Tolbert.)

Daisy Kouzel, review of *Why Do We Eat?,* pp. 92-93; February, 1985, Susan McCord, review of *The Cat Walked Through the Casserole and Other Poems,* p. 73; April, 1999, Gail Richmond, review of *What Teens Need to Succeed: Practical Ways to Shape Your Own Future,* p. 144.

OTHER

Free Spirit Publishing, http://www.freespirit.com/ (November 17, 2001).

G

GALLUP, Joan 1957-

Personal

Born November 3, 1957, in MI; daughter of Charles (self-employed) and Phyllis (a homemaker) Gallup; married Peter Grimord (an artist), May 24, 1980; children: Monique. *Education:* Eastern Michigan University, B.F.A.; Community College of Philadelphia, R.N.

Addresses

Office—2176 East York St., Philadelphia, PA 19125. *E-mail*—petejoan@earthlink.net.

Career

Self-employed artist, 1984—. Philadelphia Free Library, member of Children's Reading Round Table. *Member:* Society of Children's Book Writers and Illustrators.

Writings

(Illustrator) Jane P. Resnick, editor, *Classic Treasury of Silly Poetry,* Courage Books (Philadelphia, PA), 1995.
Silly Animal ABCs, Running Press (Philadelphia, PA), 1999.
Silly 1, 2, 3s, Courage Books (Philadelphia, PA), 2002.*

*   *   *

GAMMELL, Stephen 1943-

Personal

Born February 10, 1943, in Des Moines, IA; son of a magazine art editor and a homemaker; married; wife's name, Linda (a photographer). *Education:* Attended college in Des Moines, IA. *Hobbies and other interests:* American history; playing the guitar, banjo, mandolin, and piano—"anything with strings"; outdoor activities, including backpacking, bicycling, camping, and canoe-ing, especially in the American West; movies, especially comedies featuring Laurel and Hardy; eating big breakfasts and chocolate chip cookies.

Addresses

Agent—c/o Paula Wiseman, Harcourt, 525 B St., San Diego, CA 92101.

Career

Author and illustrator of books for children. Also worked as a freelance illustrator for book and record stores and magazines and newspapers in the 1960s and for various periodicals during the early 1970s.

Awards, Honors

Notable Book Citation, American Library Association (ALA), 1976, for *The Kelpie's Pearls;* ALA Best Books for Young Adults citation, 1978, for *The Hawks of Chelney;* Outstanding Book of the Year citation, *New York Times,* 1979, *Boston Globe/Horn Book* Award honor book designation, and ALA Notable Book citation, both 1980, all for *Stonewall;* Children's Choice citation, International Reading Association and Children's Book Council, 1980, for *Meet the Vampire; Boston Globe-Horn Book* Award honor book designation for illustration, *New York Times* Best Illustrated citation, *New York Times* Outstanding Book of the Year citation, and Parents' Choice Award, Parents' Choice Foundation, all 1981, Caldecott Award honor book designation, ALA, and American Book Award best picture book nomination, 1982, all for *Where the Buffaloes Begin;* Children's Choice Award citation, 1982, for *Wake Up, Bear . . . It's Christmas!; New York Times* Best Illustrated citation and Child Study Association of America's Children's Books of the Year citation, both 1985, and Caldecott Medal honor book designation, ALA, and *Boston Globe-Horn Book* Award honor book designation, both 1986, all for *The Relatives Came;* Children's Books of the Year citation, Child Study Association of America, 1985, for *Thanksgiving Poems;*

Boston Globe-Horn Book Award honor book citation, 1987, and Golden Sower Award nomination, Nebraska Library Commission, 1990, both for *Old Henry;* Caldecott Medal, ALA, 1988, and Society of Midlands Authors Award, 1989, both for *Song and Dance Man;* MELSA (Metropolitan Library Services Agency, Twin Cities) Summer Reading Program winner, St. Paul, MN, 1988, Minnesota Picture Book Award, Minnesota Center for the Book, 1993, for *Old Black Fly,* and 1998, for *Is That You, Winter?.* Many of the books that Gammell has illustrated have been named to best book and notable book lists by local and state library associations and also have won child-selected awards.

Writings

FOR CHILDREN; SELF-ILLUSTRATED PICTURE BOOKS

Once upon MacDonald's Farm, Four Winds (New York, NY), 1981, revised edition, Simon & Schuster (New York, NY), 2000.
Wake Up, Bear . . . It's Christmas!, Lothrop (New York, NY), 1981.
(Reteller) *The Story of Mr. and Mrs. Vinegar,* Lothrop (New York, NY), 1982.
Git Along, Old Scudder, Lothrop (New York, NY), 1983.
Is That You, Winter?, Harcourt (San Diego, CA), 1997.
Twigboy, Harcourt (San Diego, CA), 2000.
Ride, Harcourt (San Diego, CA), 2001.

ILLUSTRATOR; "SCARY STORIES" FOLKTALE SERIES

Alvin Schwartz, reteller, *Scary Stories to Tell in the Dark: Collected from American Folklore* (also see below), Lippincott (Philadelphia, PA), 1981.
Alvin Schwartz, reteller, *More Scary Stories to Tell in the Dark: Collected and Retold from Folklore* (also see below), Lippincott (Philadelphia, PA), 1984.
Alvin Schwartz, reteller, *Scary Stories Three: More Tales to Chill Your Bones* (also see below), HarperCollins (New York, NY), 1991.
Alvin Schwartz, reteller, *Scary Stories Fright Pack* (includes *Scary Stories to Tell in the Dark, More Scary Stories to Tell in the Dark,* and *Scary Stories Three*), HarperCollins (New York, NY), 1997, published as *Scary Stories Boxed Set,* 2001.

ILLUSTRATOR

Ida Chittum, *A Nutty Business,* Putnam (New York, NY), 1973.
Sara Newton Carroll, *The Search: A Biography of Leo Tolstoy,* Harper (New York, NY), 1973.
Paul Zindel, *Let Me Hear Your Whisper* (play), Harper (New York, NY), 1974.
Ramona Maher, *The Glory Horse: A Story of the Battle of San Jancinto and Texas in 1836,* Coward (New York, NY), 1974.
Patricia Lee Gauch, *Thunder at Gettsyburg,* Coward (New York, NY), 1974.
Miriam Anne Bourne, *Nabby Adams' Diary,* Coward (New York, NY), 1975.
Seymour Simon, *Ghosts,* Lippincott (Philadelphia, PA), 1976.
Georgess McHargue, *Meet the Werewolf,* Lippincott (Philadelphia, PA), 1976.

Stephen Gammell lends his illustrations to Cynthia Rylant's picture book, which describes how the lives of an Appalachian family are made more joyful by a visit from their relatives. (From The Relatives Came.*)*

Mollie Hunter, *The Kelpie's Pearls,* Harper (New York, NY), 1976.
Mollie Hunter, *A Furl of Fairy Wind: Four Stories,* Harper (New York, NY), 1977.
Ramona Maher, *Alice Yazzie's Year* (poetry), Coward (New York, NY), 1977.
Ellen Harvey Showell, *The Ghost of Tillie Jean Cassaway,* Four Winds (New York, NY), 1978.
Marietta Moskin, *Day of the Blizzard,* Coward (New York, NY), 1978.
Adrienne Jones, *The Hawks of Chelney,* Harper (New York, NY), 1978.
Dilys Owen, *Leo Possessed,* Harcourt (San Diego, CA), 1979.
Michael Fox, *Whitepaws: A Coyote-Dog,* Coward (New York, NY), 1979.
Jean Fritz, *Stonewall,* Putnam (New York, NY), 1979.
Margaret Greaves, *A Net to Catch the Wind,* Harper (New York, NY), 1979.
Georgess McHargue, *Meet the Vampire,* Lippincott (Philadelphia, PA), 1979.
David Seed, *Stream Runner,* Four Winds (New York, NY), 1979.
Eve Bunting, *Yesterday's Island,* Warne (New York, NY), 1979.
Eve Bunting, *Terrible Things: An Allegory of the Holocaust,* Harper (New York, NY), 1980.
Eve Bunting, *Blackbird Singing,* Macmillan (New York, NY), 1980.
Malcolm Hall, *And Then the Mouse . . .: Three Stories* (folktales), Four Winds (New York, NY), 1980.

Helen Reeder Cross, *The Real Tom Thumb,* Four Winds (New York, NY), 1980.

Ann Brophy, *Flash and the Swan,* Warne (New York, NY), 1981.

Olaf Baker, *Where the Buffaloes Begin,* Warne (New York, NY), 1981.

Nathaniel Benchley, *Demo and the Dolphin,* Harper (New York, NY), 1981.

Maggie S. Davis, *The Best Way to Ripton,* Holiday House (New York, NY), 1982.

Dennis Haseley, *The Old Banjo,* Macmillan (New York, NY), 1983.

Cynthia Rylant, *Waiting to Waltz: A Childhood* (poetry), Bradbury (Scarsdale, NY), 1984.

Alison C. Herzig and Jane L. Mali, *Thaddeus,* Little, Brown (Boston, MA), 1984.

Cynthia Rylant, *The Relatives Came,* Bradbury (New York, NY), 1985.

Myra Cohn Livingston, editor, *Thanksgiving Poems* (poetry), Holiday House (New York, NY), 1985.

Larry Callen, *Who Kidnapped the Sheriff? Or, Tales from Tickflaw,* Atlantic Monthly Press (New York, NY), 1985.

George Ella Lyon, *A Regular Rolling Noah,* Bradbury (Scarsdale, NY), 1986.

Joan W. Blos, *Old Henry,* Morrow (New York, NY), 1987.

Janet Taylor Lisle, *The Great Dimpole Oak,* Franklin Watts (New York, NY), 1987.

Karen Ackerman, *Song and Dance Man,* Knopf (New York, NY), 1988.

Tom Birdseye, *Airmail to the Moon,* Holiday House (New York, NY), 1988.

Virginia Driving Hawk Sneve, editor, *Dancing Teepees: Poems of American Indian Youth* (poetry), Holiday House (New York, NY), 1989.

Rafe Martin, *Will's Mammoth,* Putman (New York, NY), 1989.

Myra Cohn Livingston, editor, *Halloween Poems* (poetry), Holiday House (New York, NY), 1989.

Lyn Littlefield Hoopes, *Wing-a-Ding,* Little, Brown (Boston, MA), 1990.

George Ella Lyon, *Come a Tide,* Orchard Books (New York, NY), 1990.

Elvira Woodruff, *The Wing Shop,* Holiday House (New York, NY), 1991.

Jim Aylesworth, *Old Black Fly,* Holt (New York, NY), 1992.

Liz Rosenberg, *Monster Mama,* Putnam (New York, NY), 1993.

Jim Aylesworth, *The Burger and the Hot Dog,* Atheneum (New York, NY), 2001.

Jennifer Donnelly, *Humble Pie,* Atheneum (New York, NY), 2002.

Tamson Weston, *Hey, Pancakes!,* Harcourt (San Diego, CA), 2003.

OTHER

Books that Gammell has illustrated have been translated into Dutch, French, German, Italian, and Spanish, among other languages. Gammell was featured in *Authors for Children: A Calendar* by Sharon L. McElmeel, Hi Willow Research and Publishing, 1992. Gammell's papers are housed in permanent collections at the Mazza Collection, the University of Findlay (Findlay, OH), and the de Grummond Collection, University of Southern Mississippi. Gammell appeared as a guitarist on the sound recording *Scandinavian Fiddle* (volume three), Banjar Records (Minneapolis, MN), 1992.

Adaptations

Random House/Miller-Brody has made filmstrip/cassette sets of *Where the Buffaloes Begin,* 1982; *The Old Banjo,* 1984; and *The Relatives Came,* 1986. Miller-Brody released a video and teacher's guide of *Song and Dance Man,* 1990, and JTG released *Song and Dance Man* as part of its "Award Puzzles" series, 1991. Live Oak Media issued a combination book, cassette, and teacher's guide of *The Relatives Came,* 1999. Books on Tape, Inc., released *The Relatives Came* on cassette, 2000. PIM released a video of *Come a Tide,* read by Dixie Carter. The "Scary Stories" series has been released on audio cassette. Filmstrip adaptations have also been made of *Old Henry, Will's Mammoth, Song and Dance Man,* and *Monster Mama.* The PBS television series *Kino's Storytime* featured *The Relatives Came* (episode 103) and *Monster Mama* (episode 105).

Sidelights

An American author and illustrator of books for children and young adults, Stephen Gammell has received praise both as an artist and as the creator of original picture books. A prolific illustrator, he has provided the art for humorous tales, fantasies, picture books, nonfiction, retellings, realistic and historical fiction, poetry collections, a play, and an alphabet book. His illustrations, which range from precise pencil drawings to wildly extravagant full-page watercolors, have graced the works of such authors as Eve Bunting, Alvin Schwartz, Patricia Lee Gauch, Seymour Simon, Georgess McHargue, Mollie Hunter, Jean Fritz, Rafe Martin, Cynthia Rylant, Myra Cohn Livingston, George Ella Lyon, Joan W. Blos, Jim Aylesworth, Janet Taylor Lisle, Karen Ackerman, Tom Birdseye, and Liz Rosenberg. Gammell's self-illustrated picture books fall into two categories, pure fantasy and works that blend reality and fantasy. Generally humorous in tone, they feature unconventional protagonists—such as MacDonald, the farmer of the children's song of the same name; Scudder, a mountain man; Old Man Winter, a crusty, pint-size geezer; and Twigboy, an anthropomorphic stick—and surprise endings. Gammell is also the creator of a Christmas story about a bear who meets Santa Claus, a semi-autobiographical picture book about two siblings stuck in the back seat during a car trip, and a retelling of an old English folktale.

As an illustrator, Gammell uses the media of pencil, pastel, and watercolor, as well as a mixed-media approach that results in gleaming images—sometimes defined, sometimes impressionistic—done in scratchy line and swirling, spattered colors. Gammell is celebrated for the variety, energy, expressiveness, and distinctiveness of his art, and he is often praised for complementing, extending, and even surpassing the texts that he illustrates. Considered an interpretive artist whose pictures successfully capture the moods and emotions of the texts that he illustrates, Gammell creates works that range in effect from sensitive, haunting, and poignant to unrestrained, exaggerated, and surreal; his pictures in the latter vein have inspired favorable comparisons with popular English artist Ralph Steadman. In some of his books, especially those dealing with the supernatural such as the "Scary Stories" series of tales, poems, and songs collected by Alvin Schwartz, Gammell creates art that is considered particularly macabre and gruesome. Noted for the excellence of his work in books of American history and folklore, especially those relating to the American West, he is often acknowledged for his panoramic landscapes as well as for the accuracy of his details.

As a writer, Gammell characteristically uses brief texts in both prose and poetry to act as the jumping-off points for his illustrations. He also favors hand-lettered texts, a feature that he sometimes includes in books by other authors. Although Gammell's writing is sometimes considered less effective than his illustrations, he is generally considered a superb artist as well as an author/ illustrator whose books offer children enjoyable stories, entertaining twists, and beautiful art. A reviewer in

Gammell's drawings enhance Elvira Woodruff's imaginative tale, in which Matthew rents a pair of wings from a shop to visit his former neighborhood. (From The Wing Shop.*)*

Publishers Weekly called Gammell "one of the most gifted illustrators working today." *Horn Book* critic Annie Schwartz called the artist's work "down-to-earth, spontaneous, warm, energetic, seriously playful." Writing in *Children's Books and Their Creators,* Mary Brigid Barrett noted, "Every line in Stephen Gammell's distinctive illustrations is imbued with emotion. Every color and change of value creates mood."

Born in Des Moines, Iowa, Gammell was part of a family that fostered his artistic pursuits. His father was an art editor at Meredith Publishing, a company that produced popular magazines such as *Better Homes and Gardens.* Gammell once told *SATA,* "A big part of my childhood was spent drawing. Practically every night my father would bring home a variety of pencils and paper. These great piles of paper of many thicknesses and colors were better than any toy. Father also supplied me with magazines like *Collier's* and *Saturday Evening Post.* I remember being impressed by their illustrations and cutting them up to make scrapbooks. While I had no notion of what an artist was, I did have an awareness of illustration from an early age. I knew these magazine illustrations were with a story, but I never read them. I was only interested in the art." As a small boy, Gammell used to lie on his stomach on the floor of the solarium in the family house; there, he would draw airplanes, semaphores, soldiers, and trains, as well as, as he told *SATA,* "the usual cowboys and Indians. Now that I'm older, I stand up, use a drawing board, have better paper and pencils, and throw more drawings away than I used to, but it's still just as much fun as ever. Drawing, that is."

At the time, Gammell's favorite illustrations were of cowboys and Native Americans. Although he did not know it then, he was appreciating the works of artists such as Frederic Remington, Charles Marion Russell, and Frank Schoonover. "I also remember liking the paintings and romantic illustrations of Robert Fawcett," he told *SATA.* "I was interested in the detail of his work, the particular way he drew a dress, a window curtain, a chair." When asked to name the books that he read as a child, Gammell told online site *BookPage,* "I loved *Scuppers, the Sailor Dog,* but mostly I liked looking at the paintings and drawings in the magazines." As a child, Gammell rarely went to art museums. However, he did visit the historical museums that were located near his home in Des Moines. "I loved the stuffed animals, the American Indian artifacts, and memorabilia of the West. The exhibitions about the settling of Iowa were fascinating to me." He continued, "As years go by, you retain what is interesting from childhood and toss out the rest. Somehow the memorabilia and romance of Western history has always stayed with me. I suppose part of the lasting appeal is that artifacts are just plain fun to draw. I like the line and the form of the objects. An arrowhead, for instance, is fun to pick up, to play with, to touch, to draw. Tomahawks, hatchets, old revolvers, boots, and leather all have a certain sensual, visual appeal for me, and they, consequently, turn up in my illustrations."

Gammell received a great deal of support from his parents. "My father," he recalled, "was very encouraging. He would help me draw, supply the paper and pencils, but he would never coach me or tell me how to work. I picked up the interest on my own; my parents never pushed me. It got me through elementary school. If you could draw, the big kids were more hesitant about beating you up. I tried to make this work for me." When asked to name his childhood hero, Gammell told *BookPage,* "I had four: my Grandpa, my Mom and Dad, and Crazy Horse." Gammell attended grade school, high school, and college in Iowa. "I tried to get through high school by drawing, too," he told *SATA.* "I'd turn in book reports with illustrations, thinking the teachers would be impressed, but, of course, they weren't. After college, I drifted about for nine years. All through the sixties, I did odd jobs and continued to draw, but I never thought of myself as an artist. I wasn't intelligent enough to think about making a living or anything, much less art. I just fooled around."

During the late sixties Gammell moved to his current home state of Minnesota. While living in Minneapolis, he began to draw small ads for friends who ran neighborhood book and record stores; these ads were published in local magazines and newspapers. Gammell also created posters for music stores and signs for regional colleges and illustrated articles for local magazines. He told *SATA,* "I fell into this by accident and can't imagine what would be better suited to my personality and abilities than doing this for a living— stuck away safely in a second floor studio, out of public view and bothering no one, doing harmless drawings and paintings. Everyone's happy. Or relieved."

In the early 1970s Gammell made a pivotal trip to New York City. He noted, "Everything in my life has happened by accident. My roommate was an actor in a local theater company which was about to put on a play in New York City. This friend asked whether I'd like to tag along, and I agreed. I knew there were publishing companies in New York and that children's books, which were beginning to interest me, came out of major New York publishers. I put together some of my drawings and sketches as well as the ads and illustrations I had been doing in Minneapolis. My thought was to contact some people in publishing. I didn't want or expect to find a job. I was simply interested in getting a professional opinion of my work." Gammell visited several publishers of children's literature and asked the editors for some criticism. One of them, an editor at G. P. Putnam's Sons, liked his work and gave him a sample manuscript. Gammell recalled, "She suggested I take it home and make two or three drawings. She could see I knew how to draw, but was interested in whether I could maintain a sense of consistency and continuity from page to page. I made some drawings and brought them back several days later. To my surprise, she offered me a contract for that very book, *A Nutty Business.*" A humorous picture book by Ida Chittum that was published in 1973, *A Nutty Business* describes how the local squirrels declare war on Farmer Flint when he gathers

For the alphabet book **Old Black Fly,** *Gammell depicts the pesky insect villain who turns a household upside down with his twenty-six horrible deeds. (Written by Jim Aylesworth.)*

nuts in order to pay for the calico that he wants to buy for his wife and daughter.

Gammell continued to provide well-received pencil and charcoal illustrations for books by other authors. For example, the artist created pencil drawings for *Thunder at Gettysburg,* a fictionalized account of the Civil War battle that describes a young girl's experiences helping wounded soldiers. A reviewer in *Publishers Weekly* stated, "Gauch's dramatic, verse-like text and Gammell's somber black-and-white drawings evoke the horror of war with startling but not overpowering clarity." Writing in another issue of the same periodical, a reviewer called Gammell's drawings for *Terrible Things: An Allegory of the Holocaust* "superb."

Gammell considers *And Then the Mouse ... : Three Stories,* a collection of folktales by Malcolm Hall, to be a turning point in his work. He told *SATA,* "With it, I was finally able to get silly and free myself from inhibitions. *And Then the Mouse ...* loosened me up; I quit taking myself so seriously. As a result, I felt better about my attitude, my drawings, *myself.* From then on, I only accepted books that I really wanted to illustrate, books I could enjoy. I stopped trying to make an 'artistic statement,' and freed myself from the restrictive, self-imposed seriousness."

Where the Buffaloes Begin, a picture book by Olaf Baker, is the first of the books illustrated by Gammell to receive major awards for its art. A Native American legend that was originally published in 1915 in the children's magazine *St. Nicholas,* the story describes how ten-year-old Little Wolf travels to a legendary lake to see the sacred spot where the buffaloes begin. The boy guides the buffaloes back to his village, where the thundering herd tramples the members of an enemy tribe, thus saving his people from annihilation. The name of Little Wolf is then added to the legend of where the buffaloes begin. Writing in the *New York Times Book Review,* George A. Woods commented, "As legends go, [this] is better than most.... It is Stephen Gammell, however, who deserves the honors for his black-and-white illustrations. Working on a larger scale than customary for him, he provides spectacular scenes.... But most of all he conveys the hulking, surging, rampaging strength of the shaggy buffaloes as they rise out of a shadowy mist, the mist of legend or dream." Kate M. Flanagan, writing in *Horn Book,* called the full- and double-page pencil drawings "magnificent." *Where the Buffalo Begin* was named both a Caldecott Award honor book and a *Boston Globe-Horn Book* Award honor book; it was also nominated for an American Book Award for best picture book.

Gammell also produced his first original book, *Once upon MacDonald's Farm,* in 1981. In this picture book, which relates the "true" story behind the farmer of the beloved traditional song, Gammell discloses that, at one time, MacDonald did not have any animals on his farm. He buys an elephant, a baboon, and a lion to help him restock his land. During the day, MacDonald uses the elephant for plowing, tries to milk the lion, and attempts to get eggs from the baboon; that night, the outraged animals leave. The next day, a kindly neighbor—another farmer—gives MacDonald a horse, a cow, and a chicken. MacDonald starts again, singing "Ei-ei-oh" while plowing with his chicken. Gammell illustrates his farce with shaded pencil drawings and silhouettes. A reviewer commented in *Publishers Weekly* that the book owes its charm "to Gammell's drawings, rendered with the precision and charm that have made his illustrations distinguished additions to many books on Americana." Noting the book's "funny, slightly surrealistic mood," *New York Times Book Review* critic Karla Kuskin called Gammell's words "as silly as they are choice, and they are perfectly matched in his poker-faced, expertly penciled drawings."

After the publication of *Once upon MacDonald's Farm,* Gammell continued to create his own works while providing the pictures for works by other authors. *Wake Up, Bear ... It's Christmas!* is his first picture book in full color. In this story, which is told in rhyme, a bear who has hibernated through seven Christmases is determined to be awake for this one. Waking to his alarm on Christmas Eve, he is visited by a white-bearded man with a sleigh pulled by reindeer. The bear invites his visitor, who remains nameless, to come in and get warm; in thanks, the visitor takes the bear for a ride in his sleigh. In the end, they agree to do the same thing every year. Faith McNulty stated in the *New Yorker,* "This is a cheerful, pretty book for a child of three, four,

or five; someone older might wish for a stronger story." Writing in *Horn Book,* Ethel L. Heins commented, "No matter that the story is distinctly reminiscent of [Else Homelund Minarik's] *Little Bear's Christmas,* for with its brief text alternating between prose and verse and its luminous paintings conveying both the ingenuousness of the characters and the festivity of the season, the book is fresh and inviting."

Gammell draws upon his interest in the American West for *Git Along, Old Scudder.* In this picture book, an old mountain man gets lost and finds his way by drawing a map of the landmarks that he sees. He comes down from a mountain, goes to a fort for some rest, then heads off into the wilderness to finish his map. Spouting colorful comments in folksy dialect, he gives names such as "Sneaky Tree Road" and "Two Nose Pass" to the landmarks on the trail and asks young readers if they agree with his choices. However, readers see—before Scudder does—that the map leads the old codger in a big circle. Writing in *Booklist,* Denise M. Wilms stated that *Git Along, Old Scudder* "is set off by masterful watercolor paintings that capture the arid western landscape and startling blue skies.... Scudder himself ... casts a memorable swath." Clarissa Erwin added in *School Library Journal,* "A sense of the rich, western landscape and true grit, along with Old Scudder's drawled narrative make this a gem." Writing in *Horn Book,* Mary M. Burns called *Git Along, Old Scudder* "a handsome book that not only suggests the lure of the frontier but also offers young audiences an insight into the process by which many American landmarks acquired their colorful names."

Git Along, Old Scudder was Gammell's last self-illustrated work for fourteen years. In the interim, he continued to create pictures for books by other writers. In 1984 he produced the art for *Waiting to Waltz: A Childhood,* a collection of thirty autobiographical poems by Cynthia Rylant about growing up in a small Appalachian town during the 1960s. The next year, he illustrated another work by Rylant called *The Relatives Came.* This picture book describes how the lives of an Appalachian family are made more joyful by the arrival of their relatives from Virginia. The parents, grandparents, and children of the visiting family fill up the house; in fact, there are so many people that meals have to be eaten in rotation. The cheerful, loving relatives picnic, garden, play music, and fix things around the house, among other activities. When they leave, the family is lonely, but they know that their relatives will return the next summer. Writing in the *New York Times Book Review,* Anne Tyler stated, "If there's anything more charming than the tone of voice in this story, it's the drawings that go with it. Stephen Gammell fills the pages with bright, crayony pictures teeming with details that children should enjoy poring over for hours." Calling *The Relatives Came* a "picture book as good as country music," Ann A. Flowers of *Horn Book* noted that the illustrations, "quite different from Stephen Gammell's usual brooding, shadowy, gray drawings, are exuberant, untidy depictions of country life and down-home people in lively primary colors and quirky outlines." Gammell received his second honor book designations from the Caldecott Award and *Boston-Globe-Horn Book* Award committees for *The Relatives Came.*

In assessing his work, Gammell told *SATA* in 1988, "I'm very uncomfortable having the word 'author' with my name. Yes, I have written a few books, but the words are really nothing more than something to keep the art flowing smoothly, I hope. I hate writing and find it terribly difficult.... As long as I am given good manuscripts, I will be very happy to stick to illustration." In the same year, Gammell won the Caldecott Medal for his illustrations for *Song and Dance Man* by Karen Ackerman. Based partly on the author's childhood, this picture book features Grandpa, a retired vaudevillian, who delights his three grandchildren by recreating his act for them. Grandpa goes into the attic, dons a bowler hat and tap shoes, and picks up a gold-tipped cane to demonstrate some of the songs, dances, jokes, and banjo-playing that he used to do on stage. As he performs for them, the young narrators learn what it was like to be a real song-and-dance man. When the children tell their grandfather that they would have liked to have seen him dance in the good old days, he replies that he would not trade a million good old days for the time that he spends with them. *School Library Journal* critic Gratia Banta asserted that Gammell's "animated, crisp, colored pencil line drawings enhance this story.... The shadow and the performer, transformed by his art, complement the text tenderly."

Come a Tide, a picture book by George Ella Lyon, is one of Gammell's most popular illustrated works. Set in the hills of rural Kentucky, the story takes place in March, when the springtime combination of snow and rain brings on a natural disaster. Grandma, a feisty woman whose house is on higher ground than everyone else in the town, predicts, "It'll come a tide," and it does—a flood that washes away parts of houses and barnyard animals. Four families on the hillside—including that of the narrator, Grandma's young granddaughter—drive to Grandma's house to wait out the flood. Grandma's reassurance, wisdom, and wry wit help the narrator to cope with the flood. At the end of the story, the families emerge, safely, to begin the process of digging out. Writing in the *New York Times Book Review,* Kathleen Krull called *Come a Tide* "a complete success.... Stephen Gammell's shimmering artwork goes a long way toward making the book such pure fun." Krull concluded that Gammell and Lyon "have produced a weather-wise work of art that resonates—and exhilarates." A reviewer for *Publishers Weekly* noted, "This is a gem of a picture book, a seamless collaboration between author and artist." *Horn Book* reviewer Mary M. Burns concluded by calling *Come a Tide* "an exemplary picture book, regional in setting but universal in appeal."

During the remainder of the 1990s, Gammell continued to receive praise for his illustrations. Two of his most widely acknowledged works are *Old Black Fly,* a humorous alphabet book in rhyme by Jim Aylesworth,

and *Monster Mama,* a picture book by Liz Rosenberg. *Old Black Fly* outlines the twenty-six horrible things done by the pesky title character—a villain with bulging red eyes, in Gammell's interpretation—as he turns a household upside down before receiving his comeuppance. Writing in *Booklist,* Carolyn Phelan said, "Another artist might have depicted the fly irritating the inhabitants of the house, but in Gammell's interpretation, mere irritation gives way to frenzy as Old Black Fly unleashes page after page of household pandemonium." Margaret A. Bush observed in *Horn Book* that Gammell "spatters all of his crudely sketched watercolor scenes, creating an energetic chaos sure to invite giggles from many children." Noting Gammell's "spattery, jumpy illustrations, splashed with color, alive with movement, line, and humor, " *School Library Journal* critic Gail C. Ross called *Old Black Fly* "a book that's sure to become a classic."

Monster Mama features young Patrick Edward and his mother, a roaring, spell-casting woman "with a bad hair day and needing a manicure," as described by a reviewer in *Publishers Weekly.* In addition to her other talents, Monster Mama, who lives in a cave behind the family home, paints, bakes, gardens, and nurses Patrick Edward when he is sick. When three bullies capture Patrick Edward, he learns that he is truly his mother's son. After the older boys tie him up and taunt him about his mother, Patrick Edward roars and breaks his bonds and their baseball bat. Monster Mama hears her son, chases the bullies home, and makes them bake a new cake to replace one that they destroyed. In the end, the cake is shared, Mama gives Patrick Edward a hug, and the bullies depart with a new admiration for Monster Mama. The reviewer in *Publishers Weekly* concluded, "Gammell's trademark electric palette and airy, spattered paint technique make for illustrations that crackle with childlike energy." Writing in *Horn Book,* Nancy Vasilakis concluded, "The startling contrast between the benign, often lyrical text and Gammell's extravagant illustrations ... produce the impish dynamics that are at the heart of this original book."

In 1997, after a fourteen-year hiatus, Gammell produced his fourth self-illustrated picture book, *Is That You, Winter?* In this work Old Man Winter is a grumbling, pint-size character sporting a droopy, white mustache and wearing a ten-gallon hat. He spreads snow across the land from the back of his truck, a vehicle that, though battered, can fly. Old Man Winter wonders who is he making snow for and who is taking care of him. When he takes a tumble into the snow, he is picked up by a little girl, who defends him from the name-calling of her playmates, tells him that he makes snow for her, and assures him that he is special. Young readers learn that Old Man Winter is actually the little girl's toy—a doll. Gammell illustrates *Is That You, Winter?* with multicolored splatters and swirls; the dialogue of his text is hand-lettered, while the narrative is set in regular type. Calling the book "an ebullient tour de force," Marigny Dupuy noted in the *New York Times Book Review* that Gammell's illustrations in pencil, pastel, and watercolor are "a festival of color and image." Writing in *Booklist,*

John Peters noted, "Children will turn back to savor the sudden shifts of scale, and the girl's affection for her grizzled doll lingers past the closing scene." A reviewer for *Publishers Weekly* advised, "Forget those icy-looking fellows like Jack Frost" before calling the protagonist of *Old Man Winter* Gammell's "latest addition to his unforgettable cast of characters."

In his picture book *Ride,* Gammell addresses the theme of sibling rivalry. In this work, which draws on his childhood memories, he introduces a brother and sister who are placed in the back seat of the family car for a Sunday outing. After their mother requests that they try to get along just this once, the pair go to war with each other, setting turf limits and struggling for power. Their battle escalates, as do their imaginations. The children hit each other and call each other names while thinking of ways to obliterate their adversary. For example, the brother turns into an astronaut and shoots his sister into space while she blasts him with a tornado ("from your sister the twister"). Just as the two, now dinosaurs dressed in sneakers, are ready to make each other extinct, their mother—who remains oblivious to all off the goings-on, as does their father—brings out sandwiches from the picnic basket. It appears as if the battle is over; however, Gammell's final picture shows the brother's sandwich squirting jelly all over his sister. Sporting hand-lettered text and written totally in dialogue, *Ride* is illustrated in watercolor, pastel, and pencil with touches of bright colors such as aqua and chartreuse. Writing in the *New York Times Book Review,* Scott Veale called *Ride* "a quirky, gently subversive view of life in the rearview mirror." Veale added, "Gammell's wildly fanciful, swooshing illustrations ... are the main attraction in a narrative that pulls no punches, so to speak." A reviewer for *Horn Book* wrote, "Gammell's signature art expresses the erupting anger with panache." Writing in *Booklist,* Hazel Rochman concluded, "Kids will recognize the anger and frustration, and they will laugh, not only with one another, but also with the adults who make the decisions and trap the kids together."

In several of his works, Gammell profiles characters who play instruments. As well as being an accomplished artist and writer, Gammell is a talented musician. He told *SATA,* "Music comes naturally to me, even more naturally than drawing. I play guitar, banjo, mandolin, piano—anything with strings. I've played instruments since I was a kid, and if I hadn't become an artist, I probably would have pursued music. I have music on all the time in the studio—jazz, classical, early mountain music, bluegrass, and country music from the forties and fifties. Down in Iowa, people loved country music. I grew up with it and it was part of my environment." In 1992, Gammell appeared as a guitarist on *Scandinavian Fiddle,* a recording made with violinist Craig Ruble and other musicians and released on Banjar Records of Minneapolis.

Gammell told *SATA,* "The first time I read a manuscript, I can immediately tell whether I want to illustrate it. I may not know how the illustrations will look, but I get a certain feeling from the text. I respond to the words and, if I can respond to a story, I can illustrate it. My first concern is to serve the story. That is an illustrator's job. I don't research unless I have to because I prefer to draw from my imagination. I need to know whether a detail is anatomically correct before I can take liberties, however. If I must find out how something looks—what comes out of an animal's little paws, for instance, or which side of the face the trunk is on—I'll go to the library. But if I can get away with making up my own version, I will. It is more fun to work this way, and the illustrations are more expressive. Whatever I draw, whether it's a buffalo or a chair, I try to make it my own to satisfy myself." He continued, "I am inspired by a text which gives me the freedom to interpret. I don't like being tied to a specific historical time period, style of architecture, or costume. I like texts which take place anytime, anywhere. For this reason, I enjoy elements of fantasy in a story and turn down anything that is too literal. A careful look at my work tells the way I *interpret* a text. I take a poetic approach. The events I depict could easily be portrayed in a number of different ways."

"Much of my early work," Gammell added, "is done in pen and ink because I wasn't trained in color media. Watercolor is still difficult for me. My interest in book design has evolved over the years. I like to keep artistic control over design, especially type placement, and I

The story of Patrick Edward, who gets help from his monster mother when he is attacked by bullies, is aptly illustrated with Gammell's spattered paintings. (From Monster Mama, *written by Liz Rosenberg.)*

often make suggestions concerning overall design, quality of paper, and format." Regarding his working habits, Gammell commented, "I prefer to work alone, without feedback from the author. I believe that once a manuscript is written and accepted, the writer's work is over.... When I illustrate a story, I want to work with my ideas and my perception of the work, not with the author." Gammell keeps to a regular schedule when he is working on a book. He noted, "I work in my studio every day. Whether I accomplish my work or not, I am there. It's my job to show up, and because I like my work, I wouldn't have it any other way. I don't like to split my focus, and prefer to work on one book at a time. I would like to have the time to draw or paint outside of my illustration, but I'm at the mercy of a good manuscript. As long as they continue to come in, I will continue to work on them. I remember times when I would finish a book, turn it in, and have weeks of free time, but was so nervous about not having another book to do that I had a hard time relaxing enough to do my own drawings."

When asked to name his biggest influence on his writing and art, Gammell told *BookPage,* "My imagination, and lots of papers and pencils." He told the same source that his message for all children is, "Pay attention to your Mom and Dad (and your teachers). They're a lot smarter than you think!" When asked by *SATA* if he had any advice for aspiring artists, Gammell responded, "I haven't any advice for young artists, but make myself accessible to them. On an individual basis, I am glad to be helpful and encouraging, but am cautious about giving advice. I found my own way, and I think that is the best way." He concluded, "I think of myself as an artist—admittedly a basic term that can mean almost anything. One of the forms that my art takes is book illustration. It is very fulfilling to me. I don't feel a need to get away from my studio to rejuvenate. I love my work. I love drawing, painting, and making books. In a deep sense, I *am* my work—what is seen on the page is really me."

Biographical and Critical Sources

BOOKS

Gammell, Stephen, *Ride,* Harcourt (San Diego, CA), 2001.

Holtze, Sally Holmes, editor, *Fifth Book of Junior Authors & Illustrators,* Wilson (New York, NY), 1983.

Silvey, Anita, editor, *Children's Books and Their Creators,* Houghton (Boston, MA), 1995.

PERIODICALS

Booklist, April 1, 1983, Denise M. Wilms, review of *Git Along, Old Scudder,* p. 1033; February 15, 1992, Carolyn Phelan, review of *Old Black Fly,* p. 1106; September 1, 1997, John Peters, review of *Is That You, Winter?,* p. 132; May 1, 2001, Hazel Rochman, review of *Ride,* p. 1689.

Horn Book, June, 1981, Kate M. Flanagan, review of *Where the Buffaloes Begin,* p. 298; December, 1981, Ethel L. Heins, review of *Wake Up, Bear ... It's Christmas!,* p. 653; April, 1983, Mary M. Burns, review of *Git Along, Old Scudder,* p. 150; March,

1986, Ann A. Flowers, review of *The Relatives Came,* p. 197; July-August, 1989, Annie Schwartz, "Stephen Gammell," pp. 456-459; March-April, 1990, Mary M. Burns, review of *Come a Tide,* p. 104; May-June, 1992, Margaret A. Bush, review of *Old Black Fly,* p. 325; March-April, 1993, Nancy Vasilakis, review of *Monster Mama,* p. 200; May, 2001, review of *Ride,* p. 310.

New Yorker, December 7, 1981, Faith McNulty, review of *Wake Up, Bear ... It's Christmas!,* p. 227.

New York Times Book Review, February, 15, 1981, George A. Woods, review of *Where the Buffaloes Begin,* p. 22; June 26, 1981, Karla Kuskin, "Seeing and Reading," p. 54; November 10, 1985, Anne Tyler, "Disorder at 4 A.M.," p. 37; October 14, 1990, Kathleen Krull, review of *Come a Tide,* p. 33; February 15, 1998, Marigny Dupuy, review of *Is That You, Winter?,* p. 26; June 3, 2001, Scott Veale, "Back-Seat Warriors," p. 49.

Publishers Weekly, May 5, 1980, review of *Terrible Things,* p. 77; April 24, 1981, review of *Once upon MacDonald's Farm,* p. 75; January 23, 1987, review of *Old Henry,* p. 88; January 12, 1990, review of *Come a Tide,* p. 60; June 8, 1990, review of *Thunder at Gettysburg,* p. 54; January 25, 1993, review of *Monster Mama,* p. 87; August 11, 1997, review of *Is That You, Winter?,* p. 401.

School Library Journal, August, 1983, Clarissa Erwin, review of *Git Along, Old Scudder,* pp. 50-51; January, 1989, Gratia Banta, review of *Song and Dance Man,* p. 58; April, 1992, Gail C. Ross, review of *Old Black Fly,* p. 88.

OTHER

BookPage, http://www.bookpage.com/ (June, 2000), "Meet the Author: Stephen Gammell."

*   *   *

GARRITY, Linda K. 1947-

Personal

Born August 8, 1947; daughter of Howard and Jean (Penwell) Mosman; married Patrick Garrity, June 27, 1968; children: Meghan, Bonnie Garrity McLean. *Education:* University of Northern Colorado, B.A., 1969; University of Colorado, M.A., 1971. *Politics:* Democrat. *Religion:* Roman Catholic.

Addresses

Home—8183 South Trenton Way, Englewood, CO 80112.

Career

Cherry Creek Schools, Englewood, CO, media specialist, 1972—.

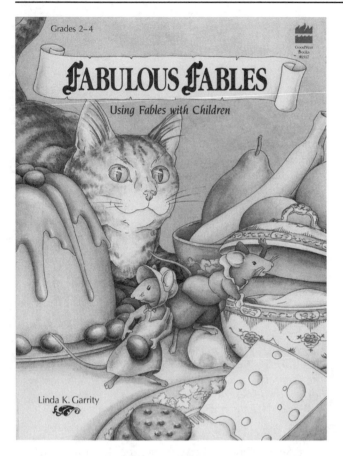

Linda K. Garrity's book offers fables from the East and West, as well as suggestions for activities, discussions, games, and other means of enhancing young readers' enjoyment and appreciation of the stories. (Cover illustration by Jackie Moore.)

Writings

The Gingerbread Guide: Using Folktales with Young Children, Good Year Books (Glendview, IL), 1987.

Fabulous Fables: Using Fables with Children, Good Year Books (Glendview, IL), 1991.

After the Story's Over: Your Enrichment Guide to Eighty-eight Read-aloud Children's Classics, Good Year Books (Glendview, IL), 1991.

The Tale Spinner: Folktales, Themes, and Activities, illustrated by Emilia Markovich, Fulcrum Publishing (Golden, CO), 1999.

Sidelights

Linda K. Garrity told *SATA:* "I have tried with my writing career to reach children through their classroom teachers and media specialists. My books are filled with rewritten folk literature from around the world and enriched with a wide array of extension activities for instructors to use with each of the tales.

"The old tales are still exciting for today's children, but are sometimes overlooked in schools because of the availability and appeal of quality contemporary literature and also because of the demands of curriculum. By

linking literature to meaningful writing, art, and drama activities, I have tried to encourage the integration of literature into the elementary school curriculum.

"I am excited by the current publication of beautifully illustrated books of folk literature for children. These books build children's awareness of the rich folklore tradition handed down through the ages by a wide range of cultures."

Biographical and Critical Sources

PERIODICALS

School Library Journal, February, 2000, Edith Ching, review of *The Tale Spinner: Folktales, Themes, and Activities,* p. 147.*

*   *   *

GELLIS, Roberta (Leah Jacobs) 1927- (Max Daniels, Leah Jacobs, Priscilla Hamilton)

Personal

Born September 27, 1927, in Brooklyn, NY; daughter of Morris B. (a chemist) and Margaret (a teacher; maiden name, Segall) Jacobs; married Charles Gellis (a teacher), April 14, 1947; children: Mark Daniel. *Education:* Hunter College (now Hunter College of the City University of New York), B.A. (chemistry), 1947; Brooklyn Polytechnic Institute, M.S. (biochemistry), 1952; New York University, M.A. (medieval literature), 1958. *Politics:* Independent. *Religion:* Jewish. *Hobbies and other interests:* Reading.

Addresses

Home and office—P.O. Box 67, Lafayette, IN 47902. *Agent*—Lucienne Diver, Spectrum Literary Agency, 320 Central Park West, Suite 1-D, New York, NY 10025. *E-mail*—robertagellis@juno.com.

Career

Novelist and editor. Foster D. Snell, Inc., New York, NY, chemist, 1947-53; McGraw-Hill, New York, NY, editor, 1953-55; New York University, New York, NY, teaching assistant in English, 1956-58; Hudson Laboratories, New York, NY, microbiologist, 1961-63; freelance author, 1964—. *Member:* Authors Guild, Authors League of America, Science Fiction and Fantasy Writers of America, Romance Writers of America, Novelists, Inc., Sisters in Crime.

Awards, Honors

Romantic Times awards, 1982 for best medieval novel, and 1983, for best historical series; Silver Medal Porgy awards, *West Coast Review of Books,* 1983, for *The Kent Heiress,* and 1984, for *Fortune's Bride; Romantic Times* reviewers awards, 1985, for *Tapestry of Dreams,* 1987,

Roberta Gellis

for *The Rope Dancer,* 1988, for *Fires of Winter,* and 1990, for *A Silver Mirror;* Lifetime Achievement award, Romance Writers of America, 1986; Golden Certificate awards, *Affaire de Coeur,* 1987, for *The Rope Dancer,* and 1988, for *Fires of Winter;* Silver Pen award, *Affaire de Coeur,* 1988; Lifetime Achievement Award for Historical Fantasy, *Romantic Times,* 1996.

Writings

Knight's Honor, Doubleday (Garden City, NY), 1964.
Bond of Blood, Doubleday (Garden City, NY), 1965.
(Under name Leah Jacobs) *The Psychiatrist's Wife,* New American Library (New York, NY), 1966.
Sing Witch, Sing Death, Bantam (New York, NY), 1975.
The Dragon and the Rose, Playboy Press (Chicago, IL), 1977.
The Sword and the Swan, Playboy Press (Chicago, IL), 1977.
(Under pseudonym Max Daniels) *Space Guardian,* Pocket Books (New York, NY), 1977.
(Under pseudonym Max Daniels) *Offworld,* Pocket Books (New York, NY), 1979.
(Under pseudonym Priscilla Hamilton) *The Love Token,* Playboy Press (Chicago, IL), 1979.
Tapestry of Dreams, Berkley (New York, NY), 1985.

The Rope Dancer, Berkley (New York, NY), 1986.
Fires of Winter (sequel to *Tapestry of Dreams*), Jove (New York, NY), 1987.
Masques of Gold, Jove (New York, NY), 1988.
A Delicate Balance, Leisure Books, 1993.
Dazzling Brightness, Pinnacle (New York, NY), 1994.
Shimmering Splendor, Pinnacle (New York, NY), 1995.
Enchanted Fire, Pinnacle (New York, NY), 1996.
Bull God, Baen (New York, NY), 2000.
Overstars Mail: Imperial Challenge (e-book), SWP, 2000.
Thrice Bound, Baen (New York, NY), 2001.
The Seven Deadly Sins, MightyWords, 2001.

"CHRONICLES OF ROSELYNDE" SERIES

Roselynde, Playboy Press (Chicago, IL), 1978.
Alinor, Playboy Press (Chicago, IL), 1978.
Joanna, Playboy Press (Chicago, IL), 1978.
Gilliane, Playboy Press (Chicago, IL), 1979.
Rhiannon, Playboy Press (Chicago, IL), 1981.
Sybelle, Jove (New York, NY), 1983.

"HEIRESS" SERIES

The English Heiress, Dell (New York, NY), 1980.
The Cornish Heiress, Dell (New York, NY), 1981.
The Kent Heiress, Dell (New York, NY), 1982.
Fortune's Bride, Dell (New York, NY), 1983.
A Woman's Estate, Dell (New York, NY), 1984.

"ROYAL DYNASTY" SERIES

Siren Song, Playboy Press (Chicago, IL), 1981.
Winter Song, Playboy Press (Chicago, IL), 1982.
Fire Song, Jove (New York, NY), 1984.
A Silver Mirror, Jove (New York, NY), 1989.

"MAGDALENE LA BÂTARD" MYSTERY SERIES

A Mortal Bane, Tor (New York, NY), 1999.
A Personal Devil, Tor (New York, NY), 2001.
Bone of Contention, Tor (New York, NY), in press.

OTHER

Contributor to *Irish Magic: Four Tales of Romance and Enchantment from Four Acclaimed Authors,* Kensington (New York, NY), 1995; *The Shadow of Doubt,* Kensington, 1996; *Irish Magic II: Four Unforgettable Novellas of Love and Enchantment,* Kensington (New York, NY), 1997; and *Millennium Magic,* Hard Shell Word Factory, 2000.

Work in Progress

Mother of Poisons, a Renaissance mystery.

Sidelights

Dubbed "one of the pioneers of the romance genre," by Jean Mason, a contributor to *Romance Reader,* Roberta Gellis is a well-respected author of historical romances that take readers back to the French Revolution, the War of the Roses, twelfth-century England, and even to ancient Greece. Praised for what Mason described as "strong characterizations, attention to historical detail, and intriguing plots," Gellis has also contributed to a number of other genres, including science fiction—

under the pseudonym Max Daniels—historical, and mythological fantasy. In Mason's opinion, the popularity of such novels as *A Tapestry of Dreams, The English Heiress,* and *Siren Song* has made Gellis's work "the standard of excellence" in the historical romance field. Reviewing her 1988 novel *Masques of Gold,* a *Publishers Weekly* critic praised Gellis for the novel's "rich tapestry of detail, well-drawn characters, suspenseful story line, . . . and fresh approach."

Born in Brooklyn, New York, in 1927, Gellis attended Hunter College, receiving a bachelor's degree in chemistry. She continued on to graduate school, earning a graduate degree in biochemistry, and then working as a chemist and microbiologist until 1954. A career change in the mid-1950s found Gellis editing scientific manuscripts, as well as attending graduate school again, this time to pursue a long-held interest in literature and history. "I always was a dichotomy in college," she recalled in an interview in *Publishers Weekly.* "While I was getting my [first] degree in chemistry, I took all my electives in English literature. I took medieval literature, and I always had a strong interest in writing. I even wrote as a child."

The knowledge she acquired during her graduate studies in medieval literature eventually combined with her skill as a writer in what became Gellis's third career as a well-respected historical novelist. Her first published book, *Knight's Honor,* was released in 1964. It would be the first of many novels in which Gellis tells a captivating story imbued with a strong sense of the historical epoch as "a thing lived and made by people, not a string of dry dates and facts," as the author once noted. In *Sing Witch, Sing Death,* her fourth novel, readers are swept back to the English coast at the turn of the twentieth century as a woman is hired to teach proper manners to a young lord's foreign-born wife. The War of the Roses is the backdrop for Gellis's 1976 novel *The Dragon and the Rose,* which a *Publishers Weekly* contributor praised as "altogether engrossing and stylish." In *The Sword and the Swan* medieval England comes to life as Gellis spins the tale of Catherine, a widow married to Rannulf, a brave but aged knight in the service of King Stephen as the English throne is threatened by Henry of Anjou. Containing what *West Coast Review of Books* contributor Henry Zorich called "excellent dramatic descriptions of jousts, swordplay and outright war," *The Sword and the Swan* reflects the author's "fine way with character and description" and, according to Zorich, proves Gellis's theory that "gaining an understanding of England's history does add more heat to the [fictional] fire."

Gellis sets most of her novels in medieval England, a period that lasted from 500 to 1500. Her lengthy research has allowed her to fill her novels with a wealth of detail that brings the era alive as she weaves within her fiction factual events, real people, and the sights and sounds of the times. Although some reviewers have criticized her heroines for being too modern in their self-assured approach to the male-dominated world around

them, Gellis explained to Mason: "Strong women were surprisingly common in the medieval period. You don't hear much about them in the chronicles or history books, of course: Nicolaa de la Hay is mentioned and Hadwissa . . . Queen Eleanor herself. But in addition there were hundreds and hundreds of women whose men were always away at war or conducting legal cases. These women were left in charge of the property and managed it and defended it in the men's absence." Mason further explained: "Gellis's view of men and women as individuals who are equal, who are able to maintain their individuality and equality in their male-female relationships, sets a different tone in the historical romance genre and places Gellis well ahead of many other authors in terms of quality."

Gellis has authored several novel series, including the "Chronicles of Roselynde," which includes the titles *Roselynde, Alinor, Joanna, Gillaine, Rhiannon,* and *Sybelle,* tracing the history of a family through the generations. From the first page of each of these novels, according to Mason, "Gellis makes it clear that she is dealing with extraordinary, rather than average, women." In *Roselynde* readers meet Eleanor of Aquitaine as she accompanies her son, Richard the Lionhearted, on a Crusade to the Holy Land, while her younger son, the less-than-goodhearted John, conspires for the throne in Richard's absence. The second volume in the series, *Alinor,* finds the queen's namesake, now a young widow, forced to marry in order to keep the avaricious king from confiscating her lands. Alinor's daughter weds King John's illegitimate nephew in *Joanna,* which a *Publishers Weekly* contributor praised for its ability to "bring a long-ago time wonderfully to life." The series continues with *Gilliane* and *Rhiannon,* the latter a love story containing "Gellis's wonderful re-enactment of Welsh-English politics of the thirteenth century," according to a *West Coast Review of Books* critic.

In an interview in *Love's Leading Ladies,* Gellis commented on the things that have most influenced her. While reading literature of the medieval period, the novelist explained, she found herself "enchanted by people who believe in honor and true love, although naturally, being human beings, they were as dishonorable and faithless then as people are now. The difference is that they had ideals, even if they did not live up to them; and when they did not live up to them, they knew they had done wrong and sometimes, tried to do better."

Gellis continues to write in her home in Lafayette, Indiana, where she lives with her husband, Charles, and their dog Taffy. Her grown son, Mark, has inherited his mother's love for words and works as a university writing instructor. In her more recent novels, she has delved into the mystery genre, while keeping her characters firmly ensconced in England's distant past. In *A Mortal Bane,* published in 1999, Magdalene la Bâtarde runs a house of ill-repute nestled in the shadows of London's St. Mary Overy Church. When a papal messenger winds up dead on the church's doorstep, all suspicion immediately falls upon Magdalene. Her only hope of escaping the blame is to discover the killer for herself. "Magdalene is a memorable character, sharp witted and strong," noted a *Publishers Weekly* contributor, "and she shines through this novel from start to unpredictable climax." Gellis's heroine returns in 2001's *A Personal Devil,* as the wife of one of her best clients is discovered murdered and Magdalene and friend Sir Bellamy of Itchen are determined to put their talent for sleuthing to the test once more.

Biographical and Critical Sources

BOOKS

Falk, Kathryn, *Love's Leading Ladies,* Pinnacle (New York, NY), 1982.
Twentieth-Century Romance and Historical Writers, St. James Press (Detroit, MI), 1994.

PERIODICALS

Booklist, April 1, 1984, Mary Banas, review of *Fire Song,* pp. 1098-1099; November 15, 1989, Mary Ellen Quinn, review of *A Silver Mirror,* p. 640.
Kirkus Reviews, September 15, 1999, review of *A Mortal Bane,* p. 1448.
Publishers Weekly, February 24, 1975, review of *Sing Witch, Sing Death,* p. 117; December 6, 1976, review of *The Dragon and the Rose,* p. 60; April 11, 1977, review of *The Sword and the Swan,* p. 76; January 2, 1978, review of *Roselynde,* p. 63; May 8, 1978, Albert H. Johnston, review of *Alinor,* p. 72; October 9, 1978, review of *Joanna,* p. 72; April 9, 1979, Sally A. Lodge, review of *Gilliane,* p. 106; August 8, 1980, review of *The English Heiress,* p. 81; November 14, 1980, review of *Siren Song,* p. 54; November 13, 1981; October 28, 1983, review of *Fortune's Bride,* p. 66; March 9, 1984, review of *Fire Song,* p. 111; October 26, 1984, review of *A Woman's Estate,* p. 99; April 26, 1985, review of *A Tapestry of Dreams,* p. 79; July 31, 1987, review of *Fires of Water,* p. 72; August 5, 1988, Peggy Kaganoff, review of *Masques of Gold,* p. 79; September 22, 1989, review of *A Silver Mirror,* p. 48; August 30, 1999, review of *A Mortal Bane,* p. 56; February 12, 2001, review of *Personal Devil,* p. 187.
Romance Reader, July 3, 1997.
West Coast Review of Books, September, 1977, Henry Zorich, review of *The Sword and the Swan,* p. 64; May, 1982, review of *Rhiannon,* p. 37; September, 1982, Henry Zorich, review of *Winter Song,* p. 65; November, 1983, Henry Zorich, review of *Fortune's Bride,* p. 45; May, 1985, review of *A Tapestry of Dreams,* p. 50.

*   *   *

GETZINGER, Donna 1968-

Personal

Born December 8, 1968, in Canoga Park, CA; daughter of James (in computer marketing) and Gerrie (a teacher) Getzinger; married David Maguire (a television editor),

September 25, 2000. *Education:* University of California—Irvine, B.A.

Addresses

Office—10061 Riverside Dr., Suite 770, Toluca Lake, CA 91602. *E-mail*—RingletRed@aol.com.

Career

Performing arts teacher at various schools, 1988-2000; freelance writer, 1998—. Tutor at Learning Center in Los Angeles, CA, 1999-2000. Also worked as a professional actress. *Member:* Society of Children's Book Writers and Illustrators, Publishers Marketing Association, Screen Actors Guild, American Federation of Television and Radio Artists, California Readers Association.

Writings

Saving Christmas Spirit, Shadowbox Media Publishing (Toluca Lake, CA), 1999.
L.A.'s Best Comedy Sketches, Meriwether Publications (Colorado Springs, CO), 1999.

Donna Getzinger

The Picture Wagon (children's historical novel; based on a story by Elaine Getzinger Callard), Denlinger's Publishers (Edgewater, FL), 2000.

For a Speck of Gold, Denlinger's Publishers (Edgewater, FL), 2001.

Contributor of articles and short stories to periodicals and books, including *Children's Digest, Story Friends, Funny Times, L.A. Parent, Cat Fancy,* and *Chicken Soup for the Mother's Soul.*

Work in Progress

Pop's Music, a historical novel; *Grand Care,* a contemporary adult novel.

Sidelights

Donna Getzinger told *SATA:* "I used to be an actress. I loved stepping on-stage and playing different characters more than anything. Writing had always been a hobby. Gradually I realized that I had a lot more fun writing than acting. Why? I get to play *all* the parts! What could be better than that? When I sold my first story in 1994, I was hooked. I knew that I wanted to be a successful writer.

"Although I write everything from health articles to fantasy novels, I like writing children's novels most. Having been a teacher for years, it just seemed natural to write for that audience. Every time I finish a story, I think of the kids out there who might read it someday, and I can't help but feel complete."

*   *   *

GILBERT, Anne Yvonne 1951-
(Yvonne Gilbert)

Personal

Born April 7, 1951, in Wallsend, Northumberland, England; daughter of Anne Dorreen Gilbert. Married David Edward Owen (deceased); married second husband, Robert Hill Tohnstonf (a gallery owner); children: Thomas Edward Gilbert Owen. *Education:* Attended Newcastle College of Art, 1969; Liverpool College of Art, B.A., 1973.

Addresses

Home—6A Bell Grove Ter., Spital Tongues, Newcastle-upon-Tyne NE2 4LL, England. *Office*—37 Highbury, Jesmond, Newcastle-upon-Tyne NE2 3EA, England. *E-mail*—enquiries@yvonnegilbert.com.

Career

Freelance illustrator of book covers, picture books, greeting cards, postage stamps, and china, 1978—. Teaches at various workshops and demonstrations,

including external assessor for the CNAA course in illustration at Manchester Polytechnic, 1981-85.

Awards, Honors

Il Fronco Bollo D'Oro (The Golden Stamp Award) and Gran Premio Del'Arte Filatelica (The World's Most Beautiful Stamp), for her postage stamps; Revel Cumberland Award for Best Use of Colored Pencils.

Illustrator

Vivian French, *A Christmas Star Called Hannah,* Candlewick Press (Cambridge, MA), 1997.

The Night Before Christmas: Classic Stories and Poems with a Christmas Message, Candlewick Press (Cambridge, MA), 2000.

Contributing illustrator to *DK Discoveries: Tutankhamun: The Life and Death of a Pharaoh,* DK Publishing, 1998.

AS YVONNE GILBERT

Katharine Mary Briggs, *Abbey Lubbers, Banshees and Beggars: An Illustrated Encyclopedia of Fairies,* Pantheon Books (New York, NY), 1979.

Baby's Book of Lullabies and Cradle Songs, Dial Books (New York, NY), 1990.

Miriam Chaikin, reteller, *Children's Bible Stories from Genesis to Daniel,* Dial Books (New York, NY), 1993.

Mary-Claire Helldorfer, *Night of the White Stag,* Doubleday (New York, NY), 1999.

Rebecca Hickox, *Per and the Dala Horse,* Doubleday (New York, NY), 1995.

Contributing illustrator to *The Iron Wolf,* Allen Lane (London, England), 1980, published as *The Unbroken Web: Stories and Fables,* Crown (New York, NY), 1980.

OTHER

Also illustrator of numerous book jackets.

Work in Progress

Writing and illustrating a book about her two dogs.

Sidelights

Anne Yvonne Gilbert's work as an illustrator ranges over a wide spectrum of advertising and design projects, including hundreds of book covers for a handful of publishers, greeting cards, limited edition china plates, and stamps issued by the British Post Office. Her original artwork is shown in exhibitions and at galleries in England. Reminiscent of the work of the early twentieth century, Gilbert uses a delicate pastel palette of colored pencils and a realistic style.

During the 1990s Gilbert illustrated several picture books for American publishers: *Per and the Dala Horse, A Christmas Star Called Hannah,* and *Night of the White Stag.* The first book tells the tale of three brothers who

Anne Yvonne Gilbert illustrates the story of Hannah, who is disappointed when she gets a minor role in the Christmas pageant but triumphs when she is able to save the play from unforeseen disaster. (From A Christmas Star Called Hannah, *written by Vivian French.)*

inherit gifts. While the oldest brother receives a farm, complete with work horse and plow, and the second brother receives a fine horse, the youngest brother inherits a dala horse, that is, a brightly painted wooden toy horse. Though the youngest brother appears to have been short changed, the dala horse saves the day when trolls steal a religious treasure. Cynthia K. Richey, writing in *School Library Journal,* likened Gilbert's work to that of Jan Brett, particularly the borders and decorative details, and noted that Gilbert's colors "effectively evoke the setting, as do the details."

A Christmas Star Called Hannah revolves around young Hannah's experience of being "just a star" in the Christmas pageant. When it is discovered that the doll that was to represent Baby Jesus has been forgotten, Hannah comes to the rescue with her own baby brother. The work caught the attention of reviewers. Gilbert's "realistic ... artwork has a photographic quality" noted *Booklist* critic Ilene Cooper, while a *School Library Journal* reviewer mentioned how the illustrations "enliven the story and lend personality to its characters."

Set in medieval times, the *Night of the White Stag* tells the story of a boy hunting rabbits in the king's woods. When he encounters a mysterious blind man, forlorn over the death of his son in the same war that orphaned the boy, man and boy become companions—and more. They hunt for a legendary white stag, which causes

miraculous changes. The illustrations, according to Tracy Taylor in *School Library Journal,* are "realistically and gracefully rendered."

Biographical and Critical Sources

PERIODICALS

Booklist, November 15, 1995, Carolyn Phelan, review of *Per and the Dala Horse,* p. 564; November 1, 1997, Ilene Cooper, review of *A Christmas Star Called Hannah,* p. 480.
Publishers Weekly, October 6, 1997, review of *A Christmas Star Called Hannah,* p. 55.
School Library Journal, January, 1996, Cynthia K. Richey, review of *Per and the Dala Horse,* pp. 84-85; October, 1997, review of *A Christmas Star Called Hannah,* p. 41; November, 1999, Tracy Taylor, review of *The Night of the White Stag;* October, 2000, Tracy Taylor, review of *The Night Before Christmas: Classic Stories and Poems with a Christmas Message,* p. 61.

OTHER

Official Yvonne Gilbert Web Site, http://www.yvonnegilbert.com/ (November 12, 2001).*

*   *   *

GILBERT, Yvonne
See GILBERT, Anne Yvonne

*   *   *

GOOBIE, Beth 1959-

Personal

Born in 1959, in Canada. *Education:* University of Winnipeg, B.A. (English literature), 1983; Mennonite Brethren Bible College, B.R.S., 1983; attended University of Alberta, 1986-88.

Addresses

Agent—c/o Author Mail, Orca Book Publishers, P.O. Box 5626, Station B, Victoria, British Columbia V8R GSR, Canada.

Career

Front line youth worker, Winnipeg, Manitoba and Edmonton, Alberta, 1984-89; freelance writer, Saskatoon, Saskatchewan, 1994—. *Member:* Writers Union of Canada, Saskatchewan Writers Guild, Canadian Children's Book Centre.

Awards, Honors

Gold Medal Award, University of Winnipeg, 1983, for academic excellence; shortlisted for Alberta Fiction Award, 1992, for *Could I Have My Body Back Now, Please?;* R. Ross Annet Award for best children's book in Alberta, and shortlisted for Governor General's Award for Children's Literature, both 1995, both for *Mission Impossible;* Pat Lowther Memorial Award for best book of poetry by a Canadian woman, and shortlisted for Gerald Lampert Award, both 1995, both for *Scars of Light;* Our Choice Award, Canadian Children's Book Center, 1995, for *Mission Impossible,* 1998, for *The Good, the Bad, and the Suicidal,* 1999, for *The Colours of Carol Moley,* 2000, for *The Dream Where the Losers Go,* and as a starred selection, 2001, for *Before Wings;* shortlisted for Canadian Library Association Young Adult Book Award, 1998, for *The Good, the Bad, and the Suicidal,* 1999, for *The Colours of Carol Moley,* and 2000, for *The Dream Where the Losers Go;* shortlisted for Saskatchewan Children's Literature Award, 1998, for *The Good, the Bad, and the Suicidal,* 1999, for *The Colours of Carol Moley,* and 2000, for *The Dream Where the Losers Go;* Joseph S. Stauffer Award for Literature, Canada Council, 1998; shortlisted for City of Saskatoon Book Award, 1999, for *The Colours of Carol Moley,* and 2000, for *The Dream Where the Losers Go;* Top Ten Poetry Books List, Literary Network, 2000, for *The Girls Who Dream Me;* Saskatchewan Children's Literature Award, 2000, for *Before Wings;* Canadian Library Association Young Adult Book Award, 2001, for *Before Wings;* Sunburst Award finalist, 2001, for *Before Wings;* Teen Top Ten List, 2001, for *Before Wings;* Best Books for Young Adults selection, American Library Association, 2002, for *Before Wings.*

Writings

Could I Have My Body Back Now, Please? (poetry and short stories), NeWest Press (Edmonton, Canada), 1991.

Dandelion Moon (radio play), commissioned and produced by Catalyst Theatre (Edmonton, Canada), 1992.

Scars of Light (poetry), NeWest Press (Edmonton, Canada), 1994.

Black Angels (screenplay), Cynthia Wells Productions, 1996.

Janine Fowler Did It (play), produced by Guelph Collegiate Vocational Institute, 1997.

The Only-Good Heart (novel), Pedlar Press (Toronto, Canada), 1998.

The Girls Who Dream Me (poetry), Pedlar Press (Toronto, Canada), 1999.

The Face is the Place (play), Blizzard (Winnipeg, Canada), 2000.

YOUNG ADULT NOVELS

Group Homes from Outer Space, illustrated by Wes Lowe, Maxwell Macmillan (Dons Mills, Canada), 1992.

Who Owns Kelly Paddik?, illustrated by Greg Ruhl, Maxwell Macmillan (Dons Mills, Canada), 1993.

Hit and Run, illustrated by David Craig, Maxwell Macmillan (Dons Mills, Canada), 1994.

Sticks and Stones, illustrated by Greg Ruhl, Maxwell Macmillan (Dons Mills, Canada), 1994.

Mission Impossible, Red Deer College Press (Alberta, Canada), 1994.

Kicked Out, Prentice-Hall (New York, NY), 1995.

I'm Not Convinced, Red Deer College Press (Alberta, Canada), 1997.

The Good, the Bad, and the Suicidal, Roussan (Montreal, Canada), 1997.

The Colours of Carol Moley, Roussan (Montreal, Canada), 1998.

The Dream Where the Losers Go, Roussan (Montreal, Canada), 1999.

Before Wings, Orca (Custer, WA), 2000.

The Lottery, Orca (Custer, WA), in press.

Work represented in anthologies, including *Under NeWest Eyes,* Thistledown Press, 1996; *Vintage 1997-1998,* League of Canadian Poets, 1998; and *Ice: New Writing in Hockey,* Spotted Cow, 1999. Contributor to periodicals, including *Canadian Review.* Also author of *Contimuum* (radio play), 1992.

Self-destructive Skey meets a boy who shares her confusion and her recurring dreams in Beth Goobie's young adult novel about sexual assault.

Resolute Jill leads protests against her high school's Lovely Legs Competition and other sexist practices in Goobie's novel. (Cover illustration by Jeffery Hitch.)

Work in Progress

"I'm always working on something—YA fiction, adult fiction, poetry, or drama. It's ongoing, full-time and ever-changing."

Sidelights

An award-winning author of young adult fiction, Beth Goobie began her publishing career with a book of short fiction and poetry, titled *Could I Have My Body Back Now, Please?* Based on Goobie's experiences working with sexually and physically abused children, the collection focuses on themes of alienation between body and self. These themes are also explored in subsequent poetry collections, including *Scars of Light,* in which Goobie reveals the existence of abuse within her own family. Her "harrowing journey" into her past, noted Marlene Cookshaw of *Books in Canada,* seems to have given Goobie "a startling clarity of vision" in order to present a powerful story of survival and insight.

In addition to writing poetry, Goobie has also penned twelve novels for young adults. One of the first books in this genre was *Group Homes from Outer Space,* a story of an abused young girl named Froggy, who eventually escapes her violent family situation and moves to a group home. Reviewing this work for *Quill and Quire,* Anne Louise Mahoney noted that although "some readers my find the subject disturbing," *Group Homes* is a very "rewarding book."

In another work, *Who Owns Kelly Paddik?,* Goobie tells the story of Kelly, a fifteen-year-old girl on the run from both her school and memories of sexual abuse by her father. Discussing this work in *Quill and Quire,* Patty Lawlor noted that Goobie's own experiences while working in group homes with young people are reflected clearly in her writing, and that the novel would work well as a "curriculum resource" as well as a reference for "girls and families who are either at risk or in crisis."

Mission Impossible focuses on a teenage protagonist struggling with issues of self-identity and was recommended by Mary Beaty in the *Quill and Quire* as a text that will "make the ... world of high school ... much more comprehensible." And Dean E. Lyons noted in *Kliatt* that the work is "tough yet sensitive," making it an appealing text for "serious young women with questioning minds."

Goobie continues her exploration of the teenage world in *The Good, the Bad, and the Suicidal* through the character of Dariel Bosma. In her school, kids are divided into categories: the Jocks, the Irregulars, and the Leftovers. Dariel knows who she is—a leftover SWFF (single white fat female)—and as Goobie traces the struggles the young heroine has to contend with, readers are given an appreciation for a "straight up and hilarious" Dariel, according to *Quill and Quire* critic Teresa Toten.

In 2000, Goobie issued her award-winning novel, *Before Wings,* a story about fifteen-year-old Adrien, who suffered a brain aneurysm two years earlier. A second episode would be fatal, and now, practically smothered by her over-protective parents, Adrien constantly mulls over the idea of her impending death. In order to escape her parent's constant worry, she escapes to a summer camp run by her aunt, who makes no allowances for Adrien's delicate state of health. While at the camp, Adrien is mesmerized by the sight of five girls dancing over the lake. Her time at the lake, both with her aunt and her new-found friend, Paul, force Adrien to grow out of her self-absorption and realize the value of living life to the fullest. Reviewing the work in *Voice of Youth Advocates,* Diane Masla wrote that despite the entertaining read, the book will also "resonate with many teens" for its "deeper message" of the need to grasp life and love completely. And a reviewer for *Horn Book* noted that the relationship between Paul and Adrien, where each finds a means to save each other, combines to make "the best kind of romance."

Beth Goobie told *SATA:* "I began writing 'full-time' when I became ill with Chronic Fatigue Syndrome in 1989. At the time, I was too ill to stand without swooning, and I had difficulty with both visual and auditory sequencing. This left me unable to read, but a dear friend gave me a tape recorder with a handheld mike. Somehow, the problems with sequencing the external world were absent when I retreated into the stories of my mind. Exhaustion allowed me to record for only five to ten minutes at a time, but I went at it three times a day, and within seven weeks, I had the novel *Mission Impossible* on tape. This young adult novel went on to be published by Red Deer Press of Alberta, edited by Tim Wynne-Jones, and shortlisted for the Governor General's Award for Children's Literature.

"I wrote myself through a complete recovery from the Chronic Fatigue Syndrome. It is my belief that creativity takes you into new areas of brain tissue, enabling both emotional and physical healing. I continue to explore stories and themes inside my own head that I hope will engage and change me as much as my favorite book of all time, *The Chocolate War* by Robert Cormier. For instance, the YA novel *I'm Not Convinced* came out of my need to affirm the difficult experience young people face in the Child Welfare system. News stories about teen curfews, gangs, and sexual harassment inspired my YA novels *The Good, the Bad, and the Suicidal* and *Sticks and Stones.* I ventured into issues of spirituality and the paranormal in *The Colours of Carol Moley,* and went deepest into myself, engaging with the issue of sexual assault in *The Dream Where the Losers Go.*

"The experience of joy, however, can challenge and change you as much as trauma. My latest YA novel, *Before Wings,* which received superlative editing from Bob Tyrell at Orca Book Publishers, came out of my need to explore joy. Once again, I was changed in the process, but then isn't creative writing fundamentally about the making and meeting of self?"

Biographical and Critical Sources

PERIODICALS

Bloomsbury Review, September, 1992, Carl V. Bankston, review of *Could I Have My Body Back Now, Please?,* p. 20.

Books in Canada, April, 1995, Marlene Cookshaw, "Patterns of Truth," pp. 55-56.

Calgary Herald, March 14, 1998, Paula E. Kirman, "Goobie Reaches Youth with Truth."

Horn Book, March-April, 2001, review of *Before Wings,* p. 205.

Kliatt, January, 1996, Dean E. Lyons, review of *Mission Impossible,* p. 8.

National Post, January 27, 2001, Elizabeth MacCullum, "Summer Camp Mirrors Life and It's Not for Sissies," p. B8.

Quill and Quire, June, 1992, Anne Louise Mahoney, review of *Group Homes from Outer Space,* p. 36; June, 1993, Patty Lawlor, review of *Who Owns Kelly Paddik,?* p. 37; February, 1995, Mary Beaty, review of

Mission Impossible, p. 36; March, 1995, Fred Boer, review of *Sticks and Stones,* p. 79; April, 1997, Janet McNaughton, review of *I'm Not Convinced,* pp. 37-38; October, 1997, Teresa Toten, review of *The Good, the Bad, and the Suicidal,* pp. 37-38; May, 1998, Suzanne Methot, review of *The Only-Good Heart,* p. 30; October, 1998, Bridget Donald, review of *The Colours of Carol Moley,* pp. 43-44; October, 2000, Philippa Shephard, review of *Before Wings,* p. 46.

Voice of Youth Advocates, April, 2001, Diane Masla, review of *Before Wings.*

*   *   *

GUTMAN, Bill

Personal

Born in New York, NY; married; wife's name, Elizabeth. *Education:* Washington College, B.A. (English), 1965; attended University of Bridgeport.

Addresses

Home—Ridgefield, CT. *Agent*—c/o Author Mail, Millbrook Press, 2 Old New Milford Rd., P.O. Box 335, Brookfield, CT 06804.

Career

Sportswriter. *Greenwich Time,* Greenwich, CT, reporter and sports editor during the late 1960s; has also worked in advertising.

Writings

NONFICTION

Great Quarterbacks, Grosset & Dunlap (New York, NY), Volume 1: *Staubach, Landry, Plunkett, Gabriel,* 1972, Volume 2: *Kilmer, Hale, Bradshaw, Phipps,* 1973, revised edition, 1974.

Pistol Pete Maravich: The Making of a Basketball Superstar, Grosset & Dunlap (New York, NY), 1972.

Hockey Explosion, Grosset & Dunlap (New York, NY), 1973.

World Series Classics, Random House (New York, NY), 1973.

Hank Aaron, Grosset & Dunlap (New York, NY), 1973.

Famous Baseball Stars, Dodd (New York, NY), 1973.

Gamebreakers of the NFL, Random House (New York, NY), 1973.

Jim Plunkett, Grosset & Dunlap (New York, NY), 1973.

Modern Baseball Superstars, Dodd (New York, NY), 1973.

At Bat, Grosset & Dunlap (New York, NY), 1973.

Great Running Backs, two volumes, Grosset & Dunlap (New York, NY), 1973-74.

New Breed Heroes in Pro Baseball, Messner (New York, NY), 1973.

New Breed Heroes of Pro Football, Messner (New York, NY), 1974.

Great Linebackers, Volume 1, Grosset & Dunlap (New York, NY), 1974.

In an informative text about motocross bicycle racing, Bill Gutman outlines the history of the sport, the types of equipment and courses, and safety precautions. (From BMX Racing.)

Csonka, Grosset & Dunlap (New York, NY), 1974.

Modern Football Superstars, Dodd (New York, NY), 1974.

O. J., Grosset & Dunlap (New York, NY), 1974.

Griese—Tarkenton, Grosset & Dunlap (New York, NY), 1974.

Jackson—Bench, Grosset & Dunlap (New York, NY), 1974.

Great Hockey Players, Volume 1, Grosset & Dunlap (New York, NY), 1974.

Aaron—Murcer, Grosset & Dunlap (New York, NY), 1974.

At Bat, No. 2: Cedeno, Rose, Bonds, and Fish, Grosset & Dunlap (New York, NY), 1974.

Modern Basketball Superstars, Dodd (New York, NY), 1975.

Football Superstars of the '70s, Messner (New York, NY), 1975.

The Front Four, Grosset & Dunlap (New York, NY), 1975.

Giants of Baseball, Grosset & Dunlap (New York, NY), 1975.

Great Receivers of the NFL, Grosset & Dunlap (New York, NY), 1975.

New Ball Game, Grosset & Dunlap (New York, NY), 1975.

Modern Hockey Superstars, Dodd (New York, NY), 1976.

Pele, Grosset & Dunlap (New York, NY), 1976.

Munson, Garvey, Brock, Carew, Grosset & Dunlap (New York, NY), 1976.

Mark Fidrych, Grosset & Dunlap (New York, NY), 1977.

Modern Women Superstars, Dodd (New York, NY), 1977.

Harlem Globetrotters: Basketball's Funniest Team, Garrard (Easton, MD), 1977.

Duke: The Musical Life of Duke Ellington, Random House (New York, NY), 1977.

Dr. J., Grosset & Dunlap (New York, NY), 1977.

Walton, Thompson, Lanier, Collins, Grosset & Dunlap (New York, NY), 1978.

Superstars of the Sports World, Messner (New York, NY), 1978.

The Picture Life of Reggie Jackson, Franklin Watts (New York, NY), 1978, published as *Reggie Jackson: The Picture Life,* Avon (New York, NY), 1978.

Great Basketball Stories: Today and Yesterday, Messner (New York, NY), 1978.

More Modern Baseball Superstars, Dodd (New York, NY), 1978.

Modern Soccer Superstars, Dodd (New York, NY), 1979.

Grand Slammers: Rice, Luzinski, Foster and Hisle, Grosset & Dunlap (New York, NY), 1979.

(Editor) Franklin Folsom, *Baseball,* revised edition, Franklin Watts (New York, NY), 1979.

Great Sports Feats of the '70s, Messner (New York, NY), 1979.

Gridiron Greats: Campbell, Zorn, Swann, Grogan, Grosset & Dunlap (New York, NY), 1979.

More Modern Women Superstars, Dodd (New York, NY), 1979.

Pro Sports Champions, Messner (New York, NY), 1981.

The Signal Callers: Sipe, Jaworski, Ferguson, Bartowski, Grosset & Dunlap (New York, NY), 1981.

Baseball's Belters: Jackson, Schmidt, Parker, Brett, Grosset & Dunlap (New York, NY), 1981.

Baseball Stars of Tomorrow: An Inside Look at the Minor Leagues, Grosset & Dunlap (New York, NY), 1982.

Women Who Work with Animals, Dodd (New York, NY), 1982.

Flame Throwers: Carlton and Gossage, Ace Books (New York, NY), 1982.

Gridiron Superstars, Ace Books (New York, NY), 1983.

Strange and Amazing Wrestling Stories, Pocket Books (New York, NY), 1986.

Refrigerator Perry and the Super Bowl Bears, Archway (New York, NY), 1987.

Sports Illustrated Great Moments in Pro Football, Archway (New York, NY), 1987.

Sports Illustrated Pro Football's Record Breakers, Archway (New York, NY), 1987.

Pictorial History of Basketball, Smith, 1988.

Great Sports Upsets, Pocket Books (New York, NY), 1988.

Sports Illustrated Baseball's Record Breakers, Archway (New York, NY), 1988.

Great World Series, Bantam (New York, NY), 1989.

Sports Illustrated Great Moments in Baseball, Pocket Books (New York, NY), 1989.

Sports Illustrated Strange and Amazing Football Stories, Pocket Books (New York, NY), 1989.

Great All-Star Games, Bantam (New York, NY), 1989.

Baseball's Hot New Stars, Pocket Books (New York, NY), 1989.

Sports Illustrated Growing Up Painfully, Simon & Schuster (New York, NY), 1990.

Pro Sports Champions, Pocket Books (New York, NY), 1990.

Sports Illustrated Baseball Records, Pocket Books (New York, NY), 1990.

(With Lee Heiman and Dave Weiner) *When the Cheering Stops: Ex-Major Leaguers Talk about Their Game and Their Lives,* Macmillan (New York, NY), 1990.

Sports Illustrated Strange and Amazing Baseball Stories, Pocket Books (New York, NY), 1990.

Bo Jackson, Pocket Books (New York, NY), 1991.

The Giants Win the Pennant! The Giants Win the Pennant! Zebra Books (New York, NY), 1991.

Micro-League Championship Baseball: Official Field Guide and Disk, Bantam (New York, NY), 1991.

Jim Abbott: Star Pitcher, Millbrook Press (Brookfield, CT), 1992.

Blazing Bladers: The Wild and Exciting World of Skating, Tor Books (New York, NY), 1992.

Mario Lemieux: Wizard with a Puck, Millbrook Press (Brookfield, CT), 1992.

This Is David Robinson, Scholastic (New York, NY), 1992.

Magic Johnson: Hero On and Off Court, Millbrook Press (Brookfield, CT), 1992.

Michael Jordan: Basketball Champ, Millbrook Press (Brookfield, CT), 1992.

Magic, More than a Legend, Harper (New York, NY), 1992.

Shaquille O'Neal, Pocket Books (New York, NY), 1993.

Jennifer Capriati, Teenage Tennis Star, Millbrook Press (Brookfield, CT), 1993.

Ken Griffey, Sr., and Ken Griffey, Jr.: Father and Teammates, Millbrook Press (Brookfield, CT), 1993.

Barry Sanders: Football's Rushing Champ, Millbrook Press (Brookfield, CT), 1993.

Great Sports Upsets 2, Pocket Books (New York, NY), 1993.

David Robinson, NBA Super Center, Millbrook Press (Brookfield, CT), 1993.

World Cup Action! Watermill Press (Mahwah, NJ), 1994.

Reggie White: Star Defensive Lineman, Millbrook Press (Brookfield, CT), 1994.

The Kids' World Almanac of Football, World Almanac Books (Mahwah, NJ), 1994.

Shaquille O'Neal: Basketball Sensation, Millbrook Press (Brookfield, CT), 1994.

Michael Jordan: Basketball to Baseball and Back, revised edition, Millbrook Press (Brookfield, CT), 1995.

BMX Racing, Capstone Press (Minneapolis, MN), 1995.

David Robinson, Rainbow Bridge (Mahwah, NJ), 1995.

Michael Jordan, revised edition, Pocket Books (New York, NY), 1995.

Sumo Wrestling, Capstone Press (Minneapolis, MN), 1995.

Kung Fu, Capstone Press (Minneapolis, MN), 1995.

Larry Johnson, King of the Court, Millbrook Press (Brookfield, CT), 1995.

The Kids' World Almanac of Basketball, World Almanac Books (Mahwah, NJ), 1995.

Roller Hockey, Capstone Press (Minneapolis, MN), 1995.

NBA High-Flyers, Pocket Books (New York, NY), 1995.

Hakeem Olajuwon: Superstar Center, Millbrook Press (Brookfield, CT), 1995.

Karate, Capstone Press (Minneapolis, MN), 1995.

Mountain Biking, Capstone Press (Minneapolis, MN), 1995.

Juan Gonzalez: Outstanding Outfielder, Millbrook Press (Brookfield, CT), 1995.

Judo, Capstone Press (Minneapolis, MN), 1995.

Emmitt Smith, NFL Super Runner, Millbrook Press (Brookfield, CT), 1995.

Bicycling, Capstone Press (Minneapolis, MN), 1995.

Julie Krone, Raintree Steck-Vaughn (Austin, TX), 1996.

Frank Thomas: Power Hitter, Millbrook Press (Brookfield, CT), 1996.

Harmful to Your Health, Twenty-First Century Books (New York, NY), 1996.

Hazards at Home, Twenty-First Century Books (New York, NY), 1996.

Recreation Can Be Risky, Twenty-First Century Books (New York, NY), 1996.

Gail Devers, Raintree Steck-Vaughn (Austin, TX), 1996.

Tae Kwon Do, Capstone Press (Minneapolis, MN), 1996.

Steve Young: NFL Passing Wizard, Millbrook Press (Brookfield, CT), 1996.

Troy Aikman: Super Quarterback, Millbrook Press (Brookfield, CT), 1996.

Jim Eisenreich, Raintree Steck-Vaughn (Austin, TX), 1996.

Grant Hill: Basketball's High Flier, Millbrook Press (Brookfield, CT), 1996.

Be Aware of Danger, Twenty-First Century Books (New York, NY), 1996.

Becoming Your Bird's Best Friend, Millbrook Press (Brookfield, CT), 1996.

Becoming Your Dog's Best Friend, Millbrook Press (Brookfield, CT), 1996.

Becoming Best Friends with Your Hamster, Guinea Pig, or Rabbit, Millbrook Press (Brookfield, CT), 1997.

Becoming Your Cat's Best Friend, Millbrook Press (Brookfield, CT), 1997.

Grant Hill: A Biography, Pocket Books (New York, NY), 1997.

Skateboarding: To the Extreme! Tor Books (New York, NY), 1997.

Snowboarding: To the Extreme! Tor Books (New York, NY), 1997.

Scottie Pippen: The Do-Everything Superstar, Millbrook Press (Brookfield, CT), 1997.

Anfernee Hardaway: Super Guard, Millbrook Press (Brookfield, CT), 1997.

Alonzo Mourning: Center of Attention, Millbrook Press (Brookfield, CT), 1997.

Deion Sanders: Mr. Prime Time, Millbrook Press (Brookfield, CT), 1997.

Baseball Bloopers: World's Funniest Errors, Troll (Mahwah, NJ), 1998.

Shooting Stars: The Women of Pro Basketball, Random House (New York, NY), 1998.

Ken Griffey, Jr.: Baseball's Best, Millbrook Press (Brookfield, CT), 1998.

Sammy Sosa: A Biography, Pocket Books (New York, NY), 1998.

Paul Azinger, Raintree Steck-Vaughn (Austin, TX), 1998.

Tiger Woods: Golf's Shining Young Star, Millbrook Press (Brookfield, CT), 1998.

Teammates: Michael Jordan, Scottie Pippen, Millbrook Press (Brookfield, CT), 1998.

Brett Favre: Leader of the Pack, Millbrook Press (Brookfield, CT), 1998.

Cap Ripken, Jr.: Baseball's Iron Man, Millbrook Press (Brookfield, CT), 1998.

Dan O'Brien, Raintree Steck-Vaughn (Austin, TX), 1998.

Brett Favre: A Biography, Pocket Books (New York, NY), 1998.

Greg LeMond, Raintree Steck-Vaughn (Austin, TX), 1998.

Tara Lipinski: Queen of the Ice, Millbrook Press (Brookfield, CT), 1999.

Greg Maddux: Master on the Mound, Millbrook Press (Brookfield, CT), 1999.

Parcells: A Biography, Carroll & Graf (New York, NY), 2000.

Adopting Pets: How to Choose Your New Best Friend, Millbrook Press (Brookfield, CT), 2001.

Becoming Best Friends with Your Iguana, Snake, or Turtle, Millbrook Press (Brookfield, CT), 2001.

Venus and Serena, Scholastic (New York, NY), 2001.

Marion Jones, Simon & Schuster (New York, NY), 2001.

The Look-It-Up Book of the Fifty States, illustrated by Anne Wertheim, Random House (New York, NY), 2002.

The Wild and Exciting World of Skateboarding, Tor (New York, NY), 2002.

Also author of *Payton, Jones, Haden, Dorsett, Baseball Super Teams,* and *Chairmen of the Boards,* 1980.

"START RIGHT AND PLAY WELL" SERIES

Football: Start Right and Play Well, illustrated by Ben Brown, Grey Castle (Freeport, NY), 1989.

Volleyball: Start Right and Play Well, illustrated by Ben Brown, Pocket Books (New York, NY), 1989, published as *Volleyball for Boys and Girls: Start Right and Play Well,* Grey Castle (Freeport, NY), 1990.

Basketball for Boys and Girls: Start Right and Play Well, illustrated by Ben Brown, Grey Castle (Freeport, NY), 1990.

Field Hockey: Start Right and Play Well, illustrated by Ben Brown, Grey Castle (Freeport, NY), 1990.

Soccer for Boys and Girls: Start Right and Play Well, illustrated by Ben Brown, Grey Castle (Freeport, NY), 1990.

Softball for Boys and Girls: Start Right and Play Well, illustrated by Ben Brown, Grey Castle (Freeport, NY), 1990.

Tennis for Boys and Girls: Start Right and Play Well, illustrated by Ben Brown, Grey Castle (Freeport, NY), 1990.

"GO FOR IT!" SERIES

Go for It! Tennis, illustrated by Ben Brown, Grey Castle (Freeport, NY), 1989.

Go for It! Softball, illustrated by Ben Brown, Grey Castle (Freeport, NY), 1989.

Go for It! Basketball, illustrated by Ben Brown, Grey Castle (Freeport, NY), 1989.

Go for It! Field Hockey, illustrated by Ben Brown, Grey Castle (Freeport, NY), 1989.

Go for It! Wrestling, illustrated by Ben Brown, Grey Castle (Freeport, NY), 1989.

Go for It! Track and Field, illustrated by Ben Brown, Grey Castle (Freeport, NY), 1989.

Go for It! Ice Hockey, illustrated by Ben Brown, Grey Castle (Freeport, NY), 1989.

Go for It! Football, illustrated by Ben Brown, Grey Castle (Freeport, NY), 1989.

Go for It! Baseball, illustrated by Ben Brown, Grey Castle (Freeport, NY), 1989.

Go for It! Soccer, illustrated by Ben Brown, Grey Castle (Freeport, NY), 1989.

Go for It! Swimming, illustrated by Ben Brown, Grey Castle (Freeport, NY), 1989.

Go for It! Volleyball, illustrated by Ben Brown, Grey Castle (Freeport, NY), 1989.

FICTION

"My Father, the Coach" and Other Sports Stories, Messner (New York, NY), 1976.

Summer Dreams, Avon (New York, NY), 1986.

Smitty, Turman, 1988.

Rookie Summer (novel), Turman, 1988.

Smitty II: The Olympics, Turman, 1990.

Along the Dangerous Trail, HarperCollins (New York, NY), 1992.

Across the Wild River, HarperCollins (New York, NY), 1993.

Over the Ragged Mountain, HarperCollins (New York, NY), 1994.

OTHER

Also contributor to *Boy's Life* and other magazines. Contributing editor, *Team!*

Work in Progress

Books on sports, sports figures, and sports history.

Sidelights

The author of almost two hundred books, sportswriter Bill Gutman has covered subjects from judo to golf, hockey to soccer, and tennis to football in his concise, informative books. Featuring sports stars such as Michael Jackson, Tiger Woods, and Steve Young, among a plethora of others, Gutman has produced biographies of such notables from contemporary news sources for over three decades. Typical of such books is Gutman's biography, *Parcells,* which is about the legendary football coach. A reviewer for *Publishers Weekly* cautioned not to "expect any blockbuster revelations" in the book, but rather a "straightforward" story of the life and times of Bill Parcells by a "capable writer who delivers an accurate overview." It is this type of overview that readers have come to expect from the prolific Gutman.

Born in New York City, Gutman grew up in Stamford, Connecticut, and planned to become a dentist, but instead he earned a bachelor's degree in English at Washington College in Chestertown, Maryland. Eventually he became a reporter and feature writer for the Greenwich, Connecticut, newspaper, *Greenwich Time.* Gutman worked briefly in advertising, then began to write nonfiction sports books full time. Since 1972 he has written scores of books about sports for readers of all ages.

Critics have recommended Gutman's biographies of sports figures as accurate and interesting depictions of the men and women who have achieved fame in all the major sports. Beginning with *Pistol Pete Maravich: The Making of a Basketball Superstar,* Gutman's books include star performers from baseball, basketball, football, hockey, tennis, wrestling, and soccer. When they were first published, his biographies were the most complete sources of information available for several sports personalities, including Greg Landry, Chris Evert, Dorothy Hamill, and Nadia Comeneci. His books appeal to readers of all ages by combining descriptions of game action and sports facts.

In *Michael Jordan: A Biography,* Gutman features the life and career of one of basketball's all-time superstars. J. J. Votapka, writing in *School Library Journal,* noted that this "readable book is filled with chatty details" that enable readers to feel as though "they are really getting to know the player." Concentrating not only on Jordan's amazing statistics, but also on the man behind them, this biography "will be enjoyed by basketball fans as well as Jordan's own fans," according to Barbara J. McKee writing in *Kliatt.* Virginia B. Moore, writing in *Voice of Youth Advocates,* found this same title to be an "action-packed biography of basketball's spectacular star for the avid reader!" Reviewing Gutman's *Magic Johnson: Hero On and Off the Court,* *Booklist*'s Ilene Cooper felt that the "clear writing, clean layout, and interesting assortment of black-and-white and color photographs" make the biography "worth a look." In his longer biography of Johnson, *Magic: More Than Just a Legend,* Gutman produced a work that is "entertaining, informative, and a winner," according to Sherri F. Ginsberg in *Kliatt.* More basketball biography is served up in *Shaquille O'Neal,* a book that will "be popular with basketball fans," according to Doris Losey writing in *Voice of Youth Advocates.* Gutman has written dozens of other titles about individual basketball players, as well as about the game of basketball itself.

Turning his hand to football, Gutman has also crafted numerous titles about the greats of the gridiron. In *Brett Favre: Leader of the Pack,* the author details Favre's youth in a small Mississippi town and how the quarterback had to overcome injuries as well as an addiction to prescription drugs as he worked his way to the top of the NFL. *Booklist* reviewer April Judge felt that Favre's biography was a "lively portrait" that will be "useful for reports and popular with young sports fans." Reviewing *Brett Favre: A Biography,* a longer study of the same subject for somewhat older readers, *Booklist* contributor Ellen Mandel wrote, "Fans will delight in the statistics, play-by-play, and game strategies that dominate the pages." Other popular football biographies from Gutman include *Steve Young: NFL Passing Wizard, Troy Aikman: Super Quarterback,* and *Emmitt Smith: NFL Super Runner,* among a score of others. In a review of *Troy Aikman,* Todd Morning commented in *School Library Journal* that the popularity of football, as well as the "short, readable format" of the book, make this biography a "hot ticket." Golf also comes to the forefront in Gutman's *Tiger Woods: Golf's Shining Young Star,* which overviews Wood's youth and then goes into detail about his professional accomplishments. A list of highlights and a bibliography also accompany the short text. Reviewing the title in *Horn Book Guide,* Jennifer M. Brabander thought that the book was "accessible and informative."

Additionally, Gutman has devoted numerous titles to America's national pastime—baseball. His *Sammy Sosa* takes an informed look at the home run slugger, from youth through his professional career and the record-breaking 1998 season. Randy Brough, reviewing the title in *Voice of Youth Advocates,* called it a "quickie" biography that should "satisfy eager fans." Other biographies include *Juan Gonzales,* outfielder for the Texas Rangers, *Jim Abbott,* a star pitcher, *Bo Jackson,* the phenomenon who played two major league sports for many years, and *Ken Griffey, Sr. and Ken Griffey, Jr.,* one of the most famous father-son match-ups in baseball history. And Gutman and coauthors Lee Heiman and Dave Weiner asked professional baseball players about their lives for *When the Cheering Stops: Ex-Major Leaguers Talk about Their Game and Their Lives.* Mark Clayton observed in the *Christian Science Monitor:* "The authors seem to have asked each of the players similar questions, which could have been a bore. But the word-for-word statements are a surprisingly interesting and spontaneous recounting of what it is like to play in the shadow of the big guys, only occasionally holding the spotlight. The answers include their impressions, their gripes, the great players they remember, and what they've been doing since hanging up their spikes."

Modern Women Sports Superstars dispels some myths about women in professional sports and provides important statistics about their accomplishments. Gutman reports, for example, that Joan Joyce was the fastest pitcher alive in 1979, with the speed of one pitch measured at one hundred and sixteen miles per hour. Female stars of tennis, golf, auto and horse racing, swimming, and softball are featured in this book and in *More Modern Women Sports Superstars.* In his 1996 *Julie Krone,* Gutman presents one of the first successful female jockeys, and one who has participated in over sixteen thousand races in her career, winning three thousand of them. Reviewing the book in *School Library Journal,* Jeanette Lambert called Gutman's narrative "absorbing," further noting that "the author brings his subject to life in a balanced portrayal of success over adversity."

In several series, Gutman also details the ins and outs of popular sports. Writing in the "Action Sports" series for Capstone Press, Gutman has authored titles on bicycling, the martial arts, wrestling, and surfing, among others. These brief introductions deal with equipment, basic skills, and the fundamentals of the sport. In the "Go for It!" series, Gutman deals with sports from field hockey to ice hockey and from football to tennis. Each volume in the series looks at the history of the sport, at the organizations that control it at the amateur level, and at instruction in the sport in question. "Gutman offers straightforward, accurate instructions, and in most cases a fairly detailed description of the basics required to succeed in each sport," according to Tom S. Hurlburt, reviewing *Field Hockey, Ice Hockey, Track and Field,* and *Wrestling* in *School Library Journal.* In a review of the entire series, a *Magpies* critic wrote, "Overall this seems like an informative series on a range of sports." A further series from Gutman is "Start Right and Play Well," an investigation of seven popular sports.

Gutman turns his attention from sports and sports figures to a famous name in the music world in *Duke Ellington: The Musical Life of Duke Ellington.* Giving more emphasis to the development of the jazz musician's musical style than to the details of his personal life, the biographer follows Ellington's rise from pianist to jazz composer of international fame. He also explains many of the social and economic conditions faced by black musicians in the United States. Critics agreed that readers can find this book a useful introductory history of American jazz presented in a format that is appealing to younger readers.

Further ventures away from sports are Gutman's books about animals and pets. *Women Who Work with Animals* looks at the careers of six women in jobs that have been dominated by men in the past. A horse trainer, two zoo workers, a show dog handler, a veterinarian, and a sea mammal trainer are featured in the book. These women tell Gutman and young readers how they became interested in working with animals and what kinds of education best prepared them for their work. They also offer advice for young women seeking similar careers. Diane Tuccillo remarked in the *High/Low Report:* "Reluctant readers who enjoy stories about animals may like this book. There is high-interest subject matter scattered throughout." For example, true stories about living with caged gorilla babies and overcoming allergies to animal hair make the book fascinating as well as readable. Patricia Manning, writing in *School Library Journal,* called *Women Who Work with Animals* a "reasonable introduction, good for Career Centers."

Gutman offers young readers advice on making their pets happy in other books, including *Becoming Your Dog's Best Friend, Becoming Your Cat's Best Friend, Becoming Your Bird's Best Friend,* and similar titles concerning small pets such as hamsters, rabbits, and various reptiles. The books in this pet series encourage young pet owners to think of life from the animal's point of view: what their natural habitat would be like, what

makes up their ideal diet, activity needs they may have, and so on. With the right information, potential pet owners can make a wise selection and minimize the stress involved in introducing an animal to a new environment. "Gutman's practical advice is laced with compassionate concerns for a pet's well-being," noted Ellen Mandel in a *Booklist* review of *Becoming Best Friends with Your Hamster, Guinea Pig, or Rabbit.* Anne Deifendeifer, reviewing *Becoming Your Cat's Best Friend* in *Horn Book Guide,* praised the "easy-to-read" text, which "offers solid advice to young animal lovers." And in a review of both titles for *School Library Journal,* Jean Pollock felt the texts were "lively and clearly written," and further commented that "these informative and appealing titles will meet the needs of curious pet lovers." In *Adopting Pets,* Gutman offers advice on how to choose a pet, emphasizing that a pet means responsibility. "There is a lot of how-to here," wrote Arwen Marshall in *School Library Journal,* "but there's an equal amount of why (insight into behavior) to help readers understand and enjoy their pets."

Gutman has also turned his attention to personal safety in some books he authored in the late 1990s. *Recreation*

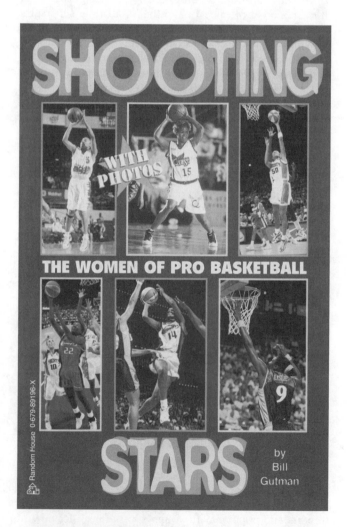

Gutman's book about women's basketball features prominent players and traces the history of women's professional leagues.

Can Be Risky takes a look at how to play hard but stay safe. Baseball, hiking, biking, and many other sports are discussed, and specific warm-ups, clothing, and appropriate gear and protective equipment are suggested for each. The particular dangers of each sport are outlined, along with ways to avoid injury. "The volume is cleanly designed and well organized," noted Susan Dove Lempke in a *Booklist* review. Writing in *Voice of Youth Advocates,* Leigh Ann Jones concluded, "This book could provide adequate information for short reports." In *Harmful to Your Health,* Gutman considers safety in a larger context, such as avoiding drugs and alcohol, disease, and violent crime. Writing in *Booklist,* Lempke praised its "appealing format and straightforward approach." *Be Aware of Danger* lists dangerous public situations and offers "concrete advice," according to *Booklist*'s Lempke, such as finding someone in uniform if you feel threatened by somebody on the streets. In *Hazards at Home,* Gutman lists numerous items at home which could prove dangerous, including firearms, tools, ladders, and poisonous materials.

The versatile Gutman has also written fiction for young readers, books dealing with sports as well as adventure tales. His *"My Father the Coach" and Other Stories* is a collection of nine tales, some of which deal with football matters. His short story "Smitty" from this collection inspired two novels, *Smitty* and *Smitty II: The Olympics.* In *Summer Dreams,* the author portrays the romance between a pair of runners, Kim and Derek. "The athletic background grounds the story in reality," noted Kathy Fritts in *School Library Journal.* And in the trilogy of books about adventures along the Oregon Trail, including *Along the Dangerous Trail, Across the Wild River,* and *Over the Ragged Mountain,* Gutman tells of twelve-year-old James Gregg, his parents, and his older brother and younger sister as the family makes the arduous and sometimes perilous journey overland to the West. Dust storms, cyclones, rampaging Indians, outlaws, and cholera are just some of the challenges the family faces. Reviewing the first two titles in the series in *Booklist,* Deborah Abbot felt the books "suffer from plot coincidences" as well as some "cardboard characterizations," but went on to comment that overall "an exciting drama unfolds."

While Gutman has shown his versatility in a wide variety of titles over a large range of subjects, his name is still mostly synonymous with sports writing. As Doris Hiatt noted in *Kliatt,* "Gutman is a one-man industry that writes sports books for young fans."

Biographical and Critical Sources

BOOKS

Authors of Books for Young People, third edition, Scarecrow Press (Metuchen, NJ), 1990.

PERIODICALS

Appraisal, fall, 1996, p. 45.
Best Sellers, October, 1978, p. 230.
Booklist, July 1, 1978, p. 1683; October 1, 1982, p. 245; November 1, 1992, Ilene Cooper, reviews of *Magic Johnson: Hero On and Off Court* and *Michael Jordan: Basketball Champ,* p. 506; March 15, 1993, p. 1344; March 1, 1994, Deborah Abbott, reviews of *Across the Wild River* and *Along the Dangerous Trail,* p. 1259; April 15, 1995, p. 1490; July, 1996, Susan Dove Lempke, review of *Recreation Can Be Risky,* p. 1823; December 1, 1996, Ellen Mandel, reviews of *Becoming Your Bird's Best Friend* and *Becoming Your Dog's Best Friend,* p. 650; February 1, 1997, Susan Dove Lempke, reviews of *Be Aware of Danger* and *Harmful to Your Health,* p. 931; August, 1997, Ellen Mandel, reviews of *Becoming Best Friends with Your Hamster, Guinea Pig, or Rabbit* and *Becoming Your Cat's Best Friend,* p. 1894; August, 1998, April Judge, reviews of *Brett Favre: Leader of the Pack* and *Tiger Woods: Golf's Shining Young Star,* p. 1993; December 1, 1998, Ellen Mandel, review of *Brett Favre: A Biography,* p. 664; June 1, 2000, p. 1834.
Book Report, November, 1992, p. 64.
Bulletin of the Center for Children's Books, June, 1997, p. 359.
Children's Book Review Service, December, 1996, p. 42.
Children's Bookwatch, July, 1995, pp. 1, 8; July, 1996, p. 8; April, 1997, p. 5.
Christian Science Monitor, May 7, 1990, Mark Clayton, review of *When the Cheering Stops,* p. 13.
High/Low Report, April, 1980, p. 3; October, 1982, Diane Tuccillo, review of *Women Who Work with Animals,* p. 6.
Horn Book Guide, spring, 1993, p. 127; fall, 1993, p. 366; spring, 1995, p. 140; fall, 1995, p. 371; spring, 1996, p. 130, p. 131; fall, 1996, p. 361; spring, 1997, p. 125, p. 144; fall, 1997, Anne Deifendeifer, review of *Becoming Best Friends with Your Hamster, Guinea Pig, or Rabbit* and *Becoming Your Cat's Best Friend,* p. 354; spring, 1998, p. 154; fall, 1998, Jennifer M. Brabander, reviews of *Brett Favre: Leader of the Pack* and *Tiger Woods: Golf's Shining Young Star,* p. 403; spring, 1999, p. 125.
Kirkus Reviews, July 1, 2000, p. 935.
Kliatt, January, 1992, Barbara J. McKee, review of *Michael Jordan: A Biography,* p. 46; April, 1992, Doris Hiatt, review of *Baseball Super Teams,* p. 46, Sherri F. Ginsberg, review of *Magic: More Than a Legend,* p. 46; September, 1992, p. 49; March, 1993, p. 48; March, 1997, p. 36; July, 1998, p. 36.
Library Journal, June 15, 2000, p. 92.
Magpies, March, 1991, review of *"Go For It!"* series, pp. 33-34.
New York Review of Books, October 11, 1990, pp. 6-7.
New York Times Book Review, October 22, 2000, p. 17.
Publishers Weekly, January 5, 1990, p. 57; July 10, 2000, review of *Parcells: A Biography,* p. 55.
Reading Teacher, May, 1994, p. 651; October, 1994, p. 156.
School Library Journal, September, 1978; November, 1982, Patricia Manning, review of *Women Who Work with Animals,* p. 84; April, 1986, Kathy Fritts, review of *Summer Dreams,* p. 103; January, 1991, Tom S. Hurlburt, reviews of *Field Hockey, Ice Hockey, Track*

and Field, and *Wrestling,* pp. 100-101; May, 1992, J. J. Votapka, review of *Michael Jordan: A Biography,* p. 122; December, 1992, p. 118; January, 1996, p. 119; June, 1996, Todd Morning, reviews of *Frank Thomas: Power Hitter* and *Troy Aikman: Super Quarterback,* p. 141; September, 1996, p. 215; November, 1996, pp. 112, 113; February, 1997, Jeanette Lambert, review of *Julie Krone,* p. 91; July, 1997, Jean Pollock, reviews of *Becoming Best Friends with Your Hamster, Guinea Pig, or Rabbit* and *Becoming Your Cat's Best Friend,* p. 105; January, 1999, p. 142; April, 2001, Arwen Marshall, review of *Adopting Pets,* p. 131.

Voice of Youth Advocates, December, 1982, p. 42; June, 1992, Virginia B. Moore, review of *Michael Jordan,* pp. 124-125; October, 1992, p. 252; August, 1993, p. 176; April, 1994, Doris Losey, review of *Shaquille O'Neal,* p. 46; October, 1995, p. 248; October, 1996, Leigh Ann Jones, review of *Recreation Can Be Risky,* p. 230; August, 1997, p. 201; April, 1999, Randy Brough, review of *Sammy Sosa: A Biography,* p. 56.*

H

HALE, Christy
See APOSTOLOU, Christine Hale

*   *   *

HAMILTON, Priscilla
See GELLIS, Roberta (Leah Jacobs)

*   *   *

HAN, Lu
See STICKLER, Soma Han

*   *   *

HAN, Soma
See STICKLER, Soma Han

*   *   *

HARRIS, Trudy 1949-

Personal

Born May 3, 1949, in UT; daughter of Myron (a rancher) and Marva (a nurse) Hanchett; married Jay M. Harris (a dentist), 1972; children: Holly Simmons, Mark, Drew, Julie, Emily. *Education:* Brigham Young University, B.S. (elementary education), 1972. *Religion:* Church of Jesus Christ of Latter-Day Saints. *Hobbies and other interests:* Painting, gardening, white-water rafting.

Addresses

Home—3125 Springwood Ln., Idaho Falls, ID 83404. *Office*—Temple View Elementary, 1500 Scorpius Drive, Idaho Falls, ID 83402. *E-mail*—trudyaharris@hotmail.com.

Career

Head Start teacher, 1972-73; elementary school teacher, 1973-75, 1992—. Author of children's books and public speaker. Cooperating teacher for Idaho State University; affiliate faculty member of Idaho State University. *Member:* Society of Children's Books Writers and Illustrators, National Education Association.

Awards, Honors

100 Days of School received the Kids Pick of the List award, 2000, from the American Booksellers Association.

Writings

(With husband, Jay Harris) *Gaining the Fullness: The Spirit-Filled Path to Exaltation* (adult nonfiction), Horizon Publishers and Distributors (Bountiful, UT), 1989.

100 Days of School (picture book), illustrated by Beth Griffis Johnson, Millbrook Press (Brookfield, CT), 1999.

Pattern Fish (picture book), illustrated by Anne Canevari Green, Millbrook Press (Brookfield, CT), 2000.

Up Bear, Down Bear (board book), Houghton Mifflin (Boston, MA), 2000.

Pattern Bugs (picture book), illustrated by Anne Canevari Green, Millbrook Press (Brookfield, CT), 2001.

Sidelights

Trudy Harris told *SATA:* "We call it the family 'illness.' For example, at eighty years of age, my teetering father would still manage to stand on his head, balancing just long enough to make the grandkids squeal with laughter. My mother's symptoms were manifest in the fact that she never could resist making up goofy words to songs that were originally meant to be perfectly serious and normal sounding. My own 'illness' worsened when I married a man who admittedly chose me 'because I was the only one' ... who always laughed at his jokes.

Trudy Harris

"Occasionally, my husband and I would lecture our children, 'Stop being silly! There is a time to be serious, you know.' Of course this was very confusing to the kids because, at home, things were seldom serious.

"If this irresistible desire to make others laugh is an 'illness,' then I suppose the affliction is evident in my writing. As a schoolteacher, I have always loved seeing children giggle (or at least smile) as they learn. My first three books (*100 Days of School, Pattern Fish,* and *Pattern Bugs*) take an important, serious subject (math) and deal with it in a bright, lighthearted, even slightly silly way.

"Along with home life, teaching has had a definite impact on my writing. Although the story for *Up Bear, Down Bear* is taken from a personal childhood incident, I chose to write this book in a style that would be perfect for a child who is just beginning to read. It is hard for me to decide which I like most—seeing a child learn or seeing a child laugh. Writing, hopefully, opens a way for me to enjoy both (and it's good medicine for my 'illness')."

Critics indeed have found Trudy Harris's picture books a lighthearted and fun way to teach children important math concepts such as patterns and multiplication. In *100 Days of School,* Harris describes a number of ways to get to the number 100, using everything from pennies, berries, bees, and peanuts to ten toes on ten barefooted children. Each way is posed as a question with the answer offered in a rhyme (often with a joke attached). So ten salty peanuts eaten every minute for ten minutes results in both one hundred peanuts ... and possibly a

stomach ache, according to one example. "Expressing one number in a variety of ways is an excellent exercise" for early math comprehension, commented Tim Arnold in *Booklist.* Other reviewers similarly found much to commend in *100 Days of School.* Beth Griffis Johnson's brightly colored cartoon illustrations of multiethnic children work in combination with the text, noted some, in allowing readers to actually count the 100 objects depicted. A reviewer for *Kirkus Reviews* proclaimed that the artwork complements "the whimsical text as it slyly works in the basics." Some predicted that though the book lacks a plot, it would work as well at story time as during a math lesson. And Lisa Gangemi Krapp called this "a solid title to read aloud on the 100th day of school—or any other day," in her review in *School Library Journal.*

For her second picture book, *Pattern Fish,* Harris took a similar approach to bringing new fun to the teaching of the concept of patterns, another mathematical basic. Each short poem describes a fish and its brightly colored pattern, leading the young audience into guessing the next element in the sequence, for example, stripe-dot-dot (or ABB). Reviewers were delighted to discover that Green's illustrations depict each fish and the surrounding aquatic flora and fauna with the same pattern-scheme. "Once children get the idea, they will enjoy discovering the repetition and looking for examples," predicted Robin L. Gibson in *School Library Journal.* As in reviews of *100 Days of School,* critics emphasized the fun and effectiveness of Harris's humorous approach to her subject, and they remarked upon how well the book with its rhyming text and bright illustrations would work in group situations other than those intent upon teaching math concepts. Thus, the reviewer in *Bulletin of the Center for Children's Books* concluded that although *Pattern Fish* may look like a math book to teachers, "kids will simply regard it as a juicy puzzle book and snap up the bait."

Biographical and Critical Sources

PERIODICALS

Book Links, November, 1999, review of *100 Days of School.*
Booklist, November 15, 1999, Tim Arnold, review of *100 Days of School,* p. 630.
Bulletin of the Center for Children's books, September, 2000, review of *Pattern Fish.*
Horn Book, September-October, 2001, review of *Up Bear, Down Bear,* p. 573.
Kirkus Reviews, August 15, 1999, review of *100 Days of School,* p. 1318.
School Library Journal, November, 1999, Lisa Gangemi Krapp, review of *100 Days of School,* p. 143; December, 2000, Robin L. Gibson, review of *Pattern Fish,* p. 133; September, 2001, Thomas Pitchford, review of *Pattern Bugs,* p. 215.

HAUTMAN, Pete(r Murray) 1952-
(Peter Murray)

Personal

Born September 29, 1952, in Berkeley, CA; son of Thomas Richard and Margaret Elaine (an artist; maiden name, Murray) Hautman; companion of Mary Louise Logue (a writer). *Education:* Attended Minneapolis College of Art and Design, 1970-72, and University of Minnesota, 1972-76.

Addresses

Agent—Jonathon Lazear, Lazear Literary Agency, 800 Washington Ave. N., #660, Minneapolis, MN 55401. *E-mail*—pete@petehautman.com.

Career

Writer. Has also worked in freelance marketing and design. *Member:* Mystery Writers of America.

Awards, Honors

New York Times Notable Book, 1993, for *Drawing Dead,* and 1996, for *The Mortal Nuts;* Edgar Allan Poe Award nomination, Mystery Writers of America, and Notable Book, American Library Association (ALA), both for *Mr. Was;* Quick Pick for Reluctant Readers, ALA, for *Stone Cold;* Minnesota Book Award for Best Popular Novel, 1999, for *Mrs. Million.*

Writings

FOR ADULTS

Drawing Dead, Simon & Schuster (New York, NY), 1993.
Short Money, Simon & Schuster (New York, NY), 1995.
The Mortal Nuts, Simon & Schuster (New York, NY), 1996.
Ring Game, Simon & Schuster (New York, NY), 1997.
Mrs. Million, Simon & Schuster (New York, NY), 1999.
Rag Man, Simon & Schuster (New York, NY), 2001.

FOR YOUNG ADULTS; FICTION

Mr. Was, Simon & Schuster (New York, NY), 1996.
Stone Cold, Simon & Schuster (New York, NY), 1998.
Hole in the Sky, Simon & Schuster (New York, NY), 2001.

CHILDREN'S NONFICTION; UNDER NAME PETER MURRAY

Beavers, Child's World (Mankato, MN), 1992.
Black Widows, Child's World (Mankato, MN), 1992.
Dogs, Child's World (Mankato, MN), 1992.
Planet Earth, Child's World (Mankato, MN), 1992.
The Planets, illustrated by Anastasia Mitchell, Child's World (Mankato, MN), 1992.
Rhinos, Child's World (Mankato, MN), 1992.
Silly Science Tricks, Child's World (Mankato, MN), 1992.
Snakes, Child's World (Mankato, MN), 1992.
Spiders, Child's World (Mankato, MN), 1992.

Pete Hautman

The World's Greatest Chocolate Chip Cookies, illustrated by Anastasia Mitchell, Child's World (Mankato, MN), 1992.
The World's Greatest Paper Airplanes, illustrated by Anastasia Mitchell, Child's World (Mankato, MN), 1992.
You Can Juggle, illustrated by Anastasia Mitchell, Child's World (Mankato, MN), 1992.
Your Bones: An Inside Look at Skeletons, illustrated by Viki Woodworth, Child's World (Mankato, MN), 1992.
The Amazon, Child's World (Mankato, MN), 1993.
Beetles, Child's World (Mankato, MN), 1993.
Chameleons, Child's World (Mankato, MN), 1993.
The Everglades, Child's World (Mankato, MN), 1993.
Frogs, Child's World (Mankato, MN), 1993.
Gorillas, Child's World (Mankato, MN), 1993.
Hummingbirds, Child's World (Mankato, MN), 1993.
Parrots, Child's World (Mankato, MN), 1993.
Porcupines, Child's World (Mankato, MN), 1993.
The Sahara, Child's World (Mankato, MN), 1993.
Saturn, Child's World (Mankato, MN), 1993.
Sea Otters, Child's World (Mankato, MN), 1993.
The Space Shuttle, Child's World (Mankato, MN), 1993.
Tarantulas, Child's World (Mankato, MN), 1993.
Silly Science Tricks: With Professor Solomon Snickerdoodle, illustrated by Anastasia Mitchell, Child's World (Mankato, MN), 1993.
Science Tricks with Air, Child's World (Mankato, MN), 1995, published as *Professor Solomon Snickerdoodle's Air Science Tricks,* 1995.
Science Tricks with Light, Child's World (Mankato, MN), 1995, *Professor Solomon Snickerdoodle's Light Science Tricks,* Child's World (Plymouth, MN), 1999.
Professor Solomon Snickerdoodle Looks at Water, illustrated by Anastasia Mitchell, Child's World (Mankato, MN), 1995, published as *Professor Solomon Snickerdoodle's Water Science Tricks,* 1998.
Dirt, Wonderful Dirt!, illustrated by Penny Dann, Child's World (Mankato, MN), 1995.

Make a Kite!, illustrated by Penny Dann, Child's World (Mankato, MN), 1995.

The Perfect Pizza, illustrated by Penny Dann, Child's World (Mankato, MN), 1995.

Sitting Bull: A Story of Bravery, Child's World (Mankato, MN), 1996.

Cactus, Child's World (Mankato, MN), 1996.

Orchids, Child's World (Mankato, MN), 1996.

Roses, Child's World (Plymouth, MN), 1996.

Earthquakes, Child's World (Plymouth, MN), 1996.

Mushrooms, Child's World (Plymouth, MN), 1996.

Hurricanes, Child's World (Plymouth, MN), 1996.

Tornadoes, Child's World (Plymouth, MN), 1996.

Volcanoes, Child's World (Plymouth, MN), 1996.

Deserts, Child's World (Plymouth, MN), 1997.

Lightning, Child's World (Plymouth, MN), 1997.

Mountains, Child's World (Plymouth, MN), 1997.

Rainforests, Child's World (Plymouth, MN), 1997.

Redwoods, Child's World (Plymouth, MN), 1997.

Prairies, Child's World (Plymouth, MN), 1997.

Floods, Child's World (Plymouth, MN), 1997.

Scorpions, Child's World (Plymouth, MN), 1997.

Pigs, Child's World (Chanhassen, MN), 1998.

Snails, Child's World (Chanhassen, MN), 1998.

Sheep, Child's World (Chanhassen, MN), 1998.

Curiosity: The Story of Marie Curie, illustrated by Leon Baxter, Child's World (Plymouth, MN), 1998.

Perseverence: The Story of Thomas Alva Edison, illustrated by Robin Lawrie, Child's World (Plymouth, MN), 1998.

Dreams: The Story of Martin Luther King, Jr., illustrated by Robin Lawrie, Child's World (Plymouth, MN), 1999.

A Sense of Humor: The Story of Mark Twain, Child's World (Chanhassen, MN), 1999.

Copper ("From the Earth" series), Smart Apple Media (North Mankato, MN), 2001.

Silver ("From the Earth" series), Smart Apple Media (North Mankato, MN), 2001.

Oil ("From the Earth" series), Smart Apple Media (North Mankato, MN), 2001.

Diamonds ("From the Earth" series), Smart Apple Media (North Mankato, MN), 2001.

Gold ("From the Earth" series), Smart Apple Media (North Mankato, MN), 2001.

Iron ("From the Earth" series), Smart Apple Media (North Mankato, MN), 2001.

Apatosaurus, Smart Apple Media (North Mankato, MN), 2001.

Stegosaurus, Smart Apple Media (North Mankato, MN), 2001.

Pterodactyls, Smart Apple Media (North Mankato, MN), 2001.

Tyrannosaurus Rex, Smart Apple Media (North Mankato, MN), 2001.

Triceratops, Smart Apple Media (North Mankato, MN), 2001.

Velociraptor, Smart Apple Media (North Mankato, MN), 2001.

Work in Progress

Two novels.

Sidelights

Pete Hautman is a prolific author who has found publishing success in not only adult novels but in several highly acclaimed works of fiction for teen readers. Lauded by critics for their imaginative, action-filled plots are *Mr. Was, Stone Cold,* and *Hole in the Sky,* all of which feature young protagonists whose confrontation with difficulties force them to follow unusual paths into adulthood. Under the pseudonym Peter Murray, Hautman has penned numerous works of juvenile nonfiction, covering everything from dinosaurs to weather to biographies of notable Americans.

Born in Berkeley, California, in 1952, Hautman attended the University of Minnesota in the early 1970s. After working for almost twenty years in advertising and design, he left that field in 1992 to begin his second

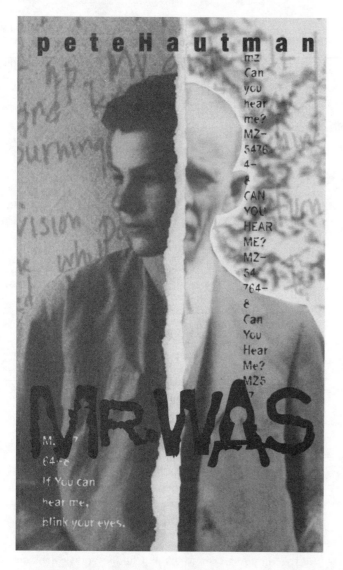

In Hautman's Mr. Was, *a portal to the past helps teenaged Jack escape his father's alcoholism and takes him to adventures in rural Minnesota and on the World War II battlefield of Guadalcanal.*

career as a freelance author. "It has turned out to be a happy decision," he once told *SATA*. "I live in a large house in south Minneapolis with mystery writer, poet, and children's author Mary Logue, and a cat named Ubik. We spend part of each summer at our second home, an old farmhouse in Stockholm, Wisconsin. Both Mary and I write every day, and we like it. We act as each other's editor, critic, and cheerleader."

Using a professional pseudonym, Hautman has published numerous nonfiction titles for the Minnesota-based publisher Child's World, covering everything from black widow spiders to the solar system in an entertaining and educational fashion. His talent for distilling scientific subjects into easy-to-understand explanations has resulted in books such as *Silly Science Tricks with Professor Solomon Snickerdoodle, Your Bones: An Inside Look at Skeletons,* and a series of books in the "From the Earth" series that examines the many resources that are hidden beneath the Earth's surface. "I never used to think of myself as a children's author," Hautman explained, "so it was with some trepidation that I undertook to author a series of books for Child's World. I found that the 'child's voice' came quite naturally to me, and that, for better or worse, the things that amused me [when I was young] *still* make me laugh."

At the same time he started authoring titles for Child's World, Hautman began working on prose fiction. *Mr. Was,* published in 1996, shows Hautman to be a compelling YA novelist, his "well-drawn problem plot mix[ing] successfully with time travel" according to *Booklist* contributor Laura Tillotson. Taking place in Hautman's home state of Minnesota, the novel finds Jack Lund moving into his late grandfather's house. While the house seems forbidding, it contains a portal that takes Jack back to 1940, allowing him to escape his brutal father's alcoholism and the death of his mother. Further twists to the plot ensue when Jack's new job as a farmhand causes him to meet the young woman who will one day become his grandmother—as long as his presence in the past doesn't disrupt his own future. Other adventures take Jack from rural Minnesota to the World War II battlefield of Guadalcanal. "Ingenious plotting and startling action combine to make [*Mr. Was*] ... a riveting read," exclaimed a *Publishers Weekly* contributor, the reviewer going on to note that Hautman's plot is "sophisticated" without becoming "overwhelming," and is "mined with surprises that explode like fireworks."

Gambling-addicted teen Denn Doyle is the troubled protagonist of Hautman's 1998 novel *Stone Cold*. Denn brushes aside the concerns of family and friends who realize his compulsion to play poker is becoming increasingly destructive, and remains hooked on the sense of power that the game gives him. The game—and the wealth it promises—becomes his life and he loses interest in his landscaping business, his family, and even his girlfriend. *Stone Cold* is "enthralling reading," in the opinion of *Horn Book* contributor Nancy Vasilakis; its "final devastating scene will ... leave readers with

When a woman wins the lottery and offers a million dollars to get her wayward husband back, several scheming individuals step up to the challenge in Hautman's novel.

something to think about." "Swift and salacious," *Stone Cold* "compellingly echoes gambling's siren call," added a reviewer in *Publishers Weekly,* while *Booklist* contributor Roger Leslie found "Denn's first-person narration ... brisk and engaging" and the novel intriguing in its focus about "the interesting intricacies of addiction" rather than a strong argument against gambling.

Taking place in the near future, *The Hole in the Sky* finds four teens among the few survivors after an outbreak of influenza depopulates most of Earth. Now living in the wilderness near the Grand Canyon, sixteen-year-old Ceej Kane, his Native American girlfriend Isabella, his sister Haryette, and his buddy Tim now find themselves battling the Survivors, a cult-like group who believe they alone are the "chosen" people of an angered God and are resolved to eliminate all living humans outside their group. While noting that the story's mysticism—involving Hopi Indian beliefs in the existence of a magical path leading to a new world—"may displease those who like their speculative fiction to remain realistic," a *Horn Book* contributor praised

Hautman's "intense action and fascinating premise." Reviewing the work for *Booklist,* Roger Leslie complimented the author as well, noting that "Thanks to Hautman's skillful storytelling," the teens' trip remains compelling; the novelist "promises much and delivers impressively," Leslie added.

In addition to his novels for teen readers, Hautman has found success as the author of thrillers for adult readers. His 1996 novel *Short Money,* about the adventures of a former cop named Joe Crow who gets caught up in the world of big-game hunting and tangled up a group of ne'er-do-wells, was called "by turns funny and soulful and always unpredictable," by a *Publishers Weekly* reviewer, while a crabby seventy-something curmudgeon named Axel Speeter is the unlikely protagonist in the 1996 whodunit *The Mortal Nuts.* Compared by *Booklist* contributor Thomas Gaughan to novels by Elmore Leonard due to his down-to-earth protagonists and gritty settings, Hautman was praised for both his "wonderful ear for low-rent dialogue" and his substantial "powers of description."

Biographical and Critical Sources

PERIODICALS

Booklist, March 15, 1993, p. 135; October 1, 1993, Donna Seaman, review of *Drawing Dead,* p. 253; April 1, 1996, Thomas Gaughan, review of *The Mortal Nuts,* p. 1346; September 15, 1996, Laura Tillotson, review of *Mr. Was,* p. 230; October 1, 1997, David Pitt, review of *Ring Game,* p. 310; September 15, 1998, Roger Leslie, review of *Stone Cold,* p. 218; April 15, 2001, Roger Leslie, review of *Hole in the Sky,* p. 1554; September 1, 2001, Joanne Wilkinson, review of *Rag Man,* p. 56.

Entertainment Weekly, July 26, 1996, Gene Lyons, review of *The Mortal Nuts,* p. 51.

Horn Book, November, 1998, Nancy Vasilakis, review of *Stone Cold,* p. 730; May, 2001, review of *Hole in the Sky,* p. 325.

Kirkus Reviews, August 15, 1993, p. 1018.

Library Journal, October 1, 1993, Erna Chamberlain, review of *Drawing Dead,* p. 126; January, 1996, Paul Kaplan, review of *Short Money,* p. 176; May 1, 1996, Rex E. Klett, review of *The Mortal Nuts,* p. 136; October 1, 1997, Jo Ann Vicarel, review of *Ring Game,* p. 122; April 1, 1999, Thomas L. Kilpatrick, review of *Mrs. Million,* p. 128.

New York Times Book Review, November 7, 1993, Marilyn Stasio, review of *Drawing Dead,* p. 24; May 21, 1995, Marilyn Stasio, review of *Short Money,* p. 39; June 23, 1996, Marilyn Stasio, review of *The Mortal Nuts,* p. 28; November 9, 1997, Marilyn Stasio, review of *Ring Game,* p. 29; April 9, 2000, John D. Thomas, review of *Mrs. Million,* p. 223; October 14, 2001, Marilyn Stasio, review of *Rag Man,* p. 26.

People Weekly, August 5, 1996, J. D. Reed, review of *The Mortal Nuts,* p. 32.

Publishers Weekly, August 30, 1993, review of *Drawing Dead,* p. 74; March 27, 1995, review of *Short Money,* p. 78; October 28, 1996, review of *Mr. Was,* p. 83;

September 1, 1997, review of *Ring Game,* p. 94; October 12, 1998, review of *Stone Cold,* p. 78; February 8, 1999, review of *Mrs. Million,* p. 196; May 14, 2001, review of *Hole in the Sky,* p. 83; August 13, 2001, review of *Rag Man,* p. 281.

School Library Journal, July, 1993, p. 77; October, 1996, John Peters, review of *Mr. Was,* p. 147; September, 1998, Joel Shoemaker, review of *Stone Cold,* p. 203; June, 2001, Steven Engelfried, review of *Hole in the Sky,* p. 149.

Wall Street Journal, November 22, 1993, p. A12.

OTHER

Pete Hautman Web Site, http://www.petehautman.com/ (February 1, 2002).*

*   *   *

HICKMAN, Pamela (M.) 1958-

Personal

Born December 4, 1958, in Ontario, Canada; daughter of Melville (an Air Canada Express manager) and Marguerite (a homemaker; maiden name, Lee) Hunter; married P. Douglas Hickman (an environmental consultant), June 27, 1981; children: Angela Lindsey, Connie Marie, Jennifer Lee. *Education:* University of Waterloo,

Pamela Hickman

B.S. (with honors), 1980. *Hobbies and other interests:* Gardening, camping, reading, travel.

Addresses

Home—Box 296, Canning, Nova Scotia B0P 1H0, Canada. *E-mail*—ph@candw.lc.

Career

Alberta Environment, mosquito control technician in Edmonton, 1979, plant sciences technician in Vegreville, 1980-81; Federation of Ontario Naturalists, Toronto, Canada, education coordinator, 1982-90; Apple Tree Landing Children's Centre, Canning, Canada, chairperson of board of directors, 1994—. Glooscap Home and School Association, member of executive committee, 1992—. *Member:* World Wildlife Fund, Canadian Children's Book Centre, Writers Federation of Nova Scotia, Federation of Ontario Naturalists.

Awards, Honors

Short-listed for Ann Connor Brimer Award, 1993, for *Wetlands,* and 1998, for *Animal Senses;* Lila Stirling Memorial Award, Canadian Authors Association, 1995, for *Habitats;* short-listed for Red Cedar Book Awards, 1998, for *Jumbo Book of Nature Science* and *Night Book;* finalist for Hackmatack Children's Choice Award, 2000, for *At the Seashore.*

Writings

Getting to Know Nature's Children: A Parent's Guide, Grolier (Danbury, CT), 1985.
Birdwise, Kids Can Press (Toronto, Canada), 1988.
Bugwise, Kids Can Press (Toronto, Canada), 1990.
Plantwise, Kids Can Press (Toronto, Canada), 1991.
Habitats, Kids Can Press (Toronto, Canada), 1993.
Wetlands, Kids Can Press (Toronto, Canada), 1993.
The Night Book, Kids Can Press (Toronto, Canada), 1996.
At the Seashore, Formac (Halifax, Canada), 1996.
The Jumbo Book of Nature Science, Kids Can Press (Toronto, Canada), 1996.
A Seed Grows: My First Look at a Plant's Life Cycle, Kids Can Press (Toronto, Canada), 1997.
Hungry Animals: My First Look at a Food Chain, Kids Can Press (Toronto, Canada), 1997.
A New Butterfly: My First Look at Metamorphosis, Kids Can Press (Toronto, Canada), 1997.
Animal Senses, Kids Can Press (Toronto, Canada), 1998.
In the Woods, Formac (Halifax, Canada), 1998.
A New Frog: My First Look at the Life Cycle of an Amphibian, Kids Can Press (Toronto, Canada), 1999.
A New Duck: My First Look at the Life Cycle of a Bird, Kids Can Press (Toronto, Canada), 1999.
Animals in Motion, Kids Can Press (Toronto, Canada), 2000.
Animals Eating, Kids Can Press (Toronto, Canada), 2001.
Animals and Their Young, Kids Can Press (Toronto, Canada), in press.

In her science book for youngsters, Hickman uses simple activities to help readers experience the world as if they had the senses of various animals. (Cover illustration by Pat Stephens.)

Writer for "The Kids Canadian Nature Series," Kids Can Press (Toronto, Canada), 1995-96.

Work in Progress

Research on the status of the endangered leatherback turtle, particularly in the Caribbean.

Sidelights

Pamela Hickman told *SATA:* "One of the most rewarding aspects of being a writer of nonfiction nature books for children is that I learn so much as I do my research. I also love the fact that I can go out birdwatching or down to the seashore, walk in the woods, or stroll through a meadow and still be working! Everything I see, smell, touch, taste, and hear can become part of a book. I find it much easier to write about something I have experienced firsthand. My main motivation for writing is to share my love and enthusiasm for nature with my readers, and I hope to kindle a similar lifelong joy in them."

HINTZ, Martin 1945-

Personal

Born June 1, 1945, in New Hampton, IA; son of Loren (an aviator) and Gertrude (an office manager; maiden name, Russell) Hintz; married Sandy Wright, May 1, 1991 (divorced, 1994); married Pam Percy (a radio producer), August 8, 1998; children: Daniel, Stephen V., Kate. *Education:* College (now University) of St. Thomas, B.A. (journalism), 1967; Northwestern University, M.S.J. (international affairs), 1968. *Religion:* Catholic.

Addresses

Office—301 North Water St., Third Floor, Milwaukee, WI 53202. *E-mail*—hintz@execpc.com.

Career

Journalist and photographer. *Milwaukee Sentinel,* Milwaukee, WI, editor and reporter, 1968-75; freelance writer, 1975—; William Eisner & Assoc., Milwaukee, WI, senior account executive, 1988-90; Hintz & Co.

Martin Hintz

(public relations), senior account executive, 1990-92; *Irish American Post,* Milwaukee, WI, publisher and editor, 1992—; Mountjoy Writers Group, manager. Broadcast journalist and manager, Hintz News/Features and Photos. Teacher of writing at schools, including University of Wisconsin—Milwaukee and Marquette University; lecturer and workshop presenter. Member, North Shore Library Board, 1999-2003. *Exhibitions:* Photography has been exhibited at the Milwaukee Press Club, 1960s to mid-1970s, Circus World Museum, 1988-98; and Milwaukee Public Library, 1988. *Member:* Society of American Travel Writers (president, 2001-02), Society of Professional Journalists, Council for Wisconsin Writers, Committee to Protect Journalists.

Awards, Honors

Inland Daily Press Association award, 1974; Council for Wisconsin Writers nonfiction awards, second place, 1979, first place, 1984; Society of American Travel Writers (Central States Chapter), second place for nonfiction, 1984, 1985, and 2000, for *America the Beautiful: Hawai'i,* and first-place book awards, 1984, for *Enchantment of the World: Finland* and *West Germany,* 1986, for *Enchantment of the World: Chile,* 1987, for *Enchantment of the World: Switzerland,* 1989, for *Enchantment of the World: Hungary,* 1990, for *Off the Beaten Path: Wisconsin,* 1995, for *Country Roads of Minnesota,* 1997, for *One Hundred and One Great Choices,* 1999, for *Enchantment of the World: Poland,* and 2001, for *America the Beautiful: Iowa;* certificate of honor, Children's Reading Roundtable of Chicago, 1985, 1986, 1989, 1997, 1998; *Writer's Digest* National Writing Competition, honorable mentions in poetry and nonfiction, 1986; certificate of appreciation from State of Wisconsin, 1987, for "contributions to Wisconsin's literary heritage"; numerous awards for photography.

Writings

FOR CHILDREN

(With wife, Sandy Hintz) *We Can't Afford It,* illustrated by Brent Jones, Reentry (Chicago, IL), 1976.

(And photographer) *Circus Workin's,* Messner (New York, NY), 1980.

Tons of Fun: Training Elephants, Messner (New York, NY), 1982.

(With wife, Sandy Hintz) *Computers in Our World, Today and Tomorrow,* F. Watts (New York, NY), 1983.

Living in the Tropics, F. Watts (New York, NY), 1986.

Michigan, F. Watts (New York, NY), 1987.

Farewell, John Barleycorn: Prohibition in the United States, Lerner (Minneapolis, MN), 1996.

(With daughter, Kate Hintz) *Motorcycle Drag Racing,* Capstone Press (Mankato, MN), 1996.

(With daughter, Kate Hintz) *Pro Stock Drag Racing,* Capstone Press (Mankato, MN), 1996.

(With daughter, Kate Hintz) *Top Fuel Drag Racing,* Capstone Press (Mankato, MN), 1996.

(With daughter, Kate Hintz) *Monster Truck Drag Racing,* Capstone Press (Mankato, MN), 1996.

Celtic Bedtime Tales, Passport (Lincolnwood, IL), 1999.

(Coauthor) *Celtic Fairy Stories,* Passport (Lincolnwood, IL), 1999.

Wisconsin Portraits: Fifty-five People Who Made a Difference, Trails Media (Madison, WI), 2000.

FOR CHILDREN; "AMERICA THE BEAUTIFUL," SECOND SERIES

Michigan, Children's Press (New York, NY), 1998.

(With son, Stephen V. Hintz) *North Carolina,* Children's Press (New York, NY), 1998.

Louisiana, Children's Press (New York, NY), 1998.

Missouri, Children's Press (New York, NY), 1999.

Hawaii, Children's Press (New York, NY), 1999.

Minnesota, Children's Press (New York, NY), 2000.

Iowa, Children's Press (New York, NY), 2000.

North Dakota, Children's Press (New York, NY), 2000.

FOR CHILDREN; "CELEBRATE" SERIES

(With daughter, Kate Hintz) *Thanksgiving: Why We Celebrate It the Way We Do,* Capstone Press (Mankato, MN), 1996.

(With daughter, Kate Hintz) *Kwanzaa: Why We Celebrate It the Way We Do,* Capstone Press (Mankato, MN), 1996.

(With daughter, Kate Hintz) *Christmas: Why We Celebrate It the Way We Do,* Capstone Press (Mankato, MN), 1996.

(With daughter, Kate Hintz) *Halloween: Why We Celebrate It the Way We Do,* Capstone Press (Mankato, MN), 1996.

FOR CHILDREN; "ENCHANTMENT OF THE WORLD" SERIES

Norway, Children's Press (Chicago, IL), 1982.

Italy, Children's Press (Chicago, IL), 1983.

West Germany, Children's Press (Chicago, IL), 1983.

Finland, Children's Press (Chicago, IL), 1983.

Sweden, Children's Press (Chicago, IL), 1985.

Morocco, Children's Press (Chicago, IL), 1985.

Chile, Children's Press (Chicago, IL), 1985.

Argentina, Children's Press (Chicago, IL), 1985, updated as *Argentina, Second Series,* 1998.

Switzerland, Children's Press (Chicago, IL), 1986.

Ghana, Children's Press (Chicago, IL), 1987.

Hungary, Children's Press (Chicago, IL), 1988.

Denmark, Children's Press (New York, NY), 1994.

(With son, Stephen Hintz) *The Bahamas,* Children's Press (New York, NY), 1997.

Haiti, Children's Press (New York, NY), 1998.

Poland, Second Series, Children's Press (New York, NY), 1998.

The Netherlands, Children's Press (New York, NY), 1999.

(With son, Stephen V. Hintz) *Israel, Second Series,* Children's Press (New York, NY), 1999.

"PORT CITIES OF NORTH AMERICA" SERIES

Destination Duluth, Lerner (Minneapolis, MN), 1997.

Destination New Orleans, Lerner (Minneapolis, MN), 1998.

Destination St. Louis, Lerner (Minneapolis, MN), 1998.

In picture book format Martin and Kate Hintz describe the African American tradition of celebrating Kwanzaa by outlining the origins of the holiday and the symbols associated with it. (Photo by Tom Wilson, from Kwanzaa: Why We Celebrate It the Way We Do.*)*

FOR ADULTS

(Coauthor) *The If I Can't Be Ordained, I'll Cook Book,* Thomas More, 1978.

(With son, Dan Hintz) *Wisconsin: Off the Beaten Path,* Globe Pequot Press (Old Saybrook, CT), 1989, fifth edition, 2000.

Country Roads of Minnesota: Drives, Day Trips, and Weekend Excursions, illustrated by Cliff Winner, Country Roads Press (Lincolnwood, IL), 1994, second edition, 1999.

Passport's Guide to Ethnic New Orleans, Passport (Lincolnwood, IL), 1995.

(With son, Stephen V. Hintz) *Wisconsin: Family Adventure Guide,* Globe Pequot Press (Guilford, CT), 1995, third edition published as *Fun with the Family in Wisconsin: Hundreds of Ideas for Day Trips with the Kids,* 2000.

One Hundred and One Great Choices—New Orleans, Passport (Lincolnwood, IL), 1996, revised edition, 2000.

Natural Wonders of Minnesota: Exploring Wild and Scenic Places, Country Roads Press (Chicago, IL), 1997, second edition, 2000.

Hiking Wisconsin, Human Kinetics (Champaign, IL), 1997.

(Coauthor) *Irish Wit and Wisdom,* Publications International, 1998.

Our Man, Sean O'Shea, County Clare Publishing, 1999.

Celtic Days, Passport (Lincolnwood, IL), 2000.

(With son, Dan Hintz) *Day Trips from Milwaukee: Getaways Less than Two Hours Away,* Globe Pequot Press (Guilford, CT), 2000.

Also author of *The Universal Story* (company history), Universal Foods, 1982; *History of the Redevelopment Authority of the City of Milwaukee,* Department of City Development, 1988; *Milwaukee,* Metropolitan Milwaukee Association of Commerce, 1990; and *The Cullen Way: 108 Years of the Cullen Construction Company,* Trails Media (Madison, WI), 2000. Contributor to books, including *Four-Wheel Drive North American Trail Guide,* Rand-McNally (Chicago, IL), 1978; *USA Guidebook,* Fisher, 1986, revised edition, 1988; *USA Travel Guide,* updated annually, Birnbaum, 1989-1997; and *Back Roads and Hidden Corners,* Reader's Digest, 1993. Contributor of articles to magazines and newspapers, including *Billboard, Travel Holiday, National Geographic World, GolfWeek, Chicago Sun-Times, New York Post, Michigan Living, Jewish Chronicle,* and *Chicago Tribune.*

Work in Progress

Wisconsin Back Roads and Places, for Voyageur Publishing; *Wisconsin Athletes: Fifty-five Sports Figures,* for Trails Media.

Hintz's **Michigan** *is a comprehensive book on various aspects of the state, from geography to culture and religion.*

Sidelights

Martin Hintz has managed to make his career as a freelance writer into almost a family affair. In addition to penning numerous travel guides that reveal the little-known wonders of the Midwestern United States, Hintz often teams with members of his own family to create well-researched works of nonfiction for a young readership. Among his titles for children are *Kwanzaa: Why We Celebrate It the Way We Do, Farewell, John Barleycorn,* and numerous titles in the "Enchantment of the World" and "America the Beautiful" series.

Born in 1945, Hintz grew up in the Midwest and attended Northwestern University, where he earned an advanced degree in journalism. Beginning his writing career by working on the copy desk of the *Milwaukee Sentinel,* Hintz later moved to the field of public relations, working for a local firm before branching out on his own in 1990. Meanwhile, by 1975 he had already begun the freelance writing that would eventually grow to fill most of his working hours, publishing the picture book *We Can't Afford It* with his first wife, Sandy Hintz, in 1976. Within a decade, Hintz would find himself in demand as an author of nonfiction for children.

Hintz's first books for young readers reflect his training in journalism in their documentary approach, and they featured photographs by the author. *Tons of Fun: Training Elephants* presents a wealth of information on elephants in the United States: where they came from, how they are trained, and which elephants have become the most well known. Calling the book "delightful," Ilene Cooper commented in her *Booklist* review that Hintz's love of his subject is obvious, "and he passes on his enthusiasm" in his "very accessible text." Other reviewers particularly enjoyed the interesting anecdotes about both elephants and the men who train them. *School Library Journal* critic Sylvie Tupacz felt that these stories "add . . . interest to his narrative." A similar journalistic approach is taken by Hintz in *Circus Workin's,* a 1980 book that Barbara Elleman cited in *Booklist* for its ability to "give [readers] a sense of being on the scene" during the run of a traveling circus.

Many of Hintz's books for children are part of a longer series, such as Children's Press's "Enchantment of the World" books, each of which profile a different country through the region's history, culture, religion, and geography. In this series, as well as in his many contributions to the "America the Beautiful" books, Hintz teams with son Stephen V. Hintz to present an intelligent overview of the world's diversity. Four volumes in Capstone Press's "Celebrate" series that Hintz coauthored with his daughter, Kate Hintz, explore the traditional celebrations revolving around a major holiday. Titles by the Hintzes include *Christmas, Halloween, Kwanzaa,* and *Thanksgiving,* and all answer the question posed by the series' collective subtitle: *Why We Celebrate It the Way We Do.*

In addition to numerous series titles, Hintz has also written some stand alone books geared for a young readership. His 1996 work *Farewell, John Barleycorn: Prohibition in the United States* presents America's long relationship to alcohol, from its use by the Pilgrims to its dispersal among the Native Americans, and through the Temperance Movement of the late 1800s to the Volstead Act. His historical overview also draws what *School Library Journal* contributor Connie Parker called "striking parallels to our own time" and the war against drugs. Praised for his detailed presentation of life during the Prohibition era of the 1920s, Hintz "goes some distance to dispel [the] simplistic treatment" given by movies and television shows featuring flappers, gangsters, and religious zealots, according to *Bulletin of the Center for Children's Books* critic Elizabeth Bush. Calling Hintz's text "well organized and informative," *Booklist* reviewer Carolyn Phelan approved *Farewell, John Barleycorn* as a welcome addition to the few books available on this fascinating period of U.S. history.

Complementing his career as a writer for young readers, Hintz has a long list of highly praised travel publications to his credit and has developed long-term professional relationships with Globe Pequot Press, Country Roads Press, and Passport, among other guidebook publishers. A skilled photographer, he also works with businesses and civic groups to develop promotional materials and media campaigns that feature his work. Also, he manages Hintz News/Features and Photos, as well as the Mountjoy Writers Group, an international news syndicate.

Biographical and Critical Sources

PERIODICALS

Booklist, February 1, 1981, Barbara Elleman, review of *Circus Workin's,* pp. 752-753; September 1, 1982, Ilene Cooper, review of *Tons of Fun: Training Elephants,* p. 44; August, 1996, Carolyn Phelan, review of *Farewell, John Barleycorn,* p. 1893.

Bulletin of the Center for Children's Books, October, 1996, Elizabeth Bush, review of *Farewell, John Barleycorn,* pp. 63-64.

School Library Journal, October, 1983, Sylvie Tupacz, review of *Tons of Fun: Training Elephants,* p. 158; October, 1996, Connie Parker, review of *Farewell, John Barleycorn,* p. 134.

*   *   *

HOLLAND, Gay W. 1941-

Personal

Born January 30, 1941, in Urbana, IL; daughter H. Bowen (a geologist) and Martha (Righter) Willman; married; children: Laura. *Education:* California State University—Long Beach, B.F.A., 1974; University of Arizona, M.F.A., 1984.

Addresses

Home—425 Chicago Ave., #C, Bandon, OR 97411. *E-mail*—hollandgw@earthlink.net.

Career

Frostburg State University, Frostburg, MD, assistant professor, 1984-1990; Southern Utah State University, Cedar City, UT, associate professor, 1990-91. *Member:* College Art Association.

Awards, Honors

Selected for publication in *American Illustration,* 1984, 1985.

Illustrator

Linda Glaser, *Spectacular Spiders,* Millbrook Press (Brookfield, CT), 1998.

Linda Glaser, *Magnificent Monarchs,* Millbrook Press (Brookfield, CT), 2000.

April Pulley Sayre, *The Hungry Hummingbird,* Millbrook Press (Brookfield, CT), 2001.

(And author) *An Introduction to Bug-Watching,* Millbrook Press (Brookfield, CT), 2002.

Contributor of illustrations to works of educational publishers, including Scholastic, and to *American Illustration* and *Print Magazine's Design Annual* 1987. Contributor of short stories for teenagers during the 1960s.

Sidelights

Illustrator-author Gay W. Holland has pursued a variety of careers. During the 1960s, she published short stories in popular magazines, while raising her daughter. Then

Using simple, realistic drawings, Gay W. Holland portrays the monarch butterflies featured in Linda Glaser's picture book about the beautiful insects. (From Magnificent Monarchs.*)*

she turned to a new attraction—graphic design. After earning a master of fine arts degree during the early 1980s, she taught graphic design and illustration at several universities for six years. Finally, Holland decided in 1991 to pursue illustrating and writing full time. Her early book illustration projects include the picture books *Spectacular Spiders* and its companion *Magnificent Monarchs,* both written by Linda Glaser for the kindergarten-to-grade-three age group. About Holland's realistic colored pencil drawings in *Spectacular Spiders, Booklist* critic Kay Weisman noted the close correlation of artwork with the text and how the "uncluttered" illustrations appeal to the readership. Karey Wehner wrote in *School Library Journal* that the drawings are "nicely varied in size and placement." So too with *Magnificent Monarchs,* according to Patricia Manning of *School Library Journal,* the "colorful, realistic illustrations ... keep step with ... the text."

Holland told *SATA:* "At twelve years old, I attempted to illustrate my first book. It was written by a family friend, an Oz enthusiast, who befriended me when I played Dorothy in a Brownie troop production of *The Wizard of Oz.* So I learned early how difficult it is to illustrate an entire book (which I never finished). However, I loved the struggle, the collaboration with the author, and the drawing and redrawing.

"I love the freedom involved in illustrating for children. Their boundless enthusiasm and imaginations allow me to experiment and play with images, which is my favorite thing to do."

Biographical and Critical Sources

PERIODICALS

Booklist, January 1, 1999, Kay Weisman, review of *Spectacular Spiders,* p. 882.
School Library Journal, March, 1999, Karey Wehner, review of *Spectacular Spiders,* pp. 193-194; January, 2001, Patricia Manning, review of *Magnificent Monarchs,* p. 117.

*   *   *

HOPKINS, Ellen L. 1955-

Personal

Born March 26, 1955, in Long Beach, CA; daughter of Albert and Valeria (Whitney) Wagner; married Jerry Vancelette (divorced); married John Hopkins (TV news assignment editor), October, 19, 1991; children: Jaysen Vancelette, Cristal Thetford, Kelly Foutz. *Politics:* "Rabid Democrat." *Religion:* Lutheran. *Hobbies and other interests:* Hiking, biking, skiing, gardening, camping, fishing, and sports.

Addresses

Home and office—220 Flicker Cr., Carson City, NV 89704. *E-mail*—e.l.hopkins@att.net.

Career

Freelance writer, 1992—. *Member:* Society of Children's Book Writers and Illustrators, Reno MOMS, Holy Cross Lutheran church choir, Blue Tahoe Schutzhund Club, New Writers of the Purple Sage.

Writings

Air Devils: Sky Racers, Sky Divers, and Stunt Pilots, Perfection Learning (Logan, IA), 2000.
Orcas, High Seas Supermen, Perfection Learning (Logan, IA), 2000.
Tarnished Legacy: The Story of the Comstock Lode, Perfection Learning (Logan, IA), 2000.
Into the Abyss: A Tour of Inner Space, Perfection Learning (Logan, IA), 2000.
Canopies in the Clouds, Perfection Learning (Logan, IA), 20001.
Countdown to Yesterday, Perfection Learning (Logan, IA), 2001.
The Thunderbirds: The U.S. Air Force Aerial Demonstration Squadron, Capstone Press (Mankato, MN), 2001.
The Golden Knights: The U.S. Army Parachute Team, Capstone Press (Mankato, MN), 2001.
Fly Fishing, Capstone Press (Mankato, MN), 2002.
Freshwater Fishing, Capstone Press (Mankato, MN), 2002.
United States Air Force, Heinemann Library (Crystal Lake, IL), 2002.
United States Air Force Fighting Vehicles, Heinemann Libarary (Crystal Lake, IL), 2002.
United States Special Forces, Heinemann Library (Crystal Lake, IL), 2002.

Work in Progress

Walking With the Monster, a young adult novel; *Women Who Made Nevada Great,* a middle reader; *Native Nevadans.*

Sidelights

Ellen L. Hopkins is the author of high-interest books for reluctant readers on such topics as airplanes and their pilots and on fishing. In *Air Devils: Sky Racers, Sky Divers, and Stunt Pilots,* Hopkins recounted the history of flight and covered such topics as dirigibles, early airplanes, military planes, and even airplane pylon races. According to *Booklist* contributor Catherine Andronik, the work is "easy to read, contemporary, and not condescending." In her next publication, *Orcas, High Seas Supermen,* Hopkins brought to readers the world of the Orca, or killer whale. Information about whale habitat, survival mechanisms, and communication is interspersed with color and black-and-white photographs, diagrams, and sidebars. Noting that whale lifestyles are "expertly explained," Roger Leslie of *Booklist* concluded, "Always captivating, this book is sure to please" Orca fans.

Hopkins told *SATA:* "As a freelance writer for a number of years, I became infatuated with several subjects and decided to carry them to the audience that most needs/

In an informative picture book, Ellen L. Hopkins explains the history and purpose of the stunt-flying U.S. Air Force Thunderbirds. (Photo by Kevin J. Gruenwald, from The Thunderbirds: The U.S. Air Force Aerial Demonstration Squadron.*)*

deserves inspiration: children. Many of my books are hi/lo, a particular challenge, but stimulating reluctant readers is especially rewarding.

"I am raising my five-year-old grandson full-time, so writing is often limited to 'nap time' or weekends, when my husband can help out with the child-rearing duties. Luckily, he is my biggest fan and best friend. Without his encouragement, I might have given up on the publishing process. Instead, I have realized many goals and set many more for the future. With my current projects, I am pushing into new arenas, guaranteed to keep me busy for years to come. In addition to my husband, I am grateful for the support of mentors and peers within the writing community, especially the Society of Children's Book Writers and Illustrators. I am also fortunate to work with some of the best editors in the business. Finally, belief in myself and my God-given talent keeps me striving to succeed and excel."

Biographical and Critical Sources

PERIODICALS

Booklist, July, 2000, Catherine Andronik, review of *Air Devils: Sky Racers, Sky Divers, and Stunt Pilots,* p. 2016; November 1, 2000, Roger Leslie, review of *Orcas: High Seas Supermen,* p. 528.

* * *

HUNDAL, Nancy 1957-

Personal

Born January 31, 1957, in Vancouver, British Columbia, Canada; daughter of John A. (a truck driver) and Doris A. (a homemaker; maiden name, Erickson) Ferguson; married Derek Hundal, August 6, 1983; children: Josh, Bianca, Lucas. *Education:* University of British Columbia, B.A., 1979, teacher's certificate, 1980. *Hobbies and other interests:* Reading, singing, running, travel.

Addresses

Home—1517 W. 58th Ave., Vancouver, British Columbia V6P 1W6, Canada. *Agent*—Melanie Colbert, 17 West St., Holland Landing, Ontario L9N 1L4, Canada.

Career

Teacher and librarian in Vancouver, British Columbia, Canada, 1981—; author, 1990—. *Member:* Children's Writers and Illustrators of British Columbia, Children's Literature Roundtable.

Awards, Honors

BC Book Prize, 1990, for *I Heard My Mother Call My Name.*

Writings

I Heard My Mother Call My Name, illustrated by Laura Fernandez, HarperCollins (Toronto, Canada), 1990.
November Boots, illustrated by Marilyn Mets, HarperCollins (Toronto, Canada), 1993.
PuddleDuck, pictures by Stephen Taylor, HarperCollins (Toronto, Canada), 1995.
Snow Story, illustrated by Kasia Charko, HarperCollins (Toronto, Canada), 1997.
Melted Star Journey, illustrated by Karen Reczuch, HarperCollins (Toronto, Canada), 1999.
Prairie Summer, illustrated by Brian Deines, Fitzhenry & Whiteside (Toronto, Canada), 1999.
Number 21, illustrated by Brian Deines, Fitzhenry & Whiteside (Toronto, Canada), 2001.

Work in Progress

Picture books tentatively titled *Once Upon a Summer* and *Camping.*

Sidelights

Nancy Hundal is the author of a number of picture books for young readers designed to capture a child's fascination with the natural world. Many of them are set in Canada, where Hundal works and lives, and reviewers have often remarked that their combination of dramatic images and poetic text would appeal to the adult reader as well. Born in 1957 in Vancouver, British Columbia, Hundal graduated from the University of British Columbia and became a teacher and librarian there. She made her literary debut in the children's picture-book field with 1990's *I Heard My Mother Call My Name.* The pages were illustrated by Laura Fernandez and show a little girl fascinated by the changing light and new sights and sounds on her street and in her garden as a summer day turns into night. At every page she repeats the title and the words, "—and I know I should go in." Here, noted *Books in Canada* reviewer Anne Denoon, "Hundal aims to create a world of meticulously heightened sensation."

In *PuddleDuck,* Hundal's 1995 picture book, a little girl named after Hundal's own daughter, Bianca, is disconsolate when her favorite stuffed animal vanishes one day on a summer picnic. Bianca is so attached to Puddle-Duck that she is convinced that he is real, and illustrations from Stephen Taylor that show PuddleDuck observing the actions on the page reinforce this belief.

Within the tale of the missing companion are several smaller stories; for example, on the day PuddleDuck disappears, Bianca's father tells her the story of how PuddleDuck came home with her from the maternity hospital. A year later finds Bianca still convinced that PuddleDuck will return, especially when she sees "gray sheets of rain slicing through the clouds." Gillian Harding-Russell, in her review for *Canadian Children's Literature,* commended the work in enthusiastic terms. "The poetic texture of the prose, the haunting structure of the story with its frames and its confusion of the real with the make-believe distinguish *PuddleDuck* from the mass of children's books turned out every year," Harding-Russell claimed.

Inclement weather plays a role in two of Hundal's other works. *November Boots,* a 1996 story illustrated by Marilyn Mets, recounts the tale of a little boy who receives a new pair of boots. Delighted, he searches in vain for puddles so that he may test them. Hundal's "writing is evocative," remarked Sandra Martin in *Quill & Quire,* and Denoon echoed that sentiment in her *Books in Canada* review, commending Hundal's "leisurely, meditative text." In Hundal's *Snow Story,* published in 1998, little Chloe finds herself housebound by a serious blizzard. For days, her school and all other appointments are canceled, and Chloe must amuse herself. On the sixth day, the sun emerges and melts it all. Maureen Garvie, writing for *Quill & Quire,* praised Hundal's prose, comparing it with the work of poet e. e. cummings. "This book has 'beautiful' written all over it, full of deep snowdrifts and cozey three-story Victorian houses with your own beautiful room at the top," Garvie asserted.

The simple beauty of a rainy night in the city becomes the focus of *Melted Star Journey,* Hundal's 1999 offering for young readers. Its story is told by Luke, who is traveling home in the back seat of a car next to his brother and sister. He struggles to keep awake to see it all—the lights of the police car that briefly, but eerily illuminate his family, the lights of the stores that "blur, like melted ice cream swished over the street." Again, Hundal won praise for her spare but lyrical style. "Hundal's text is rich and poetic in imagery," noted Joanne Findon in *Quill & Quire,* who also stated that the work's combination of artistic images and a youngster's wonder "offers a glimpse of the simple ways in which the ordinary can become extraordinary."

Hundal told *SATA:* "I write for children because I still remember very well that special world called childhood. Writing my stories puts me back in that wonderful place, and it connects me to children and to anyone who was once a child and wants to remember.

"My special interests in writing picture books are the mood of the story and its language. My aim is to use original, powerful, thought-provoking language to create a feeling in the book that leaves a lasting impression on the reader."

Biographical and Critical Sources

BOOKS

Hundal, Nancy, *I Heard My Mother Call My Name,* illustrated by Laura Fernandez, HarperCollins (Toronto, Canada), 1990.

Hundal, Nancy, *Melted Star Journey,* illustrated by Karen Reczuch, HarperCollins (Toronto, Canada), 1999.

PERIODICALS

Booklist, November 1, 1999, Carolyn Phelan, review of *Prairie Summer,* p. 520.

Books in Canada, April, 1994, Anne Denoon, review of *November Boots,* pp. 49-50; November, 1995, Phil Hall, review of *PuddleDuck,* p. 40.

Canadian Children's Literature, fall, 1997, Celeste van Vloten, review of *I Heard My Mother Call My Name* and *November Boots,* pp. 67-68; spring, 1998, Gillian Harding-Russell, review of *PuddleDuck,* pp. 56-57.

Maclean's, November 22, 1999, Patricia Chisholm and others, review of *Prairie Summer,* p. 99.

Quill & Quire, March, 1991, Frieda Wishinsky, review of *I Heard My Mother Call My Name,* pp. 20-21; September, 1993, Sandra Martin, review of *November Boots,* p. 66; October, 1997, Maureen Garvie, review of *Snow Story,* p. 39; January, 1999, Joanne Findon, review of *Melted Star Journey,* pp. 43-44.

I–J

INGOLD, Jeanette

Personal

Born in NY; married; husband's name, Kurt; children: one son, one daughter. *Hobbies and other interests:* Photography.

Addresses

Agent—c/o Author Mail, Harcourt Brace, 525 B St., Suite 1900, San Diego, CA 92101. *E-mail*—ingold@montana.com.

Career

Worked as a reporter for the *Missoulian* (Montana).

Awards, Honors

Pictures, 1918 and *Airfield* were named to the New York Public Library "Best Books for the Teen Age" list.

Writings

The Window, Harcourt Brace (San Diego, CA), 1996.
Pictures, 1918, Harcourt Brace (San Diego, CA), 1998.
Airfield, Harcourt Brace (San Diego, CA), 1999.
The Big Burn, Harcourt Brace (San Diego, CA), 2002.
Mountain Solo, Harcourt Brace (San Diego, CA), 2002.

Author of the short stories "Word Drift" in *Xanadu 3,* edited by Jane Yolen, Tor, 1995, and "Moving On" in *Time Capsule: Short Stories about Teenagers Throughout the 20th Century,* edited by Donald Gallo, Delacorte, 1999.

Sidelights

Jeanette Ingold is the author of three young adult novels that feature teen heroines confronting unusual challenges. In her 1996 debut, *The Window,* Ingold created a protagonist facing family tragedy and sudden disability; *Pictures, 1918* published two years later, portrays teens in a small Texas town worrying about World War I; *Airfield* advances to the 1930s in its tale of a young woman's fascination with flight. As Ingold once remarked, "I hope my readers will come away from my books having learned some neat things—how something works, what a particular career might be like, what life would be like in a particular time or place. I want those of my readers who are going through tough times to take courage from reading about other young people who have survived difficulties and seemingly impossible choices."

Jeanette Ingold

Ingold, married and the mother of two, lives and writes in Montana, but was born in New York. Her parents had moved east from Texas, and as a youngster Ingold occasionally traveled to their home state to visit relatives. Back at home, "I loved outdoor activities—climbing trees, trapeze stunts, and any game where the outcome hinged on fast running," she recalled. "In the Long Island neighborhood where I lived, kids gathered summer days and evenings for races, hide-and-seek, soccer baseball, capture-the-flag—all favorites of mine. My most favorite thing, though, was getting a chance to explore the woods or poke along the edges of streams, and that took a family trip or a Girl Scout outing."

Much of Ingold's work recalls a bygone era, and she recalled hearing stories about her parents' families from a very early age. "I can't remember a time when stories weren't a part of my life," she noted, "although they didn't seem like some separate thing to be identified as such—they were just always there, like family and board games and the wallpaper in my bedroom. My parents read to me, and they told me real stories of things they'd done when they were kids and of mysteries they'd come across. They passed along the family tales that had been handed down to them."

Ingold described herself as "independent" as a youngster, "and curious. Always wanting to do or try the next thing. I was blessed with parents who put challenging projects before me and helped me make them work. My mom taught me sewing. My dad and I experimented with photography and built a working radio from an oatmeal box. And they took my brother and me on lots of trips—I think we traveled between New York and Texas by every possible route, investigating all the historical sites along the way."

Like many other writers, Ingold was an avid reader as a child. "I was five when I started first grade—Stratford Elementary School in Garden City, New York—and I think that's when I started learning to read. I must have been in third grade—or maybe the end of second— before my reading ability let me get into books that told good stories—and from then on I was hooked. I went through books as fast as Mom and I could bring them home from the library. I read all over the place (which I still do)—biographies, the 'Little House' books, Nancy Drew and Cherry Ames. I must have read *Little Women* and *The Swiss Family Robinson* a half dozen times each. Then I moved on to Charles Dickens and Jane Austen, historical fiction, Mark Twain, more mysteries.

"Both of my parents encouraged my reading—Dad by discussing issues and ideas always a bit ahead of what I might find on my own; Mom by seeing that there was always a stack of books on hand," Ingold continued. "When I got too busy to visit the library, she'd go for me. Thinking back on those books I'd find waiting when I came home after school or in from a date—it seems pretty amazing how my mom always knew which books I needed or would enjoy or was ready for. All those library trips she made for me—they were probably one of the greatest gifts she gave me."

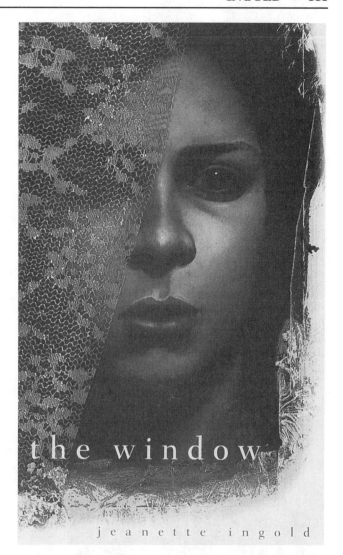

In Ingold's time-travel novel, Mandy is blinded and orphaned by a car accident and discovers her enhanced sense of hearing opens up past mysteries about her family. (Cover illustration by Joel Peter Johnson.)

Despite the fact that she "read lots and lots," Ingold also found time to pursue other hobbies as a teen. "I carried a camera and did my own darkroom work. I played violin in the school orchestra. Occasionally a girlfriend and I would go into Manhattan for lunch out and to see a matinee or go to a museum. I loved dances and going on dates. I spent a lot of time in Texas, where my grandmother and many of my relatives lived. I was an airlines kid, and once I was old enough to be allowed on a plane by myself, I flew to Texas whenever I had a chance."

She harbored some ambition for the skies herself, she admitted. "I wanted to fly, but for a variety of reasons that didn't seem to be an option. For a long time, I thought I wanted to be a nurse—all those Cherry Ames books—but eventually changed my mind about that. It never occurred to me that the things I most loved doing—reading, exploring, listening to people's stories, using my camera—might be put together in a career.

Still, I was doing them—and I was taking notes, sometimes, and beginning to try to capture on paper the things I wanted to remember."

For college, Ingold chose a school in Delaware, and was pleasantly surprised by her sudden independence. "As a freshman, I found college to be fantastic! I could not believe the freedom that college gave me (and this in an era when women's dorms had housemothers and observed curfew hours). And then by halfway through my sophomore year, I was ready to get done with college and on to the next thing. My husband, Kurt, and I were married the summer after I graduated, and the next few years were ones of rapid change and multiple moves. It all came together when we settled in Montana. We'd found the place we wanted to be, and I'd lucked into a job in the *Missoulian*'s newsroom. All it took was going out on one assignment—knowing the thrill of heading into a story not knowing what you're going to find and then the challenge of trying to tell the truth of it in a way that others can share the experience—to tell me I wanted to write."

Pictures, 1918

JEANETTE INGOLD

In Texas during World War I, fifteen-year-old Asia discovers a love for photography and the means to develop her own identity as a young artist. (Cover photo by Julie Toy.)

Eventually Ingold decided to try her hand at writing fiction. Her debut came in 1996 with *The Window,* but success "was preceded by a variety of manuscripts I think of now as my practice novels," Ingold stated. "I learned a lot writing them—craft things like handling dialog and writing scenes. They brought me enough editorial encouragement to keep me writing, and, fortunately, they didn't sell." Ingold described *The Window* as "the story of Mandy, a girl coming to grips with the realities of blindness. I didn't think the story out ahead of writing it—Mandy just appeared on my computer one day, an insistent voice that popped out when I was doing a writing exercise. Once I had her story written, I reworked it several times with the help of many people who had first-hand experience with blindness—teachers, counselors, kids attending the Montana School for the Deaf and the Blind. I'd just finished the first complete draft when I met Diane D'Andrade at a writers' conference. Diane, then a senior editor at Harcourt, suggested some revisions and said she'd like to see the manuscript again if I wanted to try making them. If! Anyway, I did, and she bought the book, and we went on to work together up until Diane retired from Harcourt."

In *The Window,* Mandy is blinded in car accident that kills her mother, a single parent. Mandy is then sent to live in Texas with relatives she has never met—and they knew nothing of her existence, either, until the tragedy. There is talk of sending her to a special school for the blind, but Mandy insists on attending the local public school, where she struggles to orient herself. She finds that heightened sense of hearing helps make up for her lack of sight. At home, she spends much time in her attic room and realizes that she seems to hear and even "see" things that may have happened long ago in the house. She starts to wonder about this branch of her family and its murky history. "The voices and time travel devices are deftly handled and make the suspension of belief workable," noted Anne O'Malley in *Booklist,* who called *The Window* "a strong and satisfying work." The challenges presented by creating a character like Mandy were particularly important to Ingold as a writer. "I love having readers who are open to stepping into the lives of people in circumstances different from their own—and I try speak to that openness by writing characters from a variety of times and places and social backgrounds."

Ingold struggled to make Mandy's challenges as realistic as possible. As the author told Teri Lesesne in an interview for *Teacher/Librarian,* "I took the draft to counselors and teachers who work with blind kids and I made changes based upon what they told me.... I learned the basics of reading Braille and I accompanied a blind teenager and her orientation and mobility instructor as she made her way from one place to another. I listened to blind kids talk about how Mandy's feelings reflected their own feelings."

Ingold has said that her success as a published author evoked many new feelings, but pointed out that "what was best—what made that first book possible—was the generous help, teaching and insights given me by other, far more experienced writers—Dorothy Hinshaw Patent, Peggy Christian, Bruce Coville, Jane Yolen. And, of course, one of the nicest things about getting that first book published was that I was suddenly no longer working alone—I had an experienced editor in my corner who helped me shape a better story than I could ever have written by myself."

Pictures, 1918, published in 1998, was Ingold's second novel for young adults. The work is set in 1918, the year after America entered the ongoing overseas conflict that came to be known as World War I. Asia is fifteen and lives in a small west Texas town called Dust Crossing. She is fascinated by new display in the window of the local pharmacy, the Kodak Autographic Camera. Asia is still sad about the mysterious fire that killed her pet rabbit, Straw Bit, and thinks that if she had had her own camera like the Kodak, then she would at least have a picture of Straw Bit by which she might remember her pet. She also thinks that a camera might have been able to yield more clues about the origin of the fire itself— Asia saw a shadowy figure running from the scene. Other suspicious fires have also occurred in Dust Crossing, and she and Nick, her friend and neighbor, wonder about them. Asia takes up photography as a hobby, and a burgeoning romance with Nick seems doomed by the possibility of his imminent draft. *Booklist* reviewer Carolyn Phelan commended the "convincing narrative" and "fine characterization" in *Pictures, 1918.* "At its best, the novel captures the nuances of ambivalent relationships," Phelan asserted.

Ingold's idea for *Pictures, 1918* was sparked by some old family photographs from that time, and she went back to Texas to research life there during the World War I era. She delved into reading materials that helped her explain the social and political climate of the time, but as she recalled on her Web site, "My absolute best resources were the microfilmed, small-town newspapers of the day. They gave me, in their headlines and personals columns, grocery ads and calls for patriotic action, the parameters of my characters' lives."

More of Ingold's own personal recollections formed the basis for her next novel, *Airfield,* published in 1999. It centers upon events at a small Texas landing strip, Muddy Springs Airport, in the early days of aviation— when planes were small, runways still ran through farmland, and sheep sometimes had to be shooed away. The story is told through Beatty, a teenager who spends much of her free time at the airport. She seems a second-generation aviator already: her father delivers mail with his plane, and her uncle manages the air field. Her friend Moss hopes to become an aviation mechanic, and both must come to terms with how dangerous air travel can be one night when her father's plane is running low on fuel, and the air strip's landing lights fail as a storm approaches. Beatty and Moss must help him land in the dark.

As Ingold recalled in the interview with Lesesne for *Teacher/Librarian,* "I got the idea for *Airfield* from stories my folks used to tell of my dad's early work for

Teenaged Beatty is fascinated by the new airport in her town and has a chance to save her father, who delivers mail by plane, when his life is in danger. (Cover illustration by Paul Lee.)

American Airlines, called American Airways back then. He and Mom would go from Texas town to Texas town where Dad would fill in for the absent airport personnel. It was do-everything work: passenger and baggage handling, radio operations, sometimes airplane refueling. The airports of 1933 were magnets to a certain kind of young person and *Airfield* is about two of them: Beatty and Moss." Ingold also noted that her father worked at New York's La Guardia airport when she was a kid, as she wrote on her Web site, "and occasionally he'd take me to see the huge hangars there, where great propeller planes shone under bright lights and mechanics worked through the night. I was enthralled by the place."

Ingold has said that in order to cultivate an idea into a story, "I write . . . and write and write. Often the writing starts with a bit of a character—a voice or line of dialog or expression I've seen on someone's face coming together with a situation or a place I've found intriguing. When that happens, usually what I do is tilt the screen on my laptop back enough that it's hard to see. Then I start asking the character questions, typing the answers without trying to control them and hoping a real—not actual, but true—person will emerge. Sometimes it works and sometimes it doesn't. And I end up with reams of stuff from which I then have to carve out the backbone of a story that I can then do more writing on to flesh out. All in all, it's not a very efficient method, and I'm working at bringing outlining and plot considerations earlier into the process. But it's also absolutely involving. Sometimes whole mornings pass in what seems like just minutes. Mornings like that, I can hardly believe how fortunate I am, to get to do what I do.

Leaving her office to investigate the details that add life to her books, however, is more immediately gratifying for Ingold. "One of the greatest joys of my writing is the excuse it gives me to do research," she asserted. "Libraries always feel like home to me, and I especially enjoy the surprises I find in archival libraries—photograph files and original correspondence, old postcards and maps, local histories. I try to find people who have experienced the lives my characters are living, and I listen to what they would like others to know. I try to know the land where my stories take place. I try to find and learn to use the objects that would have been important to my characters—learning the rudiments of reading Braille, for instance, for *The Window;* learning the mechanisms of a camera like Asia uses in *Pictures, 1918;* examining the artifacts in the basement of an aviation museum when I was working on *Airfield.* My novel, *The Big Burn,* set against the forest fires of 1910, led me into the Idaho wilderness, along abandoned railroad beds, to towns permanently changed because they lay in the path of those flames."

"I write best in solitude—when I have big spaces of time where I can get lost in my work," Ingold remarked. "Working on a novel is a kind of juggling act for me— I've got all these characters to throw up in the air and keep moving around, and all it takes is a distracting phone call to let one of them fall down. As for where I write—I migrate. Often I'll do an hour or two of work before getting out of bed. Then some more on the sofa or at my desk. Then, if the weather is nice, I'll take my laptop outside and work on the porch or in a clearing in the woods." As a wife and mother, Ingold juggles household and family duties along with her career and creative demands. "As for balancing writing with the rest of my life—how well I manage that kind of depends on where I am in a project. Sometimes, early on, I can keep pretty regular hours and do a decent job of keeping on top of my non-writing life. Other times, when a story becomes all-involving, the balance tends to get lost."

"I write for young people for lots of reasons," Ingold noted. "For starters, I enjoy trying to write what I like to read, and I think some of the best books being published today are ones written for young adults. And the YA novel is a format that allows me to try to stretch myself as a writer and to experiment with fitting form and voice to subject. Second, since YA novels are written through the lens of an adolescent seeing things for the first time, it's a great place for me to explore the new things that come my way. And, third, I love that feeling of anticipation that's inherent in my favorite YA books— that promise that there's an interesting life and an exciting world out there waiting for the person who goes after it. And, fourth, I like writing for an audience where what I have to say might make a difference. My readers are young people in the process of forming the views they'll take into adulthood. I wouldn't for one moment want to tell them what to think, but I do hope to offer them perspectives and context that might broaden their understandings.

"I like to write about young people learning to think for themselves. I like to write about teenagers learning the things they need to know to become independent, capable, responsible adults. I hope the young people who read my books will come away from them having, for a while, lived lives different from their own, and I hope that the experience will have broadened their understanding and empathy.... Maybe, most of all, I want my books to say to kids, 'Look, you don't live on this earth alone. You'll find it a great, exciting place to be, if only you'll let yourself reach out to other people and enter their lives and try to understand what you discover.'"

Ingold reaffirmed, in conclusion, her faith in the power of the written word. "I wish that all kids would understand the importance of being able to read well and would come to know the great pleasures that can be found in books," she stated. "I want our young people to be readers, and I want them to know that they can be writers, too, if they wish. I want them to know that reading and writing are just two sides of the same thing—both doable and both a joy."

Biographical and Critical Sources

PERIODICALS

Booklist, November 1, 1996, Anne O'Malley, review of *The Window,* p. 490; August, 1998, Carolyn Phelan, review of *Pictures, 1918,* p. 1990.
Teacher/Librarian, September, 1999, Teri Lesesne, "Listening to People's Stories: An Interview with Jeanette Ingold," p. 67.

OTHER

Jeanette Ingold, http://www.jeanetteingold.com (August 27, 2001).*

*   *   *

JACOBS, Leah
See GELLIS, Roberta (Leah Jacobs)

*   *   *

Autobiography Feature

Julie Johnston

1941-

I believe that if you live in a house long enough, it becomes part of your personality. When I think about my childhood I see myself in our house on William Street in Smiths Falls, a small town in eastern Ontario, or if my memory is about childhood summers, I picture myself at our cottage on Rideau Lake, half an hour's drive from Smiths Falls. Those were my first homes and belong to my first memories.

Our house was a tall, yellow brick, Victorian structure, large but not huge, with lots of rooms, some of them tucked away in surprising places, a good place to play hide-and-seek. On stormy days in the winter I was allowed to ride my tricycle along the front hall, to the back hall, through the kitchen, out the other kitchen door, through the pantry, dining room, living room, and back out to the front hall, making a complete circle. Once when we were all quarantined with mumps and not allowed to go out or have anyone in, my sisters and I dressed up in what we pretended were circus costumes. We made a parade of all our toys and went round and round the circuit on tricycles and roller skates blowing horns and dingling bells. We called ourselves the Dulmage Sisters' Circus (and still do). I expect our mother was thrilled when the quarantine was up and we were allowed to go back to school.

It was a big house to heat and a little drafty, but it had fireplaces in my father's study, in the good front room or drawing room, as it was called, and in the dining room. In the kitchen there was a wood-burning stove attached to the electric range. The lid of the woodbox beside the stove was a cozy place to sit and thaw out after an afternoon of playing in the snow and an advantageous spot if there were any icing bowls to be licked.

Writers and artists of any merit at all are thought, generally, to have suffered devastating and cruel hardships in their early lives. My childhood was embarrassingly happy and singularly free from trauma. Our family life seemed to follow a routine of rituals and traditions.

On Saturday evenings in the winter our mother would wash our hair and do it up in rags to produce curls the next day. On Sundays we went to church in the morning and had roast beef at noon. We kids went to Sunday school in the afternoon and then, when it began to get dark, we got into our pyjamas and dressing gowns and sat around the fire in my father's study, where we drew pictures or read. At supper time my mother brought in a big plate of little

Julie Johnston, 1992

triangular sandwiches, which we ate along with carrot and celery sticks and pickles and olives. It was our favourite meal of the week. We ate it listening to radio programmes beginning with *Jake and the Kid,* followed by other programmes, *Amos and Andy, Jack Benny, Charlie McCarthy.*

We continued this tradition of sandwiches around the fireplace right through our teens, but by then we were watching television instead of listening to the radio. We watched *Our Miss Brooks* and *Ed Sullivan* and *Father Knows Best,* a programme which seemed patterned, in some ways, after our own family, in which adults were

Julie with Margaret, about 1946

always right and children were expected to keep opinions, if they had any, to themselves.

In the cellar of our house were several dark and spooky rooms. In one, coal for the furnace was stored, in another, fireplace wood was piled, and in another were stored preserved chili sauce, pickles, and fruit. There was one more room, which was always kept bolted shut. I was never allowed to go in there when I was little and so it became even more mysterious. Something dark and menacing lurked there, brooding in the gloom, waiting, I was sure, to grab me and swallow me. This notion was fostered and encouraged by my older and wiser sister Diane, who even convinced me that if I stood on the cellar stairs and listened, I could hear a low, tortured moan coming from behind that bolted door.

One Saturday afternoon my father took a lamp with a long cord and let us follow him into this dungeon. It was like a cave. Its ceiling was so low that my father had to crouch. There was no floor, except for earth and ledges of rock layered almost to the ceiling at the far end. Great hulking shapes seemed to lurch and leap in the play of light and shadow cast by my father's lamp. Even though he explained that it was just a storage room for old and broken pieces of furniture and for lumber, I was not convinced. I think I have always kept that gloomy room with me, bolted most of the time, but I know it exists awaiting its chance to pull me in. Sometimes it creeps into some of the darker aspects of my writing. Some of it perhaps emerged in Sara's dark and cynical personality in *Adam and Eve and Pinch-me.*

As soon as the weather turned warm my father removed the storm windows and put the screens on and my mother would unlatch the tall glass French doors that opened onto the front veranda. Fresh air and sunshine poured into the house and we knew it was spring.

Diane once sent me a letter on my birthday describing her earliest memory of me. She was four and a half when I was brought home from the hospital in January 1941. She was waiting for me at the wrong door. Because of the blustery weather, my mother and father, and a nurse who would stay for a few days to look after my mother and me, brought me in from the garage through the attached woodshed like an armload of wood. Grandma Dulmage, who lived with us, was there too, waiting for a glimpse of the new baby.

My first memories, probably at about two or three, are of uniforms. I remember how scratchy on my bare legs my uncles' uniforms felt whenever they picked me up. They must have been on leave that summer before being sent overseas to fight in the Second World War. By comparison, my father's uniform was less abrasive. Considerably older than my uncles, he was a major in the Lanark and Renfrew Scottish Regiment and was stationed at National Defence Headquarters in Ottawa. Before the war he had practiced law and after the war he went back to his practice as Crown Attorney for Lanark County.

My next clear memory is of a stranger coming to live at our house when I was three years old, a nurse who was to sleep in our spare bedroom and look after my grandmother because she had just had a stroke and was unable to walk or to talk clearly. I remember the front doorbell ringing and Diane and I running to answer the door. There on the veranda, suitcase in hand, stood Margaret, a woman who was to become our constant companion.

As time passed, I became acquainted with Margaret's entire family and especially her brother Robert's children, who called her Aunt Peggy. I begged to be allowed to call her Aunt Peggy, too, or at least Peggy, but she insisted on Margaret, making me feel distant and a little jealous of Sheila and Myles, her niece and nephew.

One of Margaret's brothers owned a dry-cleaning business and when she had a weekend off he would pick up Margaret in the delivery van and take her "up home" to the family farm where her parents lived along with Robert and his wife and their children. Sheila and I were the same age and Myles was only a little younger so when I was about seven or eight I was sometimes invited to go along to play with them. To keep from getting carsick, which I did on a regular basis, Margaret let me stand up in the back of the van and walk around by hanging onto the rods used for hanging up the dry-cleaned clothes. I used to brag that I'd walked all the way to the farm, a trip of about sixteen kilometres (ten miles). And I never once threw up.

Part of an old tractor sat under a huge maple tree at the farm. Sometimes we climbed up into the tree or played on the swing but our favourite game was pretending we were taking produce to market. We would fill old potato sacks with sticks and stones or dead leaves and haul them onto the tractor, pretending they were bags of potatoes or corn that we were going to sell. But our game was short-lived. One day Sheila's mother caught us trying to stuff her hens into the potato sacks to sell at our imaginary market. As I recall, her mother was just about as cross as the hens.

Some of these early experiences have been modified and used in my writing. I remember hearing my mother once describe the telegram her family received saying that one of my uncles was missing during the war and presumed dead. After the war I used to imagine going to Europe and searching for my uncle and finding him and bringing him home safe and sound. Some of this re-emerges in Keely and Patrick's semi-imaginary search for Peggy's fiance in *Hero of Lesser Causes.*

In fact, Peggy in that book is very like Margaret. Margaret had apparently been engaged to a man who never came back from the war. Margaret was so strong that she could pick up my grandmother and carry her in her arms like a child. She was also superstitious and could read tea leaves. The best thing about using some of Margaret's qualities was that I finally got to call her Peggy.

Margaret had other powers which aren't described in my book. Once she brought a fresh-killed chicken back from the farm for my mother to roast. My mother was used to getting meat from the butcher and was a bit skeptical of this limp, feathery bird. Margaret told her not to worry, that she would clean it. My mother busied herself with other chores but I stayed to watch Margaret's performance. She plucked the feathers, and then reaching into the hen she pulled out the innards, among them several tiny orange eggs. Next she stoked up the fire in the kitchen stove until the flames leapt high. Wielding a cone of burning paper in one hand and the plucked bird in the other, she performed almost a sleight of hand with the bird, twisting and contorting it over and through the flames until its pin-feathers were singed completely away.

Margaret had one other dazzling accomplishment which left me believing in her superhuman power. She could sharpen a knife, a characteristic my father thought nothing short of miraculous, especially in a woman. Every Sunday before the roast beef was set in front of my father to be carved at the dining-room table, Margaret took the big carving knife in one hand and in the other a sharpening steel, a heavy cylinder set in a bone handle about the same length as the knife. She held them out in front of her broad bosom and, with her elbows pumping like pistons at a speed faster than the eye could follow, she criss-crossed the

With her cousin, Judy, and Penny the dog, about 1950

flashing weapons, carving the air into tiny brilliant sparks. In Thomas Hardy's *Far from the Madding Crowd* there is a scene in which Sergeant Troy amazes Bathsheba Everdene with what he calls the sword exercise—a dazzling exhibition of skill and mesmerizing dexterity. When I read it as an adult, I thought instantly of Margaret.

When I was nearly five my sister Kathie was born. By this time Diane was ten and although we weren't close in age, we were close as sisters. We all slept in the same room, which was called the nursery, Diane and I in twin beds and Kathie in the crib. Our grandmother's room was next to ours and if we got too noisy after lights out, she would ring her little silver bell, which would summon either Margaret or our parents.

Our mother used to read to us at night. Sometimes it would be about the Bobbsey Twins, who were always in trouble, and sometimes *Anne of Green Gables,* which made us laugh and also brought the occasional tear. She also read from the *Just Mary Stories* and from *Maggie Muggins,* both written by a Canadian woman named Mary Grannan. And we always begged for more of A. A. Milne's *Winnie the Pooh* or *Now We Are Six* or *When We Were Very Young.*

After our mother had kissed us goodnight, turned out our light, and had gone downstairs, Diane and I got out of bed and began our usual game of make-believe while Kathie lay in her crib sound asleep. Our imaginary friends were Babs and Maximilian. Babs was Diane's friend, a teenager, very sophisticated with a boyfriend. She was always talking on the telephone and using slang and saying, "Ree-aaah-lly!" My friend Max was named after a hand-knit woollen doll who could neither sit nor stand, so I gave him a life of adventure.

Diane and I would sit cross-legged on the mat on the floor between our beds along with Babs and Maximilian imagining that we were in a boat. By pushing with our hands we could propel ourselves across the nursery floor and out into the hall. During these voyages Babs would invariably fall out of our boat and have to be rescued with the help of Max. Sometimes she'd drown and we'd weep for her. Max finally got fed up with this accident-prone Babs and her simpering slang and began tossing her overboard and ignoring her drowning pleas, which caused a few noisy arguments. And then our grandmother would jingle her bell and we'd scuttle back into the nursery, hauling our boat behind us before one of the adults appeared at the top of the stairs.

By the time Kathie was big enough to play, Diane invented a new game with Kathie as her living doll. Dressing her in an elegant but ancient child's dress which had found its way into our playroom and was now somewhat faded and ratty, she would tie a wide yellow ribbon around Kathie's little bald head with the bow on top and then push her up and down the street in her stroller to show her off to the neighbours.

By now Diane had outgrown Babs and Maximilian. I wanted a game at night that would still involve me so I

Julie (second from right) with (from left) her mother, Mae Dulmage; her sister Diane; her father, Barnet Dulmage; her sister Kathie; and a family friend, Marg Fuller, 1956

started making up stories to tell my sisters. They became known as the "Patsy and Paul Stories," starring my friends who lived across the street as well as my good self. These were fantasies, often of daring climbs up to the roof of the house, and of courageous rescues by me when Patsy and Paul nearly fell off. Poor Patsy and Paul could scarcely step outside their front door without falling into a river, or out of an airplane, or getting lost in the woods. Fortunately, Julie was always there to bail them out of their predicament. I think Keely in *Hero of Lesser Causes* owes something to these early days.

My grandmother died when I was nine. I was bustled off to Perth, a nearby town, to stay with my second-cousin Judy until the day of the funeral, which took place in our house. By the time I was brought back my grandmother was in her casket in the drawing room. Relatives I had never met began arriving, the minister came, the undertaker brought folding chairs, and Margaret took me by the hand and said I should go in and say good-bye to my grandmother for the last time.

To be truthful, I had not been very close to my grandmother. I have no clear memory of her before her stroke and afterwards she seemed always to be furious with me because I couldn't make out what she was saying. Margaret and my father were the only ones who could understand her. To my everlasting shame I recall inviting school friends into her room to hear her speak gibberish and to watch her anger swell until she appeared ready to fly off the bed or burst the bulging veins at her temples. Terrified, my friends would back out of her room, stumble down the stairs, and run out the door. If my mother had known, or Margaret, they'd have tanned my hide. I said goodbye to my grandmother but not for the last time. Years later she came back to haunt me, as well she might.

Margaret stayed on with us for a short time and even though we children begged her to stay forever, she had to go somewhere else to earn her living. I think probably she was most upset at leaving Kathie, who must have seemed like her own baby. She came back often for visits, which were fun and exciting but never quite the same; she was no longer our Margaret; she had a life that didn't include us.

Before the war my father together with his cousin Gerald, Judy's father, bought an island with two cottages on it on Rideau Lake. Because of the wartime gasoline shortage and because my father was away in Ottawa, we didn't stay there much until after the war. The island was close enough to the mainland for a footbridge to be built and each June as soon as school closed for the holidays we would load up the car and proceed to the lake. All the way there we sang songs which our mother taught us, rounds like "White Coral Bells," and another which went:

To ope' their trunks the trees are never seen.
How then do they put on their robes of green?
They leave them out.

We sang partly to distract me and my sympathetic dog Queenie from getting carsick. On the way to the lake Queenie and I sat next to the window, me looking pale green and swallowing hard and Queenie trying to swallow

hard but drooling. On these trips we were known as Drooly and Jooly.

The road to the lake was very rough and twisty and at times not much more than a trail. We parked in a clearing and lugged our suitcases, baskets of canned goods, and extra blankets across the bridge to the island. There is a sensation, part smell, part sight, about a lake and an island and a cottage which you only experience when you arrive in June. It has to do with the earth stirring beneath its brown blanket of pine needles, the warm breeze bouncing across the lake as if someone were skipping diamonds over its surface, and with the inside of the frame cottage itself, cool weathered wood closed in over the winter awakening and warming to the sun as we opened windows and doors.

There were chores to be done. We had to sweep up dead wasps and flies trapped there in late fall, and droppings from mice who had vacationed in the cottage over the winter. Screens were put back on the windows and doors, a fire was lit, the hand pump in the kitchen worked up and down until icy water spurted, tables scrubbed, dishes washed.

My mother dusted and swept the outhouse and unwrapped a fresh roll of toilet paper. My father took a large pair of tongs down to the icehouse and, digging beneath the sawdust, retrieved a chunk of ice, one of many placed there during the winter by a neighbouring farmer who had chopped them out of the frozen lake. Gripping with the tongs he dipped the ice in the lake to wash off the sawdust spread over the ice to insulate it, to slow down its melting during the summer. We always had enough ice to keep our icebox cool enough to store fruit and vegetables, cheese and butter, although milk was never cold enough to taste anything but nasty. For a few years after the war a supply boat continued to cruise the shores of the lake selling fresh produce and even ice cream.

Each afternoon my sisters and I fought over whose turn it was for the hammock and with armloads of comic books, not looked at since the summer before, we had our compulsory afternoon rest. After it, our lunch well-digested, we were allowed to go swimming. Each of us could swim by the time we were four or five and would have lived in the water if we'd been allowed. We always begged for one more dip even though we shivered and shook and our lips were blue.

Our cottage had been built, decades before, as a central square cabin partially surrounded by a wide, slope-ceilinged veranda which served as both dining room and living room. On rainy days we sat around the table at one end of the veranda drawing and colouring, playing Parcheesi or endless games of cards or Monopoly.

In a cottage you feel very close to the weather, wind sighing through the trees, rain pelting the roof, drips plinking into a tin basin under a leak. When I became tired of games, I liked to curl up under a blanket with a book, feeling cozy and safe from the thunder rumbling overhead like God rearranging furniture and from the lightning sheeting the pewter sky and lake, one nearly indistinguishable from the other.

The books in the wobbly homemade bookcase constructed of cedar saplings and pine boards seemed to have been there since the beginning of time. Besides the requisite Agatha Christie murder mysteries, there were children's books, one I remember called *Stand on a*

Rainbow, in which the two main characters coincidentally were called Sheila and Myles. Another, whose title I forget, began intriguingly, "We have always lived in the castle . . . " Over the summers as I grew I ploughed through some of my father's school books which were there as well, *A Tale of Two Cities, Vanity Fair, Pride and Prejudice.*

In the early days, as evening fell my mother lit a coal-oil lamp and before bedtime we were sometimes serenaded by my father playing a mandolin and his cousin playing a ukulele, both singing the songs of their youth, songs we had on records and played on the old windup gramophone we had at the lake, "Me and My Shadow," "Peggy O'Neil," "Mr. Gallagher and Mr. Sheen." I can remember only part of a line from the latter, but a line that has always fascinated me. It goes: " . . . and they painted her bottom green. Who, the lady Mr. Gallagher? No, the rowboat Mr. Sheen." Sometimes, on a still night, we would hear the family on Birch Island across the lake singing "Sweet Adeline."

Then we would all go to bed while out on the lake loons trilled to their mates, whippoorwills in the trees behind the cottage repeated themselves endlessly, and outside our screens fireflies, jealous of the stars, twinkled in the dark. Meanwhile, inside our screens, a mosquito would whine in my ear, making me pull the sheet up over my head for protection.

My cousin Judy, who lived in the other cottage on the island, was my summertime pal. We had two particularly good climbing trees, a tall pine on the mainland across the water from our boathouse, which you could climb hand over foot through the conveniently spaced branches up to my favourite perch near the top. I loved the sensation of freedom I had up there, gripping the narrowing trunk, swaying in the wind, with a bird's-eye view of the boathouse. One day my father came out of the boathouse, looked up, and nearly fainted when he saw how high I'd climbed. I was forced to make a quick descent and to make a promise I couldn't keep, never to risk my neck again.

Judy and I began to spend more time in our other tree, safely situated about a mile away from the island. It was a monstrous old maple whose trunk had been bent as a sapling so that it formed a sort of ramp which we could easily climb. From it we could spread ourselves out into the tree's varying clusters of branches and let our imaginations go wild. Sometimes the tree was something exciting like an airplane but most of the time it was our tree house where we lived like Tarzan.

Nearby, we had other retreats: a cave, a small rocky island inhabited by one dead tree to which we liked to row for a picnic, and a dense cedar thicket as cold and sunless as any fairy-tale haunted forest. In fact, we were convinced it *was* haunted even after we saw its ghost in the guise of an owl fly away. We were both avid readers of Louisa May Alcott and L. M. Montgomery, and because we were so fond of Anne Shirley we thought we should give our hideaways romantic and imaginative names. But we couldn't think of any that we could agree on. We argued over them so much that we ended up with a prosaic "Owl Wood" for our enchanted forest, and for the tiny island "Dead Tree Island" sometimes and "Lone Tree Island" at others. Anne would have held us in deep scorn.

Judy and I were very domesticated in those days. Our other home, called "The Wee House," was a narrow point of land at the end of the island. It had a front door, rooms with walls and furniture, and the great luxury of running water on three sides. We would only let my little sister Kathie in if she rang the front doorbell and didn't step on the walls. Kathie found the front doorbell all right, a golf tee stuck into a woodpecker hole in a tree, but she had a lot of trouble with the invisible walls.

As we got bigger, Judy and I felt the need of more substantial digs. One summer we constructed a tent at the back of the island with a large piece of burlap normally used to throw over the boat in the winter. We propped up the burlap sheet with dead and broken branches until it resembled something like a cross between a tepee and a beaver lodge. We furnished it with pine bows, which we'd read native Indians found quite comfortable. They weren't, but we pretended they were. We stocked it with stolen provisions—an old saucepan which we filled with water, a potato, and a couple of matches along with some twigs and dry leaves. Stealthily we made our way to the tent with our contraband stuff, sneaked inside without anyone seeing us, and prepared to cook our meal.

We managed to get a little fire going with the smoke billowing out through the front of the tent. We thought we could hear voices but decided it was only the wind. We stuck our fingers in the pot of water with the grimy potato in it but it was barely warm. The wind shifted then and the smoke came back into the tent, choking us. Gasping, coughing, blinded by smoke, we crawled past our fire out into the air, and unluckily for us up against the legs of our parents, who, smelling smoke and fearing a forest fire, had tracked us down to our lair. Our punishment, as I recall, was swift and severe.

I grew up on the lake. In the winter growing was measured by school grades but in the summer it was measured by the next thing I was permitted to do. I graduated from swimming on the beach to diving off the dock, from the rowboat to the motorboat, from staying close to shore to taking the boat to the tiny hamlet of Rideau Ferry to buy supplies. My father taught me to shoot a rifle at a target. We reached a milestone at the cottage when we got electricity and indoor plumbing and celebrated by having a party with all the other cottagers in the bay, adults and kids.

Diane was now a teenager and had a boyfriend who would come in the evening, tie up his boat at our dock, and sit beside her on the diving board. Judy and Kathie and I hid in the bushes to spy on them until Diane heard us snickering and chased us away. Judy ended up with a very itchy case of poison ivy on the backs of her thighs. "My goodness," her mother said, "you'd almost think you'd been sitting in it."

Comic books no longer held the same appeal for me. I discovered the set of "Harvard Classics" we had at home in a bookcase and I'd lug those along to become part of my summer reading. I could not be pried loose from *Great Expectations* except to go swimming. Even then, I couldn't resist telling the story to Diane, Kathie, and Judy as we lay on the dock sunning ourselves. "And then what happened?" Diane wanted to know. I told her that was as far as I'd got. "Well," she said, "go on back up to the cottage and read some more so we can find out." And that's the way it went—read a few chapters, rehash it for the others, every day until we'd finished it.

With her husband, Basil Johnston, returning from Europe on the **Empress of Britain,** *1964*

That winter I discovered *Jane Eyre* and *Wuthering Heights* at the public library in wonderfully outsized editions with eerie black-and-white illustrations made from woodcuts. I took ages to read them, wallowing in the rich text and tingling with dread over the melancholy pictures. My mother would call up to ask what I was doing and I learned the magic response. "Homework," I called back. When Diane or Kathie got stuck with setting the table they'd look into my room and say, "Liar!"

I eventually read my way through almost the entire set of "Harvard Classics." The one that stands out most vividly in my memory was Dostoyevski's *Crime and Punishment,* which I read in my teens. I couldn't put it down and continued to read late into the night after my parents had gone to bed. My father used to have very vivid dreams which he would recount for us next day, active dreams in which he fought off intruders and kicked at menacing animals (one such was a skunk which he kicked in his dream but in reality got my mother). Anyway, sometime after midnight, with Raskolnikov poised, knife in hand, ready to commit his treacherous crime and his hapless victim about to meet her fate, a bloodcurdling scream shattered the midnight stillness and I must have jumped two feet off the bed. It was my father, of course, suffering through one of his nightmares. It was a week before I could pick up that book and even then I had to finish it in daylight hours.

We loved to hear my father tell the same stories over and over. "Tell us about when you were a little boy," we would beg. He'd say, "Did I ever tell you about a cat we had that threw fits?" He had told us but we always wanted to hear again how it ran up a drainpipe and got stuck and had to be rescued. He told us about seeing his first movie, *Birth of a Nation,* in 1915, in which a fire blazed so realistically that people ran out of the theatre. And he told us about one hot day at school when the teacher stepped out

of the classroom for a minute and all the kids climbed out through the window and went swimming. Once he told us about his uncles calling him a sissy because he wore a wristwatch instead of a pocket watch and played tennis, which, in a small town, was considered a girls' game. During the war he wrote rhymes which he kept in a book along with a series of cartoons he created. He also wrote a play for his regiment.

Playwriting appealed to me. In grade nine I wrote a play for our class to put on at assembly before the entire school. It met with enough success that I wrote another one the next year in which almost everyone in the class had a part except me. I had wanted to be in it, but the minute I thought about being on stage, my knees trembled and I became tongue-tied. I think now that this type of split personality, involving a need to say something, coupled with a need to remain hidden, might be common to more writers than just me.

In high school, writing for the yearbook and the school newspaper gave me a creative outlet, although not much scope for inventing fiction until I developed my own opportunity. The school newspaper appeared each week in the *Record News,* the Smiths Falls weekly paper. We were running short of news one spring, dances were over, sports winding down, and the school editor was away sick. He phoned me and said, "Doesn't matter what you write, Julie, just write something." So I did. I began a short novel in serial form, and soon found that people were actually reading it, not just students but townspeople as well. Occasionally they would stop me and ask what was going to happen next. I could never tell them because I was making it up as I went along. I might be writing it still if school hadn't drawn to a close. I was forced to reach a conclusion and tie up the loose ends, which I did in the car driving with my family to New Brunswick to watch Diane graduate from Mount Allison University, dispatching it by post along the way.

Judy started going off to summer camp when we were twelve or thirteen and I was left to my own devices. One summer I met a girl whose father rented horses for her and her brother to ride during their holidays. This was the beginning of a dream come true. I was wild about horses but had had no opportunity to ride one. My new friend Cathy taught me the rudiments of riding and I thought that life couldn't get much better than that. As it turned out, it could and did. That same summer of the horses was also the summer I began to fall in love. Cathy's cousin Basil arrived at the lake with his crew cut and his impish smile, and I began to grow up.

I've never lost my enthusiasm for riding. Years later we had friends who kept horses on their farm and I practiced my riding skills there, trying to improve by reading books about how to ride a horse, not unlike Keely Connor.

Judy didn't like camp very much and was not pressed to go the next summer. Suddenly, it seemed, the lake was alive with teenagers, kids who had spent their lives on the lake, but like us, I guess, were wrapped up in their own pursuits. We met Ross, a boy from Philadelphia, and together with Basil, whose home was in Toronto, we double-dated, sometimes going by boat to the dances at the Rideau Ferry Inn. Every winter from then on, Judy and I both carried on long-distance romances by letter.

"My children and nephew playing dress-up": (from left) Lauren, Andrea, John, Melissa, and Leslie

I was now getting to the stage of having to choose university courses with a view to having a career. All the while I was growing up I thought I would simply become a lawyer like my father, but he was somewhat less than encouraging. "Lady-lawyers aren't very well thought of," he told me. He was a man of his times, I guess, and being a very immature young woman of mine, I believed him. I began next to think of a career in journalism but upon sending for information to both Columbia University in New York and Carleton College, as it was then, in Ottawa, I could see that it would mean spending a very long time away from my one true love, my summer romance which had blossomed. Basil was a medical student at the University of Toronto and it was there that I went, enrolling in physical and occupational therapy.

I can't decide whether things happen for the best or whether we make the best of what happens to us. I didn't like my course; the science aspect of it didn't interest me except for anatomy classes, during which we dissected cadavers to learn about muscles, joints, and nerves. Once I stopped being squeamish about the dead body I had to cut into and once I got over the rank smell of formaldehyde used to preserve the cadaver, I became fascinated by the intricacy and design of the human body.

The theoretic aspect of occupational therapy made some sense in that it dealt with teaching disabled patients to strengthen weak muscles through specific activities. But first, we students had to master these activities ourselves, which tended to be unimaginative crafts such as glove-making, netting, and weaving. Pottery I liked; there was at least scope for creativity in working the clay into sculptures or vessels. But what irked me most was what I saw as wasted opportunity. There I was at the great University of Toronto, where people were reading the works of the most distinguished philosophers, historians, and poets while I was tracing my hand to make leather gloves.

My fellow classmates, all girls in those days, were good sports and good fun. We played bridge every chance we got, over lunch, which, after anatomy dissection, we didn't want to eat anyway, or after classes in somebody's room in our university residence (dormitory), and even during the lectures of one of our professors who was hard of hearing, and I guess had poor eyesight as well. I was never very good at sports, but I joined the girls' football and ice-hockey teams because all the other first-year girls were novices too. If I ran toward the wrong goal or skated toward the wrong net, I thought I would be forgiven, a vain hope as it turned out.

I liked the practical work we did in hospitals and rehabilitation centres. I met so many people whose lives were so different from my own that I began to feel that at last I was beginning to get an education. In *Hero of Lesser Causes,* Keely's brother Patrick falls ill with polio and becomes completely disabled. Because he is so sensitively aware that he has changed, that he can no longer be the risk-taking, fun-loving boy he once had been, he loses heart and becomes severely depressed to the point of wanting to die. I probably would not have written about such a severe disability if I hadn't had a background in rehabilitation.

In 1963 I graduated, and that October married Basil Johnston, my teenage sweetheart who had graduated in medicine the year before. (Judy and Ross were married

earlier that same year.) We went back to eastern Ontario, where we lived in Perth in Basil's grandfather's house, vacant since his death two years before.

It was a wonderful old house, white frame dating back to the 1830s or 1840s, one of the oldest in Perth and, apart from having electricity and running water, almost unchanged since Basil's mother was a baby in 1900. It sat on a large wooded lot which extended back to the next street. At one time it had boasted a beautiful rose garden and an apple orchard, but now was as overgrown as a jungle. I never saw the property in its heyday, but I think I loved that wilderness more than I could ever have loved a formal garden. I could lose myself in it and deny the neighbouring houses and paved streets while I sat on a rocky hill in the middle of it sharing a picnic with our dog, Iago. Under the gnarled apple trees amongst the wormy windfalls I once found a puffball the size of a volleyball. Puffball is a fungus, like a mushroom but almost perfectly round, and delicious fried in butter with salt and pepper.

We liked to invite friends to come for weekends so that they could share our old-fashioned atmosphere, with a candle on the dresser and an 1866 edition of *Godey's Lady's Book* for their bedtime reading. We would take them exploring through a mysterious little door in the bathroom which led into a suite of three more rooms which held family memorabilia dating back to the early 1900s.

We lived in Perth but worked in Smiths Falls at the Ontario Hospital School for Retarded Children, as it was then called. This was a low sprawling edifice, almost a village with its own shoe repair, a carpentry shop, sewing and laundry rooms, a bowling alley, a pool hall, a theatre, a gymnasium, a vegetable garden, a school wing, a hospital wing, a physio department, a huge occupational therapy department (one room filled with weaving looms and another with potters' wheels), a pharmacy, dormitories, dining rooms, and kitchens. Its central corridor was nearly a mile long.

The children ranged in age from infants to the elderly, although most were school age. In those days people were convinced that the government could look after children with emotional, learning, and physical developmental handicaps better than anyone else. In some cases this was true; the OH was the cleanest, homiest place some kids had ever known. For others, it was little more than a dumping ground, allowing their families to be free of the burden of their constant care.

Basil was one of the staff doctors and I tried to practice both occupational and physiotherapy. I was very idealistic in those days. I really thought I could make a big difference in the lives of some of those kids by practicing what I'd been taught, but it was extremely frustrating. I saw few if any sure signs of progress. About the best thing you could do was hold some of the kids on your knee and rock them. Nothing I could do would help relieve their severe and multiple handicaps. The saddest thing I learned was how quickly one can become inured to tragic circumstances. I saw acts of great kindness there but I also saw acts of extreme insensitivity. In the end, we left after less than two years.

Basil wanted to start surgical training and we both wanted adventure. We hoped to combine the two by working in London, England, for a year. Armed with letters of introduction from the heads of our departments at U of T and with what we thought were assured placements—Basil with the surgeon who had operated on King George the Sixth when he had lung cancer and I with the physio department at Great Ormond Street Children's Hospital—we packed a trunk and sailed from Montreal on the *Empress of Canada.* Carsickness had nothing on seasickness. I thought I would die and wished I would, but after about three days out, I found my sea legs and managed to enjoy the rest of the voyage.

I have been to England and other parts of Europe several times since then, but never have I experienced the excitement of landing in Liverpool and for the first time being aware of how diverse the world really is. I was bombarded by new sensations, sights, sounds, smells, tastes. I wanted to take it all in all at once and bathe myself in the exotic reality of Britain. It wasn't a place made up by writers and filmmakers; it really did exist. I wrote long descriptive letters home to my parents.

But sad news awaited us when we got to London. Sir Clement Price-Thomas, who was to have taken Basil into his surgery, was gravely ill, ironically, with lung cancer. We quickly found a cheap flat to live in while we tried to work out plan B. We sifted though all the variations of how we could support ourselves and where, and after much soul-searching decided to do, not perhaps what we should, but instead what we desired. We counted our money, put some by for our return passage, rented a car, bought a tent, sleeping bags, and a camp stove, and set off to see the world.

We travelled like gypsies for a little over three months, pitching our tent in inexpensive tourist camps which abounded in every country we visited. Some were very posh with a restaurant, grocery store, hairdresser, bank, and swimming pool; others were treeless deserts with a tank full of pea-green water to cool off in, but most were somewhere in between. Occasionally we splurged and stayed in a hotel. That trip was a three-month, hands-on, introductory course in everything from history, geography, religion, customs, cultures, and languages, to art, architecture, and culinary experimentation. We learned to like snails, oysters, squid (we tolerated squid), frogs' legs, and goat.

Our tent was called the Good Companions Tent, aptly named because there wasn't a square inch of extra space once we were inside with our gear. There were times on that trip when we were something less than good companions. Basil drove and I navigated. I sometimes have trouble with left and right, sometimes with north and south, and invariably with east and west (rightly or wrongly, I blame this handicap on being left-handed). Dialogue would run something like this:

"Maybe we were supposed to turn left at that crossroad."

"Why didn't you tell me?"

"I didn't have time."

"What do you mean? You had at least five miles."

"Well, it wasn't enough, because I have to picture myself lying on my back on the map with my arms pointing east and west and my head pointing north. That takes time. Especially in Portuguese."

"Good grief!"

"Just turn around and turn left. Or would that now be right?"

Husband, Basil Johnston

"You have the map upside down."

"I know. That's because we're heading south."

"!*&$!!#@!!"

Miraculously, our marriage survived.

Basil began his orthopaedic residency the next year in Kingston, Ontario, and I got a job in a rehabilitation centre until we began having children, our first daughter, Leslie, in 1967 and our second daughter, Lauren, in 1968. We moved to Toronto for Basil's final year and in 1970 he began his practice in Peterborough.

Then we started house hunting. We had almost no money and knew that the sensible thing was to look for a small, affordable place to tide us over until we did have some money, but we both had dreams. Our dreams were of having more children, of having space enough for them to ride tricycles, of having rooms to spread out in. Each time the real-estate agent took us through the sort of house we could afford we tried to see its possibilities but ended by shaking our heads.

Twice we drove past a big old redbrick house with a sprawling veranda across the front and a For Sale sign on the lawn. The third time we passed it I said, "Why don't we look at that one?" The real-estate agent said, "It's considerably bigger than what you said you were looking for and more expensive."

We decided it wouldn't hurt to just look. Inside we saw that it was big but not huge, with lots of rooms, some of them in surprising places, a good place to play hide-and-seek. It had fireplaces in three of the downstairs rooms (and one upstairs) and you could, if you wanted, ride a tricycle through the front hall to the back hall, through the kitchen, out the other kitchen door, through the pantry, through the dining room and the living room, and back out to the front hall, making a complete circle. We signed on the dotted line (after the promise of loans from our parents).

Our third daughter, Andrea, was born in 1972 and our fourth daughter, Melissa, in 1973. Four seemed like a good place to stop. Older people said to us, "My, my, four daughters. Think of all those weddings!" I just laughed and thought, weddings! Why would I think of weddings? They're only tiny children.

That seemed like only yesterday. Now I'm thinking about weddings!

It turned out to be a wonderful house, as I knew it would after the first night we spent in it. During the night I woke up and heard what sounded like chuckling, as if someone were being tickled. My only explanation, unscientific as it may be, is that we had a happy little ghost living with us. It was a great place for our kids, who got up to all sorts of tricks when my back was turned, some I didn't hear about until years later.

They used to take the mattress out of the crib and toboggan down the third-floor stairs on it. They used to hide in the laundry chute at a spot where it took a slight bend before the final eight-foot drop to the cellar. The laundry chute was a continuing source of exploration. A variety of things other than laundry was pitched into it, including an entire box of Kleenex, tissue by tissue, because, as they explained, they were experimenting with parachutes. Once, when Melissa, the youngest, displayed an unusual rash on her chest and tummy, we discovered that they had been playing hospital with her as the patient. The older kids had operated on her with the edge of a rock and sprayed the incision with furniture polish to cleanse it. And the two little ones once managed to get out onto the roof over the veranda and sat with their legs dangling in space until a neighbour noticed them (shades of Patsy and Paul). They were a handful, but they all turned out to be adventurous and entertaining young women. When they come home for holidays and family gatherings we spend a lot of time telling stories and laughing our heads off.

Eventually, to offset the physical and emotional stimulation provided by my children, I decided some intellectual stimulation was needed. Forthwith, and with many misgivings, I enrolled for one course only in English literature as a part-time student at Trent University in Peterborough. I felt terribly insecure, over-aged, and probably not very bright in comparison with the other students, fresh out of high school, still in the habit of writing essays and exams and answering questions in class. I felt, at first, like a tongue-tied freak.

Nine years and twenty credits later I graduated with an honors degree in English literature. My affectionate ties to

The author's daughters: Leslie, Lauren, Melissa, and Andrea

Trent University were strengthened in May 1996 when I was granted an honorary doctor of letters degree.

During the late 1970s, I began writing down my dreams, some of them every bit as bizarre as my father's had been. Once I dreamt about Margaret and my childhood and wrote down as many childhood memories as I could. All my life I have told myself stories to put myself to sleep (which doesn't say much for the excitement factor of the stories), stories without endings that drifted and changed and melted. I was still doing this but now found that the stories were firming up with something like a plot and they were keeping me awake instead of putting me to sleep. I decided to write one down.

From this tentative beginning I began to write more and more and to start sending my work to editors. My children were all in school now and one March break we invited their cousins to stay for the week, nine kids in all. If the snow remained, I thought, they could ski and go sliding and be out of doors all week. Well, it rained. The skies simply opened up and stayed open, day after sloppy day. So I wrote them a play.

There were three boys and six girls ranging in age from about four to thirteen. I wrote customized roles for each of them, typed and made copies of the script, and sent them off through the house to find costumes. Our old steamer trunk, the one that had accompanied us to London, was now used for storing Halloween costumes and old grown-up dresses, hats, and shoes we'd collected over the years for dress-up games. By rearranging some of the furniture in our front room (reminiscently called the drawing room) we had a stage for the play, a takeoff on an old-fashioned, English drawing-room mystery, appropriately enough. We were ready for production by the day the aunts and uncles came to collect their children.

Our drawing room has wide sliding doors opening into the front hall, where we seated the audience, and another door leading into what is now my study, which became the wings, the off-stage area through which the actors made their entrances and exits. We had a very enthusiastic audience who gave us rave reviews.

That summer we took the play on the road, at least as far as the lake. We did it again at the cottage with a few cast changes and a larger audience. Flushed with success I wrote another play a year later including nearly all the neighbourhood kids and this also got a repeat performance at the lake. I don't know whether this early exposure to theatre was the cause or not, but one of my daughters, Lauren, acted in high-school plays and at university intended to major in drama had she not, through a timetable fluke, become sidetracked by the study of economics. One of my nephews, David Matheson, took up serious acting and had a starring role in a movie called *The Blue Line,* as well as roles in several other screen and TV productions. He's now a member of a music group called Moxy Fruvous.

At about this time I got wind of the Canadian playwriting competition. Feeling I had nothing to lose I wrote a serious one-act play, entered it in this national contest, and to my astonishment won first prize. Three weeks later I had a letter from *Chatelaine* magazine saying that they wanted to publish a story I had sent them, and a few weeks after that a British magazine accepted another

story. It was a banner year and just as well because for about the next seven, dividing my time in three parts, family, university studies, and writing, I had very few things published, although I continued to put stories and magazine articles into the mail. The only thing that made me keep on trying was that initial good luck.

In about 1984 I took up writing in earnest. I talked to the renowned Canadian writer Timothy Findley, who encouraged me to attempt a novel. I finished writing *Hero of Lesser Causes* in 1986, sent it to a small but prestigious publisher, and waited. Weeks turned into months. When I finally heard from them they said they liked the idea and they liked the characters, but work was needed to pull the story together. I rewrote it and sent it back and again, after many weeks and months, they said it was a little better but not good enough. They said that they had very little experience with adolescent fiction and had reluctantly decided not to accept it.

I rewrote it and sent it to other publishers who sent it back eventually, saying in essence, thanks but no thanks. Personally, I thought it was a pretty good manuscript. I knew it had some strong features and I also knew it had problems. I just didn't know enough about writing to pinpoint those problems. I thought that if only I had an advisor, if only I knew an expert who could point out the weaknesses to me, I would benefit. No experts appeared on my doorstep so I stuck the manuscript in the back of a cupboard and started another novel, the one that was to become *Adam and Eve and Pinch-me.*

As time passed I met a writer named Budge Wilson who told me that the first publisher I had tried with my first manuscript had hired a children's editor and that maybe I should phone or write to her. With my fingers crossed I phoned and she asked me to send the manuscript. Many more weeks passed before I heard back from Kathy Lowinger, the new editor. Right away she said she liked the story but it needed revision and that if I wanted to continue to work on it she would be happy to have another look at it. In a letter she did exactly what I had been wishing for; she pinpointed the weaknesses and described various ways to fix them. I revised the first three chapters and sent them to her and when she phoned back she said, "If the rest is as good as this, I think we have a book here."

I put in many more months of work on it until finally in December of 1989 the publisher, Lester & Orpen Denys, sent me a contract, but before it was signed and the deal finalized, the publishing company folded. The story, however, has a happy ending. One of the publishers, Malcolm Lester, formed his own company, hired Kathy, and agreed to publish my manuscript, which he did in 1992, six years after I had first sent it out.

One of the biggest hurdles I have to overcome in my writing is structuring a suspenceful plot. It was apparent in the first book and then again with the second. I worked equally as hard on it, putting in many months revising, shifting story elements, and sharpening its focus until I was satisfied with the way it was coming together.

It's unexpected when something you've worked hard on receives recognition, but indescribably gratifying when it does. My books have won several awards, including, each of them, the Governor General's Literary Award.

"The Dulmage Sisters' Circus": Kathie, Diane, and Julie

I once made a wish that I could be a busy writer, so busy with writing and writing concerns that I wouldn't have time to agonize over trifles or analyse the state of my mental health. Most of my wish came true. My time is almost completely taken up with writing, travelling to do readings, to give speeches, and to take part in workshops. I still agonize over trivial decisions, but I have very little spare time to do anything other than write. Basil and I travel some times when we can get away. Some of our best trips have been bicycling with friends in Europe, seeing again the places we visited when we were newly married, and discovering new sights, new foods, and new cultures.

I believe I'm happiest when I'm writing and even on a holiday I take work with me, especially if I'm revising something. The first draft of a book is exciting, but hard slogging. Transferring a story from the inside of your head to what you hope will be the inside of someone else's head, weaving its intricate parts engagingly, and tying up loose ends demands extreme concentration, sharp wits, and a good memory. It seems to take forever. Revising is like taking an ordinary knife and whipping it back and forth across a steel until it has an edge, until it has a point, until it will deftly cut out and define a slice of life.

I still spend every summer at the lake. In 1986 we built our own winterized cottage on the mainland just behind one end of the island. My sisters and their families use the family cottage and we join them regularly for swims or drinks or a meal. Judy and Ross have the other cottage on the island so we see them, too. Our children grew up on the lake and still love to spend holiday time there. We still have our old boats, wooden, and not very fast, but they suit us. The maple tree house was destroyed by lightning and the pine climbing tree was cut down to widen the road. The footbridge was exchanged for a car bridge, but the shape of the land remains unchanged. The rocky shoreline still catches the setting sun and diamonds still dance on the water.

My mother sold the house on William Street in 1985 and when it came time to dispose of the furniture and dishes and all the things that were familiar to us since childhood, Diane and Kathie and I moved back into the house to sort and divide everything. Our mother was sick in hospital at the time so we were on our own, no kids, no husbands, just the Dulmage Sisters' Circus. We dredged up ancient clothes and modelled them, we pored over old pictures and letters, and ooo-ed and aah-ed sentimentally over nearly everything. We laughed and cried and laughed again until we realized that we had to get serious and get the work done.

In the attic we found a framed picture of Grandma Dulmage at about age eighteen. She was extremely pretty and soft-featured and didn't resemble the grandmother I remembered in any way. Her name was Jenny, a lighthearted name, a youthful name. That afternoon I had tried on an old pair of lace-up boots that had been hers; Diane remembered her wearing them in the garden. They fit me perfectly, right down to the bulge at the side of the big toe joint for her bunions, which I unluckily inherited.

I placed her picture on the dresser in my old room (formerly Margaret's) and spent time looking at it and trying to imagine what her life had been like. That night I awakened sensing that something had brushed the thumb of my left hand (the one I sucked as a child). I thought it might have been a bat. All the houses we've lived in from time to time have had bats; I was attuned to bats. But there was no swoop of wings, no stirring of the air. There was something, though. I was aware of pressure at the foot of the bed as if someone had just sat down. I sprang up, but could see nothing and eventually drifted off to sleep again. I like to think that the ghost of Jenny wanted to tell me something, that she hadn't always been a furious, impotent old woman and that I shouldn't look only at the surface of things, but should look deeper even if it means going down deep into the cellar of the mind.

I have one more house to describe, our winterized cottage where we spend many weekends and holidays throughout the year. It is a house of windows overlooking the lake on three sides. There is no drawing room, no cellar, as such, just open spaces and places to lounge and read and watch movies and play Scrabble. It is built up high at the front and feels like a tree house. We've had families of Canada geese, ducks, and loons as neighbours as well as beavers and muskrats, mink and otters. Deer live year round in the woods nearby and sometimes we see a fox and in winter hear wolves. Once the lake is frozen in winter my husband and I and our children when they are there like to walk at night across the ice and marvel at the abundance of stars and the cool brilliance of the moon.

This is where I come to explore the inside of my head and the depths of my soul. This is the place above all others that provides me with continuity, with a sense of well-being and with a sense of identity, things I find important to my ability to write and to live, which for me, now, are one and the same. Good fortune is a capricious, elusive thing. I'm grateful that I've had and have been able to hold so much of it.

Writings

FOR YOUNG ADULTS

There's Going to Be a Frost (one-act play), first produced at the Sears Drama Festival, 1980.

Lucid Intervals (one-act play), first produced at the Sears Drama Festival, 1984.

Hero of Lesser Causes (also see below), Lester Publishing (Toronto, Ontario, Canada), 1992, Little, Brown (Boston, MA), 1993.

Adam and Eve and Pinch-Me, Little, Brown (Boston, MA), 1994.

The Only Outcast, Tundra Books (Plattsburgh, NY), 1998.

(Editor) *Love Ya Like a Sister: A Story of Friendship: From the Journals of Katie Ouriou,* Tundra Books (Plattsburgh, NY), 1999.

In Spite of Killer Bees, McClelland & Stewart (Toronto, Ontario, Canada), 2001.

Also author of a screenplay based on *Hero of Lesser Causes,* Roy Krost Productions, 1994. Contributor of the novella *The Window Seat* to *Women's Weekly Omnibus,* 1984, and the story "Mirrors" to the anthology *The Blue Jean Collection,* Thistledown Press, 1992. Contributor of fiction to periodicals, including *Women's Weekly Buzz, Chatelaine, Woman and Home,* and *Matrix;* contributor of nonfiction to periodicals, including *Wine Tidings, Homemakers, Doctor's Review, and Canadian Author* and *Bookman.* Johnston's novels have been translated into French, Danish, Dutch, German, and Italian.

JOHNSTON, Susan Taylor 1942-
(Tony Johnston)

Personal

Born January 30, 1942, in Los Angeles, CA; daughter of David Leslie (a golf professional) and Ruth (Hunter) Taylor; married Roger D. Johnston (a banker), June 25, 1966; children: Jennifer, Samantha, Ashley. *Education:* Attended University of California—Berkeley, 1959-61; Stanford University, B.A., 1963, M.Ed., 1964. *Hobbies and other interests:* Cooking, tennis, archaeology, collecting dance masks and Latin American textiles.

Addresses

Home—2480 South Oak Knoll Ave., San Marino, CA 91108-2430.

Career

Children's author. Teacher in public elementary schools, Pasadena, CA, 1964-66; McGraw-Hill Publishing Company, New York, NY, editing supervisor, 1966-68; Harper & Row Publishers, Inc., New York, NY, copy editor of children's books, 1969.

Awards, Honors

Children's Choice Award, Harris County Public Library, 1979, for *Four Scary Stories; The Quilt Story* was named a 1986 Children's Choice Book; Outstanding Literary Quality in a Picture Book, Southern California Council on Literature for Children and Young People, 1989, for *Yonder;* Parents' Choice Award for Children's Books, 1992, for *Slither McCreep and His Brother, Joe.*

Writings

UNDER PSEUDONYM TONY JOHNSTON

The Adventures of Mole and Troll, illustrated by Wallace Tripp, Putnam (New York, NY), 1972.

Fig Tale, illustrated by Giulio Maestro, Putnam (New York, NY), 1974.

Mole and Troll Trim the Tree, illustrated by Wallace Tripp, Putnam (New York, NY), 1974.

Odd Jobs, illustrated by Tomie dePaola, Putnam (New York, NY), 1977.

Five Little Foxes and the Snow, illustrated by Cyndy Szekeres, Putnam (New York, NY), 1977.

Four Scary Stories, illustrated by Tomie dePaola, Putnam (New York, NY), 1978.

Little Mouse Nibbling, illustrated by Diane Stanley, Putnam (New York, NY), 1979.

Dedos de Luna (title means "Moon Fingers"), Secretaria de Educacion Publica (Mexico City, Mexico), 1979.

Odd Jobs and Friends, illustrated by Tomie dePaola, Putnam (New York, NY), 1982.

The Vanishing Pumpkin, illustrated by Tomie dePaola, Putnam (New York, NY), 1983.

El Regalo (title means "The Present"), Secretaria de Educacion Publica (Mexico City, Mexico), 1984.

Bestias Fantasticas (title means "Fantastic Beasts"), Secretaria de Educacion Publica (Mexico City, Mexico), 1984.

The Witch's Hat, illustrated by Margot Tomes, Bantam (New York, NY), 1984.

The Quilt Story, illustrated by Tomie dePaola, Putnam (New York, NY), 1985.

Farmer Mack Measures His Pig, illustrated by Megan Lloyd, Harper (New York, NY), 1986.

Whale Song, illustrated by Ed Young, Putnam (New York, NY), 1987.

Yonder, illustrated by Lloyd Bloom, Dial Books for Young Readers (New York, NY), 1988.

Pages of Music, illustrated by Tomie dePaola, Putnam (New York, NY), 1988.

Happy Birthday, Mole and Troll, Dell (New York, NY), 1989.

Night Noises and Other Mole and Troll Stories, illustrated by Cyndy Szekeres, Dell (New York, NY), 1989.

My Friend Bear, Ladybird Books (London, England), 1989.

The Badger and the Magic Fan: A Japanese Folktale, illustrated by Tomie dePaola, Putnam (New York, NY), 1990.

The Soup Bone, illustrated by Margot Tomes, Harcourt (San Diego, CA), 1990.

I'm Gonna Tell Mama I Want an Iguana (poems), illustrated by Lillian Hoban, Putnam (New York, NY), 1990.

Grandpa's Song, illustrated by Brad Sneed, Dial Books for Young Readers (New York, NY), 1991.

Goblin Walk, illustrated by Bruce Degen, Putnam (New York, NY), 1991.

Little Bear Sleeping, illustrated by Lillian Hoban, Putnam (New York, NY), 1991.

The Promise, illustrated by Pamela Keavney, Harper (New York, NY), 1992.

The Cowboy and the Blackeyed Pea, illustrated by Warren Ludwig, Putnam (New York, NY), 1992.

Slither McCreep and His Brother, Joe, illustrated by Victoria Chess, Harcourt (San Diego, CA), 1992.

Lorenzo, the Naughty Parrot, illustrated by Leo Politi, Harcourt (San Diego, CA), 1992.

The Last Snow of Winter, illustrated by Friso Henstra, Morrow (New York, NY), 1993, published as an electronic book, iPictureBooks (New York, NY), 2001.

The Tale of Rabbit and Coyote, illustrated by Tomie dePaola, Putnam (New York, NY), 1994.

My Mexico = Mexico mio, illustrated by John F. Sierra, Putnam (New York, NY), 1994.

Three Little Bikers, illustrated by Brian G. Karas, Knopf (New York, NY), 1994.

The Old Lady and the Birds, illustrated by Stephanie Garcia, Harcourt (San Diego, CA), 1994.

Little Rabbit Goes to Sleep, illustrated by Harvey Stevenson, HarperCollins (New York, NY), 1994.

Amber on the Mountain, illustrated by Robert Duncan, Dial Books for Young Readers (New York, NY), 1994.

Alice Nizzy Nazzy: The Witch of Santa Fe, illustrated by Tomie dePaola, Putnam (New York, NY), 1995.

The Iguana Brothers, illustrated by Mark Teague, Scholastic (New York, NY), 1995.

Very Scary, illustrated by Douglas Florian, Harcourt (San Diego, CA), 1995.

How Many Miles to Jacksonville?, illustrated by Bart Forbes, Putnam (New York, NY), 1995.

Little Wild Parrot, Tambourine Books (New York, NY), 1995.

The Bull and the Fire Truck, Scholastic (New York, NY), 1996.

Fishing Sunday, Tambourine Books (New York, NY), 1996, published as an electronic book, iPictureBook (New York, NY), 2002.

The Ghost of Nicholas Greebe, Dial Books for Young Readers, (New York, NY), 1996.

The Magic Maguey, Harcourt (San Diego, CA), 1996.

Once in the Country: Poems of a Farm, Putnam (New York, NY), 1996.

The Wagon, Tambourine Books (New York, NY), 1996.

Day of the Dead, Harcourt (San Diego, CA), 1997.

Isabel's House of Butterflies, Sierra Club Books for Children (San Francisco, CA), 1997.

We Love the Dirt, illustrated by Alexa Brandenberg, Scholastic (New York, NY), 1997.

Sparky and Eddie: The First Day of School, illustrated by Susannah Ryan, Scholastic Press (New York, NY), 1997.

Trail of Tears, Blue Sky Press (New York, NY), 1998.

The Chizzywink and the Alamagoozlum, Holiday House (New York, NY), 1998.

Boo!: A Ghost Story that Could Be True, Scholastic (New York, NY), 1998.

Sparky and Eddie: Trouble with Bugs, illustrated by Susannah Ryan, Scholastic (New York, NY), 1998.

Sparky and Eddie: Wild, Wild Rodeo! illustrated by Susannah Ryan, Scholastic (New York, NY), 1998.

Bigfoot Cinderrrrrella, Putnam (New York, NY), 1998.

An Old Shell: Poems of the Galápagos, Farrar, Straus (New York, NY), 1999.

Big Red Apple, Scholastic (New York, NY), 1999.

It's about Dogs, Harcourt (San Diego, CA), 2000.

Uncle Rain Cloud, illustrated by Fabricio Vanden Broeck, Charlesbridge (Watertown, MA), 2000.

The Barn Owls, Charlesbridge (Watertown, MA), 2000.

Any Small Goodness: A Novel of the Barrio, Blue Sky Press (New York, NY), 2000.

The Whole Green World, illustrated by Jon J. Muth, Farrar, Straus (New York, NY), 2001.

Angel City, Philomel Books (New York, NY), 2001.

Alien and Possum: Friends No Matter What, Simon & Schuster Books for Young Readers (New York, NY), 2001.

Cat, What Is That? HarperCollins (New York, NY), 2001.

My Best Friend Bear, illustrated by Joy Allen, Rising Moon (Flagstaff, AZ), 2001.

Clear Moon, Snow Soon, illustrated by Guy Porfirio, Rising Moon (Flagstaff, AZ), 2001.

Desert Dog, illustrated by Robert Weatherford, Sierra Club Books for Children (San Francisco, CA), 2001.

Gopher up Your Sleeve, illustrated by Trip Park, Rising Moon (Flagstaff, AZ), 2001.

Mummy's Mother, Blue Sky Press (New York, NY), 2002.

Sticky People, Morrow (New York, NY), 2002.

That Summer, illustrated by Barry Moser, Harcourt (San Diego, CA), 2002.

Sunsets of the West, illustrated by Ted Lewin, Putnam (New York, NY), 2002.

Alien and Possum Hanging Out, illustrated by Tony DiTerlizzi, Simon & Schuster (New York, NY), 2002.

Go Track a Yak, illustrated by Tim Raglin, Simon & Schuster (New York, NY), 2003.

Contributor to textbooks. Contributor to periodicals, including *Cricket.*

Sidelights

Susan Taylor Johnston, who writes under the pseudonym Tony Johnston, is a prolific author of books for preschool and grade school age children. Her works include fiction and nonfiction, picture books, and early readers. A number of her books feature quirky characters—both human and animal—in a variety of unusual situations. Others focus on historical or contemporary themes. Some are bilingual or feature Spanish words intermingled with the largely English texts.

Johnston was born in Los Angeles and grew up in nearby San Marino. As a child, she loved reading and books, including *The Elephant's Child, Robin Hood,* and *The Count of Monte Cristo.* But she was most impressed by the fantasies of J. R. R. Tolkien. She told a *Junior Literary Guild* contributor that her interest in writing was "partly a desire to be in that other world of fantasy and partly an attempt to transfer to paper the traces that keep popping up from time to time to take me back—traces of childhood." After graduating from Stanford University, Johnston taught for two years at a public school in Pasadena; she then moved to New York City, where she worked for a number of years as an editing supervisor and a copy editor for children's books.

One experience in particular, which involved a snowy Christmas Day in New Hampshire, was the inspiration for the popular "Mole and Troll" stories. The first book of the series, *The Adventures of Mole and Troll,* was published in 1972, followed by *Mole and Troll Trim the Tree* (which was based on the author's memories of her own real-life Christmases), *Night Noises and Other Mole and Troll Stories,* and *Happy Birthday, Mole and Troll.* A *Booklist* reviewer described the duo as "two of the more worthwhile recurring easy-reader actors: they're ingenuous and distinct, and they regularly show evidence of a remarkable likeness-of-soul to their audience."

Not all of Johnston's stories feature animals as the main character. *Odd Jobs* features an enterprising young man who will take on any job that is offered, including washing the dirtiest dog in town, standing in for a friend

Triangle eyes that stared.

Raggedy eyebrows that glared.

A delicious-looking pumpkin escapes being eaten when it is carved into a scary jack-o'lantern in Johnston's lighthearted Halloween tale. (From Very Scary, *illustrated by Douglas Florian.)*

at dance class, and guarding a balloon from a brat with a pin. A critic for *Booklist* praised the fact that Johnston had "created a resilient, inventive character and put him into laughable situations."

Animals return to the forefront in *Five Little Foxes and the Snow* (which was also inspired by the author's Christmas memories of New Hampshire) and *Little Mouse Nibbling*. The latter tells of a very shy mouse who stays inside nibbling at this and that until a cricket brings Christmas carolers to her door. A *Publishers Weekly* contributor stated that this "unabashedly sentimental Christmas fantasy should find its way under many a Yuletide tree for years to come."

The next three Johnston stories revolve around neither children nor animals, but unusual objects. In *The Vanishing Pumpkin* a seven-hundred-year-old woman and an eight-hundred-year-old man meet a ghoul, a rapscallion, and a varmint as they search for their missing Halloween pumpkin. The headgear featured in *The Witch's Hat*, a tale that *School Library Journal* contributor Kay McPherson called "fresh and funny," falls into the witch's magic pot and turns into a bat, a rat, and a cat before the story is over. *The Quilt Story* is about Abigail, a young girl who finds comfort and companionship in a midnight-blue appliqued quilt her mother made for her. She and her family travel out West via covered wagon to settle the new frontier. The quilt is eventually stored away in the attic, where, one hundred years later, it is discovered by another little girl, who finds it a comfort when her family moves.

Johnston's books are often written in a rhythmic, poetic style. *Whale Song,* which a *Kirkus Reviews* contributor deemed "a stunningly beautiful evocation of the gentle giants of the deep," is actually a counting book; the numbers represent the song that travels from whale to whale. The 1988 work *Yonder* is based on a Johnston family tradition in which trees are planted to commemorate the births and deaths of members of her family. "With the eloquent simplicity of a Shaker hymn, Tony Johnston's words capture the cyclical pattern of a farming way of life," Hanna B. Zeiger stated in *Horn Book*. Johnston's poetic efforts continued with her collection titled *I'm Gonna Tell Mama I Want an Iguana*. The mostly humorous poems on such diverse subjects as sunset, frogs' eggs, skeletons, and jellyfish were described by Tiffany Chrisman in *Children's Book Review Service* as a collection that "does much to stretch the imaginative powers" of its readers.

In 1992 Johnston's *Slither McCreep and His Brother, Joe* won a Parents' Choice Award for Children's Books. Slither and Joe have the usual problems of fighting and sharing that most siblings have. Most unusually, however, these two siblings are boa constrictors who go around squeezing, swallowing, and ruining each other's possessions. *Wilson Library Bulletin* reviewers Donnarae MacCann and Olga Richard commented that *Slither McCreep* "offers family realism plus one of the most zany, surreal settings imaginable." *Bigfoot Cinderrrrrella* tells the story of Ella the Bigfoot and her romance

with a prince in a "silly twist on a favorite fairy tale" that takes care of the romance question "with humor and style," according to a *Publishers Weekly* contributor. It is a "howlingly funny take on the original," applauded Ellen Mandel in *Booklist*. Similarly, *The Chizzywink and the Alamogoozlum* presents the tale of a marauding giant mosquito and how its intentions are foiled by a healthy dose of maple syrup. Writing in *Booklist*, Susan Dove Lempke complimented Johnston's use of "rich language and a rhythm" in a book amply suited to reading aloud. If the prospect of a giant mosquito is scary, then the *Ghost of Nicholas Greebe* is even more so. Yet this tale, in the words of Ann A. Flowers of *Horn Book,* is really a "not too spooky story" about a man whose bones are dug up by a dog and how as a ghost he must retrieve them.

The setting for several of Johnston's books, including *Lorenzo, the Naughty Parrot, The Old Lady and the Birds, My Mexico = Mexico mio, Uncle Rain Cloud, Day of the Dead,* and *The Magic Maguey,* reflects the fact that she and her family have lived in Mexico for several years. Setting is also an important component of Johnston's 1994 story *Amber on the Mountain.* Amber lives in an isolated mountain community that has no school or teacher; she has never even learned to read. However, when a man comes to build a mountain road (a seemingly impossible task), his daughter sets herself the just-as-impossible task of teaching Amber to read. When the road is completed, the man and his daughter leave, and Amber must now teach herself to write so that she can keep in touch with her new friend. A *Kirkus Reviews* critic stated that "Johnston's beautifully honed narrative glows with mountain imagery and the warmth of the girls' friendship," and a reviewer in *Publishers Weekly* called it a "heartwarming story" with "lyrical images and picturesque and convincing dialogue."

Several of Johnston's "Mexican" books are bilingual or interlace English and Spanish. *My Mexico = Mexico mio* contains eighteen short poems in English and Spanish versions, while *Uncle Rain Cloud* and *Day of the Dead* intermingle Spanish in the mostly English texts. *Uncle Rain Cloud* recounts the story of an uncle who needs his nephew to translate for him and how this difficulty causes him embarrassment. *Booklist* reviewer Hazel Rochman called the book, "funny" and "touching," adding, "Johnston's text is clear and poetic." "Brisk pacing, sympathetic characters, and clear prose ... effectively make a winner," concluded Ann Welton in *School Library Journal* about *Uncle Rain Cloud*. In *Day of the Dead* Johnston presents the customs surrounding this Mexican holiday of celebrating ancestors in a "dazzling little volume," asserted a *Publishers Weekly* reviewer.

Among Johnston's books for beginning readers are *Alien and Possum: Friends No Matter What* and *Sparky and Eddie: The First Day of School, Sparky and Eddie: Wild, Wild Rodeo, Sparky and Eddie: Trouble with Bugs,* and *The Bull and the Fire Truck.* When a possum sees a spaceship crash near his home in *Alien and Possum* he is in for excitement, befriending an alien visitor and learning about tolerance. The work elicited praise for its humor. According to a *Publishers Weekly* contributor, the "springy pace, lively dialogue and Alien's silly sound effects," will appeal to the younger set. In *Booklist,* Carolyn Phelan remarked on the author's "ready wit and understanding of a child's perspective"; "droll and expressive language helps to add a little humor," a *Kirkus Reviews* critic noted. In the first volume of the "Sparky and Eddie" series, the close friends are looking forward to the first day of school, until they learn they will be in different classes; in the second installment they compete in the class rodeo. *Booklist* reviewer Hazel Rochman described the text of *Sparky and Eddie: The First Day of School* as "exuberant," while Phelan judged *Sparky and Eddie: Wild, Wild Rodeo* to be a "highly entertaining entry in a fine series."

Johnston has also written nonfiction and poetic treatments of animals. *It's about Dogs* is a collection of forty short poems, including rhymed quatrains, haiku, and blank verse; in *Cat, What Is That?* she takes a similar poetic look at felines. According to Margaret Bush in *School Library Journal, It's about Dogs* contains "poignant moments as well as funny [moments] in this richly rendered tribute." "Johnston's compact rhymes [are] often astonishingly apt," a *Publishers Weekly* critic wrote in a review of *Cat, What Is That?.* Johnston considers mysterious creatures in *The Barn Owls,* a lyrical exploration of a family of owls living in an old barn in California. She went further afield for her *An Old Shell: Poems of the Galápagos,* a poetic look at the interesting creatures of these isolated islands.

Johnston once explained to *SATA,* "I write because I'd rather not iron (and also because I love to). My work habits are lousy. I sit either with a dog in my lap or a dog underneath me if she gets to the chair first. My goal in writing is simply to entertain—myself and someone else. If I manage to stir up a little love of language or make someone laugh or feel good about himself or go back to the library for another book along the way, well, that's all pink frosting on the cake."

Biographical and Critical Sources

BOOKS

Authors of Books for Young People, Scarecrow Press (Metuchen, NJ), 1990.

PERIODICALS

Booklist, October 15, 1974, p. 244; March 15, 1977, review of *Night Noises and Other Mole and Troll Stories,* p. 1097; November 15, 1977, review of *Odd Jobs,* p. 559; January 1, 1984, p. 682; May 1, 1990, p. 1704; December 15, 1993, p. 764; May 15, 1996, Kay Weisman, review of *Fishing Sunday,* p. 1592; July, 1996, Stephanie Zvirin, review of *The Ghost of Nicholas Greebe,* p. 1829; October 15, 1996, Annie Ayres, review of *The Magic Maguey,* pp. 435-436, and Michael Cart, review of *How Many Miles to Jacksonville?,* p. 435; January 1, 1997, Carolyn Phelan, review of *The Wagon,* p. 869; February 1, 1997, Carolyn Phelan, review of *The Bull and the Fire Truck,* p. 949; August, 1997, Carolyn Phelan, review of *Sparky and*

Eddie: The First Day of School, p. 1910; September 15, 1997, Hazel Rochman, review of *Day of the Dead,* p. 242; February 1, 1998, Hazel Rochman, review of *Sparky and Eddie: The First Day of School,* p. 926; May 1, 1998, Carolyn Phelan, review of *Sparky and Eddie: Wild, Wild Rodeo,* p. 1524; June 1, 1998, Susan Dove Lempke, review of *The Chizzywink and the Alamagoozlum,* pp. 1779-1780; December 1, 1998, Ellen Mandel, review of *Bigfoot Cinderrrrella,* p. 668; December 1, 1999, GraceAnne A. DeCandido, review of *An Old Shell: Poems of the Galápagos,* p. 700; February 15, 2000, Todd Morning, review of *The Barn Owls,* p. 1118; March 15, 2000, John Peters, review of *It's about Dogs,* p. 1383; October 1, 2000, Gillian Engberg, review of *Desert Song,* p. 336; February 15, 2001, Hazel Rochman, review of *Uncle Rain Cloud,* p. 1134; July, 2001, Carolyn Phelan, review of *Alien and Possum: Friends No Matter What,* p. 2023; November 1, 2001, Ilene Cooper, review of *Clear Moon, Snow Soon,* p. 482.

Bulletin of the Center for Children's Books, December, 1974, p. 64; May, 1995, pp. 311-312.

Catholic Library World, March, 1973, p. 512.

Children's Book Review Service, December, 1983, p. 38; December 19, 1990, review of *I'm Gonna Tell Mama I Want an Iguana,* p. 39; October, 1992, p. 19.

Horn Book, July-August, 1988, Hanna B. Zeiger, review of *Yonder,* p. 480; September, 1990, p. 610; May-June, 1996, Nancy Vasilakis, review of *My Mexico = Mexico Mio,* p. 345; November-December, 1996, Ann A. Flowers, review of *The Ghost of Nicholas Greebe,* pp. 725-726; January-February, 1997, Anne Deifendeifer, review of *Once in the Country: Poems of a Farm,* p. 74.

Junior Bookshelf, April, 1975, p. 98.

Junior Literary Guild, September, 1974, review of *Mole and Troll Trim the Tree,* p. 23.

Kirkus Reviews, August 15, 1972, p. 938; December 15, 1974, p. 1302; December 1, 1977, p. 1263; August 15, 1987, review of *Whale Song,* p. 1241; August 15, 1991, p. 1097; June 15, 1994, review of *Amber on the Mountain,* p. 847; July 15, 1994, p. 987; August 1, 2001, review of *Alien & Possum: Friends No Matter What,* p. 1126.

Library Journal, December 15, 1972, p. 4085.

New York Times Book Review, October 8, 1972, p. 8; December 11, 1977, p. 26.

Publishers Weekly, May 7, 1979, review of *Little Mouse Nibbling,* p. 83; October 19, 1984, p. 48; October 19, 1992, p. 76; June 16, 1994, review of *Amber on the Mountain,* p. 63; July 4, 1994, p. 60; October 9, 1995, review of *Little Wild Parrot,* p. 85; October 21, 1996, review of *The Magic Maguey,* p. 82; September 1, 1997, review of *Day of the Dead,* p. 103; March 30, 1998, review of *The Chizzywink and the Alamogoozlum,* p. 81; November 2, 1998, review of *Bigfoot Cinderrrrella,* p. 81; October 4, 1999, review of *The Ghost of Nicholas Greebe,* p. 77; November 8, 1999, review of *An Old Shell,* p. 67; January 31, 2000, review of *The Barn Owls,* p. 105; September 11, 2000, review of *Day of the Dead,* p. 93; September 25, 2000, review of *Desert Song,* p. 118; October 30, 2000, review of *Bigfoot Cinderrrrella,* p. 78; February 26,

2001, review of *My Best Friend Bear,* p. 84; July 30, 2001, review of *Cat, What Is That?,* p. 83; September 24, 2001, review of *Clear Moon, Snow Soon,* p. 52, review of *Alien and Possum: Friends No Matter What,* p. 93.

Quill and Quire, September, 1992, p. 78.

School Library Journal, October, 1978, p. 135; October, 1979, p. 117; December, 1984, Kay McPherson, review of *The Witch's Hat,* p. 72; June, 1990, p. 114; March, 2000, Sue Sherif, review of *The Barn Owl,* p. 208; June, 2000, Margaret Bush, review of *It's about Dogs,* p. 167; December, 2000, Daryl Grabarek, review of *Desert Song,* p. 112; April, 2001, Ann Welton, review of *Uncle Rain Cloud,* p. 113; August, 2001, Susan Marie Pitard, review of *My Best Friend Bear,* p. 154; October, 2001, review of *Clear Moon, Snow Soon,* p. 66; November, 2001, Ruth Semaru, review of *Desert Dog,* p. 126.

Teacher Librarian, March, 1999, Shirley Lewis, review of *Bigfoot Cinderrrrrella,* p. 44.

Times Educational Supplement, January 18, 1980, p. 37.

Wilson Library Bulletin, September, 1992, Donnarae MacCann and Olga Richard, review of *Slither McCreep and His Brother, Joe,* p. 90.

OTHER

Children's Literature, http://www.childrenslit.com/ (February 3, 2002), author profile of Tony Johnston.*

*   *   *

JOHNSTON, Tony
See JOHNSTON, Susan Taylor

K

KESELMAN, Gabriela 1953-

Personal

Born June 5, 1953, in Buenos Aires, Argentina; daughter of Simon Keselman (a television director) and Elsa Porter (a teacher); divorced since 1987. *Education:* Attended UBA University (Buenos Aires, Argentina), 1971-73; Cambridge Certificate of Proficiency (Madrid, Spain), 1983.

Addresses

Home—Spain and Argentina. *E-mail*—gabkesel@open-bank.es; gabkesel@ciudad.com.ar.

Career

Author; translator and critic of children's books. *Ser Padres Magazine* (*Parents Magazine*), Madrid, Spain, editor, 1987-98; conducted several kindergarten workshops on creativity, 1980-86. *Member:* Society of Children's Book Writers and Illustrators, OEPLI (Spanish association of children's books).

Awards, Honors

"Best Picture Book for Children," Generalitat de Catalunya, 1997, Honor List Book, IBBY, 1998, and "The 100 Books for Children of the Twentieth Century," GSR Foundation, all for *El Regalo; The Gift* was chosen as one of *Child* magazine's "Best of 1999," awarded a National Association of Parenting Publications (NAPPA) honor, and selected as a "The Best of Children's Media," Parent's Guide to Children's Media, all 1999; *Nadie Quiere Jugar conmigo* was honored by the Spanish Catholic Commission for Childhood (CCEI) in 1998, and *No Quiera lr al Castillo* was also honored by the CCEI in 1999.

Writings

Claudette, illustrated by Pablo Echevarria, Espasa-Calpe (Madrid, Spain), 1992.
Si Tiennes un Papá Mago . . . , illustrated by Avi, Editorial SM (Madrid, Spain), 1995.

Gabriela Keselman

El Oso Pudoroso, illustrated by Arnal Ballester, Editorial SM (Madrid, Spain), 1995.

El Regalo, illustrated by Pep Montserrat, La Galera (Barcelona, Spain), 1996, translation published as *The Gift,* Kane/Miller Book Publishers (New York, NY), 1999.

Por Qué?, illustrated by Pep Brocal and Marc Brocal, La Galera (Barcelona, Spain), 1996.

Nadie Quire Jugar Conmigo, illustrated by Pablo Echecarria, Ediciones SM (Madrid, Spain), 1997.

Hasta la Coronilla, illustrated by Carme Juliá, Grijalbo (Barcelona, Spain), 1997.

Una palabra nueva, illustrated by Sally Cutting, Círculo de Lectores SA (Spain), 1997.

El Primer dís di clase, illustrated by Sally Cutting, Círculo de Lectores (Spain), 1997.

Quién Ha Robado mi Trono?, illustrated by Anne Decis, Bruño (Madrid, Spain), 1997.

Papá se Casó con una Bruja, illustrated by María Fe Quesada, Bruño (Madrid, Spain), 1998.

No Quiera lr al Castillo, illustrated by Anne Decis, Editorial SM (Madrid, Spain), 1998.

Cuántas Cuadras Faltan?, illustrated by Jimena Tello, Alfaguara (Buenos Aires, Argentina), 1998.

Dónde Está mi Tesoro?, illustrated by Silvia Grau, Alfaguara (Buenos Aires, Argentina), 1999.

Loco por Ti, illustrated by Montse Ginesta, Espasa-Calpe (Madrid, Spain), 1999.

Pataletas, illustrated by Pau Estrada, La Galera (Barcelona, Spain), 1999.

Cuándo Viene Papá?, illustrated by Gusti, Ediciones Edebé (Barcelona, Spain), 2000.

Valeria, illustrated by Ana Azpeitia, Espasa Calpe (Madrid, Spain), 2000.

Y Ahora Traeme ..., illustrated by Marcelo Elizalde, Sudamericana (Buenos Aires, Argentina), 2000.

Penny, illustrated by Carmen Peris, Trévol Produccions (Barcelona, Spain), 2000.

Koko, illustrated by Carmen Peris, Trévol Produccions (Barcelona, Spain), 2000.

Tomás, illustrated by Carmen Peris, Trévol Produccions (Barcelona, Spain), 2000.

Monna, illustrated by Carmen Peris, Trévol Produccions (Barcelona, Spain), 2000.

El Regalo (play adaption of *El Regalo*), produced by Compañía Fantasía en Negro (Burgos, Spain), 2000.

Cinco Enfados, illustrated by Marcelo Elizalde, Anaya (Madrid, Spain), 2001.

Hasta la Coronilla, illustrated by Marcelo Elizalde, Alfaguara (Buenos Aires, Argentina), 2001.

Yo Primero, Ediciones SM (Madrid, Spain), 2001.

Ponete nos Zapatos!, Editorial Sudamericana (Buenos Aires, Argentina), 2001.

De Verdad Queno Podía, Kókinos (Madrid, Spain), 2001.

"PLASTILINA, LA SUPER SEÑO" SERIES

Me da vergüenza, illustrated by Marcelo Elizalde, Editorial Atlántida (Buenos Aires, Argentina), 2002.

Mamá llega tarde, illustrated by Marcelo Elizalde, Editorial Atlántida (Buenos Aires, Argentina), 2002.

Tomi me Pegó!, illustrated by Marcelo Elizalde, Editorial Atlántida (Buenos Aires, Argentina), 2002.

Mikie's parents cannot imagine how they can find a gift that fits the description he gives them, but they arrive at a simple, special solution. (From The Gift, *written by Keselman and illustrated by Pep Montserrat.)*

No quiero la merienda, illustrated by Marcelo Elizalde, Editorial Atlántida (Buenos Aires, Argentina), 2002.

OTHER

Keselman's work has been translated into various languages and her publications have been issued in several countries, including Mexico.

Sidelights

Gabriela Keselman told *SATA:* "Authors of children's books are often asked why we do what we do, a question seldom posed to people in other professions. I personally believe that I write in order to ask myself some fundamental questions, including why I write. Regardless, if the question is worth investigating, the clue as to *why* I write lies in *what* I write.

"My characters, boys or girls, bears or princes, live a childhood that seeks, and finds, love. In this process, they need other people, and find them. Thoughtfulness and care are the ground my heroes stand on, even though they sometimes seem to disregard them. In their world, limits are taught with hugs and kisses.

"When I can get myself to write, I prefer to position myself in such a way that I can see both the tender and humorous side of the situation. Tenderness and humor are healing. Words themselves are healing. And spelling the right words out is the greatest magic of all. I need to put that world and myself into words.

"Born and brought up in Argentina, I moved to Spain when I was young. I started out as an editor for a parents magazine and there, while giving out advice to moms and dads, I had the opportunity to write and publish stories for children themselves. In 1992, my first picture book was published and after some years of writing and submitting, this is what I can show today: a nice pile of books for children and for myself, my own collection of spells.

"I love to end my stories with surprising twists, and this reflects my own life as I have now started sharing my time between Spain and Argentina. On both shores, I write and while I'm in the air, too (twelve hour flights are most inspiring). So far, my greatest satisfaction of all was to see one of my favorite books being translated and published in the United States, Switzerland, France, and Korea. At this stage of my career, my dream is to continue publishing in the United States."

Biographical and Critical Sources

PERIODICALS

Kirkus Reviews, November 1, 1999, review of *The Gift.*
School Library Journal, December, 1999, review of *The Gift,* p. 100.

OTHER

Gabriela Keselman Web Site, http://www.gabrielakeselman. com.ar/ (January 28, 2002).

*   *   *

KETCHAM, Hank
See KETCHAM, Henry King

*   *   *

KETCHAM, Henry King 1920-2001 (Hank Ketcham)

OBITUARY NOTICE—See index for *SATA* sketch: Born March 14, 1920, in Seattle, WA; died June 1, 2001, in Pebble Beach, CA. Animator and author. Ketcham was best known for his creation of the *Dennis the Menace* comic strip. Ketcham first became interested in cartooning at the age of six. As a young man he moved to Hollywood and got a job at an advertising agency. Over time, Ketcham worked his way into Disney Studios, where he helped illustrate such works as *Pinocchio* and *Fantasia*. In 1951 Ketcham's Dennis the Menace character caught attention and was syndicated, which allowed the comic to appear in over 200 papers around the world. He wrote and illustrated numerous "Dennis" books including *Dennis the Menace: Happy Half Pint, Dennis the Menace: Short and Snappy, Dennis the Menace: Little Pip-Squeak,* and *Dennis the Menace: The Way I Look at It.* In 1953 Ketcham earned the Billy De Beck Award from the National Cartoonists Society.

OBITUARIES AND OTHER SOURCES:

PERIODICALS

Chicago Tribune, June 2, 2001, section 1 p. 25.
Los Angeles Times, June 2, 2001, pp. A1, A16.
New York Times, June 2, 2001, p. B19.
Washington Post, June 2, 2001, p. B6.

*   *   *

KINDL, Patrice 1951-

Personal

Born October 16, 1951, in Alplaus, NY; daughter of Fred Henry (a mechanical engineer) and Catherine (a homemaker; maiden name, Quinlan) Kindl; married Paul Fredrick Roediger (a mechanical designer), October 16, 1976; children: Alexander. *Education:* Attended Webster College, 1969-70. *Politics:* Democrat. *Hobbies and other interests:* Raising monkeys.

Addresses

Home—116 Middlefort Rd., Middleburgh, NY 12122.

Career

Writer. Worked with Helping Hands, a program which raises and trains monkeys to aid the disabled, 1990-2001.

Awards, Honors

Golden Kite honor book for fiction, Society of Children's Book Writers and Illustrators, 1993, Notable Book and Book for Reluctant Readers, both American Library Association (ALA), *School Library Journal* best book, *Bulletin of the Center for Children's Books* blue

Patrice Kindl

ribbon, and Book for the Teen Age selection, New York Public Library, all for *Owl in Love;* Best Book selection, ALA, Book for the Teen Age selection, New York Public Library, and Austrian Children's and Juveniles' Honor Book Award, 1999, all for *The Woman in the Wall.*

Writings

Owl in Love (young adult fantasy), Houghton Mifflin (Boston, MA), 1993.
The Woman in the Wall (young adult fantasy), Houghton Mifflin (Boston, MA), 1997.
Goose Chase (novel), Houghton Mifflin (Boston, MA), 2001.
Lost in the Labyrinth (young adult fantasy) Houghton Mifflin (Boston, MA), 2002.

Sidelights

Patrice Kindl lets her imagination roam freely in her young adult novels *Owl in Love, The Woman in the Wall,* and *Goose Chase.* In her debut, *Owl in Love,* she recounts the story of a shapeshifter who takes the form of a high school girl by day and an owl at night. Alternating between the first-person narration of both the owl and the girl, the novel centers on Owl's crush on her science teacher, Mr. Lindstrom. According to a *Publishers Weekly* reviewer, *Owl in Love* is a "highly original" debut novel that is witty, "tautly plotted," and "touching."

Kindl once told *SATA:* "When I was three years old my family moved to a Victorian house on a hill. To me it was a small country in itself. It had a cupola full of sunlight and dead flies, enormous attics suitable for imprisoning mad relatives, a butler's pantry, a grand staircase for grand entrances, and a secret, winding stair in a closet. There were miles of corridors and empty rooms, and the cellars were as dark and deep as the Minotaur's maze.

"In short, the house gave me a taste for the Gothic. We lived there for five years. When I was eight we moved to a brand-new split level. I spent the next decade sulking.

"The new house did have a forest behind it, and in the forest was a half-built log cabin. It had no door, windows, or roof, but it was some consolation for my lost kingdom. I spent hours at a time there reading, drawing, writing poetry, and eating too many apples.

"I now own a house with all the romance of my childhood home. Built in 1830, it possesses massive Greek pillars, mysterious little rooms with no obvious purpose, and a giant crypt in the basement."

Perhaps inspired by the Victorian house in which she lived for a time as a child, Kindl's *The Woman in the Wall* revolves around a reclusive young girl named Anna, who disappears metaphorically and figuratively into the walls of her family's twenty-two-room home. Transformed into a mythic figure by her family, Anna

Kindl's imaginative book is narrated by a teenaged girl who becomes an owl by night and finds her crush on her science teacher leads to nocturnal adventures to protect him. (Cover illustration by Will Hillenbrand.)

remains hidden until forced to surface due to the threat posed by her family's move to a new house and the growing emotions caused by her crush on one of the friends visiting her older sister. Calling *The Woman in the Wall* a "challenging read," Martha A. Parravano, writing in *Horn Book,* nonetheless decided that the "wit and craft of Kindl's prose keep pulling you back in."

Goose Chase, Kindl's third novel, is also in the fairy tale vein for it revolves around an orphaned Goose Girl, who happens upon a mysterious woman. In return for the girl's kindness, the old woman gives the girl three gifts. When these gifts result in her newfound beauty and wealth, the Goose Girl finds herself pursued by both a young prince and an evil king. Reviewing the novel in *Horn Book,* a reviewer noted the "appropriately archaic" first-person narration by Alexandria (a.k.a. Goose Girl), and the complex plot. In *School Library Journal,* Connie Tyrrell Burns praised the humor, imagery, alliteration, and nonsense words that "add to the fun," while *Booklist* reviewer Anne O'Malley described the novel as "a delightful, witty fairy-tale spoof," adding that the author's "humor, the strong characterizations, and vibrant action give the story wings."

"Now that I am grown up I write for children because I am still a child at heart," explained Kindl, "fond of reading, animals, and solitude. I wouldn't know how to write a book for grown-ups. I wouldn't know what to say."

Kindl finds her job as a children's writer to be enjoyable. "I can read as much as I want to and call it research," she told *SATA*. "People pay me money for the things that I write—sometimes, anyway."

Biographical and Critical Sources

PERIODICALS

Booklist, September 1, 1993, Jeanne Triner, review of *Owl in Love*, p. 51; March 15, 1997, Hazel Rochman, review of *The Woman in the Wall*, p. 1236; April 15, 2001, Anne O'Malley, review of *Goose Chase*, p. 1554.

Book Report, May-June, 1994, Kathryn Rowan, review of *Owl in Love*, p. 44; September-October, 1997, Christina H. Dorr, review of *The Woman in the Wall*, p. 37.

Bulletin of the Center for Children's Books, October, 1993.

Horn Book, July-August, 1997, Martha A. Parravano, review of *The Woman in the Wall*, pp. 458-459; July, 2001, review of *Goose Chase*, p. 454.

Kirkus Reviews, October 1, 1993, p. 1276.

Publishers Weekly, September 6, 1993, review of *Owl in Love*, p. 98; February 17, 1997, review of *The Woman in the Wall*, p. 220; March 19, 2001, review of *Goose Chase*, 99.

School Library Journal, August, 1993, Margaret A. Chang, review of *Owl in Love*, p. 186; April, 1997, Cindy Darling Codell, review of *The Woman in the Wall*, p. 138; April, 2001, Connie Tyrrell Burns, review of *Goose Chase*, p. 144.

*   *   *

KLISE, M. Sarah 1961-

Personal

Born December 31, 1961, in Peoria, IL; daughter of Thomas S. (a writer and film producer) and Marjorie A. (president of Thomas S. Klise Co.) Klise. *Education:* Attended Marquette University.

Addresses

Home and office—2830 Eighth Street, Berkeley, CA 94710. *Agent*—William Corsa, Speciality Book Marketing, Inc., 443 Park Ave. S., Suite 801, New York, NY 10016. *E-mail*—msklise@pacbell.net.

Career

Illustrator and designer of books. Teacher and founder of Chinatown Young Artists Program, San Francisco, CA.

Illustrator

Kate Klise, *Regarding the Fountain: A Tale, in Letters, of Liars and Leaks,* Avon Books (New York, NY), 1998.

Kate Klise, *Letters from Camp,* Avon Books (New York, NY), 1999.

Kate Klise, *Trial by Journal,* HarperCollins (New York, NY), 2001.

Sidelights

M. Sarah Klise told *SATA:* "As a child, I wondered if adults were paid to work or if one was required to pay for the opportunity TO work. I never could remember which way it went. Many years later, I sometimes feel the same way. It is such an honor to be able to draw pictures for children's books that I think I would PAY to do it—please don't tell our publisher this. I have to feed my three cats! I get to be part-architect, part-inventor, part-designer, and part-just-about-anything-else-you-can-think-of.

"I am also lucky to get to collaborate with my sister, Kate Klise, author. Because there are four states in between our homes, we rely on letters, packages, e-mail, phone calls, and visits to create our books. We have collaborated on books since we were children, knowing early on that Kate had a knack for telling funny stories

M. Sarah Klise

and that I could draw pictures that sort of looked how they were supposed to. In a pinch, she would write a short story for me and I would illustrate research papers for her.

"Over the years we became great pen pals. These many, many letters and the many letters from our parents and siblings became the framework for our books. Everyone loves to get a piece of mail. Correspondence can be secret and very personal. We both hope that writing letters, like making valentines and Christmas cards and sending postcards from across town, never becomes a thing of the past but remains a part of our daily lives."

M. Sarah Klise and her sister Kate's love of writing and receiving letters is at the heart of their novels for middle-grade students. In their first book, *Regarding the Fountain,* the simple job of replacing the drinking fountain at Dry Creek Middle School becomes preternaturally complicated once local fountain designer Flo Waters is called in. Flo soon invites the fifth-grade class to help design the new fountain, and various members of the community must be consulted and pacified. Flo herself, whom one critic likened to Auntie Mame of Broadway fame, moves through the town like a force of nature. The story quickly becomes a romp told through letters, memos, faxes, postcards, and newspaper clippings between the school principal, the members of Mr. Sam N.'s fifth-grade class, including Tad Poll, Gil, Lily, and Paddy, among others, president of the school board Sally Mander, and Mr. D. Eel, the owner of the municipal water company, revealing the mystery behind why the town is permanently in a state of drought and the role played by the old, leaky school water fountain in keeping it so. "The hilarious shenanigans are unremitting; the puns flow faster than the leaks in the old fountain," observed Nancy Vasilakis in *Horn Book.* M. Sarah Klise's contribution lies in creating the graphic design of the various items of correspondence that comprise each page. Though the mystery may not be too difficult to unravel, according to Rita Soltan in *School Library Journal,* "it is still fun to continue reading the diverse pages, all in different fonts with eclectic drawings, just to see how the mystery will be revealed and solved." Susan Dove Lempke, who reviewed *Regarding the Fountain* for *Booklist,* likewise wrote that while the scheme for the novel is "a trifle gimmicky," author and illustrator "carry it off extraordinarily well," and the graphic presentation of the story brings added interest for the benefit of reluctant readers.

Klise and sister Kate relied upon a similar scheme to tell the story of their next book, titled *Letters from Camp.* Like *Regarding the Fountain, Letters from Camp* is told entirely through letters, notes, newspaper articles, and other missives written by the characters themselves, and as in the earlier book, the story centers on a mystery involving characters with implausibly punning names. In *Letters from Camp,* three pairs of siblings who suffer from more than a little rivalry are sent to Camp Harmony to learn how to get along, as exemplified by the Harmony siblings, once a family singing act and now owners of the camp. As the children suffer through endless chores and terrible food, they begin to realize that the Harmonys are secretly trying to kill each other off. So they put off their own squabbling in order to join forces and solve the mystery that lies at the heart of the Harmony family ranch, inadvertently learning how to get along, just as the camp brochure promised their parents they would. Like *Regarding the Fountain, Letters from Camp* features the graphic art of M. Sarah Klise, and "each page is a collage of written evidence through which the story unfolds," according to Connie Tyrrell Burns in *School Library Journal.* Burns went on to conclude that *Letters from Camp* would appeal most to "students with a wacky sense of humor."

Using the methods of their previous two books, the Klise sisters revealed to readers the inner workings of a courtroom in *Trial by Journal.* Twelve-year-old Lily Watson faces a difficult choice of summer school or sitting as a jury member for a murder trial and writing a report about it. Because of a fictional state law in Missouri that allows juveniles to be selected to the jury in cases where a juvenile was the victim of the crime, the sixth grader decides to spend her summer with a judge, deciding the fate of Bob White, a zoo employee accused of killing eleven-year-old Perry Keet. Using their trademark puns and humor, the Klises create a "three-ring circus," according to a *Publishers Weekly* critic, that "will set in motion readers' flights of fancy from beginning to end." Claimed a *Horn Book* reviewer, "Klise matches her sister's sense of fun with outrageous layouts and sketches throughout the text."

Biographical and Critical Sources

PERIODICALS

Booklist, August, 1998, Susan Dove Lempke, review of *Regarding the Fountain,* p. 2006.
Horn Book, May-June, 1998, Nancy Vasilakis, review of *Regarding the Fountain,* p. 345; May-June, 2001, review of *Trial by Journal.*
Publishers Weekly, June, 2001, review of *Trial by Journal.*
School Library Journal, June, 1998, Rita Soltan, review of *Regarding the Fountain,* p. 147; June, 1999, Connie Tyrrell Burns, review of *Letters from Camp,* p. 132.

*   *   *

KROMMES, Beth 1956-

Personal

Born January 6, 1956, in Allentown, PA; daughter of Frederick (a professional billiards and bowling player) and Shirley (Reisenweaver) Krommes; married David Rowell (a computer programmer), September 25, 1982; children: Olivia, Marguerite. *Education:* Syracuse University, B.F.A. (painting; magna cum laude), 1977; attended St. Martin's School of Art (London, England), 1976; University of Massachusetts—Amherst, M.A.T. (art education), 1980. *Politics:* Democrat. *Religion:* Lutheran.

Beth Krommes

Addresses

Home and office—310 Old Street Rd., Peterborough, NH 03458.

Career

Worked variously as an art director and designer for a computer magazine, manager of a handicraft shop, managing director of an arts organization, and a junior and senior high school art teacher. Freelance wood engraver and illustrator, 1984—. *Exhibitions:* Has exhibited her work in Pennsylvania, Massachusetts, New Hampshire, and England. *Member:* Society of Children's Book Writers and Illustrators, Society of Wood Engravers, Wood Engravers Network.

Awards, Honors

Certificates of Design Excellence, *PRINT's Regional Design Annual,* 1985, 1986, 1987, 1988, 1990, 1991, 1994, 1999; Yankee Print Awards, League of New Hampshire Craftsmen Foundation Annual Juried Exhibit, 1986, 1987; Merit Awards in Printmaking, Annual Regional Juried Exhibitions, Sharon Arts Center (Sharon, NH), 1986, 1989; Bologna Children's Book Fair Illustrator's Exhibit selection for fiction, 2000, for *Grandmother Winter;* Bologna Children's Book Fair Illustrator's Exhibit selection for nonfiction, 2001, for *The Lamp, the Ice, and the Boat Called Fish.*

Illustrator

Ruth Adams Bronz, *Miss Ruby's American Cooking,* Harper & Row (New York, NY), 1989.

Marjorie Holmes, *At Christmas the Heart Goes Home,* Doubleday (New York, NY), 1991.

James Villas, *French Country Kitchen,* Bantam (New York, NY), 1992.

Tales of the Grizzly, Homestead Publishing (Moose, WY), 1992.

Down Home Cooking, Reader's Digest (Pleasantville, NY), 1994.

Sandra J. Taylor, editor, *Yankee Magazine's New England Innkeepers Cookbook,* Villard (New York, NY), 1996.

Tales of the Wolf, Homestead Publishing (Moose, WY), 1996.

Ric Lynden Hardman, *Sunshine Rider* (young adult novel), Bantam (New York, NY), 1998.

Phyllis Root, *Grandmother Winter* (picture book), Houghton (Boston, MA), 1999.

Carrie Young, *Prairie Cooks, Three Day Burns, and Other Reminiscences,* University of Iowa Press (Iowa City, Iowa), 1999.

Jacqueline Briggs Martin, *The Lamp, the Ice, and the Boat Called Fish* (picture book), Houghton (Boston, MA), 2001.

Judith Nicholls, *The Sun in Me: Poems about the Planet,* Barefoot Press (Bristol, England), 2002.

Sidelights

Known for her engravings, Beth Krommes's works have appeared in many exhibitions and galleries in New Hampshire, where she makes her home. Since the early 1990s, Krommes has illustrated children's books, among them the picture books *Grandmother Winter* and *The Lamp, the Ice, and the Boat Called Fish.* For *Grandmother Winter,* a lyrical tale of people's and animals' responses to the coming of winter, Krommes created suitable "delightful scratchboard illustrations, tinted with soft watercolors," noted *Booklist* reviewer Kay Weisman. So, too, a contributor to *Horn Book* commented on the bats, worms, frogs, fish, and bears among other creatures that Krommes depicted, calling them "carefully observed as well as decorative." In *The Lamp, the Ice, and the Boat Called Fish* Jacqueline Briggs Martin tells the true story of an expedition in 1913 by Arctic explorer Vilhjalmur Stefansson to prove that a continent was hidden under the Arctic ice cap. Stefansson's expedition failed when he was forced to abandon his ice-trapped fishing boat, *Karluk.* Krommes's scratchboard art "is outstanding," declared a *Horn Book* writer. "Ice, artifacts, and characters are delineated in handsome black, softened with crosshatching and a limited palette." *School Library Journal* contributor Sue Sherif added that the "evocative scratchboard illustrations show many details of the cultural and physical environment."

Biographical and Critical Sources

PERIODICALS

Booklist, November 15, 1999, Kay Weisman, review of *Grandmother Winter,* p. 637.

In scratchboard drawings that capture the essence of the Inupiaq culture, Krommes has illustrated Jacqueline Briggs Martin's true-life tale of a treacherous 1913 expedition to the Arctic ice cap. (From The Lamp, the Ice, and the Boat Called *Fish.)*

Horn Book, September, 1999, review of *Grandmother Winter,* p. 599; March, 2001, review of *The Lamp, the Ice, and the Boat Called Fish,* p. 198.

New York Times Book Review, April 15, 2001, Heather Vogel Frederick, review of *The Lamp, the Ice, and the Boat Called Fish,* p. 25.

Publishers Weekly, September 2, 1989, Molly McQuade, review of *Miss Ruby's American Cooking,* p. 54; August 30, 1999, review of *Grandmother Winter,* p. 82.

School Library Journal, July, 2001, Sue Sherif, review of *The Lamp, the Ice, and the Boat Called Fish,* p. 96.*

*   *   *

KUHARSKI, Janice 1947-

Personal

Born November 27, 1947, in Akron, OH; daughter of John (a mold maker) and Helen (a homemaker; maiden name, Alleman) Kuharski. *Education:* University of Tulsa, B.S., 1969, M.T.A., 1992. *Politics:* Democrat. *Religion:* Roman Catholic. *Hobbies and other interests:* Yoga, meditation, cooking, collecting Boyd's bears, making wreaths.

Addresses

Home—5819 East King St., Tulsa, OK 74115.

Career

Tulsa Public Schools, Tulsa, OK, language arts teacher, 1976-95; writer, 1995—. *Member:* Society of Children's Book Writers and Illustrators.

Awards, Honors

Instructional Excellence Award, Oklahoma Education Association, 1985.

Writings

Tales of China (fiction), Perfection Learning (Logan, IA), 1998.

Tales of Silliness (fiction), Perfection Learning (Logan, IA), 1998.

Tales of Yore (fiction), Perfection Learning (Logan, IA), 1999.

Raven's Gift (fiction), Richard C. Owen Publishers (Katonah, NY), 1999.

Mama's Llamas (picture book), Richard C. Owen Publishers (Katonah, NY), 2001.

Author of a play, "The Leopard's Noisy Drum," published in *Plays: Drama Magazine for Young People,*

Janice Kuharski

1996. Contributor of poems to magazines, including *Child Life, U.S. Kids, Jack and Jill, Pak-o-Fun,* and *Holidays and Seasonal Celebrations.*

Work in Progress

It's Poetry Time!, a collection of poems for babies; *Ten Cows Knocking,* a collection of ABC and counting rhymes; research on Christmas nativity legends from around the world.

Sidelights

Janice Kuharski told *SATA:* "For me, writing has always been linked to the process of discovering who I am as a person and a communicator. As a former language arts teacher, I learned that writing could be an invaluable tool to promote learning and open up the creative possibilities of teaching. I began writing to add fun and enrichment to classroom projects, but I soon discovered that writing could become addictive!

"Now that I am facing the current challenge of living with chronic fatigue syndrome (CFIDS), I find that writing has become an integral part of the healing process. I look forward to the time when I can devote my energies to writing on a regular basis. For now, however, I am happy that writing helps me stay connected to students in classrooms throughout the country.

"My advice to students and young writers is simple. Read as many books as you can, and let the styles of different writers 'sink in.' The more you read and write, the more your own unique style will begin to emerge. Soon you will be on your way to discovering how unlimited your creative potential truly is."

Biographical and Critical Sources

PERIODICALS

School Library Journal, review of *Raven's Gift,* p. 68.*

L

LANG, T. T.
See TAYLOR, Theodore

*   *   *

LEE, Lyn 1953-

Personal

Born January 31, 1953, in Sydney, Australia; daughter of Neville Walter (a naval and civil aviator) and Joan Bernadette (a homemaker; maiden name, Mednie) Lee; married Peter Simpson (a graphic artist); children: Steven, Dominic, Jesinda. *Education:* Earned diploma of art, 1979. *Hobbies and other interests:* Music, reading, writing, drawing.

Addresses

Home—134 Ingham Ave., Five Dock, New South Wales 2046, Australia. *E-mail*—entgraph@mpx.com.au.

Career

Guitarist with a rock and roll band; printer of posters and handbills for other bands; Entertainment Graphics, bookkeeper until 2001. *Member:* Australian Society of Authors.

Awards, Honors

Shortlisted for New South Wales Premier's Literary Awards and for Children's Book of the Year Award, 2001, both for *Pog.*

Writings

Pog, illustrated by Kim Gamble, Omnibus Books (Norwood, Australia), 2000.

Work in Progress

Eight, a picture book illustrated by Kim Gamble, publication expected in 2002; *Emily and the Dragon,* a picture book, 2003; a novel for young readers.

Lyn Lee

Sidelights

Lyn Lee told *SATA:* "As a child I loved to read, write, draw, sculpt, and listen to music. I still do. I climbed trees, rode my bike, and played with my brother and sister and friends. Our backyard was anything our imaginations made it. I was in the local swimming squad, so I spent a lot of time in the pool, up and down, doing laps. Swimming is a great way of making the time to dream.

"As a teenager, I wanted a life involved in the art world, I didn't care which art form. Writing, poetry, painting, music—it's all the same to me. Unfortunately it's also a hard way to make a living. Working in the food industry as a waitress, kitchen hand, or sandwich hand is enjoyable work. It pays, it's busy, and it's the sort of work that lots of interesting people go for because of the flexible hours.

"During art school I lived in a warehouse in East Sydney, an inner-city suburb which was, at the time, a sort of artists' colony. A friend had a drum kit, another a bass, so I bought a guitar and we started a rock and roll band. I met my husband, and together we set up a rehearsal studio where our band and other bands could practice, and a silkscreen studio where we printed band posters.

"After the birth of our second child, we moved to the suburbs. It was time to get serious. My husband set up a graphic arts studio, and I kept the accounts and worked freelance as a 'reader' for a publisher.

"It was when we had our first child that I became fascinated with the picture book. I fell in love with these short books full of wonderful language and fantastic illustrations. I decided I would like to try my hand at writing one. When our third child started school, I finally got the time to give it a go.

"It took a while, and a lot of rejections, before I produced *Pog*. I spent a lot of time at my children's school, reading with the kids and helping out on projects with the teachers. This was terrific for me as a writer; it reminded me that the concerns of children are very different to the concerns of adults.

"I suppose *Pog* is autobiographical in the sense that I have three children, two boys and a girl. When the children were small, my husband was busy setting up his company, and I was busy with work and the kids and my husband's mother who had Alzheimer's disease. In the end *Pog* is a story about the power of the imagination. We can either give in to fear and hide away, or use our imagination to overcome these fears and go forward."

Biographical and Critical Sources

OTHER

Scholastic Australia Web Site, http://www.scholastic. com.au/ (January 30, 2002), author profile of Lyn Lee.*

LEEDY, Loreen (Janelle) 1959-

Personal

Born June 15, 1959, in Wilmington, DE; daughter of James Allwyn (an auditor) and Grace Anne (a registered nurse) Leedy. *Education:* Attended Indiana University— Bloomington, 1978-79; University of Delaware, B.A. (cum laude), 1981.

Addresses

Agent—c/o Holiday House, 425 Madison Ave., New York, NY 10017. *E-mail*—me@loreenleedy.com.

Career

Illustrator and author. Craftsperson, specializing in jewelry, 1982-84; writer and illustrator, 1984—. Lecturer at schools and conferences. *Exhibitions:* Works have been included in Society of Illustrators' Original Art show, New York, NY, 1994. *Member:* Authors Guild, Authors League of America, Society of Children's Book Writers and Illustrators.

Awards, Honors

Parents' Choice Award for Illustration, 1987, for *Big, Small, Short, Tall;* Parents' Choice Award in Learning and Doing, 1989, for *The Dragon Halloween Party;* Ezra Jack Keats Award for excellence in the arts, 1989; Best Books citations, *Parents* magazine, 1990, for *The Furry News,* and 1992, for *The Monster Money Book;* Outstanding Science Trade Book citation, National

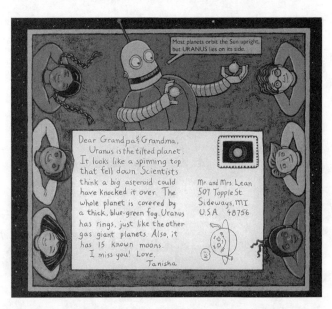

In Loreen Leedy's fun and educational book, a group of children on a field trip to outer space send postcards back to earth, relating their experiences and impressions as they visit each planet of the solar system. (From Postcards from Pluto, *written and illustrated by Leedy.)*

Science Teachers Association/Children's Book Council, 1994, for *Tracks in the Sand.*

Writings

FOR CHILDREN; SELF-ILLUSTRATED

A Number of Dragons, Holiday House (New York, NY), 1985.

The Dragon ABC Hunt, Holiday House (New York, NY), 1986.

The Dragon Halloween Party, Holiday House (New York, NY), 1986.

Big, Small, Short, Tall, Holiday House (New York, NY), 1987.

The Bunny Play, Holiday House (New York, NY), 1988.

A Dragon Christmas: Things to Make and Do, Holiday House (New York, NY), 1988.

Pingo, the Plaid Panda, Holiday House (New York, NY), 1988.

The Potato Party and Other Troll Tales, Holiday House (New York, NY), 1989.

The Dragon Thanksgiving Feast: Things to Make and Do, Holiday House (New York, NY), 1990.

The Furry News: How to Make a Newspaper, Holiday House (New York, NY), 1990.

The Great Trash Bash, Holiday House (New York, NY), 1991.

Messages in the Mailbox: How to Write a Letter, Holiday House (New York, NY), 1991.

Blast Off to Earth!: A Look at Geography, Holiday House (New York, NY), 1992.

The Monster Money Book, Holiday House (New York, NY), 1992.

Postcards from Pluto: A Tour of the Solar System, Holiday House (New York, NY), 1993.

The Race, Scott Foresman (Glenview, IL), 1993.

Tracks in the Sand, Doubleday (New York, NY), 1993.

The Edible Pyramid: Good Eating Every Day, Holiday House (New York, NY), 1994.

Fraction Action, Holiday House (New York, NY), 1994.

Who's Who in My Family?, Holiday House (New York, NY), 1995.

2 x 2 = Boo! A Set of Spooky Multiplication Stories, Holiday House (New York, NY), 1995.

Measuring Penny, Holt (New York, NY), 1997.

Mission: Addition, Holiday House (New York, NY), 1997.

Celebrate the Fifty States!, Holiday House (New York, NY), 1999.

Mapping Penny's World, Holt (New York, NY), 2000.

Subtraction Action, Holiday House (New York, NY), 2000.

Follow the Money!, Holiday House (New York, NY), 2002.

FOR CHILDREN; ILLUSTRATOR

David A. Adler, *The Dinosaur Princess and Other Prehistoric Riddles,* Holiday House (New York, NY), 1988.

Tom Birdseye, *Waiting for Baby,* Holiday House (New York, NY), 1991.

Sidelights

Author and illustrator Loreen Leedy creates picture books that are generally regarded as yet entertaining and instructive introductions to a variety of subjects. Leedy

The Edible Pyramid, *written and illustrated by Leedy, explains the basics of nutrition using the opening of a swanky new restaurant, where a variety of animal patrons turn out to sample the healthful cuisine.*

views picture books as a unique art form, and she works hard to "create a unified whole," as she once explained to *SATA.* Moving "back and forth between the text and the illustrations," she also incorporates a refreshing dash of humor as a way of engaging young imaginations. Reviewing Leedy's *Celebrate the Fifty States!,* a *Kirkus Reviews* critic praised Leedy for her ability to make "hard facts memorable" and put "information into a context that makes sense to children."

"Reading, writing, and making art have been important to me throughout my lifetime," Leedy once explained, and following her college graduation she worked for several years as a craftsperson and jewelry designer. In 1984 she turned her attention to children's books, and within the year was a published author and illustrator. Leedy's first published picture book, *A Number of Dragons,* was called "a knockout" by a *Publishers Weekly* reviewer who praised the humorous story about ten young, blue dragons. Shooed outside by their mother, the winged youngsters decide to engage in a series of activities, all of which are related by Leedy in whimsical rhymes. "The wit of both text and illustration make this an original and enjoyable counting book," noted Lisa Castillo in *School Library Journal.*

A *Number of Dragons* was followed by four more books featuring her mythic creatures. The ten little dragons return in *The Dragon ABC Hunt* as the group decides to pass the time by looking for objects that begin with all twenty-six letters of the alphabet. Leedy's "good-natured, fun loving dragons have fun on their alphabet hunt," noted *School Library Journal* contributor Anne Hoyt Sutter, "as will ... readers." The little blue fire-breathers return in *The Dragon Halloween Party* as preparations for the dragon family's holiday party are shared with readers, along with recipes, instructions for pumpkin carving, and even directions for making a costume that will transform readers into dragons. "This is a book to be relished," noted a *Publishers Weekly* contributor, "long after the last popcorn ball has been devoured."

In creating her many picture books designed to teach readers various subjects, Leedy selects a subject such as writing and then devises a set of engaging characters and a setting for the action—and education—to take place. In her *The Furry News: How to Make a Newspaper* she introduces readers to Big Bear, who decides to publish a newspaper that will cover neighborhood events not found in the city paper. Illustrating her work with a group of stylized animal characters rendered in ink and watercolor, Leedy gives the animals human characteristics and has them speak comic-book style using dialogue

For a class mapmaking assignment, Lisa decides to chart the places her dog, Penny, loves to go. (From Mapping Penny's World, *written and illustrated by Leedy.)*

balloons. As with many of her informational picture books, Leedy appends a glossary of helpful key terms. A *Publishers Weekly* contributor described the book as a "clever, irresistible introduction to the many particulars of newspaper writing and production."

Messages in the Mailbox: How to Write a Letter introduces young readers to many forms of correspondence, both formal—invitations, thank you notes, letters to the editor—and informal, such as love letters, through the actions of Mrs. Gator and her students at a swampy Florida classroom. A *Kirkus Reviews* critic noted that Leedy's "expressive characters and sample messages enliven tips on appropriate topics to write about" and other helpful information. *School Library Journal* contributor Sharon McElmeel added that *Messages in the Mailbox* is "a superb book that shouldn't be missed."

Many of Leedy's picture books address scientific matters that directly affect the everyday lives of young children. In *The Great Trash Bash* the animals in the town of Beaston follow the lead of their Mayor Hippo in confronting a rapidly growing problem: The town quite simply has too much trash. Leedy's story explores the pros and cons of each proposed solution, and she appends a list of ideas for cutting down on solid waste. *School Library Journal* contributor Ruth Smith considered the book "timely, appealing, and funny." *The Edible Pyramid: Good Eating Every Day* explains the basics of nutrition using the opening of a swanky new restaurant, where Leedy's anthropomorphized animals all turn out to sample the healthful cuisine. And in *Who's Who in My Family?*, the concepts underlying the family tree are illustrated through an animal classroom assigned to create their family trees. Uncles, aunts, half-siblings, stepchildren, and other components of modern families are illustrated on a tree that readers learn to create for themselves as a way to map their own families. Praising Leedy's gently colored illustrations, Lauren Peterson added in her *Booklist* review that "by showing families made up of different animals [the artwork] aptly reinforce[s] the book's basic theme."

Postcards from Pluto: A Tour of the Solar System explores space as the robot guide Dr. Quasar conducts a group of multicultural children on a spaceship field trip. Information is imaginatively conveyed to the reader in postcards that the young people send to Earth, relating their experiences and impressions. More down to Earth, *Blast Off to Earth! A Look at Geography* pictures alien teacher Mr. Quark and his students as they journey to Earth on a class trip. Quark's instructive comments highlight the distinguishing aspects of each continent and of the globe as a whole, prompting *Booklist* reviewer Carolyn Phelan to call it a "useful, lighthearted picture book [that] provides a new perspective on the home planet." Focusing on the United States, *Celebrate the Fifty States!* describes the fifty states of America by including little-known facts and figures on many locales. "Leedy has outdone herself with delightful illustrative details," noted *School Library Journal* contributor Jackie Hechtkopf of the book's detailed artwork, adding that the volume is a true "celebration of the diversity and wealth" of the United States. In *Booklist* Ilene Cooper also had praise for the book, calling it "brightly colored and amusingly designed" and noting its value as "a simple yet winning introduction to the U.S."

The world of mathematics is the subject of Leedy's *Fraction Action,* which a *Kirkus Reviews* critic dubbed "a lucid introduction to an often vexing topic." Composed in a comic book format, the book features a lively cast of animal students, plenty of humor, and a large variety of everyday things that can be understood in terms of halves, thirds, and fourths. *Mission: Addition* provides an entertaining follow-up in the series, as the concept of addition is illustrated with real-life examples. Teacher Miss Prime and her students tackle everything from calculating the score of a homemade bowling game to figuring out the earnings from a yard sale. Praising her explanations as "clear and concise," *School Library Journal* contributor Barbara Elleman added that "her colorful pictures feature a bevy of amusing animals." *Subtraction Action* continues in the same vein, presenting a new math problem in every story and listing all the answers in the back of the book. The world of high finance is similarly treated in Leedy's *The Monster Money Book,* as a group of monsters present an introduction to earning, saving, and spending money. Calling the monsters "outrageous" and Leedy's text "funny," *Booklist* contributor Hazel Rochman praised *The Monster Money Book* as "accessible" and "entertaining," noting that the work contains "some fascinating ideas."

Leedy's book, *The Bunny Play,* pictures the efforts of a group of rabbits to mount a musical version of *Little Red Riding Hood.* A *Publishers Weekly* reviewer noted that Leedy "delves into the behind-the-scenes information with exuberance," while the story was described by *Booklist* contributor Barbara Elleman as "a delightful entree into the theater world." Praising the bunnies for their "goofy charm," Laura McCutcheon added in her *School Library Journal* review that Leedy's "animated" ink-and-watercolor renderings "are filled with humor and an attention to detail."

The Potato Party and Other Tales is a collection of seven original stories featuring trolls. Sporting such outrageous names as Buggly and Murkle, Leedy's trolls saunter through stories with "unusual plot twists and surprise endings that add to the fun," according to a *Publishers Weekly* contributor. Calling the book "delightfully wacky" and praising the author/illustrator's "fanciful cartoons" washed with hues of lavender, blues, and earthtones, *School Library Journal* contributor Denise Anton Wright commended Leedy for a text that is "simple in sentence structure" but which uses "enough descriptive language and playful names to make" the book a good selection for reading to small children.

Biographical and Critical Sources

PERIODICALS

Appraisal, autumn, 1991, pp. 37-38; fall, 1993, pp. 33-34.

Booklist, September 15, 1986, p. 133; March 15, 1988, Barbara Elleman, review of *The Bunny Play,* p. 1264; November 1, 1988, p. 485; October 1, 1990, pp. 339-340; March 15, 1992, Hazel Rochman, *The Monster Money Book,* pp. 1388-1389; November 1, 1992, Carolyn Phelan, review of *Blast Off to Earth! A Look at Geography,* p. 516; June 1, 1993, Carolyn Phelan, review of *Tracks in the Sand,* p. 1834; October 15, 1993, p. 437; March 15, 1994, Carolyn Phelan, review of *Fraction Action,* p. 1368; November 15, 1994, Carolyn Phelan, review of *The Edible Pyramid,* p. 607; March 1, 1995, Lauren Peterson, review of *Who's Who in My Family?,* p. 1245; September 15, 1995, Hazel Rochman, review of *2 x 2 = Boo!: A Set of Spooky Multiplication Stories,* p. 171; April 1, 1996, Denia Hester, review of *How Humans Make Friends,* p. 1368; October 15, 1997, Carolyn Phelan, review of *Mission: Addition,* p. 409; April, 1998, Stephanie Zvirin, review of *Measuring Penny,* p. 1325; September 1, 1999, Ilene Cooper, review of *Celebrate the Fifty States!,* p. 136; July, 2000, Catherine Andronik, review of *Mapping Penny's World,* p. 2040.

Bulletin of the Center for Children's Books, May, 1990, p. 218; December, 1991, p. 97; March, 1992, pp. 184-185; March, 1994, pp. 224-225; February, 1995, p. 206.

Delaware Today, October, 1986.

Horn Book, July-August, 1998, Marilyn Bousquin, review of *Measuring Penny,* p. 476.

Kirkus Reviews, October 15, 1991, review of *Messages in the Mailbox: How to Write a Letter,* p. 1345; February 15, 1994, review of *Fraction Action,* p. 229; August 15, 1999, review of *Celebrate the Fifty States!,* p. 1312.

Publishers Weekly, August 9, 1985, review of *A Number of Dragons,* p. 74; August 22, 1986, review of *The Dragon Halloween Party,* p. 97; March 20, 1987, review of *Big, Small, Short, Tall,* p. 77; March 18, 1988, review of *The Bunny Play,* p. 86; October 14, 1988, review of *A Dragon Christmas,* p. 73; March 24, 1989, review of *Pingo the Plaid Panda,* p. 67; November 10, 1989, review of *The Potato Party and Other Troll Tales,* p. 60; March 30, 1990, review of *The Furry News: How to Make a Newspaper,* p. 62; November 1, 1991, review of *Messages in the Mailbox,* p. 79; November 2, 1992, review of *Blast Off to Earth!,* p. 70; February 7, 1994, review of *Fraction Action,* p. 87; December 19, 1994, review of *Who's Who in My Family?,* p. 53; September 18, 1995, review of *2 x 2 = Boo!,* p. 90; December 11, 1995, review of *The Edible Pyramid,* p. 71; March 4, 1996, review of *How Humans Make Friends,* p. 65; July 29, 1996, review of *Postcards from Pluto,* p. 89; July 28, 1997, review of *Mission: Addition,* p. 76; March 16, 1998, review of *Measuring Penny,* p. 63.

School Library Journal, February, 1986, Lisa Castillo, review of *A Number of Dragons,* p. 76; August, 1986, Anne Hoyt Sutter, review of *The Dragon ABC Hunt,* p. 84; December, 1986, Lorraine Douglas, review of *The Dragon Halloween Party,* p. 91; September, 1987, p. 166; June-July, 1988, Laura McCutcheon, review of *The Bunny Play,* p. 92; October, 1988, Susan Hepler, review of *A Dragon Christmas,* p. 35; July, 1989, Christine Behrman, review of *Pingo the Plaid Panda,* p. 68; December, 1989, Denise Anton Wright, review of *The Potato Party and Other Troll Tales,* p. 84; May, 1990, Sylvia S. Marantz, review of *The Furry News,* pp. 98-99; November, 1990, Maria B. Salvadore, review of *The Dragon Thanksgiving Feast;* May, 1991, Ruth Smith, review of *The Great Trash Bash,* pp. 80-81; September, 1991, Sharon McElmeel, review of *Messages in the Mailbox: How to Write a Letter,* p. 246; November, 1991, Virginia E. Jeschelnig, review of *Waiting for Baby,* p. 90; June, 1992, Heide Piehler, review of *The Monster Money Book,* p. 97; January, 1993, Louise L. Sherman, review of *Blast Off to Earth!,* p. 92; May, 1993, Diane Nunn, review of *Tracks in the Sand,* p. 88; October, 1993, John Peters, review of *Postcards from Pluto,* p. 119; April, 1995, Joyce Adams Burner, review of *The Edible Pyramid,* and Virginia Opocensky, review of *Who's Who in My Family?,* p. 126; November, 1995, JoAnne Rees, review of *2 x 2 = Boo!,* p. 113; July, 1996, Elaine Lesh Morgan, review of *How Humans Make Friends,* pp. 66-67; August, 1997, Barbara Elleman, review of *Mission: Addition,* p. 148; April, 1998, Jane Claes, review of *Measuring Penny,* p. 119; September, 1999, Jackie Hechtkopf, review of *Celebrate the Fifty States!,* p. 214; September, 2000, Holly T. Sneeringer, review of *Subtraction Action,* p. 219, and Louise L. Sherman, review of *Mapping Penny's World,* p. 204.

Teaching Children Mathematics, January, 1995, David J. Whitin, review of *Fraction Action,* p. 309.

OTHER

Loreen Leedy Web Site, http://www.loreenleedy.com (February 2, 2002).*

*   *   *

L'ENGLE, Madeleine (Camp Franklin) 1918-

Personal

Surname pronounced "Leng-*el*"; given name, Madeleine L'Engle Camp; born November 29, 1918, in New York, NY; daughter of Charles Wadsworth (a foreign correspondent and author) and Madeleine (a pianist; maiden name, Barnett) Camp; married Hugh Franklin (an actor), January 26, 1946 (died, September, 1986); children: Josephine (Mrs. Alan W. Jones), Maria (Mrs. John Rooney), Bion. *Education:* Smith College, A.B. (with honors), 1941; attended New School for Social Research (now New School University), 1941-42; Columbia University, graduate study, 1960-61. *Politics:* "New England." *Religion:* Anglican.

Addresses

Home—924 West End Avenue, New York, NY 10025; Crosswicks, Goshen, CT 06756. *Agent*—Robert Lescher, 155 East 71st St., New York, NY 10021.

Career

Active career in theater, 1941-47; teacher with Committee for Refugee Education during World War II; St. Hilda's and St. Hugh's School, Morningside Heights, NY, teacher, 1960-66; Cathedral of St. John the Divine, New York, NY, librarian, 1966—. University of Indiana, Bloomington, IN, member of summer faculty, 1965-66, 1971; writer-in-residence, Ohio State University, Columbus, OH, 1970, and University of Rochester, Rochester, New York, 1972. Lecturer. *Member:* Authors Guild (president), Authors League of America, PEN.

Awards, Honors

And Both Were Young was named one of the Ten Best Books of the Year, *New York Times,* 1949; Newbery Medal, American Library Association, 1963, Hans Christian Andersen Award runner-up, 1964, Sequoyah Children's Book Award, Oklahoma State Department of Education, and Lewis Carroll Shelf Award, both 1965, all for *A Wrinkle in Time; Book World* Spring Book Festival Honor Book, and *School Library Journal*'s Best Books of the Year selection, both 1968, both for *The Young Unicorns;* Austrian State Literary Prize, 1969, for *The Moon by Night;* University of Southern Mississippi Silver Medallion, 1978, for outstanding contribution to the field of children's literature; American Book Award for paperback fiction, 1980, for *A Swiftly Tilting Planet;* Smith Medal, 1980; Newbery Honor Book, 1981, for *A Ring of Endless Light;* Books for the Teen Age

Madeleine L'Engle

selections, New York Public Library, 1981, for *A Ring of Endless Light,* and 1982, for *Camilla;* Sophie Award, 1984; Regina Medal, Catholic Library Association, 1984; Adolescent Literature Assembly Award for Outstanding Contribution to Adolescent Literature, National Council of Teachers of English, and ALAN Award, both 1986; Kerlan Award, 1990; Margaret A. Edwards Award, 1998, for lifetime achievement in young adult literature; numerous honorary degrees.

Writings

The Small Rain: A Novel, Vanguard (New York, NY), 1945, published as *Prelude,* 1968, new edition published under original title, Farrar, Straus (New York, NY), 1984.

Ilsa, Vanguard (New York, NY), 1946.

And Both Were Young, Lothrop (New York, NY), 1949, reprinted, Delacorte (New York, NY), 1983.

Camilla Dickinson, Simon & Schuster (New York, NY), 1951, published as *Camilla,* Crowell (New York, NY), 1965, reprinted, Delacorte (New York, NY), 1981.

A Winter's Love, Lippincott (Philadelphia, PA), 1957, reprinted, Ballantine (New York, NY), 1983.

The Arm of the Starfish, Farrar, Straus (New York, NY), 1965.

The Love Letters, Farrar, Straus (New York, NY), 1966.

Lines Scribbled on an Envelope, and Other Poems, Farrar, Straus (New York, NY), 1969.

Dance in the Desert, illustrated by Symeon Shimin, Farrar, Straus (New York, NY), 1969.

Intergalactic P.S.3, Children's Book Council, 1970.

The Other Side of the Sun, Farrar, Straus (New York, NY), 1971.

Everyday Prayers, illustrated by Lucille Butel, Morehouse (New York, NY), 1974.

Prayers for Sunday, illustrated by Lizzie Napoli, Morehouse (New York, NY), 1974.

Dragons in the Waters (sequel to *The Arm of the Starfish*), Farrar, Straus (New York, NY), 1976.

(Editor, with William B. Green) *Spirit and Light: Essays in Historical Theology,* Seabury Press (New York, NY), 1976.

The Weather of the Heart (poetry), Harold Shaw (Wheaton, IL), 1978.

Ladder of Angels: Scenes from the Bible Illustrated by the Children of the World, Seabury Press (New York, NY), 1979.

Walking on Water: Reflections on Faith and Art (essays), Harold Shaw (Wheaton, IL), 1980.

The Anti-Muffins, illustrated by Gloria Ortiz, Pilgrim (New York, NY), 1981.

The Sphinx at Dawn: Two Stories, illustrated by Vivian Berger, Harper (New York, NY), 1982.

A Severed Wasp (sequel to *A Small Rain*), Farrar, Straus (New York, NY), 1982.

And It Was Good: Reflections on Beginnings, Harold Shaw (Wheaton, IL), 1983.

A House like a Lotus (sequel to *The Arm of the Starfish*), Farrar, Straus (New York, NY), 1984.

Dare to Be Creative, Library of Congress (Washington, DC), 1984.

Vicky is given a trip to Antarctica as a birthday gift but finds her fellow travelers suspicious and likely dangerous.

(With Avery Brooke) *Trailing Clouds of Glory: Spiritual Values in Children's Books,* Westminster (Louisville, KY), 1985.

A Stone for a Pillow: Journeys with Jacob, Harold Shaw (Wheaton, IL), 1986.

A Cry like a Bell (poetry), Harold Shaw (Wheaton, IL), 1987.

An Acceptable Time, Farrar, Straus (New York, NY), 1989.

Sold into Egypt: Joseph's Journey into Human Being, Harold Shaw (Wheaton, IL), 1989.

The Glorious Impossible, Simon & Schuster (New York, NY), 1990.

Certain Women, Farrar, Straus (New York, NY), 1992.

The Rock That Is Higher: Story as Truth, Harold Shaw (Wheaton, IL), 1993.

Anytime Prayers, Harold Shaw (Wheaton, IL), 1994.

Troubling a Star, Farrar, Straus (New York, NY), 1994.

Glimpses of Grace: Daily Thoughts and Reflections, collected by Carol Chase, Harper (San Francisco, CA), 1996.

A Live Coal in the Sea, Farrar, Straus (New York, NY), 1996.

Penguins + Golden Calves: Icons and Idols, Harold Shaw (Wheaton, IL), 1996.

(With Luci Shaw) *Wintersong: Seasonal Readings,* Harold Shaw (Wheaton, IL), 1996.

(With Luci Shaw) *Friends for the Journey: Two Extraordinary Women Celebrate Friendships Made and Sustained through the Seasons of Life,* Vine Books/Servant Publications (Ann Arbor, MI), 1997.

Bright Evening Star: Mystery of the Incarnation, Harold Shaw (Wheaton, IL), 1997.

Mothers and Daughters, Harold Shaw (Wheaton, IL), 1997.

Miracle on 10th Street and Other Christmas Writings, Harold Shaw (Wheaton, IL), 1998.

My Own Small Place: Developing the Writing Life, Harold Shaw (Wheaton, IL), 1998.

Mothers and Sons, Harold Shaw (Wheaton, IL), 1999.

(With Luci Shaw) *A Prayerbook for Spiritual Friends,* Augsburg (Minneapolis, MN), 1999.

The Other Dog, illustrated by Christine Davenier, SeaStar Books (New York, NY), 2001.

When Dr. Camilla Dickinson's teenage granddaughter attempts to unearth information about her family, a complex multigenerational story is revealed. *(Cover photo by Melissa Hayden.)*

Madeleine L'Engle Herself: Reflections on a Writing Life, collected by Carol Chase, WaterBrook Press (Colorado Springs, CO), 2001.

The Genesis Trilogy, WaterBrook Press (Colorado Springs, CO), 2001.

"THE AUSTIN FAMILY" SERIES

Meet the Austins, illustrated by Gillian Willett, Vanguard (New York, NY), 1960.

The Moon by Night, Farrar, Straus (New York, NY), 1963.

The Twenty-Four Days before Christmas: An Austin Family Story, illustrated by Inga, Farrar, Straus (New York, NY), 1964, new edition illustrated by Joe De Velasco, Harold Shaw (Wheaton, IL), 1984.

The Young Unicorns, Farrar, Straus (New York, NY), 1968.

A Ring of Endless Light, Farrar, Straus (New York, NY), 1980.

Troubling a Star, Farrar, Straus (New York, NY), 1987.

A Full House: An Austin Family Christmas, Harold Shaw (Wheaton, IL), 1999.

"TIME FANTASY" SERIES

A Wrinkle in Time, Farrar, Straus (New York, NY), 1962.

A Wind in the Door, Farrar, Straus (New York, NY), 1973.

A Swiftly Tilting Planet, Farrar, Straus (New York, NY), 1978.

Many Waters, Farrar, Straus (New York, NY), 1986.

An Acceptable Time, Farrar Straus (New York, NY), 1996.

"CROSSWICKS JOURNALS" (AUTOBIOGRAPHY)

A Circle of Quiet, Farrar, Straus (New York, NY), 1972.

The Summer of the Great-Grandmother, Farrar, Straus (New York, NY), 1974.

The Irrational Season, Seabury Press (New York, NY), 1977.

Two-Part Invention, Farrar, Straus (New York, NY), 1988.

PLAYS

Eighteen Washington Square, South: A Comedy in One Act (first produced in Northhampton, MA, 1940), Baker (New York, NY), 1944.

(With Robert Hartung) *How Now Brown Cow,* first produced in New York, 1949.

The Journey with Jonah (one-act; first produced in New York, 1970), illustrated by Leonard Everett Fisher, Farrar, Straus (New York, NY), 1967.

OTHER

Contributor of articles, stories, and poems to periodicals, including *McCall's, Christian Century, Commonweal, Christianity Today,* and *Mademoiselle.* Contributor to *Origins of Story: On Writing for Children,* edited by Barbara Harrison, Simon & Schuster, and *Watch for the Light: Reading for Advent and Christmas,* Plough Publishing, 2001. Author of foreword to *She Said Yes: The Unlikely Martyrdom of Cassie Bernall,* Plough, 1999. Collections of L'Engle's manuscripts are housed at Wheaton College, at the Kerlan Collection of the University of Minnesota, and at the de Grummond Collection of the University of Southern Mississippi.

Adaptations

A Wrinkle in Time was recorded by Newbery Award Records, 1972, adapted as a filmstrip with cassette by Miller-Brody, 1974, and adapted for a four-part mini-series for ABC, 2001; *A Wind in the Door* was recorded and adapted as a filmstrip with cassette by Miller-Brody; *Camilla* was recorded as a cassette by Listening Library; *A Ring of Endless Light* was recorded, adapted as a filmstrip with cassette by Random House, and adapted for television on the Disney Channel, 2001. *And Both Were Young, The Arm of the Starfish, Meet the Austins, The Moon by Night, A Wrinkle in Time,* and *The Young Unicorns* have been adapted into Braille; *The Arm of the Starfish, Camilla, Dragons in the Waters, A Wind in the Door,* and *A Wrinkle in Time* have been adapted into talking books; *The Summer of the Great-Grandmother* is also available on cassette.

Sidelights

Madeleine L'Engle is a writer who resists easy classification. She has successfully published plays, poems, essays, autobiographies, and novels for both children and adults. She is probably best known for her "Time Fantasy" series of children's books: *A Wrinkle in Time, A Wind in the Door, A Swiftly Tilting Planet, Many Waters,* and *An Acceptable Time.* These novels combine elements of science fiction and fantasy with L'Engle's constant themes of family love and moral responsibility.

As the daughter of a respected journalist and a gifted pianist, L'Engle was surrounded by creative people from birth. She wrote her first stories at the age of five. She was an only child; in her autobiographies she writes of how much she enjoyed her solitude and of the rich fantasy life she created for herself amid her relatively affluent surroundings. As she wrote in *The Summer of the Great-Grandmother:* "[My mother] was almost forty when I was born. . . . Once she and Father had had their long-awaited baby, I became a bone of contention between them. They disagreed completely on how I ought to be brought up. Father wanted a strict English childhood for me, and this is more or less what I got—nanny, governesses, supper on a tray in the nursery, dancing lessons, music lessons, skating lessons, art lessons."

Her father's failing health sent her parents to Switzerland and young Madeleine to a series of boarding schools, where she found herself very unpopular because of her shy, introspective ways. "I learned," L'Engle recounted in *The Summer of the Great-Grandmother,* "to put on protective coloring in order to survive in an atmosphere which was alien; and I learned to concentrate. Because I was never alone . . . I learned to shut out the sound of the school and listen to the story or poem I was writing when I should have been doing schoolwork. The result of this early lesson in concentration is that I can write anywhere."

These unpleasant boarding school memories were the ones L'Engle transformed into her first published novel,

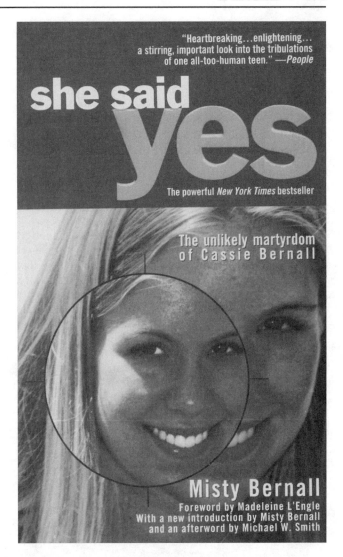

L'Engle wrote the foreword to Misty Bernall's biography of her daughter Cassie, a victim of the Columbine High School shootings who found her faith in God helped her through adolescent problems.

written in the first years after her graduation from Smith College. The novel, titled *The Small Rain,* features Katherine Forrester, a boarding-school student who finds solace in her music and becomes increasingly dedicated to her art. *The Small Rain* thus featured "one of L'Engle's predominant themes: that an artist must constantly discipline herself; otherwise her talent will become dissipated and she will never achieve her greatest potential," comments Marygail G. Parker in the *Dictionary of Literary Biography.*

After publishing several books in the late 1940s, L'Engle's career as a writer was postponed in favor of raising her own family. During the 1950s, she and her husband operated a general store in rural Connecticut. L'Engle still wrote stories in her spare time, but these were invariably rejected by magazines. As she recounted in *A Circle of Quiet:* "During the long drag of years before our youngest child went to school, my love for my family and my need to write were in acute conflict.

The problem was really that I put two things first. My husband and children came first. So did my writing." On her fortieth birthday, in 1958, discouraged by several years of rejections, she renounced writing completely, but found that she was unable to stop. She explained, "I had to write. I had no choice in the matter. It was not up to me to say I would stop, because I could not. It didn't matter how small or inadequate [was] my talent. If I never had another book published, and it was very clear to me that this was a real possibility, I still had to go on writing." Soon thereafter, things began to change for the author, and her writing began to sell again.

Selling *A Wrinkle in Time,* however, proved a challenge. The juvenile novel was rejected by twenty-six publishers in two years. Reasons given vary. The book was neither science fiction nor fantasy, impossible to pigeonhole. "Most objections," L'Engle recalled in an interview with *Children's Literature in Education,* "were that it would not be able to find an audience, that it was too difficult for children." Speaking to Michael J. Farrell in the *National Catholic Reporter,* L'Engle commented that *A Wrinkle in Time* "was written in the terms of a modern world in which children know about brainwashing and the corruption of evil. It's based on Einstein's theory of relativity and Planck's quantum theory. It's good, solid science, but also it's good, solid theology. My rebuttal to the German theologians [who] attack God with their

intellect on the assumption that the finite can comprehend the infinite, and I don't think that's possible."

The book was finally accepted by an editor at Farrar, Straus. "He had read my first book, *The Small Rain,* liked it, and asked if I had any other manuscripts," L'Engle recalled for *More Books by More People.* "I gave him *Wrinkle* and told him, 'Here's a book nobody likes.' He read it and two weeks later I signed the contract. The editors told me not to be disappointed if it doesn't do well and that they were publishing it because they loved it." The public loved the book too. *A Wrinkle in Time* won the Newbery Medal in 1963, the Lewis Carroll Shelf Award in 1965, and was a runner-up for the Hans Christian Andersen Award in 1964.

Speaking with Roy Newquist in his *Conversations,* L'Engle recalled winning the Newbery Medal: "The telephone rang. It was long distance, and an impossible connection. I couldn't hear anything. The operator told me to hang up and she'd try again. The long-distance phone ringing unexpectedly always makes me nervous: is something wrong with one of the grandparents? The phone rang again, and still the connection was full of static and roaring, so the operator told me to hang up and she'd try once more. This time I could barely hear a voice: 'This is Ruth Gagliardo, of the Newbery Caldecott committee.' There was a pause, and she asked, 'Can you hear me?' 'Yes, I can hear you.' Then she told me

Based on the experiences of her own pet, L'Engle penned a picture book about the reactions of a dog whose owner brings home a new pet from an "inferior breed." (*From* The Other Dog, *illustrated by Christine Davenier.*)

that *Wrinkle* had won the medal. My response was an inarticulate squawk; Ruth told me later that it was a special pleasure to her to have me *that* excited."

In *A Wrinkle in Time,* Meg Murry must use time travel and extrasensory perception to rescue her father, a gifted scientist, from the evil forces that hold him prisoner on another planet. To release him, Meg must learn the power of love. Writing in *A Critical History of Children's Literature,* Ruth Hill Viguers calls *A Wrinkle in Time* a "book that combines devices of fairy tales, overtones of fantasy, the philosophy of great lives, the visions of science, and the warmth of a good family story.... It is an exuberant book, original, vital, exciting. Funny ideas, fearful images, amazing characters, and beautiful concepts sweep through it. And it is full of truth."

According to L'Engle, writing *A Wrinkle in Time* was a mysterious process. "A writer of fantasy, fairy tale, or myth," she explained in *Horn Book,* "must inevitably discover that he is not writing out of his own knowledge or experience, but out of something both deeper and wider. I think that fantasy must possess the author and simply use him. I know that this is true of *A Wrinkle in Time.* I can't possibly tell you how I came to write it. It was simply a book I had to write. I had no choice. And it was only *after* it was written that I realized what some of it meant."

In his book *A Sense of Story: Essays on Contemporary Writers for Children,* John Rowe Townsend examined the themes in L'Engle's work: "L'Engle's main themes are the clash of good and evil, the difficulty and necessity of deciding which is which and of committing oneself, the search for fulfillment and self-knowledge. These themes are determined by what the author *is;* and she is a practising and active Christian. Many writers' religious beliefs appear immaterial to their work; Miss L'Engle's are crucial." Townsend saw a mystical dimension to *A Wrinkle in Time.* In that book, he wrote, "the clash of good and evil is at a cosmic level. Much of the action is concerned with the rescue by the heroine Meg and her friend Calvin O'Keefe of Meg's father and brother, prisoners of a great brain called IT which controls the lives of a zombie population on a planet called Camazotz. Here evil is obviously the reduction of people to a mindless mass, while good is individuality, art and love. It is the sheer power of love which enables Meg to triumph over IT, for love is the force that she has and IT has not."

L'Engle has gone on to write several more books featuring the characters introduced in *A Wrinkle in Time,* creating the "Time Fantasy" series. In each of these books, she further develops the theme of love as a weapon against darkness. Although the series has been criticized as too convoluted for young readers, and some reviewers have found the Murry family to be a trifle unbelievable and elitist, most critics praise the series for its willingness to take risks. Michele Murray, writing in the *New York Times Book Review,* claimed that "L'Engle mixes classical theology, contemporary family life, and

futuristic science fiction to make a completely convincing tale." Speaking of *A Wind in the Door, School Library Journal* contributor Margaret A. Dorsey asserted: "Complex and rich in mystical religious insights, this is breathtaking entertainment."

L'Engle's ability to entertain is evident in her popularity with readers. A *Publishers Weekly* survey of the nation's booksellers ranked her in the top six best-selling children's authors, while in an overview of children's book publishing, *American Bookseller* ranked L'Engle among the ten most popular children's authors in the country. Her *Wrinkle in Time* continues to be one of the best-selling children's books of all time, but it is also one of the most banned books, accused by some as providing an inaccurate portrayal of the deity. However, reviewing a year 2000 reprint of the ever-popular title, Patrick McCormick, writing in *U.S. Catholic,* felt that "this is a story that mixes mystery, science, and theology while offering a prescription of compassion and uncommon sense."

In 2001 L'Engle published her first picture book, *The Other Dog,* a poodle's account of the arrival of a new "dog" in the family. In this case, the poodle belongs to the L'Engle family, and the new arrival—which is fed on demand, does its business in something called a diaper, and is not forced to go outside for a walk in all sort of weather—is actually a baby. Our poodle narrator, Touche, however, does not yet realize this. *Booklist*'s Ilene Cooper called the picture book a "delightful offering" and further commented that young readers "who get the joke that Touche misses, will find this very funny." Starr LaTronica, writing in *School Library Journal,* called *The Other Dog* a "whimsical look at sibling rivalry from a canine point of view." And a contributor for *Publishers Weekly* dubbed the picture book an "impish, tongue-in-cheek memoir," concluding that any family "with a cosseted dog and a new baby will feel this is written just for them."

In addition to her long career as a children's book writer, L'Engle has published both adult novels and nonfiction. Her nonfiction books explore family relationships as well as religious and metaphysical subjects. *Mothers and Daughters,* produced in collaboration with her adopted daughter, is an "homage to the relationship between mothers and daughters," according to a reviewer for *Publishers Weekly.* A compilation of short prose extracts, prayers, and quotations from her earlier works, *Mothers and Daughters* explores the "ebb and flow" of such relationships, according to the writer from *Publishers Weekly.* In *Bright Evening Star,* L'Engle "offers a set of poetic meditations on the meaning and mystery of the incarnation of God in Jesus," according to a contributor for *Publishers Weekly.* The same writer concluded, "While there is nothing very theologically profound about L'Engle's meditations, her sparkling prose and ability to tell a good story about the nature of faith make the book worthwhile." Indeed, in all of L'Engle's writing, the element of religion and faith is important if not central to the story. In an interview with Dee Dee Risher of *The Other Side,* L'Engle commented, "I didn't have a Damascus-road experience. I just wandered along in the world of literature and allowed myself to see stories more and more as proof [of Christianity]. Some stories we have heard so often we've forgotten what they mean." Speaking with Charlie LeDuff of the *New York Times*, L'Engle remarked, "I'm lightly Episcopalian, but I thrive on the mystery. I don't particularly want to understand that mystery."

Biographical and Critical Sources

BOOKS

Authors and Artists for Young Adults, Volume 28, Gale (Detroit, MI), 1999.

Authors in the News, Volume 2, Gale (Detroit, MI), 1976.

Beacham's Encyclopedia of Popular Fiction, Beacham Publishing (Osprey, FL), Volume 2, 1996, Volume 8, 1996.

Beacham's Guide to Literature for Young Adults, Beacham Publishing (Osprey, FL), Volume 2, 1990, Volume 4, 1990, Volume 5, 1991, Volume 7, 1994.

Chase, Carole F., *Madeleine L'Engle, Suncatcher: Spiritual Vision of a Storyteller*, LuraMedia (San Diego, CA), 1995.

Children's Literature Review, Gale (Detroit, MI), Volume 1, 1976, Volume 14, 1988.

Contemporary Literary Criticism, Volume 12, Gale (Detroit, MI), 1980.

Dictionary of Literary Biography, Volume 52: *American Writers for Children since 1960: Fiction*, Gale (Detroit, MI), 1986.

Hopkins, Lee Bennett, *More Books by More People*, Citation, 1974.

Huck, Charlotte S., *Children's Literature in the Elementary School*, 3rd edition, Holt (New York, NY), 1976.

L'Engle, Madeleine, *A Circle of Quiet*, Farrar, Straus (New York, NY), 1972.

L'Engle, Madeleine, *The Summer of the Great-Grandmother*, Farrar, Straus (New York, NY), 1974.

Meigs, Cornelia, editor, *A Critical History of Children's Literature*, Macmillan (New York, NY), revised edition, 1969.

Newquist, Roy, *Conversations*, Rand McNally (New York, NY), 1967.

Nodelman, Perry, editor, *Touchstones: Reflections on the Best in Children's Literature*, Volume 1, Children's Library Association, 1985.

Norton, Donna E., *Through the Eyes of a Child: An Introduction to Children's Literature*, 2nd edition, Merrill Publishing (Indianapolis, IN), 1987.

St. James Guide to Children's Writers, 5th edition, St. James Press (Detroit, MI), 1999.

Townsend, John Rowe, *A Sense of Story: Essays on Contemporary Writers for Children*, Lippincott (Philadelphia, PA), 1971.

Viguers, Ruth Hill, *Margin for Surprise: About Books, Children, and Librarians*, Little, Brown (Boston, MA), 1964.

Wytenbroek, J. R., with Roger C. Schlobin, *Nothing Is Ordinary: The Extraordinary Vision of Madeleine L'Engle*, Borgo Press (San Bernardino, CA), 1995.

PERIODICALS

America, October 2, 1993; March 16, 1996, p. 19.

Booklist, September 1, 1992, p. 4; April 15, 1994, p. 1547; August, 1994, p. 2039; May 1, 1996, p. 1488; May 15, 1996, p. 1604; March 15, 1997, p. 1253; May 15, 1998, pp. 1620-1621; March 1, 2001, Ilene Cooper, review of *The Other Dog*, p. 1287.

Children's Literature in Education, winter, 1975, Ruth Rausen, "An Interview with Madeleine L'Engle"; summer, 1976, pp. 96-102, winter, 1983, pp. 195-203, spring, 1987, pp. 34-44.

Christian Century, April 6, 1977, p. 321; November 20, 1985, p. 1067.

Christianity Today, June 8, 1979.

Christian Science Monitor, February 4, 1993, p. 13; December 13, 1994, p. 11.

Horn Book, August, 1963, Madeleine L'Engle, "The Expanding Universe"; December, 1983.

Language Arts, October, 1977, pp. 812-816.

Library Journal, May 1, 1996, p. 100.

Lion and the Unicorn, fall, 1977, pp. 25-39.

Ms., July-August, 1987.

National Catholic Reporter, June 20, 1986, Michael J. Farrell, "Madeleine L'Engle: In Search of Where Lion and Lamb Abide."

New York Times, June 1, 1991, p. 9; March 15, 2001, Charlie LeDuff, "Busier than Ever at 82, and Yes, Still Writing," p. B2.

New York Times Book Review, July 8, 1973, Michele Murray, review of *A Wind in the Door*, p. 8.

The Other Side, March-April, 1998, Dee Dee Risher, "Listening to the Story," pp. 36-39; March-April, 1998, pp. 40-42.

PEN Newsletter, September, 1988, p. 18.

People Weekly, November 28, 1994, p. 47.

Publishers Weekly, July 13, 1990, p. 55; August 3, 1992, p. 58; July 4, 1994, p. 65; March 25, 1996, p. 60; May 13, 1996, p. 68; February 24, 1997, review of *Mothers and Daughters*, p. 76; September 15, 1997, review of *Bright Evening Star*, p. 70; October 18, 1999, p. 85; February 12, 2001, review of *The Other Dog*, p. 212.

School Library Journal, May, 1973, Margaret A. Dorsey, review of *A Wind in the Door*, p. 81; May, 1990, p. 66; November, 1990, p. 128; March, 1994, p. 183; June, 1995, pp. 60, 71; May, 2001, Starr LaTronica, review of *The Other Dog*, p. 126.

U.S. Catholic, August, 2000, Patrick McCormick, review of *A Wrinkle in Time*, p. 46.

OTHER

Madeleine L'Engle Web Site, http://www.madeleinelengle.com/ (September 10, 2001).*

*   *   *

LEWIS, Brian 1963-

Personal

Born May 26, 1963, in San Diego, CA; son of Martin (a college professor) and Patricia (McKenna) Lewis; married Julie Jaskol (a director of communications), January

5, 1992; children: Rose, Walker. *Education:* Occidental College, B.A., 1985. *Hobbies and other interests:* Politics, Los Angeles history, books, golf.

Addresses

Home—11759 Gateway Blvd., Los Angeles, CA 90064. *Office*—Los Angeles Independent Newspaper Group, 4201 Wilshire Blvd., Suite 600, Los Angeles, CA 90010. *E-mail*—jaskolewis@aol.com.

Career

Glendale News-Press, Glendale, CA, reporter, 1986-88; Los Angeles Independent Newspaper Group, Los Angeles, CA, reporter, 1988-94, editor, 1994—. Volunteer with local school enrichment program; volunteer coach.

Awards, Honors

Named outstanding columnist, California Newspaper Publishers Association, 1997; award from Greater Los Angeles Press Club, 1998, for best weekly newspaper.

Writings

(With wife, Julie Jaskol) *City of Angels: In and around Los Angeles,* illustrated by Elisa Kleven, Dutton (New York, NY), 1999.

LINDGREN, Astrid (Ericsson) 1907-2002

OBITUARY NOTICE—See index for *SATA* sketch: Born November 14, 1907, in Vimmerby, Sweden; died January 28, 2002, in Stockholm, Sweden. Author. Lindgren was best known for her children's books, especially her stories about a fearless, red-headed girl named "Pippi Longstocking." Lindgren wrote her first book, *Britt-Mari Opens Her Heart,* in 1944. She wrote *Pippi Longstocking* as a present for her daughter's tenth birthday. It was published in 1945. Other popular books include the "Kitty" series and *The Six Bullerby Children.* Lindgren received many awards for her work, including the Hans Christian Andersen Award in 1958 and the Lewis Carroll Shelf Award for *Pippi Longstocking* in 1973. Lindgren was an avid defender of children's rights and animal welfare. In 1998 Astrid Lindgren's Children's Hospital opened. There is a theme park devoted entirely to the author and her stories in her hometown in Sweden.

OBITUARIES AND OTHER SOURCES:

PERIODICALS

Chicago Tribune, January 29, 2002, section 2, p. 11.
Guardian (London, England), January 29, 2002.
Washington Post, January 29, 2002, p. B7.

M

MACK, Tracy 1968-

Personal

Born February 3, 1968, in Mount Vernon, NY; daughter of Stephen Jay and Elaine (Caroline) Mack; married Michael Citrin (an attorney), June 30, 2001. *Education:* University of Pennsylvania, B.A.; also attended Queen Mary College (London, England). *Politics:* Democrat. *Religion:* Jewish. *Hobbies and other interests:* Yoga, traveling, hiking, reading.

Addresses

Home—364 Clinton St., Brooklyn, NY 11231. *Office*—Scholastic, 555 Broadway, New York, NY 10012. *E-mail*—tmoaxaca@mindspring.com.

Career

Scholastic, New York, NY, executive editor, 1992—. *Member:* Society of Children's Book writers and Illustrators, Adirondack 46R Club.

Writings

Drawing Lessons (novel), Scholastic (New York, NY), 2000.

Work in Progress

Two novels.

Sidelights

Tracy Mack told *SATA:* "I have been writing for as long as I can remember. The first story I ever wrote and carefully bound between two construction-paper-blue covers was about a girl whose family moved to Minnesota. Until last year, I had never been to that lush, cold state; I just fantasized about living in a place with such a beautiful name.

"I am very influenced by beauty. The house I grew up in was surrounded by trees: towering oaks, beeches, and maples. There was even a tree growing right through the deck of our house. Because it was in front of a large window, it looked as if the tree were standing in our living room. I spent the summers of my childhood and adolescence at a wilderness camp in the Adirondack

In Tracy Mack's novel, artistic teenager Rory suffers greatly when her father leaves the family and she must divorce herself from identifying with his creative talent. (Cover photo by Marc Tauss.)

Mountains of northern New York State, where we lived in tiny wooden cabins with no electricity, nestled in pine and birch groves.

"My love for trees was (and still is) deep and all-encompassing. I climbed them, swung from their branches, made projects from their pine cone and acorn and needle offerings. From them, like Rory, the young artist in my novel *Drawing Lessons,* I learned to find solace and inspiration in the world around me.

"Today I live on the second floor of a brownstone on a tree-lined street in Brooklyn, New York. In a city known for its concrete and skyscrapers, I was fortunate enough to find an apartment overlooking a small cluster of trees, including a proud oak that stretches way above the tops of the neighboring buildings. I watch its lanky branches waving as I gaze out the window of my tiny office, and I remember how it felt to be a child. The trees remind me how important it is to surround myself with beauty.

"I am passionate about words and images, their power to heal and transform and affirm. I love describing things and trying to get at their essence. I love challenging myself to see the beauty in an object or situation that might otherwise be written off as ugly, inconsequential, or mundane.

"I'm also fascinated by the world of emotions and how we can use our feelings to create beauty. If I'm feeling angered or confused or hurt by someone, I try to explore those strong feelings within the landscape of my novel, within my characters. My aim is to reach a point of illumination—to bring out those dark, churning feelings inside me and turn them into something else, compassion, understanding.

"I hope my books illuminate for kids the strength of their internal resources and the possibility of using their feelings to create something beautiful, something uniquely their own."

Biographical and Critical Sources

PERIODICALS

Booklist, March 15, 2000, Frances Bradburn, review of *Drawing Lessons,* p. 1376; November 15, 2000, Hazel Rochman, review of *Drawing Lessons,* p. 631.
Childhood Education, winter, 2000, Lucille Fanger, review of *Drawing Lessons,* p. 108.
Publishers Weekly, March 13, 2000, review of *Drawing Lessons,* p. 85.
School Library Journal, March, 2000, Francisca Goldsmith, review of *Drawing Lessons,* p. 240.*

*   *   *

MAGORIAN, Michelle 1947-

Personal

Born November 6, 1947, in Portsmouth, England; married in 1987; children: one son. *Education:* Rose Bruford College of Speech and Drama, diploma, 1969; London University, certificate in film studies, 1984; attended École Internationale de Mime, 1969-70. *Hobbies and other interests:* Dancing, singing, reading, swimming.

Addresses

Home—803 Harrow Rd., Wembley, Middlesex HA0 2LP, England. *Agent*—Patricia White, Rogers, Coleridge & White, 20 Powis Mews, London W11 1JN, England.

Career

Writer and actress. Appeared in several television programs and the 1980 film *McVicar.* Has performed mime shows and was a member of a repertory theater group.

Awards, Honors

Carnegie Medal commendation, 1981, children's book award, International Reading Association, Best Books for Young Adults citation, American Library Association (ALA), and British Guardian Award for Children's Literature, all 1982, all for *Good Night, Mr. Tom;* West Australian Young Readers' Book Award, Library Association of Australia, 1983, for *Good Night, Mr. Tom,* and 1987, for *Back Home;* Best Book for Young Adults citation, ALA, 1984, for *Back Home.*

Writings

Good Night, Mr. Tom, Harper (New York, NY), 1982.
Back Home, Harper (New York, NY), 1984.
Waiting for My Shorts to Dry (poetry), illustrated by Jean Baylis, Kestrel (London, England), 1989.
Who's Going to Take Care of Me?, illustrated by James Graham Hale, HarperCollins (New York, NY), 1990.
A Little Love Song, Kestrel (New York, NY), 1991.
Orange Paw Marks (poetry), illustrated by Jean Baylis, Kestrel (London, England), 1991.
Not a Swan, HarperCollins (New York, NY), 1992.
Jump!, Walker Books (New York, NY), 1992.
Cuckoo in the Nest, Mammoth (London, England), 1994.
A Spoonful of Jam, Mammoth (London, England), 1998.

Author of *In Deep Water* (short stories), 1994, and the lyrics and book for the musical play, *Hello Life!* Also author of short stories appearing in books and periodicals. *Goodnight, Mr. Tom* has been translated into ten languages.

Adaptations

Back Home was adapted as a television film.

Sidelights

Michelle Magorian is a prize-winning British author of books for young adults, including *Good Night, Mr. Tom, Back Home, Not A Swan,* and *A Spoonful of Jam.* Born in 1947, in Portsmouth, England, Magorian is the daughter of a Navy man and spent much of her youth in Singapore and Australia before returning to England at age nine. By this time she was already writing stories, or, as she told *Carousel*'s Chris Stephenson, she was always "scribbling away." However, initially another career beckoned, that of the stage.

At nineteen, she began studying drama at the Rose Bruford College of Speech and Drama in London, and then later in Paris with the well-known mime, Marcel Marceau. Back in England, and working as an actress in a repertory theater, she began her literary career by writing short stories in her spare time. Eventually, she decided to attempt a children's novel, and three years later *Good Night, Mr. Tom* was published.

Both *Good Night, Mr. Tom* and *Back Home* depict the disruption to the lives of their protagonists caused by World War II. In each work, a resolution is achieved through trust and communication with an older character. Critics praise Magorian's novels for their believable characterizations, mature subject matter, and accurate portraits of England and America during the 1940s.

Magorian's first book, *Good Night, Mr. Tom*, grew out of a short story about two characters: Tom, a reclusive widower, and Willie, a young boy sent to live with Tom during the war. Although she was born after World War II ended, the author researched the era to provide her books with authentic details. The author explained that it took three years to write *Good Night, Mr. Tom* because of her work with the theater. Magorian once commented, "The story is about how [Mr. Tom] and Willie both change through living together." Hazel Rochman called this debut novel "moving" in a *Booklist* review, while Stephenson noted that it "is regarded as a modern classic."

While performing research for *Good Night, Mr. Tom*, Magorian unearthed a photograph that would haunt her and become the basis of her second young adult novel, *Back Home*. The photograph depicted a group of English children returning to England after a five-year stay in America during World War II. Magorian noticed that they looked "Americanized" and wondered how they coped with their re-integration into British society.

Back Home is the story of Rusty, an adolescent who has spent the war years with relatives in America. The story focuses on how Rusty adapts to post-war England. The story also focuses on Peggy, Rusty's mother, who discovered "new strengths and abilities" during the war and who subsequently has a more liberal view regarding traditional gender roles for her and her children, according to Caroline C. Hunt in *Twentieth-Century Young Adult Writers*. *Back Home* was also praised by critics and garnered a citation as a Best Book for Young Adults from the American Library Association in 1984. Stephenson noted of this novel that Magorian's "awesome depth of research lends a rich, resonant, never spurious authenticity" to her work.

"Although all of . . . Magorian's young adult novels take place during World War II, their subjects would have been unmentionable in juvenile fiction of the 1940s: child abuse, illegitimacy, sexuality, gender roles, and class differences," argued Hunt. "Yet these are not harsh books, thanks to Magorian's engaging protagonists, her sensitive yet powerful writing style, and her emotional honesty."

In *Not a Swan*, Magorian takes readers to the summer of 1944, the year Rose is seventeen and sent to the country while her widowed mother is off entertaining the troops. Left unchaperoned at the last moment, "Rose learns about sex and about love—in that order," according to a reviewer for *Publishers Weekly*, who also called the book "long [and] cozy," with a "plucky, just-short-of-perfect heroine."

Magorian moves on to the austerity of the postwar world in *Cuckoo in the Nest* and *A Spoonful of Jam*. In the latter novel, Elsie, the younger sister of the protagonist from *Cuckoo in the Nest*, comes into self-awareness in this world of the mid- to late-1940s, and also begins to realize her theatrical potential. *Carousel*'s Stephenson felt that *A Spoonful of Jam* "proves once again its author's enviable talent for creating and evoking . . . an enthralling, all-embracing fictional world."

Biographical and Critical Sources

BOOKS

Twentieth-Century Young Adult Writers, St. James Press (Detroit, MI), 1994, 2nd edition, 1999.

PERIODICALS

Booklist, August, 1992, p. 2005; April 1, 1999, Hazel Rochman, review of *Good Night, Mr. Tom,* p. 1429.
Book Report, March-April, 1993, p. 41.
Carousel, winter, 1998, Chris Stephenson, "Michelle Magorian."
Commonweal, March 23, 1984, p. 177.
Horn Book, June, 1982, pp. 299-300; January-February, 1985, pp. 60-61; January-February, 1991, p. 58.
New Yorker, December 6, 1982, p. 192.
New York Times Book Review, April 25, 1982, p. 34.
Publishers Weekly, October 26, 1984, p. 105; July 20, 1992, pp. 251-252.
School Library Journal, April 15, 1982, p. 73; August, 1983, p. 27; October, 1984, p. 169; September, 1992, p. 278.
Times Educational Supplement, November 1, 1991, p. 28.

OTHER

Michelle Magorian, http://www.dd.chalmers.se/ (October 20, 2001).
Michelle Magorian Web Site, http://www.michellemagorian.com/ (October 20, 2001).*

MALLORY, Kenneth 1945-

Personal

Born March 22, 1945, in Boston, MA; son of George Kenneth (a pathologist) and Carol Fisher (a homemaker) Mallory; married Margaret Thompson (a middle school teacher), September, 19, 1978. *Education:* Harvard College, B.A., 1967. *Politics:* "Independent."

Addresses

Home—37 Oak Terrace, Newton Highlands, MA 02461. *Office*—New England Aquarium, Central Wharf, Boston, MA 02110. *Agent*—Doe Coover Agency, P.O. Box 668, Winchester, MA 01890. *E-mail*—kmallory@neaq.org.

Career

MIT Press, Cambridge, MA, sales representative, 1971-74; Earthwatch, Belmont, MA, marketing director, 1975; New England Aquarium, Boston, MA, editor-in-chief of publishing programs, 1979—. *Member:* New England Science Writers, Society for Environmental Journalists.

Awards, Honors

The Last Extinction was selected by *Library Journal* as one of the 100 most important books of 1986; "Outstanding Nature Book for Children," John Burroughs Association, 1989, for *Rescue of the Stranded Whales; Search for the Right Whales* was selected as one of the sixty best children's books in 1993; *Home by the Sea*

Kenneth Mallory

was selected as one of the Smithsonian's Notable Children's Books, 1998.

Writings

(Editor, with Les Kaufman) *The Last Extinction,* MIT Press (Cambridge, MA), 1986.

(With Andrea Conley) *Rescue of the Stranded Whales,* Crown (New York, NY), 1989.

Water Hole: Life in a Rescued Tropical Forest, Franklin Watts (New York, NY), 1991.

(And photographer) *The Red Sea,* Franklin Watts (New York, NY), 1991.

(With Scott Kraus) *The Search for the Right Whale: How Scientists Rediscovered the Most Endangered Whale in the Sea,* Crown (New York, NY), 1993.

Families of the Deep Blue Sea, illustrated by Marshall Peck III, Charlesbridge (Watertown, MA), 1995.

A Home by the Sea: Protecting Coastal Wildlife, Harcourt (San Diego, CA), 1998.

(With Mark Chandler) *Lake Victoria: Africa's Inland Sea,* New England Aquarium and Lowell Institute, 2000.

(With Pamela Chanko and Susan Canzares) *Aquarium,* Scholastic (New York, NY), 2000.

Swimming with Hammerhead Sharks, Houghton Mifflin (Boston, MA), 2001.

Work in Progress

Guidebook to the Boston Harbor Islands National Park Area for Down East Books; conducting research for a book on the world's only underwater laboratory for science; a book about hydrothermal vents in the deep ocean.

Sidelights

Kenneth Mallory's educational background in literature and biology led him to begin writing as a freelance journalist for magazines. He once commented that his interest in the natural ecology of Maine, where he grew up, later led him to continue writing articles dealing with natural history, and that his experiences writing exhibit copy for the New England Aquarium helped develop a style that was suitable for children's books. He combined this writing ability with a developing interest in photography to produce nonfiction photo books that paralleled themes highlighted by the Aquarium, such as marine conservation and investigations and research into aquatic and natural life. Mallory noted that his position with the Aquarium also afforded him opportunities to travel to such destinations as New Zealand, the North Atlantic, and Costa Rica, resulting in books on the ecology and natural wildlife of these areas. Although Mallory continues to write children's books, he related that he is planning books for older audiences as well, including a work focusing on the Boston Harbor Islands National Park area.

One of the first books Mallory issued was titled *The Red Sea,* and it focused on the vast variety of species that inhabit this body of water and included several maps, a glossary, a list of further readings and index. A critic for

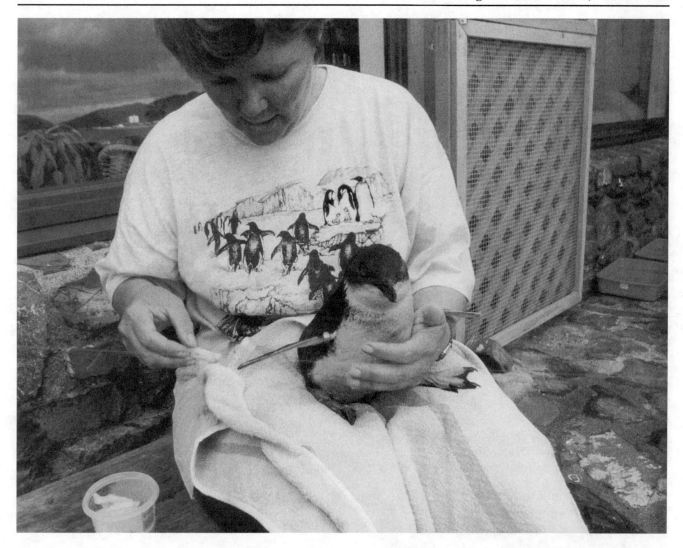

Mallory penned this tribute to three New Zealand conservation programs and enhanced his text with photographs. (From A Home by the Sea: Protecting Coastal Wildlife.*)*

Kirkus Reviews praised this book for its "vivid underwater photos" and "intriguing text." Similarly, Frances E. Millhouser praised Mallory's "fine full-color photographs" in a review for *School Library Journal,* recommending the book as one that provides a good overview of the wildlife inhabiting the Red Sea.

Mallory's position with the New England Aquarium gave him the opportunity to be at close quarters when a herd of forty pilot whales beached themselves off the coast of Cape Cod in 1986. Due to exposure and the shock the whales were subjected to, scientists were able to only save three baby whales from the group. Mallory's book, *Rescue of the Stranded Whales,* tracks these efforts on behalf of the three babies, Baby, Notch, and Tag, from the initial encounter at the beach to their final release into the wild a few months later. A critic for *Kirkus Reviews* called the book an "appealing story of scientists and conservationists in action." Phillis Wilson wrote in *Booklist* that this work is "a prime example of an informative science narrative that works as a compelling story." Mallory and coauthor Andrea Conley were also lauded in *School Library Journal* by Frances E.

Millhouser, who felt that the story told in this work was not only informative and "fascinating," but also "beautifully illustrated."

Whales are once again the focus of Mallory's *The Search for the Right Whale: How Scientists Rediscovered the Most Endangered Whale in the Sea.* Coauthored with Scott Kraus, this book contains a first-person narrative relating the search for this species of whales. Reviewing the work for *School Library Journal,* Valerie Lennox noted that the approach taken by Mallory and Kraus provides a good introduction to the events during a research expedition, and called the work a "top-notch resource for endangerment projects." Kay Weisman, writing in *Booklist,* praised the photographs and descriptions of whale sightings in particular, labeling the work "an appealing and useful addition to the animal shelf."

Mallory went to Costa Rica on assignment from the Aquarium in the late 1980s, resulting in a book about the reclaimed tropical forest in the Guanacaste National Park area. Once again, Mallory accompanied his text with colorful illustrations to produce *Water Hole: Life in a Rescued Tropical Forest,* also adding a glossary and suggested list of other titles. Focusing primarily on a small band of tropical raccoon-like animals called coatis, Mallory's text tracks these and other creatures in the forest over a course of one year. Mallory has continued writing about other geographical and aquatic regions in his books, including *Families of the Deep Blue Sea,* which focuses on fourteen different species of ocean dwellers, and *A Home by the Sea,* a book that focuses on efforts to protect coastal and marine animal life off the coast of New Zealand. Both texts have been praised for their clear text and photographs, as well as their focus on the scientists who work on these projects.

Scientist and marine biologist Pete Klimley and his IMAX film team were the focus of Mallory's *Swimming with Hammerhead Sharks,* a work that tracks the film team as much as it does the sharks they are trying to capture on camera. This combined record of investigation and biology was lauded by Patricia Manning in *School Library Journal* as an "exceptional" work that will prove to be a "useful tool for young report writers."

Biographical and Critical Sources

PERIODICALS

Booklist, July, 1989, Phillis Watson, review of *Rescue of the Stranded Whales,* p. 1905; May, 1993, Janice Del Negro, review of *Water Hole,* p. 1585; July, 1993, Kay Weisman, review of *The Search for the Right Whale,* p. 1961; April 1, 2001, Roger Leslie, review of *Swimming with Hammerhead Sharks,* p. 1462.

Horn Book Guide, fall, 1993, Kelly A. Ault, review of *Water Hole,* p. 341; spring, 1996, Peter D. Sieruta, review of *Families of the Deep Blue Sea,* p. 109.

Kirkus Reviews, June 1, 1989, review of *Rescue of the Stranded Whales,* p. 839; March 15, 1991, review of *The Red Sea,* p. 397; July 15, 1998, review of *A Home by the Sea,* p. 1038.

School Library Journal, June, 1989, Frances E. Millhouser, review of *Rescue of the Stranded Whales,* p. 119; August, 1991, Frances E. Millhouser, review of *The Red Sea,* p. 193; April, 1993, Eva Elisabeth Von Ancken, review of *Water Hole,* p. 137; August, 1993, Valerie Lenox, review of *The Search for the Right Whale,* p. 176; February, 1996, Lisa Wu Stowe, review of *Families of the Deep Blue Sea,* p. 96; September, 1998, Patricia Manning, review of *A Home by the Sea,* p. 222; July, 2001, Patricia Manning, review of *Swimming with Hammerhead Sharks,* p. 128.

*   *   *

MAXWELL, William (Keepers, Jr.) 1908-2000

Personal

Born August 16, 1908, in Lincoln, IL; died July 31, 2000, in New York, NY; son of William Keepers (an insurance executive) and Eva Blossom (Blinn) Maxwell; married Emily Gilman Noyes, May 17, 1945; children: Katharine Farrington, Emily Brooke. *Education:* University of Illinois, B.A., 1930; Harvard University, M.A., 1931.

Career

Novelist and short story writer. University of Illinois—Urbana, member of English faculty, 1931-33; *New Yorker,* New York, NY, member of editorial staff, 1936-76.

Awards, Honors

Friends of American Writers Award, 1938; National Institute of Arts and Letters grant, 1958; Howells Medal, American Academy of Arts and Letters, 1980; American Book Award, 1982, for *So Long, See You Tomorrow;* Creative Arts Award Medal for Fiction, Brandeis University, 1984; Harold Washington Award, Chicago Public Library, 1990; Heartland Award, *Chicago Tribune,* 1995; PEN/Malamud Award for the short story, 1995; Mark Twain Award, 1995; Gold Medal for Fiction, American Academy of Arts and Letters, 1995; Ivan Sandrof Award for Lifetime Achievement in Publishing, National Book Critics Circle, 1995.

Writings

Bright Center of Heaven (novel), Harper (New York, NY), 1934.

They Came like Swallows (novel), Harper (New York, NY), 1937, revised edition, Vintage (New York, NY), 1960.

The Folded Leaf (novel), Harper (New York, NY), 1945, revised edition, Vintage (New York, NY), 1959.

The Heavenly Tenants (fantasy for children), illustrated by Ilonka Karasz, Harper (New York, NY), 1946.

Time Will Darken It (novel), Harper (New York, NY), 1948.

Stories, Farrar, Straus (New York, NY), 1956.

The Chateau (novel), Knopf (New York, NY), 1961.

The Old Man at the Railroad Crossing and Other Tales (stories), Knopf (New York, NY), 1966.

Ancestors: A Family History (novel), Knopf (New York, NY), 1971.

Over by the River, and Other Stories (stories), Knopf (New York, NY), 1977.

So Long, See You Tomorrow (novel), Knopf (New York, NY), 1980, large print edition, G. K. Hall (Boston, MA), 1980.

(Editor) Charles Pratt, *The Garden and the Wilderness* (photographs), Horizon Press (New York, NY), 1980.

(Editor) Sylvia Townsend Warner, *Letters,* Chatto and Windus (London, England), 1982.

Five Tales: Written for His Family on Special Occasions and Printed to Celebrate His Eightieth Birthday, 16 August 1988 (limited edition), Cummington Press (Omaha, NE), 1988.

The Outermost Dream: Essays and Reviews, Knopf (New York, NY), 1989.

Billie Dyer and Other Stories, Knopf (New York, NY), 1992, large print edition, G. K. Hall (Thorndike, ME), 1992.

William Maxwell

Richard Bausch and William Maxwell Reading Their Short Stories (sound recording), Archive of Recorded Poetry and Literature, Library of Congress (Washington, DC), 1992.

All the Days and Nights: The Collected Stories of William Maxwell, Knopf (New York, NY), 1995.

Mrs. Donald's Dog Bun and His Home Away from Home (for children), illustrated by James Stevenson, Knopf (New York, NY), 1995.

The Happiness of Getting It down Right: Letters of Frank O'Connor and William Maxwell, 1945-1966, edited by Michael Steinman, Knopf (New York, NY), 1996.

The Element of Lavishness: Letters of Sylvia Townsend Warner and William Maxwell, Counterpoint Press (Washington, D.C.), 1997.

Contributor to *Eudora Welty: Writers' Reflections upon First Reading Welty,* Hill Street Press, 1999. Contributor of stories and book reviews to periodicals, including the *New Yorker, Paris Review, Harper's Bazaar, New England Review,* and *WigWag.*

Adaptations

So Long, See You Tomorrow was recorded on audio cassette, American Audio Prose Library (Columbus, MO), 1997.

Sidelights

Known for his work on the *New Yorker,* William Maxwell was also the author of twenty books, including a family history that traces his ancestry back to American pioneers. His novels and stories have drawn praise from critics, and he has on occasion been variously compared to Sinclair Lewis, Henry Fuller, and Sherwood Anderson. With a "gentle wit" and an appreciation of rural America, Maxwell painted a picture of small-town life in the Midwest, untouched by the worldliness and loneliness of the big city. Maxwell once said that he did not consider his books to be nostalgic "in the strict sense." "I write about the past," he stated, "not because I think it is better than the present but because of things that happened that I do not want to be forgotten."

Many of Maxwell's books and stories are set in his hometown of Lincoln, Illinois, or a fictional counterpart. *Chicago Tribune* contributor John Blades once quoted Maxwell as explaining his preoccupation with the town in this way: "To begin with, it was a very pretty town with elm trees meeting over the brick pavements, and a great deal of individuality in the houses, and the people as well. And because I left it when I was still a boy, my early memories are not overlaid by others, so the Lincoln of the first decades of this century is very vivid to me." Born there on August 16, 1908, Maxwell lived an idyllic childhood in this tree-shaded town. However, when he was ten, this abruptly changed when his mother died during the influenza epidemic following World War One. Shortly thereafter, his father remarried, sold the house in Lincoln, and moved his family to Chicago. By high school, Maxwell was deeply involved in the world of books. *Treasure Island* was the first real work of literature he got in his hands, when he was a freshman in high school. As Maxwell told David Streitfeld in the *Washington Post,* "At the last page, I turned back to the beginning. I didn't stop until I had read it five times. I've been that way ever since. I never could explain to my father what it was that I was after, not in terms he could understand." Maxwell earned his bachelor's degree at the University of Illinois, and then went on to do his master's work at Harvard. Thereafter, he taught freshman composition at the University of Illinois—Urbana. In 1933, in the midst of the Depression, Maxwell quit this job to try his own hand at writing, publishing his first novel, *Bright Center of Heaven,* the following year.

Maxwell lived most of his life in New York City, where he settled in 1936. With one book published when he arrived in the city, his publisher had given him letters of reference to three major magazines. Maxwell once commented that one letter was "to the *New Republic,* one to *Time,* and one to the *New Yorker.* I was unsuited for the *New Republic* because I was politically uninformed. I don't know if I was unsuited to *Time* as well; I got to the *New Yorker* before I got to *Time,* and they hired me, and that was that. There was a vacancy in the art department, and I found myself sitting in at the weekly art meeting, and on the following day I would tell the artists whether or not their work had been bought, and any changes in their drawings that the meeting wanted."

Maxwell eventually became one of the prestigious magazine's fiction editors, working with highly respected authors such as John O'Hara, J. D. Salinger, John Updike, and John Cheever. Maxwell once noted that there was never a conscious attempt to create a *New Yorker* fiction style; however, he allowed that "*New Yorker* editors tend to cut out unnecessary words and to punctuate according to the house rules, and most often the prose advances sentence by sentence in its effects, rather than by paragraphs in which any given sentence may not carry that much weight. The result is a certain density that may appear to be a 'style.' But when you consider the fiction writers who have appeared frequently in the magazine, for example, John Updike, John Cheever, John O'Hara, Vladimir Nabokov, Mary McCarthy, Mavis Gallant, Sylvia Townsend Warner, Shirley Hazzard, Eudora Welty, J. D. Salinger, Frank O'Connor, Maeve Brennan, and Larry Woiwode—it is immediately apparent that there is no style common to all of them."

Maxwell's trademark style has been described as "thoughtful, quiet, painfully compassionate but also painfully shy," by *Yale Review* contributor Wendy Lesser. Of his novels, *The Folded Leaf* has been singled out by a number of critics as a good example of Maxwell's "genuine artistry." A sensitive portrayal of the friendship between two adolescent boys of different temperament, the novel is, according to Diana Trilling, an "important social document." Edmund Wilson wrote that Maxwell "approaches such matters as fraternity initiations and gratuitous schoolboy fights, the traditional customs of childhood, from an anthropological point of view ... [and] with careful, unobtrusive art, [he] has made us feel all the coldness and hardness and darkness of Chicago, the prosaic surface of existence which seems to stretch about one like asphalt or ice. But there are moments when the author breaks away into a kind of poetic reverie that shows he is able to find a way out." Colby Walworth emphasized the difficulty of the book's theme, and praised Maxwell's "affectionate insight into the frailties of immaturity" in his characterizations of Lymie Peters and Spud Latham. Richard Sullivan concluded: "[The novel] does precisely, beautifully and completely what it sets out to do.... It is a satisfaction to read prose always so admirably controlled, so governed with distinction."

They Came like Swallows, an account of the effects of a Spanish influenza epidemic on a close-knit family, also drew praise from critics. David Tilden called it an "unpretentious book, simple and straightforward and natural, unspoiled by sentimentality." Fanny Butcher concurred, "The children are as real as any children in literature. There is neither oversentimentalizing nor that sometimes too obvious ... lack of sentiment in these simple and memorable pages." V. S. Pritchett mentioned the "lack of unity" in the novel, but noted that "otherwise the book is a sensitive, wistful reminiscence of family life."

Maxwell turned to a different theme in *The Chateau*—the American experience in Europe. According to Richard Gilman, Maxwell exercised "a trained, cool-tempered sensibility" in portraying the predicament of an American couple in postwar France. David Boraff called the work "a beguilingly old-fashioned novel, almost Jamesian in its restraint and in its delineation of subtle shifts in consciousness." For Naomi Bliven, "*The Chateau* ... is a large-scale work whose smallest details are beautifully made. The author has labored for the reader's case. His style is a joy—exact, moderate, from time to time amused or amusing, always compassionate, sometimes as startling as lightning.... This novel is fiction with the authenticity of a verified document, a history of what some citizens of the splintered Western World might say or mean to each other in our period." Elizabeth Bowen declared, "I can think of few novels, of my day certainly, that have such romantic authority as *The Chateau,* fewer still so adult in vitality, so alight with humor."

Miranda Seymour, reviewing a reprint of *The Chateau* in the *Times Literary Supplement,* noted that Bowen's praise of the earlier edition is included on the cover of the more recent pressing, and commented that Maxwell "was lucky to get a tribute from Bowen for a novel which must have sounded dated and quirky, and which was imprudent enough, moreover, to contemplate the poverty of postwar France, as seen through the eyes of a

In Maxwell's fantastic tale, a Wisconsin farmer with much curiosity about the universe finds his family caught up with characters from the zodiac. (Cover illustration by Ilonka Karasz.)

couple of wealthy young American tourists." Seymour asserted that Europeans of the 1960s didn't "welcome what sounded like patronage." They also didn't consider *The Chateau* to be a novel. "At the time, it flopped," wrote Seymour. "Now, it is hard not to see it as a work of genius."

In her review of *Over by the River, and Other Stories,* Joyce Carol Oates praised "Maxwell's gifts as a writer" which "allow him to impose upon his material a gentle, rather Chekhovian sense of order: whatever happens is not Fate but the inevitable working-out of character, never melodramatic, never pointedly 'symbolic.'" This collection of stories includes works written from 1941 to 1977. Oates pointed out a few stories that she especially liked, and spoke of Maxwell's "vision." "He is not unaware of what might be called evil," she commented, "and he is willing to explore the possibility that, yes, civilization is in decline."

So Long, See You Tomorrow is, according to Robert Wilson, "a summing up by Maxwell at the age of 71 of many of the most powerful experiences and concerns from his past work." In this novel, Maxwell recalls the death of his mother in the 1918 flu epidemic, and the family's subsequent move to Chicago. He also describes the tragedy which struck another Lincoln household: tenant farmer Clarence Smith finds out about his wife's love affair, kills her lover, and then commits suicide. Years later in Chicago, Maxwell comes face to face with Cletus Smith, Clarence's son, and the meeting stirs up painful memories for both men.

A *New York Post* critic noted that the book "is filled with the sense of desolation and bewilderment which adults inflict upon their young, wounds like those of war, never fully healing, aching with each twinge of recollection. There is compressed into this small work the scope of Greek tragedy, a sense of time and place and the accumulated perception of a thoughtful and moving writer. William Maxwell makes one believe that the best traditions of American fiction continue to survive." White claimed: "His accomplishment is to present a fascinating tragedy enacted by sincere, gentle, reluctant participants—and to give his account the same integrity that marks their deeds." Likewise, Wilson praised Maxwell for "a marvelously evocative prose style, which suggests in its grace and simplicity a gentle wind brushing autumn leaves across the yards of those stately old houses that seemingly exist outside time compared to the lives of the families who pass through them."

Maxwell's nonfiction collection, *The Outermost Dream: Essays and Reviews,* which covers a wide diversity of subjects, also won enthusiastic praise from book reviewers after it was published in 1989. Most of the items included in the book were previously published in the *New Yorker* magazine; many of the reviews focus on the diaries, biographies, and memoirs of nineteenth- and twentieth-century figures, including writers Virginia Woolf and E. B. White. *New York Times Book Review* contributor Judith Baumel concluded that "in this one

wonderful volume we get Mr. Maxwell's clear prose, his magical narrative and the attractions of his quirky mind."

Many of Maxwell's most widely acclaimed short stories appeared in *Billie Dyer and Other Stories* and *All the Days and Nights: The Collected Stories of William Maxwell.* Of the former, Carin Pratt remarked in the *Christian Science Monitor* that "his writing is simple and direct, poignant without being sentimental.... Reading these stories about when life was supposedly more simple than it is now makes you come away with the clear understanding that life has always been complicated and hard.... What's perhaps most appealing about this collection is that after finishing a story, you don't have to wonder what it's about.... [The author] ... doesn't make you feel stupid by obscuring the meaning."

Mary Flanagan included some rare criticism of the author's writing in her generally favorable *New York Times Book Review* assessment of *All the Days and Nights.* "Mr. Maxwell's work is throughout balanced, gentle and humane.... [His] realism is permeated by a tender lyricism. Mellow and unhurried, his warm, amiable voice mixes the cultivated with the colloquial. His powers of description are remarkable.... But he can also ramble, sacrificing structure to discursiveness and flirting with the literary equivalent of easy listening.... The last few stories are so similar that I kept wondering whether I was rereading the same one." But Penelope Mesic was unqualified in her praise for *All the Days and Nights.* She declared in the *Chicago Tribune:* "Maxwell, dealing in very ordinary days and nights, makes them luminous by the skillful use of contrasts, as the impressionists made a dull rain-washed street shine—not by using colors of garish brightness but by using one tone to bring another into prominence. We feel this is not only an esthetic but a moral choice. Maxwell's constant effort is to give to whatever he observes its true colors and just value."

An *Economist* contributor interviewed Maxwell in 1999 and noted that Maxwell was "the most sought-after fiction editor at the *New Yorker,* and he guided many young writers to literary maturity." "As a writer," commented Maxwell, "I don't very much enjoy being edited. As an editor I tried to work so slightly on the manuscript that ten years later the writer would read his story and not be aware that anybody was involved but him." When asked what he thought of recent trends in fiction, he replied, "I haven't been attentive. I am a very old man and it isn't about things that I know about or take an interest in—so long as fiction is truthful and accurate it will have value."

Maxwell died in his Manhattan home on July 31, 2000. His wife, Emily, died a week earlier, also in their home, of ovarian cancer. They had been married sixty-five years. *New York Times Book Review* contributor Daniel Menaker, who had trained to be an editor with Maxwell in 1975, said Maxwell "was widely regarded as a sweet and gentle man. And he was—sometimes, in his writing and editorial sensibility and in his personal and social loves, almost to the point of preciousness. If you told him that you had just taken your son to camp or that your wife had burned a roast the night before, his eyes might fill with tears." Menaker visited Maxwell a few days before his death. "He was impossibly thin and frail-looking," said Menaker, "but he smiled and his eyes were warm." Maxwell shared a very personal story concerning his mother's death with Menaker. "As Maxwell told me this story, all I understood about it was that it seemed at once disturbing and obliquely flattering. And that the elegant economy of its telling somehow kept me from falling apart altogether. The more I've thought about it since, the stronger it has grown in my mind as a distillation of Maxwell's character, at least as I saw it: the perduring influence of his parents; his spare, sure sense of narrative; his concern about decorum and its chronic destruction by love and hate; his capacity for blunt honesty; and the openness and trust of his friendship, which lasted through his final days."

Biographical and Critical Sources

PERIODICALS

Booklist, April 1, 1989, p. 1341; January 1, 2001, p. 902.
Boston Globe, January 7, 1986, p. 25; June 8, 1989, p. 86; February 25, 1992, p. 56; January 15, 1995, p. 62.
Chicago Daily Tribune, May 1, 1937; May 2, 1937.
Chicago Tribune, May 14, 1989, section 14, p. 7; February 9, 1992, section 14, p. 3; March 5, 1992, section 5, pp. 1-2; January 8, 1995, Penelope Mesic, review of *All the Days and Nights,* section 14, p. 3.
Christian Science Monitor, May 26, 1937; December 17, 1946; September 9, 1948; March 27, 1992, Carin Pratt, review of *Billie Dyer and Other Stories,* p. 17.
Commonweal, April 7, 1961, p. 50; December 10, 1971; May 22, 1992, pp. 2021.
Economist, June 26, 1999, "Maxwell's Silver Typewriter," p. 97.
Library Journal, June 1, 1996, p. 106; June 15, 1997, Peter Josyph, "William Maxwell Reads *So Long, See You Tomorrow:* An Interview with the Author," p. 114; February 1, 2001, pp. 41-42.
Los Angeles Times Book Review, January 22, 1995, p. 6; March 5, 1995, p. 9.
Nation, April 21, 1945; September 25, 1948, p. 353.
New Republic, September 10, 1977; January 26, 1980, pp. 39-40.
New Statesman and Nation, August 8, 1937, pp. 312-313; August 28, 1937.
New Yorker, March 31, 1945, pp. 81-82; September 4, 1948; March 25, 1961; December 27, 1999, Alec Wilkinson, "An American Original: Learning from a Literary Master," p. 68.
New York Post, January 12, 1980, review of *So Long, See You Tomorrow.*
New York Review of Books, April 28, 1966, pp. 23-24; October 8, 1992, pp. 49-50.
New York Times, April 8, 1945; September 5, 1948; April 29, 1989, p. A15; May 14, 1989, section 7, p. 23; February 16, 1992, section 7, p. 7; February 14, 1992, p. C27; December 30, 1994, p. C31.
New York Times Book Review, September 9, 1934, p. 17; April 8, 1945, p. 3; September 5, 1948, p. 4; March 26, 1961; March 13, 1966, p. 5; August 8, 1971; May 14, 1989, Judith Baumel, review of *The Outermost Dream,* p. 23; February 28, 1993, p. 32; June 6, 1993, p. 54; January 22, 1995, Mary Flanagan, review of *All the Days and Nights,* pp. 3, 20; October 15, 2000, Daniel Menaker, "The Gentle Realist."
Publishers Weekly, December 10, 1979, pp. 8-9; November 28, 1994, p. 43.
Rapport, Volume 18, number 6, p. 21.
Reporter, May 25, 1961.
Saturday Review of Literature, September 15, 1934, pp. 109-110; May 1, 1937, p. 4; November 9, 1946; September 4, 1948.
Spectator, February 14, 1998, p. 27; February 10, 2001, pp. 41-42.
Time, September 20, 1948.
Times Literary Supplement, August 21, 1937; January 21, 2000, p. 23; April 7, 2000, Miranda Seymour, "A Young Man with Money and a Wife," p. 28; February 16, 2001, p. 23.
Tribune Books, December 12, 1979; December 6, 1992, p. 13.
Vogue, June, 2001, pp. 84-86.
Washington Post, January 18, 1995, p. B2; October 26, 1997, David Streitfeld, "Maxwell the Reader," p. X15.
Washington Post Book World, January 13, 1980, pp. 1-2; April 30, 1989, p. 5; January 26, 1992, p. 1.
Weekly Book Review, April 8, 1945.
Yale Review, July, 1992, pp. 202-203.

Obituaries

PERIODICALS

Los Angeles Times, August 2, 2000, p. B6.
New York Times, August 1, 2000, p. A24.
Time, August 14, 2000, p. 25.
Times (London, England), August 2, 2000.
U.S. News and World Report, August 14, 2000, p. 10.
Washington Post, August 2, 2000, p. B7.*

*   *   *

McCAULEY, Adam 1965-

Personal

Born December 23, 1965, in Berkeley, CA; son of Gardiner (a painter, professor, and foundation director) and Nancy (an art historian, painter, and teacher; maiden name, Pohlman) McCauley. *Education:* Parsons School of Design, B.F.A., 1987. *Religion:* Independent. *Hobbies and other interests:* Playing music (drums, guitar, bass), singing.

Addresses

Home—2400 Eighth Ave., Oakland, CA 94606. *Agent*—(art) Maslov Weinberg, 608 York, San Francisco, CA 94110. *E-mail*—adam@atomicalley.com.

Career

Freelance illustrator. *Exhibitions:* Society of Illustrators Member Shows, New York, NY, 1996-98; "A Is for Alien Abduction" (group show), Osaka, Japan, 1997; and "American Pop Illustrators" (group show), Tokyo, Japan, 1999. McCauley's work has also been exhibited in San Francisco, CA, 1998.

Awards, Honors

Awards from Society of Illustrators, American Illustration, and Print.

Writings

(Self-illustrated) *My Friend Chicken,* Chronicle Books (San Francisco, CA), 1998.

ILLUSTRATOR

Jon Scieszka, *See You Later, Gladiator,* Viking (New York, NY), 2000.

Dan Yaccarino, *The Lima Bean Monster,* Walker Books (New York, NY), 2001.

Jon Scieszka, *Hey Kid, Want to Buy a Bridge?,* Viking (New York, NY), 2001.

Jon Scieszka, *Sam Samurai,* Viking (New York, NY), 2001.

Adam McCauley

Work in Progress

Illustrating *Viking It and Liking It,* by Jon Scieszka, for Viking, and *Martin MacGregor's Snowman,* by Lisa Broadie Cook, for Walker Books; a pair of self-illustrated works: *The Little Book of Solitaire* and *Snowman in a Box,* both for Running Press.

Sidelights

Adam McCauley told *SATA:* "Having been raised by two artists, my inclinations toward the visual arts have always been number one. My mother encouraged Dr. Seuss, Beatrix Potter, and Richard Scarry, while my dad pushed Maurice Sendak, Tolkien, and perhaps my favorite, the Oz books. I consider myself a far more developed illustrator than writer, so I look at writing as my big challenge. I've had the extraordinary honor now of illustrating books by Dan Yaccarino and Jon Scieszka, whose skills with words make drawing easy. In the future I hope to make books that will encourage kids to use their imaginations and learn to appreciate the world around them."

Biographical and Critical Sources

PERIODICALS

Booklist, January 1, 2001, Gillian Engberg, review of *See You Later, Gladiator,* p. 961; November 1, 2001, Gillian Engberg, review of *Sam Samurai,* p. 475.

Publishers Weekly, April 26, 1999, review of *My Friend Chicken,* p. 80; July 30, 2001, review of *The Lima Bean Monster,* p. 84.

School Library Journal, September, 2001, Sally R. Dow, review of *The Lima Bean Monster,* p. 209.

OTHER

Adam McCauley Web Site, http://www.atomicalley.com (February 2, 2002).

* * *

McCORMICK, Patricia 1956-

Personal

Born May 23, 1956, in Washington, DC; daughter of A. J. and Ann (Stapleton) McCormick; married Paul W. Critchlow (a public relations specialist), September 11, 1988; children: Meaghan, Matt. *Education:* Rosemont College, B.S., 1978; Columbia University, M.S., 1985; The New School (New York, NY), M.F.A., 1999.

Addresses

Home—85 Perry St., New York, NY 10014. *E-mail*—AMPattymac4@aol.com.

Career

New Brunswick (NJ) I Home News, crime reporter, *New York Times,* children's movie reviewer, *Parents* magazine, children's movie reviewer. Freelance writer. *Mem-*

ber: Authors Guild, Society of Children's Book Writers and Illustrators, The Writers Room (New York, NY; board member).

Awards, Honors

Books for the Teen Age, New York Public Library, 2000, Quick Pick for Reluctant Young Adult Readers, American Library Association (ALA), 2001, and Best Book for Young Adults, ALA, 2002, all for *Cut*.

Writings

(With Steven Cohen) *Parents Guide to the Best Family Videos,* St. Martin's Press (New York, NY), 1999.
Cut (young adult novel), Front Street Books (New York, NY), 2000.

Contributor of articles to periodicals, including *Parents* magazine and *New York Times*.

Work in Progress

Another young adult novel.

Sidelights

In 2000 Patricia McCormick made her entrance into children's literature with her young adult novel, *Cut*. The combination of a *New York Times Magazine* article about young women cutting themselves and the stress of her own life sparked in McCormick the idea for a novel about a girl in a residential treatment facility, kept there because she cuts herself in response to the pressures she feels at home. "I kept the article for months, then I finally threw it away," she told Elizabeth Devereaux in *Publishers Weekly*. While working toward an M.F.A. at the New School in New York City, McCormick found a voice. "I found myself writing in the voice of a girl, addressing her shrink in a loony bin." She traced the genesis of the idea back to that discarded article. During the writing of the novel that became *Cut*, McCormick had to resist the urge to over-research and smother the story and character in details. The protagonist, Callie, has chosen to be mute, except to the reader, who is privy to her memories of the family—a severely asthmatic brother, distracted mother, and non-coping father—and the events that led to her need to cut herself in order to maintain some semblance of control over her life.

Reviewers found much to praise about *Cut*, particularly its verisimilitude. Writing in *School Library Journal*, Gail Richmond called it "poignant and compelling reading" that "avoid[s] pathos and stereotypes." According to a *Publishers Weekly* critic, she does not sensationalize her story, instead presenting a "persuasive view of the teenage experience." "A too-tidy ending notwithstanding, this is an exceptional character study of a young woman," noted *Booklist* reviewer Frances Bradburn. Likewise, Lauren Adams of *Horn Book* found Callie's father's sudden understanding of his daughter's situation somewhat unrealistic; yet she praised McCormick's "sensitive portrayal of a young girl's illness and

Patricia McCormick's novel tells the story of mute, self-destructive Callie, who goes to therapy when her parents discover she is cutting herself, and who gradually unearths the causes for her behavior. (Cover photo by Helen Robinson.)

her difficult path to recovery." "I'd never understood cutting before I read *Cut*," wrote Elizabeth Crow in the *New York Times Book Review*. "The story of how Callie and some of the others begin to get well demystifies mental illness, but doesn't oversimplify or sentimentalize it," she added. "To McCormick's credit, we care—about the girls and about their clumsy, frightened parents."

McCormick told *SATA:* "We all do self-destructive or at least self-defeating things—usually at the very times when we need to take the best care of ourselves. Most times, the actions are relatively harmless: locking ourselves out of the house, forgetting an assignment, overdosing on Ben and Jerry's. They hurt us more than they hurt anyone else.

"It was at a time of great stress in my life that I began this book. I didn't cause myself bodily harm with a blade—I did do some stupid, panicky things—but all of a sudden a young girl appeared in my writing—a girl so lost she was seriously hurting herself. Obviously, I deeply identified with her.

"The challenge in writing her story was to make her experience authentic—to render it as truthfully as I knew how—without rendering her actions in a way that would frighten or offend readers. I hope I've done that. I hope that I've approached her story with empathy and integrity.

"When I read stories, I see, or hope to see, aspects of my life reflected in them. I'm always looking for answers in the books I read; if not answers, at least somebody who has the same question. I hope my book will be that kind of book for some reader."

Biographical and Critical Sources

PERIODICALS

Booklist, January 1, 2001, Frances Bradburn, review of *Cut,* p. 940.

Horn Book, November, 2000, Lauren Adams, review of *Cut,* p. 759.

New York Times Book Review, November 19, 2000, Elizabeth Crow, "Sounds of Silence," p. 38.

Publishers Weekly, October 23, 2000, review of *Cut,* p. 76; December 18, 2000, Elizabeth Devereaux, "Patricia McCormick," p. 26.

School Library Journal, December, 2000, Gail Richmond, review of *Cut,* p. 146.

OTHER

Front Street Books, http://www.frontstreetbooks.com/ (February 1, 2002), author profile of Patricia McCormick.*

*   *   *

McELMEEL, Sharron L. 1942-

Personal

Born September 13, 1942, in Cedar Rapids, IA; daughter of Leo L. (a farmer) and Helen (a farmer; birth name, Miller) Hanson; married E. J. "Jack" McElmeel (a sheet metal journeyman construction worker), January 12, 1963; children: Michael John, Deborah Lea, Thomas John, Matthew John, Steven John, Suzanne Lea. *Education:* State College of Iowa (now University of Northern Iowa), B.A., 1963; University of Iowa, M.A., 1972. *Politics:* "Democrat/independent." *Religion:* Roman Catholic.

Addresses

Home—R.R.1, Hermit's Hill, Cedar Rapids, IA 52411-9548. *Office*—3000 North Center Point Rd., Cedar Rapids, IA 52411-9548. *E-mail*—mcelmeel@mcelmeel.com.

Career

College Hill Grocery Store, checkout clerk, 1960-63; Cedar Rapids Community School District, Cedar Rapids, IA, began as classroom teacher, became library media specialist, 1964-98; Linworth Publishing, Worthington, OH, associate reviews editor, 1998—. Bookkeeper for a construction company, 1978-79; KCCK-FM Radio, book reviewer and commentator, 1979-84; Frank N. Magid Associates (media consulting firm), researcher, 1980-81; U.S. Postal Service, operator of a postal route, 1981. Grant Wood Area Education Agency, staff development instructor, 1982—, project director, 1998—; Mount Mercy College, adjunct instructor, 1988—. *Member:* International Reading Association, American Library Association, National Education Association (life member), Society of Children's Book Writers and Illustrators, Iowa Reading Association, Iowa State Education Association, Cedar Rapids Area Reading Council (vice president, 1985-86; president, 1986-87, 2001-02), Cedar Rapids Education Association.

Awards, Honors

Named Iowa Reading Teacher of the Year, 1987.

Writings

An Author a Month (for Pennies), Libraries Unlimited (Littleton, CO), 1988.

My Bag of Book Tricks, Libraries Unlimited (Littleton, CO), 1989.

Bookpeople: A First Album, Libraries Unlimited (Littleton, CO), 1990.

Bookpeople: A Second Album, Libraries Unlimited (Littleton, CO), 1990.

(Editor) *Iowa, a Place to Read: Celebrating Iowa Authors,* Iowa Reading Association, 1990.

An Author a Month (for Nickels), Libraries Unlimited (Littleton, CO), 1990.

Adventures with Social Studies (through Literature), Libraries Unlimited (Littleton, CO), 1991.

Authors for Children: A Calendar, Hi Willow (Fayetteville, AR), 1992.

Bookpeople: A Multicultural Album, Teacher Ideas Press (Englewood, CO), 1992.

Celebrating Authors: Meet Jacqueline Briggs Martin (videotape script), Hi Willow (San Jose, CA), 1992.

Celebrating Authors: Meet Carol Gorman (videotape script), Hi Willow (San Jose, CA), 1992.

An Author a Month (for Dimes), Libraries Unlimited (Littleton, CO), 1993.

The Poet Tree, Libraries Unlimited (Littleton, CO), 1993.

McElmeel Booknotes, Libraries Unlimited (Littleton, CO), 1993.

(Contributor) Ed Gorman, Martin H. Greenberg, and other editors, *The Fine Art of Murder: The Mystery Reader's Indispensable Companion,* Carroll & Graf (New York, NY), 1993.

The Latest and Greatest Read-Alouds, Libraries Unlimited (Littleton, CO), 1994.

The ABCs of an Author/Illustrator Visit, Linworth Publishing (Worthington, OH), 1994.

Sharron L. McElmeel

Great New Nonfiction Reads, Libraries Unlimited (Littleton, CO), 1994.

Educator's Companion to Children's Literature, Libraries Unlimited (Littleton, CO), Volume I: *Mysteries, Animal Tales, Books of Humor, Adventure Stories, and Historical Fiction,* 1995, Volume II: *Folklore, Contemporary Realistic Fiction, Fantasy, Biographies, and Tales from Here and There,* 1996.

(With Carol Simpson) *Internet for Schools,* Linworth Publishing (Worthington, OH), 1996.

Research Strategies for Moving beyond Reporting, Linworth Publishing (Worthington, OH), 1997.

One Hundred Most Popular Children's Authors: Biographical Sketches and Bibliographies, Libraries Unlimited (Littleton, CO), 1999.

(With Carol Smallwood) *WWW Almanac: Making Curriculum Connections to Special Days, Weeks, and Months,* Linworth Publishing (Worthington, OH), 1999.

(Editor) *Shop Talk: Ideas for Elementary School Librarians and Technology Specialists,* Linworth Publishing (Worthington, OH), 2nd edition, 2000.

(Editor) *Tips: Ideas for Secondary School Librarians and Technology Specialists,* Linworth Publishing (Worthington, OH), 2nd edition, 2000.

One Hundred Most Popular Picture Book Authors and Illustrators: Biographical Sketches and Bibliographies, Libraries Unlimited (Littleton, CO), 2000.

Character Education: A Book Guide for Teachers, Librarians, and Parents, Libraries Unlimited (Littleton, CO), 2002.

Literature Frameworks: Apples to Zoos, Linworth Publishing (Worthington, OH), 2nd edition, 2002.

Author of "McBookwords," a column in *Iowa Reading,* 1986-89, and "Cool Stuff on the Web," a column in *Library Talk* and *Book Report,* 1996-2001. Contributor of articles and reviews to magazines. Contributing editor, *See,* 1979-80, and *Iowa Reading Journal,* 1988-99; member of editorial board, *Reading Journal,* 1993-95.

Work in Progress

Starr in Beaver Creek, a book on the childhood experiences of an Arikara girl growing up on the Fort Berthold reservation in North Dakota; an educational resource book.

Sidelights

Librarian and media specialist Sharron L. McElmeel is the author of numerous books having to do with literature and curriculum as well as authors and illustrators of books for young readers. A classroom teacher and media specialist for over three decades, McElmeel brings a wealth of personal experience to her books on topics from read-alouds to author visits. McElmeel once commented: "Born in the heartland of the United States, in Iowa, I spent my childhood days on a dairy and grain farm, where three siblings and I enjoyed swimming in the farm creek, riding horses, and eating picnic lunches on the 'back forty,' enjoying idyllic days playing in an abandoned stone cabin that stood in a corn field. During my childhood, there were few books in my life; the only two books I remember were collections of Grimm's fairy tales and the tales of Hans Christian Andersen. Those tales are still among my favorites."

McElmeel attended the State College of Iowa where she graduated in 1963; she married the same year and began her career as a classroom teacher the following year. "When I married and became a parent, I wanted my children to have more exposure than I had to the literature offered to young people," McElmeel once commented. "Books by Virginia Lee Burton, Maurice Sendak, and Ezra Jack Keats became early favorites. My work as an author began after an editor at Libraries Unlimited approached me. He wanted me to put into writing the information about authors and illustrators that I had been sharing with other educators. I did, and since 1988 I have written ... reference books for educators and parents, focusing on books for children and young adults and how to use these books in the home and classroom."

Among her more recent titles is *WWW Almanac: Making Curriculum Connections to Special Days, Weeks, and*

Months. "McElmeel brings curriculum connections into the twenty-first century by providing Internet sites to link up with various important days," wrote Ilene Cooper in a *Booklist* review of the reference work. Holidays such as Halloween, New Year's Day, and Martin Luther King, Jr.'s birthday are included, among many others, with Internet sites that will provide valuable learning materials. Cooper concluded that *WWW Almanac* is a "valuable resource," while Cathy Fithian Williams, writing in *School Library Journal,* called it a "useful, reliable book."

Tips: Ideas for Secondary School Librarians and Technology Specialists includes nearly eight hundred "short, practical suggestions," according to Sandra L. Doggett in *School Library Journal.* "The collection provides a wealth of innovative recommendations that are easy to understand and implement," noted Doggett. Another four hundred tips, culled mainly from the "Shop Talk" column in the *Library Talk* magazine, are presented in McElmeel's *Shop Talk: Ideas for Elementary School Librarians and Technology Specialists.* Yapha Nussbaum Mason, reviewing the title in *School Library*

Journal, felt it "places a plethora of information right at the school librarian's fingertips."

In *One Hundred Most Popular Picture Book Authors and Illustrators: Biographical Sketches and Bibliographies,* McElmeel provides a "solid resource," according to Linda Greengrass in *School Library Journal.* Greengrass, while acknowledging other titles which introduce authors and illustrators for young readers, nevertheless felt that "McElmeel's splendid book deserves a place on library shelves." "This is a reference work that surely fills a gap in the literature about children's books," wrote Betty Ann Potter in *Reference and User Services Quarterly.*

"I have more than fourteen file drawers filled with research material about authors and books," McElmeel once commented. "My office is lined with children's and young adult books. This material all contributes to the background for the writing I do about authors and books. Since the early 1990s my life has been invaded with technology which not only aids my research but has provided new writing topics and opened the means to telecommunicate with publishers throughout the United States. For many years I described my career as a sandwich, with education being the bread and butter, the other side interests, consulting, work as a radio commentator, and so forth, and writing being the jam and jelly of the sandwich. Now the sandwich is reversed. My writing and editing provides my bread and butter, and all of the other interests, including teaching and speaking, provide the jam and jelly. I have been fortunate to have enjoyed (and continue to enjoy) a career I love for all of my adult life.

"My idea of true success as a writer will be realized when I have found a publisher for a favorite manuscript about an Arikara child in Fort Berthold, North Dakota. Until then I continue to write about books, the authors and illustrators who create them, and the children who enjoy them."

Biographical and Critical Sources

PERIODICALS

Booklist, May 1, 1994, p. 1611; May 1, 1995, p. 1596; September 15, 1996, p. 254; August, 1997, p. 1912; September 1, 1999, p. 182; March 15, 2000, Ilene Cooper, review of *WWW Almanac,* p. 1392.

Library Journal, October 15, 2000, p. 61.

Multimedia Schools, September, 2000, p. 47.

Reference and User Services Quarterly, spring, 2001, Betty Ann Porter, review of *One Hundred Most Popular Picture Book Authors and Illustrators,* p. 278.

School Library Journal, May, 1991, p. 29; August, 1993, p. 52; July, 1995, p. 28; October, 1997, p. 53; November, 1999, p. 81; July, 2000, Cathy Fithian Williams, review of *WWW Almanac,* p. 131; September, 2000, Sandra L. Doggett, review of *Tips: Ideas for Secondary School Librarians and Technology Specialists,* p. 262; September, 2000, Yapha Nussbaum Mason, review of *Shop Talk: Ideas for Elementary School Librarians and Technology Specialists,* p. 262; No-

McElmeel's text offers a compendium of biographical and bibliographical information on prominent authors for young readers. (Cover illustration by Joan Garner.)

vember, 2000, Linda Greengrass, review of *One Hundred Most Popular Picture Book Authors and Illustrators,* p. 94.

OTHER

Sharron McElmeel Web Site, http://www.mcelmeel.com/ (October 21, 2001).

* * *

McGREAL, Elizabeth
See YATES, Elizabeth

* * *

MELTZER, Milton 1915-

Personal

Born May 8, 1915, in Worcester, MA; son of Benjamin and Mary (Richter) Meltzer; married Hilda Balinky, June 22, 1941; children: Jane, Amy. *Education:* Attended Columbia University, 1932-36. *Politics:* Independent.

Addresses

Home—263 West End Ave., New York, NY 10023. *Agent*—Harold Ober Associates, 425 Madison Ave., New York, NY 10017.

Career

Federal Theatre Project of the Works Projects Administration, New York, NY, staff writer, 1936-39; Columbia Broadcasting System Inc. (CBS-Radio), New York, NY, researcher and writer, 1946; Public Relations Staff of Henry A. Wallace for President, 1947-49; Medical and Pharmaceutical Information Bureau, New York, NY, account executive, 1950-55; Pfizer Inc., New York, NY, assistant director of public relations, 1955-60; Science and Medicine Publishing Co. Inc., New York, NY, editor, 1960-68; full-time writer of books, 1968—. Consulting editor, Thomas Y. Crowell Co., 1962-74, Doubleday & Co. Inc., 1963-73, and Scholastic Book Services, 1968-72; University of Massachusetts, Amherst, adjunct professor, 1977-80; lecturer at universities in the United States and England and at professional meetings and seminars; writer of films and filmstrips. *Military service:* U.S. Army Air Force, 1942-46; became sergeant. *Member:* Authors Guild, Authors League of America, PEN, Organization of American Historians.

Awards, Honors

Thomas Alva Edison Mass Media Award for special excellence in portraying America's past, 1966, for *In Their Own Words: A History of the American Negro,* Volume 2, *1865-1916;* National Book Award nominations for children's literature, 1969, for *Langston Hughes: A Biography,* 1975, for *Remember the Days: A Short History of the Jewish American* and *World of Our Fathers: The Jews of Eastern Europe,* and 1977, for

Milton Meltzer

Never to Forget: The Jews of the Holocaust; Christopher Award, 1969, for *Brother, Can You Spare a Dime? The Great Depression, 1929-1933,* and 1980, for *All Times, All Peoples: A World History of Slavery.*

Charles Tebeau Award, Florida Historical Society, 1973, for *Hunted Like a Wolf: The Story of the Seminole War;* Jane Addams Peace Association Children's Honor Book, 1975, for *The Eye of Conscience: Photographers and Social Change,* and 1989, for *Rescue: The Story of How Gentiles Saved Jews in the Holocaust; Boston Globe-Horn Book* Nonfiction Honor Book, 1976, for *Never to Forget: The Jews of the Holocaust,* and 1983, for *The Jewish Americans: A History in Their Own Words, 1650-1950;* Association of Jewish Libraries Book Award, 1976, Jane Addams Peace Association Children's Book Award, 1977, Charles and Bertie G. Schwartz Award for Jewish Juvenile Literature, National Jewish Book Awards, 1978, Hans Christian Andersen Honor List, 1979, and American Library Association (ALA) selection as a "Best of the Best Books 1970-1983," all for *Never to Forget: The Jews of the Holocaust;* Washington Children's Book Guild Honorable Mention, 1978 and 1979, and Nonfiction Award, 1981, all for his total body of work.

American Book Award nomination, 1981, for *All Times, All Peoples: A World History of Slavery;* Carter G. Woodson Book Award, National Council for Social Studies, 1981, for *The Chinese Americans;* Jefferson Cup Award, Virginia State Library Association, 1983, for *The Jewish Americans: A History in Their Own Words, 1650-1950;* Children's Book Award special citation, Child Study Children's Book Committee, 1985, Olive Branch Award from the Writers' and Publishers' Alliance for Nuclear Disarmament, Jane Addams Peace Association Children's Book Award, and New York University Center for War, Peace, and the News Media, all 1986, all for *Ain't Gonna Study War No More: The Story of America's Peace-Seekers;* John Brubaker Memorial Award, Catholic Library Association, 1986; Golden Kite Award for nonfiction, Society of Children's Book Writers and Illustrators, 1987, for *Poverty in America;* Regina Medal, Catholic Library Association, 2000; Laura Ingalls Wilder Award, 2001.

Many of Meltzer's books have been selected as best books of the year by the American Library Association, Library of Congress, *Horn Book, School Library Journal,* and *New York Times,* and also as Notable Children's Trade Books in Social Studies, National Council for Social Studies/Children's Book Council.

Writings

NONFICTION FOR YOUNG READERS

A Light in the Dark: The Life of Samuel Gridley Howe, Crowell (New York, NY), 1964.

In Their Own Words: A History of the American Negro, Crowell (New York, NY), Volume 1: *1619-1865,* 1964, Volume 2: *1865-1916,* 1965, Volume 3: *1916-1966,* 1967, abridged edition published as *The Black Americans: A History in Their Own Words, 1619-1983,* Crowell (New York, NY), 1984.

Tongue of Flame: The Life of Lydia Maria Child, Crowell (New York, NY), 1965.

Time of Trial, Time of Hope: The Negro in America, 1919-1941 (includes teacher's guide), illustrated by Moneta Barnett, Doubleday (New York, NY), 1966.

Thaddeus Stevens and the Fight for Negro Rights, Crowell (New York, NY), 1967.

Bread—and Roses: The Struggle of American Labor, 1865-1915, Knopf (New York, NY), 1967, Facts On File (New York, NY), 1991.

Langston Hughes: A Biography, Crowell (New York, NY), 1968.

Brother, Can You Spare a Dime? The Great Depression, 1929-1933, Knopf (New York, NY), 1969.

(With Lawrence Lader) *Margaret Sanger: Pioneer of Birth Control,* Crowell (New York, NY), 1969.

Meltzer's biography heralds the accomplishments of Langston Hughes, one of the foremost African American poets of the twentieth century. (From Langston Hughes, *illustrated by Stephen Alcorn.)*

Freedom Comes to Mississippi: The Story of Reconstruction, Follett, 1970, Modern Curriculum, 1991.

Slavery, Cowles, Volume 1: *From the Rise of Western Civilization to the Renaissance,* 1971, Volume 2: *From the Renaissance to Today,* 1972, updated edition published in one volume as *Slavery: A World History,* Da Capo Press (New York, NY), 1993.

To Change the World: A Picture History of Reconstruction, Scholastic Book Services, 1971.

Hunted Like a Wolf: The Story of the Seminole War, Farrar, Straus (New York, NY), 1972.

The Right to Remain Silent, Harcourt, 1972.

(With Bernard Cole) *The Eye of Conscience: Photographers and Social Change,* Follett, 1974.

World of Our Fathers: The Jews of Eastern Europe, Farrar, Straus (New York, NY), 1974.

Remember the Days: A Short History of the Jewish American, illustrated by Harvey Dinnerstein, Doubleday (New York, NY), 1974.

Bound for the Rio Grande: The Mexican Struggle, 1845-1850, Knopf (New York, NY), 1974.

Taking Root: Jewish Immigrants in America, Farrar, Straus (New York, NY), 1974.

Violins and Shovels: The WPA Arts Projects, Delacorte (New York, NY), 1976.

Never to Forget: The Jews of the Holocaust (includes teacher's guide), Harper (New York, NY), 1976.

The Human Rights Book, Farrar, Straus (New York, NY), 1979.

All Times, All Peoples: A World History of Slavery, illustrated by Leonard Everett Fisher, Harper (New York, NY), 1980.

The Chinese Americans, Crowell (New York, NY), 1980.

The Truth about the Ku Klux Klan, F. Watts (New York, NY), 1982.

The Hispanic Americans, illustrated with photographs by Morrie Camhi and Catherine Noren, Crowell (New York, NY), 1982.

The Jewish Americans: A History in Their Own Words, 1650-1950, Crowell (New York, NY), 1982.

The Terrorists, Harper (New York, NY), 1983.

A Book about Names: In Which Custom, Tradition, Law, Myth, History, Folklore, Foolery, Legend, Fashion, Nonsense, Symbol, Taboo Help Explain How We Got Our Names and What They Mean, illustrated by Mischa Richter, Crowell (New York, NY), 1984.

Ain't Gonna Study War No More: The Story of America's Peace-Seekers, Harper (New York, NY), 1985.

Mark Twain: A Writer's Life, F. Watts (New York, NY), 1985.

Betty Friedan: A Voice for Women's Rights (part of the "Women of Our Time" series), illustrated by Stephen Marchesi, Viking (New York, NY), 1985.

Dorothea Lange: Life through the Camera (part of the "Women of Our Time" series), illustrated by Donna Diamond, photographs by Dorothea Lange, Viking (New York, NY), 1985.

The Jews in America: A Picture Album, Jewish Publication Society, 1985.

Poverty in America, Morrow (New York, NY), 1986.

Winnie Mandela: The Soul of South Africa (part of the "Women of Our Time" series), illustrated by Stephen Marchesi, Viking (New York, NY), 1986.

George Washington and the Birth of Our Nation, F. Watts (New York, NY), 1986.

Mary McLeod Bethune: Voice of Black Hope (part of the "Women of Our Time" series), illustrated by Stephen Marchesi, Viking (New York, NY), 1987.

The Landscape of Memory, Viking (New York, NY), 1987.

The American Revolutionaries: A History in Their Own Words, 1750-1800, Crowell (New York, NY), 1987.

Starting from Home: A Writer's Beginnings, Viking (New York, NY), 1988.

Rescue: The Story of How Gentiles Saved Jews in the Holocaust, Harper (New York, NY), 1988.

Benjamin Franklin: The New American, F. Watts (New York, NY), 1988.

American Politics: How It Really Works, illustrated by David Small, Morrow (New York, NY), 1989.

Voices from the Civil War: A Documentary History of the Great American Conflict, Crowell (New York, NY), 1989.

The Bill of Rights: How We Got It and What It Means, Harper (New York, NY), 1990.

Crime in America, Morrow (New York, NY), 1990.

Columbus and the World around Him, F. Watts (New York, NY), 1990.

The American Promise: Voices of a Changing Nation, 1945-Present, Bantam (New York, NY), 1990.

Thomas Jefferson: The Revolutionary Aristocrat, F. Watts (New York, NY), 1991.

The Amazing Potato: A Story in Which the Inca, Conquistadors, Marie Antoinette, Thomas Jefferson, Wars, Famines, Immigrants, and French Fries All Play a Part, HarperCollins (New York, NY), 1992.

Andrew Jackson and His America, F. Watts (New York, NY), 1993.

Lincoln: In His Own Words, illustrated by Stephen Alcorn, Harcourt (San Diego, CA), 1993.

Gold: The True Story of Why People Search for It, Mine It, Trade It, Fight for It, Mint It, Display It, Steal It, and Kill for It, HarperCollins (New York, NY), 1993.

Cheap Raw Material: How Our Youngest Workers Are Exploited and Abused, Viking (New York, NY), 1994.

The Mexican-American War, Jackdaw Publications (Amawalk, NY), 1994.

Reconstruction, Jackdaw Publications (Amawalk, NY), 1994.

Who Cares?, Walker (New York, NY), 1994.

Theodore Roosevelt and His America, F. Watts (New York, NY), 1994.

Frederick Douglass: In His Own Words, Harcourt (San Diego, CA), 1995.

Hold Your Horses!, HarperCollins (New York, NY), 1995.

A History of Jewish Life from Eastern Europe to America, Jason Aronson (New York, NY), 1996.

Tom Paine: Voice of Revolution, F. Watts (New York, NY), 1996.

Weapons and Warfare: From the Stone Age to the Space Age, illustrated by Sergio Martinez, HarperCollins, (New York, NY), 1996.

The Many Lives of Andrew Carnegie, F. Watts (New York, NY), 1997.

Langston Hughes: An Illustrated Edition, Millbrook Press (New York, NY), 1997.

Food, Millbrook Press (New York, NY), 1998.

Ten Queens: Portraits of Women in Power, Penguin Putnam (New York, NY), 1998.

Witches and Witch-hunts: A History of Persecution, Blue Sky Press, (New York, NY), 1999.

Carl Sandburg: A Biography, Millbrook Press (New York, NY), 1999.

They Came in Chains: The Story of the Slave Ships, Marshall Cavendish (Tarrytown, NY), 1999.

Driven from the Land: The Story of the Dust Bowl, Marshall Cavendish (Tarrytown, NY), 2000.

There Comes a Time: The Struggle for Civil Rights, Random House (New York, NY), 2001.

In the Days of the Pharaohs, F. Watts (New York, NY), 2001.

Ferdinand Magellan, Marshall Cavendish (Tarrytown, NY), 2001.

Captain James Cook, Marshall Cavendish (Tarrytown, NY), 2001.

Bound for America, Marshall Cavendish (Tarrytown, NY), 2001.

Piracy and Plunder, Penguin Putnam (New York, NY), 2001.

Civil Rights Landmark, Random House (New York, NY), 2001.

Walt Whitman: A Biography, Twenty-First Century Books (New York, NY), 2001.

OTHER

(With Langston Hughes) *A Pictorial History of the Negro in America,* Crown, 1956, fifth revised edition, also with C. Eric Lincoln, published as *A Pictorial History of Black Americans,* 1983, revised as *African American History: Four Centuries of Black Life,* Scholastic Textbooks (New York, NY), 1990, new revised edition, also with Jon Michael Spencer, published as *A Pictorial History of African Americans,* 1995.

Mark Twain Himself, Crowell (New York, NY), 1960, University of Missouri Press (Columbia, MO), 2002.

(Editor) *Milestones to American Liberty: The Foundations of the Republic,* Crowell (New York, NY), 1961, revised edition, 1965.

(Editor, with Walter Harding) *A Thoreau Profile,* Crowell (New York, NY), 1962.

(Editor) *Thoreau: People, Principles and Politics,* Hill & Wang (New York, NY), 1963.

(With Langston Hughes) *Black Magic: A Pictorial History of the Negro in American Entertainment,* Prentice-Hall (Englewood Cliffs, NJ), 1967, revised as *Black Magic: A Pictorial History of the African-American in the Performing Arts,* introduction by Ossie Davis, Da Capo Press (New York, NY), 1990.

Underground Man (novel), Bradbury, 1972.

Dorothea Lange: A Photographer's Life, Farrar, Straus (New York, NY), 1978.

(Editor, with Patricia G. Holland and Francine Krasno) *The Collected Correspondence of Lydia Maria Child, 1817-1880: Guide and Index to the Microfiche Edition,* Kraus Microform, 1980.

(Editor, with P. G. Holland) *Lydia Maria Child: Selected Letters, 1817-1880,* University of Massachusetts Press (Amherst, MA), 1982.

Nonfiction for the Classroom: Milton Meltzer on Writing, History, and Social Responsibility, edited by Wendy Saul, Teachers College Press (New York, NY), 1994.

Editor of "Women of America" series, Crowell, 1962-74, "Zenith Books" series, Doubleday, 1963-73, and "Firebird Books" series, Scholastic Book Services, 1968-72. Author of introduction for *Learning about Biographies: A Reading-and-Writing Approach,* by Myra Zarnowski, National Council of Teachers of English, 1990. Also script writer for documentary films, including *History of the American Negro* (series of three half-hour films), Niagara Films, 1965; *Five,* Silvermine Films, 1971; *The Bread and Roses Strike: Lawrence, 1912* (filmstrip), District 1199 Cultural Center, 1980; *The Camera of My Family,* Anti-Defamation League, 1981; *American Family: The Merlins,* Anti-Defamation League, 1982. Author of scripts for radio and television.

Contributor to periodicals, including *New York Times Magazine, New York Times Book Review, English Journal, Virginia Quarterly Review, Library Journal, Wilson Library Bulletin, School Library Journal, Microform Review, Horn Book, Children's Literature in Education, Lion and the Unicorn, Social Education, New Advocate,* and *Children's Literature Association Quarterly.* Member of U.S. editorial board of *Children's Literature in Education,* beginning in 1973, and of *Lion and the Unicorn,* beginning in 1980.

Sidelights

Winner of the 2001 Laura Ingalls Wilder Award for a career-long contribution to literature for children, Milton Meltzer is best known for his comprehensive studies of oppressed peoples, social concerns, and historical events. Much of the subject matter in his nearly one hundred titles—poverty, religion, crime, peace, discrimination, slavery—concerns injustices especially common to America. The American Library Association's Wilder Award committee noted in its presentation, reprinted on its Web site: "Meltzer's commitment to his art form, and his respect for his readers empowers young people to think creatively and critically and take an active role in a socially challenging world." Starting to write nonfiction for children at a time when such fare was typified by "invented dialogue and undocumented incident and designed largely to inspire patriotism, good character, and hard work," as noted by Wendy Saul in a profile of the author in *Horn Book,* Meltzer went against the grain, basing his histories and biographies instead on "original sources and scholarly research."

Many critics have praised Meltzer's approach to complex issues, noting that the author never "talks down" to his young audience. In an essay for the *Something about the Author Autobiography Series* (SAAS), Meltzer explained why he writes about controversial people and themes: "My subjects choose action.... Action takes commitment, the commitment of dedicated, optimistic individuals. I try to make readers understand that history isn't only what happens to us. History is what we *make* happen. Each of us. All of us."

In Witches and Witch-hunts, *Meltzer chronicles the human impulse to scapegoat, as demonstrated in medieval witch trials as well as in twentieth-century "witch-hunts" against the Jews in Nazi Germany and the communists in the postwar McCarthy era in the United States. (Cover illustration by Barry Moser.)*

Meltzer has been interested in social issues since his childhood. As a first-generation American, he was able to see firsthand the difficulties faced by many immigrants. Meltzer's parents, for example, tried to assimilate into American society as much as possible; this action would later cause identity problems for their son. An early influence on Meltzer's literary career was his introduction to the works of the American author Henry David Thoreau while in high school. Thoreau's message of simplicity and spiritual rebirth would stay with Meltzer into adulthood.

By the time Meltzer was a young adult, he began to feel a keen sense of loss with regard to his Eastern European/Jewish roots. "Perhaps [my parents] wanted to forget the world they had left behind," he writes in his essay. "Or because they knew I had no interest in their culture. I didn't realize until much later how much meaning their early life would have for me. When at last I had the

sense to want to know about it, it was too late. They were gone."

After attending Columbia University, Meltzer went to work for a time for the federal Works Projects Administration. After serving in the U. S. Army Air Force during World War II, he worked in public relations for fifteen years. This was followed by another career in editing before he finally became a full-time writer in 1968. His first publications were geared for adults, until, at the request of his daughter, he wrote a biography for younger readers, *A Light in the Dark: The Life of Samuel Gridley Howe.* This book launched a long and rewarding career as a writer of nonfiction books for children.

Meltzer has used some key periods and events in his life, such as the Great Depression and his job with the government-sponsored Works Projects Administration, as fodder for books such as *Brother, Can You Spare a Dime? The Great Depression, 1929-1933* and *Violins and Shovels: The WPA Arts Projects.* In *Brother, Can You Spare a Dime?,* which details the severe effects on millions of people of the Great Depression, Meltzer "has written a tremendously powerful and moving account of the Depression years," Judy Silverman declared in the *Voice of Youth Advocates.* Similarly, the 1986 study *Poverty in America* "goes beyond summarizing studies and quoting statistics to make the reader feel the grim reality of poverty and its related problems," *Horn Book* critic Elizabeth S. Watson observed. Using anecdotes, statistics, and the real-life experiences of America's poor, *Poverty in America* "is a marvel of succinct writing that lays bare the multi-faceted shape of economic deprival and examines its causes," *Wilson Library Bulletin* contributor Patty Campbell stated.

In his 1999 *Driven from the Land: The Story of the Dust Bowl,* Meltzer details the origins of the Dust Bowl, which forced so many farmers off their land in the early 1930s. "Meltzer offers a fascinating and well-chosen perspective," noted Steven Engelfried in a *School Library Journal* review of that book, noting also that "well-chosen statistics emphasize the destruction of the Dust Bowl." In *Cheap Raw Material: How Our Youngest Workers Are Exploited and Abused,* Meltzer looks at the phenomenon of child labor from ancient times until today. "Meltzer effectively uses quotes from numerous youngsters from different eras," wrote Marilyn Long Graham in a *School Library Journal* review. Graham further remarked that Meltzer's writing throughout is "vivid and captivating," and that his book is "an excellent resource." *Booklist*'s Stephanie Zvirin called *Cheap Raw Material* an "extraordinary book ... relevant, passionate, consciousness-raising." And in *Who Cares?* Meltzer presents a partial answer to such injustices, documenting altruism through the ages. This "may be the most comprehensive history of volunteerism ever written for young adults," declared Melissa Ducote Shepherd in *Voice of Youth Advocates.* Shepherd also thought that *Who Cares?* "should inspire more [young adults] to take part" in the volunteer effort.

Meltzer has established a reputation for effectively incorporating eyewitness accounts and personal documents, such as diaries, letters, and speeches, into his work. He noted in a *School Library Journal* article that "the use of original sources . . . is a giant step out of the textbook swamp. Working with the living expression of an era . . . you get close to reliving those experiences yourself." Starting with *In Their Own Words,* a three-volume history of African Americans, Meltzer has brought to life the stories of various ethnic groups, including Jewish, Chinese, and Hispanic Americans, as well as historical events and people, such as the American Revolution, the Civil War, and Abraham Lincoln. In *The American Revolutionaries: A History in Their Own Words, 1750-1800,* Meltzer "has been careful to incorporate various points of view and to give a balanced perspective in the narrative with which he pieces together the primary sources," *Bulletin of the Center for Children's Books* critic Betsy Hearne wrote. *Voices from the Civil War: A Documentary History of the Great American Conflict* similarly contains "a good cross-section" of Union and Confederate viewpoints, according to *School Library Journal* contributor Elizabeth M. Reardon, who also found Meltzer's narrative to be "clear, concise, and well-written, putting these turbulent times into perspective."

Meltzer's choice of material has sometimes come as a surprise to the author himself. "In those first years I wrote books without any great self-consciousness about the subjects I chose," he wrote in *SAAS.* "Then one day a reviewer described me as a writer known for his interest in the underdog. A pattern had become obvious. It was not a choice deliberately made." This interest has been manifested in several studies of oppression, such as *Slavery; All Times, All Peoples: A World History of Slavery;* and *Never to Forget: The Jews of the Holocaust.* Reviewing a 1993 revision of *Slavery,* a *Library Journal* contributor noted that Meltzer writes "directly without sentimentality." Employing primary source material, Meltzer presents the "life, hopes, and fears of the slaves themselves," according to the same reviewer. The author has also examined the various ways people have fought such oppression. *Rescue: The Story of How Gentiles Saved Jews in the Holocaust* details the efforts of non-Jews who risked their lives to protect their Jewish neighbors from the Nazi death camps of the 1940s. Including histories of anti-Semitism in Europe, *Rescue* is "a historical study as well as a series of exciting stories about individual courage," Christine Behrmann noted in *School Library Journal.*

Meltzer has continued to deal with racism and its effects throughout his career. In *They Came in Chains: The Story of the Slave Ships* he tells the story of the slave ships and slavery in America, from the capture of slaves in Africa through transportation to the Civil War and emancipation. Laura Glaser, writing in *School Library Journal,* wrote, "Firsthand accounts, black-and-white photographs and reproductions, and excerpts from newspapers and speeches dramatically convey the horrors of slavery." In his 2001 title *There Comes a Time: The Struggle for Civil Rights,* Meltzer relates the struggle for civil rights in America. The author follows the history of the movement from slavery, through Reconstruction and Jim Crow, and on to school desegregation, sit-ins, and the Martin Luther King Jr. assassination. Reviewing the title in *School Library Journal,* Eunice Weech called it a "concise, informational overview" and a "perceptive account [that] will cause readers to think critically about where we have been and where we are going as a nation." A contributor for *Publishers Weekly* called the same study an "impressive survey."

Meltzer also brings context to his studies of individual lives. *Benjamin Franklin: The New American,* which is about the noted Revolutionary American inventor and politician, "incorporates much historical background," Mary Mueller observed in *School Library Journal;* the author "shows him as a real person, pointing out many of Franklin's faults and indiscretions as well as his strengths." Meltzer's biography "is a smooth selection, condensation, and explanation of the events and significance of a complex life," *Horn Book* reviewer Mary A. Bush said. Likewise, Julie Corsaro commented in *Booklist* that in *Columbus and the World around Him* "Meltzer moves beyond his subject . . . to a well-integrated history of intellectual, scientific, and social ideas." In addition, the author includes information about the exploitation of Native Americans brought

In **Driven from the Land,** *Meltzer documents both the economic and the environmental factors that led to the Great Depression and the devastating dust storms that forced many families to move west during the 1930s.*

about by Christopher Columbus's voyages to America. "Readers cannot complete his book without an embarrassing appreciation for the great price paid by all humanity in the exploration and settlement of the new world," stated Frances Bradburn in the *Wilson Library Journal.*

In some of his biographies, Meltzer lets the subjects speak for themselves. Thus in *Lincoln: In His Own Words* and *Frederick Douglass: In His Own Words,* he presents a plethora of primary sources, including speeches and letters, woven together by brief descriptive and narrative sections, to paint a firsthand portrait. Reviewing the work on Douglass, the most renowned black leader of the nineteenth century, *Horn Book*'s Mary M. Burns noted that Meltzer brings "a historian's sensibility to his work as well as an innate sensitivity to his subject." *School Library Journal* critic Joanne Kelleher concluded of the same work, "Douglass's words live again in this volume, invoking young people to never give up the struggle for freedom and equality for all." In a review of *Lincoln,* Mueller remarked in *School Library Journal,* "This fine book introduces Lincoln to readers through his own words."

Other biographies deal with movers and shakers in the political sphere. Meltzer's *Thomas Jefferson: The Revolutionary Aristocrat* presents a "rich and multifaceted" portrait of this president and statesman, according to *Horn Book* reviewer Anita Silvey, and one that treats young readers "with respect and evidences a belief in their intelligence." Meltzer does "his usual skillful job" in a further biography of an early revolutionary, according to Nancy Eaton, reviewing *Tom Paine: Voice of Revolution* in *Voice of Youth Advocates.* "The complex ideas presented . . . are essential to understanding the background of the American Revolution and the evolution of our political system," Eaton concluded. And in *Andrew Jackson and His America,* Meltzer contextualizes his subject, creating a life-and-times approach to this military man, land-speculator, slave-holder, and president. "Meltzer's biographies always teach us as much about the history of the period as they do about his subject," commented Chris Sherman in a *Booklist* review of *Andrew Jackson. Voice of Youth Advocates* contributor Laura L. Lent declared, "Meltzer's biographical account of Andrew Jackson and the America that he lived in is fascinating and informative from start to finish." Lent also felt that Meltzer "makes the persona of Jackson come alive," warts and all.

Turning to the commercial and literary spheres, Meltzer has also provided insightful looks at personae from Andrew Carnegie to Carl Sandburg and Langston Hughes. In *The Many Lives of Andrew Carnegie,* Meltzer documents this steelmaker's rise from humble Scottish origins to wealthy U.S. captain of industry. "This fascinating portrait makes a lively read," noted *Booklist* contributor Anne O'Malley, "with no attempt to gloss over or excuse [Carnegie's] hard-driving tactics." The poet and biographer of Lincoln is profiled in *Carl Sandburg: A Biography,* a "probing, inspirational study," according to a critic for *Kirkus Reviews.* And in

the 1997 title *Langston Hughes: An Illustrated Edition,* Meltzer updates an earlier biography of this African American writer who was also a friend and collaborator of Meltzer's on several book projects.

Something of a departure for Meltzer is the 1998 book *Ten Queens: Portraits of Women in Power,* a compendium biographical account of queens from Cleopatra to Catherine the Great of Russia. The women Meltzer portrays were not accidental queens, regents who married kings, but rather women who held and wielded real power. Dubbing Meltzer "one of children's literature's foremost writers of nonfiction," *Booklist*'s Ilene Cooper went on to note in her review of *Ten Queens* that the author employs a "wonderful narrative device; he writes in a tone that is almost chatty, one that engages readers." A contributor for *Publishers Weekly* called *Ten Queens* an "enticing mix of history and biography."

In all his books, Meltzer brings a sensibility and passion to his subjects, as well as a desire to teach children about the past and its meaning for their lives. In his history of pacifism, *Ain't Gonna Study War No More,* "Meltzer is openly partisan, urging readers to learn from history and courageously oppose the false heroism of war," related Hazel Rochman in *Booklist.* Likewise, Elizabeth S. Watson observed in *Horn Book* that *American Politics: How It Really Works* "is a thoughtfully created contribution by a widely read, articulate person who has decided to share his knowledge of and views on politics with young people." With *Witches and Witch-hunts: A History of Persecution,* Meltzer chronicles the human impulse to scapegoat, from medieval witch trials to twentieth-century "witch-hunts" such as those against the Jews in Nazi Germany and against communists in postwar McCarthyite America. Kitty Flynn, writing in *Horn Book,* called *Witches and Witch-hunts* an "engaging and thought-provoking book," as well as a "provocative study from a seasoned historian." A critic for *Publishers Weekly,* in a review of the same book, felt that Meltzer "crams a lot of ideas and insights into his ambitious, unusually meaty survey."

The author has extended his interest in social issues from writing to his private life by joining unions, campaigning for political candidates, parading, and lobbying. Additionally, in titles such as *The Amazing Potato: A Story in Which the Inca, Conquistadors, Marie Antoinette, Thomas Jefferson, Wars, Famines, Immigrants, and French Fries All Play a Part; Gold: The True Story of Why People Search for It, Mine It, Trade It, Fight for It, Mint It, Display It, Steal It, and Kill for It;* and *Food,* he takes a particular topic and follows it across time and cultures to present an interdisciplinary nonfiction approach which integrates history, economics, science, and art. *The Amazing Potato* is, according to Sherman in another *Booklist* review, "a wonderful example of nonfiction writing at its best." Filled with anecdotes as well as hard research, the book traces the lowly potato from its origins in Peru through the Irish famine and on to today's french fries. Meltzer takes the same approach with *Gold,* in which the author "makes nonfiction an exciting story," according to *Booklist*'s Hazel Rochman.

"Meltzer shows that the story of gold is one of great inventiveness and also one of human cruelty and greed," Rochman concluded. A similar treatment informs Meltzer's *Food,* an "entertaining, historical overview," as Marilyn Fairbanks described it in *School Library Journal.*

"I try to be useful in the same way wherever and whenever I can," Meltzer related in his *SAAS* essay. "All my writing comes out of my convictions. I've never had to write about anything I didn't believe in." Writing from the heart as well as from the boxes of research notes he accumulates before he begins each book, Meltzer has entertained and informed an entire generation of young readers with his works. "Through his books, Meltzer asks young readers to think critically as he gives the opportunity to experience history firsthand," observed Carol Sue Harless in a *School Library Journal* review of Meltzer's *Nonfiction for the Classroom: Milton Meltzer on Writing, History, and Social Responsibility.* "It is writers like Meltzer who make the reading of history a pleasure."

Biographical and Critical Sources

BOOKS

Authors of Books for Young People, 3rd edition, Scarecrow Press (Metuchen, NJ), 1990.

Children's Books and Their Creators, edited by Anita Silvey, Houghton Mifflin (Boston, MA), 1995.

Children's Literature Review, Volume 13, Gale (Detroit, MI), 1987.

Contemporary Literary Criticism, Volume 26, Gale (Detroit, MI), 1983.

Dictionary of Literary Biography, Volume 61: *American Writers for Children since 1960: Poets, Illustrators, and Nonfiction Authors,* Gale (Detroit, MI), 1987.

Meltzer, Milton, *Starting from Home: A Writer's Beginnings,* Viking (New York, NY, 1988.

St. James Guide to Young Adult Writers, 2nd edition, St. James (Detroit, MI), 1999.

Something about the Author Autobiography Series, Volume 1, Gale (Detroit, MI), 1986.

PERIODICALS

Booklist, May 1, 1985, Hazel Rochman, review of *Ain't Gonna Study War No More: The Story of America's Peace-Seekers,* p. 1248; April 15, 1990, Julie Corsaro, review of *Columbus and the World around Him,* p. 1634; July, 1992, Chris Sherman, review of *The Amazing Potato: A Story in Which the Inca, Conquistadors, Marie Antoinette, Thomas Jefferson, Wars, Famines, Immigrants, and French Fries All Play a Part,* p. 1939; January 1, 1994, Hazel Rochman, review of *Gold: The True Story of Why People Search for It, Mine It, Trade It, Fight for It, Mint It, Display It, Steal It, and Kill for It,* p. 815; January 15, 1994, Chris Sherman, review of *Andrew Jackson and His America,* p. 924; March 1, 1994, Stephanie Zvirin, review of *Cheap Raw Material: How Our Youngest Workers Are Exploited and Abused,* p. 1261; December 15, 1996, p. 720; October 1, 1997, Anne O'Malley, review of *The Many Lives of Andrew Carnegie,* p. 316; April 15,

1998, Ilene Cooper, review of *Ten Queens: Portraits of Women in Power,* p. 1439; January 1, 1999, Stephanie Zvirin, review of *Food,* p. 868; December 15, 1999, p. 777; February 1, 2001, p. 1045; February 15, 2001, p. 1100.

Book Report, March-April, 1989, p. 39; November-December, 1991, p. 52; March-April, 1994, p. 44; May-June, 1995, p. 46; March-April, 1997, p. 46; May-June, 1998, p. 42; January-February, 1999, pp. 82-83.

Bulletin of the Center for Children's Books, December, 1985; December, 1986; July, 1987, Betsy Hearne, review of *The American Revolutionaries: A History in Their Own Words, 1750-1800,* p. 215; December, 1990, p. 94.

Horn Book, October, 1982; January-February, 1986; May-June, 1986, Elizabeth S. Watson, review of *Poverty in America,* p. 341; March-April, 1987; March-April, 1989, Mary A. Bush, review of *Benjamin Franklin: The New American,* pp. 227-228; September-October, 1989, Elizabeth S. Watson, review of *American Politics: How It Really Works,* p. 641; November-December, 1990, pp. 761-762; January-February, 1993, Anita Silvey, review of *Thomas Jefferson: The Revolutionary Aristocrat,* pp. 98-99; March-April, 1993, p. 220; March-April, 1994, p. 225; September-October, 1994, p. 6134; July-August, 1995, Mary M. Burns, review of *Frederick Douglass: In His Own Words,* pp. 480-481; March-April, 1996, p. 232; November-December, 1999, Kitty Flynn, review of *Witches and Witch-hunts: A History of Persecution,* p. 759; July-August, 2001, Wendy Saul, "Milton Meltzer," p. 431.

Kirkus Reviews, December 1, 1999, review of *Carl Sandburg: A Biography,* p. 1888.

Library Journal, February 1, 1994, review of *Slavery: A World History,* p. 116.

Los Angeles Times Book Review, April 23, 1989, p. 10.

New Yorker, October 30, 1978.

New York Times Book Review, August 6, 1978; February 20, 1983; January 14, 1990, p. 17; February 12, 1995, p. 18.

Publishers Weekly, November 10, 1989, p. 62; July 19, 1993, p. 256; April 6, 1998, review of *Ten Queens,* p. 80; September 6, 1999, review of *Witches and Witch-hunts,* p. 105; December 11, 2000, review of *There Comes a Time: The Struggle for Civil Rights,* p. 85.

School Library Journal, October, 1968, Milton Meltzer, "The Fractured Image: Distortions in Children's History Books," pp. 107-111; September, 1985, p. 147; August, 1986, p. 104; December, 1986; August, 1988, Christine Behrmann, review of *Rescue: The Story of How Gentiles Saved Jews in the Holocaust,* pp. 110-111; January, 1989, May Mueller, review of *Benjamin Franklin: The New American,* p. 101; December, 1989, Elizabeth M. Reardon, review of *Voices from the Civil War: A Documentary History of the Great American Conflict,* p. 127; May, 1991, p. 122; November, 1992, pp. 111-112; September, 1993, Mary Mueller, review of *Lincoln: In His Own Words,* p. 258; February, 1994, p. 114; July, 1994, Marilyn Long Graham, review of *Cheap Raw Material,* p. 125; February, 1995, Joanne Kelleher, review of *Frederick*

Douglass: In His Own Words, p. 121; June, 1995, Carol Sue Harless, review of *Nonfiction for the Classroom: Milton Meltzer on Writing, History, and Social Responsibility,* p. 43; December, 1995, p. 121; December, 1996, p. 148; January, 1997, p. 131; October, 1997, pp. 149-150; June, 1998, p. 164; January, 1999, Marilyn Fairbanks, review of *Food,* p. 147; December, 1999, p. 157; February, 2000, Steven Engelfried, review of *Driven from the Land: The Story of the Dust Bowl,* p. 130; February, 2000, Laura Glaser, review of *They Came in Chains: The Story of the Slave Ships,* p. 133; January, 2001, Eunice Weech, review of *There Comes a Time,* p. 151.

Voice of Youth Advocates, August, 1988, p. 148; June, 1991, Judy Silverman, review of *Brother, Can You Spare a Dime? The Great Depression, 1929-1933,* p. 128; February, 1994, Laura L. Lent, review of *Andrew Jackson and His America,* pp. 399-400; February, 1995, Melissa Ducote Shepherd, review of *Who Cares?,* p. 361; February, 1997, Nancy Eaton, review of *Tom Paine: Voice of Revolution,* p. 352.

Wilson Library Journal, April, 1987, Parry Campbell, "The Young Adult Perplex," p. 51; October, 1990, Frances Bradburn, "Middle Books," pp. 106-107; September, 1994, p. 121.

OTHER

American Library Association Web site, http://www.ala.org/ (October 3, 2001), "Milton Meltzer Wins Laura Ingalls Wilder Award."

*   *   *

MITCHELL, Lori 1961-

Personal

Born April 24, 1961, in CA; married Dean Mitchell (a graphic designer), June 25, 1988; children: April. *Education:* San Joaquin Delta Junior College, A.A.; Art Center College of Design (Pasadena, CA), B.A. (with honors). *Hobbies and other interests:* Making mosaic frames and boxes.

Addresses

Home and office—10219 Caminito Pitaya, San Diego, CA 92131. *E-mail*—lori@differentjustlikeme.cc.

Career

Illustrator in San Diego, CA, c. 1981—. Volunteer art teacher at a local school; American Vitiligo Research Foundation, volunteer. *Member:* Society of Children's Book Writers and Illustrators, Society of Illustrators.

Awards, Honors

Award for best children's book, San Diego Book Awards, 1999, cited among "Kid's Pick of the Lists," American Booksellers Association, 1999, Early Childhood News Directors Choice Award, 2000, Notable Social Studies Trade Book for Young People citation,

Lori Mitchell

National Council for the Social Studies/Children's Book Council, 2000, Best Children's Book selection, *San Diego Magazine* Book Awards, 2000, all for *Different Just like Me.*

Writings

(And illustrator) *Different Just like Me,* Charlesbridge Publishing (Watertown, MA), 1999.

Work in Progress

Illustrations for the picture book *Just Then,* publication expected in 2003.

Sidelights

Lori Mitchell told *SATA:* "Our daughter, April, had been diagnosed with vitiligo when she was only eight months old. Vitiligo is a loss of pigment or color in the skin. It started as a small dime-sized spot on her inner thigh and now looks like white clouds going across her entire body.

"At age four the vitiligo was just starting to spread to her face and hands, and people started asking more questions about why her skin looked different. April started to ask some questions of her own. We went to a baseball game, and she wanted to know why everyone else looked different. There was a man in a wheelchair next to us, a tall man behind us, a large woman down a few rows, and so on. We told her we all have something that makes us different, but we are all so much the same. We tried to find a book to help make that point and found one book about differences in race, one about the visually impaired, one about hearing loss, and so on. There wasn't one book that said we are all the same and different at the same time. So April and I decided we would create one. That's how *Different Just like Me* came to be.

"April is the main character in the book, but we left out her spots. Why, you may ask. Because not everyone can see past her spots right away. That's the point of the book. We wanted as many kids as possible to relate to her. We wanted kids to think 'I'm like her, so maybe I'm like all those other people.' We made her as generic as possible to get the point across. If we had shown her vitiligo, kids may think 'Well, I'm nothing like her, so I must not be like any of those other people,' and it would have defeated the whole purpose of the book. This way, by the end, maybe they can see that we really are all more alike than we are different.

"There is, however, a woman with vitiligo in the scene at the train station. She is also on the back cover. On the cover of the book, April has two colors of skin. If you didn't know about vitiligo, you would think it was just light and shadow on her face and arms. I wanted to do something for all of April's friends with vitiligo. She has vitiligo pen pals from all over the world.

"There is a web site with coloring book pages, lesson plans, and games to play at www.differentjustlikeme.cc. You will also find reviews, photographs, and more background about the book. The book is also available in Braille and books on tape through the Los Angeles Braille Institute."

Biographical and Critical Sources

PERIODICALS

Booklist, March 1, 1999, GraceAnne A. DeCandido, review of *Different Just like Me*, pp. 1221-1222.
Publishers Weekly, January 4, 1999, review of *Different Just like Me*, p. 88.

OTHER

Different Just like Me, http://www.differentjustlikeme.cc/ (June 21, 2001).

*   *   *

MORRIS, Oradel Nolen

Personal

Born in Austin, TX; married James Morris (a petroleum engineer), June, 1946. *Education:* University of Illinois—Urbana-Champaign, B.A., 1967.

Artwork by Oradel Nolen Morris.

Addresses

Agent—c/o Author Mail, Paupières Publishing, P.O. Box 707, Houma, LA 70361-0707.

Career

French teacher, writer. *Member:* Terrebonne Historical & Cultural Society.

Awards, Honors

Award for Excellence, Louisiana Preservation Society, for museum exhibit on native peoples of Louisiana.

Writings

Le monde acadien de Ti-Jean/The Cajun World of Ti-Jean (bilingual), Paupières Publishing (Houma, LA), 1980.
Le Reve de Ti-Jean, Paupières Publishing (Houma, LA), 1983.
(Compiler, editor, illustrator with Wylma Duplantis Dusenbery) *Wylma's La Trouvaille Cookbook: The Simple Joy of Cajun Cooking*, Paupières Publishing (Houma, LA), 1988.
I Hear the Song of the Houmas/J'entends la chanson des Houmas (bilingual), Paupières Publishing (Houma, LA), 1992.
Little Angel Dancer, Paupières Publishing (Houma, LA), 1999.

Sidelights

More than a decade after earning a bachelor's degree in French, Oradel Nolen Morris found an opportunity to put her language skills to use in teaching French in South Louisiana and writing bilingual children's books. For several years she taught French in a program sponsored through the Council for the Development of French in Louisiana. Her teaching activities allowed her to publish *Le monde acadien de Ti-Jean/The Cajun World of Ti-Jean,* with teacher handbook and student workbook, and *Le Reve de Ti-Jean,* with State Department of Education sponsorship. With her close friend, Wylma Dusenbery, owner of La Trouvaille Restaurant, Morris also compiled, edited, and illustrated a cookbook of Cajun recipes, which had enjoyed four reprintings by the year 2000.

In 1992 Morris demonstrated her long interest in another French-speaking group in Louisiana, the Houmas Indians, in *I Hear the Song of the Houmas/J'entends la chanson des Houmas,* which required nearly ten years of research in such primary sources as diaries of French explorers and priests and interaction with the contemporary Houmas tribe. This work formed part of the series "Peoples of Louisiana/Gens de la Louisiane." Morris was also active in creating a permanent exhibit on the native peoples of Louisiana, for the Terrebonne Historical & Cultural Society's Southdown Plantation Museum, which earned an award for excellence from the Louisiana Preservation Society. She has spoken on numerous occasions about the Houmas Indians and in 1999 published the story *Little Angel Dancer,* about a Houmas Indian angel who becomes a full-fledged guardian angel.

*   *   *

MORRISON, Gordon 1944-

Personal

Born June 30, 1944, in Allston, MA; son of Hugh L. and Margaret Vincent Morrison; divorced; children: Aimée Morrison-Hefron, Suzanne, John Seth. *Education:* School of the Museum of Art, Boston, 1963-64; Butera School of Art, 1964-67.

Addresses

Home and office—193 Towne St., #3, North Attleboro, MA 02760.

Career

Freelance artist and illustrator, 1967—; author and illustrator, 1991—; speaker and presenter at elementary schools, 2000—. Rhode Island School of Design, Providence, RI, instructor of biological illustration, 1985-87, independent studies mentor, 1985-91, instructor in botanical illustration studies, 1996. Guest lecturer at the Appalachian Mountain Club "Art and Nature" seminars, 1977-80; created art for the Missouri Botanical Gardens temperate forest and tropical rainforest exhibits; designed and executed diorama's for the Boston Zoological Society, Stone Zoo aviary exhibit and the Public Service Company of New Hampshire salt marsh exhibits, among others. *Exhibitions:* Has exhibited artwork in various locations, including Cross Roads of Sport, New York, NY; Left Bank Gallery, Wellfleet, MA; Marine and Science Museum, Virginia Beach, VA; and Dennison/Pequotsepos Nature Center, Mystic, CT.

Awards, Honors

Quill and Trowel, 1992; The Education Award, New England Wild Flower Society, 1996; *Bald Eagle* was selected as an "Outstanding Science Trade Books for Children" by the National Science Teachers Association and Children's Book Council, 1999; *Oak Tree* was selected for the CCBC Choices for 2001 by the Cooperative Children's Book Center in the "Natural World" section, 2001; Certificate of Merit in recognition of excellence in the category of illustration.

Writings

SELF-ILLUSTRATED

Bald Eagle, Walter Lorraine Books/Houghton Mifflin (Boston, MA), 1998.
Oak Tree, Walter Lorraine Books/Houghton Mifflin (Boston, MA), 2000.

ILLUSTRATOR

Lawrence Newcomb, *Newcomb's Wildflower Guide,* Little, Brown (Boston, MA), 1977.
Christopher Leahy, *The Birdwatcher's Companion,* Hill & Wang, 1982.
John H. Mitchell, *A Guide to the Seasons,* Massachusetts Audubon Society, 1983.
Fred Powledge, *A Forgiving Wind,* Doubleday (New York, NY), 1983.

Self-portrait of Gordon Morrison.

John H. Mitchell, *Ceremonial Times,* Doubleday (New York, NY), 1984.

Edward W. Cronin, *Getting Started in Birdwatching,* Houghton Mifflin (Boston, MA), 1986.

John Kricher, *A Field Guide to Eastern Forests,* Houghton Mifflin (Boston, MA), 1988.

Gordon Hayward, *Designing Your Own Landscape,* Whetstone Publishing (Brattleboro, VT), 1989.

Ron McAdow, *The Concord, Sudbury, and Assabet Rivers: A Guide to Canoeing, Wildlife and History,* Bliss Publishing (Marlborough, MA), 1990.

Ron McAdow, *The Charles River: Exploring Nature and History on Foot and by Canoe,* Bliss Publishing (Marlborough, MA), 1990.

Margaret Hensel, *English Cottage Gardening,* Norton (New York, NY), 1992.

Alex Wilson, *Quiet Water Canoe Guide,* Appalachian Mountain Club Books (Boston, MA), 1993.

Penelope Bass O'Sullivan and Barbara W. Ellis, *Successful Garden Plans,* Time Life Books (New York, NY), 1996.

John Kricher, *A Field Guide to Rocky Mountain and Southwest Forests,* Houghton Mifflin (Boston, MA), 1998.

John Kricher, *A Field Guide to California and Pacific Northwest Forests,* Houghton Mifflin (Boston, MA), 1998.

Gordon Hayward, *Stone in the Garden,* Norton (New York, NY), 2001.

FOR CHILDREN

John H. Mitchell, *The Curious Naturalist,* Prentice-Hall, 1982.

John Kricher, *A Field Guide to Dinosaurs Coloring Book,* Houghton Mifflin (Boston, MA), 1989.

John Kricher, *A Field Guide to Seashores Coloring Book,* Houghton Mifflin, (New York, NY), 1989.

John Kricher, *A Field Guide to Tropical Rainforests Coloring Book,* Houghton Mifflin (Boston, MA), 1991.

Richard Walton, *A Field Guide to Endangered Wildlife Coloring Book,* Houghton Mifflin (Boston, MA), 1991.

John Kricher, *Peterson First Guide to Dinosaurs,* Houghton Mifflin (Boston, MA), 1991.

John Kricher, *Peterson First Guide to Forests,* Houghton Mifflin (Boston, MA), 1995.

John Kricher, *Peterson First Guide to Seashores,* Houghton Mifflin (Boston, MA), 1995.

Contributing artist to various publications, including *First Guide to Wildflowers,* by Roger Tory Peterson, Houghton Mifflin, 1986; *Three Seasons of Bloom,* by C. Colston Burrell, Barbara W. Ellis, and Sally Roth, Time Life, 1997. Designer and illustrator for various periodicals, including *Curious Naturalist, Horticulture, Sanctuary,* and *New York Conservationist.*

Work in Progress

Pond, written and illustrated for children, fall 2002. Illustrating an ongoing series of "Rare and Endangered Plants" for the New England Wildflower Society.

Nature artist Morrison offers detailed facts about bald eagles and their habitat and portrays two eaglets as they grow and learn to fly and hunt. (From Bald Eagle, *written and illustrated by Morrison.)*

Sidelights

Gordon Morrison told *SATA:* "I grew up in Allston, Massachusetts, a part of the Greater Boston area, with very little exposure to art or to the natural world. In two specific ways, however, I was very lucky. Firstly—and perhaps most importantly—though I grew up in a family of ten children, my father still managed to give my early artistic efforts special attention, gently critiquing and encouraging me. Secondly, there was a place in my neighborhood called Little Hill, a small area of rock outcroppings and ragged trees and shrubs, where a kid such as myself could play and imagine an entirely different kind of landscape. Even as a young man, I found Little Hill to be a welcome oasis, a place of quiet where I could watch birds, insects, and the changing of the seasons. During my art school days, Little Hill's rocks, trees, and shifting patterns became the subjects of many of my drawings and photographs.

"When I left art school, I worked as a commercial illustrator for a few years, but eventually came to believe that I could do something more meaningful with my talent. For a while I tried to become an illustrator of children's books, with little success. But my growing concern for the environment compelled me to turn my attention toward nature as a subject. Educating myself about natural history turned out to be both a task, because there was so much to learn, and a pleasure, since it meant doing what came naturally to me—going out to draw. I also visited sanctuaries, zoos, museums, libraries, universities, even my own backyard. Field sketching was an especially important tool for me.

Through it, I discovered the value of learning through experience.

"Eventually natural history became the main focus of my illustration work. While my family grew, I illustrated and painted dioramas, murals, magazine articles, and several dozen books on different natural history subjects. Eventually, right around the time when my children were going off to college, I decided to try my hand at children's books again. After months of developing story ideas, and several years of searching, I finally found a publisher. Now, many years after first having decided to become a nature artist, I am writing and illustrating nature-themed children's books, and I have had the pleasure of working on various meaningful projects with many extraordinary individuals. For me, field sketching continues to be a wonderful means of understanding, appreciating, and experiencing nature.

"While being an illustrator means being able to support and clarify information, to maintain a certain level of accuracy and detail, I believe it is equally important to try to bring a certain artistic quality into one's work, to try to include balance, a sense of subject and place, perhaps even beauty. Though my father passed away a few years ago, I remain indebted to him for his gentle influence and belief in my artistic abilities; and while only a corner of Little Hill remains today, I like to think, by sharing my experiences through my work, that I may remind others to stay in touch with nature, and perhaps do their part to help protect it."

Biographical and Critical Sources

PERIODICALS

Booklist, June 1, 1998, Susan Dove Lempke, review of *Bald Eagle;* March 1, 2000, Marta Segal, review of *Oak Tree.*

Boston Globe, November 29, 1998, Stephanie Loer, review of *Oak Tree;* May 28, 2000.

Kirkus Reviews, April 1,1998, p. 498; March 1, 2000, review of *Oak Tree,* p. 304.

Library Journal, May 1, 1980, Virginia Golodetz, review of *Oak Tree,* p. 1095; May 1, 1998; June 1, 2000.

Parenting, June 1998, p. 85.

School Library Journal, November, 1992, review of *Peterson First Guide to Seashores,* p. 146.

*   *   *

MURRAY, Peter
See HAUTMAN, Pete(r Murray)

N

NEWMAN, Lesléa 1955-

Personal

Born November 5, 1995, in Brooklyn, NY. *Education:* University of Vermont, B.S. (education), 1977; Naropa Institute, certificate in poetics, 1980. *Religion:* Jewish.

Addresses

Office—Write from the Heart, P.O. Box 815, Northampton, MA 01061. *Agent*—Elizabth Harding, Cortis Brown, Ltd., 10 Astor Pl., New York, NY 10003. *E-mail*—Lezel@aol.com.

Career

Educator and author. Worked as a reader for *Mademoiselle* and *Redbook* magazines, New York, NY, 1982; *Valley Advocate,* Hatfield, MA, journalist and book reviewer, 1983-87; Mount Holyoke College, South Hadley, MA, director and teacher of writing at summer program, 1986-88; Write from the Heart: Writing Workshops for Women, Northampton, MA, founder and director, 1986—. Lectures and conducts writing workshops at colleges and universities, including Amherst College, Smith College, Swarthmore College, Trinity College, and Yale University. *Member:* Society of Children's Book Writers and Illustrators, Authors League, Author's Guild, Poets and Writers, Feminist Writers Guild, Publishing Triangle, Academy of American Poets.

Awards, Honors

Massachusetts Artists Foundation Poetry Fellowship, 1989; James Baldwin Award for Cultural Achievement, Greater Boston Area Lesbian/Gay Political Alliance, 1993; Silver Award, Parents' Choice Foundation, 1994, for *Fat Chance;* Gemini Award for Best Short Drama, Canadian Academy of Film and Television, 1995, for *Spoken Word: A Letter to Harvey Milk;* Books for the Teen Age selection, New York Public Library, 1996, for

A Loving Testimony: Remembering Loved Ones Lost to AIDS; National Endowment for the Arts Poetry Fellowship, 1997; first place winner in humor category, Vice Versa Awards for Excellence in Gay and Lesbian Press, 1999, for "Cher Heaven"; *Americus Review* Poetry Contest winner, 2000, for "The Politics of Buddy."

Writings

FOR YOUNG PEOPLE

Heather Has Two Mommies, illustrated by Diana Souza, In Other Words/Inland, 1989.

Gloria Goes to Gay Pride, Alyson Books (Los Angeles, CA), 1991.

Belinda's Bouquet, Alyson Books (Los Angeles, CA), 1991.

Saturday Is Pattyday, illustrated by Annette Hegel, New Victoria Publishers (Norwich, VT), 1993.

Lesléa Newman

184

Fat Chance (for young adults), Putnam (New York, NY), 1994.

Too Far Away to Touch, illustrated by Catherine Stock, Clarion Books (New York, NY), 1996.

Remember That, illustrated by Karen Ritz, Clarion Books (New York, NY), 1996.

Matzo Ball Moon, illustrated by Elaine Greenstein, Clarion Books (New York, NY), 1998.

Cats, Cats, Cats!, illustrated by Erika Oller, Simon & Schuster (New York, NY), 2001.

Dogs, Dogs, Dogs!, illustrated by Erika Oller, Simon & Schuster (New York, NY), 2002.

Runaway Dreidel!, illustrated by Kyrsten Brooker, Holt (New York, NY), 2002.

Felicia's Favorite Story, illustrated by Alaiyo Bradshaw, Two Lives Puplishing (Ridley Park, PA), 2003.

Pigs, Pigs, Pigs!, illustrated by Erika Oller, Simon & Schuster (New York, NY), 2003.

Daddy's Song, illustrated by Karen Ritz, Henry Holt & Co. (New York, NY), 2004.

FOR ADULTS

Just Looking for My Shoes (poetry), Back Door Press, 1980.

Good Enough to Eat (novel), Firebrand Books, 1986.

Love Me like You Mean It (poetry), HerBooks (Santa Cruz, CA), 1987.

A Letter to Harvey Milk, Firebrand Books, 1988.

(Editor) *Bubba Meisehs by Shayneh Maidelehs: An Anthology of Poetry by Jewish Granddaughters about Our Grandmothers*, HerBooks (Santa Cruz, CA), 1989.

Secrets (short stories), New Victoria Publishers (Norwich, VT), 1990.

Sweet Dark Places (poetry), HerBooks (Santa Cruz, CA), 1991.

Somebody to Love: A Guide to Loving the Body You Have, Third Side Press, 1991.

In Every Laugh a Tear (novel), New Victoria Publishers (Norwich, VT), 1992.

(Editor) *Eating Our Hearts Out: Women and Food*, Crossing Press (Freedom, CA), 1993.

Writing from the Heart: Inspiration and Exercises for Women Who Want to Write, Crossing Press (Freedom, CA), 1993.

Every Woman's Dream (essays and short fiction), New Victoria Publishers (Norwich, VT), 1994.

(Editor) *A Loving Testimony: Remembering Loved Ones Lost to AIDS*, Crossing Press (Freedom, CA), 1995.

Spoken Word: A Letter to Harvey Milk (television program; adapted from *A Letter to Harvey Milk*), Sleeping Giants Productions, 1995.

(Editor) *The Femme Mystique*, Alyson Publications (Boston, MA), 1995.

(Editor) *My Lover Is a Woman: Contemporary Lesbian Love Poems*, Ballantine Books (New York, NY), 1996.

Out of the Closet and Nothing to Wear, Alyson Books (Los Angeles, CA), 1997.

(Editor) *Pillow Talk: Lesbian Stories between the Covers*, Alyson Books (Los Angeles, CA), 1998.

Still Life with Buddy, Pride Publications (Radwor, OH), 1998.

The Little Butch Book, illustrated by Yohah Ralph, New Victoria Publishers (Norwich, VT), 1998.

Girls Will Be Girls (short fiction), Alyson Books (Los Angeles, CA), 1999.

Pillow Talk II: More Lesbian Stories between the Covers, Alyson Books (Los Angeles, CA), 2000.

Signs of Love (poetry), Windstorm Creative, 2000.

Just Like a Woman (short stories), Fluid Words, (Los Angeles, CA) 2001.

She Loves Me, She Loves Me Not (short stories), Alyson Books (Los Angeles, CA), 2002.

Contributor to magazines, including *Backbone, Common Lives, Conditions, Heresies, Sinister Wisdom,* and *Sojourner.*

Work in Progress

More children's books.

Sidelights

Lesléa Newman is an author, poet, and teacher of creative writing who is strongly motivated by her Jewish heritage and strong feminist philosophy. Among her works for young readers are the picture books *Remember That, Cats, Cats, Cats!,* and the groundbreaking *Heather Has Two Mommies,* the last a controversial book first published in 1989 that answered a growing need for literature about young children raised by same-sex couples. In addition to books for young children, Newman has authored a novel for young teens about the "thinner is better" philosophy promoted by modern culture, and has addressed similar women-focused issues through numerous essays, poetry, short stories, and works of adult nonfiction. Newman once commented: "Writing continues to teach me, surprise me, and inform me in new and exciting ways."

Deciding to become a writer after earning her bachelor's degree in education at the University of Vermont, Newman spent several years working in New York City before moving north to the college town of Northampton, Massachusetts. Active in that area's vibrant gay community, she soon realized that there was a need for books to help lesbian couples who chose to become parents deal with questions common to all children, especially the universal question: "Where did I come from?" Responding to this need, Newman wrote several books for both lesbian parents and the offspring of such non-traditional families that portray their unique circumstances in a sensitive and informed manner.

Heather Has Two Mommies answers a little girl's questions about where she came from and why she has no "Daddy." While the adult characters attempt to do so in a loving and sympathetic manner, Robert Burke took issue with Newman's approach, noting in the *Bloomsbury Review* that "on the one hand, they hope to console her with an explanation of her uniqueness. On the other hand, they also seem to be trying to convince Heather that she is just the same as everyone else." A reviewer for *Bulletin of the Center for Children's Books* was more positive, describing the book as "a positive, if idealized, portrait of a loving lesbian family," and commending it for "preach[ing] ... a respect for all kinds of families." As Heather's teacher informs the kindergarten class in *Heather Has Two Mommies,* "The most important thing about a family is that all the people in it love each other."

Unfortunately, children of lesbian or gay parents are not immune to the pain of separation or divorce, as Newman shows in *Saturday Is Pattyday.* Called "reassuring" by *Booklist* contributor Hazel Rochman, the story depicts the changing relationship between young Frankie and his mom Patty after Patty moves away from home. A more permanent loss is dealt with by Newman in *Too Far Away to Touch,* as Uncle Leonard attempts to find a way to let his young niece know that he is dying of AIDS in a text that *Horn Book* contributor Maeve Visser Knoth called "effective" and "understated." Reviewing *Too Far Away to Touch* for *Booklist,* Carolyn Phelan added that Newman's tale "has a universality that will touch readers of any age" who have experienced the death of someone close to them.

While Newman's first two picture books caused a good measure of controversy due to their focus on homosexuality and alternative families, her more recent works have been geared to a more mainstream readership. The celebration of the Jewish holiday of Passover is the focus of *Matzo Ball Moon,* as Eleanor's grandmother Bubbe makes her yearly holiday visit to help fix the holiday feast. Calling the book "a warm story of intergenerational sharing of holiday preparations within a loving family," *Booklist* contributor Ellen Mandel noted Newman's inclusion of an explanation of Passover

rituals and traditional foods. A *Publishers Weekly* reviewer had special praise for the character of Bubbe; she "says the unexpected, she is also credible and has some chutzpah." The relationship between Bubbe and her granddaughter is also the focus of *Remember That.* Taking place over several years, readers watch as the weekly Friday night Sabbath ritual they perform together is altered when the ageing Bubbe is moved to a nursing home. Including a introduction to Shabbos and translations of some of Bubbe's Yiddish expressions, Newman's book "leaves readers with a warm, happy feeling," according to Susan Scheps in *School Library Journal.* Hazel Rochman also had praise for the sentimental story, noting in her *Booklist* review that "Bubbe's story will help children cope with the changes age brings to those they love."

Cats, Cats, Cats! shows the frustrating relationship between cat owners and their beloved, but unfortunately nocturnal, felines. In swinging rhyme, Newman tells the story of Mrs. Brown, whose house full of cats does not deter her from filling her house with even more cats; "As soon as she begins to snore," Newman writes, "The fun begins with cats galore." In a starred *Publishers Weekly* review, a reviewer praised *Cats, Cats, Cats!* as "a real find for cat fanciers and their furry companions," and added that Erika Oller's illustrations, "with their indistinct edges and softly blurred colors, capture all the fuzzy charm of the capering kitties."

In conjunction with several books she has authored for adults that focus on body image, Newman published the YA novel *Fat Chance* in 1994. Written in the form of a diary, the novel is a realistic look at the effect of an eating disorder on a young girl. It follows thirteen-year-old, five-foot-four Judi, whose obsession about weight prompts her to idolize fellow student Nancy, the thinnest and most popular girl in the entire eighth grade. Discovering Nancy's trick, Judi begins the binge-purge cycle of the bulimic, and goes out of her way to keep it a secret from friends and family. A desire to fit in and be popular fuels her resolve, and the compliments that come her way as her weight begins to drop and she sheds her baggy clothes provides more encouragement. Praising Newman for her ability to create a teen voice that rings true, *Booklist* contributor Stephanie Zvirin added that *Fat Chance* "will sound achingly familiar to girls struggling with self-image." Noting that the novel goes "further than the average 'problem' novel," a *Publishers Weekly* contributor commented praised Newman for focusing on "the importance of professional help" in her "compelling, thought-provoking narrative."

Mrs. Brown's sixty cats have a party as soon as she falls asleep at night in Newman's rhyming tale. (From Cats, Cats, Cats!, *illustrated by Erika Oller.)*

Biographical and Critical Sources

BOOKS

Newman, Lesléa, *Heather Has Two Mommies,* In Other Words/Inland, 1989.

Newman, Lesléa, *Cats, Cats, Cats!,* illustrated by Erika Oller, Simon & Schuster (New York, NY), 2001.

PERIODICALS

Bloomsbury Review, June, 1992, Robert Burke, review of *Heather Has Two Mommies,* p. 19.

Booklist, November 1, 1993, Hazel Rochman, review of *Saturday Is Pattyday,* p. 531; September 1, 1994, Stephanie Zvirin, review of *Fat Chance,* p. 35; March 15, 1995, Carolyn Phelan, review of *Too Far Away to Touch,* p. 1336; February 1, 1996, Hazel Rochman, review of *Remember That,* p. 939; April, 1998, Ellen Mandel, review of *Matzo Ball Moon,* p. 1332; February 15, 2001, Helen Rosenberg, review of *Cats, Cats, Cats!,* p. 1141.

Bulletin of the Center for Children's Books, February, 1990, review of *Heather Has Two Mommies,* p. 144.

Entertainment Weekly, January 29, 1993, Rebecca Ascher-Walsh, "Writer on the Storm," and Michele Landsberg, reviews of *Heather Has Two Mommies* and *Gloria Goes to Gay Pride,* p. 66.

Horn Book, May-June, 1995, Maeve Visser Knoth, review of *Too Far Away to Touch,* p. 328.

New York Times Book Review, August 27, 1995, Roger Sutton, review of *Too Far Away to Touch,* p. 27; July 28, 1996, Judith Viorst, review of *Remember That,* p. 21.

Publishers Weekly, September 19, 1994, review of *Fat Chance,* p. 72; February 6, 1995, review of *Too Far Away to Touch,* p. 85; February 23, 1998, review of *Matzo Ball Moon,* p. 76; January 15, 2001, review of *Cats, Cats, Cats!,* p. 75.

School Library Journal, January, 1995, Melissa Yurechko, review of *Fat Chance,* p. 138; September, 1995, Mary Rinato Berman, review of *Too Far Away to Touch,* p. 183; March, 1996, Susan Scheps, review of *Remember That,* p. 179; June, 1998, Susan Pine, review of *Matzo Ball Moon,* p. 116; March, 2001, Lauralyn Persson, review of *Cats, Cats, Cats!,* p. 215.

OTHER

Lesléa Newman Web Site, http://www.lesleanewman.com (February 2, 2002).

Queer Theory, http://www.queertheory.com/ (February 2, 2002), author profile of Lesléa Newman.

*   *   *

NIEHAUS, Paddy Bouma
See BOUMA, Paddy

P

PETERS, Julie Anne 1952-

Personal

Born January 16, 1952, in Jamestown, NY. *Education:* Colorado Women's College, B.A., 1974; Metropolitan State College of Denver, B.S. (summa cum laude), 1985; University of Colorado—Denver, M.B.A. (magna cum laude), 1989. *Hobbies and other interests:* Human rights, animal rights advocacy, reading, traveling, manuscript evaluations and writing workshops, dancing, singing, musical theater.

Addresses

Home—14 Twilight Dr., Lakewood, CO 80215. *E-mail*—JuliePeters@Juno.com.

Career

Tracom Corporation, Denver, CO, secretary, research assistant, computer programmer, and systems analyst, 1975-84; Electronic Data Systems, Denver, CO, computer systems engineer, 1985-88; Jefferson County School District, Lakewood, CO, special needs educational assistant. Fifth grade teacher, 1975. *Member:* Society of Children's Book Writers and Illustrators, Authors' Guild, Colorado Authors' League, Colorado Center for the Book, Denver Zoological Society, Cat Care Society, American Civil Liberties Union, GLBT Center of Colorado.

Awards, Honors

KC3 Reading Award, Greater Kansas City Association of School Librarians, 1995, for *The Stinky Sneakers Contest;* Best Book in Language Arts: K-6 Novels, Society of School Librarians International, 1997, for *How Do You Spell GEEK?;* Top Hand Award for Young Adult Fiction, Colorado Authors' League, 1998, for *Revenge of the Snob Squad; Define "Normal"* was included by the American Library Association in the list

Julie Anne Peters

of Best Books for Young Adults and as a Quick Pick for Reluctant Young Adult Readers, both in 2000.

Writings

The Stinky Sneakers Contest, illustrated by Cat Bowman Smith, Little, Brown (Boston, MA), 1992.
Risky Friends, Willowisp Press (St. Petersburg, FL), 1993.
B. J.'s Billion-Dollar Bet, illustrated by Cynthia Fisher, Little, Brown (Boston, MA), 1994.

How Do You Spell GEEK?, Little, Brown (Boston, MA), 1996.
Revenge of the Snob Squad, Little, Brown (Boston, MA), 1998.
Romance of the Snob Squad, Little, Brown (Boston, MA), 1999.
Love Me, Love My Broccoli, Avon/HarperCollins (New York, NY), 1999.
Define "Normal," Little, Brown (Boston, MA), 2000.
A Snitch in the Snob Squad, Little, Brown (Boston, MA), 2001.
Keeping You a Secret, Little, Brown (Boston, MA), in press.

Also author of numerous articles for juvenile, young adult, and adult periodicals, including *World of Busines$ Kids, Wee Wisdom, Hopscotch, Career Woman, Purple Cow, Venture, My Friend, Free Spirit, Lollipops, Family Fun, On the Line, Touch, Guide, Children's Book Insider, Wilson Library Bulletin, Writer's Handbook, Writer, Accent on Living,* and *Good Housekeeping.* Contributing editor for *IEA News.*

Work in Progress

Two young adult novels exploring the diversity of family relationships and self-identity issues.

Sidelights

Julie Anne Peters began her writing career with the discovery of a surprising aptitude towards technical writing. This interest evolved into her exploring the possibility of writing fiction, leading her to the sale of a number of short stories as well as nonfiction articles and educational activities to various children's periodicals. Soon thereafter, Peters was able to get her first two books published, formally launching her career as a young adult and children's writer.

Her first book, *The Stinky Sneakers Contest,* is based on a combination of a real-life experience and a "grungy" shoe contest that was held out east. "Reading about the contest reminded me of my own childhood humiliation of perpetually smelly feet," Peters once told *SATA.* The plot moves far beyond the title and presents a tale of a friendship in jeopardy because of cheating. The story depicts familiar themes of winning, losing, and honesty, as Earl and Damian compete in the Feetfirst shoe company's smelly sneakers contest. An *Instructor* reviewer commented, "This pleasant, easy-to-read chapter book about two African-American boys will stimulate reflection on what it takes to be a winner." Lynnea McBurney, a reviewer for *School Library Journal,* also stated, "On the whole, this is a nicely written, humorous story. It is short enough for those just getting into transitional readers, yet there is enough here for enjoyment and food for thought."

Peters' second book, *Risky Friends,* explores the issue of choosing friends while confronting the reality of single-parent households. Two best friends, Kacie and Vicky, are at risk of losing their friendship over Kacie's

In Peters's novel, two middle-school best friends are torn apart when a spelling bee puts them and a brainy new student in competition with each other. (Cover illustration by Doran Ben-Ami.)

newfound companion, Skye, who wins Kacie's attention by buying her gifts. "As a kid, I always envied people with more money than me—thinking wealth solved the world's problems," Peters said. "That misperception, along with the inevitable growing pains accompanying young adulthood, are the themes explored in *Risky Friends.*" Sister Bernadette Marie Ondus stated in *Kliatt:* "The younger set, girls primarily, will enjoy this story since they will be able to identify closely with the characters."

Peters told *SATA:* "The most gratifying aspect of writing for young people is discovering that your books transcend storytelling to making a difference in a person's life. I cry when I receive letters like this one from Joli in New York City. 'I read your book about 3 times,' she says. 'I'm not a person to sit down and read. But your book is wonderful.' Or this from Alexandra in Denver. 'You probably don't know that I don't like to read, but your books really get me going.'"

Peters said that her response to letters like the ones quoted above "are tears of joy. Since I was a reluctant reader myself, I know how finding the one book that turns you onto reading is like being handed the keys to the kingdom. The kingdom is knowledge and adventure and self-discovery. Reading opens the realm of possibilities in life. It's life-changing, life-affirming. If my books can ignite one young person's love of reading, what greater reward could there be for a writer?"

Peters related that her book *Define "Normal"* grew out of her experiences working with special-needs children. According to her, "these kids weren't necessarily learning disabled, or intellectually challenged. They had so many family problems, so much responsibility, that school was the bottom rung on their priority ladder." Peters noted that the children she worked with struggled daily to survive, and that theirs was a far from normal childhood. "I began to examine the concept of 'normal' and how we use it to label people—particularly teens. We react so negatively to kids who choose to express themselves a bit outrageously, who dress to shock, or ornament their bodies. But this is absolutely normal behavior. Young people are trying to figure out who they are, where they fit in. And conversely, how they'll

When conservative Antonia is assigned to peer counsel outrageous Jazz, the girls recognize their similarities and Antonia finds, in a complete role reversal, that Jazz is a lifeline for her.

set themselves apart." It was this exploration of "normal" says Peters, which evolved into two of her characters in this book—Antonia and Jazz.

In *Define "Normal"* the main character, Antonia Dillon, appears to be a perfectly normal teen—healthy, happy, trouble free. She dresses conservatively, performs well in school, and never questions authority. Yet underneath her controlled exterior she is experiencing tremendous family turmoil. Peters explained to *SATA*, "Antonia has way too much responsibility for a fourteen-year-old girl. She has no time or energy to explore who she is as a person." On the other end of the spectrum is Jasmine Luther. "Jazz," noted Peters, "is all about self. She's this glorious expression of who she is. But Jazz is free to be herself because she has a solid family foundation. If she crashes and burns, she knows someone will be there to douse the flames. Antonia doesn't have this luxury." The conflict in the book occurs when Antonia is assigned to peer counsel Jazz in school, leading to a resounding clash of values. As both girls work through the counseling sessions, they each come to terms with their problems, eventually becoming friends. Reviewing this book for the *School Library Journal*, Kimberly A. Ault lauded *Define "Normal"* as "believable" and "well written."

Peters is also the author of a series of books about a group of sixth-grade girls who call themselves the Snob Squad. Each book explores aspects in the lives of these girls as they bond in friendship to combat the loneliness of being outcasts and misfits. Along the way, they fall in love, uncover mysteries, and solve crimes. In *A Snitch in the Snob Squad,* Jenny, the main character, and her friends try to discover the truth about a theft at school and its related cover-up, while also grappling with issues of trust at home and with her friends. *Romance of the Snob Squad* centers on a crush that one of the Snob Squad girls has on a classmate, while simultaneously addressing aspects of family love and loyalty to friends. Reviewing this particular work for *Booklist,* Hazel Rochman remarked that the narrator's "bossy, wry first-person narrative is candid . . . kind, and sad," predicting that many middle-graders will identify with the issues explored in this book.

Biographical and Critical Sources

PERIODICALS

Booklist, February 15, 1993, p. 1068; December 15, 1998, Ilene Cooper, review of *Revenge of the Snob Squad,* p. 751; April 1, 1999, Hazel Rochman, review of *Romance of the Snob Squad,* p. 1414; May 15, 2000, Jean Franklin, review of *Define "Normal,"* p. 1739; May 15, 2001, Hazel Rochman, review of *A Snitch in the Snob Squad,* p. 1753.
Books for Young People, June 1, 1994, p. 779.
Horn Book, September-October, 1994.
Instructor, February, 1993, review of *The Stinky Sneakers Contest,* p. 5.
Kirkus Reviews, December 15, 1992, p. 1576.

Kliatt, November, 1993, Sister Bernadette Marie Ondus, review of *Risky Friends,* p. 10.

Publishers Weekly, August 19, 1996, review of *How Do You Spell GEEK?,* p. 67; March 13, 2000, review of *Define "Normal,"* p. 85.

School Library Journal, March, 1993, Lynnea McBurney, review of *The Stinky Sneakers Contest,* p. 184; October, 1996, Harriett Fargnoli, review of *How Do You Spell GEEK?,* p. 124; July, 2000, Kimberly A. Ault, review of *Define "Normal,"* p. 108; April, 2001, Janet Hilburn, review of *A Snitch in the Snob Squad,* p. 148.

OTHER

Julie Anne Peters Web Site, http://www.JulieAnnePeters. com (January 27, 2002).

*   *   *

PINKNEY, Sandra L.

Personal

Born in Vahalla, NY; daughter of Alfred (a presser) and Frances (an insurance adjuster) McRae; married Myles C. Pinkney (a photographer); children: Myles "Leon" Pinkney, Charnelle-Rene, Rashad. *Education:* State University of New York, Empire State College, C.D.A. (early childhood education); attended Dutchess Community College. *Religion:* Baptist. *Hobbies and other interests:* Running, softball, singing, acting, crocheting, and collecting angels.

Addresses

Home—30 Spring St., Poughkeepsie, NY 12601. *Agent*—Sheldon Fogelman, 10 East 40th St., New York, NY 10016.

Career

Lil' Praiser's Christian Day-Care, Poughkeepsie, NY, director, 1996—. *Member:* National Association for the Education of Young Children, National Black Child Development Institute.

Awards, Honors

NAACP Image Award for Outstanding Children's Literary Works, for *Shades of Black: A Celebration of Our Children,* 2001.

Writings

Shades of Black: A Celebration of Our Children, photographs by Myles C. Pinkney, Scholastic (New York, NY), 2000.

A Rainbow All Around Me, photographs by Myles C. Pinkney, Scholastic (New York, NY), 2001.

Sidelights

Sandra L. Pinkney is the award-winning author of the picture book *Shades of Black: A Celebration of Our*

Sandra L. Pinkney

Children, which her husband, Myles C. Pinkney, illustrated with color photographs of children. *Shades of Black* describes the different skin, eye, and hair tones of African American children, both verbally and visually. "I came up with the idea for the book while sitting down in the library and reading a book on how to write poetry," Pinkney told *SATA.* "It started out 'I like chocolate.' I thought to myself, 'Yeah, I like chocolate.' It went on to say, 'Chocolate is sweet.' I thought again, 'Yeah, it is sweet. Hey! I could write this.' You see, one of my teachers told me that I couldn't write poetry, but I knew I could write poems like the one I was reading. But I can't write about chocolate. That's been done, I told myself. I looked around and looked at my hands and said, 'I am black.' I realized I could write about how I am black and differences and beauty in the black race. That's how the whole idea of *Shades of Black* came to be." The book caught reviewers' attention. While Tammy K. Baggett, writing in *School Library Journal,* praised the text as "vivid," a contributor to *Kirkus Reviews* noted the "patterned text full of rich vocabulary." *Shades of Black* "can certainly be appreciated by children of any color," concluded *Booklist* reviewer Denia Hester.

Pinkney told *SATA:* "My favorite time to write is early in the morning, 4:00 a.m. before the birds get up. I believe that is when God gives me my greatest inspirations. I enjoy writing poetry, but I also enjoy writing short stories and inspirational stories."

Shades of Black: A Celebration of Our Children, *written by Pinkney and illustrated with photographs by her husband Myles, describes the different skin, eye, and hair tones of African American children.*

Biographical and Critical Sources

PERIODICALS

Booklist, November 1, 2000, Denia Hester, review of *Shades of Black,* p. 548.

Instructor, January, 2001, Dana Truby, "People Are Buzzing About," p. 8.

Kirkus Reviews, December 1, 2000, review of *Shades of Black.*

Publishers Weekly, November 20, 2000, "Excursions in Diversity," p. 70.

School Library Journal, December, 2000, Tammy K. Baggett, review of *Shades of Black,* p. 135.

Skipping Stones, May-August, 2001, Paulette Ansari, review of *Shades of Black,* p. 8.*

*   *   *

PITCHER, Caroline (Nell) 1948-

Personal

Born April 16, 1948, in Grimsby, Lincolnshire, England; daughter of William George Pitcher (a marine surveyor) and Joyce (Roberts) Warner; married Richard Johnson, October 25, 1982; children: Lauren Joy Hewlett, Max

Leo. *Education:* University of Warwick, degree (with honors), 1969.

Addresses

Home—Grove Farm, Cowers Lane, Derbyshire DE56 2LS, England. *E-mail*—liney@carolinepitcher.co.uk.

Career

Worked in an art gallery, 1969-71; teacher at primary schools in East London, England, 1971-84; writer, 1985—.

Awards, Honors

Kathleen Fidler Award, 1985, for *Diamond;* story of the year award, *Independent,* 1993, for "Kevin the Blue"; shortlisted for Children's Book Award, 1996, for *The Snow Whale;* selection as one of Atop three teen books, *Times* (London), 1997, for *Mine;* Arts Council of England Writers' Award, 1999, for *Silkscreen;* Storytelling World Award, for *Mariana and the Merchild;* East Midlands Arts Council Award, for *Snow Cat;* English Association shortlist, for *The Time of the Lion.*

Writings

CHILDREN'S BOOKS

Diamond, Blackie and Son (London, England), 1987.
Gruff Treatment, Blackie and Son (London, England), 1988.
The Red-Spotted Reindeer, Blackie and Son (London, England), 1988.
Mr. Duckbody Superstar, Blackie and Son (London, England), 1988.
Gold in the Garden Shed, Blackie and Son (London, England), 1988.
The Runaway Reptiles, Blackie and Son (London, England), 1988.
The Chocolate Bar Burglar, Blackie and Son (London, England), 1988.
On the Wire, Blackie and Son (London, England), 1989.
The Sue Tribe, Blackie and Son (London, England), 1990.
Gerald and the Pelican, Transworld Yearling (London, England), 1993.
Jo's Storm, illustrated by Jackie Morris, Bodley Head (London, England), 1994.
The Snow Whale, illustrated by Jackie Morris, Frances Lincoln (London, England), 1996.
Mine (young adult novel), Mammoth Contents (London, England), 1997.
Run with the Wind, illustrated by Jane Chapman, Little Tiger Press (Waukesha, WI), 1998.
Don't Be Afraid, Little Foal, illustrated by Jane Chapman, Magi, 1998.
The Time of the Lion, illustrated by Jackie Morris, Frances Lincoln (London, England), 1998.
On the Pond, Heinemann Educational Rhymeworld (London, England), 1998.
Mariana and the Merchild, illustrated by Jackie Morris, Frances Lincoln (London, England), 2000.

Are You Spring?, illustrated by Cliff Wright, Dorling Kindersley (New York, NY), 2000.

Silkscreen, Mammoth Contents (London, England), 2000.

Cast Away, A & C Black Graffix (London, England), 2000.

Please Don't Eat My Sister, A & C Black Comix (London, England), 2001.

The Ghost in the Glass, Mammoth (London, England), 2001.

Author of activity books in the series "Make It Yourself" and "Build Your Own," F. Watts, beginning in 1984. Work represented in anthologies, including *A Moon, a Star, a Story,* Blackie and Son (London, England), 1990; *Read Aloud Storybook,* Kingfisher, 1993; *Stories for Seven-Year-Olds,* 1996; and *Quids in Surprise Surprise,* Orion. Contributor to periodicals.

Work in Progress

Eleven O'clock Chocolate Cake, for Mammoth; *Cloud Cat.*

Sidelights

British writer Caroline Pitcher is the author of twenty books for young readers, including picture books and a juvenile novel. Her themes include the world of nature

Caroline Pitcher

and humankind's relationship to it, and in her picture books she has created both original texts as well as retellings of folktales.

Married and the mother of two children, Pitcher worked in an art gallery and taught in primary schools in East London before turning to writing in 1985. Many of her award-winning titles have yet to be published in the United States. In a review of her 1996 *The Snow Whale,* a reviewer for *Plays* called the picture book an "imaginative story" which "captures the magic of winter" as well as the "loving relationship" between a young boy and his sister. In *Run with the Wind,* Pitcher presents a "tender tale [which] speaks meaningfully to the little and big separations that children and parents encounter," according to a reviewer for *Publishers Weekly.* In the story, a young foal fears the darkness but is comforted by his mother. But all the while the mother horse reminds her foal that soon she must go back to work. The foal cannot imagine being without his mother, but when the day finally comes, the young horse is off running and playing in the wind, unmindful that his mother is away and working. *Booklist*'s Linda Perkins felt that the "separation anxiety theme will strike a chord with young children."

In *The Time of the Lion,* a young boy has a secret friendship with a lion and its family in the African savanna. When traders come to the village looking for lion cubs, the boy's father misleads them, though at first his son thinks he has betrayed the lions. "Pitcher's prose is redolent with apt analogies and lyrical images," wrote a contributor for *Publishers Weekly.* And Hazel Rochman, writing in *Booklist,* described the picture book as an "elemental story of a boy and his father and their connection with the wild." In *Mariana and the Merchild,* Pitcher once again teams up with Jackie Morris, who illustrated *The Time of the Lion,* to retell a folk tale from Chile about a mythical child who washes up from the sea. Gillian Engberg, reviewing *Mariana* in *Booklist,* drew special attention to Pitcher's prose, "filled with glistening visual descriptions." And in *Are You Spring?,* Pitcher develops a "successful approach to teaching an abstract concept," in the view of Sharon R. Pearce, writing in *School Library Journal.* In this case, the concept of seasons is presented in the story of a bear cub eager to leave the den, and anxiously—though mistakenly—awaiting the arrival of an animal named Spring.

"I write children's books," Pitcher once commented. "They happen to be about children, rather than adults, that's all. Adults are obsessed by children's books—perhaps because they are about imaginative areas, feelings, and experiences that we've lost, or stifled, or yearn for. We experience the most powerful images and visions in childhood reading and give ourselves to someone else's world. The best children's books are close to poetry, rich, immediate, and clear."

In Pitcher's retelling of a South American folktale, a lonely old woman raises a merchild, knowing she will eventually lose the child to her rightful mother. (From Mariana and the Merchild, *illlustrated by Jackie Morris.)*

Biographical and Critical Sources

PERIODICALS

Booklist, August, 1998, Linda Perkins, review of *Run with the Wind,* p. 2016; January 1, 1999, Hazel Rochman, review of *The Time of the Lion,* p. 890; March 1, 2000, Gillian Engberg, review of *Mariana and the Merchild,* p. 1246; October 15, 2000, p. 446.

Plays, December, 1996, review of *The Snow Whale,* p. 64.

Publishers Weekly, June 15, 1998, review of *Run with the Wind,* p. 59; August 10, 1998, review of *The Time of the Lion,* p. 387; March 13, 2000, p. 83.

School Library Journal, March, 1984, p. 149; December, 1996, p. 103; September, 1998, p. 179; May, 2000, p. 163; September, 2000, Sharon R. Pearce, review of *Are You Spring?,* p. 206.

Times Literary Supplement, April 7, 1989, p. 379.

OTHER

Caroline Pitcher Web Site, http://www.carolinepitcher. co.uk/ (January 27, 2002).

PRICE, Susan 1955-

Personal

Born July 8, 1955, in Brades Row, Round's Green, Worcestershire, England; daughter of Alan (an electrical motor technician) and Jessy (a laborer; maiden name, Hanley) Price. *Education:* Educated in Tividale, England. *Politics:* Socialist. *Religion:* Atheist.

Addresses

Home—77 Barncroft Rd., Tividale, Oldbury, Worcestershire B69 1TU, England. *Agent*—c/o Author Mail, Faber & Faber Ltd., 3 Queen Sq., London WC1N 3AU, England.

Career

Children's book writer. Worked variously in a bakery, supermarket, warehouse, museum, and hotel, 1973-79;

North Riding College of Education, Scarborough, England, resident creative writer, 1980.

Awards, Honors

Other Award, Children's Rights Workshop, 1975, for *Twopence a Tub;* Carnegie Medal, British Library Association, 1987, for *The Ghost Drum; Guardian* Children's Fiction Prize, 1999, for *The Sterkarm Handshake.*

Writings

FOR CHILDREN

The Devil's Piper, Faber (London, England), 1973, Greenwillow Books (New York, NY), 1976.

Twopence a Tub, Faber (London, England), 1975, Merrimack, 1978.

Sticks and Stones, Faber (London, England), 1976, Merrimack, 1978.

Home from Home, Faber (London, England), 1977, Merrimack, 1978.

Christopher Uptake, Faber (London, England), 1981.

In a Nutshell, illustrated by Alison Price, Faber (London, England), 1983.

From Where I Stand, Faber (London, England), 1984.

Odin's Monster, illustrated by Patrick Lynch, Black (London, England), 1986.

The Ghost Drum: A Cat's Tale, Faber (London, England), 1987, Farrar, Straus (New York, NY), 1987.

Ghostly Tales, illustrated by Peter Stevenson, Ladybird (London, England), 1987.

Here Lies Price (stories), Faber (London, England), 1987.

Master Thomas Katt, illustrated by K. Simpson, Black (London, England), 1988.

Hauntings 6: The Bone-Dog, Hippo, 1989.

Phantom from the Past, Paperbird (London, England), 1989.

Crack a Story (stories), illustrated by Patrick Lynch, Faber (London, England), 1990.

A Feasting of Trolls, illustrated by E. Stemp, Black (London, England), 1990.

Thunderpumps, illustrated by K. Aldous, Heinemann (London, England), 1990.

Books for Life, Gondwanaland Press, 1990.

Forbidden Doors, illustrated by Patrick Lynch, Faber (London, England), 1991.

Ghost Song, Faber (London, England), 1992, Farrar, Straus (New York, NY), 1992.

Head and Tales, Faber (London, England), 1993.

Coming Down to Earth, Lions, 1994.

Ghost Dance: The Czar's Black Angel, Faber (London, England), 1994, Farrar, Straus (New York, NY), 1994.

Foiling the Dragon, Scholastic (London, England), 1994.

The Saga of Aslak, A. C. Black (London, England), 1995.

Elfgift, Scholastic (London, England), 1995.

Hauntings (stories), Hodder & Stoughton (London, England), 1996.

Elfkings, Scholastic (London, England), 1996.

The Sterkarm Handshake, Hodder & Stoughton (London, England), 1998, HarperCollins (New York, NY), 2000.

The Ghost Wife, Hodder & Stoughton (London, England), 1998.

Horror Stories, *an anthology compiled by Susan Price, features tales from such revered authors as Edgar Allan Poe, Leon Garfield, and Stephen King.* (Illustration by Harry Horse.)

Nightcomers (stories), Hodder & Stoughton (London, England), 1998.

RETELLER

The Carpenter and Other Stories, Faber (Boston, MA), 1981.

Ghosts at Large, illustrated by Allison Price, Faber (London, England), 1984.

The Kingfisher Treasury of Nursery Stories: A Collection of Traditional Favourites for the Very Young, Kingfisher (London, England), 1990.

Jack and the Beanstalk and Other Stories (includes "The Princess and the Pea" and "The Little Red Hen"), illustrated by Moira and Colin Maclean, Kingfisher (London, England), 1992, Kingfisher (New York, NY), 1993.

Little Red Riding Hood and Other Stories (includes "The Magic Porridge Pot" and "The Three Little Pigs"), illustrated by Moira and Colin Maclean, Kingfisher (London, England), 1992, Kingfisher (New York, NY), 1993.

Billy Goats Gruff and Other Stories, Kingfisher (London, England), 1992.

The Three Bears and Other Stories (includes "The Enormous Turnip" and "The Elves and the Shoemaker"), illustrated by Moira and Colin Maclean, Kingfisher (London, England), 1992, Kingfisher (New York, NY), 1993.

Goldilocks and the Three Bears (picture book), illustrated by Rosalind Beardshaw, Cambridge University Press (London, England), 1999.

The Elves and the Shoemaker (picture book), illustrated by Margaret Chamberlain, Cambridge University Press (London, England), 1999.

The Runaway Chapati (picture book), illustrated by Stephen Waterhouse, Cambridge University Press (London, England), 1999.

OTHER

(Editor) *The Kingfisher Book of Horror Stories,* illustrated by Harry Horse, Kingfisher (London, England), 1995, published as *Horror Stories,* Kingfisher (New York, NY), 1995.

Work in Progress

A novel, *The King's Head.*

Sidelights

British author Susan Price writes across several genres, dealing in realistic fiction as well as fantasies in her many titles. Price's work includes collections of macabre, ghost, and folktales, fantasy novels, and realistic, gritty stories. Her retellings of traditional tales and her own original stories such as those found in the novel *Sticks and Stones* result in unique collections for young readers. The imaginary worlds found in Price's fantasy novels, such as *Devil's Piper, Ghost Drum, Ghost Song, Ghost Dance, The Sterkarm Handshake,* and *Elfgift,* also draw on traditional writings while offering new and imaginative settings for her characters to inhabit. And in her realistic and historical novels, including *Christopher Uptake* and *From Where I Stand,* Price often draws on her own working-class background to achieve authenticity.

Born and raised in an industrialized town, Price comes from a family that owned no property and had no savings. She credits the election of the socialist Labour party in 1948 with enabling her to get the education she needed to become a writer. It is this background that is the inspiration behind Price's writings; she writes for children who have similar working-class childhoods, hoping that they will be motivated to start thinking for themselves.

This is exactly what Price did, writing her first novel, *The Devil's Piper,* at the age of sixteen. A grim fantasy featuring the evil elf Toole O'Dyna, the story begins with Toole kidnaping four children through the use of his musical pipe. He is after one child in particular, Michael, whose ancestor killed Toole's best friend over two hundred years ago. Using his pipe once again, Toole is able to pull the murderer from his grave and exchange him for Michael. In the meantime, the adults looking for the children call upon the Devil himself to help them; he agrees to help only because he wishes to punish Toole for playing with death. *The Devil's Piper* is "a complex and extremely well-written fantasy," observed Ann A. Flowers in *Horn Book.* And a *Publishers Weekly* contributor wrote of Price's first novel: "With this kind of start, she is someone to remember and expect more from in the future."

This future soon found Price drawing more from her own experiences. Graeme, the main character in her 1976 novel, *Sticks and Stones,* is a working-class youth, just as Price was. In his own words, he describes his tedious job at a local supermarket and his desire to become a gardener. Because his father wants him to have a steady job, though, Graeme feels unable to quit, so he decides to try to get fired. As his supervisor gives him chance after chance, Graeme eventually confides in him and the book ends with a bit of hope in Graeme's future. "Many, many school leavers must be faced with Graeme's problems and will be able to identify themselves with him," wrote a *Junior Bookshelf* reviewer. Cecilia Gordon maintained in the *Times Literary Supplement* that *Sticks and Stones* is a "vivid book" in which Price shows "extraordinary empathy."

Another young man in a working-class situation is found in *Christopher Uptake,* published in 1981. Set in the sixteenth century, this adventure novel begins with Christopher, a joiner's son, winning a scholarship to the university. More interested in dramatic arts, though, Christopher is expelled and makes a meager living from his writing. At the same time, he finds himself defending minorities, especially Catholics, which leads him to a spy ring that is working to expose Catholics. Forced to spy on one of his own patrons, Christopher eventually brings about the patron's and his own downfall. Although she faulted *Christopher Uptake* for starting a bit slowly, Nancy Berkowitz stated in *School Library Journal* that "the historical details are accurate and the characterizations rich." Cara Chanteau, writing in the *Times Literary Supplement,* pointed out that *Christopher Uptake* shows how successful the historical novel genre can be, adding that "the story-line is refreshingly original."

Back in modern times with her 1984 offering *From Where I Stand,* Price focuses on another form of racism. Originally from Bangladesh, teenager Kamla Momen is attending school in Great Britain, hoping to become a doctor and return to her native country. At Brownheath School, though, she endures racial slurs from her fellow classmates and prejudicial behavior from the adults. Meeting Jonathan Ullman—an alumnus of Brownheath who is obsessed with racism and genocide—Kamla joins him in his efforts to attack the prejudice surrounding them. A *Junior Bookshelf* reviewer observed that all the characters in *From Where I Stand* are unlikable, adding that "by painting the picture too black and white Susan Price produces irritation rather than sympathy for the cause." Sarah Hayes, on the other hand, maintained in the *Times Literary Supplement* that after a shaky start Price's "story works up to an excellently written dramatic confrontation between headmistress and pupil."

Drama, suspense, and conflict are also the main ingredients in the traditional stories retold by Price. *The Carpenter and Other Stories* contains nineteen medieval tales of the clash between ancient beliefs and Christianity in British and Scandinavian cultures. Introduced into this clash in several of the stories is an evil or supernatural presence, including demons, devils, elves, and trolls. "Price has recounted the tales in a straightforward and vigorous manor, combining humor and concrete details," as Anita C. Wilson described them in *School Library Journal*. The twelve stories in *Ghosts at Large* are also traditional tales; they feature a woman who boldly stands up to a ghost and wins, a man who escapes death with a riddle inspired by a corpse, and a woman who carries her head around in a basket. "It is all strong stuff not to be read lightly before going to bed unless the door can be left open and the light on the landing left burning," concluded a *Junior Bookshelf* contributor. Price has gone on to publish several more retellings, some of which look at very popular childhood tales such as "Jack and the Beanstalk," "The Three Little Pigs," and "Little Red Riding Hood." In her 1999 picture books, *Goldilocks and the Three Bears, The Elves and the Shoemaker,* and *The Runaway Chapati,* Price has created versions that "lend themselves to being read aloud with verve and feeling," according to a *Books for Keeps* reviewer.

Magical fantasy takes center stage in *The Ghost Drum: A Cat's Tale,* a novel for which Price won both critical acclaim and the 1987 Carnegie Medal. Narrated by a cat, *The Ghost Drum* is set in Czardom, where the Czar's evil sister, Margeretta, turns him against his son, Safa, who is then locked in a small, windowless room until adulthood. Safa and his nurse, Marien, cannot fight this evil alone, and it is only through the help of the powerful shaman Chingis that they are able to escape. This leads to the fall of Margeretta and the wicked witch Kuzma. *The Ghost Drum* "is shot through with magic, rendered with an incantatory repetition of both language and story patterns," asserted Roger Sutton in the *Bulletin of the Center for Children's Books*. "Price has a strong understanding of folklore," stated Susan M. Harding in her *School Library Journal* review, adding that *The Ghost Drum* "is told simply and cleanly with no excess words to mask the emotions, and still the language is lyrical and poetic."

Five years after the publication of *The Ghost Drum*, Price published its sequel, *Ghost Song*. The only character to carry over from the original story is the witch/shaman Kuzma, who claims the newborn son of a trapper to be his apprentice. The father, Malyuta, refuses to give up Ambrosi, so Kuzma promises to take revenge and a series of tragic events begins to unfold. While still trying to get Ambrosi away from his father, Kuzma approaches a nomadic tribe and asks for an apprentice. Refused, Kuzma also curses the tribe so that they all turn into wolves every winter. The spell can only be broken

when someone from the tribe agrees to serve Kuzma and help him steal Ambrosi. This is done when the wolves kill Malyuta and lure Ambrosi into the Ghost World to free his father's spirit. In the end, however, Ambrosi chooses the Ghost World and death over serving Kuzma.

"Like the previous book, this one has the feel and flavor of old folktales," related Harding in her *School Library Journal* review of *Ghost Song*. "There is a purity and a beauty to the language; every word, every phrase, is perfectly placed, like an exquisite ice sculpture," she concluded. *Ghost Song* "is a saga that requires the reader to be willing to . . . surrender the imagination to the word magic of Susan Price's story-telling," praised a *Junior Bookshelf* contributor. And Hanna B. Zeigler concluded in *Horn Book:* "The beauty of the descriptive language of this tragic tale adds to the folkloric quality of the story—which incorporates the Norse myth of the death of Balder—leaving a haunting memory for the reader."

The trio of "Ghost" novels is rounded off with *Ghost Dance: The Czar's Black Angel*. In this tale, a young shaman's apprentice, Shingebiss, feels real concern for the situation of the Northmen, whose lands are being destroyed at the order of the Czar. Young Shingebiss disregards the warnings of her dying shaman and goes to the capital to confront the Czar. The Czar is a tortured individual, controlled largely by an English wizard, Master Jenkins; when the Czar sees Shingebiss, a shapechanger, he thinks at first that she is the Dark Angel sent by God. In order to get the Czar to stop despoiling the lovely natural beauty of the Northlands, Shingebiss must first deal with Master Jenkins. Ultimately, Shingebiss overthrows the corrupt Czar, but the price is high for the country is thrown for a time into political chaos. Critics were as full of praise for the third book in the "Ghost" cycle as they were for the others. For example, writing in *Booklist*, Ilene Cooper called *Ghost Dance* "ambitious" and a "dazzling offering," while a reviewer for *Publishers Weekly* noted that Price "crafts a rich, vivid fantasy about spirits and ghosts." The same reviewer concluded: "A writer with an impressive range and an expansive imagination, Price has truly mastered her idiom."

In *Here Lies Price,* the author creates a bond with her readers by starting each of the scary stories with an explanation of why the story is true. *Crack a Story* uses a red stone squirrel who lives in a nut tree to start each story; every time the squirrel cracks open and eats a nut, a new story begins. "Susan Price is an engaging and gifted writer for children," maintained Iain Bamforth in a *Times Literary Supplement* review of *Here Lies Price,* concluding: "This book should delight any child who has learned to think for him or herself, and any adult who is honest enough to admit to childish origins." Elizabeth J. King, writing in *School Librarian,* asserted that in *Crack a Story* "the writing is full of imagery and poetry. . . . Susan Price has always been an interesting and challenging writer." *Hauntings* is an "excellent collection" of ghost tales, according to *School Librarian* critic Robert Dunbar; it is a grouping of ten stories whose "power to disturb," as Dunbar put it, lies in the stories' "subtlety of characterization and in the restrained tone of their telling." In *Nightcomers,* Price deals in what *Magpies* contributor Helen Purdie felt are ghost stories "aimed at an older, even adult audience." Ranging in subject matter from a graveyard vigil to a vampire tale with "homo-erotic undertones," and from stories reminiscent of Poe to one that talks about the price of fame, the collection of tales "provides excitement for the older reader," concluded Purdie, "but has a depth of emotion that is at times disturbing."

Throughout the 1990s, Price continued to publish fantasy and horror novels in her native England, many of which have not seen U.S. publication. *Foiling the Dragon, Elfgift, Elfkings,* and *The Ghost Wife* are among such titles. Price's *Elfgift* is set in ancient Britain and deals with dynastic strife in a gritty, realistic manner on one level, while incorporating elements of fantasy. Elfgift, the spawn of a kingly coupling with an elven woman, inherits the throne from his royal father, a transference of power that initiates court intrigue and

Andrea Mitchell, an anthropologist from the twenty-first century, travels back in time and becomes involved with a sixteenth-century barbaric clan from the borderlands between Scotland and England. (Cover illustration by Peter Bollinger.)

ultimately summons up supernatural powers. A reviewer for *Books for Keeps* found *Elfgift* to be a "bleak, bloody and enthralling book." Price's 1999 horror novel, *The Ghost Wife,* deals with family history and the tug between the present and the past. Set at the dawn of the industrial age, the novel employs "strongly drawn characters," according to Catherine Sack writing in *School Librarian.*

With *The Sterkarm Handshake* Price secured a larger readership in the United States. Originally published in England in 1998, the 2000 publication in the United States brought Price's name to the forefront of fantasy writers. Her tale is set in a mythical sixteenth century on the borderlands between Scotland and England. There the Sterkarms have managed to plunder the land for generations, but suddenly they are confronted with intruders who call themselves Elves and have time-traveled from the twenty-first century. These invaders now plan to do their own bit of plundering of the region's natural resources. But when the Elves take on the Sterkarms, they dangerously underestimate their enemy.

These future Elves are actually surveyors from the twenty-first century, employees of a British company, FUP, which has developed a Time Tube. The director of the company is the evil Mr. Windsor, who plans to take all the natural resources he can and turn the place into a tourist attraction. Andrea Mitchell, a modern day linguist, accompanies the FUP survey team in their travel to the past and becomes caught in the middle between the FUP people and the Sterkarm clan. Falling in love with the handsome son of the leader of the clan only complicates things for Andrea.

Taking as inspiration the ancient family of Armstrong ("Sterkarm" is a direct translation into Danish of this name) who roved the border country in the sixteenth century, Price blends history and fantasy in this "dazzling story," as Steven Engelfried described it in *School Library Journal.* The "way of life portrayed in the book is broadly true," Price noted on *HarperChildrens.com.* "Though it was a little more political than I've shown it. I simplified things and made them more personal. In fact, both Scotland and England, in their endless wars, made use of the Border families as mercenaries—they made superb light cavalry. Both countries tacitly encouraged the raiding, as the constant skirmishing kept enemy resources tied up." Price also revealed on the *Harper-Childrens.com* site that she even learned how to ride a horse—and fall off of one—"in order to lend the Sterkarms more reality." Such verisimilitude did not go unnoticed with reviewers. Engelfried further commented on Price's combination of "time travel, romance, and action, along with thought-provoking ideas and memorable characters" which make the book an "excellent choice for adventure lovers." *Booklist* critic Sally Estes felt that the novel is a "gripping story, filled with realistic details of sixteenth-century life in all its harshness." And announcing Price's winning of the *Guardian* Children's Fiction Prize for 1999, a reviewer for *Magpies* called the author a "master storyteller" and her novel "simply stunning."

Price's range encompasses history, fantasy, science fiction, and myth, as well as more realistic fiction. Yet in the end it is the story that counts for her, and the honesty of the enterprise. As she noted in the *St. James Guide to Children's Writers:* "The more I write, the less I feel I want to make any 'personal statement.' I write for money; it's my living. I try to do my job as well as I can. That's all."

Biographical and Critical Sources

BOOKS

St. James Guide to Children's Writers, 5th edition, St. James (Detroit, MI), 1999.

PERIODICALS

Booklist, September 15, 1992, p. 147; November 15, 1994, Ilene Cooper, review of *Ghost Dance,* p. 590; October 15, 1995, Chris Sherman, review of *Horror Stories,* p. 396; October 1, 2000, Sally Estes, review of *The Sterkarm Handshake,* p. 332.

Book Report, May-June, 1993, p. 43.

Books for Keeps, July, 1989, p. 11; March, 1991, p. 10l; January, 1996, review of *Elfgift,* p. 13; July, 1999, reviews of *Goldilocks and the Three Bears, The Elves and the Shoemaker,* and *The Runaway Chapati,* p. 19.

Bulletin of the Center for Children's Books, October, 1987, Roger Sutton, review of *The Ghost Drum: A Cat's Tale,* p. 36.

Horn Book, June, 1976, Ann A. Flowers, review of *The Devil's Piper,* p. 292; January-February, 1993, Hanna B. Zeigler, review of *Ghost Song,* p. 87.

Junior Bookshelf, June, 1975, p. 203; October, 1976, review of *Sticks and Stones,* pp. 285-286; June, 1977, p. 183; June, 1984, review of *From Where I Stand,* pp. 146-147; February, 1985, review of *Ghosts at Large,* p. 44; August, 1986, p. 151; December, 1988, pp. 293-294; August, 1990, p. 177; December, 1990,

p. 283; October, 1991, p. 227; August, 1992, review of *Ghost Song,* pp. 165-166; December, 1992, p. 231; December, 1993, p. 243.

Magpies, May, 1998, Helen Purdie, review of *Nightcomers,* p. 39; November, 1999, review of *The Sterkarm Handshake,* p. 7.

New Statesman, May 31, 1999, p. 50.

Publishers Weekly, April 19, 1976, review of *The Devil's Piper,* p. 85; November 14, 1994, review of *Ghost Dance,* p. 69.

School Librarian, December, 1983, p. 361; May, 1990, Elizabeth J. King, review of *Crack a Story,* p. 68; February, 1996, p. 32; May, 1996, Robert Dunbar, review of *Hauntings,* p. 78; summer, 1999, p. 101; autumn, 1999, Catherine Stack, review of *The Ghost Wife,* p. 158.

School Library Journal, September, 1982, Anita C. Wilson, review of *The Carpenter and Other Stories,* p. 126; October, 1982, Nancy Berkowitz, review of *Christopher Uptake,* p. 163; September, 1987, Susan M. Harding, review of *The Ghost Drum: A Cat's Tale,* p. 182; January, 1993, Susan M. Harding, review of *Ghost Song,* p. 102; December, 1994, p. 130; December, 2000, Steven Engelfried, review of *The Sterkarm Handshake,* p. 148.

Times Educational Supplement, February 23, 1990, p. 34; November 8, 1991, p. 41; July 24, 1992, p. 20; March 25, 1994, p. R3.

Times Literary Supplement, July 16, 1976, Cecilia Gordon, "Communication Problems," p. 884; July 24, 1981, Cara Chanteau, "The Stuff of Fiction," p. 842; March 30, 1984, Sarah Hayes, "In the Real World," p. 336; January 15, 1988, Iain Bamforth, "Supping with the Devil," p. 70.

OTHER

HarperChildrens.com, http://www.harperchildrens.com/ (May 19, 2001).

Susan Price Home Page, http://www.susanprice.org.uk/ (May 19, 2001).*

R

RAINES, Shirley C. 1945-
(Shirley Raines Smith)

Personal

Born April 15, 1945, in Jackson, TN; married Robert J. Canady (an educator and author); children: Brian; stepchildren: Lynnette, Scott, Lark. *Education:* University of Tennessee—Martin, B.S. (child development), 1967; University of Tennessee—Knoxville, M.S. (child development), 1972, Ed.D. (early childhood education), 1979.

Addresses

Office—Office of the President, University of Memphis, Memphis, TN 38152-3370.

Career

Jefferson County Schools, Louisville, KY, teacher, 1967-68; West Clark Community Schools, Sellersberg, IN, teacher, 1968-70; Knox County Schools, Knoxville, TN, director of Head Start Centers, 1972-76; Roane State Community College, Harriman, TN, director and founder of Community Child Center, instructor, 1976-78; University of Alabama, Tuscaloosa, AL, instructor, 1978-79, assistant professor, 1979-82, chair, Elementary and Early Childhood, 1981-82; North Carolina Wesleyan, Rocky Mount, NC, associate professor and coordinator of Early Childhood Education, 1982-83; George Mason University, Fairfax, VA, assistant professor, 1983-84, associate professor, 1984-87, associate professor of Curriculum and Instruction, 1987-92; University of South Florida, Tampa, FL, professor and chair of Childhood/Language Arts/Reading Education, 1992-95; University of Kentucky, Lexington, KY, professor and dean of the College of Education, 1995-2001, vice chancellor for Academic Services, 1998-2001; University of Memphis, Memphis, TN, president, 2001—.

International Studies Program, Bogota, Colombia, summer, 1979, Mexico City, Mexico, summer, 1980, Quito,

Shirley C. Raines

Ecuador, summer, 1981; visiting professor, State University of New York—Oneonta, summer, 1982; National Teacher of the Year Selection Committee, 1990, 1991, 1992, 1999; associate editor, *Journal of Early Childhood Teacher Education,* 1990-92. Speaker at local, national, and international conferences and venues. *Member:* Association for Childhood Education International (international/intercultural committee, 1982-86; presidents' council, 1985-87; publications committee, 1986-91; teacher education committee, 1990-92; member-at-large,

1992-95; president-elect, 1998-99; president, 1999-2001), National Association for the Education of Young Children (representative to Association for Childhood Education International, 1989-92; Teacher Education Review Panel, 1991-94), National Association of Early Childhood Teacher Educators (chair of resolutions committee, 1986-89; treasurer, 1987-89; research network, 1989-91; editorial board, 1989-92), International Reading Association, Southern Early Childhood Association, Omicron Delta Kappa Leadership Society, Phi Delta Kappa.

Awards, Honors

Outstanding Woman in the Arts, Delta Kappa Gamma State Convention, 1984; Instructional Excellence Award for Teachers of Teachers, Northeastern State University/ Oklahoma Education Association, 1986; Outstanding Member Award, Association for Childhood Education International, 1987, 1996; Faculty Award for Outstanding Teaching, Student Education Association, George Mason University; Distinguished Faculty Award, College of Education and Human Services, George Mason University, 1991.

Writings

A Guide to Early Learning, R. and E. Research Associates (Palo Alto, CA), 1982.

(Editor) *Keeping the Child in Childhood,* Wesleyan College Press (Rocky Mount, NC), 1983.

(With Robert J. Canady) *Story S-t-r-e-t-c-h-e-r-s: Activities to Expand Children's Favorite Books,* Gryphon House (Mt. Rainier, MD), 1989.

(With Robert J. Canady) *The Whole Language Kindergarten,* foreword by Bill Martin, Teachers College Press (New York, NY), 1990.

(With Robert J. Canady) *More Story S-t-r-e-t-c-h-e-r-s: Activities to Expand Children's Favorite Books,* Gryphon House (Mt. Rainier, MD), 1991.

(With Robert J. Canady) *Story S-t-r-e-t-c-h-e-r-s for the Primary Grades: Activities to Expand Children's Favorite Books,* Gryphon House (Mt. Rainier, MD), 1992.

(With Rebecca T. Isbell) *Stories: Children's Literature in Early Education,* Delmar Publishers (Albany, NY), 1994.

450 More Story S-t-r-e-t-c-h-e-r-s for the Primary Grades: Activities to Expand Children's Favorite Books, Gryphon House (Mt. Rainier, MD), 1994.

(With Rebecca T. Isbell) *Children's Literature in Early Education,* Delmar Publishers (Albany, NY), 1994.

(Editor and contributor) *Whole Language across the Curriculum: Grades 1, 2, 3,* foreword by Dorothy S. Strickland, Teachers College Press (New York, NY), 1995.

Never, Ever, Serve Sugary Snacks on Rainy Days: The Official Little Instruction Book for Teachers of Young Children, Gryphon House (Beltsville, MD), 1995.

(With Rebecca T. Isbell) *Tell It Again! Easy-to-Tell Stories with Activities for Young Children,* illustrated by Joan Waites, Gryphon House (Beltsville, MD), 1999.

The authors of **The Whole Language Kindergarten** *discuss how to incorporate the traditional elements of a kindergarten setting with a program based on the practice of literacy skills.*

(With Rebecca T. Isbell) *Tell It Again! 2: Easy-to-Tell Stories with Activities for Young Children,* illustrated by Joan Waites, Gryphon House (Beltsville, MD), 1999.

Contributor to *Parenting Resource Guide,* edited by B. L. Walden, State Department of Education (Montgomery, AL) 1982; *Early Childhood Education,* 1985 and 1986 annual editions, edited by J. S. McKee, Dushkin Publishing Group (Guildford, CT), 1985, 1986; *Ideas and Insights: Language Arts in the Elementary School,* edited by D. Watson, National Council of Teachers of English (Urbana, IL), 1987; *Leaders in Education: Their Views on Controversial Issues,* edited by G. Roberson and B. Johnson, University Press (Lanham, MD), 1988; *Annual Review of Conflict Knowledge and Conflict Resolution,* Volume 3, edited by J. Gittler and L. Bowen, Garland Press (New York, NY), 1991; *School Library Media Annual,* Volume 10, edited by J. Bandy Smith and J. G. Colemen, Libraries Unlimited (Littleton, CO), 1992; *New Perspectives in Early Childhood Teacher Education,* edited by S. G. Goffin and D. E. Day, Teachers College Press (New York, NY), 1994; *Inte-*

grating School Restructuring and Special Education Reform, edited by J. L. Paul, H. Rosselli, and D. Evans, Harcourt, Brace (Orlando, FL), 1995; *The Professional Collection for Elementary Educators,* edited by P. P. Wilson, H. W. Wilson (New York, NY), 1996; *Major Trends and Issues in Early Childhood Education: Challenges, Controversies, and Insights,* edited by J. P. Isenberg and M. R. Jalongo, Teachers College Press (New York, NY), 1997.

Articles and book reviews published in *Teacher Education and Special Education, Childhood Education, Journal for Research in Childhood Education, Dimensions, Young Children, Reading Teacher, Education Digest, Child Care Information Exchange, Journal of Early Childhood Teacher Education, Resources in Education, National Association of Early Childhood Teacher Educators Conference Report, Oklahoma Children, Livewire, Journal of Educational Leadership, Rocky Mount Telegram, North Carolina Association for Young Children, Classroom Activities from Heath, Dissertation Abstracts International, Tennessee Education, Record, National Association of Early Childhood Teacher Educators' Bulletin, Young Children,* and *Capstone Journal of Education.*

Sidelights

Shirley C. Raines is an educator who has written extensively in her field of early childhood development. Her books include theoretical treatises on the whole language educational environment as well as practical guides that reviewers praise for their usefulness in classroom and home-teaching situations. Raines and her husband, Robert J. Canady, have co-authored several works, including a series called "Story S-t-r-e-t-c-h-e-r-s," in which popular children's books are brought into the classroom for lessons in math, art, science, imaginative play, writing, and cooking. Beginning with *Story S-t-r-e-t-c-h-e-r-s: Activities to Expand Children's Favorite Books,* geared toward preschool and kindergartners, and its sequel, *More Story S-t-r-e-t-c-h-e-r-s,* and continuing with *Story S-t-r-e-t-c-h-e-r-s for the Primary Grades,* and its sequel, *450 More Story S-t-r-e-t-c-h-e-r-s for the Primary Grades,* reviewers commended the authors for their clear organization of a wealth of practical information on how to get children excited about reading. *Booklist* reviewer Janice Del Negro concluded her review of the fourth book in this series: "A solid, well-designed work, this will be a valuable resource for teachers as well as librarians." And *Language Arts* reviewer Kathleen Chang recounted her own experience using the first book at home with her own children as well as in the classroom and concluded: "There are so many opportunities to use this book. You can adopt the suggestions or use them as models to create your own. I highly recommend this book as a mother and educator of young children."

Raines and Canady teamed up again for *The Whole Language Kindergarten,* which "provides a balance of theory, research, and kindergarten applications," according to the reviewers in *Language Arts.* Here, the authors explain the whole language approach to teaching, and discuss how to incorporate the traditional elements of a kindergarten setting into a classroom based on the whole language philosophy, in which children are surrounded by opportunities to practice literacy skills. The authors offer practical examples of how to use themes to expand the opportunities for learning. "The chapter on theme units is especially helpful," felt the reviewers in *Language Arts.* "It demonstrates the importance of integrating a topic by giving students a variety of activities throughout the day that incorporate many opportunities to listen, speak, read, and write about a theme," they continued. *The Whole Language Kindergarten* concludes with a chapter on the parents of kindergartners and the importance of educating them on the whole language approach. "The authors have done an outstanding job in providing a complete picture on the whole language kindergarten," concluded the reviewers in *Language Arts.*

Biographical and Critical Sources

PERIODICALS

Booklist, April 1, 1993, Janice Del Negro, review of *Story Stretchers for the Primary Grades,* p. 1445; January 1, 1995, Janice Del Negro, review of *450 More Story Stretchers for the Primary Grades,* p. 831.

Language Arts, December, 1990, Kathleen Chang, Madeline Oshiro, and Judith Scheu, review of *Story Stretchers,* pp. 868-869; April, 1993, Jacqueline H. Carroll, Joyce Ahuna-Ka-ai-ai, Kathleen S. Chang, and Joann Wong-Kam, review of *The Whole Language Kindergarten,* p. 310.

OTHER

University of Memphis Web Site, http://www.memphis.edu/ (February 2, 2002).*

*   *   *

REEF, Catherine 1951-

Personal

Born April 28, 1951, in New York, NY; daughter of Walter H. Preston, Jr. (an advertising executive) and Patricia Preziosi (a teacher; maiden name, Deeley); married John W. Reef (a physical scientist), March 13, 1971; children: John Stephen. *Education:* Washington State University, B.A., 1983. *Hobbies and other interests:* Reading, music, handicrafts.

Addresses

Home and office—4613 Amherst Rd., College Park, MD 20740.

Career

Taking Care (a health education newsletter), Reston, VA, editor, 1985-90; children's book author, 1990—. *Member:* Society of Children's Book Writers and Illustrators.

Awards, Honors

Joan G. Sugarman Children's Book Award, 1994-95, Notable Children's Trade Book in the Field of Social Studies, National Council for the Social Studies/Children's Book Council (NCSS/CBC), 1996, Books for the Teen Age selection, New York Public Library (NYPL), 1996, and One Hundred Titles for Reading and Sharing, NYPL, all for *Walt Whitman;* Notable Children's Book selection, American Library Association (ALA), and Books for the Teen Age selection, NYPL, 1997, both for *John Steinbeck;* Society of School Librarians International Honor Book, and Books for the Teen Age selection, NYPL, both 1997, both for *Black Explorers;* Books for the Teen Age selection, NYPL, 2000, for *Africans in America: The Spread of People and Culture;* Notable Children's Trade Book in the Field of Social Studies, NCSS/CBC, 2001, for *Paul Laurence Dunbar: Portrait of a Poet;* One Hundred Titles for Reading and Sharing, NYPL, 2001, for *Sigmund Freud: Pioneer of the Mind.*

Writings

Washington, DC, Dillon (Parsippany, NJ), 1990.
Baltimore, Dillon (Parsippany, NJ), 1990.
Albert Einstein: Scientist of the Twentieth Century, Dillon (Parsippany, NJ), 1991.
Arlington National Cemetery, Dillon (Parsippany, NJ), 1991.
Monticello, Dillon (Parsippany, NJ), 1991.
Ellis Island, Dillon (Parsippany, NJ), 1991.
Rachel Carson: The Wonder of Nature, Twenty-First Century Books (New York, NY), 1992.
Henry David Thoreau: A Neighbor to Nature, Twenty-First Century Books (New York, NY), 1992.
Jacques Cousteau: Champion of the Sea, Twenty-First Century Books (New York, NY), 1992.
Gettysburg, Dillon (Parsippany, NJ), 1992.
Mount Vernon, Dillon (Parsippany, NJ), 1992.
Benjamin Davis, Jr., Twenty-First Century Books (New York, NY), 1992.
Colin Powell, Twenty-First Century Books (New York, NY), 1992.
Buffalo Soldiers, Twenty-First Century Books (New York, NY), 1993.
Civil War Soldiers, Twenty-First Century Books (New York, NY), 1993.
Eat the Right Stuff: Food Facts, Twenty-First Century Books (New York, NY), 1993.
Stay Fit: Build a Strong Body, Twenty-First Century Books (New York, NY), 1993.
Think Positive: Cope with Stress, Twenty-First Century Books, 1993.
Black Fighting Men: A Proud History, Twenty-First Century Books (New York, NY), 1994.
The Lincoln Memorial, Dillon (Parsippany, NJ), 1994.
Ralph David Abernathy, Dillon (Parsippany, NJ), 1995.
The Supreme Court, Dillon (Parsippany, NJ), 1995.
Walt Whitman, Clarion Books (New York, NY), 1995.
John Steinbeck, Clarion Books (New York, NY), 1996.
Black Explorers, Facts On File (New York, NY), 1996.

Catherine Reef

Africans in America: The Spread of People and Culture, Facts On File (New York, NY), 1999.
Working in America: An Eyewitness History, Facts On File (New York, NY), 2000.
George Gershwin: American Composer, Morgan Reynolds (Greensboro, NC), 2000.
Paul Laurence Dunbar: Portrait of a Poet, Enslow (Berkeley Heights, NJ), 2000.
A. Philip Randolph: Union Leader and Civil Rights Crusader, Enslow (Berkeley Heights, NJ), 2001.
Sigmund Freud: Pioneer of the Mind, Clarion Books (New York, NY), 2001.
Childhood in America: An Eyewitness History, Facts On File (New York, NY), 2002.
This Our Dark Country: The American Settlers of Liberia, Clarion Books (New York, NY), 2002.

Sidelights

Catherine Reef is a nonfiction writer for children and young adults whose biographies, social histories, health books, and descriptions of famous buildings and monuments both inform and entertain young readers. Notable among her biographical subjects are writers such as John Steinbeck and Walt Whitman, scientists such as Albert Einstein and Sigmund Freud, and outstanding African Americans from Colin Powell to the poet Paul Laurence Dunbar. Writing of the spirit of place in America, Reef has presented such monuments to history as Monticello, Mount Vernon, and the Lincoln Memorial. Among her books of social history are those dealing with African

Americans, such as *Africans in America: The Spread of People and Culture*, as well as several detailing the African American military contribution, including *Buffalo Soldiers* and *Civil War Soldiers*.

Reef once described her childhood for *SATA:* "I grew up in Commack, New York, a flat, spreading Long Island town, during the 1950s and 1960s. It was a town where most people lived in clean, new split-level or ranch houses on treeless land that had been farmers' fields. My house was different. I lived in one of Commack's few old houses, a place with carved woodwork and a yard full of trees. That backyard seemed enormous, and it beckoned my friends and me to imaginative play. There was an ancient apple tree, bent-over and climber-friendly, where we acted out stories of loss and rescue. There was a sky-high pine tree from which a tire hung on a rope. We often would swing, heads leaning back and faces pointing up through the branches, and imagine that we could fly.

"Sometimes I played indoors on my bedroom floor with my dolls and stuffed animals lined up in front of me. The game was school, and it could last for hours. The dolls and toys were the pupils, and I was their teacher. If there ever was an energetic teacher, I was she! I planned lessons and lectured to my students on science and geography. I taught them to form letters and numbers, and to add and subtract. I made all of their textbooks and work sheets by hand, and I completed every assignment for everyone in my class. Then I corrected all of the work and handed it back."

Such childhood games fostered an early love of reading in Reef, as she once explained to *SATA:* "I read to my class, too, because I loved to read stories and poems. Literature never meant more to me than when I was a child. Dr. Seuss's books were among my early favorites, and I read them so often that I committed them to memory. (I can still recite long sections of *The Cat in the Hat* and *Happy Birthday to You!*) I loved the poems of English fiction writer and playwright A. A. Milne and turned my favorites into songs. I delighted in the silly, unreal characters of American journalist and playwright L. Frank Baum's Oz stories. Books brought scenes and characters to life in my imagination. They expressed wonder, love, humor, and sorrow. They taught me that language is a powerful tool. Words are an artist's medium. Like clay, they can be molded into something beautiful."

From a love of reading, it was a short jump to experimenting with writing. "I also wrote poems and stories of my own," Reef told *SATA*. "Some high-school boys I knew printed a small newspaper. How proud I was when they published one of my stories—the all-but-forgotten 'I Am a Dishwasher'! I kept on reading and writing as I got older, but I developed other interests as well. As a teenager I loved to draw with pastels, pencils, and charcoal. I acted in two school plays. I listened to music for hours at a time. I learned to knit and sew."

However, Reef was about to learn the truth of the old adage "Jack of all trades, master of none." "By the time I reached college, I had so many interests that I couldn't decide what to do—and so I did nothing," Reef once told *SATA*. "I felt bored with college and left after my first classes ended. I took a job as a secretary and soon got married. Then, nearly a decade later, when I was twenty-eight years old and the mother of a young son, I decided that I wanted an education. I was finally ready to go to college. I still didn't know what to choose as a major, or main subject of study, but this time I didn't worry about it. I took classes in a variety of subjects, and I developed even more interests than I already had. I studied history, psychology, anthropology, and science. I also took courses in literature and writing, and I found that I liked writing best of all. Creating with the English language offered greater possibilities and deeper satisfaction than working with pastels or yarn or fabric. I realized, too, that my many interests stem from the fact that I love to learn—and so writing was right up my alley.

"I never became the classroom teacher that I pretended to be as a child, but I work as a teacher through my writing. For five years I wrote a newsletter about health for adults called *Taking Care*. My articles gave people information they needed to stay healthy. It was an interesting job that taught me a lot, but I wanted to do something more. When I tried writing a book for children, I liked it right away. Here was something that would enable me to keep on learning—about all kinds of subjects—for the rest of my life. By writing children's books, I could remain a teacher and share what I had learned with a very important group of readers."

Reef began her writing career with *Washington, D.C.*, a "brief history and description of the nation's capital with emphasis on the federal government and its buildings," as Margaret C. Howell described the book in *School Library Journal*. She followed this early portrait with other books dealing with monuments, memorials, and buildings. In *Mount Vernon* Reef tells the story of George Washington and his famous home. Reviewing several books in the "Places in American History" series, including *Mount Vernon, School Library Journal* critic Pamela K. Bomboy called the books "attractive and informative glimpses of the past." Reviewing Reef's *Arlington National Cemetery* and *Monticello*, Susan Nemeth McCarthy noted in *School Library Journal* that they would be useful "as supplements to encyclopedia information for reports." And another *School Library Journal* contributor, Joyce Adams Burner, felt that Reef's *The Lincoln Memorial* is a "clearly written and well-illustrated" introduction to this famous American landmark. In other books, such as *The Supreme Court* and *Ellis Island*, Reef blends history with architecture and even tour information to introduce young readers to some of the famous places in American history.

"To me, one of the best parts of writing nonfiction is doing the necessary research," Reef once explained to *SATA*. "I feel lucky to spend my time gathering information on the lives and work of famous people, learning about life in years gone by, talking with scientists and historians, and traveling to historic places. Writing lets me learn in other ways as well. As I organize and evaluate the facts that I have gathered, I gain insights into human nature and my own beliefs. I better understand the time in which I live by understanding times gone by. As I write, I continue to learn about using the language. I continue to become a more competent, more creative writer."

Reef has also written many biographies, dealing with writers, composers, scientists, military figures, and civic leaders. One of her earliest biographical efforts is *Albert Einstein: Scientist of the Twentieth Century,* "a smooth and balanced integration of Einstein's life and accomplishments," according to Tatiana Castleton in *School Library Journal.* Another twentieth-century intellectual revolutionary is presented in Reef's *Sigmund Freud: Pioneer of the Mind.* A reviewer for *Horn Book* felt that Reef "depicts a complex, brilliant, and human man," and also "presents his seminal ideas and the objections, refinements and alternatives to them ... [with] admirable clarity."

American writers and composers are presented in several further biographies. Reef's *John Steinbeck* chronicles the life and works of the Nobel Prize-winning writer of such classics as *The Grapes of Wrath* and *East of Eden.* "Reef captures the quintessential twentieth-century American writer," observed a reviewer for *Booklist.* A *Publishers Weekly* contributor called *John Steinbeck* a "thoughtful story" and as "nonjudgmental and upbeat as Steinbeck himself strove to be." Mary M. Burns, writing in *Horn Book,* found the biography to be "an accessible introduction to a significant literary figure" despite the "somewhat sporadic" documentation. Another blend of image and text is Reef's *Walt Whitman,* chronicling the life of that nineteenth-century bard and author of the ever-expanding *Leaves of Grass. Horn Book*'s Burns felt this title was "handsomely produced" and includes a "thoughtfully composed introduction to Whitman's work and life that neither sensationalizes nor diminishes the controversial aspects of his oeuvre." A writer for *Publishers Weekly* noted that even readers already familiar with Whitman "will find much to ponder in this forthright biography." Turning to musicians, Reef presents the life of a composer in *George Gershwin: American Composer.* Creator of the opera *Porgy and Bess* and the symphonic *Rhapsody in Blue,* among other well-known pieces, Gershwin comes alive in Reef's biography because "the writing gives a sense of [his] personality, his family, and his times," according to *Booklist*'s Carolyn Phelan.

Movers and shakers in ecology and the environment are dealt with in other biographies from Reef. *Rachel Carson: The Wonder of Nature* takes a look at the author of *Silent Spring,* a book that awoke the world to the dangers of the pesticide DDT and other environmental concerns. In *Henry David Thoreau: A Neighbor to Nature* Reef introduces the great nineteenth-century nonconformist and writer, author of the classic description of living the simple life, *Walden.* Reviewing both these titles in *School Library Journal,* Burner called

them "two nicely drawn and organized biographies that convey their subjects' personal philosophies, politics, and actions in a highly readable manner." In *Jacques Cousteau: Champion of the Sea,* Reef plumbs the depths of the man who explored the ocean's underworld using diving inventions he himself created. "The story this book begins will continue to be written by the generations to come," opined James H. Wandersee in *Science Books and Films,* for Cousteau "is one champion of the biosphere whom every child should learn to know."

"I have always been interested in the human side of history," Reef once commented to *SATA.* "I prefer to read about how people lived and thought in the past than to memorize dates or pore over accounts of battles. I try, in my books, to bring the human stories in history to life. When I write about a famous person, whether it's George Washington ... or French oceanographer Jacques Cousteau, I try to give a complete portrait of the person. I emphasize not just his or her outstanding accomplishments, but his or her activities outside of public life as well—how the person played as a child, what he or she was like as a parent, what kinds of hobbies the person enjoyed."

Additionally, Reef has penned a number of biographies of eminent African Americans. Looking at military men, she wrote *Benjamin Davis, Jr.* and *Colin Powell.* In the latter, Reef traces the future secretary of state's life from his South Bronx youth to his rise to chairman of the Joint Chiefs of Staff in a narrative "simply phrased and clearly organized," according to a critic for *Kirkus Reviews.* In *Ralph David Abernathy,* Reef takes a look at that civil rights leader with a book that "fills a void," according to Kay McPherson in *School Library Journal.* In *Paul Laurence Dunbar* Reef presents a portrait of a black poet whose life ended early because of tuberculosis. Janet Woodward, reviewing the biography in *School Library Journal,* felt it provided an "accessible introductory biography of this African American writer" who later influenced the works of Langston Hughes and Maya Angelou, among others.

Reef has also written more broadly about African Americans in several more volumes. In *Civil War Soldiers* and *Buffalo Soldiers* she details the military contributions of black soldiers during and after the Civil War, while in *Black Fighting Men* she gives an overview of African Americans in the military. Reviewing *Civil War Soldiers* and *Buffalo Soldiers* in *School Library Journal,* David A. Lindsey noted that these "concise works," written in "clear, interest-holding prose ... bring to life two little-known aspects of American history." *Booklist*'s Janice Del Negro called the same two titles "engagingly written." In *Black Fighting Men,* Reef chronicles the acts of fourteen black soldiers in the major conflicts America has fought, from the American Revolution to the Gulf War. "Reef's appreciation for her subjects comes through loud and clear," wrote a critic for *Kirkus Reviews.* Of more sociological interest is Reef's *Africans in America: The Spread of People and Culture,* a book "written with clarity and depth," according to *Booklist*'s Hazel Rochman, and an "excellent account of the 'African diaspora.'" Blending general history with individual accounts, Reef follows the history of Africans in America from the slave trade through emancipation and northern migration to the present.

Reef concluded to *SATA*, "I like to think about the many young people I've never met who will gain knowledge and pleasure from my books. But I also write for another person—the girl who climbed the crooked apple tree and read out loud to her dolls. I get to know her better as I think about what she would like to read; at the same time, I get a deeper understanding of the woman I am today."

Biographical and Critical Sources

PERIODICALS

Booklist, March 15, 1992, p. 1353; August, 1993, Janice Del Negro, reviews of *Buffalo Soldiers* and *Civil War Soldiers*, p. 2056; January 1, 1995, p. 817; May 1, 1995, p. 1559; May 1, 1996, pp. 1496-1497; April 1, 1997, review of *John Steinbeck*, p. 1305; December 1, 1998, p. 680; February 15, 1999, Hazel Rochman, review of *Africans in America*, p. 1058; February 15, 2000, Carolyn Phelan, review of *George Gershwin*, p. 1110.

Book Report, November-December, 1995, p. 48; September-October, 1996, p. 50.

Horn Book, September-October, 1995, Mary M. Burns, review of *Walt Whitman*, pp. 622-623; September-October, 1996, Mary M. Burns, review of *John Steinbeck*, p. 624; July-August, 2001, review of *Sigmund Freud*, p. 475.

Kirkus Reviews, July 1, 1992, review of *Colin Powell*, p. 854; June 1, 1993, p. 727; December 15, 1993, p. 1596; May 15, 1994, review of *Black Fighting Men*, p. 705.

Kliatt, January, 1995, p. 36.

New York Times Book Review, August 12, 2001, Patricia McCormick, "Children's Books: *Sigmund Freud*."

Publishers Weekly, May 8, 1995, review of *Walt Whitman*, p. 298; May 6, 1996, review of *John Steinbeck*, p. 82.

School Library Journal, April, 1990, Margaret C. Howell, review of *Washington, DC*, p. 137; December, 1991, Tatiana Castleton, review of *Albert Einstein*, p. 127; March, 1992, Susan Nemeth McCarthy, reviews of *Arlington National Cemetery* and *Monticello*, p. 250; April, 1992, p. 134; May, 1992, Joyce Adams Burner, reviews of *Henry David Thoreau* and *Rachel Carson*, p. 126; July, 1992, p. 87; August, 1992, Pamela K. Bomboy, review of *Mount Vernon*, pp. 171-172; November, 1992, pp. 122-123; August, 1993, David A. Lindsey, reviews of *Buffalo Soldiers* and *Civil War Soldiers*, p. 201; January, 1994, p. 128; March, 1994, p. 233; August, 1994, Joyce Adams Burner, review of *The Lincoln Memorial*, p. 166; November, 1994, p. 116; May, 1995, p. 115; October, 1995, Kay McPherson, review of *Ralph David Abernathy*, p. 150; March, 1996, pp. 229-230; June, 1999, p. 152; March, 2000, p. 261; September, 2000, Janet Woodward,

review of *Paul Laurence Dunbar*, p. 254; February, 2001, p. 84.

Science Books and Films, August-September, 1992, James H. Wandersee, review of *Jacques Cousteau*, p. 173; January-February, 1994, p. 20.

*   *   *

REYNOLDS, Peter H. 1961-

Personal

Born March 16, 1961, in Weston, Ontario, Canada; son of Keith H. (a treasurer) and Hazel E. (a bookkeeper; maiden name, Gasson) Reynolds; children: Sarah. *Education:* Attended Fitchburg State College, 1978-83, and Massachusetts College of Art, 1979-80.

Addresses

Home—462 Washington St., Dedham, MA 02026. *Agent*—Paul Reynolds, 47 Fairfield, Dedham, MA 02026. *E-mail*—petefable@aol.com; Pete@Fablevision.com.

Career

Tom Snyder Productions, Cambridge, MA, vice president and creative director, for thirteen years; cofounder (with brother, Paul Reynolds) and creative director of FabelVision Studios.

Awards, Honors

Earned awards, including Media and Methods Excellence in Education Award, Parenting Magazine Award, Parents' Choice Award, Educom Distinguished Software award, and Technology and Learning Award of Excellence, for his work as a creative director on several Tom Snyder Productions projects; 1999 Telly Award, second place, ASIFA-East, and 1999 BDA International Design Silver Award, all for *The Blue Shoe;* third place, ASIFA-East, and 1999 ASIFA-Hollywood Annie nominee, both for *Living Forever; The North Star*, was selected by the National Education Association for its Top 100 Books List, 2000; "Shaper of the Future 2000," *Converge Magazine; Judy Moody* was selected by *Publishers Weekly* for its Best Children's Books 2000 list.

Writings

(And illustrator) *Fizz and Martina in the Incredible Not-for-Profit Pet Resort Mystery*, Tom Snyder Productions (Watertown, MA), 1993.

(And illustrator) *The North Star*, FabelVision Press (Watertown, MA), 1997.

(With Sue Pandiani, and illustrator) *North Star Inspiration for the Classroom*, FableVision Press (Watertown, MA), 1999.

(And illustrator) *Sydney's Star*, Simon & Schuster (New York, NY), 2001.

Has created more than twenty interactive children's stories for the online service Prodigy, including *The Three Wolf Architects, The Adventures of Pewter Pan, Snow White and the Seven Accounts, Hilary and the Beast,* and *The Gingerbread Channel.*

ILLUSTRATOR

Megan McDonald, *Judy Moody,* Candlewick Press (Cambridge, MA), 1999.

Donald H. Graves, *The Portfolio Standard,* Heinemann (Portsmouth, NH), 2000.

Tobi Tobias, *Serendipity,* Simon & Schuster (New York, NY), 2000.

Megan McDonald, *Judy Moody Gets Famous!,* Candlewick Press (Cambridge, MA), 2001.

Megan McDonald, *Judy Moody Saves the World,* Candlewick Press (Cambridge, MA), 2002.

Also illustrator and creative director for "Misfit Mansion," a prototype, for FableVision Studios, 1996; "Fatherhood," a public service announcement, Fast Forward Productions, 1997; and two short films, *The Blue Shoe,* 1997-98, and *Living Forever,* 1998-99, both for FableVision Studios.

Peter H. Reynolds

Sidelights

Peter H. Reynolds began his career in advertising, but quickly moved on to become a pivotal player in Tom Snyder Productions, one of the early computer software companies to specialize in educational products. As creative director, author, and/or artist, Reynolds contributed to short films, public service announcements, interactive software programs, and online stories, all with a goal of encouraging creativity in young people while making learning fun. Reynolds wrote down his ideal of life as a journey of learning in the book *The North Star,* which eventually inspired a guidebook for teachers interested in bringing the North Star approach into their classrooms. Not long after, Reynolds began illustrating children's books written by others. His first, *Judy Moody,* written by Megan McDonald, was welcomed as the inaugural appearance of a likeable new heroine for first readers.

In *Judy Moody,* McDonald introduces a character who is "independent, feisty, and full of energy," according to Janie Schomberg, writing in *School Library Journal.* Judy is just starting the third grade, and her expectations for fun are low. They only get lower on the first day of school, when she is seated next to the boy most famous for eating paste. Judy typically makes a wise-crack about how bad things are and then inventively sets about making them better, as when her brother spills grape juice all over her "me" collage for school and Judy figures out how to save her project from ruin. McDonald's ability to capture both the way children think and the way they talk makes for an entertaining read, remarked Shelle Rosenfeld in *Booklist,* adding that children will "also like the witty, detailed drawings (especially the picture of Judy's unique collage)." Janice M. Del Negro, writing in the *Bulletin of the Center for Children's Books,* similarly commented: "Each chapter is amiably illustrated with ... full-page and spot art that extends the friendly feeling of the humorous text."

Reynolds also contributed the illustrations to Tobi Tobias's *Serendipity,* a picture book that defines the tongue-twisting word of the title with both humor and sentimentality, according to critics. For example, one definition explains that serendipity is when you meet a squirrel on the day you just happen to have a peanut in your pocket. For his part, "Reynolds provides sweetnatured and airy watercolor and ink cartoons," according to a reviewer in *Publishers Weekly.* And Sue Sherif, writing in *School Library Journal,* concluded that "teachers will undoubtedly use this picture book as a starting point for writing exercises."

Biographical and Critical Sources

PERIODICALS

Booklist, July, 2000, Shelle Rosenfeld, review of *Judy Moody,* pp. 2028, 2030; December 15, 2001, Todd Morning, review of *Sydney's Star,* p. 741.

Bulletin of the Center for Children's Books, May, 2000, Janice M. Del Negro, review of *Judy Moody,* pp. 324-325.

Family Fun, June-July, 2000, review of *Judy Moody.*

Horn Book, September, 2001, review of *Judy Moody Gets Famous!,* p. 589.

Kirkus Reviews, April 15, 2000, review of *Judy Moody,* p. 564.

Pittsburgh Post-Gazette, May 21, 2000, review of *Judy Moody.*

Publishers Weekly, April 17, 2000, review of *Judy Moody,* p. 81; August 28, 2000, review of *Serendipity,* p. 82; July 30, 2001, review of *Judy Moody Gets Famous!,* p. 85; November 12, 2001, review of *Sydney's Star,* p. 59.

School Library Journal, July, 2000, Janie Schomberg, review of *Judy Moody,* p. 83; Sue Sherif, November, 2000, review of *Serendipity,* p. 135; October, 2001, Sharon R. Pearce, review of *Judy Moody Gets Famous!,* p. 124; December, 2001, Maryann H. Owen, review of *Sydney's Star,* p. 110.

OTHER

Digital MASS, http://www.boston.com (April, 2000), Tim Allik, "Peter Reynolds, FableVision: He Hasn't Forgotten the 'Little' People."

FableVision, http://www.fablevision.com/ (February 2, 2002), profile of Peter Reynolds.*

* * *

ROOS, Stephen 1945-

Personal

Born February 9, 1945, in New York, NY; son of William Ernest (a writer) and Audrey (a writer; maiden name, Kelley) Roos. *Education:* Yale University, A.B. (history), 1967. *Politics:* Democrat.

Addresses

Home—R.R. 2, Box 706, Banks Hill Rd., Pawling, NY 12564. *Agent*—Writers House, 21 West 26th St., New York, NY 10010.

Career

Children's book author. Harper & Row Publishers (now HarperCollins), New York, NY, copywriter in marketing department for children's books, 1968-76, junior editor of adult trade fiction, 1976-80; writer, 1980—. Institute for Children's Literature, Redding Ridge, CT, instructor, 1983-89.

Awards, Honors

Charlie May Simon Award, 1986, for *My Horrible Secret.*

Writings

My Horrible Secret, Delacorte (New York, NY), 1983.
My Terrible Truth, Delacorte (New York, NY), 1983.
My Secret Admirer, Delacorte (New York, NY), 1984.

(With parents, who write under the joint pseudonym Kelley Roos) *The Incredible Cat Caper,* Delacorte (New York, NY), 1985.

Confessions of a Wayward Preppie, Delacorte (New York, NY), 1986.

The Fair-Weather Friends, illustrated by Dee deRosa, Atheneum (New York, NY), 1987.

Thirteenth Summer, Atheneum (New York, NY), 1987.

My Favorite Ghost, Atheneum (New York, NY), 1988.

You'll Miss Me When I'm Gone, Delacorte (New York, NY), 1988.

And the Winner Is . . . , Atheneum (New York, NY), 1989.

Twelve-Year-Old Vows Revenge! after Being Dumped by Extraterrestrial on First Date, Delacorte (New York, NY), 1990.

A Young Person's Guide to the Twelve Steps (nonfiction), Hazelden (Center City, MN), 1992.

Never Trust a Sister over Twelve, Delacorte (New York, NY), 1993.

Who's Been Sleeping in My Grave? ("Ghosts of Fear Street" series), Pocket Books (New York, NY), 1995.

The Ooze ("Ghosts of Fear Street" series), Pocket Books (New York, NY), 1996.

The Gypsies Never Came, Simon & Schuster (New York, NY), 2001.

Recycling George, Simon & Schuster (New York, NY), 2002.

"MAPLE STREET KIDS" SERIES

Silver Secrets, Hazelden (Center City, MN), 1991.
Leave It to Augie, Hazelden (Center City, MN), 1991.
My Blue Tongue, Hazelden (Center City, MN), 1991.
Dear Santa: Make Me a Star, Hazelden (Center City, MN), 1991.

"PET LOVERS CLUB" SERIES

Love Me, Love My Werewolf, Delacorte (New York, NY), 1991.

The Cottontail Caper, Delacorte (New York, NY), 1992.

Crocodile Christmas, Delacorte (New York, NY), 1992.

Sidelights

Although Stephen Roos never intended to be a writer, and certainly never intended to be an author of children's books, that is just what happened. Roos's first published book, *My Horrible Secret,* won him the Charlie May Simon Medallion, and his novel about a teenage alcoholic, *You'll Miss Me When I'm Gone,* quickly started him on a fiction series about children growing up in alcoholic or other dysfunctional homes. Roos is particularly noted for his handling of young people's problems, from school bullies to teen suicide. In a *Horn Book* review of *My Terrible Truth,* Kate M. Flanagan observed that the humor in Roos's writing "stems from the wry characterizations of a group of typical middle-school students with their not-so-earth-shattering concerns and dilemmas."

Born in 1945, in New York City, Roos spent his early years in the city's Upper East Side, where he met his writer parents' many friends, most of them theatrical and literary types. In New Canaan, where the family moved

Stephen Roos

in 1950, Roos discovered the quiet, affluent small-town life that was to figure in many of his books. Even in such staid New England surroundings, Roos's parents remained free-spirited and nontraditional. They collaborated on writing mystery novels under the joint pseudonym Kelley Roos, while his father also wrote for musical theater. Around age ten, he started reading his parents' books, which he loved. He also was stagestruck from an early age.

Around the time Roos was in fifth or sixth grade, his family began traveling around Europe, leaving behind the stable environment Stephen had come to love. He expressed his unhappiness by writing a story about a family that moved around too much and gave it to his parents. They loved the story and encouraged his obvious writing talent. They also ultimately got their son's point, and Roos returned to Connecticut and enrolled at a prep school. His parents, meanwhile, remained in Europe until after Roos had graduated from college.

Roos's experiences at prep school became the basis for his first book for older kids, *Confessions of a Wayward Preppie,* which Mary M. Burns called "wryly touching, sometimes humorous" in her *Horn Book* review. In the

story, a freshman student trying to fit in at his new school finds himself in a compromising situation when he is asked to help an upperclassman pass French by doing the older student's homework. The story is about the crime of cheating, but as Burns noted, while the novel is "readable and fast-moving," it is also "a fascinating consideration of responsibility—to oneself, one's friends, and to the larger community." Also noting the way social class plays in the story, *School Library Journal* contributor Phyllis Graves added that *Confessions of a Wayward Preppie* is "an accurate, if somewhat simplistic portrayal of the pressurized world in which today's privileged teen is expected to succeed."

Enrolling at Yale University after prep school, Roos earned a degree in history. He also penned the book and lyrics to two college musicals, although a career in writing seemed out of the question at the time. After graduation he attended the Radcliffe Publishing Procedures course and spent some time in Europe. Returning to the United States, he started writing ad copy for the marketing department of Harper & Row (now Harper-Collins) publishers in New York City. "That was really my introduction to children's books," he once explained to *SATA*. At Harper's Roos read all the books from their children's list, which included works from authors like E. B. White and Maurice Sendak. Roos enjoyed reading children's books so much that he decided to try his hand at writing one. His first effort was in the form of trying to "write a good version of a bad book," a plan that had "terribly embarrassing, horrible, horrible" results.

Meanwhile, Roos moved from marketing to the editorial department of the adult trade division. After four years he reviewed his career and decided to take a chance and just write. He quit his job and decided to try writing until the money ran out. "I gave myself a year," he recalled, "to get one nice word, from anybody, about my writing, and then I would continue." Roos first attempted to tackle an adult novel, but never finished it. He also started a book for teens but dropped it because it was too flat. Then he came up with the idea for a story about a boy who cannot throw a baseball. Despite doubts about the worthiness of his subject, Roos started putting it together, and in less than four months he had a completed manuscript. About five days before Roos' self-imposed, one-year deadline, Delacorte accepted *My Horrible Secret* for publication.

My Horrible Secret proved to be a successful debut and won its first-time author the Charlie May Simon Award. In the story fifth grader Warren Fingler not only must deal with his fear of playing ball, but also with the never ending comparisons to his popular and athletic older brother, Roger. In trying to find an alternative to baseball, Warren further embarrasses himself by falling off a horse. He redeems himself, however, by arranging a charity all-star baseball game and overcoming his fear to make a game-saving catch. While noting that some of Roos's characters tell jokes "too sophisticated to be made by most fifth graders," *School Library Journal* contributor Caroline S. Parr praised *My Horrible Secret* for its "breezy," first-person style. A *Publishers Weekly* reviewer called Roos "a fluent, humorous writer, tuned in to the concerns of kids like his hero-narrator."

Roos followed up the success of his first book with a pair of sequels, *The Terrible Truth* and *My Secret Admirer,* both of which take place in the same small town as *My Horrible Secret.* In *The Terrible Truth* the focus is on Shirley Garfield, Roger Fingler's sixth-grade classmate, who is tormented by the bossy Claire Van Kemp and preoccupied over her social life. Trying to create some order and goals in her life, Shirley is derailed in her efforts by Claire's constant interference, so she decides to start an anti-Claire club. *The Terrible Truth* is a comic look at affluent, small-town life, and Roos veers into satire with certain characters, such as the sixth-grade girl who has a nervous breakdown when the stripes on her sheets are not straight. His follow-up effort, *My Secret Admirer,* finds the ambitious Claire suddenly sidelined in her efforts to win the Junior Chamber of Commerce Award when she receives a valentine from ... who? "Roos' deadpan humor skillfully offsets Claire's intensity as she tries to uncover the identity of her admirer," commented *Horn Book* contrib-

In this work by Roos from the "Ghosts of Fear Street" series, Al creates a stink bomb but it fails to explode; instead it oozes, permanently changing everything it touches. (Cover illustration by Mark Garro.)

utor Charlotte W. Draper in a review of *My Secret Admirer.*

With two published books under his belt, Roos felt like a professional writer. He started writing a book and a half each year, most of them humorous in tone. In 1988 Roos's fans were in for a change when he published *You'll Miss Me When I'm Gone.* Sixteen-year-old Marcus, the protagonist of the novel, seems to have it all: he gets along at school with an enjoyable position on the school newspaper, and he has a girlfriend and a car. After wrecking his car, however, and facing the loss of his friends, Marcus must come to terms with his drinking. With the aid of an understanding school psychologist, Marcus accepts that he is an alcoholic and begins to move forward with his life. In *Voice of Youth Advocates,* Becki George commended the author for creating "a very believable character and plot.... Readers will recognize the excuses and rationalizing Marcus uses to justify why and when he drinks." *Horn Book* contributor Elizabeth S. Watson similarly observed that Marcus's problems "are real ones for today's adolescent and believable as part of the plot." Roos would deal with similar issues in his "Maple Street Kids" series, "positive and hopeful" books geared for younger readers who, as Pamela K. Bomboy noted in *School Library Journal,* "may be overwhelmed by adult problems."

The four-book "Maple Street Kids" series is drawn from some of the family situations Roos encountered through his friends and acquaintances while growing up. Tara's parents in *Dear Santa: Make Me a Star* are recovering alcoholics, and Tara, in response, becomes the "perfect daughter." Rooney in *My Blue Tongue* is always playing outrageous pranks and telling huge lies to distract herself and everyone else from her father's gambling addiction. Families in the other books include a mother addicted to prescription drugs and a boy whose much-loved uncle is an alcoholic. *School Library Journal* contributor Kenneth E. Kowen called *My Blue Tongue* "a commendable undertaking," but felt that Roos "takes the easy way out" since problems are resolved "with speed and ease." However, Bomboy commented in *School Library Journal* that the books are "written with a great deal of warmth and care."

The experience of growing up in a small New England town continued to serve as Roos's focus through several book series. *The Fair-Weather Friends* introduces a collection of four novels that take place in Plymouth Island. Twelve-year-old Kit is excited to return to the island for the summer and visit her good friend Phoebe. However, Phoebe has changed over the year—now all she can think about are boys and fashion—and several months will pass before the girls reconcile their differences in interests. Calling *The Fair Weather Friends* "a perfect vacation book," *Horn Book* contributor Elizabeth S. Watson went on to note that Roos "tells a funny, poignant story of growing up that will ring very true" to preteens not yet fully engaged in adolescence.

Flamboyant Lydie Rose convinces deformed and fatherless Augie to wish for a visit from the Gypsies, who will celebrate his specialness. (Cover photo by Peter Liepke.)

Thirteenth Summer also takes place on Plymouth Island, where thirteen-year-old, year-round islander "Pink" Cunningham becomes torn between following his dad's wishes of his going into the family boatyard business and leaving the island like his friend Mackie, a wealthy mainlander who visits Plymouth Island during the summer. Praising Roos for his well-rounded characters, Denise A. Anton noted in her *School Library Journal* review that *Thirteenth Summer* presents "a thoughtful and sensitive study of a young boy faced with the choices that come with maturity." The island's historic side is revealed in *My Favorite Ghost,* as the ghost of long-dead Evangeline Coffin is just the ticket newly unemployed teen Derek Malloy needs to regain his job at the local theater. An attempt to cash in on Evangeline's ghostly visits by creating some special effects of his own become Derek's undoing in a novel boasting what *Horn Book* reviewer Nancy Vasilakis dubbed "a rollicking plot, passable characterizations, and a brisk, offhand style." "The lesson in this humorous account of the consequences of deception won't be lost on young readers," added Connie Tyrell Burns in a *School Library Journal* review. Winding up the series, Phoebe returns in

And the Winner Is ..., as a change in family circumstances inspires the preteen to stage a talent show to help her parents keep their Plymouth Island summer house. *School Library Journal* contributor Nancy P. Reeder predicted that the final installment of the series would not disappoint Roos's fans, and she praised in particular the "well developed" main characters and the "realistic" dialogue.

While Roos has continued to specialize in writing books about preteen protagonists, he has also veered into the world of younger children with his three-volume "Pet Lovers' Club" series. Including the novels *Love Me, Love My Werewolf, The Cottontail Caper,* and *Crocodile Christmas,* the series revolves around a group of third-grade animal lovers whose relationships with favorite dogs, cats, rabbits, and assorted reptiles affect the traumas encountered in making it through elementary school in one piece. Comparing the series to Patricia Reilly Giff's popular "Polk Street School" books, *School Library Journal* contributor Andrew W. Hunter praised Roos for his "quickly paced" plots and noted that he "integrates information about ... the value of animals without being too heavy handed."

Throughout his long and prolific career Roos has found that the opportunity to be creative remains the most important aspect of his life as a professional writer.

Biographical and Critical Sources

PERIODICALS

Bulletin of the Center for Children's Books, March, 1983, p. 132.
Booklist, March 1, 2001, Michael Cart, review of *The Gypsies Never Came,* p. 1281.
Horn Book, February, 1984, Kate M. Flanagan, review of *My Terrible Truth,* p. 55; March-April, 1985, Charlotte W. Draper, review of *My Secret Admirer,* p. 182; September-October, 1986, Mary M. Burns, review of *Confessions of a Wayward Preppie,* p. 593; July-August, 1987, Elizabeth S. Watson, review of *The Fair-Weather Friends,* p. 465; March-April, 1988, Elizabeth S. Watson, review of *You'll Miss Me When I'm Gone,* p. 211; May-June, 1988, Nancy Vasilakis, review of *My Favorite Ghost,* p. 355; May, 2001, review of *The Gypsies Never Came,* p. 336.
Publishers Weekly, May 6, 1983, review of *My Horrible Secret,* p. 98; May 8, 1987, review of *The Fair-Weather Friends,* p. 70; July 24, 1987, review of *Thirteenth Summer,* p. 187; September 20, 1991; October 18, 1993, p. 73; February 12, 2001, review of *The Gypsies Never Came,* p. 213.
School Library Journal, May, 1983, Caroline S. Parr, review of *My Horrible Secret,* p. 76; January, 1984, Elaine E. Knight, review of *The Terrible Truth,* pp. 80-81; March, 1985, David Gale, review of *My Secret Admirer,* p. 171; December, 1985, Elizabeth Mellett, review of *The Incredible Cat Caper,* p. 93; May, 1986, Phyllis Graves, review of *Confessions of a Wayward Preppie,* p. 109; November, 1987, Denise A. Anton, review of *Thirteenth Summer,* p. 128; April, 1988, Connie Tyrell Burns, review of *My Favorite*

Ghost, p. 104; March, 1989, Nancy P. Reeder, review of *And the Winner Is . . . ,* pp. 178, 183; July, 1990, Nancy P. Reeder, review of *Twelve-Year-Old Vows Revenge!,* p. 78; August, 1991, Andrew W. Hunter, review of *Love Me, Love My Werewolf,* p. 168; June, 1992, Pamela K. Bomboy, review of the "Maple Street Kids" series, and Kenneth E. Kowen, review of *My Blue Tongue,* pp. 124-125; July, 1992, Florence M. Brems, review of *The Cottontail Caper,* p. 64; September, 1993, Cindy Darling Codell, review of *Never Trust a Sister over Twelve,* pp. 234-235; February, 2001, Coop Renner, review of *The Gypsies Never Came,* p. 122.

Voice of Youth Advocates, April, 1988, Becki George, review of *You'll Miss Me When I'm Gone,* p. 29.*

S

SCILLIAN, Devin

Personal

Son of Bill (a career Army officer) and Betti Scillian; married; wife's name, Corey; children: Griffin, Quinn, Madison, Christian. *Education:* University of Kansas, B.A. (journalism), 1985. *Hobbies and other interests:* Playing the guitar and piano, basketball, tennis, golf, drawing and painting, and coaching his children's soccer teams.

Addresses

Home—Grosse Pointe, MI. *Office*—WDIV-TV, 550 West Lafayette Blvd., Detroit, MI 48226-3140. *E-mail*—devins@clickondetroit.com.

Career

Television journalist, singer-songwriter, and children's book author.

Awards, Honors

Peabody Award, for news coverage of the Murrah Federal Building bombing in Oklahoma City, OK, provided by KFOR-TV; Emmy Awards for Best Anchor, Best Writing, and Best Documentary; Best Country Performer, Detroit Music Awards, 2001.

Writings

Tulsa (sound recording), High Heel Records, 1999.
Fibblestax, illustrated by Kathryn Darnell, Sleeping Bear Press (Chelsea, MI), 2000.
A Is for America: An American Alphabet (picture book and musical compact disc), illustrated by Pamela Carroll, Sleeping Bear Press (Chelsea, MI), 2001.
S Is for Sunflower: A Kansas Alphabet, Sleeping Bear Press (Chelsea, MI), 2002.
P Is for Panhandle: An Oklahoma Alphabet, Sleeping Bear Press (Chelsea, MI), 2002.

One Nation: An American Counting Book, Sleeping Bear Press (Chelsea, MI), 2002.

Also singer-songwriter for the album *Argentina,* 1994.

Biographical and Critical Sources

PERIODICALS

Publishers Weekly, June 11, 2001, review of *A Is for America,* p. 85.

OTHER

DetroitCountryMusic.com, http://www.detroitcountrymusic.com/ (March 8, 2002).

Devin Scillian

Scillian's alphabet book celebrates, in verse, various aspects of America and her people. (*From* A Is for America, *illustrated by Pamela Carroll.*)

Radio-Television News Directors Association and Foundation, http://www.rtnda.org/september11th/special.shtml (March 8, 2002), Jill Geisler, "Covering Terror and Tragedy."

Sleeping Bear Press, http://www.sleepingbearpress.com/ (March 8, 2002).

WDIV-TV, http://www.clickondetroit.com/ (March 8, 2002).

*   *   *

SIMPSON, Margaret 1943-

Personal

Born February 15, 1943, in Liverpool, England; daughter of Kenneth (a sea captain) and Mary (a nurse) Simpson; married Jeremy Holmes, 1965 (divorced, 1975); children: Jacob, Matthew, Lydia. *Education:* Attended Merchant Taylors' Girls' School, and Newnham College, Cambridge University. *Politics:* "Left of centre." *Religion:* "SYM" (Siddha Yoga Meditation).

Addresses

Agent—MBA Literary Agents, 62 Grafton Way, London W1P 5LD, England.

Career

Writer, meditation teacher.

Awards, Honors

Earthworm Award, Friends of the Earth, and Fiction Prize shortlist, *Guardian,* both 1993, both for *Strange Orbit.*

Writings

Strange Orbit, SUNY Press (Albany, NY), 1992.

A Perfect Life: The Story of Swami Muktananda Paramahamsa, SYDA Foundation (South Fallsburg, NY), 1996.

Top 10 Arthurian Legends, Scholastic (New York, NY), 1998.

Top 10 Irish Legends, Scholastic (New York, NY), 2000.

Cleopatra and Her Asp, Scholastic (New York, NY), 2000.

Mary Queen of Scots and Her Hopeless Husbands, Scholastic (New York, NY), 2001.

Elizabeth I and Her Conquests, Scholastic (New York, NY), 2001.

Also author of *Sorry Wrong Number* (novel); contributing writer to several television series, including *Grange Hill.*

Work in Progress

Currently a regular writer on the television series, *Emmerdale;* writing a timeslip novel; research on Romania and stories of Krishna.

Sidelights

Margaret Simpson told *SATA:* "I remember as a child, the joy of learning to read, and shortly thereafter the fun of inventing stories, the first of which impressed my kindergarten teacher. When I left school, aged nineteen, with a place at Cambridge to read English Literature, my headmistress embarrassed me by telling the whole assembly that at aged seven I had said that when I grew up I wanted to be another Enid Blyton.

"My writing took back seat to acting while I was at university, and I did not return to it until I was a young mother, at home with small children. I wrote my first novel (*Sorry Wrong Number,* for adults) over a period of two years, in snatched hours when the children were sleeping. There followed a second novel, and then on the strength of the dialogue in those books, I was invited to try my hand at writing for television. For many years I did little else, contributing to many series, including *Grange Hill,* which is a famous, award-winning children's programme on British television.

"Over the years my spiritual life became increasingly important to me. I had begun to meditate in 1975, or thereabouts, and in 1984 I read an article on Siddha Yoga Meditation. This appealed to me so much that I found my way to a public programme, and I have been attending Siddha Yoga Ashrams and centres ever since. In 1992 I published a space fantasy for young people entitled *Strange Orbit,* born of a longing to bring the ideas and experiences of my spiritual life into a book for young people. It is about a group of teenagers who go on a trip to the moon, but stray through a black hole and encounter not only the laws of physics and the terrible effects of global warming some centuries hence, but also, on one of the moons of Saturn, a yogi deep in meditation, who helps them back through eternity into the present. It has a very matter-of-fact and savvy fourteen-year-old girl as its narrator, which gives it a comic edge. *Strange Orbit* was awarded the 1993 Earthworm prize by Friends of the Earth and was short-listed for the *Guardian* newspaper Fiction Prize in the same year.

"My retelling of the *Mahabharata* was born of the same longing to make the teachings and stories which have meant so much to me available to Western youngsters in an accessible, entertaining form. The story of the dynastic feud between two sets of cousins, the Kauravas and the Pandavas, has been told in India for millennia, yet it is utterly relevant today. Just as Shakespeare's *Macbeth* leaves us—or me, anyway—with the feeling that there is nothing more to say on the subject of tyranny as it corrodes the tyrant, so the *Mahabharata* offers a comprehensive account of the way in which war follows inexorably from ambition, cruelty, and injustice. It could be a tale of Kosovo or the Middle East today except that it is lit by the spiritual truths, the higher perspective of Indian philosophy. And it is full of magic, faith, humanity, humour and love. It was a privilege to work with such material."

A British writer of both fiction and nonfiction, Simpson is best known for her young adult science-fiction fantasy, *Strange Orbit.* In this novel, teenager Jessica is invited to join the crew of the first space expedition to be manned by children. Simpson lingers over the rigorous

training the children undergo as they prepare for their perilous adventure, and a contributor to *Kirkus Reviews* called this "the most satisfying section of the novel, partly because Simpson has stuffed it full of facts and realistic scenarios drawn from NASA's astronaut training program." The journey itself quickly goes awry as the rocket ship is drawn off course by the force field of a black hole, which catapults them forward in time some three hundred years. From that perspective they get a firsthand glimpse of the consequences of the environmental devastation wrought in their own century. The children end up on Titan, one of Saturn's moons, where they encounter Yogi Shantih Baba, who explains what they have seen and helps them find the Earth's moon, their original destination. While the reviewer for *Kirkus Reviews* was disappointed by the ending, a contributor to *Books for Keeps* commended *Strange Orbit* for its intriguing combination of science, humor, spiritualism, and environmentalism, and recommended the book for reluctant readers, "although its appeal is by no means limited to them," this reviewer concluded.

Biographical and Critical Sources

PERIODICALS

Books for Keeps, September, 1992, review of *Strange Orbit,* p. 13.
Kirkus Reviews, June 15, 1995, review of *Strange Orbit,* p. 863.*

*   *   *

SMITH, Shirley Raines
See RAINES, Shirley C.

*   *   *

STEVENS, Chambers 1968-

Personal

Born June 10, 1968; son of Austin (a car salesman) and Norma (Stevens) Chambers; married Betsy Sullenger (a film producer), December 16, 1989. *Education:* The Conservatory of Theatre Arts at Webster University (Webster Groves, MO), B.F.A. (regional theater performance). *Politics:* "Blue Dog Democrat (which means I would rather vote for a blue dog than a Republican)."

Addresses

Office—7425 Hollywood Blvd., Los Angeles, CA 90046. *E-mail*—chambersontheroad@hotmail.com.

Career

Writer, actor, theater director, standup comedian, playwright, storyteller, and children's acting coach. *Member:* Screen Actors Guild, American Federation of Television and Radio Artists, Society of Children's Book Writers and Illustrators, Dramatist's Guild, Authors League of

Chambers Stevens

America, Independent Film Project, People for the American Way, American Civil Liberties Union.

Awards, Honors

Ingram Fellowship for Outstanding Playwright, State of Tennessee, 1989; Backstage West Garland Award, 1994, for *Desperate for Magic;* Emmy nomination, National Academy of Television Arts and Sciences, 1997, for Outstanding Achievement—Individual Excellence Performer.

Writings

Magnificent Monologues for Kids, Sandcastle Publishing (South Pasadena, CA), 1999.

24-Carat Commercials for Kids, illustrated by Jeremy Cohen, Sandcastle Publishing (South Pasadena, CA), 1999.

Sensational Scenes for Teens, Sandcastle Publishing (South Pasadena, CA), 2001.

Magnificent Monologues for Teens, Sandcastle Publishing (South Pasadena, CA), 2001.

Sensational Scenes for Kids, Sandcastle Publishing (South Pasadena, CA), 2002.

24-Carat Commercials for Teens, illustrated by Jeremy Cohen, Sandcastle Publishing (South Pasadena, CA), 2002.

PLAYS

Biff and Charlie (first produced in St. Louis, MO, 1985), The Green Fuse, c. 1985.

The Kount of Monty Krisco (one act), first produced in St. Louis, MO, 1986, full-length version produced in Nashville, TN, 1987.

Drink?, Family and Children's Service (Nashville, TN), 1988.

Desperate for Magic, first produced in Los Angeles, CA, 1994.

Plum Pink Pedicure, first produced in Los Angeles, CA, 1995.

Bing Bang Boom, produced in Los Angeles, CA, 1996.

Work in Progress

A play, *Travels with Jack Lemmon's Dog,* "based on a real-life experience of driving Jack Lemmon's black standard poodle, Chloe, to Canada"; a one-man show, *Super Kid,* based on eleven years spent as a children's acting coach in Hollywood; a picture/chapter book series called *The Escapades of Eugenie,* about a young girl who finds a genie in her milk carton while eating in the school cafeteria; and two picture books, one on the annual presidential pardoning of the Thanksgiving turkey called *Pardon Me!,* and the other based on the song "Santa's Got the Flu," written by Trent Walker and Joe Patrick for Stevens' play *Plum Pink Pedicure.*

Sidelights

Chambers Stevens is a comedic actor whose experience as a children's acting coach has led him to write a series of books for would-be child actors. In works such as *Magnificent Monologues for Kids* and *Sensational Scenes for Teens,* Stevens provides short, original scenes that actors can memorize and use in audition situations. In *Magnificent Monologues for Kids,* for example, Stevens offers fifty-one short pieces, each a monologue ranging from half a page to a page and a half, dealing with issues of concern to children. The monologues are divided into those appropriate for girls and those appropriate for boys, though Darcy Schild, writing in *School Library Journal,* contended that many of the monologues would be appropriate for either gender. And while both Schild and *Booklist* reviewer Susan Dove Lempke noted that Stevens's reference to popular culture icons such as brand names and cartoon characters will make the book seem dated in a short time, Lempke praised Stevens for providing a myriad of choices in his material, all of which "represent a good range of emotion and contain natural-sounding language."

Sensational Scenes for Teens is a similar offering, providing more than thirty short scenes for young actors working in pairs, either boy-boy, boy-girl, or girl-girl. As in his earlier books for younger actors, Stevens's scenes draw upon issues commonly of concern to the age of his intended audience and use language that sounds natural to young adults. Though reviewers agreed that older high school students may find the scenes simplistic or juvenile, the general use of the book to a wide array of students and teachers with an interest in acting and performance was asserted. *Sensational Scenes for Teens* concludes with a bibliography of plays that teenagers interested in the theater should become familiar with, interviews with a casting agent and a television writer, acting exercises, and a glossary of stage terms.

"I am a college graduate," Chambers Stevens told *SATA.* "And in my sixteen years of education I have failed only three classes. Ninth grade: drama class. Eleventh grade: creative writing. And in my junior year of college I failed a film class. Since I graduated from college I have made my living solely from acting, writing, and directing. Passion can not be put in a box.

"In college I met this playwright, if you could call him that. He was seven years older than I and knew more about the German playwright Brecht than anyone on the planet. I petitioned the dean of the university to let him teach a class. He did and he was horrible. On the last day of class the teacher/playwright gave me a play of his to read. It was supposed to be a children's play but the characters kept discussing Karl Marx. I hated it. To the best of my knowledge it was never performed. But this playwright, Tony Kushner, went on to write *Angels in America* and won back-to-back Pulitzer Prizes. The night I saw *Angels* performed I cried for an hour. Passion can not be put in a box.

"I started to write because of a girl. She was a writer. I was an actor and we dated for couple of months. And then she dumped me. Wrote me a 'Dear John' letter. (It was the only writing of hers I liked.) Made me so mad I decided to write my first play. I bet you can guess what about. If you guessed it was about a guy who gets dumped, you're right. The play, *Biff and Charlie*, was very well received. And before I knew it strangers started calling me a writer. Being from the South I refrained from correcting them. Eight plays and ten books later I'm still writing.

"I don't write every day. I *think* about writing every day. I walk down the street talking to myself. Throwing ideas out into the universe. Bouncing things off God. Most of the time She doesn't respond. But every once in a while I feel a force dragging me back home. Where my Mac and I duke it out. Writing is hard. Writing is lonely.

"That's why after I finished my second book, I begged my publisher, Renee Whatley, to send me on a book tour. In the summer of 1999 I signed books in thirty-six cities from Nashville to Boston. Since my books are about performing I led workshops in the stores (Borders and Barnes & Noble). In Greenville, North Carolina, three hundred kids showed up. In Columbus, Ohio, a twelve-year-old boy showed up and recited my entire first chapter, word for word! In Connecticut, the store didn't order enough books and two parents got in a fist fight. On my first day in Maryland I opened the local paper to find a bad review of my newest book. Not just a bad review. It was really, really bad. That night I signed books at the local Borders. Four hundred people came! They had read the review and didn't believe any book could be that bad. The next day I called the reviewer and thanked him for the horrible notice. He was shocked at first. But then ended up apologizing and confessed to me that he was mad because his son had read the book before he did and loved it.

"If you've always wanted to be a children's writer then write. But first take a kid to lunch. Kids need food as well as literature. And then go home and write. Don't put your passion in a box."

"What to write about is always a challenge," Stevens told *SATA*. "So many ideas rolling around in my little brain. I've learned to trust that the best ones will, like a gum ball machine, fall out when their time is right. Currently, a number of ideas are pushing their way forward. One is a love story about string-theory physics, another is on the non-violence movement. And behind them is just a title that every once in a while raises its ugly head, *Bucknekid Buckdancing*."

Biographical and Critical Sources

PERIODICALS

Back Stage West, February 10, 1994, Liz Braunstein, review of *Desperate for Magic,* p. 9; December 21, 1995, Rob Kendt, review of *Plum Pink Pedicure,* p. 7; September 7, 2000, Brad Schreiber, review of *Chesapeake,* p. 19.

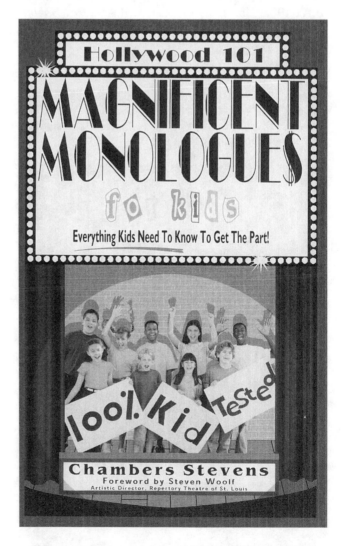

Stevens, an acting coach for young people, has collected short monologues designed to help young readers master the craft of performing. (Cover photo by Karl Preston.)

Booklist, April 1, 1999, Susan Dove Lempke, review of *Magnificent Monologues for Kids,* p. 1410; May 15, 2001, Karen Simoneti, review of *Sensational Scenes for Teens,* p. 1742.

School Library Journal, August, 1999, Darcy Schild, review of *Magnificent Monologues for Kids,* p. 150; April, 2001, Toni D. Moore, review of *Sensational Scenes for Teens,* p. 168.

*   *   *

STEWART, Jennifer J(enkins) 1960-

Personal

Born September 21, 1960, in East Patchogue, NY; daughter of Edgar William (a professor of physics) and Beverly Fern (a stockbroker; maiden name, Waggoner) Jenkins; married Bruce Edwin Stewart (a physician), May 28, 1983; children: Miranda Elizabeth, Robin Marjorie, Amy Caroline. *Education:* Wellesley College, B.A., 1982; University of Utah, M.B.A., 1985. *Hobbies and other interests:* Hiking, snorkeling, reading.

Addresses

Home—11825 East Elin Ranch Rd., Tucson, AZ 85749-8798. *Office*—Make Way for Books, 4713 East Camp Lowell Dr., Tucson, AZ 85712. *E-mail*—jenniferj-stewart@mindspring.com.

Jennifer J. Stewart

Career

American Express TRS, Inc., Salt Lake City, UT, manager of inventory services, 1985-88; writer in Tucson, AZ, 1988—. Make Way for Books, associate director, 1998—. Harry and Marjorie Stewart Foundation, secretary, 1990—. Pima County Medical Society Alliance, treasurer, 1989-90; Helping Hands, medical volunteer in Nepal, 1999. *Member:* Authors Guild, Society of Children's Book Writers and Illustrators, Society of Southwestern Authors (vice president, 1999-2001).

Awards, Honors

First place award, children's novel category, Deep South Writer's Contest, 1997; second place award, juvenile fiction category, Southwest Writer's Workshop, 1997; Sequoyah Book Award master list, Oklahoma Library Association, 1999-2000, for *If That Breathes Fire, We're Toast!;* awards from short story and poetry contests.

Writings

If That Breathes Fire, We're Toast!, Holiday House (New York, NY), 1999.

Contributor of stories, poems, and columns for both adults and children to periodicals.

Work in Progress

A middle grade novel, *The Bean King's Daughter,* for Holiday House; middle-grade fiction, stories, poems, and essays.

Sidelights

Jennifer J. Stewart told *SATA:* "I've wanted to be a writer since second grade, when I figured out that librarians didn't write the books and that maybe I could. Up until then, I'd thought of libraries as extensive supermarkets, where you could find any kind of exotic ingredient on the shelves. That's still true, luckily. I love libraries!

"As a child, I read everything I could get my hands on. At school, if I cracked the lid of my desk slightly, I could hide a book inside and read it when I was supposed to be doing something else. I missed a fair number of tests that way.

"I believe very much in adventures. My motto: have lots of them! For instance, I worked as a medical volunteer in Nepal for three months in the spring of 1999, alongside my surgeon husband. We took our three girls, then ages ten, eight, and five, halfway around the world. We worked in primitive rural hospitals a day's hike from the nearest road or airstrip, using Nepali school children as translators. Someday our experiences—both funny and hair-raising—will find their way into a book of mine."

STICKLER, Soma Han 1942-
(Lu Han, Soma Han)

Personal

Born January 13, 1942, in Choongnam-do, Korea; daughter of Tok-Kyo (a tao master) and Tok-Myong (a storyteller; maiden name, Song) Han; married John Stickler (a journalist), 1964; children: Stephen, Alexander. *Education:* California College of Arts and Crafts, B.F.A., 1978. *Hobbies and other interests:* Feng shui, residential design.

Soma Han Stickler

Addresses

Home—P.O. Box 1543, Wildomar, CA 92595. *E-mail*—jstick@ix.netcom.com.

Career

Fine artist and children's book illustrator, 1978—. Art work exhibited at galleries in New York City and in Arizona, California, Korea, and Hong Kong, sometimes under the names Lu Han or Soma Han; represented in national registry, National Museum of Women in the Arts. Very Special Arts Arizona, member of board of directors, 1995-96. *Member:* Society of Children's Book Writers and Illustrators.

Illustrator

Dan Holt, editor and translator, *Tigers, Frogs, and Rice Cakes: A Book of Korean Proverbs,* Shen's Books (Auburn, CA), 1999.

Work in Progress

Writing and illustrating *A Glimpse into the Hermit Kingdom,* for Shen's Books (Auburn, CA), completion expected in 2002; research on Korean history and culture.

Biographical and Critical Sources

PERIODICALS

School Library Journal, June, 1999, DeAnn Tabuchi, review of *Tigers, Frogs, and Rice Cakes: A Book of Korean Proverbs,* p. 116.
U.S.-Korea Review, January-February, 1999, review of *Tigers, Frogs, and Rice Cakes,* p. 10.*

T

TAYLOR, Theodore 1921-
(T. T. Lang)

Personal

Born June 23, 1921, in Statesville, NC; son of Edward Riley (a molder) and Elnora Alma (a homemaker; maiden name, Langhans) Taylor; married Gweneth Goodwin, October 25, 1946 (divorced, 1979); married Flora Gray Schoenleber (an elementary school librarian and library clerk), April 18, 1981; children: (first marriage) Mark, Wendy, Michael. *Education:* Attended Fork Union Military Academy, VA, 1939-40, U.S. Merchant Marine Academy, Kings Point, NY, 1942, and

Theodore Taylor

Columbia University, 1948; studied with American Theatre Wing, 1947-48. *Politics:* Republican. *Religion:* Protestant. *Hobbies and other interests:* Travel, ocean fishing, watching football, playing with his dog, listening to classical music, collecting foreign menus.

Addresses

Home—1856 Catalina St., Laguna Beach, CA 92651. *Agent*—Gloria Loomis, Watkins Loomis Agency, Inc., 133 East 35th St., Suite 530, New York, NY 10016.

Career

Author, editor, screenwriter, journalist, publicist, producer, and director. *Portsmouth Star,* Portsmouth, VA, cub reporter, 1934-38, sports editor, 1941; *Washington Daily News,* Washington, DC, copy boy, 1940-41; National Broadcasting Company Radio, New York, NY, sports writer, 1942; *Sunset News,* Bluefield, WV, sports editor, 1946-47; New York University, New York, NY, assistant director of public relations, 1947-48; YMCA schools and colleges, New York, NY, director of public relations, 1948-49; *Orlando Sentinel Star,* Orlando, FL, reporter, 1949-50; Paramount Pictures, Hollywood, CA, publicist, 1955-56; Perlberg-Seaton Productions, Hollywood, CA, story editor, writer, and associate producer, 1956-61; freelance press agent for Hollywood studios, 1961-68; Twentieth Century-Fox, Hollywood, CA, screenwriter, 1965-68; full-time writer, 1970—. *Military service:* U.S. Merchant Marines, 1942-44; U.S. Naval Reserve, active duty, 1944-46, 1950-55; became lieutenant. *Member:* Academy of Motion Picture Arts and Sciences, Mystery Guild, Mystery Writers of America, Society of Children's Book Writers and Illustrators, Writers Guild.

Awards, Honors

Silver Medal, Commonwealth Club of California, 1969, Jane Addams Children's Book Award, 1970, Women's International League for Peace and Freedom (returned, 1975), Lewis Carroll Shelf Award, Southern California

Council on Literature for Children and Young People Notable Book Award, Woodward Park School Annual Book Award, California Literature Medal Award, and Best Book Award, University of California—Irvine, all 1970, all for *The Cay;* Outstanding Book of the Year, *New York Times,* 1976, for *Battle in the Arctic Seas: The Story of PQ 17;* Spur Award for Best Western for Young People, Western Writers of America, and Silver Medal, Commonwealth Club of California, for the best juvenile book by a California author, both 1977, both for *A Shepherd Watches, A Shepherd Sings;* Mark Twain Award nomination, 1977, for *Teetoncey,* and 1978, for *Teetoncey and Ben O'Neal;* Young Reader's Medal, California Reading Association, and Mark Twain Award nomination, both 1984, both for *The Trouble with Tuck;* Jefferson Cup Honor Book, Virginia Library Association, 1987, for *Walking Up a Rainbow;* Best Book Award, American Library Association (ALA), 1989, and Best Middle Grade Book Award, Maryland Reading Association, 1994, both for *Sniper;* Edgar Allan Poe Award and Best Book Award, ALA, both 1992, both for *The Weirdo;* Best Book Award, ALA, 1993, and Mark Twain Award nomination, 1996, for *Timothy of the Cay;* Mark Twain Award nomination, 1994, for *Tuck Triumphant;* Scott O' Dell Historical Fiction Award, University of Central Florida Libraries, and Children's Literature Council of Southern California Book Award, both 1996, both for *The Bomb;* South Carolina Book Award nomination, 2000, for *A Rogue Wave and Other Red-Blooded Sea Stories.* Taylor has also won three awards for his body of work: the Southern California Council on Literature for Children and Young People Award, 1977, for distinguished contributions to the field of children's literature, and the George G. Stone Center for Children's Books Recognition of Merit Award, 1980; The Kerlan Collection Award, University of Minnesota, 1996.

Writings

"CAPE HATTERAS" TRILOGY (ALSO CALLED THE "OUTER BANKS" TRILOGY); YOUNG ADULT NOVELS

Teetoncey, illustrated by Richard Cuffari, Doubleday (Garden City, NY), 1974, also published as *Stranger from the Sea: Teetoncey.*

Teetoncey and Ben O'Neal, illustrated by Richard Cuffari, Doubleday (Garden City, NY), 1975, also published as *Box of Treasures: Teetoncey and Ben O'Neal.*

The Odyssey of Ben O'Neal, illustrated by Richard Cuffari, Doubleday (Garden City, NY), 1977, also published as *Into the Wind: The Odyssey of Ben O'Neal.*

FICTION; FOR CHILDREN

The Cay, Doubleday (Garden City, NY), 1969, published as *The Cay: With Connections,* Holt (Austin, TX), 2000.

The Children's War, Doubleday (Garden City, NY), 1971.

The Maldonado Miracle, Doubleday (Garden City, NY), 1971.

The Trouble with Tuck, Doubleday (Garden City, NY), 1981.

Sweet Friday Island, Scholastic (New York, NY), 1984.

Walking Up a Rainbow: Being the True Version of the Long and Hazardous Journey of Susan D. Carlisle, Mrs. Myrtle Dessery, Drover Bert Pettit, and Cowboy

Left alone to guard his family's nature preserve, fifteen-year-old Ben Jepson must save the big cats that inhabit the land from a deadly sniper.

Clay Carmer and Others, Delacorte (New York, NY), 1986.

The Hostage, illustrated by Darrell Sweet, Delacorte (New York, NY), 1987.

Sniper, Harcourt (San Diego, CA), 1989.

Tuck Triumphant (sequel to *The Trouble with Tuck*), Doubleday (New York, NY), 1991.

The Weirdo, Harcourt (San Diego, CA), 1991.

Maria: A Christmas Story, Harcourt (San Diego, CA), 1992.

Timothy of the Cay (sequel to *The Cay*), Harcourt (San Diego, CA), 1993.

The Bomb, Harcourt (San Diego, CA), 1995.

Rogue Wave and Other Red-Blooded Sea Stories (short stories), Harcourt (San Diego, CA), 1996.

A Sailor Returns, Scholastic (New York, NY), 2001.

Hello, Arctic! (picture book for younger children), illustrated by Margaret Chodos-Irvine, Harcourt (San Diego, CA), 2002.

Lord of the Kill (sequel to *Sniper*), Scholastic (New York, NY), 2002.

The Boy Who Could Fly without a Motor (fantasy), Harcourt (San Diego, CA), 2002.

NONFICTION; FOR CHILDREN

People Who Make Movies, Doubleday (Garden City, NY), 1967.
Air Raid—Pearl Harbor! The Story of December 7, 1941, illustrated by W. T. Mars, Crowell (New York, NY), 1971, revised edition, Harcourt (San Diego, CA), 2001.
Rebellion Town, Williamsburg, 1776, illustrated by Richard Cuffari, Crowell (New York, NY), 1973.
Battle in the Arctic Seas: The Story of Convoy PQ 17, illustrated by Robert Andrew Parker, Crowell (New York, NY), 1976.
(With Louis Irigaray) *A Shepherd Watches, A Shepherd Sings,* Doubleday (New York, NY), 1977.
Rocket Island, Avon (New York, NY), 1983.

"BATTLE" SERIES; NONFICTION FOR CHILDREN

The Battle Off Midway Island, illustrated by Andrew Glass, Avon (New York, NY), 1981.
H.M.S. Hood vs. Bismarck: The Battleship Battle, illustrated by Andrew Glass, Avon (New York, NY), 1982.
Battle in the English Channel, illustrated by Andrew Glass, Avon (New York, NY), 1983.

NOVELS; FOR ADULTS

The Stalker, Donald I. Fine (New York, NY), 1987.
Monocolo, Donald I. Fine (New York, NY), 1989.
To Kill the Leopard, Harcourt (San Diego, CA), 1993.

NONFICTION

The Magnificent Mitscher (biography), Norton (New York, NY), 1954, Naval Institute Press (Annapolis, MD), 1997.
Fire on the Beaches, Norton (New York, NY), 1958.
The Body Trade, Fawcett (New York, NY), 1968.
(With Robert A. Houghton) *Special Unit Senator: The Investigation of the Assassination of Senator Robert F. Kennedy,* Random House (New York, NY), 1970.
(With Kreskin) *The Amazing World of Kreskin,* Random House (New York, NY), 1973.
Jule: The Story of Composer Jule Styne, Random House (New York, NY), 1978.
(With Tippi Hedren) *The Cats of Shambala,* Simon & Schuster (New York, NY), 1985.
The Flight of Jesse Leroy Brown (biography), Avon (New York, NY), 1998.

OTHER

Showdown (screenplay), Universal, 1973.
The Stalker (screenplay; based on Taylor's novel of the same name), Home Box Office, 1988.

Also author of television plays, including *Tom Threepersons* (adult mystery), TV Mystery Theatre, 1964, *Sunshine the Whale* (juvenile), 1974, and *The Girl Who Whistled the River Kwai,* 1980; author of screenplays, including *Night without End,* 1959, *The Hold-Up,* and seventeen documentaries. Also author of books under the pseudonym T. T. Lang and as a ghostwriter for other authors. Contributor of short stories and novelettes to periodicals, including *Argosy, Collier's, Ladies' Home Journal, Look, McCall's,* the *New York Times, Redbook,* and the *Saturday Evening Post.* Taylor's books have been published in eighteen other languages and forms, including Hebrew and Braille. Taylor's manuscripts are housed in a permanent collection at the Kerlan Collection at the University of Minnesota.

Adaptations

The Cay was adapted as a movie by NBC-TV, 1974, and was broadcast on the Bell System Family Theater; it was also released as a filmstrip by Pied Piper Productions, 1975; *The Trouble with Tuck* was adapted as a filmstrip by Pied Piper Productions, 1986; *The Cay* was released on audio cassette by Bantam Audio Publishing, 1992; Recorded Books Library Service has released audio cassettes of several of Taylor's works, including *Timothy of the Cay, Sweet Friday Island,* and *Tuck Triumphant* in 1994; *The Hostage* and *The Weirdo* in 1995; *The Bomb* in 1996; and *The Trouble with Tuck* in 1997. *The Cay on Stage,* a theatrical production for schools, was created by the California Theatre Center, Sunnyvale, CA. Teacher's guides for Taylor's works also have been published, including *The Cay/Timothy of the Cay Curriculum Unit* by the Center for Learning Network Staff, The Center for Learning, 1995; *The Cay—Literature Unit,* Teacher Created Units, Inc., 1995; and *A Guide for Using "The Cay" in the Classroom.* Taylor is also the subject of the video *A Talk with Theodore Taylor,* Good Conversations! Series, Tim Podell Production, 1998.

Work in Progress

Excelsior, Excelsior, an autobiography; *Ice Drift,* historical fiction for young adults; an adult novel, a sequel to *Monocolo.*

Sidelights

A prolific, popular American author of fiction and nonfiction for children and adults, Theodore Taylor is acclaimed for writing works that are both action-filled and thought-provoking. He is considered a distinguished author for young people as well as an accomplished historian, especially of naval history, for both children and adults. As a writer for the young, Taylor has written realistic, historical fiction and informational books, most of which he addresses to middle-graders and young adults. His fiction characteristically features young protagonists—preteen or adolescent boys and girls of varying ethnic backgrounds—who cope with challenges that often concern their physical survival. Through their experiences, these characters, who sometimes have lost their senses, such as sight and speech, or have physical disabilities, stand up for their values and learn independence and self-reliance as well as acceptance of other people and cultures. In his nonfiction, Taylor addresses important events in World War II, both successes and failures, that relate to the U.S. Navy, such as Pearl Harbor, the Battle of Midway, and the sinking of Germany's greatest battleship, the *Bismarck.* He has also written well-received biographies of Jesse Leroy Brown, the first African American naval aviator, and of a second-generation Basque shepherd in California. In addition, Taylor recreated a pivotal year in American history (1775-76) by focusing on the events in Williamsburg, Virginia; wrote a behind-the-scenes survey of the motion picture industry; and created an account of the secret research done by Germany on rocket weaponry. As a writer for adults, Taylor has penned mysteries and thrillers as well as nonfiction. In the latter genre, he has collaborated with actress Tippi Hedren and mentalist The Amazing Kreskin, has written biographies of composer Jule Stein and Admiral Marc Andrew "Pete" Mitscher of the U.S. Navy, and has investigated the assassination of Senator Robert Kennedy, among other works. Taylor is also a screenwriter for children and adults and has written, produced, and/or directed seventeen documentaries.

Taylor is well known as the author of *The Cay,* a young adult novel that relates how a prejudiced eleven-year-old American boy is shipwrecked on a small deserted cay, or low island, with a seventy-year-old, black, West Indian man during World War II. Through his experiences the boy, Phillip Enright, learns to love and respect the man, Timothy (no last name), and to learn that friendship is color blind. *The Cay* is one of the most successful and controversial novels in children's literature. It has sold over four million copies world-wide, but has been criticized as racist by both black and white organizations. Consequently, it has been banned by some schools and libraries. Taylor is also the creator of *Timothy of the Cay,* which is both a prequel and a sequel to *The Cay.*

In addition, Taylor is well known as the creator of the "Cape Hatteras" trilogy (also called the "Outer Banks" trilogy), a trio of historical novels for children set in the late 1800s on the Hatteras Banks of North Carolina. In these works, the author outlines the adventures of Ben O'Neal, a fatherless boy who wants to go to sea, and Wendy Lynn Appleton, a mute young English girl who is the sole survivor of a shipwreck and is nicknamed "Teetoncey," or teeny-tiny, by the residents of the island on which she and Ben live. Taylor is also the creator of the "Tuck" books, two popular stories about an adolescent girl and her beloved blind dog, Friar Tuck, and two young adult novels, *Sniper* and *Lord of the Kill,* that feature teenage protagonist Ben Jepson, a young man who encounters kidnaping and murder when his parents leave him to manage Los Coyotes Preserve, a refuge for big cats near Los Angeles.

As a literary stylist, Taylor favors fast-paced narratives written in spare but descriptive language. The author includes various techniques in his works, such as alternating chapters, interior monologues, flashbacks, epilogues, use of present tense and third person, and inclusion of dialect and words in other languages. Thematically, Taylor's works reflect his environmental, political, and social consciousness as well as his interest in nature lore, dogs, islands, and, especially, the sea. Acknowledged for his respect for and understanding of both people and animals, he blends history, psychology, and suspense to promote tolerance, freedom, independence, respect for the natural world, and connections among people of all ages and races. As a writer of nonfiction, Taylor is credited for the dramatic quality of his works as well as for their thorough research and balanced presentation of both sides of an issue. Although he has been criticized for some of his portrayals of minorities, women, and secondary characters, the author is generally lauded as one whose compelling books provide readers with both insight and entertainment. "A fine sense of dramatic action propels Taylor's fiction," a contributor to *Children's Books and Their Creators* noted, "making his fast-paced novels exciting and readable"; Carol Clark, writing in *School Library Journal,* called Taylor's nonfiction "as absorbing as his fiction."

Taylor presents both the American and the Japanese perspective on the bombing of Pearl Harbor and the events just prior to December 7, 1941. (Cover illustration by James Dietz.)

Taylor's experiences and interests inform much of his writing. Born in Statesville, North Carolina, in the center of the Piedmont area, he is the youngest of six children; his only brother died before Taylor's birth, leaving Theodore, called Ted, the only boy among four sisters.

His father, Edward Riley Taylor, was described by the author in his *Something about the Author Autobiography Series* (*SAAS*) entry as "a blue-collar workingman's working man." Edward Taylor never finished grade school, leaving at twelve to become a molder in a Pittsburgh foundry. Later, he served in the Spanish-American War. In the 1920s, Edward Taylor became involved in the International Workers of the World, a left-wing labor organization that was nicknamed "the Wobblies." In his essay, Taylor recalled that, as a preschooler, he saw his father coming home one night "bloodied and bruised, results of tangling with police during a strike." Taylor's mother, Elnora Alma Langhans, was, according to her son, so different from her husband that he and his sisters "could never understand how these two people got together and got married. She, delicate and fragile; he, stocky and muscular. Mother, reciting poetry; father, talking about the 'working man' endlessly.... She was so gentle and creative; he was so ungentle and so uncreative." Elnora Langhans had wanted to be an actress and had won contests in elocution. Writing on his Web site, Taylor recalled how his mother would stop in the making of a pie. She would, the author wrote, "dramatically throw an arm into the air in a final curtain flourish, shouting 'Excelsior! Excelsior!' Ever higher. Onward." Taylor recalled, "Somewhat afraid of my father and his Irish temper, I worshiped my mother except for her religiosity." The family (except Edward, who was Roman Catholic) attended Lutheran church services all day on Sundays as well as on Wednesday nights. Taylor also credits his four sisters—Norma, Eleanor, Louise, and Mary—for providing him with a connection to a world outside of his own. One lived in London, another was in New York, and a third was a schoolteacher in the Carolina foothills who was living with a "moonshiner" family. The youngest girl, Mary, lived at home, but had sophisticated literary taste; she introduced young Ted to the writings of Ernest Hemingway, an influential experience for the would-be writer. Taylor said, "All of them enriched me, but John Steinbeck was my favorite author." Taylor told SATA that "his first and most unforgettable childhood memory occurred when he was three or four perched on his father's shoulder, mother and sister Mary standing alongside." Up the dirt road to pass them on the hard-crabble front yard came nearly a dozen hooded men in white robes, mounted on horses, carrying pine-knot torches. "It was my first, but not last sight of the Ku Klux Klan. I remember the horses, most of them big and black, steam puffing from their nostrils on that wintry night. I remember the eyes of the riders. Seventy-six years have gone by but I think I could paint that scene if I had the talent." His mother later told him the KKK had burned a black family's house.

Taylor's very first introduction to literature came mainly from the stories in an illustrated children's edition of the Bible. "Action," he noted in *SAAS,* "was what I liked—David slaying Goliath; Samson and Delilah; Samson pulling down the Philistine temple.... I still prefer action stories, both to read and to write." He added, "I was a dreamer when a child, and had a good imagination then, much better than now." He also noted, "I'm told

In his second book about the blind dog Tuck, Taylor portrays Tuck's heroism and loyalty to his young mistress and her new adopted brother, an orphaned mute Korean boy.

that I was very shy as a child, the kind that clung to Mother's skirt. And in certain situations I remain shy to this day." When he was about five or six, Taylor became friends with a boy named Phillip. The author stated, "We had fun together but I remembered, later on, his absolute hatred of black people. Man, woman, or child. Tragically, his mother had taught him that hatred. He became the 'Phillip' of *The Cay.*" At around the same time, Taylor started school. He commented, "I never was a very good student and my memories of Mulberry Street School and Davie Avenue School are more of endurance than anything else." Fascinated with World War I, Taylor filled sheets of paper with war scenes while his teachers droned on. After school and during summer vacations, Taylor, as he noted, "excelled in the practice of freedom." He roamed through fields, creeks, and abandoned buildings and flirted with danger, all with the implicit approval of his mother, who, as a religious woman, believed that God would deliver him home safely. Taylor commented, "I had remarkable freedom for a kid curious about most things." He wrote on his Web site, "The fields and creeks of North Carolina were my playgrounds. I roamed as free as rabbits and birds and deer.... Exploration! A writer needs to explore, mentally and physically."

At the age of eight, Taylor got his first library card, although his mother had been reading to him for years. By the time he was nine, Taylor had read *Huckleberry Finn,* the stories of L. Frank Baum, the "Tom Swift" series, and adult mysteries and detective stories. He noted in *SAAS,* "I read both *Frankenstein* and *Dracula* about then. Heady stuff." At around this time, Taylor was introduced to Hugh Beam, a teacher and ex-football tackle who had married one of his sisters, Louise. According to Taylor, Hugh Beam "was a merry farmer's son who occasionally wrestled a black bear and did other feats of strength that held me in awe. Visiting them in Marion during summers, I spent some of my happiest days in the company of this huge man." Eventually, Hugh Beam went into politics, serving in the state assembly and becoming a judge. He also turned Taylor into a rabid football fan and, as the author revealed, "I remain one to this day."

At nine Taylor and his family moved to Johnson City, Tennessee, where his father, as a war veteran, entered the Soldier's Home to receive free meals. Taylor and his mother occupied two rooms in a private home. During this period, Taylor and his father went fishing frequently. As he did in Statesville, Taylor explored the countryside in and around Johnson City. After about a year, Edward Taylor left the Soldier's Home and went off to find part-time work, while Taylor and his mother returned to Statesville. During the Depression, Taylor had a paper route—getting up at four-thirty in the morning to deliver papers—and sold candy by the box; he also picked up scrap metal to sell at the local junkyard. The author commented, "I wasn't alone in these endeavors and I'm not the least sorry that I went through them." At around this time, Taylor acquired Napoleon, a mongrel pup that, the author noted, "began my long love affair with dogs."

In 1933 Taylor and some friends went down the Catawba River on a raft that they had made. "My parents," he told Norma Bagnall in *Language Arts,* "knew I was going and they didn't tell me I couldn't. They depended on me to use my head, not to do anything foolish, not to get myself drowned." In 1934 Edward Taylor got his first full-time job in years as a molder's helper at the Norfolk Navy Yard in Portsmouth, Virginia. Taylor and his mother took the train to Portsmouth, then traveled a few miles outside of it to make their home in Cradock, a comfortable village built in 1918 to house blue-collar workers during World War I. "I'd never been so excited," Taylor recalled. "Another state; a town near water, near ships." He added, "Somewhere in me is a considerable dollop of salt.... I had a hankering for the water long before we moved to Virginia." He wrote on his Web site, "I wanted to be aboard [ships], to be a sailor, go to London and Conakry and Durban and Hong Kong and the Java Sea. With the Second World War, that dream came true." Taylor told *SATA* that he used Portsmouth as the background for *A Sailor Returns.*

In Cradock, Taylor explored the area and, for once, enjoyed school. At Cradock High School he met an English teacher, Caroline Hardy, who encouraged him to write. He also went down to the Hatteras Banks to fish with his father or with his high-school friends; his trips to the Banks, which were peopled by descendants of shipwreck survivors, many of whom still spoke in Elizabethan dialect, were later to result in the "Cape Hatteras" trilogy. In 1935 Taylor was offered the chance to write a sports column, for fifty cents a week, on the weekly athletic events at his high school for the *Portsmouth Star.* He wrote in *SAAS,* "Never had I thought about writing of any sort. And, to my knowledge, I had no talent for it. But I was certainly willing to gamble that I could put a story together." For the next three years, Pete Glazer, the sports editor of the *Star,* was Taylor's "patient teacher," as the author called him. The editorial staff at the *Star* doubled as general assignment reporters." It was the perfect learning institution for me," Taylor recalled. After delivering his stories, Taylor would listen to eye-opening newsroom conversations. He commented that the *Star* and "another paper, a fast-paced metropolitan tabloid, were to be my college, my seamy-side university, my graduate schools. I've often regretted I didn't attend college. City rooms were the substitutes, newsmen were the teachers."

A boyhood friend of Taylor's, Lou Bass, was a talented amateur boxer. Taylor came along regularly as a "second" for Lou and his fellow boxers, earning several dollars per week at amateur fights in Virginia, Pennsylvania, and the District of Columbia. Of Lou Bass, Taylor stated, "I loved him as I loved a brother. I also used my slowly growing ability as a sports reporter to enhance his career." Bass became a champion fighter, winning titles in Virginia and the District of Columbia. Both Taylor and Lou Bass left Cradock for Washington, D.C., although Taylor had to return to satisfy a math requirement at his high school before being allowed to graduate. He went to Fork Union Military Academy in Virginia in order to obtain the credit and, after finishing the requirement, headed for Washington. Taylor arrived on crutches, having damaged his knee while playing touch football. His pitiful appearance, plus his tenacity on traveling the Chesapeake Bay Steamer on crutches to get a copy boy's job, landed him an engagement with the *Washington Daily News.* Taylor wrote in *SAAS,* "A metropolitan newspaper! A Washington paper! Abode of the blessed, the Elysian fields to which most reporters longed to go, and there I was happily answering to the yell of 'copy' or 'boy.'" After about a month, Taylor began writing entertainment features and reviews of movies and plays for the *Star.* After his first story, an interview with bandleader Charlie Spivak, was published, Taylor wrote, "I kept looking at that 'by Ted Taylor' in that metropolitan paper and thought I, too, had gone to the Elysian fields." His first assignment on the sports desk was a true learning experience: using big words like "erudite' and "hirsute" got his article thrown back in his face by the editor, Rocky Riley, who told Taylor to write simply. "I've never forgotten his advice," the author noted.

When Taylor's mentor at the *Portsmouth Star,* Pete Glazer, joined the navy in 1941, he offered the job of sports editor to the cub reporter. Taylor moved back to Virginia and became a one-man sports department; he also worked general news: "courts, accidents, sometimes the police beat—fine training for a young reporter," he wrote in *SAAS.* After Pearl Harbor, Taylor began covering stories concerning the war. His brother-in-law, who worked for NBC, recommended Taylor as the scriptwriter for Bill Stern, a nationally known radio sportscaster. Taylor got the job and began living the high life in New York City. "I couldn't believe my luck," he commented. In September 1942, Taylor joined the Merchant Marines and became a member of the naval reserve. He served as a deck cadet and then as an able-bodied seaman aboard a gasoline tanker in the Atlantic and Pacific areas as well as on a freighter in the European theater. Then Taylor obtained a third-mate's license, sailing for two trips on other ships. Returning to the United States in 1944, he was called by the U.S. Navy as a cargo officer. Taylor became a U.S. Naval Reserve ensign on a cargo attack vessel in the Pacific. Seventeen of his books are about ships and the sea, including *Rogue Wave and Other Red-Blooded Sea Stories.*

Following the Japanese surrender, he volunteered for duty, out of curiosity, in Operation Crossroads, the nuclear experiment on Bikini Atoll. Two atomic bombs were set to be tested on this idyllic island in the western Pacific. Two atomic bombs, originally scheduled for explosion over Japan, would be used on a fleet of one hundred obsolete warships. In a 1999 History Channel documentary, Taylor lamented: "I was shocked when I first saw the quiet beauty of the lagoon, knowing what would happen there. The gentle islanders would be forced to leave their homeland, by Marine gunpoint, if necessary. As a North Carolinian I was well acquainted with the Cherokee Trail of Tears. Now, our government was going to do it again. For what purpose? Everyone already knew what would occur when you drop a nuclear weapon." The experience served as a background for the young adult novel, *The Bomb.*

Taylor met his first wife, Gweneth Goodwin, in San Francisco, while he was in the service. They were married in 1946 in Bluefield, West Virginia, where Taylor had become the sports editor of the *Sunset News.* Less than a year later, the couple was back in New York, where Taylor became the assistant director of public relations at the Washington Square campus of New York University. Thinking that he might want to become a playwright or an author of fiction, Taylor took classes at the American Theatre Wing and at Columbia University. "I knew I wanted to write," he wrote in *SAAS.* "I didn't know exactly *what* I wanted to write. My strong suit was reportorial, nonfiction, so I tried that." Taylor began selling travel articles and other informational pieces to magazines; however, several dozen short stories came back with rejection slips. A few months after his first son, Mark, was born, Taylor got a job with the *Orlando Sentinel* as its "space" reporter, covering activities at the new space center in Cape Canaveral. Joining a naval

reserve unit, Taylor was called back into the navy at the onset of the Korean War in 1950. While serving at the Pentagon, he became friendly with a writer for the *New York Times* who had a contract to do a book on Admiral Marc Andrew "Pete" Mitscher, whom Taylor called in *SAAS* "a wizened, tough little carrier group commander in World War II." Taylor took over the contract and wrote the book, hurriedly, on nights and weekends; it was rejected. On Christmas Eve, Taylor learned that he had to return the five hundred dollar advance to publisher E. P. Dutton. After extensive rewriting, *The Magnificent Mitscher* was published by W. W. Norton in 1954. Taylor commented in *SAAS,* "I learned from the Dutton Christmas Eve catastrophe to take my time, be careful, write simply. Above all, write well."

After their daughter, Wendy, was born, Taylor and his wife took their children to the Caribbean, where Taylor was a public information officer for the Caribbean Sea Frontier. He acted as an aide to the admiral, who also headed up the naval district centered in San Juan, Puerto Rico, and went on several hurricane missions. "I sponged up background and atmosphere," Taylor noted in *SAAS,* "little knowing that *The Cay* was fourteen years up the path." After his release from the navy, Taylor was hired as a press agent by Perlberg-Seaton Productions, an independent Hollywood company that worked with Paramount Pictures. On his way to California, he stopped off to research his next book, *Fire on the Beaches,* the story of the ships that tried to avoid German submarines along the East Coast during World War II. While at Coast Guard headquarters in Washington, D.C., Taylor came across a paragraph that described the sinking of a small Dutch vessel. An eleven-year-old boy survived the sinking but was eventually lost at sea, floating alone on a life raft. Taylor wrote in *SAAS,* "That paragraph became *The Cay,* years later."

Taylor worked as a publicist for Paramount for three years. During that time, he worked with actors such as Clark Gable, Henry Fonda, Doris Day, Frank Sinatra, Fred Astaire, William Holden, Debbie Reynolds, and Charlton Heston before becoming story editor and assistant to producer William Perlberg and director George Seaton. While working for Perlberg-Seaton, Taylor wrote his first screenplay and completed *Fire on the Beaches.* After his son Michael was born, Taylor decided to leave Hollywood and make documentary films. After moving his family to Laguna Beach, sixty miles down the coast from Hollywood, he began filming documentaries. He created several behind-the-scenes documentaries on the making of feature films that were shown on television and made a total of seventeen documentaries. Between assignments, he wrote fiction and nonfiction for magazines. He also began to work as a freelance press agent for Hollywood studios, as a screenwriter for Twentieth Century-Fox, and as a ghostwriter for such notable figures as comedian Jerry Lewis.

In 1966, after living in Taiwan and Hong Kong while shooting a movie, Taylor decided to write a book for young readers. He wrote in *SAAS,* "My own children were interested in how motion pictures were made and I thought others might be, too." The result was *People Who Make Movies,* an informational book published the next year that describes the various parts of the industry. Taylor explains the background behind acting, makeup, sets, stunts, publicity, and visual and sound effects, among other aspects of production and direction. After the book began circulating in schools, Taylor was amazed to receive more than three thousand letters from young readers, many of whom wanted to be actors. In 1968, after hearing a black choral group sing spirituals in the lobby of a Miami hotel, Taylor was inspired to begin writing *The Cay.* His manuscript was completed in just three weeks. "By far," Taylor noted in *SAAS,* "it was the quickest and easiest book I've ever written, yet twelve years of occasional thought had gone into the work." Taylor based his characters on people from his childhood and on an old black schoonerman named Robbert, a man whom he met while doing research in St. Croix. In an essay on the *For the Middle Grades Only* Web site, Taylor noted that Robbert "couldn't read or write, yet he was one of the wisest men I'd ever talked to. He became 'Timothy,' ... though, in fact, the fictional character had parts and pieces of other sailors I'd met, too. The physical Timothy—the way he looked, the way he walked, the way he talked—was Robbert. He knew more about the Caribbean Sea than anyone I'd been around, on land or on the decks of ships."

Set in the Caribbean Sea in 1942 and dedicated to "Dr. King's dream, which can only come true if the very young know and understand," *The Cay* is both a survival tale in the vein of Daniel Defoe's *Robinson Crusoe* and a story about the defeat of prejudice. Taylor outlines how Phillip Enright, a eleven-year-old boy who lives on the island of Curacao off the coast of Venezuela, meets Timothy, the West Indian sailor. Phillip has been raised by his Virginia-born mother to dislike and distrust people of color. When German submarines begin to sink oil tankers and threaten the refinery on Curacao, Mrs. Enright decides to take her son back to the United States. The pair board a freighter bound for America; however, the ship sinks after being struck by German torpedoes. After being separated from his mother, Phillip jumps overboard and is hit by falling debris. Timothy, a seaman on board, rescues Phillip by pulling him onto one of the rafts. By the time the castaways arrive at a cay, or small island, Phillip is blind. With only a few supplies, Timothy and Phillip try to survive on the island. Although Phillip acts hatefully to Timothy, Timothy is patient, kind, and wise. He slowly teaches Phillip how to survive on the island. Over a period of three months, Phillip's anger and racist attitudes dissipate, and he begins to see Timothy as a man of strength and compassion. After Timothy sacrifices his life to save Phillip during a hurricane, the boy is able to live alone successfully, thanks to Timothy's tutelage, until his rescue a few weeks later. Reunited with his parents, Phillip returns to Curacao, where his vision is restored slightly. At the end of the novel, Phillip vows to return to the cay.

The Cay was both a critical and popular success and established Taylor as a writer of juvenile fiction. Initially, the novel was acclaimed for its successful rendering of Phillip's growth as well as for its powerful storytelling. Writing in *Book World,* Polly Goodwin called *The Cay* an "immensely moving novel" and "unforgettable reading" before concluding, "Phillip, who survived to tell the story, would never forget his friend. Nor will the reader." Marilyn Singer commented in *School Library Journal* that the book's essential value lies "in the representation of a hauntingly deep love, the poignancy of which is rarely achieved in children's literature." Writing in *Children's Literature in the Elementary School,* Charlotte S. Huck and Doris Young Kuhn called *The Cay* "one of the few stories that details the gradual loss of prejudice." *The Cay* received several awards, including the Jane Addams Children's Book Award from the Women's International League for Peace and Freedom, a prize that Taylor received in 1970. "But," the author noted, "*The Cay* soon came under attack as a 'racist' book, a charge which I believe is untrue." Taylor told *SATA,* "five years later, the Jane Addams Book Award committee decided that the book was racist and requested return of the plaque. I shipped it back to San Francisco COD, without comment."

In the mid-1970s *The Cay* began to be charged with racism by various organizations connected with children and their literature, most notably the now-defunct Council on Interracial Books for Children. Critics of the novel charged that Timothy is a stereotypical character, an ignorant, superstitious caricature who confirms the negative assessment of black people being subservient to whites. In addition, Taylor was criticized for introducing young people to a colonialist way of life and for using dialect for Timothy's speech. The controversy reached its peak in 1975 when Taylor was asked to return the Jane Addams Award that he had won five years earlier; the author complied. In a letter to *Top of the News,* Taylor commented that in writing *The Cay,* "I hoped to achieve a subtle plea for better race relations and more understanding,." Margery Fisher of *Growing Point* quoted the author as saying, "I wanted young readers to understand that color is simply a matter of vision in its basic form." Writing in *SAAS,* Taylor concluded, "*The Cay* is *not* racist, in my firm belief, and the character of Timothy, the old black man, modeled after a real person and several composites, is 'heroic' and not a stereotype. Would the critics have had him speak Brooklynese instead of Creole? Nonsense!" Currently, reviewers generally take a more balanced view of *The Cay.* The subservience for which the character of Timothy was criticized is now seen most often as a product of his historical era than of his low self-esteem. *The Cay* is usually recognized as an potent coming-of-age story, one that reflects its time and setting accurately. In addition, the novel is regarded as an example of exceptional storytelling and expression of truth and honesty. Many reviewers now consider *The Cay* to be a classic of children's literature, and it has become required readings in several schools. However, *The Cay* continues to be banned occasionally by schools and libraries. In an interview in *People Weekly,* Taylor noted that he has not let the critics of *The Cay* deter him. "I was stunned at first," he noted, "but time heals. And for every detractor, I have letters from black children who view Timothy as a hero."

Before retiring from the motion picture industry in 1970, Taylor worked on one more film, *Tora! Tora! Tora!*, which he described in *SAAS* as "draining and disastrous." In 1973 Universal Pictures released *Showdown,* a film with a screenplay by Taylor; the movie, a Western, features Rock Hudson and Dean Martin. Later, in 1988, Taylor was to write another screenplay, *The Stalker,* a television movie for HBO that was based on his adult novel of the same name.

Shortly after leaving the film industry, Taylor began to work on his "Cape Hatteras" trilogy. This series, which includes *Teetoncey, Teetoncey and Ben O'Neal,* and *The Odyssey of Ben O'Neal,* outlines the growing relationship of Ben and Teetoncey, a character modeled on Taylor's daughter, Wendy, as well as his desire to become a sailor. Writing in *SAAS,* Taylor called this series "a work which I favor." He added, "The charac-

In this tale of forgiveness and familial loyalty, Taylor depicts young Evan, whose wayward grandfather returns home unexpectedly, harboring a troubling secret. (Cover illustration by John Thompson.)

ters were drawn from real-life, as they are in all my books. I stress that I don't have a very good imagination. I'm still basically a reporter, finding it easier to work from real-life models."

In 1974, shortly after the publication of the first novel in the trilogy, Taylor heard a story from Tony Orser, a lawyer who was the stepson of one of his friends. Orser told Taylor about his blind dog; this story became the inspiration for *The Trouble with Tuck* and *Tuck Triumphant.* In the first book, teenager Helen Ogden trains Tuck, who has lost his sight, to work with Lady Daisy, a retired Seeing Eye Dog. In the second novel, Helen seeks to train the orphaned, mute Korean boy whom her family has adopted. Tuck rescues Helen and the boy during a thunderstorm while recovering from the death of Lady Daisy.

In January 1979, Taylor and his wife, Gweneth, were divorced. Shortly thereafter, Taylor was walking on the beach with two of his dogs when one of them attacked another dog. Its owner, Flora Schoenleber, became Taylor's second wife. The author wrote, "We were married in April, 1981, and I'm now enjoying the happiest and most productive years of my life."

In 1993, twenty-four years after the publication of *The Cay,* Taylor produced *Timothy of the Cay,* which is both a prequel and a sequel to the first novel. Although readers—including his own children—had urged Taylor to let them know what happened to Phillip after he was rescued from the cay, he refused to oblige. Finally, after his publisher suggested that he write Timothy's life as a prequel in third person, Taylor relented. The author decided to write his book in alternating chapters, with Phillip continuing his own story in first person. *Timothy of the Cay* begins in 1942, with Phillip in the sick bay of the ship that rescued him. The story then flashes back to 1884, as twelve-year-old Timothy, who longs to be a ship's captain, seeks work on a sailing vessel. The story continues to alternate between Phillip's struggle to regain his sight and Timothy's life as a sailor until he meets Phillip on the raft. Abandoned as a child and raised by his aunt on St. Thomas, Timothy is determined to own his own ship. Phillip, who is set on regaining his sight completely, faces an extensive operation that could leave him paralyzed—or dead. He also faces a world where prejudice is a commonplace thing. Finally, Phillip returns with his father to the cay, where his friend Timothy lost his life.

Critics generally were enthusiastic about *Timothy of the Cay.* A reviewer for *Publishers Weekly* wrote, "In the tradition of its predecessor, the 'prequel/sequel' explores social and racial imbalances and draws a graceful parallel between Timothy's youthful struggle to achieve an unheard-of dream—the captaincy of his own boat—and Phillip's courage in choosing to undergo a risky operation to restore his vision.... Somewhat more thoughtful than its well-loved antecedent, this boldly drawn novel is no less commanding." *Horn Book* critic Kristi Beavin called *Timothy of the Cay* an example of "the book that breaks the rules—and wins. *Timothy of the Cay* is such a book: weaving two separate plots, two separate time periods, and two separate voices together."

Taylor told Norma Bagnall in *Language Arts,* "I think young people need to learn at an early age the satisfaction of relying on themselves.... Every story I have written is about real people and stems from real-life events. They include kids who have figured out things for themselves because kids like that really exist." He concluded, "I'm proud to write for young people, but when I sit down to write, I do not consciously think, 'Now, you're writing for young people.' I let the story go the way that story should go; the worst thing a writer can do is write down to children. I am just not conscious of whether I am writing for young people or for adults. But I will probably do other books with characters like Ben O'Neal, Jose, Phillip, and Teetoncey. They are the kind of peer models children can like and respect." He wrote on his Web site, "I tell aspiring writers to do diverse things, to go to as many places as possible, to watch and listen.... I look back on a lifetime at the typewriter, many typewriters in many places, and marvel at how lucky I've been. On those keys I have two-fingered sports and crime and love and death. I've pecked out books for adults and young readers as well as scripts for radio, TV, and feature films. I've been so very, very lucky. Here I am, still learning the three C's of good storytelling: character, conflict, and construction. And I'm still pecking away. Excelsior! Excelsior!"

Biographical and Critical Sources

BOOKS

Children's Literature in the Elementary School, third edition, Holt (New York, NY), 1979.
Children's Literature Review, Volume 30, Gale (Detroit, MI), 1993.
Drew, Bernard A., *The One Hundred Most Popular Young Adult Authors,* Libraries Unlimited, 1996.
Hipple, Ted, editor, *Writers for Young Adults,* Scribner's (New York, NY), 1997.
St. James Guide to Young Adult Writers, second edition, St. James Press (Detroit, MI), 1999.
Silvey, Anita, editor, *Children's Books and Their Creators,* Houghton (Boston, MA), 1995.
Something about the Author Autobiography Series, Volume 4, Gale (Detroit, MI), 1987.
Speaking for Ourselves, Too: More Autobiographical Sketches by Notable Authors of Books for Young Adults, National Council of Teachers of English (Urbana, IL), 1993.
Twentieth-Century Children's Writers, third edition, St. James Press (Detroit, MI), 1989.

PERIODICALS

Booklist, September 15, 1992, Chris Sherman, review of *Maria: A Christmas Story,* p. 104; September 15, 1993, Stephanie Zvirin, review of *Timothy of the Cay,* p. 153; October 1, 1995, Susan Dove Lempke, review of *The Bomb,* p. 309; November 1, 1996, Susan Dove Lempke, review of *Rogue Wave and Other Red-Blooded Sea Stories,* p. 491; May 1, 2001, Carolyn Phelan, review of *A Sailor Returns,* p. 1684.

Book World, May 4, 1969, Polly Goodwin, review of *The Cay,* p. 36.
Growing Point, January, 1971, Margery Fisher, p. 1669.
Horn Book, April, 1982, review of *The Trouble with Tuck,* p. 170; January-February, 1990, Nancy Vasilakis, review of *Sniper,* p. 72; March-April, 1992, Margaret A. Bush, review of *The Weirdo,* p. 211; May-June, 1995, Kristi Beavin, review of *Timothy of the Cay* (sound recording), p. 318.
Language Arts, January, 1980, Norma Bagnall, "Theodore Taylor: His Models of Self-Reliance," pp. 86-91.
Library Journal, August, 1985, review of *The Cats of Shambala,* p. 106.
New York Times Book Review, January 29, 1995, review of *Walking Up a Rainbow,* p. 20.
People Weekly, May 3, 1993, review of *To Kill the Leopard,* p. 294; December 20, 1993, Kim Hubbard, "Return to the Cay: Theodore Taylor Reprises His Controversial Classic," p. 105.
Publishers Weekly, July 16, 1982, review of *H.M.S. Hood vs. Bismarck,* p. 79; June 7, 1985, review of *The Cats of Shambala,* p. 72; April 25, 1986, Diane Roback, review of *Walking Up a Rainbow,* p. 84; April 10, 1987, Sybil Steinberg, review of *The Stalker,* p. 85; December 11, 1987, Diane Roback, review of *The Hostage,* p. 66; August 11, 1989, Sybil Steinberg, review of *Give My Heart Ease,* p. 441; December 14, 1990, Diane Roback and Richard Donahue, review of *Tuck Triumphant,* p. 67; November 22, 1991, review of *The Weirdo,* p. 57; September 7, 1992, Elizabeth Devereaux, review of *Maria: A Christmas Story,* p. 69; September 6, 1993, review of *Timothy of the Cay,* p. 98; September 18, 1995, review of *The Bomb,* p. 133; October 12, 1998, review of *The Flight of Jesse Leroy Brown,* p. 65; May 21, 2001, review of *A Sailor Returns,* p. 108.
School Library Journal, September, 1969, Marilyn Singer, review of *The Cay,* p. 162; January, 1982, review of *The Trouble with Tuck,* p. 82; May, 1982, review of *The Battle Off Midway Island,* p. 75; April, 1984, Civia M. Tuteur, review of *Battle in the English Channel,* p. 127; August, 1986, Dorcas Hand, review of *Walking Up a Rainbow,* p. 107; March, 1988, Patricia Manning, review of *The Hostage,* p. 200; November, 1989, Susan Schuller, review of *Sniper,* p. 115; March, 1991, Ellen Ramsay, review of *Tuck Triumphant,* p. 196; December, 1991, Eldon Younce, review of *Air Raid—Pearl Harbor: The Story of December 7, 1941,* p. 130; January, 1992, Yvonne Frey, review of *The Weirdo,* p. 137; January, 1993, Ruth Semrau, review of *Maria: A Christmas Story,* p. 104; October, 1993, Susan Knorr, review of *Timothy of the Cay,* p. 132; May, 1994, Susan Knorr, review of *Sweet Friday Island,* p. 135; July, 1996, Stephanie Gall Miller, review of *The Hostage,* p. 51; August, 1996, Pat Griffith, review of *The Weirdo,* p. 64; April, 1997, Melissa Hudak, review of *Rogue Wave,* p. 142; April, 1999, Carol Clark, review of *The Flight of Jesse Leroy Brown,* p. 166; April, 2001, Tim Rausch, review of *A Sailor Returns,* p. 150.
Top of the News, April, 1975, Theodore Taylor, letter to the editor, pp. 284-288.

Wilson Library Bulletin, March, 1990, Lesley S. J. Farmer, review of *Sniper,* p. S13; September, 1992, Frances Bradburn, review of *The Weirdo,* p. 93.

OTHER

ALAN Review, http://scholar.lib.vt.edu/ (November 18, 2001), Theodore Taylor, "Exploding the Literary Canon."

For the Middle Grades Only, http://www.kidstrek.com/ (November 18, 2001), Theodore Taylor, "On Writing *Timothy of the Cay.*"

The Scoop, http://www.friend.ly.net/ (November 18, 2001), Theodore Taylor, "On Writing *The Bomb.*"

Theodore Taylor Home Page, http://www.theodoretaylor.com/ (November 18, 2001).

W

WHELAN, Gloria (Ann) 1923-

Personal

Born November 23, 1923, in Detroit, MI; daughter of William Joseph (a contractor) and Hildegarde (Kilwinski) Rewoldt; married Joseph L. Whelan (a physician), June 12, 1948; children: Joseph William, Jennifer Nolan. *Education:* University of Michigan, B.S., 1945, M.S.W., 1948.

Addresses

Home—9797 North Twin Lake Rd. N.E., Mancelona, MI 49659. *Agent*—Liza Vogues, 866 United Nations Plaza, New York, NY 10017.

Career

Writer. Minneapolis Family and Children's Service, Minneapolis, MN, social worker, 1948-49; Children's Center of Wayne County, Detroit, MI, supervisor of group services and day care program, 1963-68; Spring Arbor College, Spring Arbor, MI, instructor in American literature, beginning 1979. Writer in residence, Interlochen Academy for the Arts; instructor in writing workshops.

Awards, Honors

Juvenile Book Merit Award (older), Friends of American Writers, 1979, for *A Clearing in the Forest;* Juvenile Fiction Award, Society of Midland Authors, 1994; Great Lakes Book Award, 1996, for *Once on This Island;* named Michigan Author of the Year, Michigan Library Association/Michigan Center for the Book, 1998; National Book Award, and Best Books citation, *School Library Journal,* both 2000, both for *Homeless Bird;* Best Books of the Year citation, Bank Street College of Education; Edgar Award nomination, Mystery Writers of America; four Pushcart Prize nominations; Creative Artist Award, Michigan Council for the Arts; Master List finalist, Florida Sunshine State Young Readers

Award; citations for Texas Lone Star Reading List and International Reading Association (IRA) Children's Choices List; nominations for Dorothy Canfield Fisher Award, Georgia Children's Book Award, and Mark Twain Award.

Writings

A Clearing in the Forest, Putnam (New York, NY), 1978.

A Time to Keep Silent, Putnam (New York, NY), 1979.

Next Spring an Oriole, illustrated by Pamela Johnson, Random House (New York, NY), 1987.

Playing with Shadows (short-story collection; for adults), University of Illinois Press (Champaign, IL), 1988.

Silver, illustrated by Stephen Marchesi, Random House (New York, NY), 1988.

A Week of Raccoons, illustrated by Lynn Munsinger, Knopf (New York, NY), 1988.

The Secret Keeper, Knopf (New York, NY), 1990.

Hannah, illustrated by Leslie Bowman, Knopf (New York, NY), 1991.

Bringing the Farmhouse Home, illustrated by Jada Rowland, Simon & Schuster (New York, NY), 1992.

Goodbye, Vietnam, Knopf (New York, NY), 1992.

Night of the Full Moon (sequel to *Next Spring an Oriole*), illustrated by Leslie Bowman, Knopf (New York, NY), 1993.

That Wild Berries Should Grow: The Diary of a Summer, Eerdmans (Grand Rapids, MI), 1994.

Once on This Island, HarperCollins (New York, NY), 1995.

The Indian School, HarperCollins (New York, NY), 1996.

The President's Mother (adult novel), Servant Publications, 1996.

The Miracle of Saint Nicholas (picture book), Ignatius, 1997.

Forgive the River, Forgive the Sky, Eerdmans (Grand Rapids, MI), 1998.

Farewell to the Island (sequel to *Once on This Island*), HarperCollins (New York, NY), 1998.

Miranda's Last Stand, HarperCollins (New York, NY), 1999.

Homeless Bird, HarperCollins (New York, NY), 2000.

Welcome to Starvation Lake (chapter book), illustrated by Lynne Cravath, Golden (New York, NY), 2000.

Return to the Island (sequel to *Once on This Island* and *Farewell to the Island*), HarperCollins (New York, NY), 2000.

Angel on the Square, HarperCollins (New York, NY), 2001.

Rich and Famous in Starvation Lake, illustrated by Lynne Cravath, Golden (New York, NY), 2001.

The Wanigan: A Life on the River, Knopf (New York, NY), 2002.

Are There Bears in Starvation Lake?, illustrated by Lynne Cravath, Golden (New York, NY), 2002.

Also contributor of short stories to anthologies, including *O. Henry Prize Stories.* Contributor of adult fiction to periodicals, including *Michigan Quarterly, Virginia Quarterly, Story Quarterly, Missouri Review, Gettysburg Review, Detroit Monthly,* and *Ontario Review.* Contributor of poetry to periodicals, including *Ontario Review* and *Country Life.*

Sidelights

Winner of the National Book Award for young people's literature for her novel *Homeless Bird,* Gloria Whelan is a late bloomer as far as publication is concerned. Fifty-five years of age when her first novel, *A Clearing in the Forest,* was published, Whelan has made up for lost time with two dozen offerings in as many years. A versatile author of historical and contemporary fiction for children and young adults, as well as short stories and poetry for adults, Whelan is, according to Liz Rosenberg in the *Chicago Tribune,* "an accomplished, graceful, and intelligent writer."

Whelan told the National Book Award committee, "Books saved my life.... I think they save the lives of lots of children." As reported in a *Booklist* article by Renee Olson, that award committee felt that Whelan's tale of a thirteen-year-old Indian girl who is married and then quickly widowed was "told clearly and without extravagance, somber in the way in which it confronts the difficulties ... and yet radiant with hope." Previous to winning the National Book Award, Whelan was known primarily as a regional author, writing tales often set in Michigan, such as *A Clearing in the Forest, Hannah,* and *Once on This Island* and its sequels, although she had also written books with a more international flavor before *Homeless Bird.* Her 1992 novel, *Goodbye, Vietnam,* for instance, deals with the plight of the Vietnamese boat people fleeing their country for a new life abroad. But with the winning of the National Book Award, Whelan moved out of the category of local or regional author and stepped on a national and international stage. Receiving the award set a new standard for Whelan, as she explained to Elizabeth Farnsworth on the Public Broadcasting Service's *News Hour:* "It pushes me to try and do better. It's a kind of responsibility, and it's also a kind of affirmation. It makes me feel that somehow the stories that I'm writing are stories that are being received by somebody."

Born an only child in Detroit, Michigan, in 1923, Whelan has been writing stories "as long as I can remember," as she told Kathleen T. Isaacs in a *School Library Journal* interview. "I used to dictate stories to my baby-sitter and she would type them up." Such stories would often be about having a brother or sister. Books were, as she noted in her speech to the National Book Award committee, an early friend and solace. One of her role models while growing up was Jo March from *Little Women.* Whelan's love of books and writing continued through high school, and entering the University of Michigan, she felt she wanted to write "the great American novel." Short stories also occupied Whelan's attention for a time as did poetry, but nothing came of her ambitions to be a novelist for many years.

In the intervening years, Whelan married and had two children. She also worked as a social worker and a supervisor of group services and a day care program in Detroit. Then, in 1977 she and her doctor husband decided to leave the hustle and bustle of Detroit behind and settle at a house situated on a small lake in northern Michigan. "Our family had been coming up here for years in the summertime," Whelan told Isaacs. "I came up here as a child with my father, who was an enthusiastic fisherman." Whelan's husband, from Minnesota, was also fond of the north country, so they finally decided to make the move.

Their remote country location was quickly disturbed, however, when one day the representative of an oil drilling company told them they intended to drill for oil on their property as the Whelan's did not own the mineral rights to the land. The workers bulldozed three acres and put up a derrick and began drilling, but the Whelan's were lucky: the well came in dry and the oil people left Whelan in peace once again. However, the entire process so fascinated Whelan that she began writing about an imaginary young boy who works on an oilrig. "Because he was a young boy and I was telling his story, somehow it turned into a young adult novel," Whelan explained to Isaacs. That novel, *A Clearing in the Forest,* was Whelan's first book and it started her on a long journey of writing discovery, often using the background of her chosen rural world around Oxbow Lake in northern Michigan.

One of Whelan's earliest books is the contemporary novel *A Time to Keep Silent,* first published in 1979. The novel focuses on thirteen-year-old Clair, who reacts to her mother's death by withdrawing into herself and refusing to speak to anyone. To make matters worse, Clair's father, a minister in an affluent suburban community, decides to uproot the family in order to build a mission church in a poor rural area. After moving to their new home, Clair meets independent and adventurous Dorrie, who uses her wits to survive alone in an unfinished house in the woods. When Dorrie's violent father comes looking for her after his release from prison, Clair must speak in order to help her friend. Writing in *Kliatt,* Claire Rosser called the book "strong and life-affirming" and noted that "there is suspense amidst the story of emotional healing."

In this early title, Whelan displays her love of the natural world and uses material at hand—her own cabin in the remote woods—for color. The Whelans have several hundred acres of land; their nearest house is a mile distant and their mailbox is a half-mile down the road. "I look out my window when I'm writing," Whelan told Isaacs, "and I see herons and beaver and deer and fox trotting around the lake." Whelan enjoys her woods at firsthand, too, walking through them daily and fly-fishing in nearby streams.

Another of Whelan's books for young readers, *Next Spring an Oriole,* is a historical novel set in 1837. The narrator, ten-year-old Libby, tells the story of her family's difficult move from Virginia to Michigan on a wagon train. After Libby's parents help Fawn, a Potawatomi Indian girl, to survive the measles, Fawn's family returns the favor by providing food during a long winter. Betsy Hearne of *Bulletin of the Center for Children's Books* found the story "smoothly written and appealing," and a *Kirkus Reviews* writer remarked that it seemed "historically authentic." Whelan published a sequel to this book in 1993, *Night of the Full Moon.* Disappointed that her father cannot take her to visit Fawn's village, Libby sneaks away by herself. While she is there, however, the U.S. Army arrives to forcibly relocate the Potawatomi, and Libby is included by mistake. Her struggle to return home makes for "very readable historical fiction," according to Maeve Visser Knoth in the *Horn Book Guide.* "Whelan packs quite a story into this brief sequel to *Next Spring an Oriole,*" wrote a reviewer for *Publishers Weekly.* The same writer felt that Whelan's book, told in "simple, well-chosen language," was as "captivating" as any of the "Little House" series, but "far more insightful and thought-provoking" as regards historical events. Whelan did not know much Native American history before moving to the woods, but she researched the subject thoroughly in preparation for her books, in particular the tribes that once flourished in northern Michigan.

Whelan returned to contemporary fiction with *Silver,* the story of nine-year-old Rachel growing up in rural Alaska. Rachel's father, an avid dogsled racer, allows her to raise the runt of the litter produced by his best lead dog. Rachel rescues Silver from wolves as a pup and then raises him to be a champion. A *Kirkus Reviews* contributor praised the book as "a charming, unassuming narrative that authentically conveys its setting." Likewise, *School Library Journal* reviewer Hayden E. Atwood called *Silver* "a lively, thoroughly credible story emphasizing the loneliness and excitement of Alaskan living for a young girl."

A Week of Raccoons is a whimsical tale that helps children learn the days of the week. It describes a week at the Twerkles' cottage in which each day is disrupted by a clever raccoon. Each night Mr. Twerkle captures one of the five raccoons and transports it deep into the forest, only to have a different raccoon cause mischief the next day. Finally, all the raccoons find other places to live, and the Twerkles enjoy a peaceful Saturday at their cottage. Writing in *School Library Journal,* Marga-

ret Bush found the tale "entertaining" and "moderately humorous," though she commented that "the extension of the cycle to five repetitions prolongs the gimmick a bit too long." A further excursion into picture books came in 1997 with *The Miracle of Saint Nicholas,* a parable for Christmas set in Communist Russia.

Whelan ventured into the suspense genre with *The Secret Keeper,* published in 1990. The story is told from the perspective of Annie, who is hired to take care of ten-year-old Matt for a summer at the Beaches, a private Lake Michigan resort. Annie finds it mysterious that Matt's grandparents refuse to let him see his father, Bryce, and seem unwilling to discuss his mother's death. When Bryce kidnaps Matt, Annie discovers the terrible family secret that the entire resort community has conspired to conceal, and thus puts herself in danger. In a *School Library Journal* review, Kathryn Havris commented that "the element of lurking evil is there, making this a book that will hold readers' interest and provoke discussions on vigilante justice and just who is above the law." A reviewer for *Publishers Weekly* also felt Whelan's book had merit: "Containing many elements of a modern-day Gothic, Whelan's thoroughly satisfying novel is sure to produce shivers."

In Whelan's historical novel *Hannah,* the title character is a blind girl living on a farm in 1887. A new teacher convinces her mother that she should attend school, and the story follows Hannah's hardships and successes as she learns. *Hannah* is "a gentle story that sensitively portrays Hannah's feelings," Margaret C. Howell said in *School Library Journal,* though she concluded that the happy ending is "not really believable." In the nostalgic *Bringing the Farmhouse Home,* a family of five adult siblings and their children gathers to divide up the treasured belongings of a deceased grandmother. They share their memories of the grandmother and the farm, and then devise a fair method of allocating the contents of the farmhouse. In the end, seven-year-old Sarah's mother trades a beautiful platter for the quilt that Sarah hoped to keep. A *Kirkus Reviews* contributor claimed that people dividing up possessions "are faced with an experience that's in some ways like preschoolers' first bouts with sharing," so the successful conclusion provides a positive example for children. A writer for *Publishers Weekly* called the picture book "unusually atmospheric," and one that "celebrates the passage of traditions from one generation to the next."

Whelan again expanded her impressive range with the 1992 publication of *Goodbye, Vietnam.* This book tells the story of thirteen-year-old Mai, whose family is forced to leave its village because her grandmother was accused of practicing folk medicine and following the old religion. They endure a dangerous journey on a small, crowded boat to seek freedom in Hong Kong and eventually in the United States. Diane S. Marton noted in *School Library Journal* that the book "describes well the hardships many of America's newest refugees have endured," while Roger Sutton, in a *Bulletin of the Center for Children's Books* review, stated that it has "a rare simplicity and sharp focus." Reviewing the same title in

In the mid-1800s, young Libby attempts to visit her friend's Potawatomi settlement, is forced to relocate with the villagers, and labors to return to her family. (From Night of the Full Moon, *written by Whelan and illustrated by Leslie Bowman.)*

Horn Book, Carolyn K. Jenks noted that "Mai's stark, straightforward narration" lets the reader bring his or her own feelings into the plight of the Vietnamese boat people. Jenks also felt that the conclusion of the book "ties together a few too many loose ends to be completely realistic, but the people and the journey are compelling." "Mai is the perfect narrator through whom to introduce a large cast of unusual, sympathetic characters," commented a contributor for *Publishers Weekly,* who further observed that her "emotional control and keen observations prove to be a source of calm in the storm that swirls around her."

Another tale of northern Michigan is served up in *That Wild Berries Should Grow: The Diary of a Summer.* It is the fictional diary of Elsa, a young girl who is sent away from her home in Detroit to live with her German-born grandparents at their lake house. Set in 1933, the story includes references to the Depression and the mounting concern about Adolf Hitler's activities in Germany leading up to World War II. In her *School Library Journal* article, Sally Bates Goodroe noted that Elsa gains an understanding of herself and others in this "gentle, authentic slice of childhood with the timeless feel of summer." *Booklist* contributor Carolyn Phelan noted that Elsa's transformation "is gradual enough to be convincing," and that Whelan's novel was "a good portrayal of a child growing up during the Depression."

Whelan's three-part series about a young woman who lived during the early 1800s on an island between Lake Michigan and Lake Huron includes the titles *Once on This Island, Farewell to the Island,* and *Return to the Island.* In the first book, Mary, age twelve, is living on a small farm on Mackinac Island. The year is 1812, and when the invading British capture her island, Mary's father goes off to fight for the Americans. "Through Mary's narration, the everyday details of life in 1812 intertwine with larger events," commented *Booklist*'s Susan Dove Lempke. Mary and her two siblings must survive the vicissitudes of the next three years on their own. The local fort is taken by the British and Mary's sister Angelique flirts with a British lieutenant, while their brother Jacques must escape from the British. And through it all, Mary is worried sick that her father will never return from the war. "Whelan's smooth writing, vivid characters, and strong sense of place make this a good choice for libraries," Lempke concluded.

Whelan reprised the characters of this 1995 novel three years later with *Farewell to the Island,* in which Mary leaves her island to visit Angelique, now married and living in London. She leaves her hotheaded brother behind and his new wife, Little Cloud. Her father has given the farm to the son, rather than to Mary who worked so hard to keep it together during the war. She also leaves behind White Hawk, a Native American with whom she has grown close. On the voyage to England, she meets a handsome young sailor who turns out to be the son of a duke, Lord Lindsay. England, however, is a disappointment, as plucky Mary is always a bit too brash for the locals. Lempke, again writing in *Booklist,* felt this first sequel "is not as strong historically as the first book," though she did feel "it will satisfy young readers with a taste for romance." In *Return to the Island,* Mary is back on her beloved farm, working with brother Jacques and the gentle White Hawk, when James, an English painter she met while in England arrives to paint on the island and to woo Mary. "[R]eaders of the first two books will want this one," wrote *Booklist* critic GraceAnne A. DeCandido, while Carrie Lynn Cooper commented in *School Library Journal* that "Whelan writes a convincing third novel in her series.... deftly integrat[ing] history into the novel."

In *The Indian School,* Whelan depicts with "eloquent if predictable precision ... the tensions of early 19th-century Michigan," according to a writer for *Publishers Weekly.* When her parents are both killed in a wagon accident, eleven-year-old Lucy is sent from Detroit to live with her aunt and uncle at a mission school for Indian children. There Lucy must earn her keep and meanwhile learns about Native American culture from the other children before her Aunt Emma can Americanize them. One of the children, Raven, however, refuses to adapt and runs away, leaving Lucy with her secret. The *Publishers Weekly* reviewer concluded that Whelan manages to "transport the reader into a believable and complex past" despite a climax that is "frustrating in its patness." Lauren Peterson, writing in *Booklist*, felt that teachers "in search of fiction tie-ins to Native American units will welcome this."

A further title with a Native American theme is *Miranda's Last Stand*, an account of "one young girl's gradual coming to terms with the loss of her father and understanding the plight of the Sioux," according to Carol A. Edwards writing in *School Library Journal*. Miranda, like Lucy in *The Indian School*, learns what it means to be Indian when her mother takes a job with William Cody's Wild West Show. Miranda, whose father was killed at Custer's Last Stand, has always been taught that Indians are bad, but when she comes into contact with some Lakota Sioux children firsthand, and with Sitting Bull when he joins the show, the young girl is forced to reassess her feelings. "Miranda's story, filled with characters from the American West, will fascinate middle readers," observed Karen Hutt in *Booklist*, while a contributor for *Publishers Weekly* felt Whelan "uses an accessible first-person narrative and polished, easy prose filled with behind-the-scenes detail."

Nothing in Whelan's repertoire quite prepared her or her readers for her year 2000 title, *Homeless Bird*. Inspired by a newspaper article Whelan read about an Indian city where widows as young as thirteen are abandoned by their in-laws, the novel tells the story of young Koly who is simply an extra mouth to feed in her own family. Thus she is, like many young women in contemporary India, married off as early as possible. However, Koly's arranged marriage with Hari does not go as planned. The youth is younger than promised and also sickly. In fact, Koly has been married off for her dowry, which Hari's family uses in a vain attempt at medical treatment for the young man. When Hari dies, Koly finds herself penniless and homeless, abandoned by her in-laws. She must find her own way in the city and does so, partly through the intercession of a mysterious and handsome young man, but mainly through her own will and drive.

Alice Stern, reviewing the book in *Voice of Youth Advocates*, called the novel "beautifully written" with all the elements of a great read: "a strong, empathic heroine, a fascinating culture, triumph over adversity ... romance, and hope for the future." Other reviewers followed in such high praise. Shelle Rosenfeld, for example, writing in *Booklist*, called *Homeless Bird* a "beautifully told, inspiring story" that takes readers on "a fascinating journey through modern India." Rosenfeld also pointed out for commendation Whelan's "lyrical, poetic prose, interwoven with Hindi words and terms." An accompanying glossary helps readers to find their way through such terminology and is just one more sign of the prodigious amount of research Whelan did for the book. "Whelan has enhanced a simple but satisfying story with loving detail," noted Isaacs in a review of the novel. Isaacs went on to conclude, "Readers with a

curiosity about other worlds and other ways will find Koly's story fascinating."

Homeless Bird won the National Book Award in 2000 in addition to bountiful critical acclaim. But for Whelan, nothing has changed regarding her writing. Her ambition still is summed up in the Latin "nulla dies sine linea"— "no day without a line." "The Greek Pythagoras could draw a perfect line," Whelan told Isaacs, "but he said if he didn't draw it every day, he would lose the skill. So on my computer I have 'no day without a line,' and I really make myself write every day. It's what I like best to do, and it's what I do."

Biographical and Critical Sources

PERIODICALS

Booklist, December 1, 1988, p. 656; October 15, 1992, p. 443; May 1, 1994, Carolyn Phelan, review of *That Wild Berries Should Grow: The Diary of a Summer,* p. 1602; October 1, 1995, Susan Dove Lempke, review of *Once on This Island*, p. 321; December 1, 1995, Susan Dove Lempke, review of *Farewell to the Island,* p. 667; October 15, 1996, Lauren Peterson, review of *The Indian School,* p. 425; November 1, 1997, p. 485; November 1, 1999, Karen Hutt, review of *Miranda's Last Stand,* p. 531; March 1, 2000, Shelle Rosenfeld, review of *Homeless Bird,* p. 1243; December 1, 2000, p. 713; January 1, 2001, Renee Olson, "Of Satin and Surprises: The 2000 National Book Awards," p. 874, and GraceAnne A. DeCandido, review of *Return to the Island,* p. 961; August, 2001, GraceAnne A. DeCandido, review of *Rich and Famous in Starvation Lake,* p. 2123; September 15, 2001, Gillian Engberg, review of *Angel on the Square,* p. 215.

Book Report, January-February, 1993, pp. 49-50; March-April, 1996, p. 39; November-December, 2000, p. 64.

Bulletin of the Center for Children's Books, October, 1987, Betsy Hearne, review of *Next Spring an Oriole,* p. 39; June, 1991, p. 252; October, 1992, Roger Sutton, review of *Goodbye, Vietnam,* p. 57.

Chicago Tribune, January 15, 1989, Liz Rosenberg, "Consistent Strength: Four New Volumes in the University of Illinois' Short Fiction Series," sec. 14, p. 3.

Christian Science Monitor, December 14, 2000, p. 21.

Five Owls, September-October, 1994, p. 5.

Horn Book, January-February, 1993, Carolyn K. Jenks, review of *Goodbye, Vietnam,* p. 87.

Horn Book Guide, July-December, 1993, Maeve Visser Knoth, review of *Night of the Full Moon,* p. 183.

Kirkus Reviews, November 1, 1987, review of *Next Spring an Oriole,* p. 1682; April 15, 1988, p. 570; May 15, 1988, review of *Silver,* p. 768; July 1, 1992, review of *Bringing the Farmhouse Home,* p. 856.

Kliatt, November, 1993, Claire Rosser, review of *A Time to Keep Silent,* p. 12.

Publishers Weekly, June 24, 1988, p. 95; October 28, 1988, p. 77; February 9, 1990, review of *The Secret Keeper,* p. 64; July 10, 1992, review of *Bringing the Farm-house Home,* p. 247; July 27, 1992, review of *Good-*

bye, Vietnam, p. 63; November 8, 1993, review of *Night of the Full Moon,* p. 77; March 24, 1994, p. 73; September 23, 1996, review of *The Indian School,* p. 77; October 6, 1997, p. 56; October 11, 1999, review of *Miranda's Last Stand,* p. 76; January 31, 2000, p. 107; July 16, 2001, review of *Angel on the Square,* p. 182.

Reading Teacher, January, 1998, pp. 333-334.

School Library Journal, February, 1988, p. 65; October, 1988, Hayden E. Atwood, review of *Silver,* p. 129; December, 1988, Margaret Bush, review of *A Week of Raccoons,* p. 95; May, 1990, Kathryn Havris, review of *The Secret Keeper,* pp. 128-129; June, 1991, Margaret C. Howell, review of *Hannah,* p. 113; September, 1992, Diane S. Marton, review of *Goodbye, Vietnam,* p. 262; January, 1993, p. 88; March, 1994, p. 239; July, 1994, Sally Bates Goodroe, review of *That Wild Berries Should Grow: The Diary of a Summer,* pp. 104-105; September, 1998, p. 212; November, 1999, Carol A. Edwards, review of *Miranda's*

Last Stand, p. 166; February, 2000, Kathleen Isaacs, review of *Homeless Bird,* p. 127; December, 2000, Carrie Lynn Cooper, review of *Return to the Island,* p. 150; January, 2001, Rick Margolis, "The Bird Is the Word," p. 17; March, 2001, Kathleen T. Isaacs, "Flying High," pp. 52-56; October, 2001, Lisa Prolman, review of *Angel on the Square,* p. 175; November, 2001, Blair Christolon, review of *Rich and Famous in Starvation Lake,* p. 123.

Voice of Youth Advocates, August, 1990, p. 164; February, 2001, Alice Stern, review of *Homeless Bird,* pp. 428-429; April, 2001, Leslie Carter, review of *Return to the Island,* p. 47.

OTHER

News Hour Online, http://www.pbs.org/newshour/ (November 23, 2000), transcript of interview with Gloria Whelan.*

*   *   *

Autobiography Feature

Ellen Wittlinger

1948-

I was born on October 21, 1948, in a small town in southern Illinois just across the great Mississippi River from St. Louis, Missouri. (And isn't this, after all, where an autobiography ought to begin, with that helpless baby brought into daylight in strange surroundings that it will soon call "home"?) Belleville, Illinois, was a manufacturing town founded in the early nineteenth century by a combination of French settlers and pioneers from the eastern states. But it was the wave of German immigrants in 1832-33 who settled in and gave the place its flavor. By the time I was a youngster most of the stove foundries, which employed many local people, had closed and the manufacture of shoes and farm equipment had fallen off as well. Men (and the occasional woman) often worked across the river in St. Louis, unless of course they had jobs in one of Belleville's most thriving industries: its breweries.

One of my favorite childhood memories is of seeing men walking home from work after stopping by a local tavern to have their tin buckets filled with foamy Stag beer. Although my parents didn't take part in this local custom (my mother never cared for beer, and my father, born in Canada, preferred his beer in bottles), I knew from days spent with older relatives that the bucket would be passed around the living room later that evening, each family

member or visiting friend drinking from its rim as it passed. Even children would wait for the big silver goblet to come their way so they could sip a few bitter swallows.

I was my parents' only child, which I never appreciated and still don't. Families in those days tended to be large, and having no siblings made me feel like an oddball. I was always jealous of my friends who got called home for supper or from an evening's outdoor play and ran inside yelling and arguing with their sisters and brothers. It seemed to make for a lively life very different from my own quiet one.

My parents both worked (unusual in those days—most mothers didn't), managing a grocery store for an old German gentleman, and I stayed home with my paternal grandmother, who lived with us until her death in 1953, just about the time I was ready to start school. Because I'd spent so much of my young life with her, her death left me miserable and frightened; it made going off to school by myself for the first time a torment. I was very shy and easily upset for a few years, but as I was fortunate enough to have caring teachers, I found solace in their attention and became an eager student.

For several years after my grandmother's death it was common for me to have nightmares that woke me up in terror. People still spoke often of World War II, during which my father had been a soldier in the army, and many of my dreams involved some kind of enemy sneaking into my bedroom with a bayonet. But one night I had a very vivid dream which put an end to the frightening ones. Or maybe it wasn't a dream—I didn't think it was at the time. What I believed was that I woke up in the middle of the night to find my beloved (and dead) grandmother sitting calmly at the foot of my bed. She looked just as she always had, her gray hair in a neat bun, her hands folded in the lap of her navy blue dress, her black, clunky shoes set flat against the floor. I was so happy to see her! She didn't say anything, and I don't think I did either, but her presence was thrilling. It wasn't at all frightening to me; I felt she was telling me that she was still around, still taking care of me, watching over me. And although I never saw her again, I slept much better after that night.

After-school time was now spent with my other grandparents, whose vegetable garden ended in an alley through which the Illinois Central trains chugged every few hours. And, as if waving to strangers on their way to foreign places wasn't exotic enough, one could also (from time to time—if Grandma wasn't being vigilant) sneak down the block and peek in the windows of the Holy Roller church. Over the years I heard the congregation singing many a time but, to my great disappointment, never saw anybody rolling on the floor.

I remember the day I stopped halfway down Bristow Street to pet a big dog and was spied by my great-aunt Emma from her sitting-room window. She called my grandmother, and the two of them ran out onto their front porches and began screaming at me to get away from the friendly pooch they feared would eat me alive. In this way I felt always under surveillance—safe, but too safe. Early on I longed for more freedom, for adventure, although the fear of it was instilled in my heart too by the succession of well-meaning old ladies who guarded my early life.

The most thrilling moments in those years were when my Uncle Walter, my mother's younger brother, would suddenly show up on his parents' doorstep as if dropped from a cloud, carrying only his trombone case and an old valise, to take a temporary break from his life on the road with one dance band or another. He was always full of stories about the strange characters and fellow travelers he encountered as he crossed the country back and forth. Grandma sighed proudly when he talked about Harry James and Woody Herman, the famous and semifamous people he'd met on the big band circuit. He described dance halls in Chicago and hotels in New York City, places I could hardly believe real. Uncle Walter would play his horn at Grandma's request, and it too told beautiful stories of how far away from Belleville it was possible to go.

When Walt finally married, his wife too was exotic, at least to me. An ice skater with a Tennessee accent, Jackie had been traveling the world since age sixteen with

Ellen Wittlinger, 1996

Olympic gold medal winner Sonja Henie's ice show. She had scrapbooks full of clippings and photos, and a large oil painting of herself balanced on one thin leg, short skirt flipping in the wind, ice chips scattering behind her. She smoked cigarettes and tied scarves around her blonde hair and talked Walt into buying two big poodles to which she gave odd-sounding French names. (My grandmother eventually accepted Jackie, but never those dogs.)

I have always thought these reports of a life in art, a life outside the early-to-bed, early-to-rise world in which I'd grown up, reports of a world so big it scared the rest of the family, took root in me then and helped me to believe in larger possibilities than our small town could offer. I saw there were other paths to take, and that, like Walt, like Jackie, I could find one that suited me too. Someday it might be me on the Illinois Central or the Wabash Cannonball, waving to dreamy kids in their grandma's backyard. (When my mother got wind of my grandiose traveling plans, she'd shake her head and say, "You didn't get that wanderlust from me. You must have inherited it from your Uncle Walter." That was just what I wanted to hear—there was a reason for me to be like him!)

For children who find themselves alone a good deal and thrown back on their own resources, reading often becomes their escape, their friend, their adventure, their imaginary life. This was also true for me. I had only a very few books of my own as a young child, as we were far from wealthy, but I was taken regularly to the public library and allowed to bring home the maximum number of books the library allowed. As I grew older I could visit the library on my own, and it became a beloved refuge. I moved from the children's room to the young reader section, full in those days of dog and horse stories, all of which I loved.

I had gotten a dog, Penny, a Welsh corgi mix, when I was seven, a necessary companion for a child so often on her own, and a love of all animals sprang from my attachment to her. As many only children will do, I made my dog a kind of sibling, telling her my deepest secrets. I think having the dog helped me move from loneliness to an enjoyment of being alone; I was learning to talk (and to listen) to myself while pretending Penny could understand what I was saying. On the night my grandfather died, my parents ran down the alley to deal with the crisis while I huddled in the hallway with my dog, discussing the meaning of life and death from a twelve-year-old's perspective. How could I have sorted all this out without her help? (Penny died when I was a teenager. A friend who was amazed at my daylong crying jag told me, "It's only a dog, Ellen!" I've never really forgiven her.)

At about the same time we got Penny, my parents bought a small grocery store of their own which had living quarters attached to the side and behind it. The building sat on a corner lot with four or five large elm trees in the yard in a residential neighborhood. Within a few weeks of the move my father had ordered a sign to be up across the entire front of the store, just over the big picture windows: WITTLINGER MARKET. It made me proud to see my name written so large, announcing to everyone who drove by that we owned this store and every candy bar and Popsicle in it! (Of course there was also milk and meat and canned goods and thread and all the other things you buy in a store, but in those days it was the penny candy counter and the ice cream freezer which impressed me and my friends the most. And indeed, I became quite popular in the neighborhood. What other parents had such a choice of afternoon snacks to offer?)

By this time I was happier in school; my friends and I rode our bicycles to the Jefferson School every morning or, in cold weather, took the bus. Because our house was attached to the store, my parents were now more available to me, if always busy. The store opened at 8:00 a.m., and my father started cutting and grinding meat an hour before that. In the early days they stayed open until eight in the evening, after which my mother did the bookkeeping and ordering. Of course we were open on Saturdays too, and though we were closed on Sundays, neighbors would often knock on the back door to get another bottle of milk or loaf of bread. There were seldom vacations for more than two or three days at a time, and these were usually to visit relatives. Still, life at the grocery store was pleasant for me. The constant noise of chatty customers and wrangling children just the other side of the screen door compensated a little bit for the modest size of our immediate family. And I made spending money by stocking the shelves once a week and sometimes, on Saturdays, packing up orders or even working at the cash register.

The store gave me an identity. Everyone in the neighborhood knew me. Elderly ladies with German accents, toddlers clutching sweaty pennies, even the older boys who bought sodas and sat swigging them down on the front steps knew who I was. One year, as a promotional gimmick, my parents had pencils made with the name and address of the store printed on them. WITTLINGER MARKET stood out in red ink on the bright white pencils. We had to make thousands of them to get a reasonable price, and those pencils stayed around for years. We gave them out in the store but never seemed to get to the bottom of the boxes. By the time I left for college the store had closed, forced out of business by the new, large supermarkets going in all over town, and my parents had both gotten other jobs. But there were still pencils left, so I took them with me and distributed them to college friends. For years those pencils would turn up when I least expected them—sometimes I'd see someone I didn't even know writing with one! They were very good pencils. Even now a stubby, chewed-up leftover will surface from time to time and make me think back fondly on that little store just a screen door away from our dining room. (I even wrote a poem about those pencils, published in my book of poetry for adults called *Breakers*.)

By the time I got to junior high school my closest friends were the other girls in the club we'd formed: the Horse and Pony Club. The funny thing about this club was that none of us owned horses and only one girl had a rather nasty pony that even she didn't seem to ride much. And while we did go out to the farm and visit Alana's pony once in a while, our primary activities were collecting and trading ceramic horse statues, reading books about horses, and drawing pictures of the handsome creatures. Most of these activities took place during slumber parties at Alana's house, her mother being the least likely to get angry at late-night noise. Sandy was a few years older than the rest of us and indisputably the best horse artist. When her interest in horses began to wane (about the time her interest in boys

With parents, Karl and Doris Wittlinger, 1950

began to wax), the group gradually disbanded, but I could never get rid of my horse statues even though my own children showed no interest in displaying the unbroken ones in their rooms. Today the old mares and stallions and colts are wrapped in tissue paper and stored in the attic, some of them with severed legs or tails, and none of them more beautiful than the palomino I got from Sandy in the best trade I ever made.

As a teenager I dreamed of becoming an artist, a painter, and spent long afternoons and evenings sitting at a card table which my parents let me set up in the middle of their living room, the only place in the house big enough for it, painting stylized renditions of landscapes and still lifes. My parents took me to the St. Louis Art Museum, and I stood for a long time before some of those paintings, especially one called *The Red Stairway* by Ben Shahn, stunned by the emotional impact to be made by oil on canvas. I read about Michelangelo and Gauguin and Picasso, living on the edges of normal society, not bound

by the rules of regular people. Like many a young person, the independence of the artist's life appealed to me.

I began writing poems during this period too and was always praised by my English teachers for my style. But somehow writing didn't have the same allure as painting. It seemed like such a stodgy thing to do, and the writers I knew about, in their suits and glasses, were not nearly as romantic as painters, who got to wear old clothes all the time and smear them with colorful reminders of their work!

And I was certainly a romantic. At thirteen I fell in love with the boy across the street. Fell madly and for several years. He had black hair and a crooked smile (just like Elvis, I thought!) and was a little bit wild, not interested in being more than friends with the quiet, buck-toothed, bespectacled girl at the grocery store. But I spent my spare time staring up at his bedroom windows, the blue curtains matching exactly the color of the paper cover on my favorite sappy record, "Johnny Angel," the story of a girl desperately mired in unrequited love. How often now, in the midst of writing a scene in a young adult novel, do I think back to those moments and how tragically romantic and marvelously painful it was to daydream about Mike!

Sometimes I hear people say about teenagers that they're in "puppy love," by which they seem to mean a lesser kind of emotion than that felt by more mature people. I always disagree. How can it be other than spectacular, that first emotional experience, the first time you say to yourself, "I would give all that I am to this person," and if you're a very lucky teenager, having that feeling returned to you? Precisely because it's not weighted with the knowledge of former loves or future prospects, I think that first love is the most thrilling (if often most poignant) period of life many people will ever experience. At this age we are discovering emotions we didn't know we possessed. When I write a "love scene," a deeply felt moment between two young people, I try to put myself back into those terrifying times when I felt the ground was hardly stable under my feet, when it seemed that the way this person reacted to my feelings would change my life forever. (And in a way, it did.)

I get a little aggravated when people label my books "romances." A romance is a book for adults and frequently is based more in fantasy than in reality. And to call them "love stories" is not correct either, because in the midst of the purity of that first experience, it doesn't really matter if it's "love" or not. I prefer to think of my books as coming-of-age stories, books that remember what it feels like to be thirteen or fifteen or seventeen and to feel for the first time the tumult of adult emotions.

I sometimes tell people I never got over being thirteen—I got kind of stuck back there. But I don't only mean stuck with that feeling of being an oddball kid, with not quite the right looks or interests to fit in (the square-peg-in-a-round-hole feeling I that I think most teenagers have at some time), but also I never got over what's so good about being thirteen. At that age (unless a child is very unlucky) we're still optimistic; the world is right in front of us waiting to be embraced, and we have unlimited hope that it will open its arms to us as well. We're just beginning to feel our own strength, to notice our own abilities. The challenges and decisions ahead seem like marvelous opportunities. And at thirteen or fifteen or even seventeen we're still willing to be vulnerable, to open ourselves to new people, to fall in love without first checking whether there's a net hanging below.

This is why I love writing young adult novels. Who lives a more exciting life than a teenager just moving from the safety of home and family into the wide world of emotional possibilities? It's the equivalent of boarding one of the first manned spacecrafts. And yet teenagers rush enthusiastically into this rare atmosphere, as they have always done and will always do. I hope only to show them there have been others there before them and they have survived.

Yes, I read "love stories" when I was a teenager. The only authors' names I recall now are Betty Cavanna and Maureen Daly, author of the famous pillow-soaker *Seventeenth Summer.* Of course in those days "girls' books," as they were called, weren't as steeped in reality as modern

"My favorite picture of myself, age two or three"

YAs are. The biggest problem most of these protagonists faced was getting a date to the prom or breaking up with Todd, the handsome, but shallow captain of the football team. And in fact I moved rather quickly past these books and began, purely by chance (they were kept in a pleasant alcove in the library), to read plays. I became particularly interested in the bizarre world of Eugene O'Neill's characters, ravaged by drink or drugs and tied to each other by the bandages of love and need. I'm quite sure O'Neill and after him Tennessee Williams formed my ideas of what a great character should be: strange and almost unknowable, yet crying out for someone to *try.*

The high school I attended was very large, almost four thousand baby boomers stuffed into a facility built for half that many. There were so many students, I was never quite sure which group I belonged with. In classes I was with the smart kids, but almost none of them were friends of mine. Most of them were "popular" (or at least I thought they were at the time—I wonder if that's the way they felt?), cheerleaders and class officers and kids who got dates. They were always friendly to me, but friendship didn't extend outside the classroom.

Many of the kids in my "advanced" classes lived in the newer, wealthier parts of town and belonged to one of the country clubs that had just recently opened. Their families all knew one another; they went to parties and dinners together and spent their summers hanging around the pool at the club instead of the public pool my friends and I frequented. Their lifestyle was alien to my family (I'd never even *seen* my parents in swimming suits), whose financial problems were getting worse and worse as Piggly Wiggly and Kroger supermarkets opened up all over town. (It became a particularly guilty thrill for me to actually go inside these places with their aisles full of choices, more kinds of cookies than we'd ever have room for in our market. It seemed to me my parents would die if they ever found out I'd committed such treason, but at least, I told myself, I never *bought* anything there. I am still a little shocked to realize my parents themselves shop in supermarkets now.)

The friends I ended up with were an eclectic bunch who didn't really fit in anywhere else either. One was quite overweight and a loud-mouth to boot, but her jokes kept us in stitches. Another was an introverted, violin-playing valedictorian who was never allowed to have friends inside her house. A third was obsessed with her tattooed, out-of-town boyfriend, and a fourth was happily flunking most of her classes and driving her parents to distraction. But perhaps the kids I was most drawn to were the Scott Field kids, the ones whose fathers were air force personnel, who transferred in and out of the local air base every year or so. These kids had lived all over—California, Colorado, Germany—and they were unimpressed by almost everything. They weren't in a big hurry to find friends. Why bother? They'd just have to leave them behind anyway. They weren't even interested in getting to know each other, much less kids from a hick town like Belleville, Illinois.

Air Force Brats, as they were known, fascinated me. (Even Mike was one!) They wore their outsider status like an invisible shield. They were proud to be able to keep us away, such naive, small-town kids, and most people were happy to stay away from them. But not me. Like Walt, they'd been out in the world and they *knew* things, had *seen* things the rest of us hadn't. I courted several Air Force Brats over the years and eventually managed to become their friend. They were, every one of them, important people in my life, and all of them moved on, and I lost track of them forever. Even now, looking back, they seem elevated somehow, so aloof, so self-sufficient, and, as it usually turned out, so happy to find a real friend.

The times I remember as being the most fun in high school were when one or two kids could get the family car for the evening and the rest of us would pile inside, the radio blasting KXOK, the St. Louis rock station, and head for a drive-in movie. (Almost all these marvelous places have closed down now, a terrible loss.) The movie would start around nine o'clock, or whenever it got dark enough—things were pretty loose at the drive-in. Since you were never quite sure when things would get going, you'd come early and make your first tour through the snack bar, then walk past all the parked cars, looking for familiar faces.

The movie itself was actually just an excuse to park in a big field with lots of other people and eat junk food. Since the speakers that hung on your window were pretty squeaky, you usually couldn't hear the movie all that well. We'd always try to park near a car with other kids we knew because much time at a drive-in could be spent running back and forth between cars and into the snack bar, causing us to miss large portions of the movie anyway (and probably annoy all the adult moviegoers).

There were always two movies, lasting late into the night, but sometimes we'd leave after the first one so we'd have time to stop at one or two drive-in hamburger stands too. (Everything was drive-in in those days.) The A&W root beer stand was good, but so were some of the local places where the teenage waitresses would hook the silver trays right onto your car window and you could get your fries and cherry Cokes without getting out of your Chevy (or Nash Rambler).

But the biggest thrill was driving into St. Louis late at night (strictly forbidden by *everyone's* parents) and sitting out underneath the just-completed Arch, an enormous silver croquet hoop towering over the Mississippi River, reflecting in the moonlight. Of course we'd all been there with our parents during the daytime, but to sit beneath it at night was eerie and wonderful. You felt all sparkling, like you'd been dusted by fairies. It was especially nice to have boys along on this trip, even if they weren't your boyfriends (and they were never mine in those days), because the setting was so romantic and you could pretend you were with the one you liked best. (It's good training for a writer to be a great pretender!) I'm sure the consequences for going on this trip would have been tremendous if we'd ever been caught, but we never were. It was the kind of adventure (just dangerous enough to make you feel *very* grown up) that, once you're a parent yourself, you pray your own kids never dream up.

I left Belleville at seventeen for Millikin University in Decatur, Illinois. It wasn't as far as I'd planned to go, but my parents had nixed the notion of going to either coast for an education (too expensive and dangerous flying back and forth!), and the Kansas City Art Institute (my closer-to-home choice) had not granted me a scholarship. Millikin did, and so I settled there, unsure even as I registered for

"At age five, on a pony that was brought around for the purpose of taking pictures. That's our house on Church Street, behind me to the left."

classes whether I ought to be signing up as an art major or an English major. But the frightening amount of reading (I've always been slow at it) one had to do for an English major decided me: art it was. Now I realize one should never make decisions based on fear of hard work. I should have been an English major. I enjoyed the English classes I took and continued to write poetry. I never had much talent for painting, though I loved the technical aspects of it, the study of its history, and the smell of the studios. I limped through and got my degree with a double major in art and sociology. (The sociology major was to satisfy my mother, who feared, correctly, that a degree in art would not make me a hot commodity in the job market. What she didn't know was, neither would sociology.)

However, my college years were not entirely wasted: I became more politically aware (the Vietnam War did that to many of us in those years), attended civil rights rallies and marches (especially when the charismatic Reverend Jesse Jackson came down from Chicago to speak), and became a hippie (the fun part of political awareness). In the spring of 1970, when campuses across the country were in an uproar over student protests against the war, Millikin also faced a series of traumatic events which eventually shut down the campus for several days. It began with bomb threats being called into classroom buildings, escalated with a fiery rag being thrown into a dormitory basement, and finally peaked with the burning of an old classroom building in the middle of the night. For this last event the girls in my dorm, just across the street from the engulfed building, were routed from bed at 3:00 a.m.; we spent the sunrise in robes and pajamas on the front lawn watching brick walls collapse, flames leap up to dance again through broken windows, contemplating how we'd ever have the nerve to fall asleep again. The police were never able to pin these crimes on any person or group, but the relations between the college and the working-class community of Decatur were strained as many accusations were made.

Then in early May four students were shot and killed by National Guardsmen at Kent State University in Ohio. This was a defining moment, I think, for many people my age who, up until then, still felt like children, felt our chanting and marching and raggedy clothes would eventually be understood and even embraced by our parents' generation. We had been so sure of ourselves, of the rightness of our beliefs; we had thought our hippie revolution would transform the world into a peaceful and harmonious sphere. But now that hope had crumbled away. Older people, especially the ones in power, would never hear our message. In fact, they hated us so much, our youth and idealism, they hardly needed an excuse to open fire and kill us. Or at least that was how it seemed that sad and frightening spring.

And in fact there was a change after 1970. Many people gave up their idealism and replaced it with cynicism. They didn't want to be caught out again, didn't want to have their hopefulness shattered once more by hatred. After that, to be a hippie was little more than a fashion statement or a way to drop out of the mainstream. People turned the revolution inward; if they couldn't change the world, at least they'd change themselves.

But something else also happened in my senior year of college, an event which ultimately had a greater impact on my personal life than anything else that took place in those four years: I became friends with a young teacher and his wife, Kelly and Pamela Yenser, who were poets. They lent me books by poets I'd never heard of, and we discussed what I'd read. They invited me to dinner and taught me to play poker and treated me as an equal. They read my work and made suggestions and encouraged me to keep writing. Suddenly everything fell into place. *This* was who I was supposed to be: a writer. Maybe it wasn't quite as glamorous as painting, but it was a lot better than becoming a secretary (always my fallback job because I could type quickly), which seemed to be about the only position my degrees in art and sociology were going to get me. This was perhaps the first time I understood how my life would be divided: a job would be what I did for money; writing would be what I did for love.

I graduated from Millikin in 1970, and because a college friend lived there and raved about it, I moved

"With Uncle Walter, Penn, and our '56 Chevy, in front of Wittlinger Market," 1959

across the country to Ashland, Oregon, a beautiful little town with which I fell instantly in love. Finally I had gotten free of the Midwest—I was living surrounded by mountain ranges, two hours from the Pacific Ocean, putting together ads for the local newspaper and writing poems the rest of the time. The town was home to a small college, a thriving Shakespeare festival, a beautiful park, and a good book-store. A perfect place. My friends were mountain climbers and Quakers and guitar players who performed in coffee-houses. I had found, it seemed, the life I'd always wanted, and I vowed only one thing could get me to leave Ashland—an acceptance to the graduate school Pam and Kelly had recommended as the best, the University of Iowa Writers' Workshop.

I've lived in many places over the years, but none was harder to leave than Ashland. I was in Iowa City, Iowa, for two years. No place could have been more different from easygoing Ashland. The Writers' Workshop was full of students from the East Coast, many of them older and almost all of them more confident of their writing skills than I was. The competition was fierce, and the workshop classes often critical to the point of brutality. Many students gave up midyear; I'm not sure why I wasn't one of them. I think, frightening as the company was, it was the first time I'd been surrounded by other writers, and the stimulation afforded by so many people pushing and shoving towards the same goal was very exciting. This was also the first time in my life I had been *identified* as a writer. Just the fact of being in the program at Iowa empowered me to be able to say to people, "I'm a writer." And as I believed it, I worked at it, and as I worked at it, I became one. I made many close friends during those two years, and one whom I would marry a few years later, David Pritchard, a short-story writer and Spanish-language translator.

With a master of fine arts degree, I was eligible to teach college courses in writing, but as most of us soon found out, it wasn't enough. Colleges wanted their instructors to have a book published, preferably two, and so I was now unemployed (and in my field, unemployable), with college and graduate school debts to be paid back. I had no urge to stay in Iowa City—most of my friends were moving on, and besides, the winters were, to me, unendurable. I thought of course of returning to Ashland, but all around me the writers were going east. "If you want to write, you *have* to be on the East Coast," a friend told me. (This of course is not true—writers live everywhere, including Ashland, Oregon—but she was right that there are more contacts to be made and probably more jobs that employ writers in the eastern cities.) And because New York City seemed just *too* big for a girl from Belleville, Illinois, I chose Boston, which people assured me was smaller and friendlier.

I moved to Boston (actually, across the Charles River to the college town of Cambridge) in the fall of 1973 and have lived in eastern Massachusetts ever since. I have been a temporary secretary, a chambermaid, a pasteup artist for a commercial typesetting firm, a layout artist for a weekly newspaper, a library assistant for a large college library, a jewelry maker, a computer typesetter for the Boston Public Library (briefly), a substitute teacher (even more briefly—these people deserve combat pay), a mother (the job with

"In hippie garb," Ashland, Oregon, 1970

the longest hours), and a children's librarian in a small-town library. And while I was doing all those other things, I was also being a writer.

From 1974 to 1976 I enjoyed the benefits of two fellowships from the Fine Arts Work Center in Provincetown, Massachusetts, a wonderful organization that gives a room and bare-bones living expenses to twenty writers and visual artists for seven months at a time from October through April. Provincetown sits at the very end of the long, skinny peninsula that is Cape Cod, land's end in every respect. It's a town full of artists, old hippies, fishermen, gay people, and anybody else smart enough to figure out a way to stay in such a beautiful place year-round. There is not much work to be had outside of the summer tourist season (unless you fish), and a good deal of the town closes up between October and June, but I don't know of a spot more enchanted on the entire East Coast. Tiny clapboard houses with immaculate, picket-fenced yards nestle close to one another on narrow streets, most of which run right down to the bay. In Provincetown a good day's work (whatever that might be) is often capped, winter or summer, by watching the sun go down at Herring Cove Beach. In the off-season, summer resorts boarded up and only a dozen stores still open for the reduced population, the town becomes an ideal working environment: silent and beautiful. I had found another heavenly spot—not the same as Ashland, but with the same spirit—another place I felt completely at home.

More than just the necessary dollars of the fellowship, the Fine Arts Work Center also gave me real fellowship. Unlike the competitive atmosphere of graduate school, the writers here were a cohesive group, helpful and interested in each other's work rather than jealous of it. Many of the people I met at FAWC remain my close friends even now, more than twenty years later. In Provincetown I grew comfortable with my writing self and came to respect myself as a writer.

But the rewards of writing are seldom monetary ones, so David (who had joined me in Provincetown) and I moved back to Cambridge to find jobs. I hated having, once again, to leave a place that seemed so right to me, but we wanted to have children and were afraid we'd never find secure employment on Cape Cod. My first book, the book of poetry *Breakers,* was published not long before our first child, Kate, was born. It was a surprise to me (who believed herself a feminist, and still do) that of the two events, it was the birth of my child—not holding that hardcover baby in my hands—which filled me with the most complete joy.

Before long we moved again, this time to Swampscott, a suburban town on the ocean, and within a few years our son, Morgan, joined the family. David was working (as he still is) as a reference editor for Houghton Mifflin Publishing Company, and I was happy to be able to quit working outside our home for a few years, not only because I wanted to be with my children when they were young, but also because I could sometimes still sneak in a few hours of writing now and then, when they napped or on those brief occasions when they played happily together or with a visiting friend.

I was still writing poetry, but for several years another genre of writing had been of interest to me too: playwriting. Several of my plays had been given staged readings in

The author with her husband, David Pritchard, in the dunes of Provincetown, Massachusetts, 1976

Boston by a group called Playwright's Platform. Finally one of them was given a limited performance—two evenings in a small, dark space with room for an audience of no more than one hundred people. But the play was well reviewed by a local newspaper and eventually was optioned by a New York producer. Oh, I was very excited—I thought I was going to be on Broadway!

I know now that getting a play produced is perhaps the most difficult task any writer faces. So many people must be involved: a director, a producer, actors, people to put up money for the project, set and lighting and costume designers (and all of them with an opinion on how your play should be changed!). It's a wonder to me now that, any plays actually get on stage at all. For a beginning playwright the road is a long one, and you must be able to travel around the country with your play, writing and rewriting for each new director and theater that is interested. It's a frustrating process, and as the mother of small children, I found it an impossible one.

When Morgan started school, I took a part-time job as the children's librarian in the Swampscott Public Library. It was a job which required me to be a performer, a singer, a caretaker of books, an obsessive organizer, a parent-child negotiator, a computer operator, and often a baby-sitter. But the part of the job I soon loved the most was the job of salesman. It seemed that once I'd established any sort of relationship with the older children, those who chose their own books, they would come to me for advice, for recommendations on what they should read. In order to prepare myself, I read as many of the best chapter books and young adult novels as I could and found, to my delight, that many of them were wonderful books I could heartily recommend, and did.

Not only did I recommend the books to children; I tried to interest my adult friends in them too. Unfortunately, this is hard work. (Adults, it seems, will go to see movies about teenagers, but they don't want to read books about them.) In my reading I found several books that went beyond the others, inspirational books: my favorites were *Celine* and *The Goats* by Brock Cole; the Fell series and *Dinky Hocker Shoots Smack* by M. E. Kerr; *Jacob Have I Loved* by Katharine Paterson; *Hatchet* and *Dogsong* by Gary Paulson; *Nothing but the Truth* by Avi; and *Rabble Starkey* by Lois Lowry. It seemed to me they took the YA genre and pulled it in new directions. And I wanted to try it too.

The great surprise to me when I began to write *Lombardo's Law* was that writing a YA novel was as munch fun as writing a play! Well, there was all that *talking* going on, all those wacky characters who would only come alive for the reader if something interesting came out of their mouths, so it better be good. I had always loved writing dialogue—it was the thing that first got me started on plays years before. If it's done well, it's exciting and unpredictable, sometimes even for the author! You think you know where your story is headed, but darned if that Justine doesn't start it going in another direction with some insightful comment no one can ignore.

Young adult novels are like plays in other ways too. The plot is usually tight and comes to a satisfying (if not always happy) conclusion. Because teenagers tend to be

"With David, Kate, Morgan, and our dog, Ruby Tuesday," Swampscott, Massachusetts, 1989

emotional creatures (not stifled as we adults learn to be), the situation in a YA is usually highly charged, as it is in most plays. A play needs action, momentum to carry an audience along; YAs also depend on a rather quick introduction of the problem and then a swirl of activity surrounding it. So you see, my transition from writing plays to writing young adult novels was not a difficult one. I loved them immediately.

My first YA, *Lombardo's Law,* was published in 1993 to good reviews. It was named to the ALA Best Young Adult Novels for 1994 list, the ALA Best Reluctant Reader list for the same year, and several state book lists. *Lombardo's Law* is the story of two kids who are on the outskirts of teenage society and find solace in each other and in making a movie together. I began this book knowing only one of my two main characters: Justine Trainor, a fifteen-year-old sophomore in high school, an introvert with virtually no friends but a good sense of humor and a strong sense of herself. Listen to Justine explain lunchtime at her new school in Massachusetts. "These two girls used to sit with me at lunch and constantly ask me what I liked best about living in New England, and beg me to admit how superior it is to Iowa. I got tired of them and moved to the table with kids who read while they eat. No talking allowed."

Justine's voice is a combination of my daughter's self-confident one and the voice that lived in my head during my own high school years but was seldom allowed to speak. I made Justine a secret writer (like me) and a lover of old movies so she'd have strong passions of her own before she even knows my second protagonist, Mike Lombardo (remember the name of *my* first love?), a mere thirteen-year-old eighth grader but clearly Justine's mismatched soul mate from the moment they meet. And then she has a problem—what do you do when your best friend (and maybe *more* than friend) is a boy two years younger and two inches shorter than you? When the only *other* friend you have asks you if you're baby-sitting for him when she sees you together?

Mike is even more outspoken than Justine. Listen to what he has to say the second time she runs into him and admits she can't remember his name. "As usual. Reach into my backpack—I've got some paper towels. You're covered with chocolate." I wanted Mike to be audacious, but still realistic. He's not afraid of what people might think of him, but he sometimes has to pay for his truth-telling, as when he's taunted by a group of boys for being a teacher's favorite. He turns on the group and asks them, "You think it's so damn cool to be dumb?," for which he receives a punch in the stomach.

Heartened by the publication of *Lombardo's Law,* I decided to give up my librarian job and write full-time once again. The result was *Noticing Paradise* (1995), which was inspired by a family trip to Ecuador and the Galapagos Islands. *Noticing Paradise* takes place on a boat in the Galapagos, involves the mysterious disappearance of endangered tortoises, and allows two lonely sixteen-year-olds, Cat and Noah, to fall in love in one of the most romantic spots on earth.

Noah's life has been flowing along quite smoothly until he suddenly washes up on the shores of his parents' divorce and begins to question what he's always believed. Cat has never had much confidence in herself, except as a photographer, able to order the universe through the viewfinder of her camera. Can Cat notice what's around her without a camera to her face? Can Noah separate himself from his father's legacy of unfaithfulness so he can recognize the paradise he's fallen into? These two find the emotional currents they must ride as frightening as the storm they weather in a small rubber boat in their efforts to save endangered Galapagos tortoises.

In these books and others I'm currently working on, I find I'm most interested in those kids who are on the fringes, the slight oddballs and lovable misfits who aren't quite comfortable in their own skins, or if they are, their differentness makes those around them uncomfortable. I want to celebrate their differences because they are likely to be the most fascinating people the rest of us will ever know. (Of course the kids they go to high school with won't know that until they summon the nerve to show up at a reunion years hence!) Many of my characters also seem to turn into artists—writers, photographers, filmmakers—and that's because I'm most interested in the kids with their ears to the ground, the ones who can tell us secrets, and in

my experience that kind of person is often an artist of one kind or another.

Writers are often asked where their ideas come from. The answer is both simple and complicated. I do write about things I know: kids who are like I was, or like I wished I was (bright, thoughtful, artistic), whose problems I'm familiar with (being odd person out, misunderstood, sometimes lonely). I make them crazy about the boy across the street (like I was), I send them to places I've been (small towns, exotic islands, even Italy), and sometimes they even say something I've really heard someone say (maybe one of my own kids!).

But these ideas are just the beginning of the story. You need to use *some* familiar ideas so you can get a grasp on your characters and their situation. But if you rely too much on what really happened, you won't (usually) have a very interesting story. So what you're doing is taking a character you know something about and stretching him or her to find out their secrets—what it is you *don't* know about them. After all, you don't want to just write about the same characters over and over.

Then you decide what needs to happen to them. They need to grow and change during the course of the story, or there's not much of a plot to keep the reader reading. For example, our family had a wonderful trip to the Galapagos Islands, but if I had just written a story about two kids doing the things we did, it would have been a travel article, not a YA novel. So I had to figure out what would make those islands really come alive for my readers. I decided to combine two lonely teenagers with a plot involving the disappearance of four endangered tortoises, the last of their species on earth. This idea allowed me to tell something about the rare and unusual animal life on the islands and at the same time draw a parallel between the endangered animals and the teenagers who felt equally isolated in their own lives.

In 1996 our family took a summer trip to Italy. My children particularly loved Venice where, as my son put it, "you never know what you'll see when you turn the corner." My writer's instinct sharpened when I heard that: what a great setting for a mystery! I like my books to have both a male and a female protagonist, so I decided an Italian boy with a secret would be necessary, and maybe an American girl spending the summer with a very strange aunt she's never met before. The aunt would be the key to everything, so she'd have to be a great character. No, I haven't written this book yet—I'm still thinking about that aunt. Will she be based on a woman I worked for twenty years ago or an elderly neighbor I don't really know much about? How does she know the Italian boy? Is she in on his secret? Or is the secret hers? How will the characters feel about each other in the beginning? What happens to change that? I'll be writing down ideas for a few more months, but with any luck someday there will be a young adult mystery set in Venice with my name on it. Unless of course I take another trip (maybe to Mexico, or maybe just to the supermarket) and a better story jumps up and demands to be told.

I have recently taught writing at Emerson College in Boston. Because I am a writer and a teacher, I am often asked to give advice on how to become a writer. The advice

Ellen and David, on a gondola in Venice, 1996

sounds simple, but carrying it through takes a lot of discipline and hard work. Often people decide to become writers because they've been told they are "talented"—they have an ear for dialogue or an easy, flowing style of writing. Some amount of talent is probably necessary, but there's a long road between having talent and becoming a writer. Talent is just your car. It's very shiny sitting there in the driveway, but if you actually want it to *get* you somewhere; you better put gas in it and learn how to drive. What I mean is, you'll have to work hard to figure out how to use your talent.

My advice is not unusual; you will hear almost all published writers say the same thing. First you must read and read and read—all kinds of things, poems and plays, children's books and adult books, fiction and nonfiction, everything you can get your hands on. Read it as a writer, so you can figure out how it *works.* And then of course you must write. Every day. Just the way you would practice piano or tennis. Every day. Even if it sounds so awful it makes you sick. Even when you feel hopeless about the words you're able to put down on the paper. Put those pages aside and write some more. Do it again. And again. And tomorrow. And the next day. And one day it will be very good.

Writings

FOR YOUNG ADULTS

Lombardo's Law, Houghton (Boston, MA), 1993.
Noticing Paradise, Houghton (Boston, MA), 1995.
Hard Love, Simon and Schuster (New York, NY), 1999.
Gracie's Girl, Simon and Schuster (New York, NY), 2000.
What's in a Name?, Simon and Schuster (New York, NY), 2000.
Razzle, Simon and Schuster (New York, NY), 2001.
The Long Night of Leo and Bree, Simon and Schuster (New York, NY), 2002.

FOR ADULTS

Breakers (poetry), Sheep Meadow Press (Bronx, NY), 1979.
One Civilized Person (play), first produced by Playwright's Platform, Boston, MA, 1982.
Coffee (play), produced by Egg Rock Players, Swampscott, MA, 1985.

Contributor of short stories and poems to periodicals, including *Ploughshares, Antioch Review,* and *Iowa Review.*

Y

YATES, Elizabeth 1905-2001
(Elizabeth McGreal)

OBITUARY NOTICE—See index for *SATA* sketch: Born December 6, 1905, in Buffalo, NY; died July 29, 2001, in Concord, NH. Author. Yates is best remembered as an author of children's books, though she also published works for adults. She began her writing career while living in Europe, where she met her husband, William McGreal, and wrote travel articles for American newspapers such as the *New York Times*. Her first book, *High Holiday,* a novel for adults, was published in 1938. Thereafter followed a prolific writing career; she earned great acclaim in 1950 with her children's book *Amos Fortune,* based on the true story of an African prince who becomes a slave in America and later gains his freedom. The book won a John Newbery Award in 1951. Yates wrote over fifty other books, including *Mountain Born* (1943), *Patterns on the Wall* (1943), *A Place for Peter* (1953), *Prudence Crandall, Woman of Courage* (1955), and *Carolina's Courage* (1964), as well as an autobiographical trilogy. Her most recent book, *Open the Door* (1999), includes prose and poetry selections. Yates was also an active lecturer, writers conference organizer, and environmentalist.

OBITUARIES AND OTHER SOURCES:

PERIODICALS

Los Angeles Times, August 4, 2001, p. B14.
New York Times, August 2, 2001, p. C12.
Washington Post, August 4, 2001, p. B7.